T5-DIG-486

Psychology In Progress

Psychology In Progress

William Epstein
University of Wisconsin

Franklin Shontz
University of Kansas

HOLT, RINEHART AND WINSTON, INC.
New York Chicago San Francisco Atlanta
Dallas Montreal Toronto London Sydney

Grateful acknowledgement is made for cover and chapter opening illustrations reproduced in the text.

Cover stamping: Ernest Trova: Falling Man Suspended Relief. Bronze in Lucite 1969.
Published by Pace Editions, Inc. N.Y.
Chapters 2, 3, 6, 7, 10, 13: Ernest Trova's Falling Man Manscapes Portfolio, 1969.
Published by Pace Editions, Inc. N.Y.
Chapters 1, 4, 5, 8, 11, 12, and 15: Trova's Index, 1970.
Published by Pace Editions Inc., and Harry N. Abrams Inc. N.Y.

Library of Congress Catalog Card Number 75-151152
SBN: 03-081387-S
Printed in the United States of America
1 2 3 4 5 039 9 8 7 6 5 4 3 2 1

Preface

We have chosen an approach that differs markedly from approaches used in other introductory texts. We have deliberately avoided the encyclopedic tendency of many psychology textbooks and have elected instead to examine in depth certain specific problems that interest modern investigators.

Several considerations guided our choice of problems. First, the topics had to cover enough of the ground of general psychology to insure that students would obtain a sampling of a variety of content and methods. Second, each topic had to represent a problem that has been or promises to be of relatively enduring interest to psychology; the topics are not of a sort that we regarded as simply faddish in their appeal. Third, within each topic, it had to be possible to find some consistent thread of investigative development, so that the student could be shown how scientific knowledge grows through consistent and determined application of logic to the interpretation of empirical data. Finally, at least one of the authors had to feel competent and sufficiently interested in the topic to write an accurate, representative, and instructive chapter.

Our approach assumes that problems that interest psychologists will also interest students of psychology. Our own experiences as teachers has convinced us that this is so. We have tried to embed in our matrix of topics a consistent thread of emphasis on the processes of scientific inquiry. Every chapter tells the student not only what is interesting about a subject but how the curious psychologist sets to work to formulate questions about the subject and to seek answers to them.

A few words about the ordering of the chapters. Following the introduction, which provides background for the rest of the book, the chapters are arranged according to the following plan. In general, matters that are currently being dealt with exclusively in the carefully controlled environment of the experimental laboratory are presented early in the text. Chapters 2 and 3 cover topics in perception, a subject of enduring interest in experimental psychology. Chapters 4 and 5 concern memory and language, with an emphasis upon how these are studied in the laboratory. Chapter 6, on feeding behavior, shows how precise investigation is accomplished in physiological psychology. Chapters 7 (Sleep and Dreams) and 8 (Stress) are transitional, since they show how laboratory techniques are brought to bear on some of the more complex processes of behavior. In the material described in these two chapters, inference is somewhat further removed from data than is the case in the chapters that go before.

The next two chapters (Chapter 9, Models of Aggression; Chapter 10, Decision and Dissonance) present topics in social psychology and personality that reveal some of the characteristic modes of research in those fields and the difficulties as well as the possibilities of systematic investigation of interpersonal processes.

The next two chapters describe possible answers to two questions students often ask. First, how can psychology hope to explain not just how people act in laboratories but how they deal with the complexity of the extralaboratory world in which they spend most of their time? (Chapter 11, The Psychological World: Naturalism in Psychology). And second, how may psychology be used to improve the human condition? (Chapter 12, The Control of Behavior).

The last three chapters deal with some of the "softer" issues, from the study of the not-too-clearly-understood subjects of body experience (Chapter 13) and personality defenses (Chapter 14) to the ultimate enigma of seriously abnormal behavior (Chapter 15, The World of Schizophrenia).

There is nothing binding about this arrangement of chapters. The text may be used effectively if chapters are assigned in a completely different order, or even if a few chapters are omitted.

We hope that students who are introduced to psychology by way of this textbook will become excited about the subject. We also hope that they will appreciate the complexity of the problems psychologists are trying to solve and will have a reasonably clear idea of how the scientific process operates. Not the least of our hopes is that students who learn from this book will have a better idea of what psychology courses they want to take in the future. Although our chapter on feeding behavior treats only a small segment of the field of physiological psychology, it does represent some of the best research this specialized study has to offer. Research on one hypothesis about the motives of patients with schizophrenia scarcely exhausts the field of abnormal psychology. Nevertheless, we are convinced that it is more helpful for the student to learn, step-by-step, how one problem is solved in a field than to be engulfed by a massive array of findings, principles, and classification schemes that seem to come from nowhere in particular and everywhere in general. Advanced courses in personality, in experimental, physiological, social, abnormal, and developmental psychology, will provide the supplementary content the student needs to complete his education. One of the most valuable functions the instructor can serve is that of guiding students who show special interest or aptitude in particular chapters to appropriate future studies.

Acknowledgments

Many individuals served as expert readers for chapters dealing with topics in their special fields of competence: Ralph N. Haber (Chapter 2), Sheldon Ebenholtz (Chapter 3), John Jung (Chapter 4), Richard Keesey (Chapter 6), David Foulkes (Chapter 7), Sheldon Korchin (Chapter 8), Ross Parke (Chapter 9), Elliot Aronson (Chapter 10), Edwin Willems (Chapter 11), Richard J. Herrnstein (Chapter 12), Donn Byrne (Chapter 14), Benjamin Braginsky (Chapter 15). In addition, the entire manuscript was read by Ralph N. Haber. All these reviewers made valuable suggestions and corrections to the text. We have done our best to incorporate their ideas as completely as possible. All omissions and errors that may remain are our responsibility.

Mrs. Lee Dulin spent many long hours typing the manuscript, with extraordinary accuracy, speed, and skill. We greatly appreciate her work and the pleasant manner with which she did it.

Finally, a debt of gratitude is owed to our wives and families, who bore up well and cheerfully under the strain we necessarily imposed upon them.

William Epstein
Franklin Shontz

Madison, Wisc.
Lawrence, Kans.
January, 1971

CONTENTS

Chapter 1 The Science of Psychology 1
Early Experimental Psychology 4
Later Developments 14
Definitions of Psychology 17
Strong Inference 19

Chapter 2 The Perceptual World of the Infant 29
Form and Pattern Perception 31
Visual Space Perception 42
Nativism versus Empiricism 53

Chapter 3 Perceptual Adaptation to a Transformed World 57
Adaptation 58
The Effective Stimulus 61
Movement and Intention 69

The Locus of Change 73
Adaptation and Perceptual Development 76
Open Questions 78

Chapter 4 Remembering and Forgetting 81
Aspects of Forgetting 82
Passive Forgetting 85
Active Forgetting 94
Not Remembering 103
The Organization of Memory 106

Chapter 5 Syntax and Cognition 113
Concepts of Syntax 114
The Perceptual Reality of Syntax 117
Syntax and Memory 123
Syntax, Comprehension and Reasoning 134
Linguistic Relativity and Determinism 137

Chapter 6 Regulatory Centers in the Brain: Central Mechanisms of Feeding 143
Central and Peripheral Factors 144
The Hypothalamus 146
The Feeding Center 150
The Satiety Center 156
Stop and Go Signals 159
An Alternative Viewpoint 162
Centrally Elicited Reinforcement and Feeding 164
Olds' Theory of Reinforcement 166
Summary of Progress 167
Obesity in Humans 168

Chapter 7 Sleep and Dreams 175
Dreams and Mental Life: Psychoanalysis Sleep 179
Rapid Eye Movements and Dreams 185
REM Deprivation 193
Eye Movements and Conscious Mental Acitivity 196
What Is a Dream? 199

Chapter 8 Stress: Things Are Not as Simple as They Seem 205
Two Points of View 206
Some Physiological Research 208
The Psychological Approach 214
Reactions to Films of Body Mutilation 216
Related Research 227
Ethical Consideration 231

Chapter 9 Models of Aggression 237
Aspects of Aggression 238

The Instinct to Aggress 239
Models of Aggression 240
Conditions of Aggression 251
Vicarious Aggression: Catharsis or Stimulation? 257
Violence and the Mass Media 262

Chapter 10 Decision and Dissonance 267
The Theory of Cognitive Dissonance 270
Research on Cognitive Dissonance 273
Criticisms of the Theory 280
Conditions Affecting the Magnitude of Dissonance 283

Chapter 11 Naturalism in Psychology 289
Environmentalism in Psychology 290
Behavior in Natural Settings 291
Ecological Units: Behavior Settings 300
Other Matters of Interest 306

Chapter 12 The Control of Behavior 315
Operant Conditioning 316
Characteristics of Operant Analysis 325
Modification of Human Behavior 328
Evaluations 334

Chapter 13 Body Experience 343
Disturbances of Body Experience 344
Draw-a-Person Technique (DAP) 351
Body Image Boundaries 359
Verbal Measures 361
Perception of Body Parts 362

Chapter 14 Individual Differences in Repression-Sensitization 371
Background 373
Measurement of Repression-Sensitization 375
Testing the Test 377
Future Research 382

Chapter 15 The World of Schizophrenia 393
The Disease Model 394
Schizophrenia A Case in Point 396
Similarities Between Schizophrenics and Normals 402
Retorts and Counterarguments 409
Author Index 417
Subject Index 425

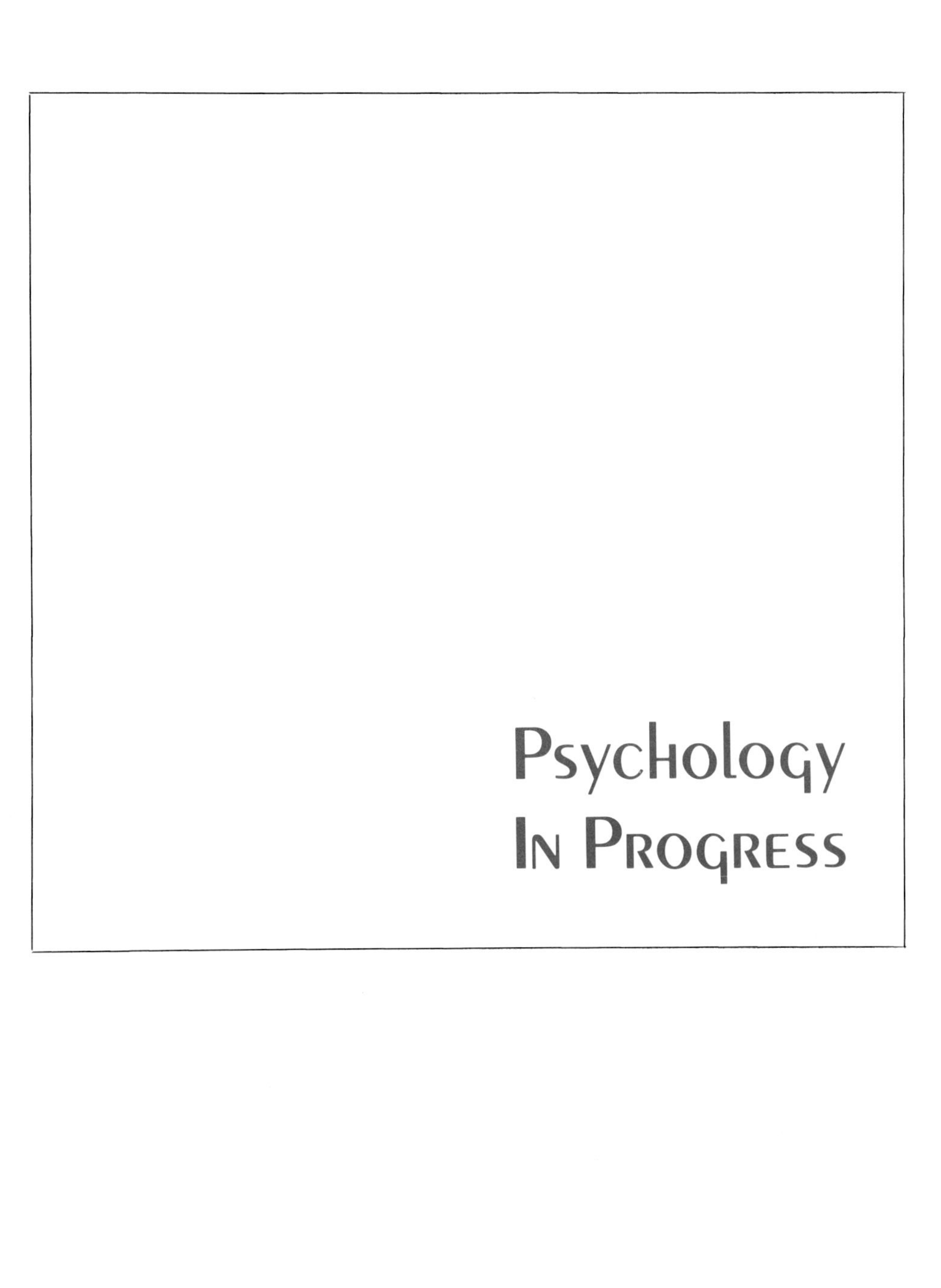

Psychology In Progress

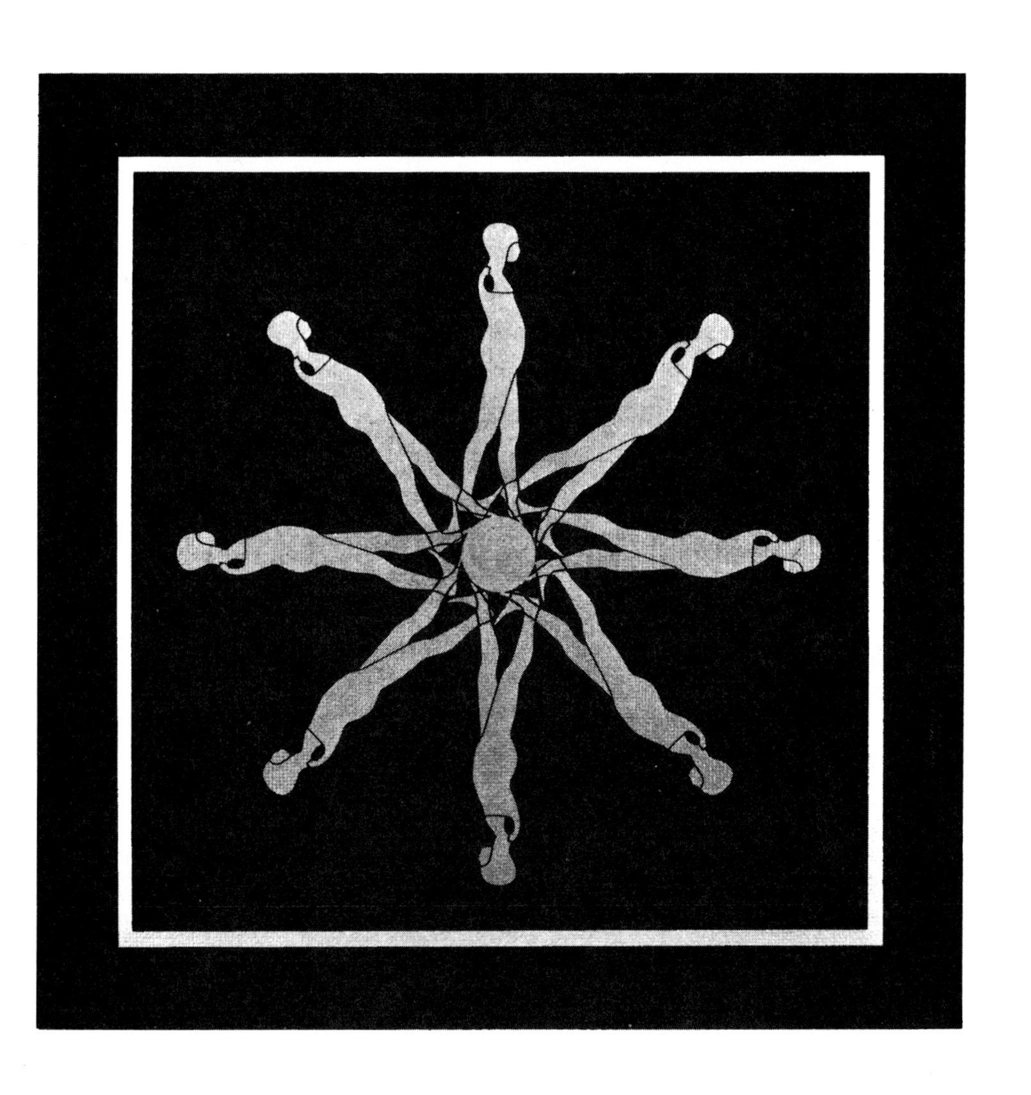

1 The Science of Psychology

In the myths of the ancient Greeks, Psyche was a mortal woman of such rare loveliness that the admiration and attention she inspired in men detracted from their worship of Venus, the goddess of beauty. Jealous over her loss of affection, the angry goddess dispatched her son, Cupid, to wreak vengeance upon the unlucky girl. But Cupid failed to complete his mission, for he too found Psyche extraordinarily attractive, and fell in love with her. Instead of punishing her, Cupid arranged a secret dwelling place where he visited her every night. His only command was that she must never try to look at him.

For a while Psyche obeyed and was happy, but her sisters, whom Cupid had reluctantly allowed to keep her company during the lonely daylight hours, aroused her curiosity. They suggested that her ardent lover was not a handsome god, but some ugly creature who hid his repulsiveness in the darkness. Unable to resist temptation, she looked at Cupid by candlelight while he slept. Although she was delighted with what she saw, Psyche carelessly awakened her lover by spilling hot candle wax on him. Because she had disobeyed his command, Cupid left her.

Psyche despairingly set out to search for her godly lover, at last coming before Venus herself to plead for reunion with Cupid. The goddess set for Psyche a series of tasks and trials that seemed impossible to complete successfully, including a journey to the underworld to bring back a box of beauty from the queen of Hades. The tasks were too hard for a mortal to accomplish; just when it seemed that Psyche was failing utterly, Cupid begged Jupiter to take a benevolent hand in the matter. Jupiter granted Psyche immortality and equal status with the gods, Cupid and Psyche were reunited forever, and the ancient story comes to a happy end.

In about the fifth century B.C., the figure of Psyche came to personify for the Greeks the human soul, a ghostly immortal substance within the individual. Later, the word *psyche* came to mean not only *soul* but also *mind:* a spiritual entity within the person that perceives, thinks, wills, and remembers. Mind, in turn, was commonly equated with consciousness or awareness.

Today the term *psychology* has lost the romance of its association with the myth of the immortal lovers, but still reflects, albeit often dimly, its early significance as the study of mind, soul, or consciousness. The notion that he has a mind or psyche often implies to western man that the power of thought endows him with godlike status and enables him to transcend the limits of nature and mortality, as Psyche ultimately achieved equality with the gods and goddesses of ancient Greece.

Mind and Early Science

Mental processes have long been identified with consciousness and with the idea that man possesses an immortal soul. Such a soul hardly seems a fit subject for the cold scrutiny of science, and it was late in the development of modern technology before serious effort was made toward systematic study of psychology.

Aristotle (384–322 B.C.) was the first of the early Greek philosophers to advocate careful observation and description of nature, and he is generally regarded as the first true scientist. But experimental science in its present familiar form was not born until the Renaissance, more than 1,500 years later, when the writings of the ancient Greeks, which had been lost to Europe since the fall of the Roman Empire, were rediscovered by western scholars.

The attentions of early investigators were drawn to physical more than psychological phenomena, and remarkable advances were made early in the development of Renaissance science. Galileo (1564–1642) formulated the basic laws of the motion of physical bodies. Copernicus in 1543 replaced the belief that the sun moves around the earth (the *geocentric* theory) with the *heliocentric* theory (that the earth orbits the sun). In the early sixteenth century, Vesalius violated the alleged sanctity of the human body by developing methods for its systematic dissection and study; later, William Harvey (1578–1657) demonstrated conclusively by experimental methods that the blood circulates through a closed hydraulic system in which the heart functions as a pump.

So effective was science, and so impressive were its innovations, that 400 years ago Francis Bacon (1561—1626) proposed the revolutionary idea of establishing a university wholly devoted to study and experimentation in natural science. (All universities of the time concentrated solely on the teaching of the classics.) With this enthusiasm over the successes of science, it seems strange that psychology did not appear until the middle of the nineteenth century. While man had made important advances in unravelling the riddles of the physical universe by 1700, he did not undertake to solve the riddle of his own behavior for still another 150 years.

Mind and matter; soul and substance. Probably the most important reason for delay in the development of psychology was the generally accepted belief that the properties of the mind are fundamentally so different from the properties of material objects that the methods of natural science could not be expected to apply to the study of mental states and processes. What greater contrast can be imagined than that between ideas and material things? To the earliest Greek philosophers such as Plato, as well as to others who came later, the soul and its products—ideas and thoughts—seemed spiritual, eternal, absolute, and, most important of all, free, while mere matter seemed transient, unstable, and subject to growth and decay. That soul and matter were entirely different kinds of reality was as obvious to the ancients as the then indisputable facts that the sun moves around the earth and that a heavier object falls faster than a lighter one.

Furthermore, just as natural science began to challenge ancient conceptions about the universe, a highly influential philosopher stated a strong case against the development of a science of the soul. René Descartes (1596–1650) argued that many of the phenomena that we now call psychological cannot be studied by empirical means (that is, by direct observation). Descartes maintained that, while all material things, including the human body, are subject to mechanical laws which can be scientifically understood, the human soul is not controlled or limited by such laws and is therefore not a fit or proper subject for science. In Descartes' day, most of the activities or functions that were thought to come from and belong to the *soul* (for example, acts of choice, decision, or will) could just as easily be said to be operations of the *mind,* as we use that term today. Descartes' doctrine therefore made "off limits" much of what psychologists now investigate routinely; it is sometimes said that Cartesian dualism was responsible for delaying the growth of scientific psychology for centuries.

Evolutionary doctrine. An event of utmost importance to psychology occurred in 1859, when Charles Darwin (1809–1882) published his most influential work: *On the Origin of Species by Means of Natural Selection, or the Preservation of Favoured Races in the Struggle for Life.* Darwin had observed interspecies consistency of organic structure that led him to conclude that man is a product of a continuous, long-term structural adaptation to the demands of biological survival. Darwin's views had the shocking effect of removing man from the pedestal of superiority to nature that he had occupied for thousands of years. They denied that all-important qualitative difference between man and other creatures—man's rational soul—that had been assumed to exist since the days of the early Greek philosophers. They despiritualized the human creature and seemed to make man nothing more than a complex animal struggling for existence in a hostile world.

Darwin's theories brought to the study of man the concept of *functionalism,* an emphasis on goals and on the process of adaptation to the environment. For Darwin, the primary problem of living creatures is that of *survival,* and the primary question is inherently practical: How does any organic structure or action serve to insure survival? The question cannot be answered by saying "man can reason," but only by showing how the power to reason makes man fit to survive in the world of nature, and by describing how this form of adaptation evolved through genetic change and natural selection.

Darwinism contributed to psychology a matured biological concept of man, with an emphasis on instincts and drives. This concept legitimized comparative research, in which knowledge of man is gained through the study of other animals. It supported the growing interest in maladaptive behavior (abnormal psychology) and fostered research into individual differences. Perhaps most important of all, the concept avoided metaphysical disputes by posing an entirely new set of questions to be answered by the science of man.

Early Experimental Psychology

Weber's Law

Psychological science may be said to have begun with the work of Gustav Fechner (1801–1887), who instituted the systematic empirical study of aesthetics and formulated a famous psychophysical law which he hoped would specify in a mathematical equation the relationship between mind and matter. Fechner's contribution was a development and expansion of earlier studies by E.H. Weber (1795–1878). Weber, a physiologist, had observed that a change in the magnitude of a physical stimulus can be detected by a human observer only if that change bears a constant relationship to the value of the original stimulation. Weber's law may be expressed as:

$$\frac{ds}{S} = k$$

or as its algebraic equivalent:

$$ds = kS$$

where ds is the barely detectable change in a stimulus of original magnitude S. Thus, if the value of k in this equation were known by experiment to be .05, the formula would indicate that any given stimulus S (which might be measured in centimeters, grams, or lumens, depending on the type of stimulation involved) must be increased or decreased by one-twentieth (.05 = 1/20) of its original value before most people can observe that a change has taken place. Since one-twentieth of a low number is less than one-twentieth of a high one, the formula states that different amounts of change are required for different stimulus values. A weak or low level of original stimulation does not have to be changed as much as a strong one in order for the change to be observed. It is easier to detect the addition or subtraction of one ounce when a half-pound weight is involved than when the weight is 20 pounds, and it is easier to detect a half-inch change in a line two inches long than in a line ten feet long.

Weber's law applies to many kinds of perceptual judgments, from estimation of the brightnesses of lights and the lengths of lines to detection of differences in the loudness of sounds or the weights of objects. Fechner's modification of Weber's law changed its form and added an important term, but did not cast doubt on the fundamental relationship that Weber had discovered. Fechner merely recast the equation in a form that seemed to make possible the measurement of mental experience.

Fechner's Restatement

Weber's formula does not contain any "mental" terms. Both ds and S are measured in physical stimulus units, and k is a unitless constant, a pure number. Fechner changed this by considering that, subjectively speaking, it is possible to think of all *just noticeable differences* (*jnd*'s) as being *psychologically* or mentally equal, despite the fact that (as Weber's law states) the physical size of the jnd for a stimulus of low magnitude is smaller than the physical size of a jnd for a stimulus of high magnitude.

If Fechner's assumption is correct, the jnd may be used as a unit of mental measurement, and the subjective experience of a stimulus can be specified by the number of mental jnd units it contains. Fechner applied the methods of calculus to Weber's law and restated it to specify the relationship between mental events and stimulus magnitudes (material events). Fechner's law took the form:

$$R = c \log S + a$$

where R is a measure of subjective intensity (in mental units, or jnd's), S is a measure of stimulus magnitude (in appropriate physical units), and c and a are constants. Like the constant in Weber's law, the values of c and a are determined experimentally.

To demonstrate how changes in jnd units (the values of R) depend upon the initial value of S in Fechner's law, arbitrary values may be assigned to the terms on the right-hand side of Fechner's equation. Assume, for example, that the constants c and a equal 3 and 20, respectively. (These values are selected for convenience only; they are not likely to occur in an actual experiment.) A stimulus of 10 units yields a value of 23 perceptual units for R, since the logarithm of 10 to the base 10 is 1.0:

$$R = c \log_{10} 10 + a$$
$$R = 3 \times 1 + 20$$
$$R = 23$$

A stimulus of 100 units yields a value of 26 for R, since the logarithm of 100 to the base 10 is 2.0:

$$R = 3 \times 2 + 20$$
$$R = 26$$

This represents an increase of 3 units (from 23 to 26) in perceptual response. In other words, an increase of 90 *stimulus* units (from 10 to 100) produces an increase of 3 *perceptual* units.

By how many units must the stimulus be further increased to raise the value of R another 3 perceptual units, to 29? The answer is not 90 again, but 900, because the logarithm of S must equal 3:

$$R = 3 \times 3 + 20$$

$$R = 29$$

S must therefore be raised from 100 (log = 2.0) to 1,000 (log = 3.0). It is obvious that equal changes in perceptual responses (R) are not produced by equal changes in stimulus magnitudes (S), and it is the nature of the relationship between the two that both Weber's and Fechner's laws were designed to express.

Fechner felt that his equation demonstrated the unity of mind and body by showing how at least one class of mental events (perceptions) can be measured objectively. His thinking reflected contemporary optimism that ancient philosophical questions would finally yield to the methods of science and mathematics. However, if Fechner had merely dabbled with interesting mathematical and philosophical ideas, he would not be regarded as one of the founders of psychological science. Fortunately, he was not content with sheer speculation. The methods he developed, by which measurements of perception could be made, proved to be valuable in virtually all fields of psychology.

Psychophysical Methods

Fechner developed several techniques for determining absolute thresholds and just noticeable differences (difference thresholds). An examination of one of his methods, the *method of constant stimuli,* will serve to convey the general characteristics of the classical psychophysical approach to these problems.

Method of constant stimuli. In this method, the subject makes a series of judgments about stimuli (such as lights, tones, and weights) that are presented to him in pairs. One member of each pair, the *standard,* remains the same throughout the series. The other member is variable and can be set by the experimenter to higher and lower levels of intensity.

The subject is first presented with the standard and with one setting of the variable stimulus. He reports whether the variable stimulus is greater than, less than, or the same as the standard in magnitude. This process is repeated many times over the whole range of settings of the variable stimulus. The experimenter may present the various settings of the variable stimulus in any order, so long as he covers a range well above and well below the probable threshold value.

After obtaining several judgments at each setting of the variable stimulus, the investigator counts the number of times each setting is reported to be smaller than, larger than, or the same as the standard. Naturally, the subject's responses are accurate and reliable at extreme stimulus settings; at settings more nearly equal to that of the standard stimulus, they are less consistently correct. A common procedure is to identify as *transition points* those stimulus settings at which the subject judges the variable and the standard stimulus to be *the same* 50 per cent of the time. These are the settings at which his reports are wrong as often as they are right.

There are two transition points. One represents the change of response (from *greater than* to *the same*) when the variable stimulus is of greater magnitude than the standard. The other represents the change of response (from *less than* to *the*

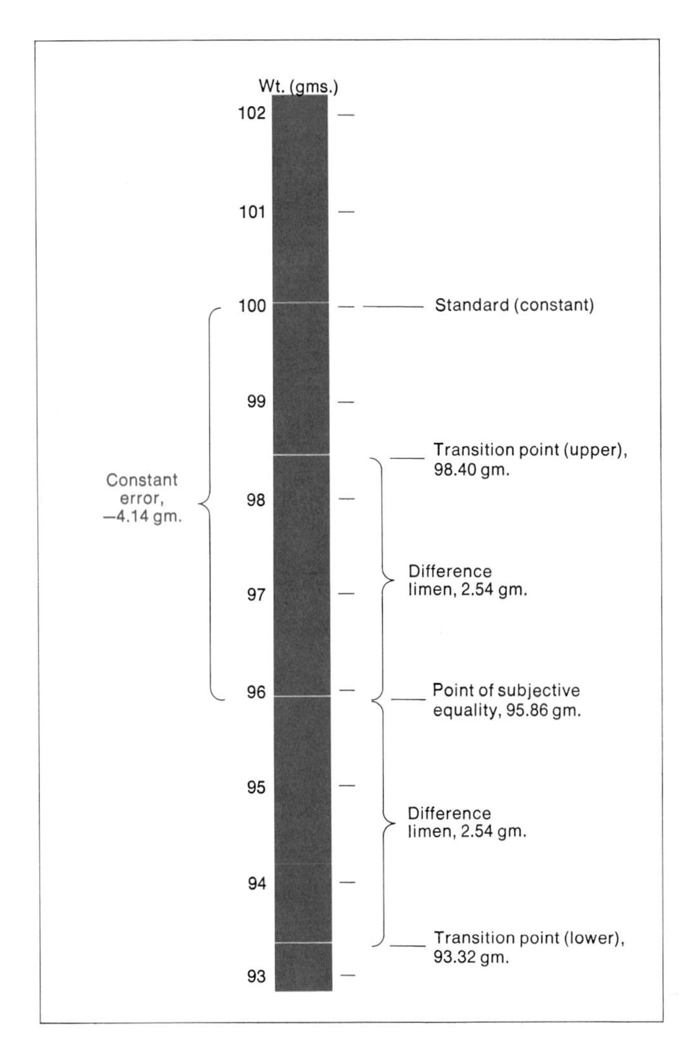

Fig. 1.1. Point of subjective equality, constant error, and difference limen for data from lifted weights. (Data from Woodworth, 1938)

same) when the variable is of lesser magnitude than the standard. Halfway between these points lies the *point of subjective equality*, the setting at which the subject presumably perceives the variable and the standard stimuli to be of the same magnitude. The difference between the actual magnitude of the standard stimulus and the point of subjective equality defines the *constant error*, which tells the extent to which the subject typically overestimated or underestimated the standard stimulus.

These relations are shown graphically in Figure 1.1, which uses data reported by Woodworth in 1938. The subject generally underestimated the weight of the 100 gm. standard. The point of subjective equality is at 95.86 gm., and the constant error is −4.14 gm. (95.86–100.00). The difference limen (or threshold) specifies the region of uncertainty of judgment, the range within which the subject's responses are unreliable and vary from trial to trial.

The method of constant stimuli may also be used to determine an absolute threshold. In this case, there is no standard stimulus; the subject is simply presented with settings of the variable stimulus above and below the probable threshold value and asked to report whether or not he perceives the stimulus. The absolute threshold is usually defined as the point on the physical scale where perception is reported 50 per cent of the time.

Other classical psychophysical methods. When Weber first studied sensory discrimination, he set the variable stimulus equal to the standard stimulus. He then changed the variable stimulus slightly and asked the subject to report whether he could detect a difference between the two. For obvious reasons, Weber's method came to be called the *method of just noticeable differences.*

Fechner realized that the same problem could be approached by setting the variable stimulus at an initial level obviously different from that of the standard. The experimenter could then make a small adjustment of the variable stimulus in the direction of the standard and ask the subject to report whether it still appeared to be different from the standard. By noting when judgments changed from *different* to *the same,* the experimenter could determine transition points, the point of subjective equality, the constant error, and the difference limen, just as in the method of constant stimuli. This method came to be called the *method of limits,* which differs from the method of constant stimuli mainly in that it requires that the variable stimulus be made progressively more similar to the standard; in the method of constant stimuli, settings of the variable stimulus may be administered in any order.

Finally, in the *method of adjustment,* the subject is provided with a standard stimulus and with a variable stimulus that he can adjust himself. In a typical experiment, the variable stimulus is set by the experimenter at a level obviously different from that of the standard, and the subject adjusts the variable stimulus to apparent equality with the standard. The average setting of the variable stimulus defines the point of subjective equality. Since there are no transition points, a difference threshold cannot be obtained from the method of adjustment.

Variations on a theme. The method of constant stimuli is the most versatile of the classical psychophysical methods. It may be used even though the experimenter does not know in advance the actual stimulus values of the variable stimulus. Suppose you wished to study the expressive intensity of several words, all of which mean nearly the same thing; such words might be respect, love, like, revere, cherish, idolize, and appreciate. One of these words could be made a standard stimulus (for example love). The others could then be presented one at a time to a subject, who would report whether each word expresses more attraction than does the word *love,* less attraction, or about the same degree of attraction. By examining the proportion of responses of *more, less,* and the *same* to each stimulus word, you would be able to arrange them in order of their expression of attraction of one person for another.

A few more techniques. Another approach to the same problem is to use each word as a standard for all the rest, so that every word is ultimately compared to every other word. Each word is compared to the stimulus *love,* to the stimulus *like,* and so on. This is the *method of paired comparisons.*

Still another approach is to present all words together and to ask the subject to identify the one that expresses the greatest attraction of one person for another,

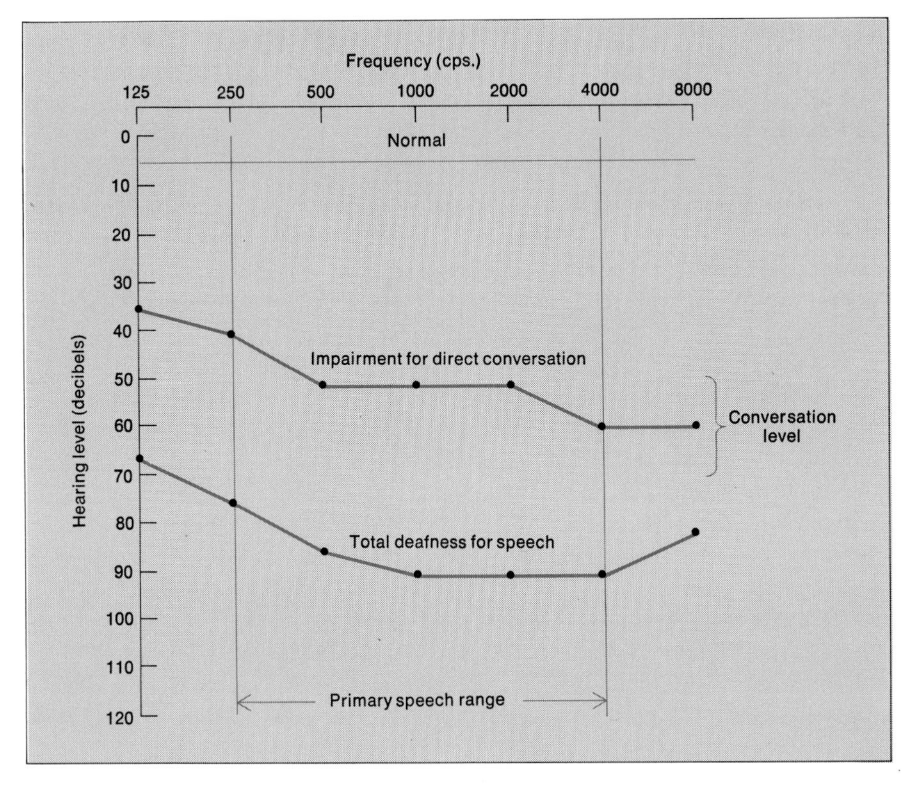

Fig. 1.2. Audiograms, showing approximate threshold values in persons with hearing losses. Plotted points represent absolute thresholds for pure tones (air conduction).

the one that expresses the next greatest attraction, and so on, down to the one that expresses the least attraction of all. This is the *ranking* method.

Yet another approach is to present the words one at a time and ask the subject to assign each stimulus a number, say from one to ten, to show the degree of attraction the word expresses. In the language of classical psychophysics, this is the *method of single stimuli,* but its more common name is the *rating* method.

The same methods can be used to study samples of handwriting, written essays, Playboy foldouts, popular songs, or any other stimuli that may be assumed to vary along a single dimension. That is really why Fechner is so important to psychology. His influence began with his contribution to (indeed, his initiation of) the study of perception and continues in contemporary psychology as the foundation upon which nearly all *psychometric methods* (techniques of psychological measurement) are built (see Chap. 14).

Most people today are familiar with at least one application of results from classical psychophysics. The well-known scale of *decibels,* a measure of subjective loudness, is derived from Fechner's law. Decibels are used to measure noise levels in cities and in buildings, and to evaluate the output of high fidelity music systems and other devices for the transmission and reproduction of sound.

By presenting sounds of known frequency and loudness to a patient and by recording whether or not they are heard, a speech pathologist can draw a profile or *audiogram* of that person's ability to hear tones of different pitches (Fig. 1.2). An audiogram not only identifies the existence of deafness, but also in skilled hands

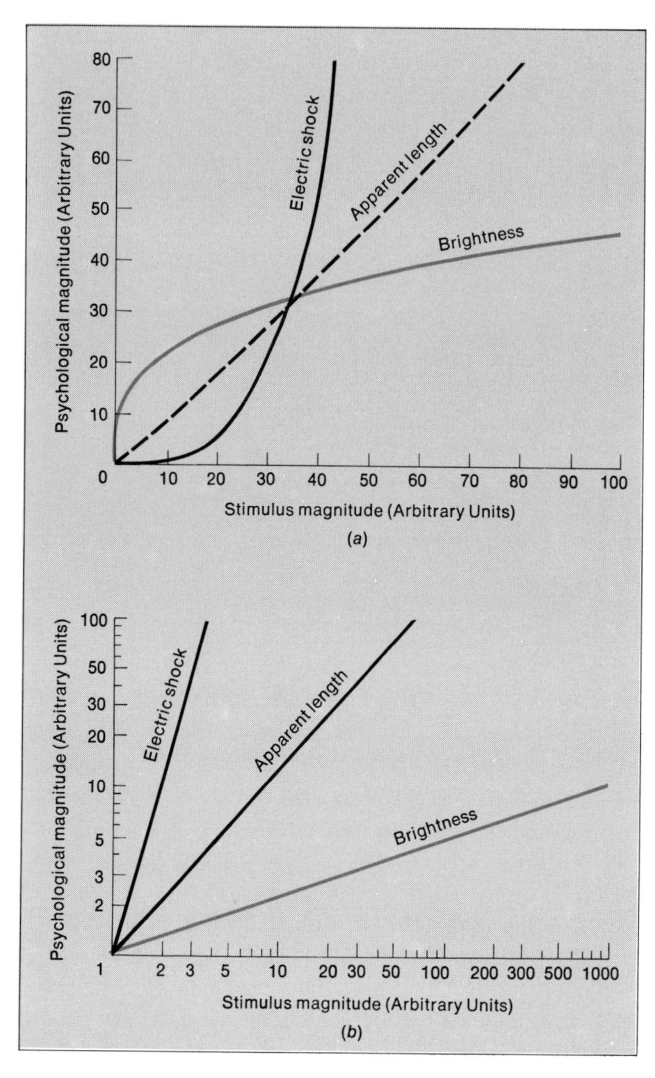

Fig. 1.3. Plots of Stevens' power function on linear–linear coordinates (a) and log–log coordinates (b). (From Stevens, 1962)

it provides clues to the cause of deafness, since hearing losses from different sources often produce audiograms with quite different characteristics.

Modern Psychophysics

Stevens' Law. S.S. Stevens has recently proposed a different equation to link apparent intensities of stimuli to physically measured stimulus magnitudes. Stevens had subjects assign numbers to stimuli which would express their impressions of the magnitudes of stimulation. He found that a *power function* expresses the relationship between reports of stimulus intensities and actual stimulus magnitudes better than a logarithmic function. That is:

$$R = kS^n$$

where R is the report of apparent magnitude, S is the stimulus magnitude measured in physical units, and k and n are experimentally determined constants. When data obtained by Stevens' method are plotted on an ordinary graph, they yield rather complex curves, like those shown in Figure 1.3a. However, when the data are plotted on log-log coordinates, they produce simple straight lines, like those shown in Figure 1.3b. The slopes (tangents) of the lines are equal to the values of n in Stevens' equation. (A *log coordinate* is a line on which the distances between numbers represent the logarithmic instead of the ordinary arithmetic relationships among them.)

Stevens' work has led to the production of several new psychophysical scales. One of the most interesting is a scale of loudness based on the newly defined unit, the *sone,* which was developed because acoustical engineers found the decibel scale unsatisfactory. They needed a scale which reflected more accurately the loudness of sounds to the typical listener (Stevens, 1957, p. 163). These developments clearly reflect renewed experimental interest in a problem that was for many years regarded as permanently solved.

A new look. Although psychophysical research can become very complex, the fundamental problem of classical psychophysics can be simply stated. It is the problem of measurement.

The most sophisticated measures in science have a meaningful zero point and a sequence of equally spaced units extending from that point. A measure of this type is called a *ratio scale* because the relationship between two measurements on the scale can be expressed by dividing one by the other (Stevens, 1951). An example of a ratio scale is the scale of inches, used to measure length. It has equal units and a meaningful zero point, and we can describe the relationship between 12 units and 8 units on the scale by saying that 12 inches is 1.5 times as long as 8 inches, or by saying that 8 inches is two-thirds as long as 12 inches.

Classical psychophysicists viewed their assignment as the invention of sophisticated scales for measuring perception. It is for this reason that so much time and effort has been spent measuring absolute thresholds and just noticeable differences, and Fechner's and Stevens' contributions to psychology show that the approach of classical psychophysics still yields useful outcomes. However, modern psychophysics does not always see its task in quite that way. Present-day psychologists realize that absolute thresholds and difference thresholds are not fixed quantities, but are more like regions within which response probability varies systematically. Look again at the transition points in Figure 1.1, and recall that these points are defined as stimulus settings at which the subject judges the variable stimulus and the standard stimulus to be the same 50 per cent of the time.

Although it may seem reasonable to suppose that the subject is 50 per cent certain of his response at this point, he does not actually say that he is 50 per cent sure the stimuli are the same. What he says is that one-half of the time he perceives the stimuli to be the same, while the other half of the time he perceives them to be different. Similarly, the point of subjective equality, which is arbitrarily located halfway between the two transition points, is not a point at which the subject suddenly says the stimuli always appear to be the same. It is merely the center of the stimulus region within which the probability of occurrence of the response, *the same,* is greater than .50.

Similar considerations apply to the determination of absolute thresholds. An absolute threshold is not a sharply defined point, below which subjects always say

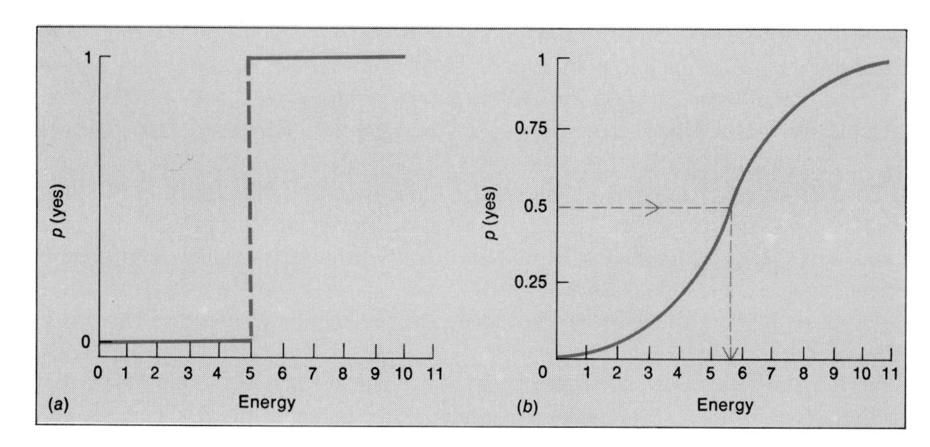

Fig. 1.4. Threshold functions: (a) is what classical psychophysics might lead us to expect; (b) is what is actually found. (From Galanter, 1962)

they do not perceive the stimulus and above which they always say they do perceive the stimulus. It, too, is a region in which response probabilities vary as a function of stimulus strength. Figure 1.4a shows what classical psychophysical theory might lead one to expect: a sharp change in response from *no* (I do not perceive it) to *yes* (I do perceive it) when the stimulus reaches a certain specific intensity. Fig. 1.4b shows what actually happens. The probability of a *yes* response increases gradually over a portion of the stimulus range, and the threshold is arbitrarily defined as the point on the scale of physical energy at which that probability is .50. Since there is nothing absolute about the threshold value, the study of absolute thresholds is now called *signal detection*, and the 50 per cent point is often referred to as the *detection threshold* (Galanter, 1962).

In a typical modern experiment on the detection threshold, the constant stimulus is so weak that the subject cannot report its presence with complete certainty. On some trials, the stimulus is actually presented; on some trials it is not. The subject's task on each trial is to report whether or not he perceives a stimulus. When the frequency of presentation is systematically varied, from close to zero per cent (the stimulus is rarely if ever presented), to close to 100 per cent (the stimulus is presented on all or nearly all trials), the detection threshold is found to shift considerably. In general, when the probability of a stimulus being presented is objectively high, signal detection is more accurate; the type of error in which the subject incorrectly says that no stimulus is present tends to occur a small proportion of the time (upper right, Fig. 1.5a). However, when the stimulus is presented only infrequently, signal detection is less accurate, and the proportion of errors in which the subject fails to report the presence of the stimulus rises sharply (upper right, Fig. 1.5b). Figure 1.5 shows how the proportions of correct responses (in the upper left and lower right of each diagram) and the proportions of the two types of errors possible in both experiments change with different signal presentation probabilities; the energy value of the stimulus is the same in both cases.

Results such as these suggest that detection thresholds are determined by the subject's expectations as to whether a stimulus will or will not be presented. Other experiments have shown that motivational factors also influence detection thresholds. When the subject is paid for correct responses and penalized for incorrect

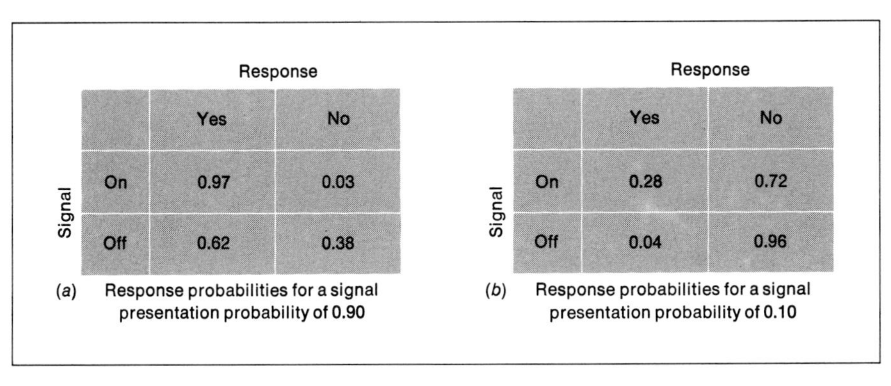

Response

Signal	Yes	No
On	0.97	0.03
Off	0.62	0.38

(*a*) Response probabilities for a signal presentation probability of 0.90

Response

Signal	Yes	No
On	0.28	0.72
Off	0.04	0.96

(*b*) Response probabilities for a signal presentation probability of 0.10

Fig. 1.5. Outcomes of an experiment on signal detection with high (a) and low (b) probabilities of signal presentation. (From Galanter, 1962)

ones, he is more accurate than when his reports have no reward consequences (see Chap. 12). The presence of background stimuli, or "noise," also influences subjects' abilities to detect stimuli, as does the subject's ability to recognize the specific type of stimulus presented to him. In some experiments, in which subjects are required both to detect and identify the source of threshold stimuli of different kinds (for instance, sounds and lights), sensitivity deteriorates markedly (see Chap. 8, pp. 212-213). It is fair to say, then, that the modern psychophysical investigator views the detection threshold in terms of response probabilities and sees his task as determining the ways in which these probabilities vary as the conditions under which they are measured are systematically manipulated.

The modern psychophysicist may question whether it is reasonable to speak of thresholds at all. Even if he believes that they exist, he is not convinced that there is only one. There may be as many as three: one below which a signal is never detected (low threshold), one at which the signal is detected with a specified degree of probability, and one at which the subject becomes completely certain that a signal is present (high threshold) (Krantz, 1969).

Similar considerations apply to what the modern psychophysicist calls the problems of *discrimination* (determination of difference thresholds) and *scaling* (accurate expression in mathematical language of the relationship between perceptual experience and the magnitudes of physical stimuli). Since the organism is variably sensitive to many factors in addition to stimulus energy at the detection threshold, there is reason to suppose that discrimination thresholds are also unstable. That being the case, it will doubtless be necessary in the future to revise our thinking about the problem of scaling. Much experimental work needs to be conducted before this can be accomplished.

Finally, modern psychophysics has found a helpful partner in information theory, which has opened for investigation the new and challenging problem of *recognition*. In its simplest form, the question it poses is: How do we know which of several possible detectable stimuli that might have been presented actually was presented? Generally, this question is answered in terms of the amount of information the stimulus contains and the amount of information the observer can process at one time.

Information theory tells the investigator how much information is contained in a stimulus display. Experimentation that uses controlled stimulus displays tells the psychophysicist how much information his observer can handle and still produce accurate responses. With stimuli on a single sensory dimension (such as pitch of a tone, brightness of light, or weight of an object), subjects can learn to recognize perfectly only about seven alternatives. That is a little less than three *bits* of information (a *bit* is the logarithm to the base 2 of the number of alternatives that can be processed).

When complex stimuli are used instead of simple stimuli, recognition is somewhat easier, and the number of bits that can be successfully managed is relatively higher. But a process of diminishing returns sets in as stimuli become more complex, and the absolute limit for *equally likely* stimuli of any complexity is probably not greater than 10 or 11 bits, i.e., one to two thousand alternatives (Galanter, 1962, p. 119). Of course, people manage many more alternatives than this in real life, but that is partly because stimuli in real life are not equally likely. It is improbable that you would hear the squeal of a pig while sitting in a classroom studying psychology, and if you did you would probably have trouble recognizing the sound for what it was.

Psychophysics has come a long way since Weber and Fechner. Fundamental laws have been challenged, basic problems have been reformulated, and totally new questions have been asked. Historically, psychophysics is the cornerstone upon which much of experimental psychology has been built. But it is not to be studied out of mere historical curiosity. For a good many years to come, psychophysical research will remain theoretically constructive, intellectually challenging, and eminently practical in its application.

Introspection

Despite the significance of their work, neither Weber nor Fechner actually founded the science of psychology. Weber was a physiologist, and Fechner was more interested in solving philosophical problems than in establishing a new branch of science. In about 1860, Wilhelm Wundt publicly identified experimental psychology as a scientific discipline in its own right. Both Wundt and William James, an American psychologist of exceptional ability, founded psychological laboratories in 1875, primarily for demonstration purposes. Wundt began a program of original psychological research in 1879, building upon the work of Weber and Fechner. He also founded the approach to psychology known as *introspectionism.*

Introspectionism is a strategy of research that requires subjects to examine and report upon their own experiences. In its early form introspectionism reflected the notion that mind and consciousness are identical, implying that subjects are capable of knowing and describing their own thoughts. Later developments in psychology established the weaknesses of the introspective method for the study of many phenomena, such as personality, motivation, and emotion. The limits of introspective data are more clearly understood today than they were a century ago, but the method is still used, directly or indirectly, in much important psychological research.

Later Developments

The work of Wundt and his followers dominated psychology at first, but after a few decades others developed new and exciting methods and ideas. Although it is not possible to describe them all, a few examples of the more important will show how psychology expanded into other fields of investigation.

Psychoanalysis

One of the most important of the innovators was Sigmund Freud (1856–1939), a Viennese physician and neurologist strongly influenced by evolutionary doctrine, who developed the theory and methods of psychoanalysis. Freud's assertion that the most important mental activities are those of which the person is not aware (unconscious) was revolutionary, contributing to the end of classical introspectionism as the dominant method of psychology. Freud's studies of the meanings of dreams and of the use of hypnosis in the treatment of hysteria led him to develop the method of *free association* as a means for probing the depths of the unconscious. In free association, the subject, usually a patient seeking psychological help, lies on a couch, with the psychoanalyst seated behind him, out of sight. The subject then reports everything that comes into his mind, no matter how trivial or how embarrassing it may seem. The analyst helps by remaining uncritical and aiding the subject to overcome the resistances or mental blocks that prevent him from being completely honest about his thoughts and feelings. Freud found that most unconscious thoughts were sexual in character, and that most emotional problems resulted from conflicts over sexual impulses. More recent theories of psychoanalysis stress the importance of aggression and hostility as additional sources of psychological disturbance.

Freud used free association as a method of therapy and as a source of data about psychological processes and structures. From his observations of behavior in the therapeutic setting, he gradually built the first comprehensive theory of personality. We will have much to say about some of Freud's ideas in later chapters of this book (Chap. 4, pp. 84, 94; Chap. 7, pp. 176–178; Chap. 9, p. 239; Chap. 14). The apparent success of Freud's methods for treating psychological disturbances helped set the pattern for the development of a new professional specialty, clinical psychology, which came into its own during and after World War II, when its techniques were widely applied in the treatment and rehabilitation of those who broke down under the strain of military service.

Mental Testing

Another important innovator was Alfred Binet (1857–1911), a French psychologist. Binet, along with Théodore Simon, undertook the task of identifying school children who would have difficulty benefiting from ordinary classroom education. The work of Binet and Simon resulted in the publication of the first successful scale of intelligence, and was responsible, in large measure, for launching the mental testing movement as well as the more general study of individual differences (Chap. 14). Mental testing (a term suggested by James M. Cattell, one of Wundt's American students) first proved its worth in World War I, and psychological tests are routinely used today in schools, clinics, industries, and the military services for selection, placement, and guidance.

Gestalt Psychology

Max Wertheimer (1880–1943) developed the Gestalt school of psychology. The Gestalt psychologists were dissatisfied with the attempts of introspectionists to break down mental events into their component parts; they rejected the doctrine of *elementarism,* which sought to explain experience by searching out its simplest units. Instead, they argued that experience occurs as a differentiated totality, which takes the form it does because all the parts within it are organized in a specific way. The elementarist might describe facial expression, for example, by analyzing the position of the mouth, the dilation or constriction of the nostrils, the slant of the eyes, and the wrinkles on the forehead. But the Gestalt psychologist would point out that facial expression is not perceived piece by piece. Usually, we respond to the face as a whole, its global characteristics, its gestalt, or overall form. We may easily recognize sadness in the face of a friend without being able to specify whether it is his mouth or eyes that reveal it (cf. also the contrast between the molecular and molar approaches, Chap. 11, pp.).

Gestalt psychology had an immediate impact upon the study of perception, and provided the foundation for Kurt Lewin's (1890–1947) formulation of a comprehensive theory, which has extensive application in the studies of learning, thinking, perception, memory, motivation, personality, social psychology, and human development. The influence of Gestalt psychology can also be seen in the theories of the *holists*, particularly Kurt Goldstein (1878–1965) and Andras Angyal (1902–1960), who argued that the human organism is not divisible into special psychological and physiological structures, but functions as a total, integrated entity—as an *organism*, in the truest sense of the word.

Learning

Psychology developed an interest in *learning* from the research and theories of two outstanding scientists, one Russian, the other American. The Russian, Ivan Pavlov (1849–1936), was a physiologist who identified and described the principles of what is now called *classical conditioning*. Pavlov demonstrated that a normal (*unconditional* or *unconditioned*) reflex, such as an increase in a hungry dog's salivation when food is placed in his mouth (*the unconditional* or *unconditioned stimulus*), could eventually be aroused by an ordinarily nonarousing (*conditional* or *conditioning*) stimulus, such as the sound of a bell.

The usual procedure for demonstrating the conditioning process is to present first the conditioning stimulus (the bell), and shortly thereafter the unconditional stimulus (food). In early trials, the *unconditional* or *unconditioned response* (salivation) occurs only after the animal has been given food. As experimentation progresses, however, salivation begins after the sounding of the bell but before presentation of the food. This salivation represents a *conditional* or *conditioned response* because it is aroused by presenting only the conditional stimulus. Eventually it becomes possible for the experimenter to withhold food altogether after the bell has been sounded; the conditional response will continue to appear for a number of trials. Of course, nothing lasts forever, and the conditional response becomes weaker (undergoes *extinction*) unless it is occasionally *reinforced* by presentation of the unconditional stimulus.

Pavlov preferred to explain these phenomena in physiological terms. Clark Hull (1884–1952), the American scientist, developed a truly psychological theory of learning, founded on the premise that conditioning is the basic process by which habits are formed. Hull's theory reflects the influence of evolutionary doctrine in its emphasis on the fundamental importance of biological *drives* (like hunger and thirst) in behavior. Hull felt that learning takes place only when a response brings about drive-reduction; the process by which reduction of drive causes strengthening of a learned response he called *reinforcement*. Hull's theory is mathematical and *hypothetico-deductive* in character. That is, hypotheses to be tested by experiments are derived logically from a limited number of assumptions and postulates. The theory is validated by testing the accuracy of these derivations in predicting the outcome of controlled observations in the laboratory.

Behaviorism

Finally, it is essential to mention the work of another psychologist, John B. Watson (1878–1958), founder of the still highly influential school of *behaviorism.* Watson was thoroughly anti-introspectionistic. He objected to any reference to "mental processes" in the scientific study of psychology, which he felt was exclusively the study of *behavior,* not of thoughts, ideas, or other subjective events. What we commonly regard as thought or imagery is merely verbal behavior. If communicated to others, such behavior is a *verbal report;* if not communicated it remains *subvocal* (at such a low level of intensity that it does not result in speech). Similarly, to Watson and his followers, perception is not a mental experience, but consists entirely of behavioral discriminations among stimuli. An emotion is not a feeling but a state of the glands and of body chemistry.

Watson stressed the importance of learning in human growth and development. He was a thorough environmentalist, believing that the behavior of the adult human being is entirely the product of the experiences to which he was exposed as a child. Thus, Watson could claim that if he were given complete control of a child's environment, he could produce any kind of adult he wished.

The behaviorist point of view is represented today by B.F. Skinner, whose work with operant conditioning is known to all modern psychologists (Chap. 12). Skinner's development of teaching machines and of the associated concept of programmed learning is familiar to most of the general public in America.

Like Watson, Skinner and his disciples attempt to reduce all of psychology to the study of observable stimulus–response relations. Skinner, however, uses systematically presented reinforcing stimuli to guide or *shape* behavior to desired ends. In his system, a *positive reinforcement* is a stimulus that tends to increase the rate of occurrence of any behavior that immediately precedes its administration. If relations between behavior and reinforcements (reinforcement contingencies) are properly arranged and administered according to a well-planned schedule, very complex sequences of behavior may be shaped. Sometimes they can be made self-sustaining, so that externally administered reinforcement is no longer required for their continuation.

Skinner and his disciples are just as thorough (though far more sophisticated) about their behaviorism as was Watson. To Skinner and many of his followers, even a motivational state is not a subjective phenomenon or feeling or driving force. A motive is merely the set of environmental conditions that produces behavior. Hunger and thirst can be differentiated not by the fact that they feel different, but in that to produce the former the organism must be deprived of food, while to produce the latter it must be deprived of water. Much more is said of these matters in Chapter 12 of this book.

If the reader supposes that the intention of behaviorism is to remove entirely from psychology the troublesome concept of *mind*, he is correct.

Definitions of Psychology

Psychologists have long searched for a completely satisfactory definition of the subject matter of their science. William James (1842–1910), one of the earliest and most famous of American psychologists, called it "the science of mental life." Others, such as the behaviorists, object to use of the word "mental" and prefer to think of it as the "science of observable behavior." Of course, it was John B. Watson who first maintained that psychologists must restrict their attention to things that can be studied directly—observable responses produced by the organism in the presence of known physical stimulation.

The Content of Psychology

Most definitions of psychology attempt to identify the range of phenomena that lie within its province, and every such definition encounters difficulties when it is made to apply to the field as a whole. For example, the behaviorists' definition says that psychology, like all other natural sciences, studies only that which can be observed; it does not deal in such unscientific matters as the study of the soul, which no one can see, touch, or even prove exists. Yet the behaviorists' definition excludes such very real psychological phenomena as dreams, images, pains, and thoughts.

Indeed, any delimiting of psychology can usually be attacked on the grounds that it is not inclusive enough to do justice to the field. Even the apparently broad statement that "psychology is the study of human behavior" suffers because psychologists conduct extensive research with animals. The argument that they study animals only to find out about human beings does not fare too well either, for there will always be someone to argue, with complete justification, that animal behavior is interesting and worth studying in its own right.

There is presently no definition of psychology that describes clearly its entire content and subject matter. Probably the best that can be done is to say that psychology examines the behavior of organisms, with *behavior* taken to include almost all possible forms of activity, and *organisms* taken to include virtually all living creatures. Psychologists are already studying some of the most primitive of creatures, like flatworms and paramecia (Jacobson, 1963), and it is not beyond the realm of possibility that certain psychological laws (perhaps, for instance, the principles of conditioning) will be found to apply not only to animals but to plants as well.

But even the definition of psychology as the study of the behavior of organisms has certain weaknesses. For example, it does not distinguish clearly between psychology and other legitimate fields of investigation (such as biology, physiology, and anthropology) that also study organismic behavior. Nonetheless, it has the considerable advantage of breadth and reflects the scope of psychologists' actual interests.

The Methods of Psychology

Perhaps the major objection of many psychologists to the definition as it now stands is that it does not clearly identify psychology as a science, as a method of study that involves observation, experimentation, and the testing of theories. However, there are eminent authorities who argue that many problems of psychology cannot presently be solved by applying the methods of science. The well-known theory of psychoanalysis, for instance, poses challenging ideas, but the theory itself has certain logical characteristics that not everyone will accept as scientific

(Bronowski, 1966). (See also the discussion of the theory of repression in Chapter 14.)

Actually, it is as difficult to form a precise definition of science as it is to define psychology. Extreme cases of failure to employ scientific methods, such as a gambler placing bets according to intuitive hunches, may be easily recognized, but it is usually difficult to determine exactly where scientific method begins and idle speculation ends. To complicate the problem, psychologists use so many individual methods that the task of evaluating the scientific merits of each would be overwhelming. Some psychologists perform carefully controlled experiments on rats or pigeons in laboratories; some use clinical methods to study the behaviorally disturbed in mental hospitals; some observe people in the everyday environment of the street, the office, and the grocery store; some turn to the analysis of artistic and literary works, as Henry Murray turned to Melville's *Moby Dick* (1951), to verify their points of view.

The variety of methods used by psychologists makes it almost impossible to say whether all can be properly regarded as scientific. However, we can examine some of the most important features of the methods of science and speak, at least in general terms, about what scientists do and how they go about doing it.

Strong Inference

Put most simply, science is a way to answer questions about nature. Fundamentally, science attempts to answer such questions by combining observation with logic; that is, by collecting empirical data and drawing inferences about them.

To improve their ability to observe natural events, scientists invent measuring instruments, like the microscope, to extend and expand the ranges of their sense organs. To improve the accuracy and objectivity of their observations, they record their data as accurately as possible, often employing photography, tape recordings, and automatic timers or counters which virtually eliminate the possibility of human error. Recent studies have shown that the results of psychological research can be strongly influenced by the expectations of the investigator, even when he appears to have gone to great lengths to insure the objectivity of his methods (Rosenthal, 1963, 1966).

To make sense out of their data, scientists classify their observations and relate them to each other. For this purpose, they develop *theories*, tentative explanations of observed facts. Usually, several theories can be used to explain the same set of facts.

Suppose you hear a dog barking. You might propose several possible explanations, and each would constitute a primitive theory. The dog may be hungry; he may have just seen a cat; he may be barking at a stranger walking past his house; or perhaps he is barking at another dog. Nature does not usually make it easy to decide among alternatives. If you were to learn more about the situation and what preceded it, you might find that the barking dog, who had not been fed for 24 hours, is now standing at the base of a fence, on a post of which a cat is sitting, while a stranger is walking by with a dog on a leash.

In such a case, it would obviously be impossible to decide which alternative is correct unless you could somehow control the conditions under which your observations are made. Among several things you could do, one of the easiest would be to wait until the stranger and his dog have passed and are out of sight or smell of the barking dog. If the dog continues to bark, then two of your alternatives (barking at a stranger and barking at another dog) may be regarded as unlikely explanations of the dog's behavior. Another possibility would be to remove the cat from the fence post. Still another would be to offer the dog food.

These attempts to find out which explanation is correct (or, just as important, which are incorrect) are simple *experiments*. An experiment consists of observations made under conditions which are controlled so that the number of explanations for a given phenomenon may be reduced to a minimum. Experimentation is the basic tool of the scientific investigator; it is the method by which he seeks to unify theory and observation. Given the task of explaining why an event occurs, the scientist first tries to imagine as many possibilities as he can. Then he devises experiments with alternative possible outcomes (for example, the dog will continue to bark or he will stop). If the investigator designs his experiments well, each should tell him whether a particular theory may be rejected as a possible explanation for the event he is studying. After a long series of investigations, the careful scientist will be in a position to say that, of all the conceivable explanations, only one is consistent with the facts.

Consider the barking dog. Suppose you remove the cat from the fence post and the dog continues to bark just as vigorously and loudly. You may now reasonably reject any explanation of the dog's barking that depends upon that cat's presence in the dog's visual field. Now, however, the idea may occur that the dog hates the cat so much that even the memory of the cat sitting on the fence infuriates him. This new alternative opens up possibilities for several new experiments to find out why the dog barks.

Although it may come as something of a surprise to learn that science progresses, not by proving that its theories are true, but by deciding that they are false, such is the case. Science advances only when there is vigorous competition among alternative theories and scientists are stimulated to attempt to eliminate existing alternatives and to generate new ones.

The process by which alternative explanations are systematically excluded through experimentation was first described by Francis Bacon (1561–1626), often thought of as the father of modern science. In 1879 it was elaborated by T.C. Chamberlin, an American geologist, who described the "method of multiple hypotheses." More recently, in 1964, it was restated by J.R. Platt, a professor of biophysics at the University of Chicago. Platt calls the process the method of *strong inference*. He complains that many who call themselves scientists do not use it, but he feels strongly that it is the only strategy that deserves to be called the method of science.

Strong Inference in Psychological Research

A series of investigations conducted in the 1940s shows the power of the method of strong inference in answering psychological questions. These investigations concerned the perception of obstacles by the blind. Details may be found in the original references (Supa, Cotzin, and Dallenbach, 1944; Worchel and Dallenbach, 1947; Cotzin and Dallenbach, 1950), and a complete summary of the studies is available in Crafts, Schnierla, Robinson, and Gilbert (1950, pp. 137–169). The interested student may also wish to examine more recent articles by Kellogg (1962) and Rice (1967).

It had long been known that blind persons are frequently capable of detecting obstacles in their paths. The question to be answered by research was: How do they do it? It would seem that all one would have to do is ask blind people directly. Unfortunately, they do not give consistent answers to the question; some of them do not know how they do it.

Supa, Cotzin, and Dallenbach (1944) decided to attack the problem experimentally. As subjects they used four young adults, two of whom had been blind from early life and two of whom had normal vision. The first few experiments were conducted to generate hypotheses, to determine whether the blind subjects were actually better at obstacle perception than the sighted subjects, and to find whether sighted persons could improve in their ability to detect obstacles without vision. If differences did exist, and if sighted subjects performed poorly at first but improved with practice to the point where their performances matched those of the blind, the hypothesis—that the blind possess some unique sensory powers not commanded by sighted people—could be rejected with a high degree of certainty.

Each subject was placed in a long hall and asked to approach an obstacle at a distance of from 6 to 36 feet. The subject reported when he first perceived the obstacle and when he was next to, but not touching, it. Both the blind and the sighted subjects were fitted with blindfolds, to equalize the amount of facial area exposed. This was necessary because one hypothesis was that obstacle perception occurs through the perception of air currents on exposed skin. Failure to reduce the amount of exposed skin of the blind subjects would have given them an extra advantage over the sighted subjects, if that hypothesis were correct.

Are the blind actually better than the sighted in obstacle perception? In the first experiment, in which all subjects walked on a hardwood floor toward the obstacle, the blind were successful on every trial. They did not bump into the obstacle (the end wall of the hallway) even once in 25 trials. The sighted subjects achieved no successes on the first 8 or 9 trials, and took 40 or more trials to accumulate 25 successes each. To the extent that these performances are representative of the performances of blind and sighted persons in general, they encourage rejection of the proposition that the blind are really no better at obstacle perception than sighted subjects would be if they did not use vision to guide them.

Can obstacle perception be learned? This question can be answered by examining overall changes in performance during the course of the investigation. It has already been noted that the successes of the sighted subjects increased after 8 or 9 trials. Their performances continued to improve throughout the research, and by the time of the third experiment they were doing almost as well as the blind. The data therefore contradict the hypothesis that the blind possess special sensory powers that cannot be used by sighted persons.

Does the sound of footsteps facilitate obstacle perception? When blind and sighted subjects performed the same task, but walked without shoes on a soft carpet, the accuracy of their judgments decreased. They shuffled their feet to make noise, and they complained about the loss of sound (Fig. 1.6).

Since it is possible that the blind may have had some advantage by virtue of their ability to orient themselves more accurately to walls parallel to their path of movement, the experimental situation was altered slightly. A large masonite board

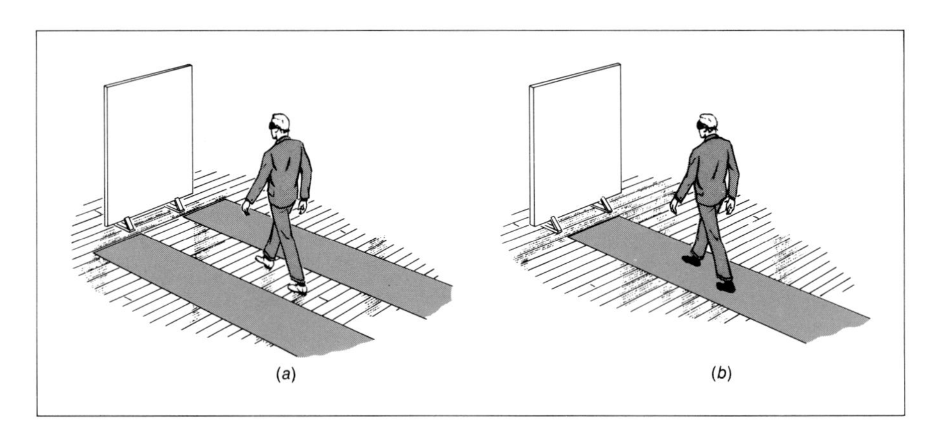

Fig. 1.6. Tests of obstacle perception: (a) Subject walks on hardwood floor, guided by two carpet runners; (b) Subject walks without shoes on carpet. (From Crafts, Schneirla, Robinson, and Gilbert, 1950)

was mounted on a stand and used as a portable obstacle (Fig. 1.6) which could be placed anywhere in the hallway, at any angle to the walls. Tests showed that the performance of the blind subjects was adversely affected by this change, and the screen was used in all subsequent experiments.

Are cutaneously perceived air currents necessary for successful obstacle perception? To answer this question, subjects' skins were completely covered by a heavy felt veil, leather gloves, and, of course, their own clothing. The subject could still hear almost as well as he could without the veil, but he was not able to feel air currents.

The effect of this arrangement was very slight; all four subjects were almost always successful in perceiving the obstacle both from a distance and up close. It was concluded that it is not necessary to perceive air currents in order to avoid obstacles in the absence of vision.

Is it possible to perceive obstacles using skin perception alone? Suppose the subject is allowed to feel air currents but not to hear sounds—will he still perceive obstacles successfully? In the next experiment, subjects' ears were plugged, but their faces (except for the part covered by the blindfold), hands, and arms were left exposed. Under these conditions, all subjects collided with the screen on every one of 100 trials. It seems, then, that cutaneous cues are not sufficient to produce successful avoidance of obstacles.

The hypothesis that obstacle perception is determined by cutaneous cues seems fairly clearly disproved. But what about the objection that plugging the ears or eliminating hearing altogether might somehow adversely affect a subject's ability to respond to cutaneous cues? Can auditory cues be eliminated without actually eliminating hearing?

To accomplish this, one needs to introduce into the subjects' ears a sound that masks all other sounds. This was done with a 1,000 cycle tone, delivered through earphones during the tests. Again it was found that the subjects uniformly and regularly collided with the obstacle.

It appears that reliance on skin perception does not permit subjects to perceive obstacles correctly, and that hearing alone is both necessary and sufficient to the task. But have the experiments yet proved that hearing is critical? Have they completely eliminated the skin as a possible source of perceptual information? In the experiment in which the body was completely covered, subjects were successful in locating the obstacle, but that does not prove that they did it by hearing alone. Air currents did not penetrate to the body in that experiment, but sound waves did. Perhaps subjects responded to the effect of these waves on their skins. In other words, perhaps it is not hearing per se that enables one to perceive obstacles, but sound waves acting on the rest of the body. The preceding experiments make this possibility seem unlikely, but it is nonetheless possible that plugs in the ears or a masking tone make the subject less sensitive to cutaneous effects of sound waves.

To answer this objection, the experimenters isolated each subject in a soundproof room. An experimenter then carried a microphone with him and walked toward the obstacle while the subject listened via earphones to the sound of the experimenter's footsteps. The subject reported his perception of the obstacle over a sound system.

The results were unambiguous; perception was as accurate under these conditions as it was when subjects had both auditory and cutaneous cues available. It therefore can be concluded that sound is both a necessary and sufficient condition for perception of obstacles by the blind. Repetition of the same experiment, using pure tones of various frequencies instead of footsteps, produced the same findings (Cotzin and Dallenbach, 1950). However, it was noted that success rates were much higher with high-pitched tones (10,000 cps or higher) than with low-pitched tones.

Obstacle perception in the deaf-blind. The ultimate test of these findings would be to use subjects who are both deaf and blind. Ten such subjects were found and examined by Worchel and Dallenbach (1947). Even under the most favorable conditions these subjects did poorly in the test situation. Collisions with the obstacle were frequent, and improvement in performance was slight. Subjects with limited hearing or vision showed some success, but others with more complete losses did not.

Behavior in Extralaboratory Settings

This series of experiments shows how experimental manipulations may be used to provide answers to questions about behavior. At first, the question was simply: Can obstacles be perceived without sight? An affirmative answer led to a more specific question: Can the ability to perceive obstacles without vision be learned? An affirmative answer led to a still more specific question: How are obstacles perceived in the absence of vision? This question was reduced to the alternate possibilities—by hearing or by means of the cutaneous senses. A series of experiments then eliminated the alternative of skin senses as the crucial factor. These findings have obvious practical implications for training of the blind. They imply that such training should emphasize substitution of auditory cues for visual cues, and place little or no emphasis on factors such as perception of air currents or temperature differentials.

Can we now conclude that blind persons actually detect obstacles in extralaboratory settings only through hearing? If you are acquainted with people who are blind, you will know that the answer to this is *no;* they do not rely solely on hearing for perceiving obstacles any more than sighted people rely solely on vision. Some evidence supporting this is available from parts of the research described previously which have not yet been mentioned.

When Supa, Cotzin, and Dallenbach were preparing their portable obstacle, they tried several materials before settling on masonite. The others (plywood, whether unfinished or finished with shellac, varnish, paint, or wax) were unsatisfactory because subjects detected their odors even at a distance. Masonite was selected because it is odor free. However, for a blind person in a natural situation, odor may often provide useful information about the structure of his environment, and the investigators' observations reveal that when such information is available it is used effectively.

Then, too, many blind persons use canes, even for travel in familiar environments, because the tactile cues provided by the cane are useful in exploring the space ahead of them. (The white cane is also useful because it identifies the walker as blind and informs others of his special problems, but that lies outside of this investigation.)

In the blind, as in the sighted, perception is almost always overdetermined. That is, there are many different kinds of cues which work together to determine how something is perceived with regard to motivation, and with regard to stimulus–response relations in general). You can identify fresh bread by its smell, texture, and taste as well as by its visual characteristics, and you can identify a trumpet by how it sounds as well as how it looks.

Experimentation and the method of strong inference enable the scientist to analyze complex situations, pitting one factor against another, so that he can answer such questions as: "Which is most important in determining sales of a food product—how it tastes, how it smells, what it looks like, how much it costs, what kind of package it comes in, or how difficult it is to prepare?" To accomplish his purpose he must often create situations of a type that would rarely occur in real life (Chap. 11, pp. 307–11). He sacrifices the naturalness of the real situation for the precision of the laboratory. Nevertheless, as you can see, his finds may have important practical implications.

Preview

In the final analysis, psychology is what psychologists do; there is no better way to approach the subject than by discovering what it is that these investigators find so worth the doing. It is therefore appropriate now to examine the things that make this subject worth studying—the thought and work of psychologists.

Succeeding chapters examine a variety of subjects and problems whose investigation psychologists currently find interesting and rewarding. Each of these problems is examined in some detail and depth, and every chapter emphasizes the ways in which psychologists seek answers to questions about experience and behavior by employing the methods of science.

The next two chapters take up problems in the field of perception: the perceptual world of the infant (Chap. 2) and seeing in a transformed world (Chap. 3). Following these are chapters on remembering and forgetting (Chap. 4) and psycholinguistics (the psychological study of language, Chap. 5). Chapter 6 turns to a problem in physiological psychology, the central regulation of feeding behavior, a subject studied primarily through research on rats. Chapter 7, on sleep and dreams, shows how methods of physiological research are used to study an important human psychological process. The next three chapters show how psychologists study such complex phenomena as stress (Chap. 8), aggression (Chap. 9), and decision making (Chap. 10). Two chapters are then devoted to describing general approaches to the study of psychology that have become important in recent years: naturalism (Chap. 11) is a reaction against traditional efforts to confine scientific psychology to research in the laboratory; operant methodology (Chap. 12) is an attempt to use knowledge of behavior gained in the laboratory to solve practical problems of the sort that often appear in education, industry, and the psychological clinic. The last three chapters cover topics in the general fields of personality and clinical psychology. Chapter 13 describes research on the body image and shows how intriguing and difficult it is to investigate complex personality processes. Chapter 14 uses research on the concept of repression to show how psychologists build tests to evaluate theories and measure individual differences. Finally, Chapter 15 describes research on a rather unconventional approach to the study of an age-old problem in abnormal psychology, schizophrenia.

The 14 chapters which follow offer a selected sample of problems upon which psychologists are actively working. All of these are important, but of course all the significant problems of psychology are not exhausted by the materials in this text. Psychology has long passed the stage in which a full summarization of its subject matter could be contained in a single volume. Study of this book will give you a good idea of what psychologists are doing, and, more importantly, how and why they are doing it. We hope it will encourage you to pursue the subject even more thoroughly in the future.

Glossary

Behaviorism: an approach that stresses the study of observable behavior only; a reaction against introspectionism.

Conditioning (classical): a procedure by which a neutral stimulus (the conditional or contioning stimulus) is made to elicit a response (the conditional or conditioned response) that previously occurred only in the presence of another stimulus (the unconditional or unconditioned stimulus).

Conditioning (operant): a procedure in which reinforcement is systematically applied or withheld to increase or decrease the probability of occurrence of a preceding behavioral act.

Constant error: in psychophysics, the magnitude of the difference between the setting at which the subject typically reports two stimuli to be of the same intensity and the setting at which the stimuli are objectively equivalent.

Constant stimuli: in psychophysics, a method for determining absolute and difference thresholds. The subject judges stimuli presented in pairs. One stimulus is standard, the other is variable.

Detection threshold: modern term for the absolute threshold (*see* threshold).

Elementarism: a viewpoint that emphasizes the necessity for psychology to discover and study the simplest possible units of behavior or experience (*see* Glossary, Chap. 11, molecular).

Extinction: reduction of the probability of occurrence of a conditioned response by the removal of reinforcement.

Functionalism: the view that behavior is adaptive, useful in the process of survival and adjustment to the environment.

Gestalt psychology: an approach to psychology that emphasizes the study of wholes, configurations, and global units of behavior and experience; a reaction against elementarism.

Holism: a viewpoint that emphasizes the organismic unity of living creatures, particularly the inseparability of mind and body in human beings.

Introspection: an approach to psychology that emphasizes the study of experience through subjects' reports of sensations, thoughts, or emotions.

JND: just noticeable difference; a difference threshold (see threshold).

Just noticeable differences (method of): Weber's approach to the study of sensory discrimination, in which the variable stimulus is initially equivalent to the standard stimulus. The subject reports when he detects a difference between the two.

Limen: See threshold.

Method of adjustment: in psychophysics, a method in which the subject adjusts the variable stimulus to apparent equality with the standard stimulus.

Method of limits: Fechner's approach to the study of sensory discrimination, in which the variable stimulus is initially set to noticeable nonequivalence with the standard. The subject reports when the two appear to be equivalent.

Method of single stimuli: in psychophysics, a method in which the subject assigns numbers to stimuli according to their apparent magnitudes.

Point of subjective equality: in psychophysics, the setting at which the subject typically reports two stimuli to be of the same magnitude.

Psychoanalysis: a theory of personality and a method for treating abnormalities of behavior, developed by Sigmund Freud in the early twentieth century.

Psychometrics: the techniques and procedures of psychological measurement.

Psychophysics: the study of relations between perceptual responses and physical stimuli.

Reinforcement: a stimulus that alters the probability of occurrence of a response.

Strong inference: the strategy of science which uses experimentation as a means for reducing the number of possible explanations of a phenomenon.

Threshold: the minimum stimulus value at which a response will occur. In psychophysics, the *absolute threshold* is the minimum value at which the presence of a stimulus is detected; the *difference threshold* is the minimum detectable change in the stimulus.

Transition point: in psychophysics, the stimulus setting at which a subject's responses change from reports of stimulus equivalence to reports of nonequivalence, or vice versa.

References

Bronowski, J. The logic of the mind. *Amer. Scientist,* 1966, **54,** 1–14.

Cotzin, M., and K.M. Dallenbach. "Facial vision": The role of pitch and loudness in the perception of obstacles by the blind. *Amer. J. Psychol.,* 1950, **63,** 484–515.

Crafts, L.W., T.D. Schneirla, E.E. Robinson, and R.W. Gilbert. *Recent experiments in psychology.* (2nd ed.) New York: McGraw-Hill, 1950.

Galanter, E. Contemporary psychophysics. In R. Brown, E. Galanter, E.H. Hess, and G. Mandler, *New directions in psychology I.* New York: Holt, Rinehart and Winston, 1962.

Jacobson, A.L. Learning in flatworms and annelids. *Psychol. Bull.,* 1963, **60,** 74–94.

Kellogg, W.N. Sonar system of the blind. *Science,* 1962, **137,** 399–404.

Krantz, D.H. Threshold theories of signal detection. *Psychol. Rev.,* 1969, **76,** 308–324.

Murray, H.A. *In Nomine Diaboli. New England Quarterly,* 1951, **24,** 435–452. (Reprinted in *Psychology Today,* 1968, **2,** September, 64-69.)

Platt, J.R. Strong inference. *Science,* 1964, **146,** 347–353.

Rice, C.E. Human echo perception. *Science,* 1967, **155,** 656–664.

Rosenthal, R. *Experimenter effects in behavioral research.* New York: Appleton-Century-Crofts, 1966.

______. On the social psychology of the psychological experiment: The experimenter's hypothesis as unintended determinant of experimental results. *Amer. Scientist,* 1963, **51,** 268–283.

Stevens, S.S. Mathematics, measurement, and psychophysics. In S.S. Stevens (Ed.), *Handbook of experimental psychology.* New York: Wiley, 1951.

———. The surprising simplicity of sensory metrics. *Amer. Psychologist*, 1962, **17,** 29–39.
———. On the psychophysical law. *Psychol. Rev.*, 1957, **64,** 153–181.
———. To honor Fechner and repeal his law. *Science,* 1961, **133,** 80–86.
Supa, M., M. Cotzin, and K.M. Dallenbach. "Facial vision"; the perception of obstacles by the blind. *Amer. J. Psychol.,* 1944, **57,** 133–183.
Woodworth, R.S. *Experimental psychology.* New York: Holt, Rinehart and Winston, 1938.
Worchel, P., and K.M. Dallenbach. "Facial vision": Perception of obstacles by the deaf-blind. *Amer. J. Psychol.*, 1947, **60,** 502–533.

Recommended General Readings

Boring, E.G. *A history of experimental psychology.* (2nd ed.) New York: Appleton-Century-Crofts, 1950.
Hall, C.S., and G. Lindzey. *Theories of personality.* New York: Wiley, 1957.
Herrnstein, R.J., and E.G. Boring (Eds.) *A source book in the history of psychology.* Cambridge, Mass.: Harvard University Press, 1966.
Hilgard, E.R., and G.H. Bower. *Theories of learning.* (3rd ed.) New York: Appleton-Century-Crofts, 1966.
Marx, M.H., and W.A. Hillix. *Systems and theories in psychology.* New York: McGraw-Hill, 1963.
Murphy, G. *Historical introduction to modern psychology.* (Rev. ed.) New York: Harcourt, Brace & World, 1949.
Watson, R.I. *The great psychologists: From Aristotle to Freud.* Philadelphia: Lippincott, 1963.

2 The Perceptual World of the Infant

William James (1890) speculated that the perceptual world of the newborn infant is a "blooming, buzzing confusion," a chaotic conglomeration of light points, unorganized and continuously changing. Speculation about the infant's perceptual world was popular in philosophy and early scientific psychology, but the absence of empirical investigations made these speculations pointless and inconclusive; after a while, interest in them abated.

Unlike old soldiers, engaging scientific questions neither die nor fade away, but enter a state of temporary retirement, eventually to return in slightly new dress. Interest in the origins of perception has been true to form. The question was rediscovered in the decade of the sixties. Unlike the earlier history, however, the new interest has been marked by ingenious and instructive experimental investigation.

At best, the investigation of perception is difficult, since perception is essentially a private event and perceptual experience cannot be observed directly. Perception is the process that intervenes between the impingement of physical stimulation on the sensory receptors and the report of what is perceived. If the process of perception is hidden from view, how can the experimental psychologist investigate it? The investigator must depend on indirect observations which are assumed to indicate the nature of the observer's perceptual experience. On the simplest level, the observer's verbal description may be accepted as a perceptual report. If an observer says that one form looks like a circle and a second looks like a triangle, we may decide to accept this report as an accurate indication of the observer's perceptual experience. However, on most occasions, the experimenter tries to ascertain what the observer perceives with the help of a nonverbal perceptual indicator, thus avoiding difficulties that may arise from variations and imprecisions in the subject's verbal repertoire. For example, suppose an experimenter wants to determine whether the perceived size of an object depends on its distance from the observer. With the psychophysical procedure called the *method of adjustment,* the subject is instructed to adjust the size of a nearby variable-size comparator to match the size of the more distant object. Some of the psychophysical procedures for assessing perception have been described in Chapter 1 (see also Kling and Riggs, 1971).

What procedures are available for determining what an infant perceives? Obviously, verbal perceptual report is eliminated from consideration. In this respect, the infant and animal subject present similar difficulties. However, from another viewpoint, the animal is easier to study, because many animals possess a stable repertoire of motor responses soon after birth, while the human infant lacks coordinated motor responses. Periods of random free ranging movement, such as hand waving, alternate with periods of profound sleep. Indeed, occasionally one gets the impression that the infant is sleeping with eyes open, thus posing peculiar problems in the interpretation of his activities. (The infant loses this special ability, but apparently it is recovered sometime during the first two years of undergraduate life.)

The impossibility of verbal communication coupled with a high level of random motor behavior are obvious obstacles in the study of infant perception. Those interested in answering questions about the genesis of perception looked to other kinds of evidence. One possibility, first mentioned prominently by the eighteenth century French philosophers Molyneaux and Descartes, called for the study of people who had been born blind and had their sight restored surgically. In 1932 Senden published a compilation of such cases, and there have been a number of new reports since then, most recently by Gregory and Wallace (1963). Although study of the newly-seeing might appear to be a promising approach, many serious difficulties attend it, and consequently the results of various studies have been contradictory (Epstein, 1964).

Another alternative to the study of infants is to introduce experimental procedures that presumably restore the adult to the earlier primal state of perception. This may seem to require rather drastic experimental intervention, but investigators have relied simply on interposing a special optical medium between the environment and the eyes of the observers. The favorite medium for this purpose has been the prism, mounted in eyeglass frames (Chap. 3). The wedge prism, mounted with base in a vertical orientation, bends the incoming light toward the base and makes objects appear to be displaced in the direction of the prism apex. Thus, if you wore a base-right wedge prism, the pencil on your desk would look to the left of its true location. If you were to reach for it without seeing your hand, you would fail to make contact because you would reach too far to the left. The right-angle prism, properly oriented, produces a left-right inversion and a tilting of the visual scene by as much as 180 degrees; the visual scene would therefore appear upside down and right-left reversed.

It is presumed that the interposition of prisms which alter the usual relationships between environment and the *optic array* (the light that impinges on the retina), as well as the relationships between action and perception, reinstates the original conditions of infant perception. Observers who wear these distorting prisms *adapt* and regain normal preexperimental perception after the prisms are removed. The process of adaptation may be analogous to development of perception in the infant, but the relevance of adaptation phenomena for questions concerning the growth of perception can be questioned. In spite of the difficulties, we have no recourse but to study the infant himself in order to gain an understanding of the genesis of perception.

Form and Pattern Perception

An inspection of my writing desk reveals a typical collection of objects resting on a continuous surface. This low-level articulation of the visual field into objects and background is often called *figure-ground* perception. At the same time, in addition to distinguishing between figure and ground, I perceive the different forms or shapes of specific objects; square, circular, and rectangular shapes are distinguished effortlessly. Furthermore, if I change my viewing position, or if the positions of the objects are changed, the perceived shapes of the objects are unaffected. A coin does not assume a variety of elliptical perceived shapes as changes in viewing angle are introduced: the perceived shape remains constant. Would the foregoing descriptions of the perceptual world apply equally to the newborn infant, or does the infant experience a "blooming, buzzing confusion"? The next section describes several experiments which help to answer this question.

The Stimulus-Preference Method

The only evidence that an infant can discriminate between two forms that are different for the adult would be for the infant to be observed to behave differently toward the two forms. There is no differential or preferential responding without prior perceptual discrimination.

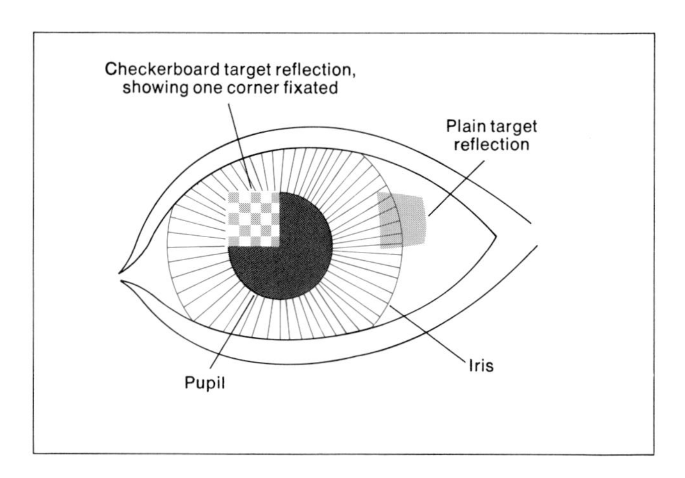

Fig. 2.1. Schematic drawing of infant's eye as seen by the experimenter when checked and plain squares are exposed. Generally the target reflection overlaps the pupil to a greater degree than shown here. (From Fantz, 1965)

The difficulty in securing evidence of this sort lies in the fact that the very young infant has very few stable behaviors. Fortunately, there is one spontaneous, stable, observable response that appears very early. The infant will turn his eyes to direct his gaze at visual stimuli. Suppose two different visual forms, such as a triangle and circle, are presented simultaneously, side by side. The infant might respond in a number of ways: he might look at the blank background and at the figures for equal amounts of time; he might look at the figures most of the time, dividing his looking evenly between the two forms; he might look at the figures most of the time, but divide his looking disproportionately, favoring one or the other form. The last outcome is especially interesting. If the infant directs his gaze more often at either the circle or the triangle, then he must be able to discriminate between them. Differential or preferential direction of gaze presupposes discrimination.

This application of the stimulus-preference method requires a procedure for determining the direction of gaze. There is an objective indicator which can be easily recorded: the position of the corneal reflection (those images you can see when you look into someone's eyes) relative to the pupil indicates the direction of gaze. When a target is being fixated (looked at directly), its corneal reflection is centered on the pupil. Figure 2.1 will help you understand this measure of fixation. It shows the positions on the eye of a checkerboard target and a plain target when the lower left corner of the checkerboard is fixated. The position of the target relative to the pupil can be reliably detected from direct observation of the infant's eyes, or an automatic photographic system can photograph the infant's eyes at regular intervals, such as once each second, securing a practically continuous record of looking behavior. The position of the corneal reflection shows how the infant has distributed its gaze between alternative targets or among the several parts of one target.

In order for the investigator to record corneal reflection, the infant lies on his back in a cradle with a comfortable head restraining device. At a short distance above the infant's head and in his frontal parallel plane (parallel with his forehead), two targets are presented for simultaneous side by side viewing. At regular intervals

Fig. 2.2. Visual acuity was tested with stripes: 1/8, 1/16, 1/32, and 1/64 of an inch wide similar to those illustrated above. Each pattern was displayed with a gray square of equal brightness 10 inches from the infant's eyes. The finest pattern consistently preferred to gray showed how narrow a stripe the infant could perceive.

the two targets are interchanged to guard against misinterpretation of a position preference for a form preference. For example, if the infant looks to the left on 80 per cent of the observations, and the triangle has always been the left-hand member of the pair, we cannot decide whether the infant's preference is based on position or form. Alternating the positions of the forms permits separation of form and position preference.

The findings obtained with this method will now be brought to bear on three questions: (1) How acute is the infant's vision? (2) Can infants discriminate between forms? (3) Do infants exhibit a consistent preference for certain types of form?

Visual Acuity

The ability to discriminate between patterned stimuli presupposes the capacity to resolve their details. This capacity to resolve visual details is called *visual acuity*. Everyone who has undergone an ophthalmological examination has been subjected to tests of visual acuity, the most familiar of which is the Snellen eye chart, which contains rows of letters of various sizes. Another test measures acuity by examining responses to a series of graded *acuity gratings*. This test is designed to determine how far apart two points must be separated in order to be seen as two, rather than one. The smaller the minimal separation required, the better the individual's acuity. The acuity grating consists of alternating black and white stripes of varying width. The subject is required to indicate the orientation of the lines, for example, upright, horizontal, oblique. Obviously, at the point where the observer cannot resolve the detail of the grating, the stripes merge into a uniform gray and he is unable to designate their orientation.

Fantz, Ordy, and Udelf (1962) adapted the acuity grating test to study the acuity of 37 infants of one to 22 weeks of age. Each test trial consisted of the presentation of a square grating with vertical black and white stripes of equal width paired with a uniform gray square, matched in luminous reflectance (brightness). Figure 2.2 shows four of the test gratings. The rationale of the test follows from the preceding discussion of the stimulus-preference method. If the infant directs his gaze more often or for greater duration at the grating or the paired gray square, we can infer that visual acuity is at least as fine as the separation indicated by that grating.

You would be correct in inferring that the hedging at the end of that last sentence means that some qualification is intended. The usefulness of the stimu-

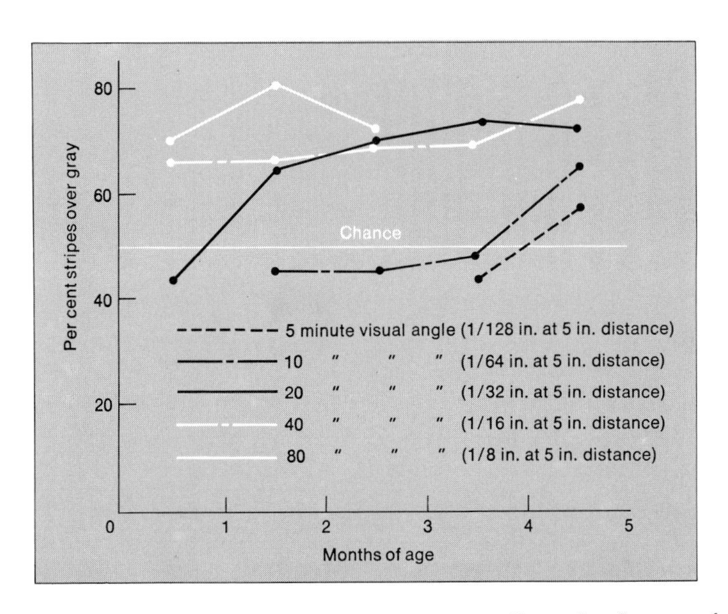

Fig. 2.3. Differential strength of visual fixation to squares with varying fineness of pattern, averaged for tests at three distances for all infants at a given age. (Encircled points indicate that 75 per cent of individual tests showed predominant response to pattern.) (From Fantz, Ordy, and Udelf, 1962)

lus-preference method is qualified by the fact that *absence* of differential looking does not logically lead to any conclusions about the ability to discriminate. Absence of differential responding does *not* imply absence of discrimination. If the infant directs his gaze equally often to two forms, we cannot know whether he is unable to see the difference or merely does not care about the difference. Usually this limitation is not critical. Nevertheless, we must confine our conclusions to specifying what the infant can see, omitting statements regarding failure to discriminate.

Figure 2.3 shows the results of the experiment described above. The per cent of test trials on which the infants looked predominantly at the grating is plotted against ages of the infants. In Figure 2.3 the width of the stripe in the grating is specified as the visual angle subtended by the stripe at the eye. For present purposes you may understand this to mean the width of the retinal image of the stripe. Thus, smaller visual angles mean finer gratings. A grating with stripes of width 1/128 of an inch at a distance of 5 inches subtends an angle of 5 minutes (one-twelfth of a degree), and a grating with stripes of width 1/8 of an inch at the same distance subtends an angle of 80 minutes (one degree plus 20 minutes). Figure 2.3 shows that between the ages of one and two months, infants make differential responses to gratings with widths of 40 minutes (stripe widths of 1/16 of an inch at a distance of 5 inches). Note also that acuity increases as the infant matures. By the fourth month, a grating with stripes of width 1/32 of an inch at 5 inches (20 minutes) can be resolved. (The standard for adults is one minute.)

Subsequent studies under optimal conditions of illumination have given evidence of even finer acuity. Three month old infants responded differentially to 3.5-minute stripes, 1/64 of an inch stripes viewed from a distance of 15 inches. Seven infants under 24 hours old fixated 1/8 of an inch stripes longer than a solid gray area at a distance of 9 inches.

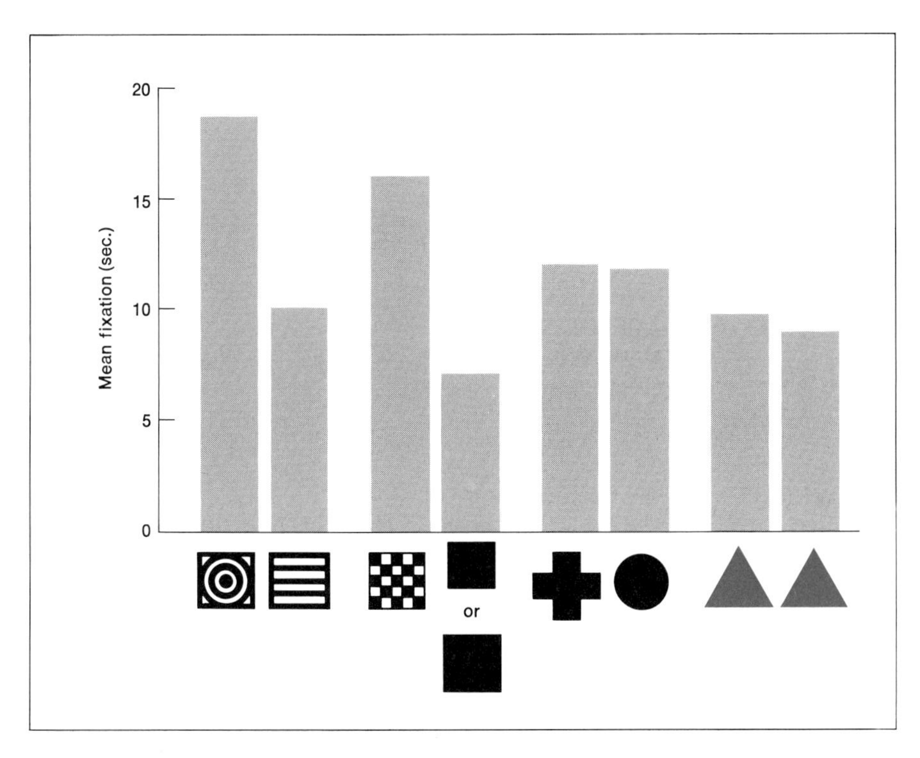

Fig. 2.4. Visual preference among eight stimulus targets presented in pairs, showing the fixation time during one minute for each pair, averaged for repeated tests of 22 infants ranging from one week to six months of age. White areas were gray to match the inside of the stimulus chamber. The checked pattern was paired on two successive exposures with squares of the same area of red and of same overall size; other pairs were equated in area of red. The large squares measured five inches; others are to scale. (Adapted from Fantz, 1965)

These results give evidence of adequate visual acuity early in life. The infant does not see amorphous masses of light and dark; he perceives a field of articulated patterns. This experiment also suggests that the infant prefers striped patterns to the gray square, since the infants tended to look more often and for longer durations at the striped gratings. In other words, they displayed not only differential fixation, but also preferential fixation. We will return to the question of visual preference later in this chapter.

Form Discrimination

The acuity study shows that the visual system functions effectively soon after birth. Evidence from recent studies suggests that the infant also can discriminate between forms. The procedure in these studies is similar to that followed in the acuity study. A pair of visual targets is exposed, and a record is kept of the infant's direction of gaze. If the infant looks more often or longer at one member of the pair, we can conclude that he can discriminate between them.

The results of one experiment (Fantz, 1961) are shown in Figure 2.4, with the paired targets illustrated at the bottom of the bar graph. The data are the mean number of seconds that each member of the pair was fixated during a one minute test. The infants give evidence of discriminating between a bullseye and a striped pattern and between a checkerboard and a solid square. Surprisingly, there is no evidence of discrimination between a cross and a circle, but other investigators (for example, Saayman *et al.*, 1964) have shown that three month old infants can discriminate between these forms.

Form Preference

The two experiments we have described provide a small sample of the increasing evidence that form perception is highly organized early in life. Even more interesting is the possibility that, in addition to the capability for form discrimination, there may also exist form preference; the infant may not only be able to see the difference between forms, but may have preferences for one form over another.

Novelty. Experiments by Saayman *et al.* (1964) and Fantz (1964) give evidence of preference for novel visual forms over familiar ones. The study consisted of three stages: (1) a pair of targets was presented to determine the infant's spontaneous looking behavior; (2) one member of the pair was presented alone for a relatively extended period; (3) the pair of targets was presented again. The critical data involve the differences in distribution of looking between the first and third stages. Saayman *et al.* tested three month old infants with three pairs of targets: *form only*—red cross vs. red circle; *color only*—red circle vs. black circle; *form and color*—red cross vs. black circle. In the first stage, Saayman *et al.* recorded the distribution of looking time between the two forms of each pair on a 60 second exposure. In the second stage, from each pair, the stimulus at which the infant had looked *longest* was exposed alone for four and one-half minutes. In addition to these familiarization exposures involving preferred forms, a fourth familiarization trial was included which presented the nonpreferred member of the third pair, that is, the stimulus from the third pair at which the infant had looked *least*. In the third stage the original pairs were presented again.

Look at the bar graph in Figure 2.5, which shows the mean looking time before and after the second stage (familiarization) for the nonfamiliarized stimulus (upper half) and the familiarized stimulus (lower half), in other words, the stimulus presented in the second stage. Results indicate that the effect of familiarizing a stimulus was to shift the infant's looking in the direction of the nonfamiliarized stimulus; the infant preferred the novel form. Fantz (1964) reported similar results, and also found that this preference for novelty increases with age. It is not present in one to two month old infants, appearing first between the ages of two and three months.

Complexity. Visual forms and patterns differ in complexity. Everyone would probably agree that a striped grating is more complex than a uniformly gray square. The results of the acuity and form discrimination studies suggest that complexity of form may be a dimension that controls the infant's looking. The unresolved problem has been to determine the exact relationship between level of complexity and preference. Different investigators have reported evidence of preference for high, medium, and low complexity, an inconsistency which may be due to the lack of standard measures of complexity which can be used to scale visual forms. In addition, there is the possibility that preferences for complexity change very rapidly

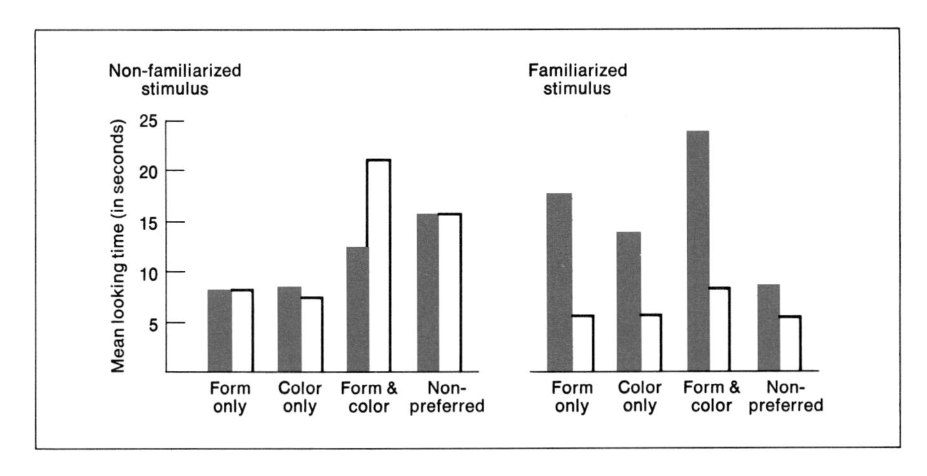

Fig. 2.5. Mean time looking at familiarized and nonfamiliarized stimuli pre- and postfamiliarization, under four conditions. Shaded bars indicate prefamiliarization; unshaded bars represent postfamiliarization. (From Saayman, Ames, and Moffett, 1964)

during the first several months of life (Brennan, Ames, and Moore, 1966), so that studies yield different outcomes depending on the age of the infants.

An example of the efforts to determine the relationship between complexity and preference is the study of seventeen newborn infants, two to four days old, reported by Hershenson, Munsinger, and Kessen (1965). They prepared three irregularly contoured shapes whose complexity was defined by the number of independent turns or angles in the contour. The three shapes, from least to most complex, had 5, 10, or 20 independent turns. All possible pairings of the three shapes were presented. Hershenson *et al.* found that newborns looked most frequently at the form of intermediate complexity (10 turns). Other investigators (such as Fantz, 1966; Lewis *et al.*, 1963) have found preference for the most complex of several patterns, and Hershenson, in another study (1964), for the least complex. Only future research can resolve this confusing state of affairs. This research will probably be a longitudinal study (that is, it will follow the same infants through the first six months of life) and will use a wide range of degrees of stimulus complexity.

Determination of the dimensions of stimulation that control preferential looking will contribute importantly to our understanding of the early development of form perception. We know now that very young infants can discriminate form. Subsequent development of form and pattern perception probably depends on exploration of the visual field. A preference for novelty would insure that exploration will occur, and a preference for complexity may determine the order in which different parts of the field are explored. These preferences may provide the opportunity for development of preferences on other bases. For example, Stechler (1964) has reported that infants two to four days old, exhibit a preference for a schematic face, compared to a die pattern or blank card. This may reflect an initial preference based on complexity. For this reason, the infant may favor the mother's face over other visual stimuli. This favoritism may provide the opportunity for establishing the relationship between mother and positive reinforcement that maintains and strengthens the preference.

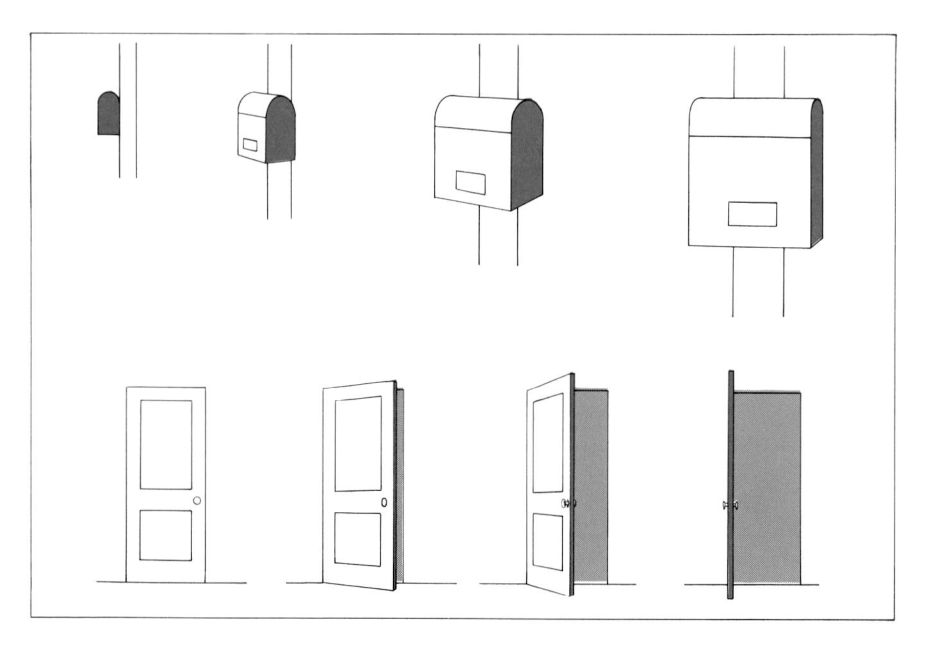

Fig. 2.6. Changes of projective (retinal image) shape that occur when the observer moves (mailbox) or when the object changes its orientation (door). (From J.J. Gibson, 1950)

The Perception of Shapes in Space

The studies we have described have examined the infant's responses to visual forms oriented in the frontal parallel plane, parallel to the subject's forehead. In this position an object will project a retinal image fairly faithful to the shape of the object. A square shape will project a square image, a circular shape a circular image, and so on. As long as we confine ourselves to two-dimensional targets oriented in the frontal plane, we may conclude erroneously that projective (retinal image) shape is always an undistorted miniature copy of the objective shape. Observing only projections of frontal plane shapes, we may infer that there is a one-to-one relationship between projective and objective shape, and that the latter is the sole determinant of the former. But as soon as we widen our consideration to include targets that are displaced from the frontal plane, we find that both of these conclusions are false. For every new orientation of the target, resulting from rotation of the target or movement of the observer, there is a different projective shape. Thus a circle projects a whole family of retinal shapes, ranging from a very narrow ellipse to a circle, depending on its orientation to the observer. This fact of geometry is illustrated in Figure 2.6. Therefore, contrary to the expectations we might derive from the frontal parallel case, projective shape is not determined solely by physical shape, and there are many different projective shapes that can be produced by one constant physical shape.

From a description of the relationship between retinal (projective) shape and physical (objective) shape, let us move to the relationship between objective shape and perceived shape. Under normal conditions of viewing, what happens to perceived shape when we view an object from different positions? The simple answer can be easily confirmed—there is very little change of perceived shape. The rectangular picture frame hanging on the wall looks rectangular whether we face it head-on

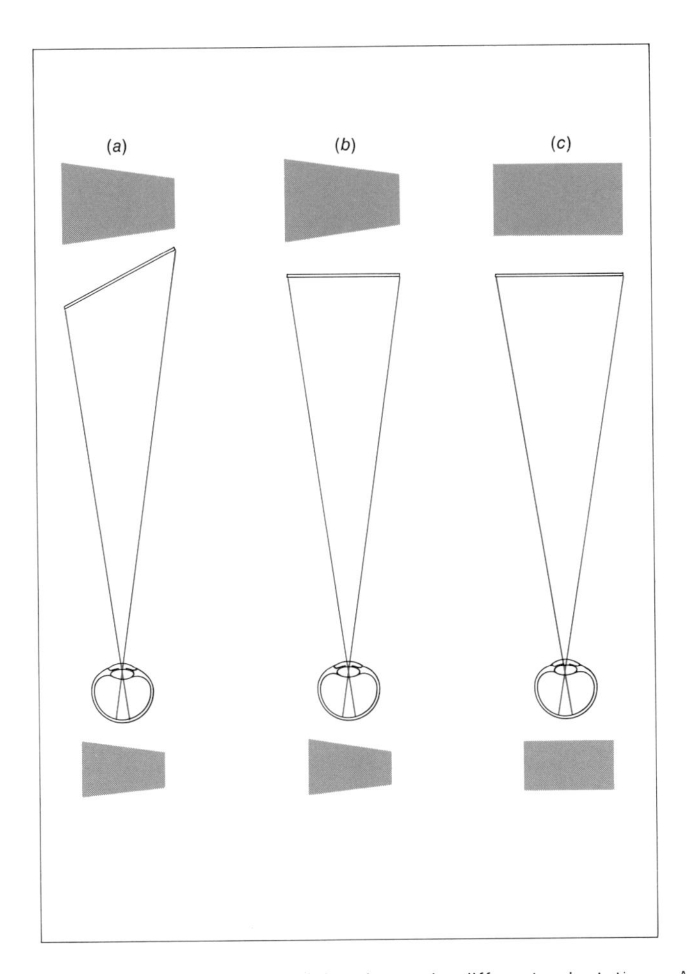

Fig. 2.7. Shape constancy is illustrated by shapes in different orientations. A rectangle presented in the parallel plane (c) projects a rectangular image on the retina (bottom) and is seen as a rectangle. Presented at a slant, it projects a trapezoidal image (a), yet is usually seen as a rectangle. A trapezoid in the parallel plane projects the same shape (b), but it is seen as a trapezoid. (From Bower, 1966b)

or view it from an angle. Similarly, as we walk around a table, it appears to maintain a constant shape. With a special attitude of observation it is possible to see the shape becoming deformed, but if we assume the "natural" object-oriented attitude, perceived shape appears constant despite variations in the retinal image. Shape constancy is defined graphically in Figure 2.7.

The initial response of many readers is to dismiss the commonplace fact of shape constancy as too simple to require discussion. After all, the shapes of objects do not in fact change when the viewing orientation changes, so constancy of perceived shape is only to be expected. A moment's consideration will convince you that this claim is based on the mistaken premise that the shapes of objects affect us directly, that they are impressed on the retina of the eyes much like the shape of an object grasped in the hand will impress itself on the skin. However, the perceived shape of the object is mediated by its retinal image shape. If the retinal shape of the object remained constant when orientation changed, the occurrence of shape constancy could indeed be explained simply (although we would need a complicated theory of light propagation). But projective shape changes when orientation varies, and since perceived shape is mediated by projective shape we might expect perceived shape to be highly variable.

If you have been convinced by this counterargument, you may entertain another seemingly obvious explanation of shape constancy. The shapes of most objects are familiar to us from frequent experience with the shape in various orientations. Having learned the true physical shape of the object, we become invulnerable to projective shape changes that accompany changes in orientation and see the shape in conformity with its remembered frontal parallel shape. Despite the apparent validity of this claim, it is incorrect. Laboratory studies of perceived shape have found that shape constancy prevails for unfamiliar nonrepresentative shapes, and since in such cases memories of shapes past could not have determined perceived shape, it is unlikely that prior knowledge is the explanation of constancy.

The explanation is that shape constancy is possible because, along with projective shape, the observer also has information about the orientation of the object. Perceived shape is determined by an integration of projective shape and perceived slant. When cues for slant are available, the combination of a specific projective shape and a specific perceived slant determines what shape is perceived. When the cues lead to accurate slant perception, changes in orientation that produce changes in projective shape are seen as the changing orientation of a *constant shape*. It has been demonstrated that reducing the information available for determining slant leads to a breakdown of constancy (so that slanted rectangles look trapezoidal), and experimental manipulation of slant cues leads to predictable errors of shape perception (Epstein and Park, 1963).

We have been describing the perceptual experience of an adult. How much of this is true for the newborn infant? When forms turn from the infant's frontal plane, or when the infant changes his viewing position, do the objects in his visual field seem plastic, their shapes changing with every new orientation, or do they appear to have a constant shape? Is the infant able to integrate projective shape changes and changes in perceived slant to achieve shape constancy?

Before we describe experiments bearing on these questions, it would be best to make explicit that the shape–slant integration is not a conscious act of judgment. As a rule, we are aware only of the product of perceptual processes, such as perceived shape, and not the processes leading to the percept. Nor does the process require a high level act of reasoning. A variety of animals, including rats, chickens, and monkeys, have been shown to possess perceptual constancy, so there is little reason to believe that intellect is critically involved. Therefore, in raising our question regarding shape constancy in infants, we need not fear that we are imputing to the infant intellectual feats that exceed his capacity. In any event, evidence of shape constancy would answer our main question, and judgment may be reserved about the nature of the process that underlies it.

The stimulus-preference method used in the studies described earlier involves minimal experimental intervention and manipulation of the observer. The response occurs spontaneously, and the investigator does not attempt to control it experimentally. The study we will consider next (Bower, 1966a, b) is different in that *operant conditioning* procedures are used to shape the infant's response. The classical model of operant conditioning is the pigeon in the Skinner-box, named after the famous investigator of operant behavior, B.F. Skinner (see Chap. 12). The box contains a key which, when pressed, delivers a food pellet. The food pellet is the reinforcement, and the rate of key pressing can be regulated by controlling the frequency and distribution of reinforcement. Operant conditioning techniques have proven powerful means for controlling many types of behaviors in animals and humans.

Bower set out to determine if the young infant perceives shape as constant despite variations in orientation. Suppose a visual form is exposed, displaced from the infant's frontal parallel plane, slanted with one side farther away. Does the infant see a shape that corresponds to the projective, retinal image shape? To find an answer, operant procedures were used to condition a response to the slanted form. Then the infant was tested with new stimuli that were identical to the training form in either objective or projective shape, or both. If the infant has the capacity for shape constancy, the conditioned response (CR) should be elicited by identical objective shapes with the same frequency regardless of their projective shape. If the infant does not have the capability for constancy, the identical objective shape should elicit the conditioned response with significantly reduced frequency when the shape is not presented in the original orientation.

The subjects were infants 50 to 60 days old. The infant lay on his back in a special cradle, his head clasped between two yielding pads. The left pad contained a microswitch which operated an event recorder. Every time the infant turned his head to the left he closed the microswitch and a record of the movement was automatically made. During the first stage a slanted rectangle was the conditioned stimulus (CS). Initially the infants were trained to make a leftward head movement (CR) only when the CS was present; the CR was reinforced only in the presence of the CS. The reinforcer was the momentary appearance of the experimenter's face and a cheerful "peekaboo." Then the infant was gradually put on a variable-ratio schedule on which every fifth response on the average was reinforced. When the first stage was completed, the infant was performing one CR every two seconds.

Next were the generalization tests, which consisted of the presentation of four forms, one at a time. Each form of the following four was presented *without* reinforcement for four 30 second periods in counterbalanced order: (1) The training rectangle at 45 degrees (Fig. 2.7a). Since in this case there is no change between the training and generalization stimuli, this test simply measures the rate of extinction of the CR when reinforcement is withdrawn. (2) A trapezoid in the frontal plane which projected the same retinal shape as the slanted rectangle (Fig. 2.7.b). (3) The training rectangle in the frontal plane (Fig. 2.7c). If shape constancy prevails, this stimulus should elicit the same number of CRs as 1. On the other hand, stimulus 2, which is a different objective shape, should elicit significantly fewer CRs even though it is projectively equivalent to 1 and the training stimulus. (4) The trapezoid at an angle of 45 degrees. Since this stimulus differs from the training form both objectively and projectively, very few responses should be elicited. Table 2.1 summarizes the similarity relationships between each test stimulus and the conditioned training stimulus. The last column in Table 2.1 shows the number of CRs elicited by each test stimulus.

The results were unambiguous. Stimuli 1 and 3 elicited approximately the same number of CRs, indicating that the training stimulus (1) was perceived as a rectangle despite the fact that it was slanted and projected a trapezoidal shape. Stimuli 2 and 4 elicited significantly fewer responses. The trapezoidal shape (2) was not confused with the training shape, although they are projectively equivalent.

These findings answer our main question; they show that shape constancy

Test Stimulus	Shape			No. of CRs on Test
	Objective	Projective	Slant	
1	same	same	same	51.00
2	different	same	different	28.50
3	same	different	different	45.13
4	different	different	same	26.00

Table 2.1 *Relationship between the Test Stimuli and Training Stimuli and Number of CRs to Test Stimuli*

is a feature of the infant's perceptual world. But the results are also puzzling in one respect. If an adult were shown stimuli 1 and 3 he would describe 1 as a slanted rectangle and 3 as the same rectangle in the frontal plane. For the adult, the two stimuli are different. If he had been trained exclusively with stimulus 1, it is reasonable to expect that he would emit fewer CRs for stimulus 3 than for stimulus 1. The infants, however, did not emit significantly different numbers of CRs for the slanted and unslanted stimuli. Granted this implies shape constancy, what does it imply for slant discrimination? It seems to suggest accurate shape perception *without* slant discrimination. This is contrary to the hypothesis that shape constancy depends on an integration of projective shape and perceived slant. Another possibility is that infants do discriminate both shape and slant, but that shape is more impressive and controls the response. This would be consistent with the results for stimulus 4. In this case, similarity of slant was not sufficient to elicit a significant number of CRs.

Visual Space Perception

Every person with an intact visual system is endowed with space perception. The three-dimensional arrangement of the environment is mapped pretty faithfully in the perceptual world. The size, solidity, and distances of objects are perceived effortlessly. Nothing could seem less puzzling. Nevertheless, questions concerning the basis of space perception have challenged students of perception for centuries (Boring, 1942, Chaps. 1, 7, 8).

In the classical statement of the problem, the principal difficulty arises from the fact that retinal images are two-dimensional; they lack depth. The retina is a slightly curved carpet of photosensitive elements at the back of each eye; light entering the eye is focused by the lens of the eye as an image on the retina. Like the movie screen, the retina is two-dimensional, and there is no provision for reproducing a three-dimensional array of surfaces. Therefore, although the environment is a three-dimensional distribution of objects and surfaces, the retinal image is necessarily flat. How do we see a three-dimensional world if the retinal image can only provide us with two-dimensional versions of it?

As a first step toward resolution of this problem, we must abandon the assumption, implicit in the classical formulation, that three-dimensional retinal replicas are required to explain perception of a three-dimensional world. Even if 3D miniature replicas were available, there is no eye behind the retina to see them.

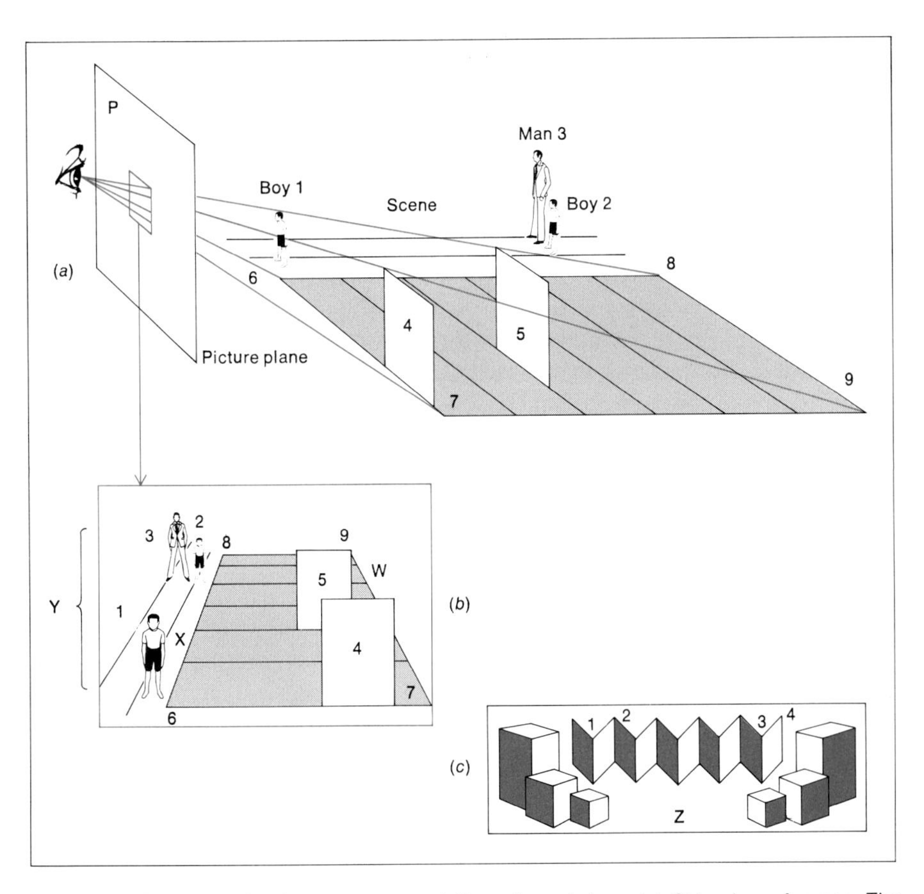

Fig. 2.8. Monocular depth cues as prescriptions for painters. (a) Side view of scene. The means of portraying three-dimensional space on flat canvas were discovered by tracing the view on a "picture plane" of glass (P) held between the eye and the scene. Examining the tracings on the picture plane shows the cues that should be employed by the painter; some of these are listed below and are displayed at (b), front view of scene. (c) A demonstration of the cue of illumination.

Monocular depth cues: (W) Interposition. Notice that rectangle 4 interrupts the outline of 5; this is a strong and effective depth cue, but it only indicates which of the objects is in front, not how much distance there is between them. (X) Linear and size perspective. Although lines 7–9, 6–8 are parallel on the ground, their tracings converge in the picture plane; similarly, 6–8–9–7 is a trapezoid on the picture plane, though it depicts a rectangle on the ground. Following the same geometry, the same-sized boy (1,2) and the same-sized rectangles (4,5) produce smaller tracings when they are at a greater distance: this is called size perspective, or the cue of relative size. Both of these sets of cues are effective. (Y) Familiar size. We know that the man (3) must be physically taller than the boy (1), yet they produce images of the same size; therefore, knowing their true sizes, we might deduce on the basis of their tracing sizes (b1, 3) that the man is more distant than the boy. This is a weak or ineffective cue. (Z) Illumination direction. Cover the right half of the picture in (c): which corner looks nearer, 1 or 2? Now cover the left half; which looks nearer, 3 or 4? Uncover both halves. What was responsible for the differences between 1 and 2, 3 and 4? (From Hochberg, 1964)

Although the formation of retinal images is an important step in seeing, we do not see them directly.

However, there are retinal correlates of the three-dimensional world. A retinal correlate is some variable of the retinal image which varies systematically with changes in the spatial properties of the three-dimensional world. Often called *depth cues*, these correlates have been identified by experimental research. They are useful because the perceptual system is sensitive to their variations. The list of depth cues is extensive. Some, like those illustrated in Figure 2.8, have been known since ancient times, while others, such as *binocular disparity*, are still incompletely understood. The two eyes are separated in the head by an interocular distance of about 6.5 cm. As a result, when a three-dimensional arrangement is viewed, the images in the two eyes are slightly disparate. This disparity is an important determinant of perceived solidity and the perceived depth between objects. Contemporary research is directed to determining exactly what differences are processed to yield single vision of a three-dimensional configuration (for example, Julesz, 1964). For purposes of our discussion we may concentrate on two important cues: optical texture and movement parallax.

Optical Texture

Figure 2.9a represents a typical distribution of surfaces in the environment, a floor extending in the distance until it joins a frontal parallel wall. Part b represents the relation between the orientation of the floor and wall and the density of the optical array projected to the retina. Examine the optic array as represented in Figure 2.9b. The portion of the optic array correlated with the wall is of uniform density, while this is not the case for the portion correlated with the floor. In this latter instance the optic array exhibits a gradual change of density of texture, due to the increasing distance of the parts of the floor closer to the wall, and also to the fact that the angle of viewing becomes increasingly oblique as a function of the distance of the floor from the observer. Similar differences in the gradient of optical texture are associated with every difference in the orientation of textured surfaces. In other words, whenever a surface is displaced in depth, or changes its slant relative to you, the gradient of optical texture changes correspondingly. In this way, the gradient of optical texture can provide information about the distribution of surfaces in depth.

Movement Parallax

Relative motion of objects in the visual field can supply accurate information about their relative positions in space. Move your head to the right or left while keeping your gaze fixed on some point in the middle distance. Closer objects will appear to move in the direction opposite that of your head movement, whereas far objects will appear to move in the same direction as the head displacement. Objects in the vicinity of the fixation will appear to remain stationary. In cases involving far fixation at the horizon, all objects in view seem to move against the head motion. The direction, extent, and speed of the apparent movement is correlated with the actual relative distance of the objects and can serve as a depth cue. Objects nearest the observer are most rapidly displaced from the line of sight; objects farther away seem to move more slowly and to a lesser extent. Figure 2.10 presents an idealized description of movement parallax.

A stroll in a wooded area provides an excellent opportunity for noting the effectiveness of motion parallax. Intermingled leaves, perceived as somewhat indeterminate in relative distance when you stand motionless, immediately separate

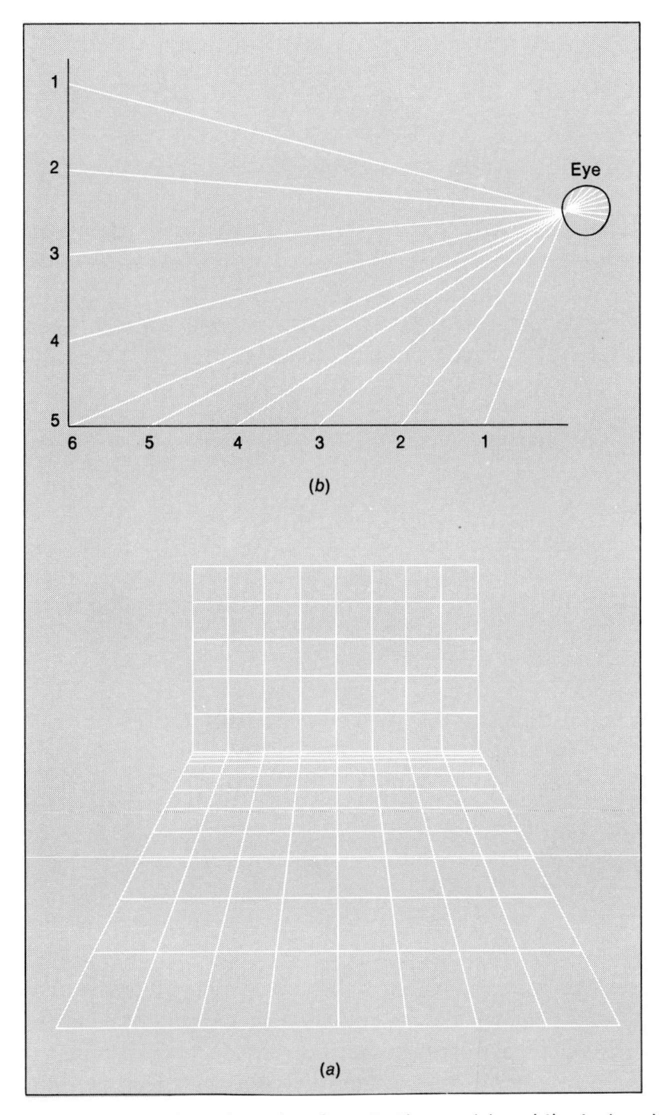

Fig. 2.9. Relation between orientation of surfaces to the eye (a) and the texture they present to it (b). Frontal plane surfaces present a uniform texture when the target field is uniform. The same surfaces oriented obliquely present a graded texture. (From J.J. Gibson, 1950)

in depth when you move your head laterally or resume walking. It is also possible to observe the effects of parallax on apparent motion when you look at animated cartoons in the movies or on television. Some cartoonists simply draw their figures going through appropriate motions as a scenic screen slides by in the background, thereby producing a flat and artificial effect. Other artists paint a series of background scenes on transparent material, each layer representing objects at a different distance from the moving character. The scenes are placed over one another to produce the total background of the picture. To create the impression of movement to the left, the scenes are moved to the right between successive exposures of the film. Scenes representing near objects are moved further each time than are scenes representing more distant objects, the result being a far more realistic illusion of movement through three-dimensional space.

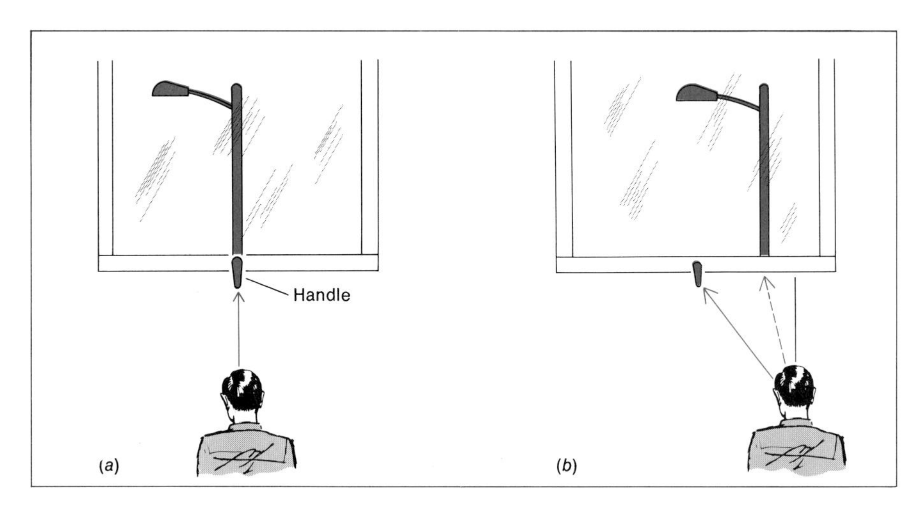

Fig. 2.10. Motion parallax. (a) When I face my wall I see a metal window frame with a handle in the middle; it is perhaps three feet from my eyes. The handle lines up perfectly with a light pole outside, about 100 ft. away. Now, I move my chair to the right about 18 inches, with the result shown in (b). The handle appears far to the left of its original position; the solid arrow shows how far it has been displaced in the visual field. The light pole appears to be almost straight ahead, as it was before. Although it has actually been displaced to the left in the visual field (dashed arrow), its movement to the right *relative to the window frame* has been much greater. Hence I have the visual impression that the pole has moved to the right with me, while the frame and handle have passed to the left. Similar effects may be observed from an automobile window while the car is in motion.

The gradient of optical texture and motion parallax are two retinal correlates of extension in space. Correlates such as these do not provide exact copies of the spatial arrangement of the environment, but they do provide reliable information about it, and our capacity for space perception depends on this information. Do we learn to use this information, or is this ability inherent in the nervous system? Is space perception among the perceptual abilities of the naive organism with no history of exposure to these correlates, or is it a product of accumulated experience? Progress toward an answer to this question has been provided by investigation of the responses of animals and young infants to the *visual cliff* (Walk and Gibson, 1961).

The Visual Cliff

The starting point for visual cliff studies is the observation that most land animals display a fear of falling. Falling from high places is obviously dangerous, so it is not surprising that avoidance of loss of support should have developed in terrestrial creatures over the course of evolution. An animal given a choice between movement in a direction which will culminate in falling and a direction which will provide continued support will choose support; an animal placed on the edge of a sheer cliff will move away from the edge. This behavior is only possible because the animal can perceive the difference between the sheer drop and the level terrain. He is able to discriminate depth.

The visual cliff simulates a natural cliff setting. The subject may choose between movement leading to a sheer drop and movement leading to a shallow

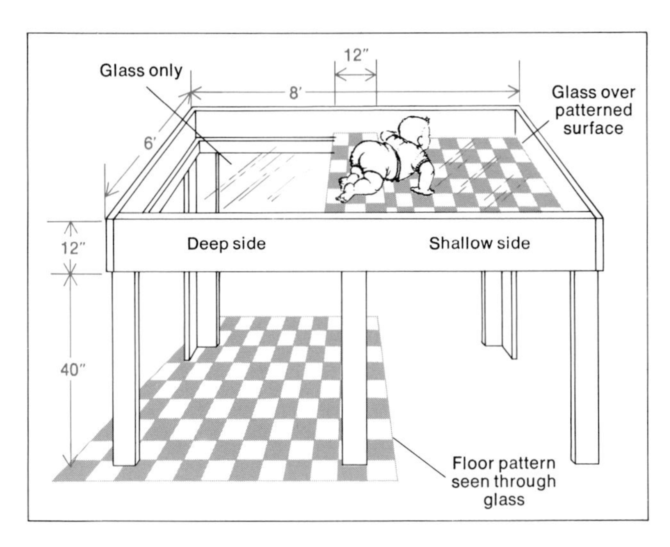

Fig. 2.11. Drawing of the visual cliff. An infant is starting from the center board toward the shallow side. The entire floor of the room is covered with checkerboard linoleum identical with that on the cliff. (From Walk and Gibson, 1961)

descent. The critical differences between the visual cliff and the natural setting are that there is no actual danger of falling, and the retinal correlates or cues for depth are controlled experimentally.

Figure 2.11 shows a model of the visual cliff apparatus. It consists of a center runway board bisecting a sheet of heavy glass which is supported 40 inches above the floor. On one side of the runway a checkerboard sheet of linoleum is placed flush against the underside of the glass; on the other side the same linoleum is placed on the floor. The subject is placed on the center board and the side to which he descends is recorded.

The adult has no difficulty discriminating the difference in depth between the two sides because of the effectiveness of two cues present in the visual cliff arrangement. First is the gradient of optical texture. The pattern on the cliff side, being more distant, projects a more dense optical array than the pattern on the shallow side (see Fig. 2.12). Second, the cue of motion parallax is available. When the head is moved during observation of the two sides, the pattern elements on the shallow side move more rapidly across the field of vision than do those on the cliff side.

When an infant is placed on the runway, to which side will he descend? Given the fear of falling and the availability of depth cues, he should avoid the cliff side and go toward the shallow side; this would be evidence of depth discrimination. Infants between the ages of 6 and 14 months have been tested on the visual cliff. The standard procedure is pictured in Figure 2.13. The infant's mother stands twice at each end of the apparatus, alternating between the cliff side and the shallow side, beckoning to her infant. The results were unambiguous: 67 per cent of the 36 infants went to their mothers *only* when they were on the shallow side. These infants, like the one in Figure 2.13, refused to approach their mothers when they were called from the cliff side. Only 8 per cent went over the cliff on some trials, and 25 per cent found the center runway so appealing that they would not move in either direction.

These results show that infants can discriminate depth on the basis of optical

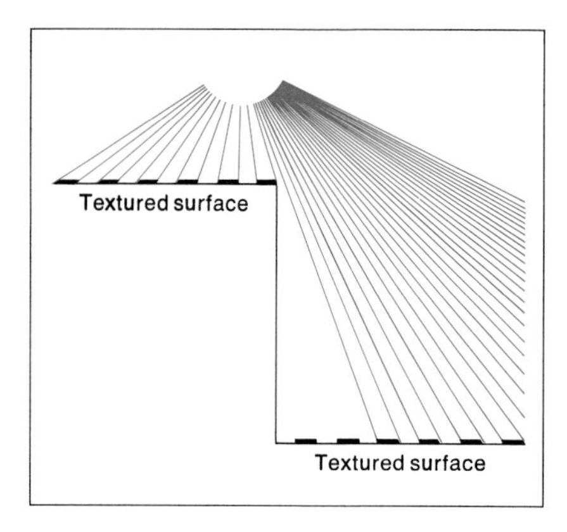

Fig. 2.12. If an animal stands on the raised floor on the left, with an identically textured surface below on the right, the light rays reaching his eyes will differ in intensity, a finer density characterizing the surface farthest below the eye. (From Walk and Gibson, 1961)

texture gradients and motion parallax. But even the youngest of the infants were too old to serve as subjects in an investigation of the origin of space perception. As all parents can testify, six month old infants have had more than ample opportunity to learn that falling is dangerous. They also have had the chance to learn the relationship among optical texture, motion parallax, and differences in depth. We need to test much younger infants, a procedure not possible with the visual cliff apparatus. Only subjects who can walk or crawl can be tested, and human infants are slow in developing these skills. All we can say for certain is that human infants exhibit depth perception as soon as they can crawl; other tests are needed for any further assertions about perception in younger infants.

Size Constancy in Premotor Infants

Both the stimulus-preference method and the operant conditioning procedure can be applied to questions about space perception. As an example, we may consider a study of size constancy, which involves the tendency for the perceived size of an object to remain constant over a considerable range of distances from the observer. If you place this book at various distances from yourself in the room, the perceived size will remain the same. Perceived constancy of size is the rule despite the fact that every change in distance of the book is accompanied by a change of its retinal image size. Retinal image size is inversely proportional to distance (becomes smaller as distance increases), but perceived size is invariant with changing distance.

It is fortunate that size constancy prevails, because adaptive behavior would be difficult in its absence. Does the infant enjoy size constancy, or does the perceived size of an object change every time the distance between him and the object changes? An experiment to answer the question has been conducted by Bower (1964), following the model of the shape constancy experiment described in the preceding section.

Infants between six and eight weeks old were conditioned to make a sideways head movement (CR) in the presence of a white cube, 12 inches on a side, placed 3 feet from the infant's eyes (CS). Then the generalization tests began. Four test stimuli were presented: (1) the original CS, (2) the original cube placed 9 feet from the infant, (3) a cube three times as large as the original cube, but at the original distance, and (4) the large cube placed three times the distance of the

Fig. 2.13. Child's depth perception is tested on the visual cliff. Placed on the center board, the child crawls to its mother across the "shallow" side. Called from the "deep" side he pats the glass, but despite this tactual evidence that the "cliff" is in fact a solid surface he refuses to cross over to the mother. (From Gibson and Walk, 1961)

original cube. Figure 2.14 represents the five stimulus conditions, and Table 2.2 summarizes the relationships between each test stimulus and the conditioned, training stimulus. The last column in Table 2.2 shows the number of CRs elicited by each test stimulus.

The four generalization tests were designed to separate objective size from retinal size, and to determine whether it is the former or the latter which controls the CR. If it is the former, we may conclude that the infant has the capacity for size constancy. As shown in Table 2.2, the CS elicited 102.70 CRs, stimuli 2 and 3 elicited 66.03 and 54.10 responses, respectively, and stimulus 4 elicited only 22.92 responses.

The significance of these findings for our question is most easily understood by comparing the results for stimuli 2 and 3 with the results for stimulus 4. Stimulus

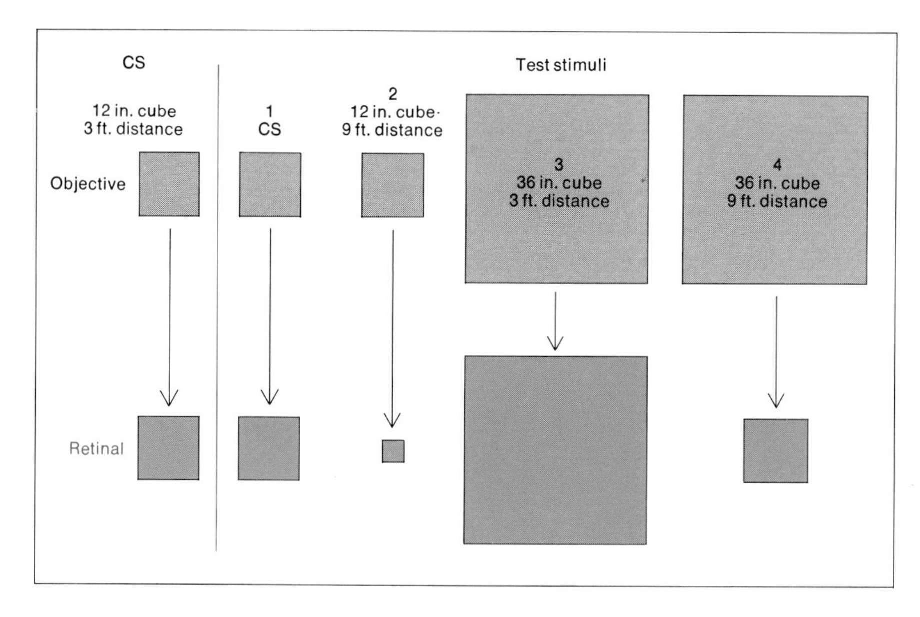

Fig. 2.14. This figure represents the five stimulus conditions (CS) and four test conditions in Bower's size constancy experiment. The upper row represents the objective stimuli and the lower row the corresponding retinal stimuli, i.e., retinal image size.

2 provides the same objective size as the CS, and stimulus 4 the same retinal image size. If perceived size in the infant conforms to objective size, the number of CRs to stimulus 2 should exceed the number elicited by stimulus 4. On the other hand, if perceived size is governed by retinal size, the reverse should occur. The results confirmed the first prediction.

At this point an objection may be raised. If the infant is responding to objective size, why were there fewer CRs to stimulus 2 than to the CS? The answer is suggested by the results for stimulus 3, which yielded the same number of CRs as stimulus 2 but more than twice as many as stimulus 4. This latter result must be due to the fact that stimulus 3 was placed at the same distance as the CS, while stimulus 4 was not. Therefore, we can conclude that the young infant discriminates both size and distance correctly. During the original training, the head turning response is conditioned to both perceived size and distance, so testing with a stimulus which is different in size or distance will elicit fewer CRs.

The generally accepted explanation of size constancy is that perceived size remains constant over changes in distance because the changes are perceived correctly and taken into account in evaluating retinal image size. This explanation has been tested and found satisfactory with adults (Epstein, Park, and Casey, 1961). The fact that the infants in the Bower experiment gave evidence of perceiving *both* size and distance correctly suggests that they use distance information similarly to adults.

Visual Deprivation

The visual cliff test is unsuitable for the study of space perception in young human infants because the discriminatory response, descending to one side, re-

Test Stimulus	Size Objective	Retinal	Distance	No. of CRs on Test
1	same	same	same	102.70
2	same	different	different	66.03
3	different	different	same	54.10
4	different	same	different	22.92

Table 2.2 *The Relationship between the Test Stimuli and Training Stimuli and Number of CRs to Test Stimuli*

quires motor coordination that is late in maturing. But there are many terrestrial animals capable of perambulation on the first occasion of visual experience. Studies of newborn animals have been conducted. Their results cannot be generalized for human infants, but they are instructive, and we will conclude this section by describing one of the animal studies.

The study we have selected employed a procedure which can be applied experimentally only with animals. The procedure provides an experimental analogue of clinical cases of newly seeing persons whose sight has been restored surgically. Animals born in the laboratory are reared from birth until the time of testing in total darkness. This eliminates all prior visual experience, so that at the time of testing the animal is being observed on the very first occasion of visual experience. Can animals reared in the dark discriminate depth as well as can normal light-reared animals? Experiments of this type have been conducted with rats and kittens.

Walk and Gibson (1961) tested three groups of rats. One group was reared in total darkness until the age of 90 days (when they were adult). A second group was reared in the normal, lighted laboratory environment. These animals were able to see the interiors of their home cages and also the interior of the laboratory room which housed them. The experimenters called this group the "light-reared, full vision" group. A third group was also light-reared, but the environment outside their cages extended only four inches from the cages.

We noted earlier that the standard visual cliff provides two depth cues—optical texture and motion parallax. When a subject avoids the cliff side, his choice may be due to the joint effects of both cues. But it is also possible that depth discrimination is controlled by only one of the cues, while the other is ineffective. In order to assess this possibility we need to separate the two cues and test the subject with only one cue present. To retain differential texture density and eliminate motion parallax, the pattern on the cliff side is placed flush on the undersurface of the glass, but the size of the elements is reduced and the pattern is made objectively more dense than on the shallow side. Under this condition, the same difference in optical texture that exists in the standard cliff is present, but since the distances of the patterns on the two sides are the same, there is no motion parallax. The reverse procedure is necessary to produce motion parallax without an accompanying gradient of optical texture. The pattern on the cliff side remains on the floor, but the sizes of the elements are increased to compensate for the difference in distance between the sides, thus equating the textural density.

The experiment was designed to determine whether dark-reared rats can

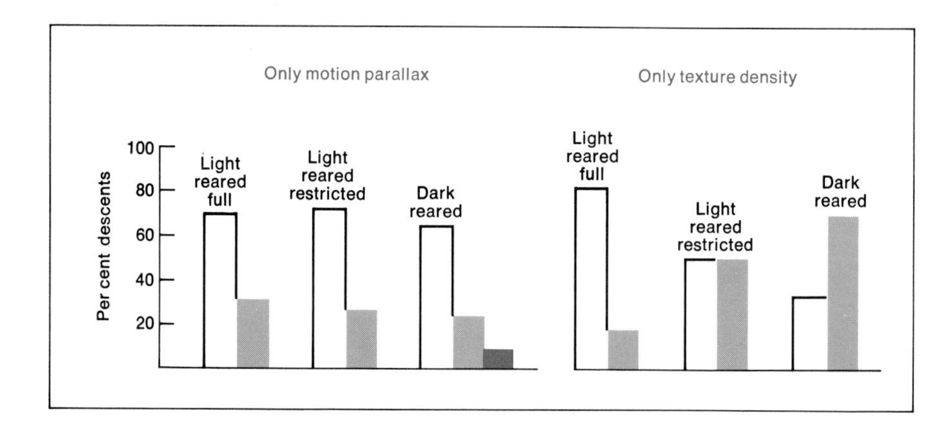

Fig. 2.15. Unfilled bars show percentage of descents to the shallow side. Hatched bars show percentage of descents to cliff side. Filled bar shows percentage of trials on which rats did not descend to either side.

discriminate depth as well as normal light-reared rats. The results, graphed in Figure 2.15, show that there is no single answer; the outcome depends on specific cues. If motion parallax is present, dark-reared rats with no visual experience prior to testing perform just as well as light-reared rats. Nor does it matter whether light-rearing included exposures to long distances or was confined to short distances. Under all three conditions the rats avoided the cliff side; depth discrimination was equally good for all three groups.

When motion parallax is absent, leaving only texture density, the picture is different. Rats reared in the light with full vision avoid the cliff side, just as they did when only motion parallax was present. But rats reared in the dark fail to avoid the cliff side. These rats are unable to discriminate depth with only the optical density cue available. Since the light-reared unrestricted rats are able to use texture density as a cue, we can only conclude that the opportunity for learning the relationship between texture density and depth is a necessary condition for the effectiveness of this cue.

This experiment shows that depth discrimination is part of the natural endowment of the rat, but we should reiterate that this conclusion may not be generalized for human infants. In fact, it should not be uncritically applied to all terrestrial animals. Nevertheless, the experiment demonstrates the valuable lesson that a careful analysis of stimulation can lead to more precise conclusions. Many perceptual discriminations are overdetermined. There are more *potential* sources of information than are required for the discrimination. In the case of the visual cliff, both optical texture and motion parallax are potential cues. If we wish to state conclusions about the effective stimulus for the discrimination, we need to perform analytic experiments which permit us to assess the separate effects of several potential cues. Sometimes the results of the analysis are unexpected and lead to a more precise conclusion. In the present case, instead of concluding that, for the rat, depth discrimination is unlearned, we must restrict our conclusion to the statement that when motion parallax is available, the rat can discriminate depth without prior experience. The analytic experiment allows us to avoid the error of overstating our conclusion.

Nativism versus Empiricism

What does the world look like to the very young infant? The current status of research does not allow us to answer this question in detail, but one assertion can be made confidently. James' characterization is decidedly wrong—the infant's perceptual world is not a "blooming, buzzing confusion." To a degree that has surprised most psychologists, the infant gives evidence of being able to make many of the kinds of discriminations that are crucial for adaptive behavior.

There is a hoary controversy, predating the nineteenth century beginnings of scientific psychology by at least 2,500 years, between adherents of nativism and of empiricism (Hochberg, 1962). Proponents of nativism claim that most perceptual functioning is innate. Perception is part of the unlearned natural endowment of the organism. Empiricists claim that there are no innate perceptual capabilities. All perceptual functioning is the product of learning and experience. Many of the great figures in philosophy and science have been associated with the nativism–empiricism controversy. As a rule, the positions adopted were part of a general philosophical orientation concerning the origins and possibility of attaining true knowledge. The methods brought to bear on the question were usually those of philosophy, logical analysis supported by informal empirical observation.

The status of this controversy in the experimental psychology of perception is difficult to describe. While the doctrines of nativism and empiricism are too general and loosely stated to have much predictive value, the controversy does seem related to issues about which a scientific theory of perception cannot be completely silent. Indeed, experimental psychology has been providing data that are relevant to these issues. Nevertheless, it is doubtful that the efforts of the experimentalist are motivated by the wish to contribute toward a resolution of the nativism–empiricism controversy. The question he asks is usually a straightforward empirical one, without the theoretical charge of the mutually exclusive alternatives. His general aim is to identify the variables that control perception. The discovery that a newborn infant displays space perception is important, but it is not an end in itself. The next step is to identify the variables of optical stimulation or central activity that govern the perception of space. Neither would evidence of perception in the absence of prior experience bar from active consideration the possibility that subsequent experience affects perception significantly. Establishment of the fact that many perceptual capabilities are unlearned components of the infant's perceptual system is not the end of the investigation; it is only part of the continuing effort to understand the psychology of perception.

Although we have just asserted that resolution of the nativism–empiricism controversy is not the principal objective of investigations of infant perception, let us admit that the question still stirs interest among psychologists. It is appropriate that this chapter be concluded with a speculative statement on this matter. A reasonable statement would have to reconcile evidence of the very early appearance of perceptual discrimination with the evidence of many investigations that perception is modifiable and influenced by learning and past experience (Epstein, 1967). The following statement takes note of these findings: The original appearance of much of the normal repertoire of perceptual discriminations does not depend on a prior history of visual experience. These discriminations are innate, unlearned principles of processing visual input. As the infant accumulates a history of visual experience, this history begins to exert an important influence on the way visual input is processed. Past experience and learned principles of processing interact with visual input (optical stimulation) in determining our perceptual world.

Glossary

Constancy: the tendency for perceived attributes to remain constant despite variations of local retinal stimulation when the position of an object is changed relative to the observer. Shape constancy and size constancy are discussed in this chapter.

Corneal reflection: a reflection of the scene from the corneal surface of the eye. The location of the reflection relative to the pupil has been used to determine the target of an observer's gaze.

Empiricism: in the context of the psychology of perception, refers to the view that the infant is born with very limited perceptual capabilities. Perception is acquired by learning and experience.

Fixation: to fixate an object is to look directly at the object; to bring the image of the object over the central foveal region of the retina, where vision for detail is best.

Fovea: a central part of the retina which affords the greatest visual acuity. This is due to the special composition of the fovea, which consists of closely packed cones, each with its own connection to the optic nerve.

Frontal parallel: parallel to the observer's forehead; in a plane perpendicular to the observer's line of sight.

Motion (movement) parallax: a cue consisting of the differential angular velocity between the line of sight to the fixated object and any other object in the visual field, and serving as an indication of the relative distance of points in the visual field when an observer moves with respect to the environment, or when parts of the environment move with respect to the observer.

Nativism: in the context of the psychology of perception, refers to the view that human organisms are born with an organized repertoire of perceptual capabilities. The role of learning is deemphasized.

Optical texture: a term introduced by J.J. Gibson to describe the retinal correlate of an environmental surface that normally is textured. The gradient of optical texture is a determinant of the perceived orientation of surfaces.

Projective: in geometry, pertaining to the projection of one surface onto another. If the two surfaces are not parallel, the projection will result in a projective transformation. Thus, a circle projected onto a surface, such as the retina, that is not parallel to the plane of the circle will result in an elliptical projective shape.

Pupil: the circular opening in the center of the iris.

Retina: a layer of light-sensitive elements (rods and cones) and nerve fibers which lines the inner walls of the large chamber of the eyeball.

Shape constancy: tendency of perceived shape to remain constant when orientation (and, therefore, projective shape) is varied.

Size constancy: tendency of perceived size to remain constant when distance (and, therefore, retinal image size) is varied.

Stimulus-preference method: a method for assessing the perceptual capabilities of young infants. A pair of stimuli, e.g., geometric forms, is presented, and the investigator records the amount of time, or number of fixations, devoted to each member of the pair.

Veridical: a term for which several definitions may be presented. The most common usage is in reference to perceptual reports which agree with the properties of the environment as determined by conventional physical measurement. Such perceptual reports are labeled as "veridical perception."

Visual acuity: the capability for seeing fine detail.

Visual angle: the angle subtended by an object in the visual field at the nodal point of the eye. (The front surface of the cornea is the most frequently used point.) Visual angle is directly proportional to the size (e) of the object (e.g., length, diameter) and inversely proportional to the distance (*R*) of the object along the line of regard. It is expressed in the form of a simple equation; $\Theta = e/R$ in radians or $\Theta = 57 \cdot Be/R$ in degrees.

Visual cliff: an experimental arrangement designed to test depth discrimination in animals and human infants.

References

Bartley, S.H. *Principles of perception.* New York: Harper & Row, 1958.

Boring, E.G. *Sensation and perception in the history of experimental psychology.* New York: Appleton-Century-Crofts, 1942.

Bower, T.G.R. Discrimination of depth in premotor infants. *Psychon. Sci.*, 1964, **1,** 368.

________. Slant perception and shape constancy in infants. *Science*, 1966, **151,** 832–834.(a)

________. The visual world of infants. *Scientific Amer.*, Dec. 1966, **215,** 80–92.(b)

Brennan, W.M., E.W. Ames, and R.W. Moore. Age differences in infants' attention to patterns of different complexity. *Science*, 1966, **151,** 354–356.

Epstein, W. Experimental investigations of the genesis of space perception. *Psychol. Bull.*, 1964, **61,** 115–128.

________. *Varieties of perceptual learning.* New York: McGraw-Hill, 1967.

________, and J. Park. Shape constancy: Theoretical formulations and functional relationships. *Psychol. Bull.* 1963, **60,** 265–288.

________, and A. Casey. The current status of the size-distance hypothesis. *Psychol. Bull.*, 1961, **58,** 491–514.

Fantz, R.L. The origin of form perception. *Scientific Amer.*, 1961, **204** (5), 66–72.

________. Pattern discrimination and selective attention as determinants of perceptual development. In A.H. Kidd and J.L. Rivoire (Eds.), *Perceptual development in children.* New York: International University Press, 1966.

________. Visual experience in infants: Decreased attention to familiar patterns relative to novel ones. *Science*, 1964, **146,** 668–670.

________. Visual perception from birth shown by pattern selectivity. *Ann. N. Y. Acad. Sciences*, 1965, **118** (21), 793–814.

________, J.M. Ordy, and M.S. Udelf. Maturation of pattern vision in infants during the first six months. *J. comp. physiol. Psychol.*, 1962, **55,** 907–917.

Gibson, E.J., and R. Walk. The "visual cliff." *Scientific Amer.*, 1960, **202,** 4, 64–71.

Gibson, J.J., *The perception of the visual world.* Boston: Houghton Mifflin, 1950.

Gregory, R.L., and J.G. Wallace. Recovery from early blindness: A case study. *Exper. Psychol. Social Monogr.*, 1963, No. 2 (Cambridge).

Hershenson, M. Visual discrimination in the human infant. *J. comp. physiol. Psychol.*, 1964, **58,** 270–276.

________, H. Munsinger, and W. Kessen. Preference for shapes of intermediate variable in the newborn human. *Science*, 1965, **147,** 630–631.

Hochberg, J.E. Nativism and empiricism in perception. In L. Postman (Ed.), *Psychology in the making.* New York: Knopf, 1962.

________. *Perception.* Englewood Cliffs, N.J.: Prentice-Hall, 1964.

James, W. *Principles of psychology.* New York: Holt, Rinehart and Winston, 1890.

Julesz, B. Binocular depth perception without familiarity cues. *Science*, 1964, **145,** 356–362.

Kling, J.W., and L.A. Riggs (Eds.), *Woodworth and Schlosberg's Experimental Psychology.* 3d Ed. New York: Holt, Rinehart and Winston, 1971.

Lewis, M., W. Meyers, J. Kagan, and R. Grossberg. Attention to visual patterns in infants. *Amer. Psychologist*, 1963, **18,** 357.

Saayman, G., E.W. Ames, and A. Moffett. Response to novelty as an indicator of visual discrimination in the human infant. *J. exp. child Psychol.*, 1964, **1** (2), 189–198.

Senden, M. von. Raum-und Gestalt-auffasung bei Operierten Blindgeborenen. 1932. Trans. by P. Heath in *Space and sight.* London: Methuen, 1960.

Stechler, G. The effect of medication during labor on newborn infants. *Science*, 1964, **144,** 315–317.

Walk, R., and E.J. Gibson. A comparative and analytical study of visual depth perception. Psychol. Monogr., 1961, **75** (Whole No. 519).

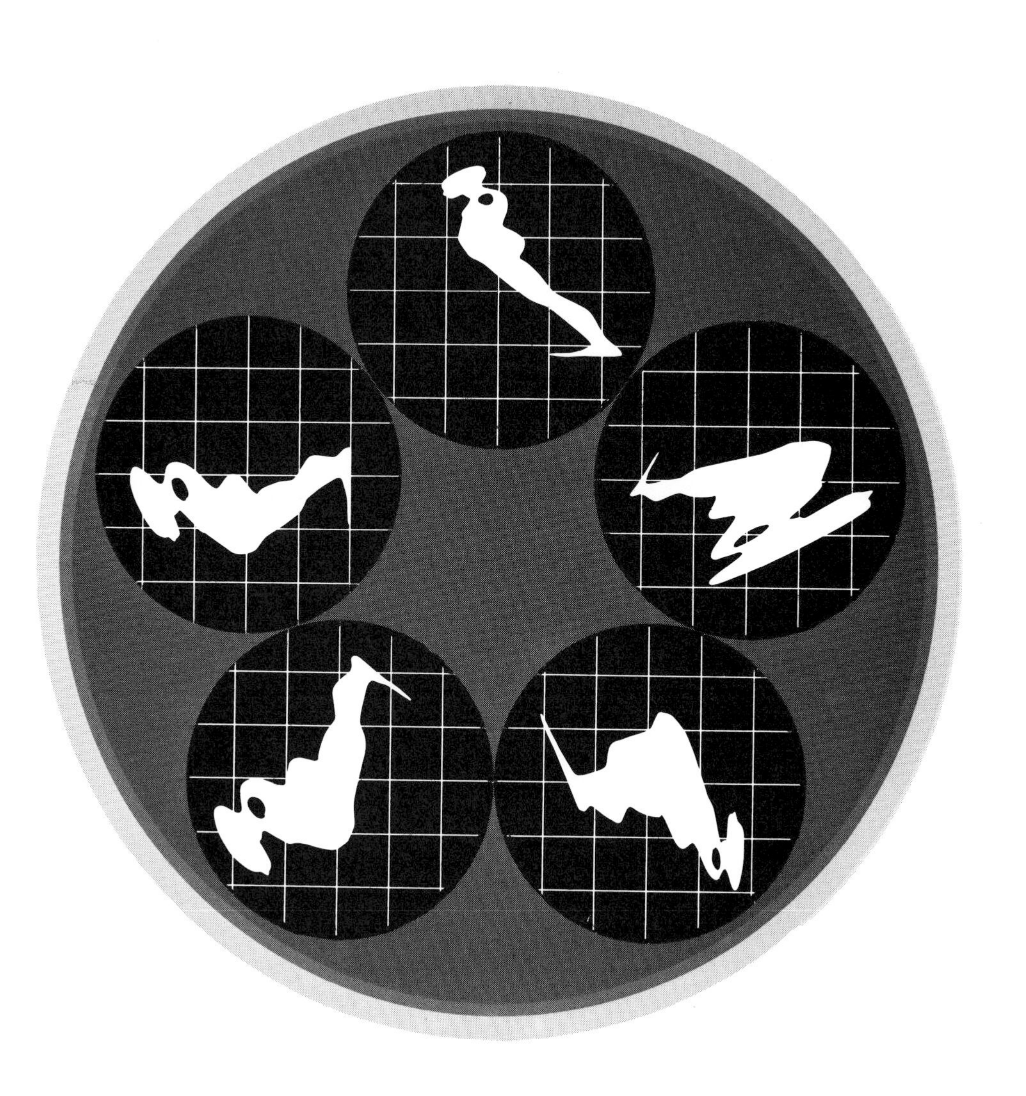

3 Perceptual Adaptation to a Transformed World

> The room and all in it seemed upside down. The hands when stretched out from below into the visual field seemed to enter from above. Yet although all these images were clear and definite, they did not at first seem to be real things, like the things we see in normal vision, but they seem to be misplaced, false, or illusory *images* between (myself) and the objects or things themselves. . . . All movements of the body at this time were awkward, uncertain, and full of surprises. Only when the movement was made regardless of visual images . . .—as when one moves in the dark—could walking or movements of the hand be performed with reasonable security and directness. Otherwise, the movement was a series of errors and attempts at correction . . . (Stratton, 1896, pp. 613–614).

With these words, George Stratton described his perceptual experience on the first day of an experiment conducted in 1896. On that day and for seven succeeding days, Stratton wore during all his waking hours a specially designed optical system which produced complete up-down inversion and a right-left reversal of the normal orientation of the retinal image. Figure 3.1 illustrates the normal and reinverted orientations of the image.

The question that interested Stratton has a long history, dating back to Kepler (1571–1630) and Scheiner's (1575–1650) conclusive demonstration that the retinal image is inverted with respect to the external scene. Berkeley (1709) raised the question in his *Essay Towards a New Theory of Vision:*

> . . . there occurs one mighty difficulty. Objects are painted in an inverted order on the bottom of the eye: the upper part of any object being painted on the lower part of the eye, and the lower part of the object on the upper part of the eye: and so also as to right and left. Since therefore the pictures are thus inverted, it is demanded how it comes to pass that we see the objects erect and in their natural posture?

If the retinal image is "upside down," how is it that the visual world is "rightside up"? One answer is that the orientation of the image is irrelevant, so long as a consistent relationship is maintained between the orientation of the image and the orientation of the scene. We learn to perceive the visual directions of the external world correctly on the basis of association between retinal orientation and other information, such as touch and felt positions of parts of the body. If this is the case, then it matters little whether the image is inverted or "rightside up" with respect to the environment; in both instances we would learn to see the world in the same orientation.

At this point you may be able to guess the purpose of Stratton's experiment. The optical system which he wore reerected the image, so that it was upright with respect to the external environment, rotated 180 degrees with respect to the normal, preexperimental orientation of the image. (see Fig. 3.1). One would expect that upon first looking through the optical system (a small astronomical telescope of unit magnification) the world should appear drastically altered, and, as Stratton's description reveals, this is indeed the case. But what happens if the optical system is worn continuously for an extended period? Will the world continue to look distorted, or upside down? It might, if there are fixed, immutable connections between retinal locations and perceived directions. But if the associations between retinal position and visual direction are learned, then it is possible that continued exposure

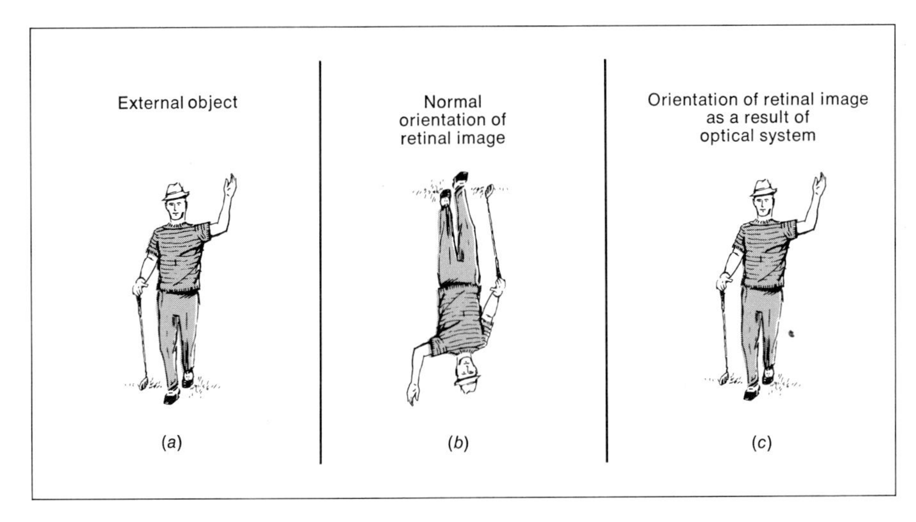

Fig. 3.1. This figure illustrates the relationship among the orientation of an object in the external environment (a) and the orientation of the retinal image in normal vision (b) and in Stratton's experiment (c).

might teach the subject new associations, and gradually the world would come to appear normal, not different from its preexperimental appearance.

Let us return to Stratton's description of his experience. On each succeeding day his movements grew less laborious and Stratton reported that he began to feel more at home in the new situation. On the fourth day, "actions appropriate to the new visual perceptions frequently occurred without any conflict or apparent tendency to react by misinterpretation of visual positions." During the sixth day, Stratton reported further development of normalcy. "There was perfect reality in my visual surroundings, and I gave myself up to them without reserve and without being conscious of a single note of discord with what I saw."

When the time came to remove the inverting system at the conclusion of the experiment, Stratton closed his eyes while an assistant replaced the optical system with a lensless tube that provided the same field of vision. Upon opening his eyes ". . . the scene had a strange familiarity. The visual arrangement was immediately recognized as the old one of preexperimental days; yet the reversal of everything from the order to which I had grown accustomed during the past week, gave the scene a surprising, bewildering air which lasted for several hours."

It is obvious that Stratton's experience and behavior changed significantly over the course of the exposure period. On the first day, the visual scene looked strange, objects appeared in unexpected places, and normal behaviors failed to yield their expected consequences. By the eighth day the world looked normal, and behavior was effective. In fact, a later investigator, Ivo Kohler (1951), reported that adaptation to inversion was so complete that in the latter stages of his experiment he was able to ski on the Austrian Alps while wearing the inverting system.

There is no question that experience and behavior changed significantly. What does remain open to question is the correct designation of the change. Did a genuine change in visual perception occur? Was the underlying shift an alteration in the relationship between retinal position and visual direction, so that points imaged on the lower part of the retina signified "down" and points imaged on the upper part "up"? This possibility, illustrated in Figure 3.2, was favored by Stratton. But

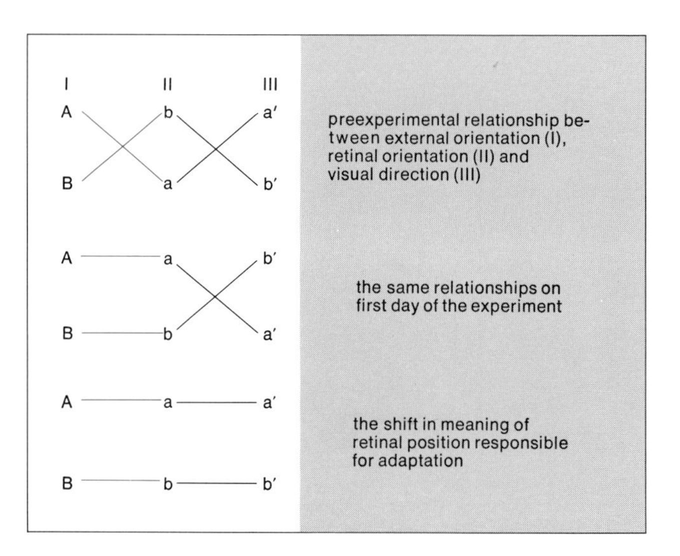

Fig. 3.2. A schematic representation of one interpretation of the underlying change in Stratton's experiment. *A* and *B* are two points in the environment, one above the other; *a* and *b* are the retinal positions of *A* and *B;* and *a′* and *b′* are the perceived directions of *A* and *B.*

there is another equally plausible interpretation. Perhaps Stratton learned to accept the upside down world as normal, *and* to adopt a new rule of responding, such as reaching down for objects that appeared in the upper part of the visual scene. A simple rule would suffice to restore effective behavior: reverse the preexperimental relationship between perceived direction and visually guided behavior. This is not the only possible alternative to Stratton's conclusion, and we will return to this matter in our discussion of the locus of adaptation.

Adaptation

The process that Stratton studied is now called *adaptation.* The general procedure for its study is to introduce an optical device that produces known transformations of optical stimulation, and to record changes in the subject's response on a controlled test. The favorite optical medium has been the prism. Prisms have been used to transform straight lines into curved lines, vertical scenes into tilted scenes, and to produce sideways displacements of visual targets.

Consider the case of a subject who wears wedge prisms. Figure 3.3 shows that the wedge prism produces a sideways displacement of the visual scene. Light passing through the prism is bent in the direction of the prism base, and the apparent location of targets is displaced in the direction of the prism apex. Consequently, when a base-right prism is placed before the eye, an object will appear to the left of its actual position. Our purpose is to learn whether adaptation to sideways displacement occurs when a subject wears base-right prisms continuously for several hours. With this goal in mind, a test of visual direction is designed. A single luminous point is presented in total darkness. The subject, seated in a fixed position with his head facing forward, is to move the luminous point into a position directly in line with his nose, egocentric straight ahead. By depressing a key, the subject can transport the point across his field of vision by remote control.

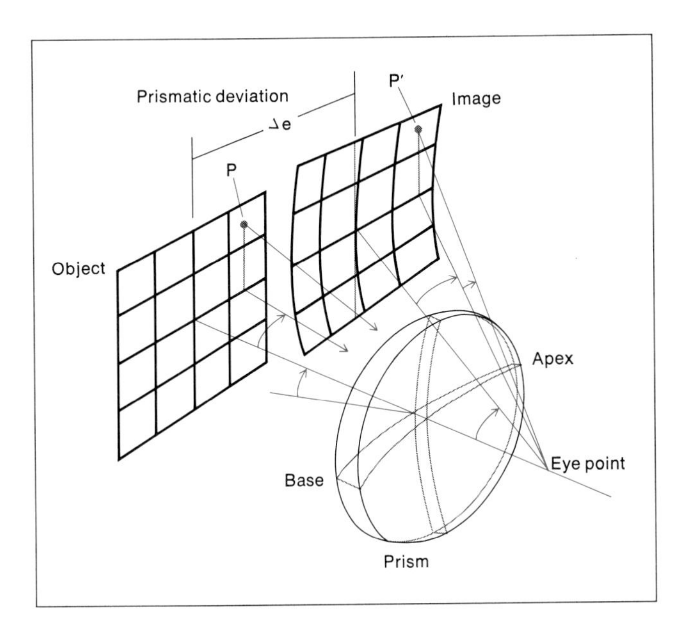

Fig. 3.3. The light passing through a wedge prism is bent toward the base. As a result, the perceived location of the target is displaced toward the apex. In addition, lines entering the prism obliquely are bent more than those entering at right angles, resulting in apparent curvature of vertical lines. (Adapted from Ogle, 1961)

A test administered during the initial moments of prism exposure reveals predictable error in localization of the straight ahead. If the base-right prism produced a leftward displacement of 11 degrees, the point is judged to be straight ahead when it is in fact 11 degrees *right* of the true straight ahead. The error is equal in magnitude to the prism displacement. We want to determine whether continued exposure is accompanied by adaptation, whether the perceived visual direction of the point gradually comes to correspond to its true direction. Therefore, we plan to test the subject at half-hour intervals over the duration of exposure.

Measuring Adaptation

At this juncture in planning the experiment, a decision has to be made concerning the conditions of testing. We can try to secure a direct measure of adaptation by testing with the prisms on, or we can secure an indirect measure by having the subject remove the prism spectacles during testing. In the latter case we would be measuring the *aftereffect* of adaptation. When we use the direct measure, adaptation would be evidenced if, on successive tests, the subject's error in setting the point to the right of true straight ahead gradually *diminished.* This is represented in the negatively decelerated curve labeled "adaptation" in Figure 3.4. Evidence of adaptation would be indicated with the aftereffect measure if the subject's error in setting the point to the left of the true straight ahead *increased* on successive tests. This is represented in the negatively accelerated curve labeled "aftereffect" in Figure 3.4

The rationale underlying the aftereffect measure needs to be made explicit. Consider the performance of an ideal subject. *Prior* to introduction of the prisms,

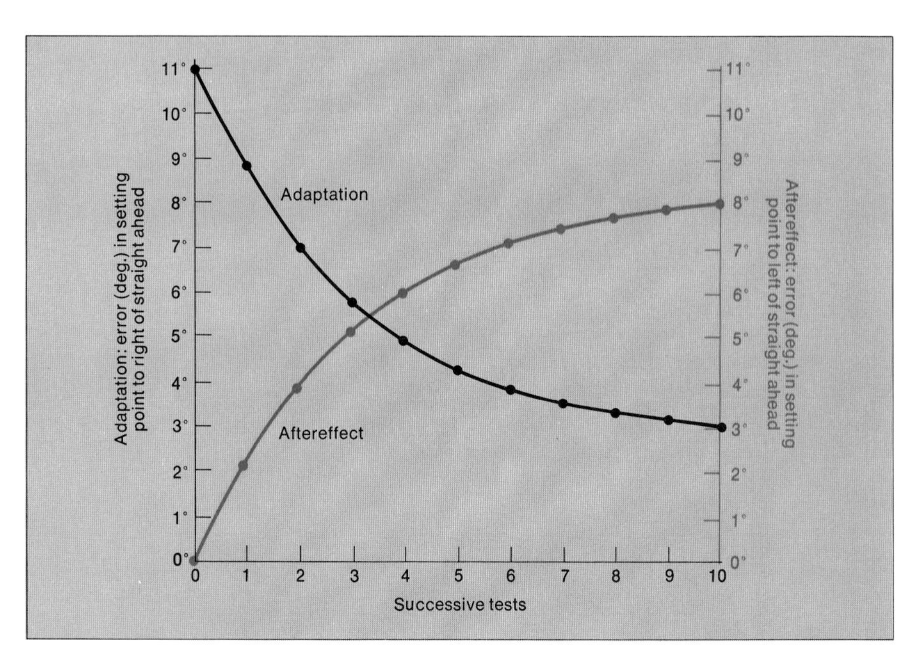

Fig. 3.4. The subject wears base right prisms that produce sideways displacements of 11 degrees. The curve labeled *adaptation* shows the diminishing rightward error when tests are administered with prisms on. The curve labeled *aftereffect* shows the increasing leftward error when tests are administered with prisms off.

he sets the point with perfect accuracy. Immediately following introduction of 11 degree base-right prisms, and with the prisms in place, the subject sets the point 11 degrees to the right of its true position. Assume that at the end of the exposure period 100 per cent adaptation has occurred—with prisms in place, the subject judges the point to be straight ahead when it is indeed straight ahead. This means that a target imaged in the right half of the retina now appears straight ahead. If we remove the prisms, the subject will persist in judging a point to be straight ahead when it is imaged in the right half of the retina. In other words, he will judge that the point seen with prisms on and the point seen with prisms removed have the same visual direction when it is imaged in the same retinal location. However, for the point to occupy the same retinal location, both with and without prisms in place, it must hold different objective positions. With the prisms off, the point must be located to the left of straight ahead. For this reason an aftereffect is observed. Figure 3.5 will help you retrace this argument.

Faced with a choice between direct measure and aftereffect measure, contemporary investigators have been almost unanimous in preferring the aftereffect measure. The aftereffect test is preferred because it reduces the concern that observed changes merely represent conscious correction for prism effects. Suppose that during the exposure intervals between tests the subject goes about his normal routine. In the course of this activity he learns that the prism causes objects to appear to the left of their accustomed position. If the test is administered with prisms on, the subject will compensate deliberately for the prism effects. This type of compensation would be analogous to the conscious correction that spear-fishermen employ to strike underwater targets. The aftereffect measure alleviates our concern on this point. By testing with the prisms off, we are looking for changes

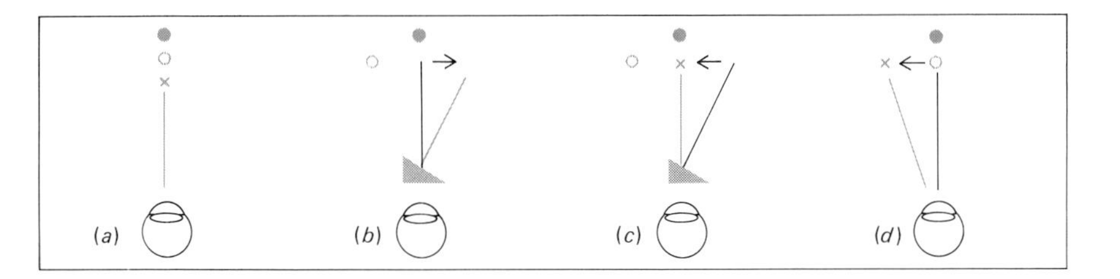

Fig. 3.5. In this drawing, the true straight ahead is indicated by the solid circle, the displacement effect of the prism by the open circle, and the setting of the point to apparent straight ahead by the x. Arrows are used to show the effect on x of introducing the prism (b); of adaptation (c); and of removing the prism following adaptation (d). In (a), prior to introduction of prisms, the subject's setting of the point corresponds to the true straight ahead. In (b), the prism has just been introduced, so that the objectively straight-ahead point appears to the left. Therefore, the subject moves the point to the right to make it appear straight ahead. In (c), the subject has fully adapted; now the judged and true straight ahead coincide. (d), shows that the subject will persist in judging the point as straight ahead when it stimulates the same retinal point as in (c). But this requires that the points be moved to the left of straight ahead by 11 degrees.

which are not likely to be products of conscious correction. If adaptation is simply deliberate compensation, aftereffects should not occur, since there is no reason to introduce a correction in the absence of prisms. The spear-fisherman abandons his compensatory responses when he returns to the land.

Motivation for the Study of Adaptation

Investigations of adaptation have been prominent in the experimental literature of perception since 1960 (for reviews see Epstein, 1967, Chap. 9; Howard and Templeton, 1966, Chap. 15; Rock, 1966). Research on adaptation has been spurred by diverse motives.

Investigators interested in examining the relationships between perception and learning or memory have seen the adaptation experiment as a promising tool for the study of perceptual learning.

The developmental psychologist views the introduction of optical systems which rearrange relationships between external environment and optical stimulation and between the latter and perception as a tool for recreating an earlier developmental stage of perception. The variables and conditions that control adaptation may provide leads in the search for the variables that control early developmental changes in perception.

Perceptual theorists consider the study of adaptation important because accounts of adaptation have led to more detailed consideration of the way in which intentions, behavior, and intersensory relationships are involved in visual perception.

The Effective Stimulus

The early experiments reported by Stratton (1896, 1897) and Ivo Kohler (1951) are important contributions to the study of adaptation. These investigators reported

Fig. 3.6. The appearance of the world viewed through Dove prisms. The visual scene is rotated or tilted. There is *no* lateral displacement. The lateral displacement in this drawing is only an artistic convenience. (Courtesy S.M. Ebenholtz)

many provocative findings, and Kohler must be given a large share of the credit for reintroducing the question into contemporary psychology. But in several respects these studies were deficient. Most disappointing is the absence of experiments designed to establish the functional relationships between amount of adaptation and precisely defined independent variables. Data of this nature are essential to an understanding of adaptation. We will describe an experiment by Ebenholtz (1966) which examines two important determinants: duration of exposure and degree of optical transformation.

The Experimental Situation

If you view the world through a Dove prism which has been rotated around its long axis, the visual scene will appear to be rotated or tilted. (A right-left reversal is also produced, but this is eliminated by having the subject look through two Dove prisms mounted in tandem, thereby rereversing the image and leaving only

Fig. 3.7. In the aftereffect test, the subject instructs the examiner to adjust the orientation of a luminous line so that it appears perfectly upright. The room is totally dark so that only the luminous line is visible. (Courtesy S.M. Ebenholtz)

a tilt transformation.) Any desired amount of optical tilt can be produced simply by rotating the prism to the appropriate position. Figure 3.6 shows an artist's rendition of the appearance of a typical scene when tilting prisms are worn. This drawing, which represents the perceptual world of the *stationary* subject, cannot convey a picture of the changes in stimulation and perception that accompany the subject's movement.

Will a person who wears tilting prisms for several hours adapt to optical tilt? As a measure of adaptation, Ebenholtz used the aftereffect of prism exposure, observed in the subject's judgment of the vertical. In a completely dark room with the prisms removed, the subject adjusted the orientation of a single luminous line until it appeared upright. Figure 3.7 shows the test arrangement. Assume that a subject, immediately prior to donning the prisms, judges the upright with perfect accuracy. Next the subject wears prisms that tilt the visual scene by 30 degrees counterclockwise (Fig. 3.6). Suppose he adapts fully to the optical tilt; immediately prior to removal of the prisms, lines that are tilted retinally 30 degrees appear upright. Therefore, when the prisms are removed, the subject should judge the luminous test line to be upright when the top of it is in fact tilted 30 degrees counterclockwise. The difference between the preexposure and postexposure settings is the aftereffect, and the magnitude of the aftereffect is the measure of adaptation.

The Effect of Optical Tilt and Exposure Time

The question of interest was not simply whether adaptation occurs, but how the magnitude of adaptation is related to the amount of exposure time and the degree of optical tilt produced by the prisms. Three groups of subjects wore prisms that produced 10, 20, or 32 degrees of optical tilt for four hours. Each subject was tested four times, at one hour intervals. During the prism exposure periods, the subject's activity consisted chiefly of walking about the inside of the laboratory building. Brief periods were devoted to a variety of other filler tasks.

Optical tilt. The aftereffect is expressed as the mean deviation of the subject's setting from the true vertical in the direction of the prism tilt. The effect of optical tilt is shown in Figure 3.8a. The greater the optical tilt to which the subject had been exposed, the greater was the amount of adaptation attained in a given period of exposure. The mean level of adaptation averaged over the four exposure intervals was 3.50, 5.59, and 8.24 degrees at 10, 20, and 32 degrees of optical tilt.

Exposure time. The effect of exposure time is shown in Figure 3.8b. The aftereffect is plotted as a function of exposure time for the three optical tilts. All three curves show the same trend. Adaptation develops rapidly during the first hour and then proceeds at an extremely slow rate.

What Is the Effective Stimulus?

These two findings fit well with the view that adaptation is a form of learning. The negatively accelerated function relating adaptation to exposure duration is typical of data in experiments on learning. The typical learning curve, which plots performance as a function of number of learning trials, shows the same trend. Learning proceeds rapidly during the early trials, and then more slowly until mastery is achieved. The positive relationship between adaptation and amount of tilt can be viewed as another instance of the common observation that the more there is to learn, the greater will be the amount learned.

The analogy between adaptation and learning is useful, but we need to go much further before we have an adequate explanation of the data. Let us consider what more can be said about the relationship between adaptation and exposure duration. There are two alternatives that may be advanced.

The *dependence hypothesis* holds that the effective stimulus for adaptation is the difference between the *prism tilt* and the current *level of adaptation.* The amount of adaptation in a given unit of time will be a constant fraction of the difference between the *prism tilt* and the current *level of adaptation.* Suppose that this constant is 0.25. When 20° prisms are first introduced, *prism tilt* – *level of adaptation* = 20° – 0° = 20°, and the adaptive shift will be (.25) (20°) = 5°. In the second hour, *prism tilt* – *level of adaptation* = 20° – 5° = 15°, and the adaptive shift during the second hour will be (.25) (15°), or 3.75°. In the third hour, *prism tilt* – *level of adaptation* = 20° – (5° + 3.75°) = 11.25°; the adaptive shift will be (.25) (11.25°) = 2.81°. You will note that each successive hour yields smaller adaptive shifts; repeated applications of this computational procedure would yield a curve of the general form shown in Figure 3.8b.

The *independence hypothesis* holds that the effective stimulus for adaptation is the difference between the *prism tilt* and the preexperimental optical tilt. For example, when the subject moves his head sideways, the direction of flow of the retinal pattern is different when prisms are worn. In normal, preexperimental viewing, the direction of retinal flow is parallel with the direction of head movement; with prisms on, sideways movement of the head is accompanied by retinal motion in a direction determined by the *prism tilt.* The independence hypothesis suggests that this difference is the stimulus for adaptation. In order to account for the

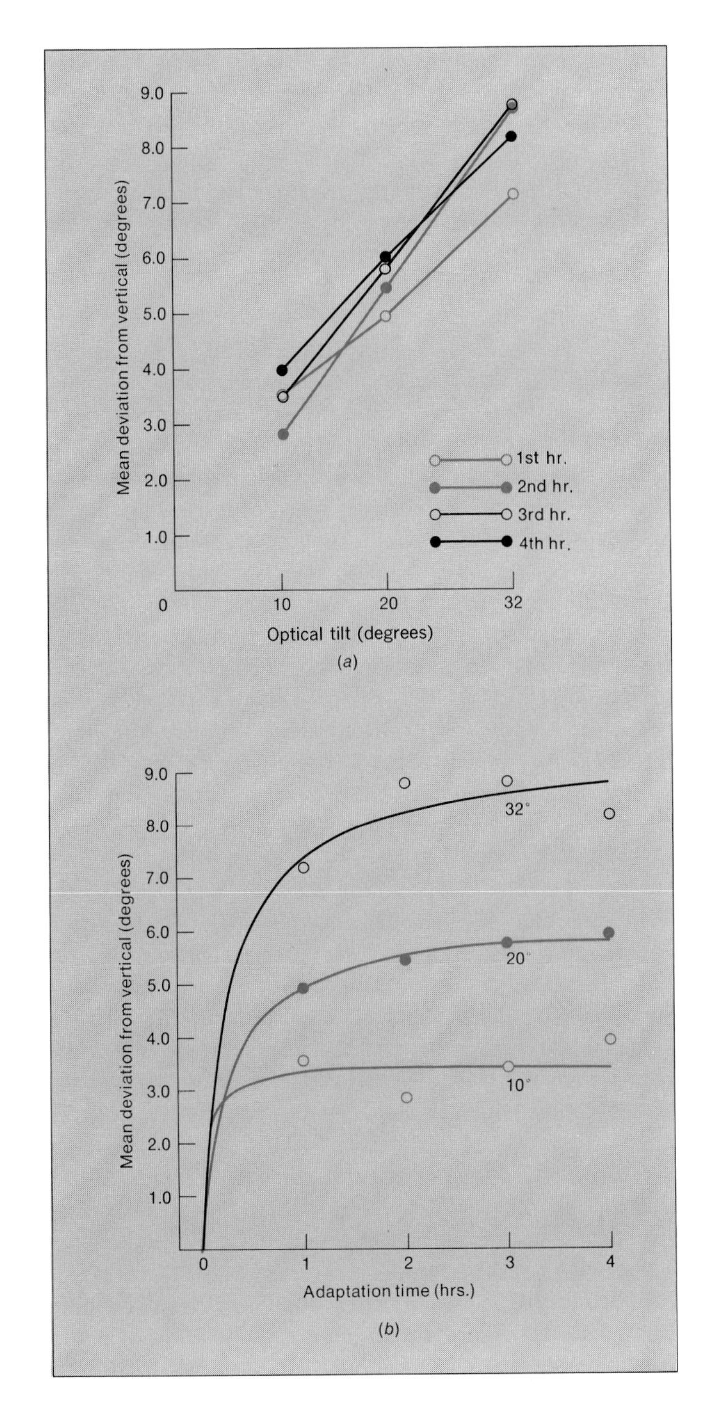

Fig. 3.8. Magnitude of adaptation as a function of optical tilt (a) and exposure duration (b). (Adapted from Ebenholtz, 1966)

negatively accelerated function in Figure 3.8b, the assumption is made that, as duration of exposure is extended, the preexperimental standard of optical tilt is gradually replaced by the current *prism tilt*. As a consequence, the difference responsible for adaptation is gradually reduced and adaptation slows.

How can we decide between these two hypotheses? There is a preferred procedure in experimental science for arriving at a decision between competing hypotheses. If the hypotheses are genuine alternatives, they should yield distinctive implications or predictions. If we can identify these, an experiment may be designed to determine which of them is borne out by data. To identify these implications, we need to make explicit the way in which the alternative hypotheses actually differ. In our case, the difference is clear. The dependence hypothesis claims that the magnitude of adaptive shift *depends* on the current *level of adaptation*; the independence hypothesis is correct, the reduction of *prism tilt* necessary to match the *of adaptation.* This difference provides a basis for deciding between the hypotheses.

Ebenholtz (1968) designed a set of experiments to decide between the two alternatives. The logic of the experiments was as follows: If the effective stimulus for an adaptive shift is the difference between *prism tilt* and current *level of adaptation*, then adjustment of the amount of *prism tilt* to match the *level of adaptation* should arrest adaptation. In the terms of the previous discussion, the effective stimulus is *prism tilt* − *level of adaptation*, so if *prism tilt* − *level of adaptation* = 0, no further adaptation should occur. On the other hand, if the independence hypothesis is correct, the reduction of *prism tilt* necessary to match the *level of adaptation* should still leave an effective difference between current optical tilt and preexperimental tilt, so adaptation should continue.

Let's see how this logical analysis was translated into experimental operations. Two conditions were compared. In the experimental condition (*E*) the subject was first exposed to 30 degree prism tilt for 30 minutes; then the aftereffect test was administered. The average aftereffect was 8.1 degrees. In other words, the subject judged the luminous line to be upright when it was tilted 8.1 degrees in the direction of *prism tilt.* Next, the *prism tilt* was adjusted to equal 8.1 degrees and the subject wore the prism for another 30 minutes, after which the aftereffect test was administered again. In the second condition (*C*), subjects wore only 22 degree prisms for 30 minutes, followed by a test.

The two hypotheses involve contrasting expectations about the outcome of this experiment. The dependence hypothesis predicts that no further adaptive shift should occur during the second half hour of condition *E*. This is deduced from the fact that *prism tilt* was set to match the *level of adaptation,* so that *prism tilt* − *level of adaptation* = 0. The independence hypothesis predicts that further adaptation should occur, since a difference (22 degrees) remains between the current tilt of 8 degrees and the immediately preceding tilt of 30 degrees. Furthermore, the prediction is that the amount of shift exhibited in the second phase of condition *E* should equal the shift under condition *C*, since under both conditions the effective difference was 22 degrees.

The results conformed to the independence hypothesis. Condition *E* yielded continued adaptation in the second half hour in the amount of 5.4 degrees, and condition *C* yielded 5.3 degrees of adaptation.

Since one experiment is rarely sufficient to transform a hypothesis into a definitive conclusion, Ebenholtz (1968, 1969) has conducted additional experiments to establish the independence hypothesis on firm ground. We will not discuss these studies, except to say that the overall picture is consistent with the view that the effective stimulus is the difference between current input and stored traces of preceding inputs. Of the many questions that remain for future study, two of the more intriguing have to do with the nature of the comparison between current and past inputs. What are the characteristics of the mechanism that does the comparing? What determines the state of the stored trace with which the current prism input is compared? The fact that rate of adaptation slows as exposure duration is extended suggests that something is happening to the stored standard. Has the standard faded, erased like the chalk marks on a board? This seems unlikely. A person who exhibits adaptation on an aftereffect test and then sits in the dark shows diminishing aftereffects with the passage of time, finally returning to his preexperimental setting. Restoration of preexperimental perception without intervening exposure to nonprism stimulation is a strong argument that the preexperimental standard remains intact. It is more likely that the preexperimental standard has been temporarily replaced by the current *prism tilt.* We will see in Chapter 4 that contemporary explanations of forgetting attribute a large share of forgetting to replacement resulting from interference between successive inputs.

Movement and Intention

In the experiments considered thus far, the subject moves about freely in a normal environment during the exposure period. Are there characteristics of this activity which are necessary, or at least conducive, to the occurrence of adaptation? We can feel certain that some form of interpolated activity is necessary. A person would never adapt during an exposure period in which he sat absolutely still in the dark, looking through prisms at a stationary luminous line or point, because such conditions would contain no stimulus for adaptation. The fact that the perceived orientation of the line or location of the point would not agree with its true orientation or location is not relevant. In any event, this discrepancy would not be a fact available to the visual system.

Let us look more carefully at the activity during the period of prism exposure, in order to identify tentatively those features which may be important. First, the subject engages in active, self-initiated movement. Second, these movements are accompanied by atypical changes of optical stimulation. Third, familiar objects appear to be distorted: the sides of a bookcase appear to be curved, the walls of the corridor appear tilted. Finally, visually guided behavior does not have its expected consequences; for example, the person reaches normally for an object only to find that it is to the side of where it appeared. The way to find which of these features is important for the occurrence of adaptation is to conduct experiments that compare different conditions of activity during exposure.

Held, with various associates (1958, 1961, 1963, 1965), has reported an extensive series of experiments dealing with this subject. The studies have focused on the first two factors listed above, but have also provided incidental information about the remaining factors. Commonly, these studies have compared two conditions of movement: (1) active movement by the subject, and (2) passive movement of a second subject simulating the activity of the first, to whom he may be yoked. The earliest experiment (Held and Gottlieb, 1958) deals with adaptation to the sideways displacement produced by wedge prisms. The experimental apparatus (shown in Fig. 3.9) was designed to test target localization. In the preexposure and postexposure tests, the subject was required to mark the four intersections of the target grid. During these tests, the subject could not see his hand; during the exposure period, he could see his hand, but no targets were visible. The prism was in place only during the three minute exposure period. Since the subject could not see his hand during the localization test, he had no way of knowing whether

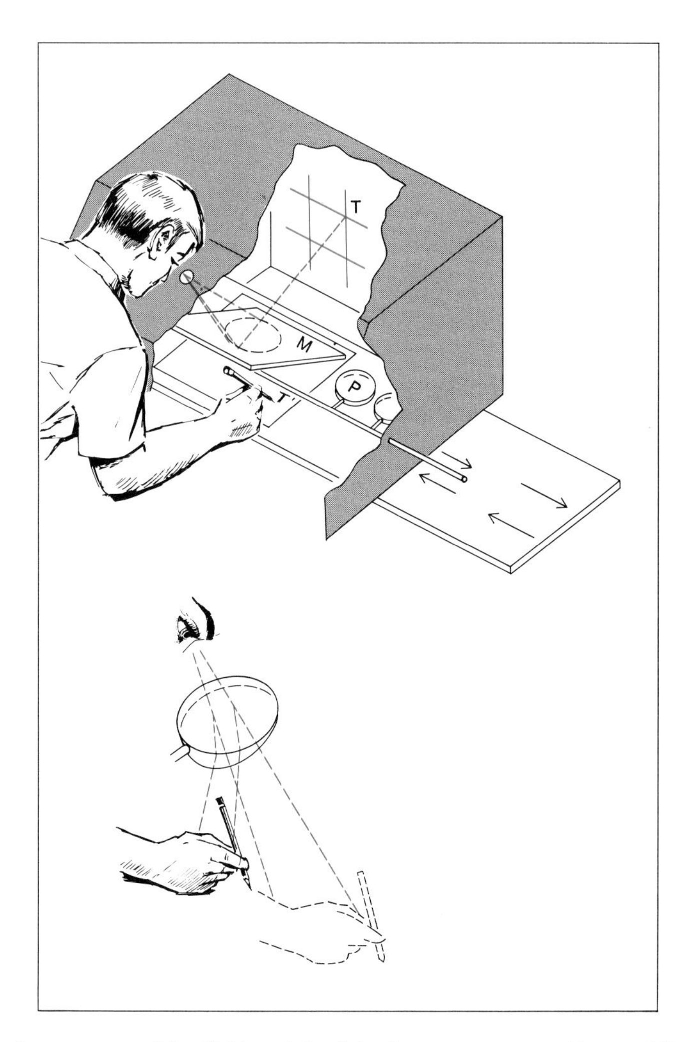

Fig. 3.9. Apparatus used by Held and Gottlieb. Apparatus tests subject's ability to guide his unseen hand to a visible target (T). The subject first marks the apparent location of the corners of the square as he sees them in the mirror. Note that the subject's hand is under the mirror and is not visible during target marking. The mirror can be replaced by a prism, (P). Now the subject sees his hand but not the target. The prism produces an apparent displacement of the hand, as shown. (From Held and Gottlieb, 1958)

he had marked the target accurately. He had no way of assessing the normalcy of his visually guided reaching.

After the preexposure target localization, the subjects were assigned to one of three conditions: (1) No movement—the subject looked through the prism at his stationary hand. (2) Active movement—the subject looked through the prism at his hand, which he moved back and forth in a left-right arc. (3) Passive movement—the subject's arm was secured on a mechanical pivoting device, and the arm was moved by the experimenter to simulate the movements of the active subject.

Figure 3.10 is an idealized representation of the results. The target marking before and after prism exposure can be compared for the three movement conditions. When no movement was allowed to occur (panel *b*), no evidence of adaptation

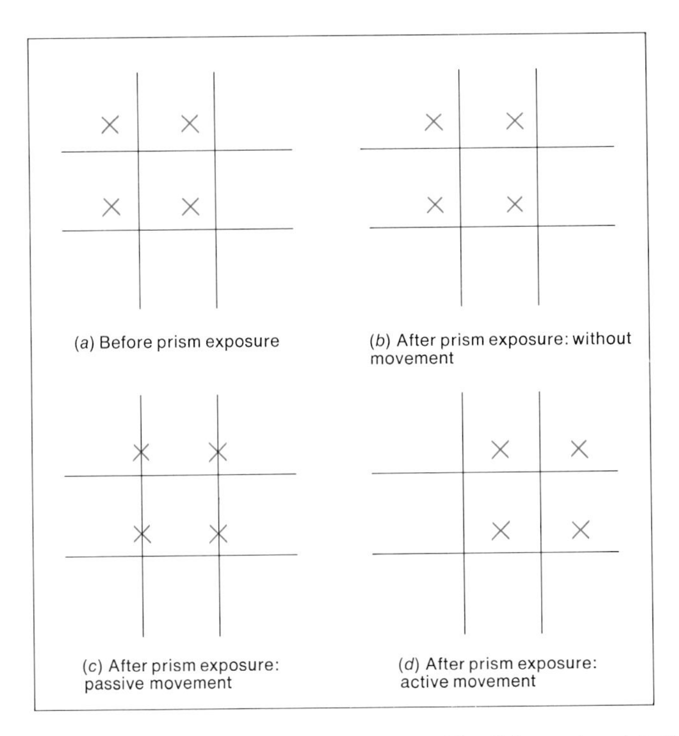

Fig. 3.10. Idealized representation of the results of the Held-Gottlieb experiment. In this example the subject has been exposed to a base-right prism.

was obtained; there was no shift in the target marking. The passive movement condition (panel c) yielded a slight shift. But the outcome for active movement (panel *d*) differed significantly from the other two conditions, evidencing an adaptive shift in target localization.

This experiment, involving only movements of the arm and very brief exposure durations, seems very different from the studies considered earlier. Would similar results be obtained for longer durations of movements of the entire body? Held and Bossom's (1963) experiment answers this question. In this study, a test of egocentric localization was administered. The subject sat in a rotating chair and tried to position himself so that a luminous target was directly in front of him. Suppose that a subject accomplishes this task without error, and then wears base-right wedge prisms that produce an apparent leftward displacement of 11 degrees. If he adapts completely to the prisms, he will come to accept the new retinal location as signifying straight ahead. Therefore, when he is tested after prism exposure he will shift his position 11 degrees to the right of his preexposure position. In other words, he will judge himself to be straight ahead of the target when his nose is actually pointing 11 degrees to its right.

During the exposure periods, which lasted several hours on each of four successive days, the subjects engaged in one of two forms of movement. Under the condition of active movement, they walked about outdoors. Under the condition of passive movement, they sat in wheelchairs and were transported over the same route as the active subjects.

The results of this experiment were consistent with the previous experiment. Significantly greater amounts of adaptation were obtained for the active subjects;

a number of active subjects exhibited 100 per cent adaptation on the fourth day. The passive subjects showed little adaptation; a number of them gave no evidence of any adaptation after 15 hours of exposure.

Held's results and similar findings by other investigators have helped to identify the features of the exposure condition that are involved in adaptation. First, it is not necessary that there be a discrepancy between the appearance of the visual scene and its expected appearance. The fact that adaptation continues after optical input has been adjusted to match the subject's level of adaptation supports this statement. In addition, investigations have demonstrated adaptation when the exposure activity has occurred in an experimentally created random environment (Held and Rekosh, 1963) that does not appear any more or less strange or distorted with or without prisms. Second, the optical transformations produced by the prisms may not be sufficient in and of themselves to induce adaptation. Held's passive subjects' frequent failure to adapt is evidence for this statement. But we must qualify this assertion, since other investigators (for example, Mack, 1967) have reported evidence of adaptation under conditions of passive movement. At present, we are unable to state the precise conditions under which adaptation will occur purely on the basis of optical stimulation, without active movement.

Third, active movement correlated with optical input is a condition which favors adaptation. Why should active movement be so important? One possibility is that this condition guarantees that the subject will sample the full range of stimulation. If the subject is moved passively, there is little motivation to engage in visual exploration. Passive movement might be equivalent to active movement if subjects under both conditions were instructed to look constantly at directional arrows painted on the floor. The subjects would engage in very little visual exploration, since in neither case would visual exploration have any consequences for guiding behavior.

Another possibility, currently under investigation, has broad implications for a theory of perception (Festinger *et al.,* 1967; Taylor, 1962). According to this interpretation, perceptual experience depends on the readiness or intention to respond motorically (*efferent readiness*) that is elicited by the optical input. In the absence of a readiness to respond, perception deteriorates, becoming dysfunctional or nonveridical. For this reason, there is little adaptation to prism rearrangement under the condition of passive movement. The condition evokes no readiness to respond, since the person does not control his own behavior.

The arguments for the efferent readiness hypothesis are too complex to review here. However, we will pause briefly to acquaint you with a striking phenomenon that seems to be compatible with the hypothesis.

Typically, the visual field is variegated, presenting various contours and areas that differ in brightness, hue, and other attributes. But sometimes nature provides an atypical visual scene of uniform, homogeneous stimulation (a snow storm in the arctic presents such a field). There are also various laboratory techniques for producing a field of uniform homogeneous stimulation. The term *Ganzfeld* is used to refer to a field of this nature. Continued inspection of a Ganzfeld leads to dramatic perceptual effects. At first the subject reports that he sees a kind of space-filling, surfaceless fog. After a while, he reports that he feels as if he has become blind, as if his visual sense has ceased functioning. In fact, recordings of cortical activity during these periods of "blank-out" look like recordings obtained when the eyes are closed. Arctic explorers have referred to this traumatic experience as "white-out."

The cessation of vision can be understood with the help of the efferent readiness hypothesis. In a Ganzfeld, the person receives the same optical stimulation wherever he directs his gaze. Eye movements have no perceptible consequences; therefore, the person may give up his normal readiness to respond to optical input.

The Locus of Change

In the first section of this chapter we described the classical study of adaptation to up-down inversion reported by Stratton. The discussion was concluded with a question concerning the nature of the adaptation he reported. Did he actually come to see the world upright, or did he merely accept an inverted scene as normal, and respond adaptively to the inverted scene? These two alternatives do not exhaust the list of possible interpretations. A number of authors (including Walls, 1951; Harris, 1965) have argued that Stratton came to feel *himself* to be inverted relative to his preexperimental body orientation, and to accept his new body image as normal. This would bring his felt body position and the orientation of the visual scene into a harmonious relationship. Stratton died in 1957, 60 years after completion of the inversion experiment. Friends of his reported that he lived in daily dread of being asked for the thousandth time to clarify his experience. It might not be presumptuous to suppose that by that time Stratton was as uncertain as his readers. Subsequent experiments have not succeeded in bringing about unanimity concerning the changes that take place when inverting prisms are worn (Harris, 1965; Rock, 1966; Epstein, 1967; Ewert, 1930; Kohler, 1951).

Questions concerning the locus of adaptation can be raised in connection with all cases of adaptation. The matter has been studied experimentally, fortunately with better results than those described for Stratton's case. In what follows we will consider one experiment designed to determine the locus of change in adaptation to sideways displacement produced by wedge prisms. An experiment similar to this one, but aimed at adaptation to inversion, could contribute significantly to settling the 75 year old Stratton controversy.

Look back to the Held–Gottlieb experiment, which used the eye-hand coordination test (Fig. 3.9) to measure adaptation to sideways displacement. Under the condition of active movement, subjects showed significant shifts in target marking following exposure to the prism, and we concluded that adaptation had occurred. Our present aim is not to question this conclusion, but to refine it by specifying *what* has been changed during adaptation. There are two main alternatives:

1. The locus of change is *visual.* Retinal locations, or combinations of retinal location and eye position, which specified a particular visual direction prior to prism exposure, specify a different visual direction after adaptation. This interpretation has been illustrated in our earlier discussions of adaptation to inversion and optical tilt.

2. The locus of change is *proprioceptive.* This hypothesis is most easily understood in the context of a specific example. Consider the target markings shown in Figure 3.10. Prior to prism exposure, the subject exhibits a tendency to mark the location somewhat to the left of the target. Next, during the period in which he views his moving hand through base-right prisms, the subject sees his hand in one place, but feels it to be in a different place. The discrepancy arises because the prism produces a sideways displacement of the visually perceived location of the hand. This atypical discrepancy between the felt and seen positions of the hand can be resolved in one of two ways. The hand can come to be seen where

it is felt to be—vision conforms to proprioception—or the hand can come to feel to be where it is seen—proprioception conforms to vision. What would be the consequences of a proprioceptive shift of the second sort? Since base-right prisms produce an apparent visual displacement to the left, the subject feels his hand to be to the left of its true position. In the aftereffect test, when the subject marks the target with his unseen hand, he will continue to feel that his hand is to the left of its actual position. As a result, he will shift his hand objectively to the right in order to mark a target whose visually perceived location has not changed.

How can we determine which of these alternatives is a correct interpretation of the adaptive shift? Since both are equally compatible with the results of the eye-hand coordination test, we cannot use this test to distinguish between the alternatives. We need a test for which the two hypotheses have contrasting expectations. For example, suppose that a blindfolded person is asked to point at the location of an *auditory* signal before and after prism exposure. Since this *ear-hand* coordination test does not involve vision, the visual shift hypothesis predicts that no change in auditory target localization will occur. The proprioceptive shift hypothesis would predict that any test which requires utilization of the hand to localize a target will show a shift equal to that exhibited on the *eye-hand* coordination test.

Hay and Pick (1966) designed an experiment which followed the logic of this example. Six tests were administered prior to prism exposure and at various intervals during 144 hours of exposure to prisms that produced an 11 degree sideways displacement.

The *eye-hand test* was the target marking task used by Held and Gottlieb.

The *ear-eye and eye-head tests* were designed to measure visual shift; adaptive shift on these tests would imply that the locus of adaptation is visual. In the ear-eye test the subject turned his head to a position straight ahead of a concealed sound source, and then indicated the visual direction of the source by calling out a number which designated its location. In the eye-head test, the subject turned his head so that he was directly facing a visible target. This test, like the one used by Held and Bossom (1961), identifies the combination of eye position and retinal position that elicits the visual impression of straight ahead.

The *ear-hand and head-hand tests* were designed to measure proprioceptive shift. The ear-hand test required the subject to point to the location of a sound source (signal) while blindfolded. The head-hand test required the subject to point straight ahead of his nose, with his eyes shut. Changes on these tests would imply that the adaptive shifts are due to alterations in the felt position of the body.

The *ear-head test* was designed to determine whether a shift in auditory localization had occurred. The subject was instructed to turn his head so that he was directly facing a concealed sound source.

Figure 3.11 shows the shifts obtained with the four types of tests. First, we may note that the eye-hand coordination test, which theoretically taps both visual and proprioceptive shifts, shows the greatest change. Next, we may observe that there is evidence of both visual and proprioceptive shifts in the other tests, but that these two types of shift follow different time courses. The proprioceptive shift develops rapidly, then dissipates with continued exposure. The visual shift grows less rapidly, but continues to increase up to 72 hours, remaining stable up to 144 hours. Finally, if you examine the curves for the visual and proprioceptive shifts and sum the curves at each exposure interval, you will arrive at the conclusion that the two curves add up to the curve for the eye-hand coordination test.

We initiated this discussion by proposing two alternative hypotheses to account

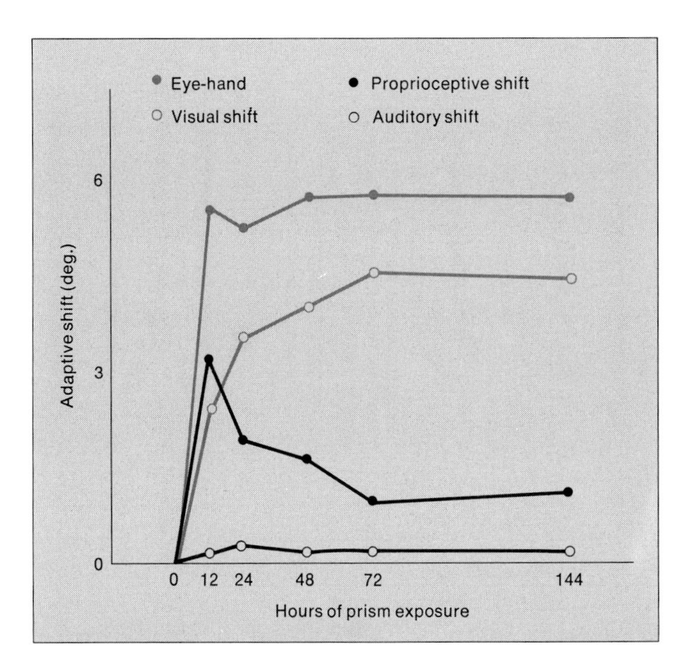

Fig. 3.11. Shifts on four types of test in Hay and Pick's experiment. The visual shift curve represents the average for the ear-eye and eye-head tests. The proprioceptive shift curve represents the average for the ear-hand and head-hand tests. (Adapted from Hay and Pick, 1966)

for adaptation to sideways displacement, but the results of the Hay–Pick experiment show that our original formulation was too simple. Adaptation is based on *both* proprioceptive and visual shift. During the early exposure period adaptation depends on proprioceptive shift; as exposure continues, alterations in vision occur which are largely responsible for the continued growth of adaptation.

Another way of interpreting the Hay–Pick results emphasizes the vital role of visual changes. This interpretation assumes that proprioceptive shift reflects "visual capture." Proprioception conforms to vision; the hand feels as though it is where it is seen. Therefore, early during exposure, when there has been little visual shift, the hand will look off to the side, and its felt position, conforming to vision, will feel off to the side. With the development of visual changes, the seen position of the hand agrees more with its true position, and if proprioception conforms to vision, the hand will begin to feel to be where it actually is. As a result, a test of proprioceptive shift will indicate a reduction in the magnitude of the effect. Thus, the visual test and proprioceptive test are providing tied measures. When the visual test shows little change, the proprioceptive test will show large changes; the converse will also be true. This was the case in Hay and Pick's experiment.

The Hay–Pick study illustrates the strategy that may be used to identify the locus of change in adaptation. Successful implementation of this strategy presupposes the availability of tests that provide independent measures of potential changes underlying the adaptive shift. These tests administered at regular intervals can assess the possibility that diverse changes are responsible for adaptation. Future research in this area is likely to resolve the question concerning the locus of adaptation.

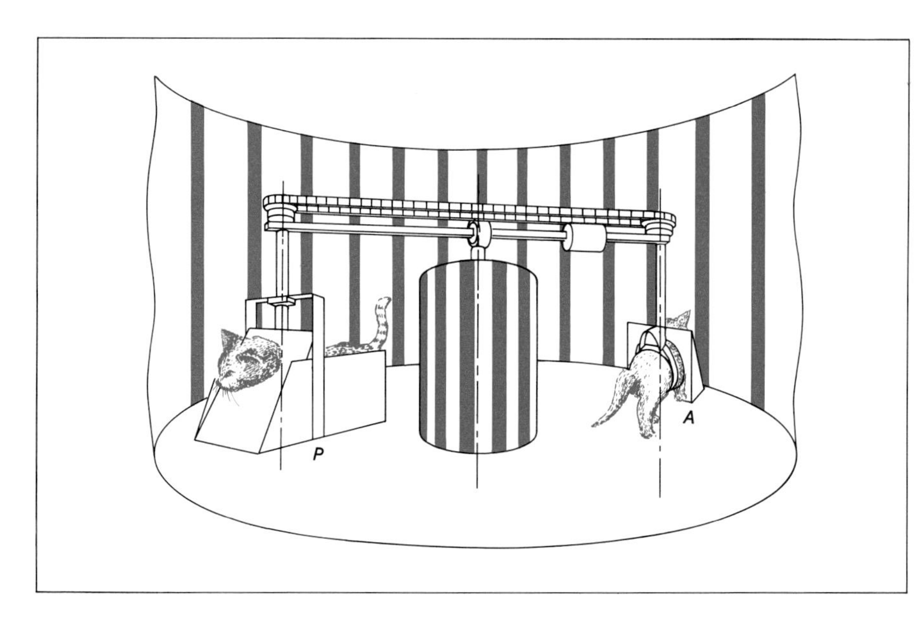

Fig. 3.12. Apparatus for equating motion and consequent visual feedback for an actively moving (A) and a passively moved (P) subject. (From Held and Hein, 1963)

Adaptation and Perceptual Development

Earlier in this chapter we remarked that interest in adaptation has been stimulated by a variety of underlying motivations, one of which has been the wish to identify variables that influence developmental changes in perception. The argument has been that the intervention of optical systems that disrupt normal retinal-perceptual and perceptual-behavioral correlations tends to create a condition somewhat like that which prevails in infancy. Therefore, if we discover the variables that control adaptation, we may also have identified the variables that regulate development.

Two aspects of this argument can be usefully distinguished. One is simply the claim that the proponent of the argument is impressed by apparent similarities between the original state of perception and the prism exposure state. Little would be gained by debating this position. Whether or not you too are impressed will depend on your picture of the perceptual world of the infant. The second aspect of the argument draws an implication that is empirically testable. Can it be demonstrated experimentally that variables important for adaptation are also important for development?

Of the few experiments addressed to this question, one of the most widely cited is the "kitten-carousel" experiment reported by Held and Hein (1963). The objective was to determine whether self-produced movement, which figures so prominently as a factor in adaptation, is also vital for development. The experimental subjects were kittens born and reared in the laboratory. Sixteen kittens were divided into eight pairs. One kitten in each pair was assigned to the active movement (A) condition, while its mate was assigned to the passive movement (P) condition. The kittens were reared in darkness from birth until member A of a pair attained the size and coordination necessary for the experimental task. At that time, between

Pair Number	Age in Weeks[a]	Exposure in Apparatus (in hr.) A	P	Ratio of Descents Shallow/Deep A	P
1X	8	33	33	12/0	6/6
2X	8	33	33	12/0	4/8
3X	8	30	30	12/0	7/5
4X	9	63	63	12/0	6/6
5X	10	33	33	12/0	7/5
6X	10	21	21	12/0	7/5
7X	12	9	9	12/0	5/7
8X	12	15	15	12/0	8/4

[a] *At the beginning of exposure in the experimental apparatus.*

Table 3.1 *Ratio of Descents to Shallow and Deep Sides of Visual Cliff (From Held and Hein, 1963, p. 875)*

8 and 12 weeks, the pair of kittens was removed from the dark for three hours daily and placed in the "kitten carousel."

The apparatus (Fig. 3.12) is designed to provide equivalent optical stimulation to each member of the pair—with active movement for kitten A, and with passive movement for kitten P. Pictured in Figure 3.12, the kittens are inside a cylinder whose interior is painted with vertical stripes. Kitten A is in a harness that permits it to move freely along a circular path; kitten P is restrained in a gondola which prohibits self-produced locomotion. The kittens are in a yoked arrangement, so that the self-produced movements of kitten A are mechanically transferred to P. Thus, when A moves, P is moved in the opposite direction by the same amount, to provide equivalent optical stimulation to both members of each pair. In the case of A this stimulation is correlated with self-produced movement, while for P the same stimulation is not associated with self-produced movement.

If optical stimulation correlated with self-produced movement is important for development, as it is for adaptation, differences should be observed between the performances of kittens A and P on a relevant test of perception. The test selected for this purpose was the visual cliff described in Chapter 2. On the first day that Kitten A gave evidence of normal depth discrimination (by exhibiting visually mediated anticipation of contact with a surface by extending its paws as it was brought nearer to the surface), both kittens were tested on the visual cliff.

As you will recall, the visual cliff provides evidence of depth discrimination if the subject shows a significant preference for the shallow side; normally reared animals almost never descend on the cliff side. Table 3.1, which shows the number of descents to the shallow and cliff sides, makes it evident that kittens A and P differed greatly. The A kittens performed like normally reared kittens, avoiding the cliffs on every trial. The P kittens, on the other hand, gave no evidence of depth discrimination, and descended to the two sides equally often. Thus, although kittens A and P have equivalent histories of exposure to optical stimulation, kitten P, which did not engage in self-produced movement, failed to develop normal depth perception.

Held and Hein (1963) conclude that these findings demonstrate the complementarity of experiments on adaptation and on development. Furthermore, there is the implication that the processes of adaptation and development may have common characteristics. If apparently disparate phenomena are affected in the same way by a given experimental variable, then the processes underlying these phenomena may be similar. This is a not uncommon argument in scientific reasoning (see, for example, Underwood, 1957, Chap. 8).

Open Questions

Adaptation has been studied intensively in the decade of the sixties, and significant contributions have been made to our knowledge about it. Nevertheless, many questions remain to be answered. We would like to understand better the way in which movement affects adaptation. We would like to explain the rate of adaptation. This area is complicated by the fact that adaptation for different kinds of optical transformation, such as curvature, sideways displacement, or tilt, proceeds at different rates. An additional complication is the existence of individual differences among subjects. Some adapt fully, some partially, while others give no evidence of adaptation. These differences, although they are concealed in the group averages reported in this chapter, do exist.

The study of adaptation can be viewed as a self-contained field of investigation, but eventually we will want to spell out the relevance of the adaptation phenomena to other questions in the psychology of perception. Consider the perceptual constancies discussed in Chapter 2. As an example, perceived size tends to remain constant despite variations of retinal image size and perceived shape tends to remain constant despite variations of retinal image shape. Stated in this way, perceptual constancy and perceptual adaptation appear to have common characteristics. In both cases, perception is relatively unaffected by transformations of optical stimulation. Would it be useful to consider the perceptual constancies as the product of an adaptation process? This is a theoretical and empirical question which we cannot answer at present.

In connection with the above question, you may also wish to consider the implications of findings reported in studies of *sensory deprivation* (Zubek, 1969). In these studies, the subject is deprived of all sensory stimulation for long periods of time. A typical arrangement has him lying on a bed in a soundproof chamber. His eyes are blindfolded and a steady sound is transmitted through earphones. He wears a specially designed suit which prevents him from receiving tactual stimulation through parts of his body. As you might expect, the experience is not pleasant, and paid volunteers will rarely submit to this treatment for more than several days. A variety of cognitive and emotional effects are observed (see Chap. 8), but our concern is with the perceptual effects of sensory deprivation. Several investigators have reported that a breakdown of the perceptual constancies occurs. When the blindfold is removed at the end of the deprivation period, the subject reports a plastic world in which sizes and shapes change when distance and orientation are varied. One way to interpret this breakdown is in terms of a loss of adaptation.

We should make explicit one question which may have been troubling those of you who have read this chapter soon after completing Chapter 2. In that chapter we presented evidence that the young infant, perhaps even the newborn infant, perceives the world not too differently from the adult. This implies the presence of unlearned processes of perception which operate to produce a stable perceptual world. Now we have presented evidence that the perceptual world is highly modifiable—that organisms can adapt to a wide variety of optical transformations. Is there some way of combining these two pictures of the perceptual world into a single consistent view? This is one of the tasks facing perceptual theory.

Glossary

Adaptation: the perceptual shift that occurs during the course of continuous exposure to prismatic transformation. The term is also used more generally to refer to a perceptual shift that occurs when the observer is exposed continuously to an unvarying stimulus.

Aftereffect: the perceptual effects observed after continuous and extended exposure to a specific condition of stimulation has been terminated. In this chapter, it is the difference between a judgment made before and after prism exposure.

Efferent readiness: certain analyses of perception assume that programs stored in the brain issue commands to the motoric system to execute specific movement patterns in response to optical input. Signals issued by the brain to the motoric system are called efferent signals, or efference, and the visual system is said to be in a state of readiness to issue efferent signals.

Egocentric localization: localization with respect to the position of the body. Thus, if S is asked to point straight ahead, egocentric localization is being tested.

Proprioceptive: pertaining to the position sense, or the sense by which we know the relative locations of various parts of our body even without the aid of vision. Changes in the position sense may be called proprioceptive changes.

References

Berkeley, G. An essay towards a new theory of vision. In A.A. Luce and T.E. Jessop (Eds.), *The works of George Berkeley, Bishop of Cloyne.* New York: Nelson, 1948.

Ebenholtz, S.M. Adaptation to a rotated visual field as a function of degree of optical tilt and exposure time. *J. exp. Psychol.*, 1966, **72,** 629–634.

———. Some evidence for a comparator in adaptation to optical tilt. *J. exp. Psychol.*, 1968, **77,** 94–100.

———. Transfer and decay functions in adaptation to optical tilt. *J. exp. Psychol.*, 1969, **81,** 170–173.

Epstein, W. *Varieties of perceptual learning.* New York: McGraw-Hill, 1967.

Ewert, P.H. A study of the effect of inverted retinal stimulation upon spatially coordinated behavior. *Genet. Psychol. Monogr.*, 1930, **7,** 177–363.

Festinger, L., H. Ono, C. Burnham, and D. Bamber. Efference and the conscious experience of perception. *J. exp. Psychol.*, 1967, **74** (Whole No. 4).

Harris, C.S. Perceptual adaptation to inverted, reversed and displaced vision. *Psychol. Rev.*, 1965, **72,** 419–444.

Hay, J., and H. Pick, Jr. Visual and proprioceptive adaptation to optical displacement of the visual stimulus. *J. exp. Psychol.*, 1966, **71,** 150–158.

Held, R. Plasticity in sensory-motor systems. *Scientific Amer.*, 1965, **213,** 5, 84–94.

Held, R., and J. Bossom. Neonatal deprivation and adult rearrangement: Complementary techniques for analyzing plastic sensory-motor coordinations. *J. comp. physiol. Psychol.*, 1961, **54,** 33–37.

Held, R., and N. Gottlieb. Technique for studying adaptation to disarranged hand-eye coordination. *Perceptual and Motor Skills*, 1958, **8,** 83–86.

Held, R., and A. Hein. Movement-produced stimulation in the development of visually guided behavior. *J. comp. physiol. Psychol.*, 1963, **56,** 872–876.

Held, R., and J. Rekosh. Motor sensory feedback and the geometry of visual space. *Science*, 1963, **141,** 722–723.

Howard, I.P., and W.B. Templeton. *Human spatial orientation.* New York: John Wiley, 1966.

Kohler, I. Experiments with goggles. *Scientific Amer.*, 1962, **206,** 562–84.
_______. Uber und Wandlungen der Wahrnehmungswelt. *SB Ost. Akad. Wiss.*, 1951, **227,** 1–118. Trans. by H. Fiss, The formation and transformation of the perceptual world. *Psychol. Issues*, 1964, **3** (Whole No. 4).
Mack, A. The role of movement in perceptual adaptation to a tilted retinal image. *Perception and Psychophysics*, 1967, **2,** 65–69.
Ogle, K.N. *Optics: An introduction for ophthalmologists.* New York: CC Thomas, 1961.
_______. Upright vision and the retinal image. *Psychol. Rev.*, 1897, **4,** 182–187. (a)
_______. Vision without inversion of the retinal image. *Psychol. Rev.*, 1897, **4,** 341–360; 463–481. (b)
Rock, I. *The nature of perceptual adaptation.* New York: Basic Books, 1966.
Stratton, G.M. Some preliminary experiments on vision without inversion of the retinal image. *Psychol. Rev.*, 1896, **3,** 611–617.
Taylor, J.G. *The behavioral basis of perception.* New Haven, Conn.: Yale University Press, 1962.
Underwood, B.J. *Psychological research.* New York: Appleton-Century-Crofts, 1957.
Walls, G.L. The problem of visual direction. Part III. Experimental attacks and their results. *Amer. J. Optometry*, 1951, **28,** 173–212.
Zubek, J.P. (Ed.) *Sensory deprivation: Fifteen years of research.* New York: Appleton-Century-Crofts, 1969.

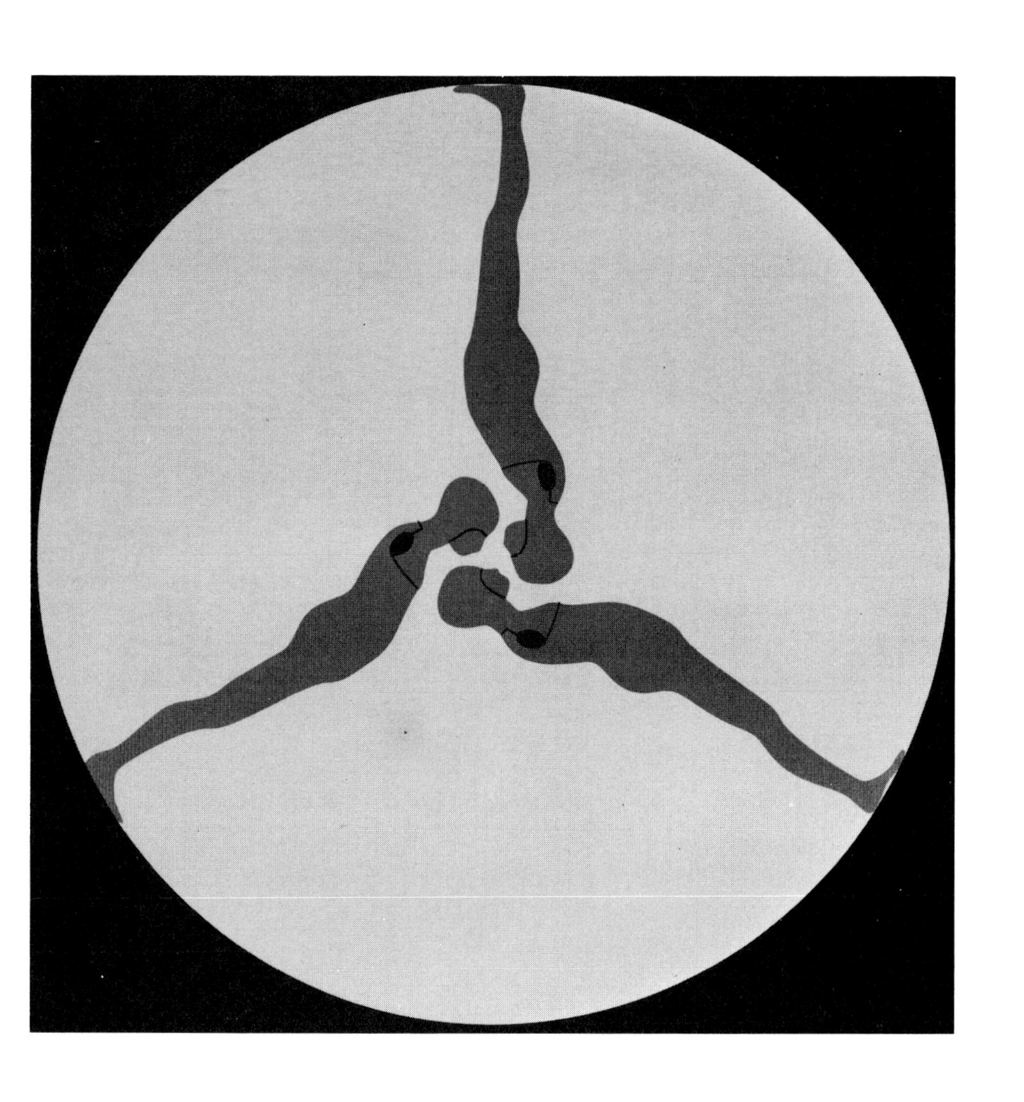

4 Remembering and Forgetting

Like death, taxes, and final examinations, forgetting is always with us. Although we are reconciled to the fact of forgetting, occasionally we are tempted by the prospect of a memory system that will eliminate it. Memory systems are not recent inventions; their greatest development and popularity was during the period preceding widespread availability of printed matter. A memory system was indispensable to the practice of rhetoric, and a number of elaborate systems existed in ancient Rome. The concluding section of this chapter will be devoted to a discussion of mnemonic devices and memory systems. However, for the most part our attention will be concentrated on an examination of forgetting, by which we mean the difference between what has been learned originally and what can be remembered: amount forgotten = amount learned − amount retained.

Aspects of Forgetting

Short-Term and Long-Term Memory

A number of distinctions will facilitate our exploration of forgetting. The first concerns the length of the retention interval, that is, the time elapsed between original learning and the attempt to recall. The term *short-term memory* (STM) is used when the learned material has been in the memory store only a brief interval prior to the recall effort; *long-term memory* (LTM) is used when the learned material has been acquired at a relatively longer interval prior to the recall effort.

Short-term memory (STM). Short-term memory typically refers to retention intervals counted in seconds. Everyday experience provides many examples of our forgetting after very brief retention intervals. We consult the directory for an unfamiliar telephone number, intending to dial the number immediately, but our attention is deflected by a momentary distraction. When we return to the phone, the number has been forgotten. A similar instance is the rapid forgetting of names of newly introduced people. Sometimes names are forgotten at the same rate as new names are introduced, so that at the end of a sequence only the last name can be remembered. In these cases, our inability to reproduce the desired material represents a failure to retrieve stored information, forgetting rather than failure to learn.

A simple procedure, which tests the subject's retention of a single nonsense syllable over spans of time shorter than one minute, demonstrates the occurrence of forgetting after brief retention intervals. The experimenter spells aloud a three consonant nonsense syllable, such as CHJ, and immediately following the last letter gives a three digit number, such as 506. The subject has been instructed that his task is to remember CHJ, but that during the retention interval he is to count backwards by threes from 506 in time with a metronome. The counting task minimizes the subject's opportunity to engage in covert rehearsal of the syllable during the retention interval. At a signal he is to stop counting and recall the syllable.

Figure 4.la reviews the procedure of an early experiment of this sort reported by Peterson and Peterson (1959). Figure 4.lb plots the frequency of recall of nonsense syllables for retention intervals ranging in duration from 0 to 18 seconds. The probability of correct recall decreases with increases in the recall interval. At 18 seconds, less than 10 per cent of the syllables are correctly remembered.

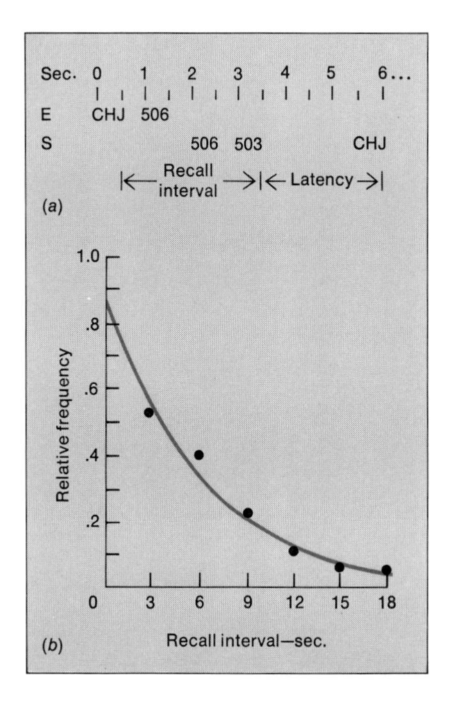

Fig. 4.1. (a) Sequence of events for a recall interval of 3 seconds. (b) Correct recalls with latencies below 2.83 seconds as a function of recall interval. (From Peterson and Peterson, 1959)

Long-term memory (LTM). Studies of long-term memory examine retention after longer elapsed intervals. In one experimental procedure the subject is required to learn a list of unrelated verbal items; then he leaves the laboratory with instructions to return at a prescribed time. Upon returning he is asked to relearn the original list. Consider two extreme subjects, one who has forgotten nothing during the retention interval, another who has forgotten everything. Obviously, the first subject will relearn the list on a single trial, while the second may need as many trials to relearn it as he needed during original learning. Generalizing from this hypothetical situation, we may assert that the difference between original and relearning performance is a measure of forgetting. The smaller the difference, the greater the amount of forgetting. This measure is usually called a *savings* measure, because it expresses forgetting in terms of the amount of work saved in relearning compared to the amount of work required in original learning:

$$\text{per cent savings} = \frac{\text{number trials to learn} - \text{number trials to relearn}}{\text{number trials to learn}} \times 100$$

The savings measure was introduced by Ebbinghaus (1885), the first experimental psychologist to study memory. Figure 4.2 is his classic curve of retention. Although this curve is based on the data of only one subject (Ebbinghaus was both experimenter and subject), its general features are typical of retention curves for lists of nonsense syllables. In agreement with Ebbinghaus' data, contemporary investigations have found that the curve of retention falls very rapidly; most forgetting occurs in the first few hours after learning.

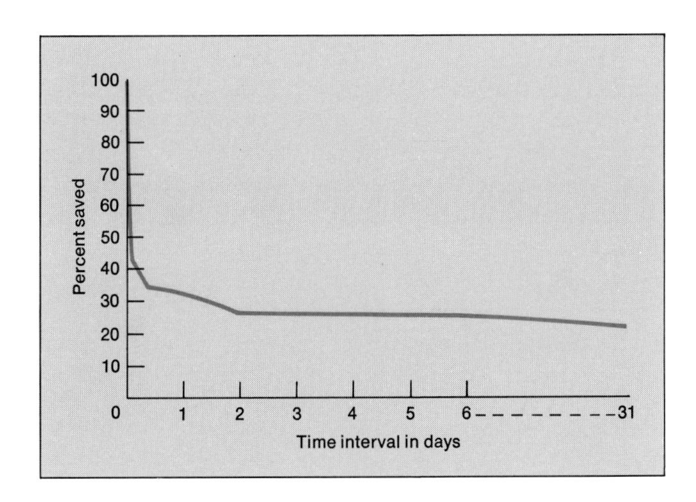

Fig. 4.2. Ebbinghaus' curve of retention by the savings method. (From data of Ebbinghaus, 1885)

Passive Forgetting, Active Forgetting, and Not Remembering

The distinction between STM and LTM is based on an objective feature of the experimental procedure, length of the retention interval. Our next distinction is derived from the way in which forgetting is commonly experienced. The experience of forgetting may be classified into three broad categories: passive forgetting, active forgetting, and not remembering.

Passive forgetting. Most forgetting seems to occur without our involvement. We neither seek to forget nor try to guarantee that we will remember. As a consequence of disuse the originally learned material fades from memory.

Active forgetting. In other cases, the occurrence of forgetting appears due to active involvement. We exercise an ill-defined, but effective, ability to put things out of mind—we actively forget. Two types of active forgetting may be distinguished. One involves forgetting as the result of deliberate suppression. The material is voluntarily put out of mind, usually to allow us to acquire new information. When we return to the "excluded" material we may discover that it is no longer accessible. The other type of active forgetting was central to Freud's (1904) analysis of psychological functioning. He claimed that forgetting is often motivated by the need to repress memories that are likely to evoke anxiety (Chap. 14). Unlike deliberate suppression, this type of forgetting is the result of unconscious repression. We need not share Freud's unbounded enthusiasm for the repression hypothesis in order to agree that everyday experience confirms the existence of motivated forgetting.

Not remembering. In normal language, there are two common ways of reporting forgetting: "I forgot," and "I can't remember." It is instructive that ordinarily the two are not used interchangeably. A variety of factors are undoubtedly responsible for this, but here we will propose that they are used distinctively because they refer to two distinctive states of memory. "I forgot" reports the impression that the previously acquired material is erased from memory and is no longer accessible. "I can't remember" reports the impression that the material is present in memory, but cannot be retrieved or remembered. The first phrase suggests a disturbance in *storage*, the second a disturbance in *retrieval* from storage. "I can't remember" often implies that if the right hint or retrieval cue were provided, we would remember.

Probably the most common and vexatious example of not remembering is the "tip of the tongue" phenomenon, in which the sought-after material is almost within reach. William James (1893, p. 251) described the phenomenon this way:

> Suppose we try to recall a forgotten name. The state of our consciousness is peculiar. There is a gap therein; but no mere gap. It is a gap that is intensely active. A sort of wraith of the name is in it, beckoning us in a given direction, making us at moments tingle with the sense of our closeness and then letting us sink back without the longed-for term. If wrong names are proposed to us, this singularly defined gap acts immediately so as to negate them. They do not fit into its mould.

While few of us could match James' prose, all of us can recognize the experience.

Passive Forgetting

Most forgetting is probably passive forgetting. We learn something today, then after a period of nonrehearsal or disuse discover that the material has been forgotten. In this section we describe the progress that has been made in understanding this phenomenon.

Disuse Hypothesis

Our first impulse might be to explain forgetting by restating its defining conditions: inasmuch as forgetting follows a period of disuse, we might be inclined to claim disuse as its cause. Although it is evident that no forgetting would occur if we engaged in continuous rehearsal, it is not the absence of practice or rehearsal that produces forgetting. There are a number of logical arguments for rejecting the hypothesis of disuse (Osgood, 1953, p. 549), but we will confine our objections to a single argument based on experimental data.

If the hypothesis is correct, then whenever retention is tested after equal periods of disuse, the amount of forgetting should be the same. To test this, experimenters are investigating the effect of sleep on forgetting. In a recent experiment, Ekstrand (1967) had two groups of subjects learn a list of 12 pairs of words. Practice continued until the subjects could provide the right-hand member of each pair as a response to the left-hand member as a stimulus. Group S learned the list immediately prior to retiring for a night of sleep in the laboratory. Group A learned the list in the morning prior to beginning their normal round of activities. Both groups were instructed not to rehearse the list after learning was concluded. Eight hours after the completion of their learning, both groups were tested for retention. Group S showed 89 per cent recall, forgetting 11 per cent, and Group A showed 77 per cent recall, forgetting 23 per cent. The subjects who spent the retention interval in sleep forgot only half as much as the awake subjects. Similar results had been reported earlier by Jenkins and Dallenbach (1924) and Van Ormer (1932).

The fact that *less* forgetting is observed following sleep contradicts the hypothesis of disuse. First, equal periods of disuse produced unequal amounts of forgetting. Moreover, if disuse were responsible for forgetting, we would expect more to be forgotten following a period of sleep; there is certainly less opportunity for active rehearsal during sleep than during waking hours.

Interference Theory

The sleep study is instructive not only because it demonstrates the weakness of the disuse hypothesis, but also because the results suggest an alternative. Forgetting is due to interference from other activities. The level and diversity of intervening activity is significantly reduced during sleep; consequently, less is forgotten.

The interference theory is now the dominant explanation of forgetting. The status of this theory rests on findings from two types of experiments which demonstrate the effects of two kinds of interference, retroactive and proactive, and elucidate the processes by which interference produces forgetting.

Retroactive Interference (RI)

Retroactive interference (RI) refers to interference with retention produced by activities interpolated between original learning and recall. The experimental plan for demonstrating RI compares retention under two conditions: an experimental condition which interpolates a task between original learning and the test of retention, and a control condition that omits the interpolated task.

A favorite laboratory task for the analysis of RI is paired associate learning, which requires the subject to learn associations between arbitrarily combined pairs of verbal items. A list of pairs is presented in a memory drum, a device that exposes elements of the list singly for controlled durations. A typical order of presentation exposes the left-hand member of each pair alone for two seconds, followed by an exposure of the whole pair for two seconds. When the entire list of pairs has been presented in this alternating order, a trial has been completed. The subject's task is to learn the associations between the members of each pair so that he can anticipate the right-hand item as a response to the left-hand item.

Many studies of paired associate learning and RI have used nonsense syllables as learning materials. The three letter nonsense syllable, consonant-vowel-consonant, was introduced by Ebbinghaus in an effort to minimize the role of meaningfulness in learning. However, modern investigators who use nonsense syllables do not assume that they are meaningless or nonsensical. On the contrary, considerable effort has been devoted to scaling their meaningfulness (for example, Archer, 1960; Noble, 1952), which varies greatly. This factor is always taken into account in selecting the materials for an experiment in verbal learning.

The RI paradigm. Table 4.1 represents a typical plan for demonstrating the effects of retroactive interference on retention of a list of paired associates. A–B represents one list, and A–C a second list of paired associates which is formed by pairing the left-hand members (stimuli) of list A–B with new right-hand members (responses). For the experimental condition, learning of A–C is interpolated between

Condition	Task 1	Task 2	Task 3
Control	Learn list A–B	Rest	Test for A–B
Experimental	Learn list A–B	Learn list A–C	Test for A–B

Table 4.1 *Experimental Plan for Demonstration of Retroactive Interference*

the original learning of A–B and the test for its retention, while for the control condition no relevant activity is interpolated.

The retroactive interference produced by A–C is manifested on the retention test; retention of A–B will be significantly lower under the experimental condition. The measure of retroactive interference is the difference between retention levels under the two conditions. In appropriate conditions, forgetting of A–B may be complete.

When does RI occur? The decrement in recall under the experimental condition is attributable to the interference produced by the interpolated list A–C. However, it is important to make explicit that, despite the convention of designating the effect as retroactive, the interpolated list cannot in fact act retroactively to affect a preceding event. Interference of list A–C with A–B must occur during a stage in the experiment when the two are concurrent. This is possible at two stages: during the learning of A–C, the first list, A–B, may intrude, and during the test stage for retention of A–B, list A–C may intrude. In other words, interference may occur either during the interpolated learning or at the time of A–B recall.

Early investigators of RI localized the effects exclusively in the test stage. They proposed that, at the time of A–B recall, responses from A–C intruded and competed with the correct response. The decrement in retention was attributed to *response competition.* The occurrence of interlist intrusions was cited as evidence of the influence of response competition. In a number of cases the subject gave a response from A–C instead of the prescribed response from A–B, and everyday descriptions also frequently attribute forgetting to response competition: "When I try to recall X, Y comes to mind instead."

While the contemporary analysis of RI agrees with the older view in assigning an important role to response competition, it also claims a second locus of interference at the time of A–C learning. According to this hypothesis of *unlearning*, inappropriate responses from list A–B that occur during the learning of A–C are rapidly unlearned and forgotten. The interpolated task leads to a retention decrement in part because it is a condition conducive to unlearning of the original material. The contemporary view can be described as a *two factor theory* of retroactive inhibition: response competition at the time of recall and unlearning at the time of interpolated activity.

Experimental Evidence

Our exposition of the theory of RI has made scant reference to data, fostering the false impression that the two factor theory is the product of armchair theorizing. In fact, theorizing in the field of verbal learning and retention has probably been

Condition	Original Learning	Interpolated Learning	Rest	Relearning
0	5 trials	None	30 min.	Two perfect trials
5	5 trials	5 trials	25.5 min.	Two perfect trials
10	5 trials	10 trials	22.0 min.	Two perfect trials
20	5 trials	20 trials	15.0 min.	Two perfect trials
40	5 trials	40 trials	1.0 min.	Two perfect trials

Table 4.2 *Design of Melton-Irwin Experiment (From Melton and Irwin, 1940)*

more closely tied to experimental data than in any other field of psychology. Therefore, we should turn without delay to consideration of a selected sample of the experimental data that led to the two factor theory. These experiments produced two important findings. First, response competition cannot be the sole cause of forgetting in the RI paradigm, because increasing amounts of RI are not accompanied by evidence of increasing response competition. Second, even when the effects of response competition are not in evidence, significant amounts of forgetting occur in the RI paradigm.

Intrusions and RI. The objective index of response competition is the occurrence of intrusions from list A–C during the recall of list A–B. If the sole source of interference is response competition, then an experimental variable that affects the magnitude of RI should produce correlated variations in the frequency of interlist intrusions. If variations of X increase RI, then these variations should also be accompanied by increases in the frequency of intrusions. If variations in the magnitude of RI are not accompanied by congruent variations in the frequency of intrusions, we cannot expect to account for the observed RI solely in terms of response competition. The most widely cited experimental exploration of this question is Melton and Irwin's (1940) study of the influence of degree of interpolated learning on retroactive inhibition.

Look once more at the experimental paradigm presented in Table 4.1. An examination of this model suggests some of the variables that may affect the magnitude of RI: the time allowed to elapse between successive stages; the degree of similarity between the original (A–B) and interpolated (A–C) tasks; and the relative degree of learning of the original and interpolated variable. Melton and Irwin examined this last variable by varying the number of practice trials on the interpolated list.

Melton and Irwin's subjects learned lists of single nonsense syllables. List 1 was learned for five trials, followed by a rest period without additional learning, or by 5, 10, 20, or 40 learning trials with a second list of syllables. Finally, all subjects relearned the original list. The plan of the experiment is reviewed in Table 4.2.

Figure 4.3 shows the mean number of correct responses on the first four relearning trials for all subjects combined. In order to determine the absolute magnitude of retroactive interference, we need to compare the mean number of

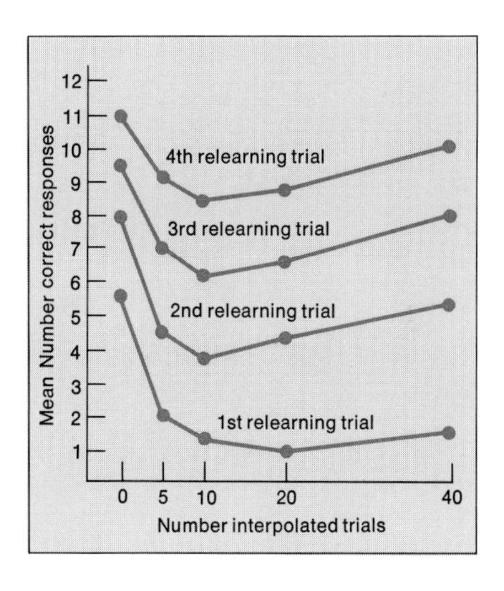

Fig. 4.3. Retroactive inhibition as a function of degree of interpolated learning. (Data from Melton and Irwin, 1940)

items recalled under each condition of interpolated learning with the mean number recalled under the control condition (zero interpolated trials): absolute RI = (recall zero) − (recall interpolated). The results of these calculations are plotted on the solid line curve of Figure 4.4, showing how the magnitude of RI increases as the number of interpolated trials is increased from 5 to 20. Increasing the number of interpolated trials to beyond 20 does not further increase RI.

Having established the effect of degree of interpolated learning on RI, we turn next to a consideration of the intrusion data. Does the frequency of intrusions mirror the observed RI effects? The bottom line in Figure 4.4 plots the frequency of intrusions at each level of interpolated learning. Two facts are immediately obvious: overt intrusions occur very infrequently, and frequency of intrusions does not vary in correspondence with variations of RI. The first observation makes clear that response competition cannot be the sole determinant of RI, while the second indicates that response competition cannot even account for a constant proportion of RI. Some additional factor must be postulated to account for the discrepancy between RI attributable to response competition and total obtained RI. This factor (labeled factor X in Figure 4.4) was identified as *unlearning*.

Retroactive inhibition in the absence of effective response competition. If the retention decrement observed following interpolated learning is due in part to unlearning of A–B associations, then a decrement should be observed even under conditions that minimize potential interference from response competition. A reduction in effectiveness of response competition may be achieved by modifying the conditions of the retention test. The recall test and relearning test provide the subject with the stimulus and require him to supply a *single* response. Response competition may lead to overt intrusions from the interpolated list, or complete omission of both responses resulting from uncertainty about which of them is correct. Both of these will result in a decrement in retention. However, suppose the retention test is modified to allow the subject to give *both* of the responses, B and C, previously associated with the common stimulus, A. This procedure will not eliminate response competition, but it will nullify the effects of competition

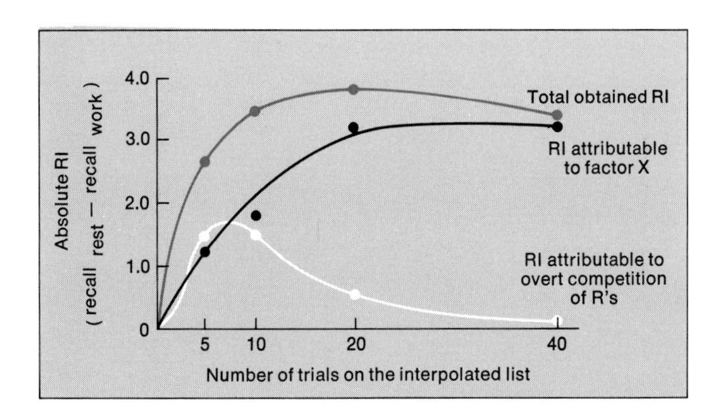

Fig. 4.4. Relationship between the amount of retroactive inhibition and the degree of learning of the interpolated material. The total obtained RI is the number of syllables forgotten as a consequence of the interpolated learning. The curve for factor X represents the absolute decrement in recall attributable to the factor or factors other than the overt competition of original and interpolated responses. (From Melton and Irwin, 1940)

on the recall of A–B. Now the competing response can occur without precluding occurrence of the correct response.

A procedure to accomplish this end was introduced by Briggs (1954) and Barnes and Underwood (1959). In the Barnes–Underwood experiment, four groups of subjects learned two lists of eight paired associates in the A–B, A–C, A–B paradigm (Table 4.1), using the method of paced anticipation described earlier. The stimuli were nonsense syllables and the responses were adjectives (e.g., vax-royal). All four groups learned list A–B to the criterion of one errorless trial. Then list A–C was presented for a specified number of trials, 1, 5, 10, or 20 for each of the four groups. After A–C practice was completed, the memory drum was stopped and the retention test administered. The complete list of the eight stimuli was provided and the subject was asked to write from memory the two responses associated with each stimulus. In addition, the subject was asked to identify the list, first or second, to which each of the two responses belonged.

Figure 4.5 shows the mean number of responses correctly recalled from list 1 (A–B) and list 2 (A–C) for the four levels of interpolated learning. Recall from list A–C increased with increasing practice on it, approaching the maximum possible after 20 trials of practice. At the same time, the number recalled from list A–B declined with increased practice on list A–C. In order to establish that the forgetting of list A–B was actually attributable to the interpolated A–C trials, a control group was tested after a rest interval (13 minutes) equal to the length of time required by the group that received 20 trials of A–C practice. The control group showed almost perfect A–B recall. This finding demonstrates that the forgetting of A–B under the experimental conditions was due to the interpolated activity.

Since the method of testing minimized the effectiveness of response competition, and since the subjects also identified the list membership of the responses with a high degree of accuracy, the decline of A–B recall strongly implicates unlearning. This gives rise to two questions. What is unlearned, and what is the mechanism of unlearning?

What is unlearned? The answer which seems obvious—that the first list as-

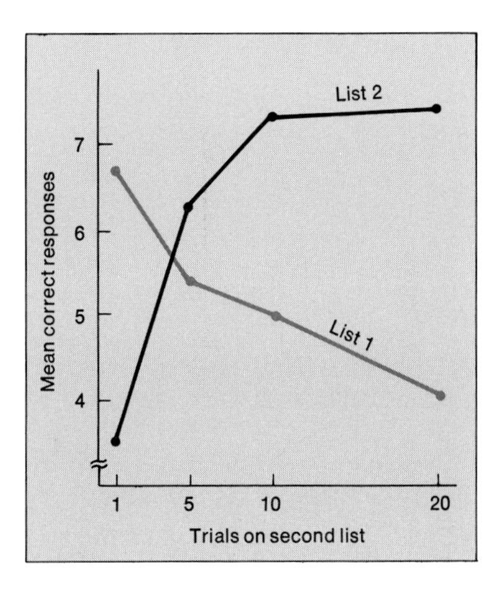

Fig. 4.5. Mean number of responses correctly recalled and identified with stimulus and list in the A–B, A–C paradigm. (From Barnes and Underwood, 1959)

sociations, A–B, are unlearned—is correct but incomplete. It fails to account for the fact that interpolated learning produces RI even when the two lists have no repeated items. This case is typically referred to as the A–B, C–D paradigm. Since list C–D has no items in common with list A–B, the association A–B will not be evoked and no opportunity for unlearning A–B should be present. If, nevertheless, there is evidence of unlearning in the A–B, C–D paradigm, it must involve another type of association. It is possible that this is a "contextual association," an association between the experimental context, such as the lab room or apparatus, and the response term. During original learning, B is associated with specific stimulus A and also with the general experimental context. Since the experimental context is maintained during C–D learning, B is evoked, but since B is incorrect, it is unlearned. Thus, two main types of unlearning have been proposed: unlearning of specific associations, and unlearning of associations between the response terms and the context. An excellent exposition of these ideas may be found in McGovern (1964).

Mechanisms of unlearning. Why does unlearning occur? We have suggested that the mechanism of unlearning is analogous to the gradual extinction of conditioned responses (see Chap. 12), when reinforcement is terminated. List 1 associations in the RI paradigm may be unlearned because their evocation during interpolated learning is not reinforced. Unfortunately, this interpretation encounters difficulties similar to those that affected the analysis of response competition, when there was little evidence of overt response competition. List 2 intrusions were infrequent during the relearning of list 1. In the present case, the frequency of overt list 1 intrusions during list 2 learning is very slight. If A–B is unlearned or extinguished in the course of A–C learning, we should expect to find B as a frequent response during the early stages of A–C learning. The fact that such errors are infrequent poses a difficulty for interpreting unlearning as extinction. How can a response be unlearned if it does not occur? Furthermore, if the subjects are encouraged to guess during interpolated learning, thereby leading to an increase in the frequency of occurrence of list 1 responses, there is no correlated decrease of first list recall attributable to unlearning (Keppel and Rausch, 1966; Houston

Condition	Task 1	Task 2	Task 3
Experimental	Learn A–C	Learn A–B	Recall A–B
Control	Rest	Learn A–B	Recall A–B

Table 4.3 *Plan of Experiment To Demonstrate Proactive Inhibition*

and Johnson, 1967). In summary, there is no evidence that *overt* elicitation of list 1 responses is essential for unlearning.

It would appear that an impasse has been reached in the development of the two factor theory. Introduction of the unlearning concept was necessitated by the demonstration that response competition could not account for failure to recall A–B (Melton and Irwin, 1940), and that recall of A–B declined with increasing interpolated learning in the absence of response competition (Barnes and Underwood, 1959). But attempts to provide direct evidence of unlearning in the form of a correlation between frequency of occurrence of intrusions during interpolated learning and magnitude of unlearning have failed. Faced with this crisis, advocates of interference theory have sought to salvage the situation by proposing that the elicitation of list 1 responses is *covert* rather than overt (Keppel, 1968, pp. 182–185). According to this view, the subject recognizes intrusions from list 1 and rejects them as overt, but since these responses do occur covertly they are unlearned.

The covert elicitation notion is not a very happy resolution, since it removes the unlearning mechanism from direct observation. Proponents of interference theory (Keppel, 1968; Postman, 1961) recognize this weakness and have tried to shore up the concept in a series of experiments which show that conditions that reduce the likelihood of covert list 1 intrusions also reduce the magnitude of unlearning. For example, Postman and Stark (1965) compared unlearning in the A–B, A–C paradigm under two conditions. Lists were composed of numbers as stimuli and either letters or adjectives as responses. Under condition S, both lists had responses from the same class, either letters or adjectives. Under condition D the lists had responses from different classes—list A–B: number–letter, list A–C, number–adjective. After learning the second list, subjects were given a list of the stimuli *and the correct list 2 responses* (C terms), and were required to provide the list 1 responses. Since the C terms are provided, response competition is eliminated and unlearning effects can be measured. It was assumed that there would be fewer covert instrusions under condition D than under condition S, since with the former the response terms B and C obviously come from different categories. Therefore, there would be less unlearning under condition D and better recall of list 1. The experimental results confirmed this prediction.

Proactive Inhibition (PI)

The second source of interference originates in material that has been learned prior to the task for which retention is measured. The laboratory model for demonstrating proactive inhibition (PI) is shown in Table 4.3. Under the experimental condition two lists of paired associates, A–C and A–B, are learned; then retention of the second list is tested. Under the control condition A–B is learned without

Condition	Task 1	Task 2	Task 3
RI: Experimental	Learn A–B	Learn A–C	Recall A–B
RI: Control	Learn A–B	Rest	Recall A–B
PI: Experimental	Learn A–C	Learn A–B	Recall A–B
PI: Control	Rest	Learn A–B	Recall A–B

Table 4.4 *Plan of Experiment To Compare Magnitude of Retroactive and Proactive Inhibition*

the prior learning of list A–C. Proactive interference is manifested in the poorer recall of A–B under the experimental condition.

The recall decrement under the experimental condition is due to the interfering effects of the first list. Of the two processes of interference we identified earlier—response competition and unlearning—only response competition is directly responsible for the decrement in A–B recall. Unlearning of A–B will not have taken place since it was learned after A–C. This conclusion leads to an interesting prediction. Since both unlearning and response competition are involved in RI, but only response competition is involved in PI, the decrement in recall in an RI paradigm should be greater than the decrement in recall in a PI paradigm. The plan for making this comparison is shown in Table 4.4; the difference between the RI experimental and RI control conditions should be greater than the difference between the PI experimental and PI control conditions. This prediction, a straightforward derivation from interference theory, has been confirmed for a recall test administered soon after completion of list 2 learning.

Interference and Forgetting

Laboratory studies of retroactive and proactive inhibition have bolstered the interference theory of forgetting. According to this theory, forgetting in everyday situations results from interference between associations. Associations that have been stored in memory prior to learning compete with retrieval of the desired material at the time of recall. Acquisition of new material following the learning of the material which we seek to retrieve results in unlearning of the desired material as well as competition at the time of recall.

A great deal remains to be investigated before we can be satisfied with interference theory. Most important is our need for a better understanding of the processes through which interference operates. The task is made difficult because directly observable manifestations of the component processes are not available. (Restrictions apply similar to those in our discussion of unlearning.) Indirect strategies must be adopted, but these do not always work out. For example, if PI is exclusively the result of response competition, a test which eliminates response competition should eliminate PI. Experiments along these lines have been performed, using techniques like those in the Barnes–Underwood and Postman *et al.* studies. But PI was not eliminated. What are we to deduce from this result? Did the test allow the occurrence of response competition, despite the experimenter's intentions, or is some component other than response competition involved in proactive inhibition? Difficulties of this sort, which are not uncommon in the literature on interference theory, testify to the need for more exact analytic techniques for isolating the components of interference and describing the way in which they affect retention.

Active Forgetting

In introducing our discussion of forgetting we distinguished between passive and active forgetting. We also distinguished between two kinds of active forgetting: repression and voluntary or intentional forgetting.

Freud (1925, p. 86) wrote that ". . . the essence of repression lies simply in the function of rejecting and keeping something out of consciousness." This expulsion from consciousness is not deliberate suppression, but an unconscious rejection motivated by the need to defend the ego against anxiety inducing memories (Chap. 14). Most readers will be familiar with Freud's hypothesis that repressed memories and conflicts lie at the root of psychopathological symptoms. But Freud did not intend to reserve the repression hypothesis for clinical examples of forgetting. In his view, all forgetting is motivated, and his *Psychopathology of Everyday Life* is devoted to vigorous advocacy of this thesis.

The practicing psychoanalyst is convinced of the validity of the hypothesis of repression. Daily clinical observations provide all the evidence he requires, and he is inclined to view as unnecessary the experimental efforts to verify the concept. In 1934, Freud responded to one of the earliest laboratory studies of repression (Rosenzweig and Mason, 1934) with the following evaluation: "I have examined your experimental studies for the verification of the psychoanalytic assertions with interest. I cannot put much value on these confirmations because the wealth of reliable observations on which these assertions rest make them independent of experimental verification. Still, it [experimental verification] can do no harm."

Despite Freud's judgment, efforts continued to demonstrate repression in the laboratory. Many of these studies have been reviewed by Rapaport (1950), Mackinnon and Dukes (1962), Weiner (1966), and Zeller (1950). Our discussion of repression has two objectives. First, we will identify the requirements of a sound experimental demonstration of repression. Then we will consider two recent studies in light of this analysis.

Methodological Considerations

To test the repression hypothesis we need to state it more explicitly: given that two equivalent forms of material (such as two lists of words) have been learned equally well, the probability of recalling or retrieving material that has threatening connotations will be less than the probability of recalling neutral material. This statement asserts that the repression hypothesis is concerned with retention or retrieval, and not with learning. The claim is also made that, in order to demonstrate that retrieval is affected, we have to ascertain that the different materials have been equally well learned prior to the retention test. If degree of learning has not been equated we will be uncertain whether differences on a retention test reflect genuine differences in retrieval, differences in original learning, or both.

The following example will make this clear. Suppose a subject is asked to learn a list of affectively neutral nonsense syllables. During learning, half of the items are accompanied by an unpleasant electric shock, while the remaining items are presented without any accompanying treatment. Then the subject leaves the laboratory and returns a day later for a retention test, on which he shows significantly poorer retention of the shocked items. Is this evidence of repression? Not necessarily, since it seems likely that the shock treatment has had an adverse effect on learning. Any time experimental manipulations of affect or threat accompany learning, there is the risk that subsequent differences in retention reflect differences in learning rather than in retention.

A second methodological concern is the nature of the experimental operations for manipulating the affective connotations of material that has been made to be anxiety inducing. Two general procedures have been adopted—one attempts to identify material that has preexperimental associations with anxiety, the other tries to develop associations between initially neutral material and threat or anxiety. The second procedure calls for administration of an experimental treatment that on a priori considerations seems to have threatening connotations, such as electric shock. We will shortly describe an example of each procedure, but first we simply wish to raise a question often asked in evaluations of these procedures. How intense does the threat or anxiety associated with a memory have to be before it will affect retention? Do some experiments to demonstrate repression fail because the experimental procedures are manipulating superficial and transitory anxieties? It is a weakness of the repression hypothesis that it does not specify in an objective manner the level of anxiety that can be expected to affect memory.

Experimental Studies

We have selected two very different types of studies to illustrate the variety of laboratory investigations of repression. Clemes' (1964) study uses the first procedure described above to demonstrate repression during posthypnotic amnesia. The study by Glucksberg and King (1967) uses the second procedure to demonstrate repression in the recall of paired associates.

Repression and posthypnotic amnesia. Hypnosis is a procedure for inducing a subject to accept and act in accordance with suggestions advanced by the hypnotist. Probably the most important factor in the hypnotic interaction is the subject's willingness and aptitude for role-playing. Given a subject with high motivation and aptitude, the experienced hypnotist can help him act prescribed roles and perform tasks at greater than typical levels of performance. (A very good introduction to hypnosis is provided by Moss, 1965.) Clemes used hypnosis to bring about partial posthypnotic amnesia—the subject was induced to forget part of what he had learned during the hypnotic trance.

The hypothesis under investigation was that, following equal mastery of critical and neutral words, subjects under partial hypnotic amnesia will forget a significantly greater number of critical words. The subjects in the experimental condition were selected on the basis of their performance on the *Stanford Hypnotic Susceptibility Scale*, which showed them to be highly susceptible to hypnotic induction and hypnotic amnesia. The control subjects were randomly selected or had given earlier evidence of low susceptibility to hypnotic suggestion.

The first step was to identify words which were neutral or related to repressed

Group	Number of Cases	Mean Words Forgotten Critical	Mean Words Forgotten Neutral	Difference Favoring Critical Words
Experimental (under partial hypnotic amnesia instructions)				
More critical words forgotten	15	4.1	2.3	+1.8
Critical and neutral words equally forgotten	7	1.1	1.1	0.0
More neutral words forgotten	4	1.3	2.5	−1.2
Total	26	3.2	2.3	+0.9
Control (not hypnotized)				
More critical words forgotten	6	1.7	0.5	+1.2
Critical and neutral words equally forgotten	15	0.1	0.1	0.0
More neutral words forgotten	6	0.3	1.5	−1.2
Total	27	0.6	0.6	0.0

Table 4.5. *Selective Amnesia for Critical versus Neutral Words* (*From Clemes, 1964, p. 65*)

conflicts for the individual subject. A word association test was administered to each subject. They were asked to respond with the first word that came to mind to each of the words on the list of stimulus words. Reaction time was measured. The theory of the word association test was that those words to which the subject's reaction time was far above his own mean reaction time for the list were anxiety inducing. Those words to which the reaction time did not exceed the mean were considered neutral. With this procedure a list of 18 words, 9 *neutral* and 9 *critical*, was selected for each subject.

On the second day of the experiment, subjects in the experimental group were hypnotized. While under hypnosis each subject learned his list of 18 words. The entire list was presented, one word at a time, and then the subject attempted to recall the list. Practice continued until he recalled each word at least twice. The subject was then told that when he was asked later to recall the list he would be able to remember *only ten words,* no matter how hard he tried, until the experimenter said, "Now you can remember everything." These instructions induced *partial* posthypnotic amnesia, with the further suggestion that the experimenter would also release the subject from the amnesic state. The control subjects were not hypnotized, but half of them were given the partial amnesia instructions.

After completion of learning, the experimental subjects were released from the trance state and asked to recall the list. When the subject signified that he could not remember any more words, the hypnotic amnesia was lifted and he made a second attempt to recall the list. The control subjects also made two recall efforts.

Before reporting the outcome of this experiment, let us be more explicit about the underlying rationale. Repression is alleged to operate by expelling threatening memories; it is *selective* forgetting. The partial amnesia instructions given to the hypnotized subjects were intended to produce partial forgetting, with the aim of

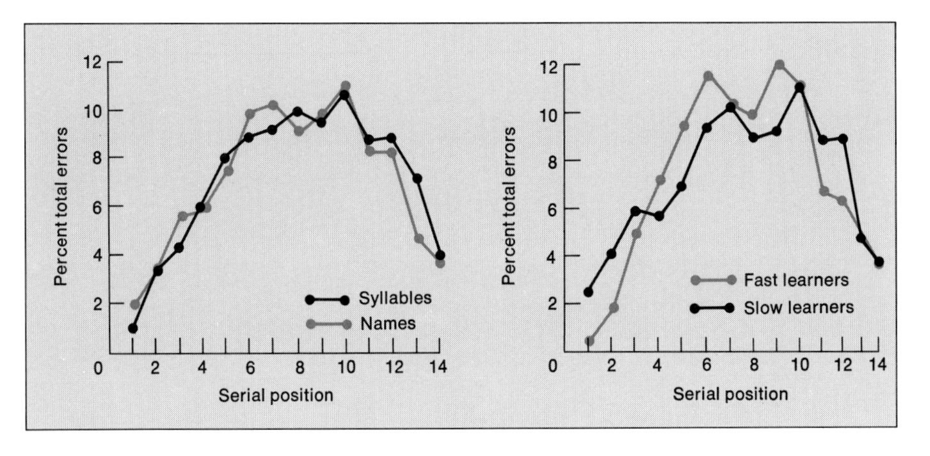

Fig. 4.6. The left-hand panel shows two serial position curves for lists of nonsense syllables and lists of first names. The right-hand panel shows curves for fast and slow learners. (From McCrary and Hunter, 1953)

demonstrating that the amnesia would provoke the selective influence of repression; in other words, more critical than neutral words would be forgotten.

Earlier we noted the serious interpretive problem that arises in experiments on repression. How can we be sure that differences in retention are not due to differences in learning? Clemes dealt with this matter in two ways. First, the learning data were analyzed for evidence of differences between the learning of neutral and critical words. The mean number of correct recalls for critical and neutral words during original learning was compared, and no differences were found. Second, the data which were examined for evidence of repression were restricted to the words that were *forgotten* on the first test, but *remembered on the second test.* A word that is remembered on the second test obviously has been learned, so it seems unlikely that lack of recall on the first test represents failure to learn. It is more plausible to attribute differences between the recall of critical and neutral items on the first test to failure of retrieval.

Table 4.5 shows the main results of Clemes' experiment. Most of the experimental subjects, 15 of 26, forgot more critical than neutral words. Only 4 of 26 experimental subjects forgot more neutral words. The control subjects behaved differently. Only 6 of 27 subjects forgot more critical than neutral words. Most of the control subjects forgot an equal number of critical and neutral words. These results conform to the experimental hypothesis in showing that the subjects under partial hypnotic amnesia forgot more of the threatening than the neutral words. At this point a question may arise. Inasmuch as the lists learned by the control subjects also contained nine words related to anxiety, why didn't the control subjects exhibit selective forgetting of the critical words (Table 4.5 shows that the control subjects recalled exactly the same number of critical and neutral words)?

Perhaps repression acts chiefly as a selective principle of forgetting operating not so much as a primary cause but as a factor that determines *what* is forgotten. If conditions for forgetting exist, such as interference, then the mechanism of repression exercises selection in determining what is forgotten. Since the recall test for the control subjects followed immediately after learning, forgetting was minimal, and the opportunity for observing the selective effect of repression was

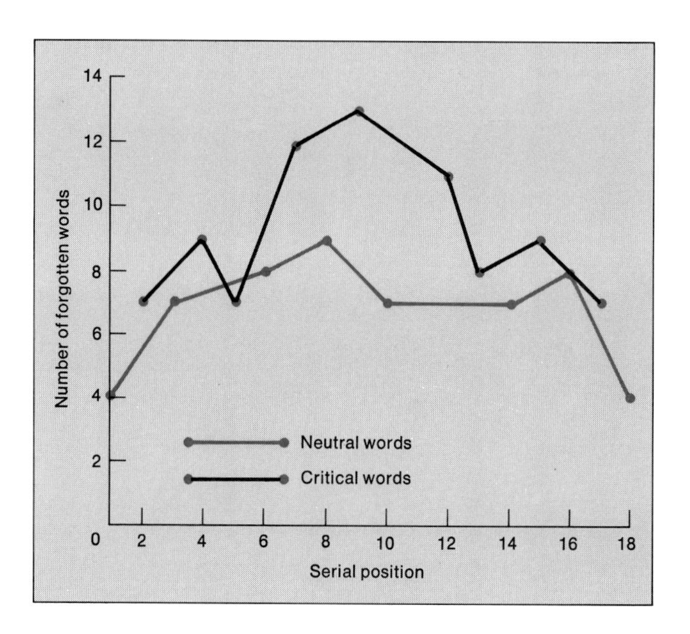

Fig. 4.7. Relationship between number of words forgotten and serial position for the experimental group ($N = 26$). (From Clemes, 1964)

absent. In the experimental condition, forgetting occurred (because of the hypnotic suggestion) and the effect of repression was observed.

Although Clemes did not raise the question, he does present data compatible with our answer. A digression is necessary before these data can be described. In serial learning tasks of the sort assigned to the subjects in Clemes' experiment, items in the list differ in difficulty as a function of their positions in the list. Items at the beginning and end of the list will be learned faster; items in the middle will be learned last. The curves in Figure 4.6 are examples of the conventional serial position curve. The curve shows the percentage of errors during learning for the items at each position in the list. Fewest errors occur at the ends of the list, while the positions of maximal difficulty are in the center.

We have suggested that repression may act as a selective principle when conditions for forgetting are present. If the middle of the list is most difficult, we may assume that forgetting is most likely for this part of the list. Therefore, we should expect that the difference between the number of critical and neutral words that are forgotten will be greatest for words in the middle of the list. Figure 4.7 shows the relationship between number of words forgotten and serial position of the items; the greatest difference between critical and neutral items was in fact localized in the middle of the list.

Repression and mediated associative learning. A subject may learn to associate two items, such as A and C, in one of two ways. He may form a direct association between A and C, or he may join A and C by associating each term with a third term (B) which serves as a link between the two. In this case, the stimulus A will elicit B as a covert response, and B will act as a stimulus that elicits C (this chain of events is diagramed in the upper row of Table 4.6). The association A–C is said to be a *mediated association,* and B is called a mediator.

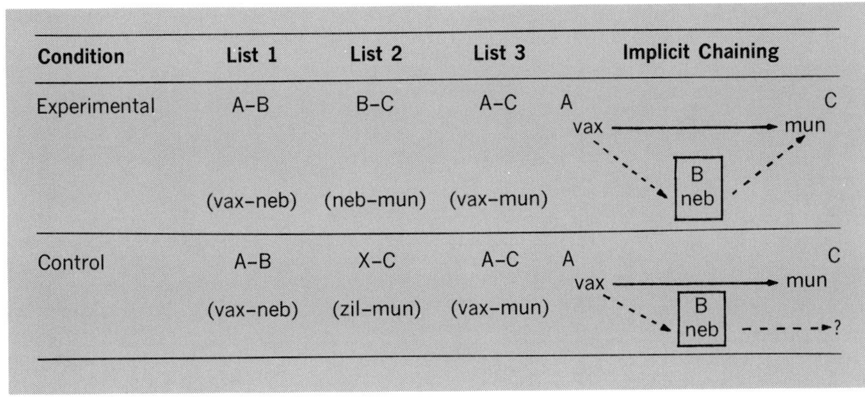

Condition	List 1	List 2	List 3	Implicit Chaining
Experimental	A–B (vax–neb)	B–C (neb–mun)	A–C (vax–mun)	A vax → C mun B neb
Control	A–B (vax–neb)	X–C (zil–mun)	A–C (vax–mun)	A vax → C mun B neb → ?

Table 4.6 *Plan of Mediation Experiment Using Laboratory Established Linkages*

Table 4.6 represents one laboratory procedure for demonstrating mediated association. The experimental subjects learn list A—C after learning two preceding lists which form an A→B→C chain. The control subjects learn list A—C after learning two lists which do not form a chain linking A with C. The effect of mediation is to facilitate the acquisition of A—C for the experimental subjects.

In the experiment diagramed in Table 4.6, nonsense syllables were used, and the chain of associations was constructed in the laboratory. The effect of mediation can also be demonstrated with natural language mediators. Consult Table 4.7, in which columns A and B constitute a list of paired associates, with nonsense syllables as stimuli and real words as responses. Each of the words in column C is the most common response to the adjacent word in column B. On a free association test, for example, "flower" is the most frequent response to "stem." Each of the words in column D is the most common response to the adjacent word in column C (for example, "flower"—"smell"). Therefore, A and D are associated by way of the mediating links B–C and C–D. The effects of these mediators can be demonstrated in the manner outlined in Table 4.8. First the experimental subjects learn A–B, then they learn A–D. It is assumed that, in learning A–D, the common associations B–C and C–D will occur covertly and facilitate its acquisition. The control subjects begin with A–X, in which X does *not* lead to D. Russell and Storms (1955), among others (e.g., Jenkins, 1963), have shown that mediation produces faster A–D learning.

Now we return to the question of repression. Glucksberg and King (1967) had subjects learn list A–B of Table 4.7 until they could go through the whole list without error. Then list A–D was presented. Electrodes were attached to the subject's fingers and he was told that some of the words in list D would be accompanied by electric shock. The subject's task was to learn which words would be followed by shock. He was instructed to press a buzzer key whenever he anticipated a shock. This action did not eliminate the shock; it only provided evidence of learning. For half of the subjects, the shock-paired D words were *smell, war,* and *tree;* for the other half, *brain, good,* and *take.* This phase of the experiment continued until the subject had correctly anticipated shock for three successive trials. When the subject achieved this criterion, the A items were presented again and he was asked to recall the B items.

List 1		Inferred chained word	List 2	
A	B	C	D	
CEF	stem	flower	smell	(1)
DAX	memory	mind	brain	(2)
YOV	soldier	army	navy	
VUX	trouble	bad	good	(2)
WUB	wish	want	need	
GEX	justice	peace	war	(1)
JID	thief	steal	take	(2)
ZIL	ocean	water	drink	
LAJ	command	order	disorder	
MYV	fruit	apple	tree	(1)

Table 4.7 *Stimulus Words Used and Inferred Associative Responses*

The D words followed by (1) were the critical, shock-paired words for half the subjects; those followed by (2) were the crtitical, shock-paired words for the remaining subjects. From Glucksberg and King, 1967. p. 518.

The rationale of this study is based on the analysis of mediated chaining of associations. Glucksberg and King (1967, p. 518) assumed that B would occur as an implicit mediating response during the presentation of A–D.

> If the D word is associated with an unpleasant event, such as electric shock, then the likelihood of saying, or thinking of, the associated B response has an unpleasant consequence, namely, thinking of the D word, which presumably elicits fear. Thus, pairing specific D words with electric shock should cause differential forgetting of A–B pairs learned prior to the D word presentations. The B words associated with shock-paired D words should be forgotten more often than the B words associated with neutral D words.

Unlike the Clemes experiment, this study tries to manipulate anxiety experimentally, rather than depending on preexperimentally established associations. The experiment is also noteworthy because the anxiety inducing treatment is introduced *after* learning has been completed, which eliminates concern that the treatment may affect learning as well as retrieval. In fact, an analysis of the learning data showed that the critical and neutral A–B pairs did not differ in the number of trials required to learn them, or in the number of times they were anticipated correctly during original learning.

The results of the recall test showed that 29 per cent of the critical A–B pairs (those mediating shocked A–D associations) were forgotten, while only 6.7 per cent of the neutral A–B pairs were forgotten. The hypothesis based on the concept of repression was confirmed.

Voluntary Forgetting

Although repression is an instance of active involvement in forgetting, the individual does not exercise deliberate control over the process. The second type

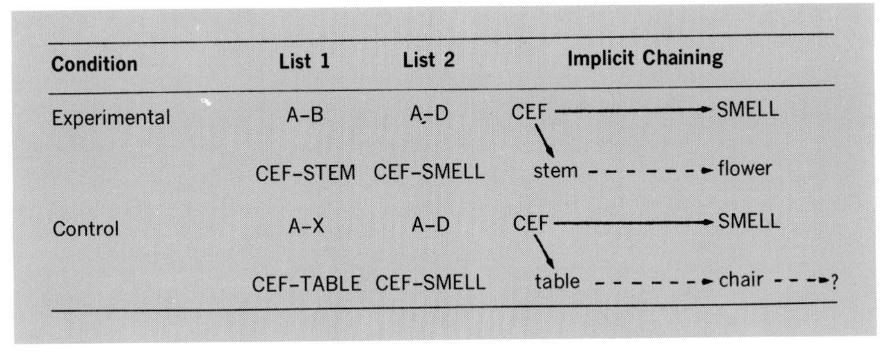

Condition	List 1	List 2	Implicit Chaining
Experimental	A–B	A–D	CEF ——→ SMELL
	CEF–STEM	CEF–SMELL	stem - - - - - - → flower
Control	A–X	A–D	CEF ——→ SMELL
	CEF–TABLE	CEF–SMELL	table - - - - - - → chair - - - → ?

Table 4.8 *Plan of Mediation Experiment Using Natural Language Linkages*

of active forgetting differs from repression in this respect. Voluntary forgetting is the product of an intentional effort to forget.

Although voluntary forgetting is a common experience, it has rarely been studied in the laboratory; primary attention has been focused on passive forgetting. Nevertheless, there is a stirring of interest in voluntary forgetting. The experiments reported thus far (for example, Bjork, LaBerge, and Legrand 1968; Elmes, 1969; Epstein, 1969; Turvey and Wittlinger, 1969; Weiner and Reed, 1969) represent a first step toward an analysis of this phenomen. We will describe two of these experiments which demonstrate voluntary forgetting in short-term memory.

The experiments follow different procedures but are based on the same underlying reasoning. If a subject who learns two lists or two items is subsequently induced to forget one of the lists or items, then when he has to recall the retained list, the list that has been deliberately forgotten should interfere less, and recall should be enhanced. As an illustration, suppose you memorize two new telephone numbers in succession, and then are asked to dial both numbers, beginning with the second. While dialing the second number, the first will interfere and may produce errors. However, suppose that prior to dialing the second number you are told that the other number is no longer required, and you may safely forget it. To the degree that you succeed in forgetting the first number, deliberately excluding it from memory, interference with the second number will be reduced, and performance improved.

Note that the example provides an *indirect* measure of voluntary forgetting. The effect of a subject's intention to forget X is not sought in recall of X, but in the influence that forgetting of X has on recall of Y. The indirect approach is adopted because if we were to look for the effect of voluntary forgetting of X in the recall of X, all we might get is evidence that the subject is a cooperative, compliant person. For example, if we instruct the subject to forget X, and at a recall test he does not recall X, has X been forgotten, or is the subject simply complying with instructions? The indirect measure avoids this problem, since the evidence of voluntary forgetting is sought in recall of a task which the subject has *not* been asked to forget.

On each of a long series of trials, Bjork *et al.* (1968) presented a different list of digits plus one or two consonant quadrograms (CCCC), e.g., DBRF. The subject's task was to shadow the digits, that is, to repeat them aloud as they appeared, and also to memorize the CCCC items for subsequent recall. After the last digit, the subject was asked to recall the CCCC items. There were three types of trials: (1) The list contained two CCCC items and the subject was asked to recall them both, second item first. (2) The list contained two CCCC items, but prior to exposure of the second the subject was signalled that he could forget the first item because he would have to recall only the second item. (3) A control list contained only one CCCC item at the position that matched the position of the second CCCC item in the other lists. The retention intervals (the time between presentation of the second CCCC and the recall test) never exceeded 12 seconds.

Let us examine the purpose of this study in the context of the rationale presented above. Condition 3 is a baseline condition that tells us how much will be retained in the absence of proactive inhibition from similar preceding items. In terms of our hypothetical example, we want to know how well a single telephone number will be recalled when a second number is not presented. Condition 1 gives us a measure of proactive interference with recall of the second CCCC resulting from the first CCCC. Recall should be poorer under condition 1 as compared with condition 3. Condition 2 provides the data for critical comparison. Under this condition the subject is instructed to forget the first CCCC. As in our hypothetical example, voluntary forgetting should lead to a reduction in proactive interference. Therefore, recall of the second CCCC should be better under condition 2 than under condition 1.

The results of the study by Bjork *et al.* confirmed these expectations. For example, after a 12 second retention interval the percentage of items recalled correctly was 40 per cent, 35 per cent, and 19 per cent for conditions 3, 2, and 1, respectively. Voluntary forgetting of the first CCCC reduced the amount of forgetting of the second CCCC from 81 per cent (100% − 19%) under condition 1 to 65 per cent (100% − 35%) under condition 2. The latter figure is not much different from the 60 per cent forgetting when only a single CCCC was presented.

The second study we will consider differs in detail from Bjork's, but the underlying logic is the same. On each of eight trials, Epstein (1969) presented a list of common words, one at a time, followed by a list of two digit numbers, one at a time. Each trial presented completely different lists. The subject was instructed to memorize both lists in preparation for a test of free recall that would follow immediately after the last number. The subject was told that the test would vary from trial to trial. On some trials he would be asked to recall only *one* list, words or numbers, while on others he would be asked to recall *both* lists, words or numbers first. He would not know until after the last number which of the four tests would be administered, and therefore would have to treat each learning trial the same way, trying to memorize both lists. The four tests, "words only," "numbers only," "words then numbers," and "numbers then words," were distributed randomly among the trials so that the subject could not successfully anticipate the type of test.

The reasoning behind this experimental plan can be understood by comparing two of the trials. Compare the trial on which the subject is asked to recall only numbers (N_0) and the trial on which recall of both lists is required, numbers first (NW). On trial N_0 the subject can forget the words, but on trial NW he must keep the words in mind while recalling the numbers. The experimental situation is similar to our telephone number example. Therefore, we would predict that if the subject can voluntarily forget the word list, he will display better recall on trial N_0 than on trial NW. The results of Epstein's (1969) experiment confirmed this prediction. This finding is noteworthy because, prior to the recall signal, the number lists on trial N_0

and trial NW are treated identically. On both trials the number list is memorized to the same degree; the same length of time intervenes between learning and recall and no prior recall test is administered. There is no way to distinguish between the number lists on trial N_0 and trial NW prior to the signal to drop the word list. Only after the signal is given to forget the words can an advantage accrue to trial N_0. Recall of the number list, relieved of the interference associated with the word list, is then enhanced.

Future Experimental Directions

Although the study of active forgetting has not previously been a principal concern of experimental psychologists, everyday experience testifies to its reality. As our discussion has illustrated, active forgetting can be studied experimentally. The current literature on the problem represents only a beginning, but even now it is possible to discern the outlines of questions that future investigators must pursue.

What are the conditions that govern our ability to forget? For example, is the degree to which material has been learned an important condition? Extralaboratory experience suggests that all material is not equally susceptible to exclusion from memory. Some matters are remarkably persistent, while others are easily discarded. What conditions determine these differences?

What is the mechanism of active forgetting? We would like to know the best way to characterize the process. As illustration, consider the following two possibilities. The mechanism of active forgetting may operate analogously to the "clear" key on a cash register. When the key is punched, the register is cleared, leaving a clean slate. Another possible conceptualization of active forgetting is modeled after a filing system that includes a "dead" file. Active forgetting in this event would consist of transferring material from the active file to the dead file. Experimental procedures for evaluating these models as well as others will probably involve a third question.

What is the fate of the forgotten material? Has it been erased like chalk marks on a blackboard so that it is beyond recovery, or is its status such that it can be entirely or partially recovered? This question is closely related to discovery of the mechanism. All three questions need to be answered before we can claim an adequate understanding of active forgetting.

Not Remembering

We turn next to our third type of forgetting—*not remembering*. In this state, recall fails despite the strong subjective impression that the sought-after material is present in memory. The difficulty is in retrieval; we cannot find the key that will enable us to gain access to the stored material.

The tip of the tongue (TOT) phenomenon is a familiar example. Earlier we presented James' description of the experience. The TOT state involves "a failure to recall a word of which one has knowledge. The evidence of knowledge is either an eventually successful recall or else an act of recognition that occurs, without additional training, when recall has failed" (Brown and McNeill, 1966, p. 325).

The TOT state, while relatively infrequent, is such a striking example of not remembering that it is worthwhile to look at one of the handful of experimental

Definitions
1. A navigational instrument used in measuring angular distances, especially the altitude of sun, moon, and stars at sea
2. The practice of showing special favor to nephews (or other relatives) in conferring office; unfair preferment of relatives to other qualified persons
3. A semi-circular or polygonal recess, arched or dome-roofed in a building, especially at the nave of a church

Inquiry
How many syllables does the word have?
What is the first letter of the word?
What words come to mind?
Separate the words that come to mind into those you believe to be similar to the target word in (a) sound, and (b) meaning.

Table 4.9 *The TOT Experiment*

studies of the phenomenon. The infrequency and unpredictability of the TOT state suggest that a study of naturally occurring TOT states would be unprofitable; an experimental procedure that precipitates the TOT state is preferable. Brown and McNeill (1966) invented an ingenious but simple procedure which satisfies this need.

Table 4.9 presents dictionary definitions of three relatively uncommon words. Read the first definition. Do you know the word that fits this definition? If not, do you feel certain that you do *not* know the word? If you answered the first question negatively and the second question affirmatively, proceed to the second definition. You may find that, for at least one of the definitions, you neither know the word nor feel certain that you do not know it. Although you are unable to recall it at the moment, you may feel that it is on the verge of coming back to you. In this case, you will be in the TOT state. If one of the definitions does precipitate a TOT state, answer the questions found in the inquiry in Table 4.9.

Brown and McNeill used the foregoing procedure to generate TOT states. They presented definitions of 49 uncommon words to a large group of subjects (words that do not occur more often than once per million words). Although none of the definitions generated the TOT state in all subjects, and some target words failed entirely to generate the TOT state, the procedure did succeed in precipitating 360 instances of the TOT state. For each instance, the subject responded to the inquiry.

Brown and McNeill found that the subjective impression that one knows the word despite failure to recall was confirmed by the inquiry. For example, the actual number of syllables in the target word and the guessed number of syllables were correlated perfectly. In addition, the initial letter was guessed correctly 57 per cent of the time. Considering the probability of guessing correctly from a pool of 26 letters, this figure is significantly high. These are only two of the findings reported by Brown and McNeill. If you experienced the TOT state and responded to the inquiry, you will be interested in checking your results; the target words are (1) sextant, (2) nepotism, (3) apse. If one of your wrong guesses was similar in sound to the target word and had the same number of syllables, was the syllable receiving primary stress the same in your guess and in the target? Do your guesses reveal any other type of knowledge of the target word?

Brown and McNeill's study of the TOT state shows that the state of not remembering is not an illusion—one can know without recalling. Material can be in storage without being accessible, in which case forgetting is due to a failure of retrieval. As we have mentioned, this is characteristic of the state of not remembering. We believe that the proper retrieval cue would lead to recall. For evidence that supports this belief in the efficacy of retrieval cues, we will turn to another type of experiment.

In the general experimental plan, two groups of subjects are instructed to learn a list of words in preparation for a subsequent recall test. The groups are treated identically in every respect up to the beginning of the recall period. However, at the time of the recall test, one group is supplied a retrieval cue.

Tulving (Tulving and Pearlstone, 1966; Tulving and Osler, 1968) has reported experiments that follow this plan. In one experiment categorized word lists consisting of *category names* and *words representing instances of categories* were presented to subjects once only. The following list is an illustration: four footed animals—cow, rat; weapons—bomb, cannon; crimes—treason, theft; entertainment—theatre, movies; food flavoring—cinnamon, pepper; professions—engineer, lawyer. The lists varied in length (12, 24, and 48 categories) and number of items per category (1, 2, and 4 words). Immediately after the list was presented, two recall tests were given in succession. The subjects were instructed to try to remember as many words as possible. On the first recall test half of the subjects were tested without any aids (unaided free recall) while the other half were provided with retrieval cues (the category names). On the second test all subjects received the retrieval cues.

The object of this experiment was to provide evidence to substantiate the distinction between the presence or availability of material in memory storage and its accessibility for recall. Tulving's two main findings seem to provide such evidence. First, subjects who received the retrieval cues recalled significantly more words on the first test than those who did not. Second, presentation of retrieval cues on the second test significantly increased recall for subjects who had not received the cues on the first test. The first finding shows that retrieval cues, which facilitate access to storage, enhance recall; the second shows that failure of recall can be due to failure of retrieval rather than fading or displacement from storage.

What are the characteristics of an effective retrieval cue? In our illustrative experiment, the cue was part of the original learning task. Is this an essential condition? Suppose the category names were not presented along with the list, but were introduced for the first time on the recall test. Would the cue be effective? (See Tulving and Osler, 1968.)

Given a set of retrieval cues that are demonstrated to be effective, why do the cues themselves vary in effectiveness? For example, Horowitz and Prytulak (1969) had subjects memorize sentences and then tested them by cued recall. For some subjects the cue was the subject of the sentence, for others the verb, and for others the object. Horowitz and Prytulak found that the subject of the sentence is the most effective cue for eliciting recall of the sentence, and the verb is the poorest.

Our discussion of the state of not remembering has been brief, largely because investigators have only recently recognized the possibility that failures of retrieval or loss of accessibility may account for much of forgetting. The literature is not very extensive. The bulk of the task is still ahead of us.

The Organization of Memory

Experimental psychologists have contributed very little to our understanding of memory systems. The current status of the matter has been summarized aptly by Miller, Galanter, and Pribram (1960, p. 134) in *Plans and the Structure of Behavior:*

> The antagonistic attitude of experimental psychologists toward mnemonic devices is even more violent than their attitude toward their subject's word associations; mnemonic devices are immoral tricks suitable only for evil gypsies and stage magicians. As a result of this attitude almost nothing is known by psychologists about the remarkable feats of memory that are so easily performed when you have a Plan ready in advance.

Despite this attitude, there can be no doubt that memory systems are effective, and that well-established memory systems retard forgetting. Skillful practitioners can perform prodigious feats of memory. Therefore, it is entirely appropriate that we consider the matter briefly as part of this examination of forgetting. Our discussion will be based primarily on treatments of the question provided by Norman (1969), an experimental psychologist, and Yates (1966), an English historian.

Most memory systems are applications of one of two methods, the *method of loci* and the *method of analytic substitutions;* the former is the oldest. The basic idea of the method of loci (locations, places) is to impress on memory a mental image of some architectural structure, such as a cathedral or theatre, or some neighborhood, such as Capitol Square, and then store information in well-defined loci. Recall is accomplished by visualizing each location and retrieving its contents. Yates (1966, pp. 1–2) cites Cicero as his source for attributing the invention of the method of loci to the ancient Greek poet Simonides.

> At a banquet given by a nobleman of Thessaly named Scopas, the poet Simonides of Ceos chanted a lyric poem in honour of his host but including a passage in praise of Castor and Pollux. Scopas meanly told the poet that he would only pay him half the sum agreed upon for the panegyric and that he must obtain the balance from the twin gods to whom he had devoted half the poem. A little later, a message was brought in to Simonides that two young men were waiting outside who wished to see him. He rose from the banquet and went out but could find no one. During his absence the roof of the banqueting hall fell in, crushing Scopas and all the guests to death beneath the ruins; the corpses were so mangled that the relatives who came to take them away for burial were unable to identify them. But Simonides remembered the places at which they had been sitting at the table and was therefore able to indicate to the relatives which were their dead. The invisible callers, Castor and Pollux, had handsomely paid for their share in the panegyric by drawing Simonides away from the banquet just before the crash. And this experience suggested to the poet the principles of the art of memory of which he is said to have been the inventor. Noting that it was through his memory of the places at which the guests had been sitting that he had been able to identify the bodies, he realized that orderly arrangement is essential for good memory.
>
> He inferred that persons desiring to train this faculty [of memory] must select places and form mental images of the things they wish to remember and store those images in the places, so that the order of the places will preserve the order of the things, and the images of the things will denote

the things themselves, and we shall employ the places and images respectively as a wax writing-tablet and the letters written on it.

Elaborate memory systems based on the method of loci were developed as late as the Renaissance period. Detailed prescriptions were worked out concerning the kinds of architectural structures best suited for the task and the conditions for impressing the structure on memory. It would not have been unusual to observe a new devotee of the system engaged in intent study of the interior of a cathedral in order to establish his cathedral of memory. Eventually it occurred to masters of the art that the ultimate step would be construction of an edifice designed to maximize its effectiveness as the architectural model for memory. Several plans or scale models were actually constructed.

The method of loci enhances recall by fitting the material to be remembered into a previously learned organizational scheme. The method of analytic substitutions is based on the same principle, but the organizational scheme is different. The method is popularly used to develop a system for memorization of unrelated lists of items, such as social security or selective service numbers. The first step is to invent a code that substitutes more easily recalled symbols for numbers. Suppose consonants are selected for this purpose, with S, Z, and C = 0, T = 1, N = 2, M = 3, R = 4, L = 5, G, K, Q = 7, and so on. When this code has been memorized, a sequence of numbers slated for memorization is translated into a sequence of consonants. Then, to make this code sequence resistant to forgetting, the letters are transformed into an organized sequence of words containing the consonants. The procedure seems more trouble than it is worth, but practiced users apparently can implement it without great investment of effort, allowing them to perform dramatic feats of memory.

The key to the success of memory systems is organization. The systems provide organizational structures for storage of material and for processing the material as it is learned. Successful systems merit more attention from experimental psychologists than they have received thus far, since the study of memory systems is relevant to an analysis of the role of organization in memory. Until recently, psychologists have ignored questions concerning organized memory, but a new body of experimental data and theoretical opinion makes continued neglect impossible. Some examples of this data are discussed on the following pages.

Clustering

The clustering phenomenon, first described by Bousfield (1953), refers to the clustering of words in free recall. The clustering or grouping of words reflects the organization of the list. In a typical procedure for demonstrating clustering, the experimenter selects four conceptual categories (for example, animals, names, professions, and vegetables) and chooses ten words belonging to each category. The 40 words are then randomly mixed to form a single list of 40 words which is read to the subject once, or several times in varying random order. The subject is instructed to memorize the list. After the learning phase is concluded, the subject is instructed to recall the list unaided in any order that he wishes.

The records reveal that the subject tends to recall the list in clusters of words from the same category. Not all of the recalled words are clustered together in categories, but the tendency toward clustering is significant. Clustering occurs despite the fact that the words from different categories are randomly mixed together on the learning trial. Also noteworthy is that nothing in the instructions encourages the subject to emit the words in any particular order. The clustering phenomenon seems to reflect organized memory and organized retrieval.

Subjective Organization

In the examination of the clustering phenomenon, the experimenter has provided a basis for organization in the form of categories. However, if the hypothesis of organized memory is to have general validity, organizational tendencies should be observed in the recall of material that had no discernible structure. Under such conditions, does the subject impose his own organization on memory and recall?

Consider the performance of a subject required to learn and recall a list of totally unrelated words. Will recall of this list, which has no inherent organization, exhibit organizational tendencies? This would be a case of subjective organization, imposed by the subject and not introduced by the experimenter. Tulving (1962) has provided evidence that organization is exhibited under these conditions. He presented a list of 16 *unrelated* nouns for 16 alternating study and recall test trials. On each study trial the list was presented in a different order, and the subject told that he was free to recall the words in any order.

Organization in the clustering experiment was defined in terms of category membership. In Tulving's experiment a different measure of organization was required. Tulving's measure was the subject's tendency to recall items in the same order on different trials. He reasoned that if memory is organized into units or chunks, each containing several items, then as the units are organized the subject should recall the words that comprise them in the same order from trial to trial. Despite the absence of any experimentally manipulated sequential organization among words in the list, subjective organization would lead to invariant sequences in recall. Tulving found that this did occur. The subjects repeated sequences of items from trial to trial, and this tendency grew greater with increasing trials.

Organization and Memory

The previous sections have provided illustrations of the evidence that memory and recall are organized. Mandler (1967) has gone a step further, arguing that organization is necessary for recall. Furthermore, he proposes that "organization is a sufficient condition for recall and that asking subjects to remember something implies that they are instructed to organize" (p. 355). In order to examine this proposal, Mandler compared recall following two kinds of instructions.

Categorization instructions asked the subject to categorize a list of unrelated words. A list of 52 words was read to the subject, who was instructed to sort the words into from one to seven categories (columns), using any basis he wished for categorization. There were five trials and the subject was asked to try to use the same organization on successive trials. There was no mention of a recall test. *Recall instructions* informed the subject that he would have to recall the words after the fifth presentation. No mention was made of categorization. Following the fifth trial, both groups were tested by free recall.

Mandler's experiment compares recall following instructions to organize with recall following instructions to memorize. If organization is a sufficient condition for recall, the two groups should perform equally well on the recall test. The results showed 32.8 and 32.9 words recalled for the categorization and recall conditions, respectively. Obviously the expectation was confirmed.

We began this section with a description of two types of memory systems. The key to the success of these systems is that they establish an organizational scheme into which new material can be fitted. We next described illustrative experimental evidence of organization in memory. There are many questions that remain to be answered concerning the structure of organization in memory. What form or structure does the organization of memory assume in the absence of experimental manipulations? This is a most important theoretical question. In addition, determination of the type of organizational structure which is most effective in enhancing recall would lead to a useful, experimentally based memory system.

Conclusion

Why do we forget? One answer is that "all forgetting results basically from interference between the associations a man carries in his memory system" (Underwood, 1964). As long as we restrict ourselves to laboratory studies of retroactive and proactive inhibition, this confidence in interference is amply justified. But we do not have to deviate very much from the standard laboratory interference model before encountering difficulties. For example, if a subject learns one list of words in the laboratory and then leaves the laboratory to return 24 hours later for a recall test, he will show approximately 25 per cent forgetting. According to interference theory, this is the result of proactive and retroactive interference caused by extralaboratory experience preceding and following learning. Unfortunately, experiments designed to test the notion of extralaboratory interference have failed to provide conclusive evidence to support the hypothesis (Keppel, 1968). When positive demonstrations of active forgetting and not remembering are added to this failure, there is sufficient ground for doubting that interference theory can account for all forgetting.

We offer the following guess about future developments in the study of forgetting. There will be an increasing emphasis on the study of the organization of memory, retrieval schemes, and control mechanisms such as voluntary forgetting. At the same time, the more established views, such as interference theory, will be modified to cope with the findings of the newer experiments. The psychology of forgetting in 1975 will look very different than it did in 1965.

Glossary

Clustering: the tendency for items that belong to the same category in a list to occur successively, in clusters, on a test of *free recall*.

Disuse hypothesis: the hypothesis that forgetting occurs because the forgotten material has not been used (practiced) during the retention interval.

Free recall: when a subject is instructed to recall the items in a list in any order that he wishes, he is engaged in free recall.

Interference theory: the theory that forgetting is due to interference from learning activities preceding and subsequent to the acquisition of the forgotten material.

Intrusions: wrong responses during acquisition or retention that can be identified as members of another list that the subject has learned are called *interlist* intrusions; if the wrong response is from another part of the same list the error is called an *intralist* intrusion.

Mediated association: two items that are indirectly associated by virtue of their direct association with a third item are said to constitute a mediated association. Thus if A→B and B→C, then A and C are associated by virtue of the mediator B.

Posthypnotic amnesia: a suggestion to the hypnotic subject while he is in a trance may produce amnesia for the events that occurred during the trance state.

Response competition: competition between responses at the time of recall. Competition is most obvious when two different responses have been associated with the same stimulus, as in A–B and A–C. If the recall test calls for one of the responses, the other will compete and interfere with performance.

Retroactive interference: interference with recall of originally learned material stemming from the acquisition of different material between the original occasion of learning and the time of the recall test.

Serial position curve: the curve representing the proportions of the total number of errors that are observed at each position in a serial list.

Short-term memory: memory over very brief retention intervals. In one of the best known experiments the retention intervals ranged from 0 to 18 seconds.

Subjective organization: observed in free recall of an unrelated list of words, when the subject tends to recall the items in the same order on different trials.

Tip of the tongue (TOT) phenomenon: failure to recall a word of which one has knowledge. The evidence of knowledge is either an eventually successful recall or an act of recognition that occurs, without additional training, when recall has failed.

Two factor theory: the interference theory of forgetting that attributes forgetting to two factors, unlearning and response competition.

Unlearning: in the interference theory of forgetting, disruption of originally learned material during the course of learning new material. In the retroactive inhibition paradigm, unlearning of an original list is presumed to occur during acquisition of an intervening list.

References

Archer, J.E. A re-evaluation of the meaningfulness of all possible CVC trigrams. *Psychol. Monogr.*, 1960, **74** (Whole No. 497).

Barnes, J.M., and B.J. Underwood. "Fate" of first-list associations in transfer theory. *J. exp. Psychol.*, 1959, **58,** 97–105.

Bjork, R.A., D. LaBerge, and R. Legrand. The modification of short-term memory through instructions to forget. *Psychon. Sci.*, 1968, **10,** 55–56.

Bousfield, W.A. The occurrence of clustering in the recall of randomly arranged associates. *J. gen. Psychol.*, 1953, **49,** 229–240.

Briggs, G.E. Acquisition, extinction, and recovery functions in retroactive inhibition. *J. exp. Psychol.*, 1954, **47,** 285–293.

Brown, R., and D. McNeill. The "tip of the tongue" phenomenon. *Journal of Verbal Learning and Verbal Behavior,* 1966, **5,** 325–337.

Clemes, S. Repression and hypnotic amnesia. *J. abnorm. soc. Psychol.*, 1964, **69,** 62–69.

Ebbinghaus, H. *Uber das Gedächtnis: Untersuchungen zur experimentelen Psychologie.* Leipzig: Duncker und Humboldt, 1885. Trans. by H.A. Ruger and C.E. Bussenius, *Memory,* 1913. Reissued New York: Dover Press, 1964.

Ekstrand, B.R. Effect of sleep on memory. *J. exp. Psychol.*, 1967, **75,** 64–72.

Elmes, D.G. Cuing to forget in short-term memory. *J. exp. Psychol.*, 1969, **80,** 561–562.

Epstein, W. Poststimulus output specification and differential retrieval from short-term memory. *J. exp. Psychol.*, 1969, **82,** 168–174.

Freud, S. *Psychopathology of everyday life.* In *The basic writings of Sigmund Freud.* New York: Random House, 1938 (first German edition, 1904).

———. Repression. In Alex and James Strachey (Trans.), *Collected Papers.* Vol. IV. London: Hogarth, 1925.
Glucksberg, S., and L.J. King. Motivated forgetting mediated by implicit verbal chaining: A laboratory analog of repression. *Science,* 1967, **158,** 517–519.
Horowitz, L.M., and L.S. Prytulak. Redintegrative memory. *Psychol. Rev.,* 1969, **76,** 519–531.
Houston, J.P., and O. Johnson. Unlearning and the reinforced evocation of first-list responses. *Journal of Verbal Learning and Verbal Behavior,* 1967, **6,** 451–453.
James, W. *The principles of psychology.* Vol. 1. New York: Holt, Rinehart and Winston, 1893.
Jenkins, J.G., and K.M. Dallenbach. Obliviscence during sleep and waking. *Amer. J. Psychol.,* 1924, **35,** 605–612.
Jenkins, J.J. Mediated associations: Paradigms and situations. In C.N. Cofer and B.S. Musgrave (Eds.), *Verbal behavior and learning.* New York: McGraw-Hill, 1963.
Keppel, G. Retroactive and proactive inhibition. In T. R. Dixon and D. L. Dixon (Eds.), *Verbal behavior and general behavior theory.* Englewood Cliffs, N.J.: Prentice-Hall, 1968.
———, and D.S. Rausch. Unlearning as a function of second-list error instructions. *Journal of Verbal Learning and Verbal Behavior,* 1966, **5,** 50–58.
MacKinnon, D.W., and W.F. Dukes. Repression. In L. Postman (Ed.), *Psychology in the making.* New York: Alfred A. Knopf, 1962.
Mandler, G. Organization and memory. In K.W. Spence and J.T. Spence (Eds.), *Psychology of learning and motivation.* Vol. 1. New York: Academic Press, 1967.
McCrary, J.W., and W.S. Hunter. Serial position curves in verbal learning. *Science,* 1953, **117,** 131–134.
McGovern, J.M. Extinction of associations in four transfer paradigms. *Psychol. Monogr.,* 1964, **78,** (Whole No. 593).
Melton, A.W., and J.M. Irwin. The influence of degree of interpolated learning on retroactive inhibition and the overt transfer of specific responses. *Amer. J. Psychol.,* 1940, **53,** 173–203.
Miller, G.A., E. Galanter, and K.H. Pribram. *Plans and the structure of behavior.* New York: Holt, Rinehart and Winston, 1960.
Moss, C.S. *Hypnosis in perspective.* New York: Macmillan, 1965.
Noble, C.E. An analysis of meaning. *Psychol. Rev.,* 1952, **59,** 421–430.
Norman, D.A. *Memory and attention.* New York: John Wiley & Sons, 1969.
Osgood, C.E. *Method and theory in experimental psychology.* New York: Oxford University Press, 1953.
Peterson, L., and M.J. Peterson. Short-term retention of individual verbal items. *J. exp. Psychol.,* 1959, **58,** 193–198.
Postman, L. The present status of interference theory. In C.N. Cofer (Ed.), *Verbal learning and verbal behavior.* New York: McGraw-Hill, 1961.
———, and K. Stark. Unlearning as a function of the relationship between successive response classes. *J. exp. Psychol.,* 1965, **69,** 111–118.
Rapaport, D. *Emotions and memory.* New York: International University Press, 1950.
Rosenzweig, S., and G. Mason. An experimental study of memory in relation to the theory of repression. *Brit. J. Psychol.,* 1934, **24,** 247–265.
Russell, W.A., and L.H. Storms. Implicit verbal chaining in paired associate learning. *J. exp. Psychol.,* 1955, **49,** 287–293.
Tulving, E. Subjective organization in free recall of "unrelated" words. *Psychol. Rev.,* 1962, **69,** 344–354.
Tulving, E., and S. Osler. Effectiveness of retrieval cues in memory for words. *J. exp. Psychol.,* 1968, **77,** 593–601.
Tulving, E., and Z. Pearlstone. Availability versus accessibility of information in memory for words. *Journal of Verbal Learning and Verbal Behavior,* 1966, **5,** 381–391.
Turvey, M.T., and R.P. Wittlinger. Attenuation of proactive interference in short-term memory as a function of cuing to forget. *J. exp. Psychol.,* 1969, **80,** 295–298.
Underwood, B.J. *Experimental psychology.* (2nd ed.) New York: Appleton-Century-Crofts, 1966.

———. Forgetting. *Scientific Amer.,* 1964, **210,** 91–94.

Van Ormer, E.B. Retention after intervals of sleep and waking. *Arch. Psychol.,* New York, 1932, No. 137.

Weiner, B. Effects of motivation on the availability and retrieval of memory traces. *Psychol. Bull.,* 1966, **65,** 24–37.

———, and H. Reed. Effects of the instructional sets to remember and to forget on short-term retention. *J. exp. Psychol.,* 1969, **79,** 226–232.

Yates, F.A. *The art of memory.* Chicago: University of Chicago Press, 1966.

Zeller, A.F. An experimental analogue of repression: I. Historical summary. *Psychol. Bull.,* 1950, **47,** 39–51.

5 Syntax and Cognition

Language plays a vital role in directing and maintaining behavior. No single scientific discipline can claim the study of language as its exclusive privilege, since the students of language come from such diverse parent disciplines as anthropology, biology, education, linguistics, and psychology. When two of these disciplines converge, a new specialty may be formed. *Psycholinguistics,* the intersection of psychology and linguistics, is an example.

Linguists are concerned with the description of language at various levels. At the phonetic level, the emphasis is on the distinctive units of sound (phonemes) of language. At the morphemic level, the description seeks to isolate the smallest units of meaning (morphemes). At the most complex level, the linguist attempts to describe the structure of language, emphasizing grammar or syntax. The ideal description at this level would be a set of rules, a grammar, that would generate all of the syntactically acceptable sentences of the language and none of the unacceptable ones.

Psycholinguists are concerned primarily with a description of the *language user.* They study the relationships among the formal phonemic, morphemic, and syntactic features of language and the way in which the language user processes linguistic information. The linguist may feel his task to be complete when he has written a generative grammar, but this achievement may only set the stage for the psycholinguist's efforts. For example, developmental psycholinguists will be interested in identifying the stages of development of the grammar and the processes that make it possible for the child to acquire syntactical language.

This chapter examines one aspect of psycholinguistic endeavor, the attempt to exhibit and explain the effects of linguistic variables on the basic cognitive processes of perception, memory, comprehension, and reasoning. Although a number of different linguistic variables will be mentioned, the principal aim is to describe and analyze the relationship between syntax (grammar) and cognition. Does syntactical structure affect memory for sequential strings of verbal items? Is our willingness to accept the truth of a statement affected by its syntactical organization? Does successful reasoning depend in some measure on the way the problem is presented grammatically? For example, the following are two formulations of the same "three term" reasoning problem:

1. If John is better than Dick, and Pete is worse than Dick, then who is best?
2. If Dick is worse than John, and Dick is better than Pete, then who is best?

Even though both problems present exactly the same information, most people find the second formulation more difficult. Is the difference in difficulty related to differences in the linguistic structure of the alternative formulations? These are the questions that will occupy our attention in this chapter.

Concepts of Syntax

If we are to examine the relationship between syntax and cognition, we must first describe the conceptualization of syntax that has provided the starting point for many of our studies. Linguists frequently distinguish two main tasks comprising grammatical analysis. One is to identify the morphemes of a language, in other words, the smallest meaningful units; this branch of grammatical analysis is called *morphology* (Gleason, 1961). Morphemes do not occur in a language in any order. Only some sequences are found, while others (is clear section this?) never occur. The second task of grammatical analysis is to describe the rules that govern the arrangement or order of morphemes. The branch that deals with this question is *syntax*. Let us consider two alternative conceptualizations of syntax.

Left-to-Right Model

The left-to-right model, sometimes called the Markov model, proposes that the only prescriptions concerning what may be said are the words that have already been said. The next word in this sentence will depend only upon the words preceding it. Such a grammar might have a rule like: "After the sequence *The man* . . . , continue with *is, who, that* . . . but not with *the, ball, am*. . . ." The complete grammar would be the list of all the prescribed and proscribed sequences.

This model of syntax has very few adherents. Objections to it, presented in detail by Miller *et al.* (1960, pp. 146–148) and Miller and Chomsky (1963), fall into two chief categories. One argument shows that it would be impossible to learn to speak acceptable English if acquisition of a left-to-right grammar were required. It is estimated that a left-to-right grammar would require a century of undisturbed exposure to spoken English before the listener could be expected to have received the information necessary for the production of sentences. Yet many children speak syntactically acceptable English before the age of three.

The other major argument against the Markov model is that it would not generate an important class of sentences—sentences that have other sentences embedded in them. Consider the sentence, "The man who said give me liberty or give me death bought a farm in Virginia after the war was won." This sentence contains grammatical dependencies that extend across the embedded sentence. Of course there is no limit, except taste and the burden on memory, to the number of nested sentences that may be included. It is hard to conceive of a left-to-right rule that could prescribe embedded sentences.

Generative Model

The generative model differs from the left-to-right model in two ways. Instead of treating sentences as strings of independent elements, connected only by word-word associative links, the generative grammar offers a structural analysis of the sentence. Instead of treating sentences as independent entities, the generative grammar stresses the relationships among sentences, or more precisely the relationships among underlying sentence structures. In a sense, the generative grammar exploits what every native speaker of a language knows intuitively: that language is structured.

One aspect of the structure of a sentence is described by a phrase structure analysis of the sentence itself. This is a sophisticated form of assigning grammatical labels to parts of a sentence to break it down into subparts that are grammatically relevant. The parts are called constituents. An *immediate constituent* is one of the two (or several) constituents of which any given sentence is formed. Analysis of phrase structure consists of developing a hierararchy of successive levels of constituents showing the relationships among them.

Consider the simple sentence: *A man read the book.* There would probably be general agreement about the appropriate way to segment this sentence. The two immediate constituents are *A man* and *read the book;* the last two words seem to comprise a unit within the latter constituent. This simple analysis was guided

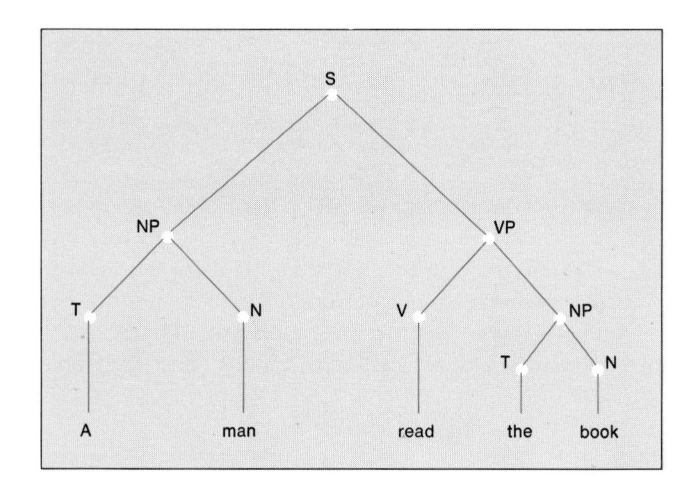

Fig. 5.1 A tree diagram to represent phrase structure.

partly by semantic considerations, but the formal grammatical analysis of phrase structure is guided by more abstract principles called *rewrite rules.* The rewrite rule has the general form X → Y, which is read "X is to be rewritten as Y," where to rewrite means to replace or expand. For example, the following rewrite rules guide the phrase structure analysis of our illustrative sentence:

1. Sentence → Noun Phrase + Verb Phrase, in symbolic form S → NP + VP, which means that a sentence may be rewritten (expanded) as two terms, a noun phrase plus a verb phrase.
2. Noun Phrase → Determiner + Noun, or NP → T + N.
3. Verb Phrase → Verb + Noun Phrase, or VP → V + NP.
4. T → a, the, this, that, some, which means that T may be replaced by *a, the,* etc.
5. N → man, boy, book, train.
6. V → read, gave, sat.

Figure 5.1 represents the hierarchical phrase structure of this type of sentence in the form of a tree diagram. One aim of the generative grammar is to provide complete phrase structure rules which would generate the phrase structure of all acceptable sentences without generating any unacceptable structures.

Consider the sentences in Table 5.1. A phrase structure analysis could be provided for each of them, but plainly this analysis would fail to represent one vital aspect—these sentences comprise a family. Each one is related to the others by virtue of the relationships among their phrase structures. Each phrase structure is *transformationally* related to every other. A transformation rule is a rewrite rule that allows an *entire* sentence to be rewritten as a different sentence. For example, the SAAD sentence is related to the P sentence by a passive transformation, and the P sentence is related to the PNQ by two transformations. Figure 5.2 is a graphic representation of the transformational relationships among the sentences in Table 5.1. Each of the eight sentences is located at one of the eight corners of the cube. The closeness of the vertices occupied by two sentences is a measure of the transformational distance between them. Thus K (kernel, SAAD) is separated from P by a single transformation and from PN by two transformations. It is also implied

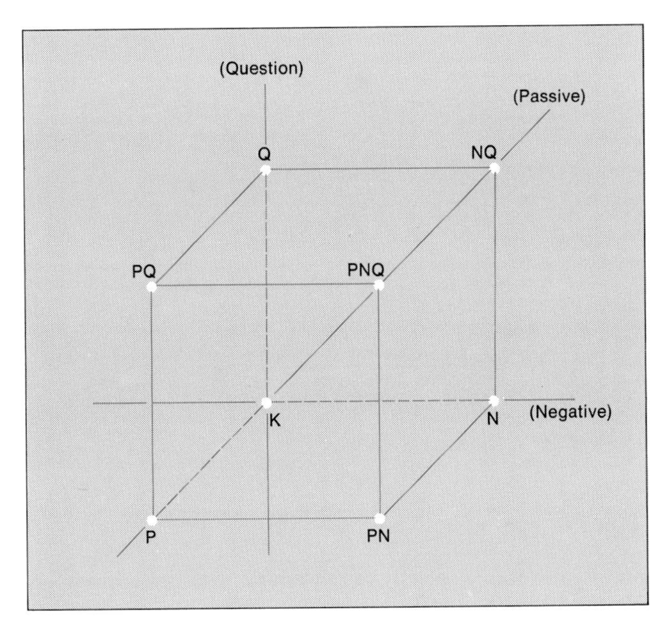

Fig. 5.2. Cube representing transformational relationships among sentences. (From Clifton and Odom, 1966)

that to rewrite K as PN the K → P transform or the K → N transform must first be completed. This property of the cube reflects the step-wise character of transformational rules.

In summation, the generative grammar emphasizes a structural analysis. The grammar is a set of rules that generate structural descriptions of all acceptable sentences. At the level of relationships among words, phrase structure rules are proposed; at the level of relationships among sentences (deep structure), transformational rules are proposed.

The Perceptual Reality of Syntax

The linguist does not offer his grammar as a description of the process followed by a speaker in constructing a sentence, or by a listener in decoding a sentence. The linguist's grammar is a statement about language, not about language users. His position is analogous to the logician's who offers an analysis of syllogistic structures without intending any claims about the way people reason. Unlike the linguist, the psychologist's chief concern *is* with the language user. Our analysis begins by examining the relationship between syntax and perception. Although the experiments we have selected employ different procedures, they can be arranged progressively. The first study, by Miller and Isard (1963), shows that syntactical structure does have perceptual consequences. The second series of studies (Fodor and Bever, 1965; Garret *et al.*, 1965; Bever *et al.*, 1969) examines the influence of phrase structure on perception. The third study (Mehler and Carey, 1967) is aimed at exhibiting the role of transformational relationships in the perception of sentences.

Sentence	
The boy closed the door.	Simple Active Declarative (SAAD or K)
The door was closed by the boy.	Passive (P)
The boy didn't close the door.	Negative (N)
Did the boy close the door?	Question (Q)
The door wasn't closed by the boy.	PN
Was the door closed by the boy?	PQ
Didn't the boy close the door?	NQ
Wasn't the door closed by the boy?	PNQ

Table 5.1 *Example of P, N, Q Sentence Family*

Syntax and Intelligibility

Miller and Isard (1963) set out to determine whether grammatical structure contributes to the intelligibility or successful perception of a sentence. As a measure of successful perception they determined the subject's ability to "shadow"—to repeat aloud immediately afterward—exactly what the speaker was saying. Consider the first example in Table 5.2. This sentence was tape-recorded and played into a subject's earphones at the rate of two words per second. The subject's task was to repeat the sentence. Compare this sentence with the second string, labelled *ungrammatical.* No one would be surprised to discover that the ungrammatical string is shadowed less successfully than the grammatical string. But this comparison is not very informative, since the two strings differ in too many ways to allow us to isolate the contribution of syntax. However, consider the third string, which is semantically *anomalous* and does not seem to include highly probable sequences of words. (How many times would "earrings" follow "legal" in normal English discourse?) In these respects, the anomalous string differs from the sentence and resembles the ungrammatical string. But upon closer examination it will be noted that the anomalous string is like the sentence in one important respect: it is grammatical.

Suppose that a subject is required to shadow grammatical sentences, anomalous strings, and ungrammatical strings like those presented in Table 5.2. We have already noted that shadowing should be more successful with sentences than with ungrammatical strings. But how will anomalous strings fare? Will the fact that they are grammatical make them easier to hear?

Figure 5.3 shows the per cent of each type of string that was shadowed without error. The specification of speech-to-noise ratio refers to the fact that the presentation of the strings was accompanied by a masking noise ranging in intensity from +15 to −5 db relative to the level of speech. The experiment was also performed without masking noise; these data are shown on the right side of Figure 5.3a. In one experiment the three types of strings were presented in a mixed list of 150 strings (Fig. 5.3a). In another experiment the three types were represented in three unmixed blocks, each containing 50 strings. Comparing Figures 5.3a and 5.3b shows that the ordering of results was the same under all conditions: sentences were shadowed best, ungrammatical strings poorest, and anomalous strings were

Grammatical:	A witness signed the official legal document.
Ungrammatical:	A legal glittering the exposed picnic knight.
Anomalous:	A magazine prevented the ferocious legal earrings.

Table 5.2 *Sample Verbal Strings from the Study by Miller and Isard (1963)*

intermediate. Anomalous strings, which reflect the syntactical structure of English, are easier to perceive than ungrammatical sequences, despite the fact that both types of strings are semantically anomalous. The superiority of sentences over anomalous strings reflects the special contribution of semantic rules.

Phrase Structure

Earlier we noted that a sentence may be subjected to a phrase structure analysis that identifies its constituents. For present purposes we can limit our attention to segmentation of the sentence into its major constituents or phrases. Consider the following sentence:

(That he was happy) (was evident from the way he smiled.)

The major constituent break or phrase boundary is between "happy" and "was." We could continue this analysis, dividing the first phrase into the constituents *That* and *he was happy,* and so on, but the present discussion will be confined to the major constituents.

The question under consideration is whether the units of a sentence marked off by phrase structure analysis correspond to the perceptual units into which sentences are encoded by the hearer. Are the rules of syntactical organization also the rules of perceptual organization? To answer this question, Fodor and Bever (1965) assumed an analogy between auditory speech perception and visual form perception. The Gestalt psychologists have frequently noted that an organized perceptual unit resists interruption (illustrations of this principle are shown in Fig. 5.4). Fodor and Bever assumed that the perceptual units in language exhibit the same tendency, and therefore reasoned that if the segments isolated by phrase structure analysis function as perceptual units, then they should resist intrusions.

The experimental procedure will help clarify this reasoning. The subjects were presented with the stimulus materials through earphones. One ear received a sentence, such as "That he was happy. . . ." The other ear received a click, equal in intensity to the most intense speech sound and lasting 25 msec. Each of 30 different sentences was recorded nine times with the click superimposed in nine different locations. The locations of the clicks were balanced around the major phrase boundary. For example:

(That he was happy) (was evident from the way he smiled.)

c c c c c c c c

The subject's task was to write each sentence immediately following its presentation, and to mark the location of the click.

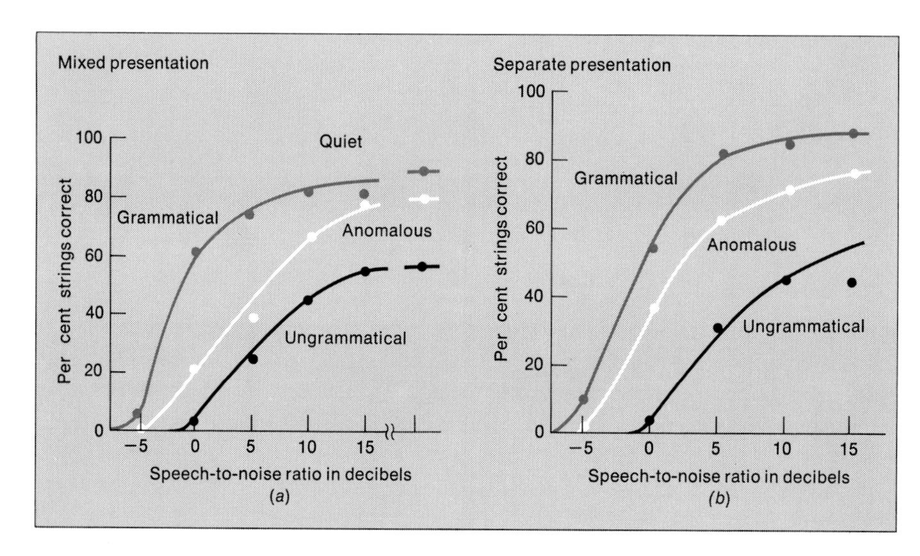

Fig. 5.3. (a) Per cent strings heard correctly as a function of speech-to-noise ratio when the three types of test strings are presented in mixed order. (b) Per cent strings heard correctly as a function of speech-to-noise ratio when each type of test material is presented separately. (From Miller and Isard, 1963)

The crucial datum is perceived location of the click. If the syntactical segments are perceptual units they should resist intrusion, and clicks that interrupt them should be mislocated. The clicks should appear to be located where they interfere least, in the boundary between phrases. More specifically, clicks occurring earlier than the major segment boundary should be perceived to have occurred later than their objective position, and clicks occurring later than the major boundary should be perceived to have occurred earlier than their objective position. Apparent displacement should occur toward the major boundary. This hypothesis was confirmed for all 30 sentences.

You will note that in the sample sentence one of the clicks is located in the boundary between phrases. This click should be located more accurately than clicks whose objective position is within segments. This follows from the thesis that a significant factor in producing click displacement is the tendency to maintain the integrity of the segments as perceptual units. This prediction was also confirmed.

This last finding fits well into the general picture, but it also raises another possibility. Read the sentence aloud with normal intonation. The major boundary will be accompanied by a slightly longer pause than that between other adjacent words. It is possible that clicks are located more accurately in the phrase boundary because this location provides a quiet interval. It is equally possible that some acoustic feature also attracts the clicks from other positions. Can we rule out the effect of acoustic correlates of phrase structure in interpreting the click displacement data?

Fortunately, an experiment by Garret *et al.* (1965) answers this question. Consider the following two sentences:

A. (In her hope of marrying) (Anna was surely impractical.)
B. (Your hope of marrying Anna) (was surely impractical.)

First, sentence A was taped. Then sentence B was prepared by splicing the already

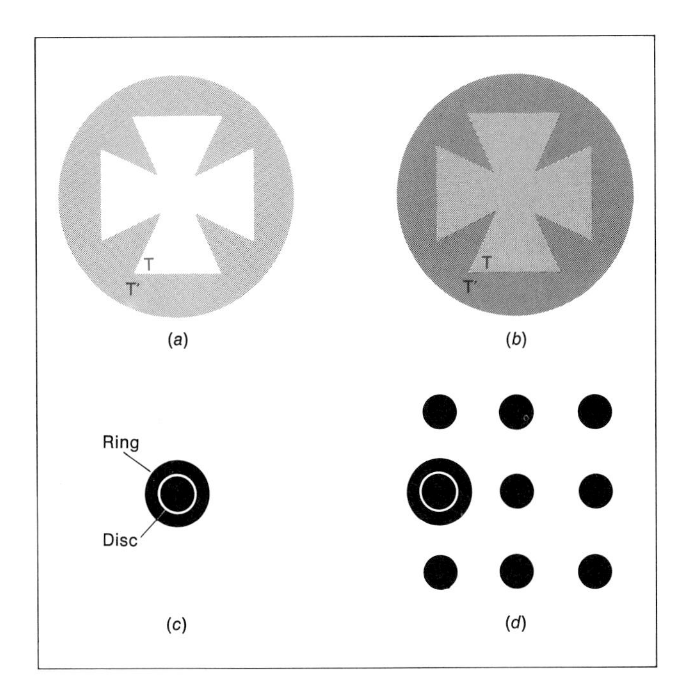

Fig. 5.4. Two illustrations of the tendency of a visual form to resist interruption. In (a) and (b), T and T′ are colored spots of light that are projected either on the lower arm of the figure (cross) or on the background. The intensity of light required to make the spot visible is higher on the figure than on the ground. The cross resists interruption. In (c) and (d) this tendency is illustrated in a case of visual masking. A black disc is flashed briefly and followed shortly after by a concentric black ring. The effect is to mask the disc so that it is not detected by the subject. But if the disc is part of a configuration, as in (d), it is more difficult to mask the disc.

taped common portion of the two sentences, *hope . . . impractical*, to the word *Your*. This means that the common portion of the two sentences was acoustically identical. However, as the parentheses indicate, the location of the major constituent boundary is not the same in the two sentences, preceding *Anna* in A and following *Anna* in B. Suppose a click is presented along with *Anna*. According to the main hypothesis, the click should be displaced in opposite directions in the two sentences, despite the fact that this portion of the sentence is acoustically identical in the two recordings. The results agreed with the hypothesis. Additional evidence resulting from these procedures has been reported by Bever, Lackner, and Stolz (1969) and Bever, Lackner, and Kirk (1969). Together they support the conclusion that the linguistic units identified by description of the phrase structure of sentences function as units in the perception of language.

Deep Structure

A distinction was made earlier between phrase structure and deep structure. Consider the following two sentences:

1. They are reluctant to consent.
2. They are troublesome to employ.

These sentences have the same phrase structure, but note that to paraphrase the first, one may say, *They are reluctant about consenting,* but for the second, *To employ them is troublesome. They* is the subject of the verb in the first sentence type and the object in the second. This difference is not represented in the phrase structure, as you may confirm by segmenting the sentences.

The study we consider next seeks to determine whether deep structure influences perception. The experimental procedure takes advantage of the well-established relationship between *set* (readiness to respond) and perception. If you are shown a serial sequence of ten letters—X, A, Z, L, V, N, T, Q, F, and D—you may develop a set to process all letterlike stimuli as letters. Consequently, the eleventh stimulus, 13, will look like the letter B and not the numeral 13. The effect of set is thus two-sided: stimuli consonant with the set are perceived more easily, and stimuli that are dissonant are more difficult to perceive.

Mehler and Carey (1967) utilized this fact in their study of sentence perception. Two series of sentences were composed which differed only in their deep structure. One series had the deep structure of sentence 1 above, and one series had the structure of sentence 2. The plan of the experiment was to set the subject to hear sentences of one type and then, without notice, to present the other type. The set was established by presenting ten successive sentences with the same base structure, each sentence's presentation accompanied by white noise. The subject's task was to listen to each sentence and write it down immediately after it was presented. The eleventh sentence, selected from the other deep structure set, provided the test.

This experiment assumes that when the listener hears a sentence, the perceptual organization of the input is determined partly by its deep structure. As a consequence of the preparatory sequence of ten sentences, the subject develops a readiness to recognize sentences with one type of base structure. If this is correct, perception of the test sentence should be impeded. The effect would be analogous to the failure to identify the numeral 13 following a sequence of letters.

To determine whether perception of the test sentence has been impeded by the shift to a different base structure, we need a standard for comparison, that is, a control condition that shows the level of correct perception of the test sentence in the absence of set. Most suitable for this purpose would have been a randomly ordered sequence of 11 sentences of several different base structures, with the test sentence of the experimental sequence as the eleventh sentence. Mehler and Carey used a less exacting standard. They compared perception of the set-breaking test sentence with perception of the same sentence when it was tenth in the sequence of set-inducing sentences presented to another group of subjects. The results confirmed the hypothesis: The sentence was correctly perceived less frequently when it followed ten sentences of different base structure than when it followed a sequence of sentences of the same base structure.

The conclusions drawn by Garret *et al.* (1965, p. 32) from their own study provide an apt summarization of the implications of the research considered in this section:

> The primary significance of these results is the support they provide for a view of sentence decoding as an active process in which the listener provides the structural analysis of the sentence rather than responding passively to to some acoustic cues which mark the structure. It is clear that the differential response of subjects in these experiments cannot be accounted for with any

"passive" theory of speech perception. The results here provide added evidence of the operation of an active process of perception at the level of the grammar's syntactic component.

Syntax and Memory

In this section our concern shifts to the storage (memorization) and retrieval (recall) of linguistic sequences. Does syntax affect these processes? As in the previous section, we begin by describing an experiment that exhibits an effect of syntax in general; then we look at experiments designed to examine the role of phrase structure and base structure.

Syntax and Learning

Suppose a subject is asked to memorize the following sentence: *A happy boy delivered the pup quickly to warm quarters.* Most people could successfully reproduce this sentence from memory after only a single exposure. Next, the same subject is asked to memorize the following sequence: *vax koob a um nerf citar desak molent glox the.* This sequence will prove difficult, and many trials will be required before the subject can reproduce it without error.

Why is the sentence so much easier to memorize than the nonsense string? Obviously, many aspects of the sentence may be involved:

1. *Semantic aspects.* The sentence has semantic structure; it conveys meaningful information. In addition, the components of the sentence are familiar words that are individually meaningful.
2. *Statistical (probabilistic) aspects.* The sentence is composed of a sequence of words that have followed each other frequently in previous experience with English. The conditional probability (the probability of *boy* given *happy,* or the probability of *the* given *delivered*) between adjacent words is high. (Refer to the Markov model, above.) Presumably, the subject can draw on these preexperimentally established associations to facilitate current learning.
3. *Syntactical aspects.* The sentence is syntactically structured. Aspects of syntax may also facilitate learning.

These three types of factors are present in every sentence, but at the moment our interest is exclusively in the syntactical aspects. As a first step, it would be useful to establish that, in the absence of semantic and statistical factors, syntactical structure affects learning. This objective requires a rather special type of linguistic sequence. Normal English sentences are unsuitable because they invariably entail semantic and statistical constraints. A comparison between anomalous and ungrammatical strings of the sort used by Miller and Isard would be better suited (Table 5.2). However, these strings contain different words, and this difference might conceivably result in effects on learning independent of syntax.

The solution may be seen in the four types of verbal strings reproduced in Table 5.3. Type S–N, syntactical nonsense, was inspired by Lewis Carroll's "Jabberwocky" poem: "Twas brilling, and the slithy toves did gyre and gimble in the wabe. . . ." Like Jaberwocky, string S–N is semantic nonsense that sounds reas-

Type	String
S–N	A vapy koob desaked the citar molently um glox nerfs.
US–N	koob vapy the desaked um glox citar nerfs a molently
S–W	Cruel tables sang falling circles to empty bitter pencils.
US–W	sang tables bitter empty cruel to circles pencils falling

Table 5.3 *Syntactical and Unsyntactical Strings for the Study of the Influence of Syntax on Learning (From Epstein, 1961, Table 1, p. 82)*

suringly familiar and acceptable. In addition to lacking meaning as a sentence, S–N is not likely to have incorporated preexperimental statistical dependencies between individual items. String S–N sounds acceptable because the string simulates the syntactical structure of English by appending grammatical tags (like *ed* and *ly*) to some of the nonsense syllable stems, and arranging the items, together with two articles, in the order specified by English grammar. String S–N, therefore, meets our requirement for a sequence that is structured syntactically but lacks other constraints. String US–N, unstructured nonsense, is the appropriate comparison for S–N. It is a scrambled version of S–N, containing the same items in an unsyntactical order. The remaining two strings, S–W, syntactical words, and US–W, unsyntactical words, are like Miller and Isard's (1963) anomalous (S–W) and ungrammatical (US–W) strings.

Epstein (1961) had different subjects learn the four types of strings shown in Table 5.3. The procedure was simple. The complete string was presented for a seven second period, then the subject had 30 seconds to reproduce the string from memory. Study and test trials alternated until the subject could reproduce the string perfectly. The object of the experiment was to determine if syntactical structure would facilitate learning, a conclusion that would be implied if S–N and S–W were learned more rapidly than US–N and US–W, respectively. The mean number of study trials required to achieve perfect reproduction is shown in Table 5.4. Strings S–N and S–W were learned in fewer trials than their unsyntactical equivalents, showing that syntax facilitates learning.

Many additional studies employing these types of materials have been reported by investigators (see O'Connell, 1970). Although these studies have clarified the role of syntax in learning language-like strings, they have not changed the basic conclusion that syntax facilitates learning.

Phrase Structure and Recoding

How does syntax facilitate learning? One possibility is that syntactical structure provides the learner with a readily available *recoding* plan. Recoding is the label for the variety of organizational schemes that a subject may adopt in coping with a memory task. The most common scheme is to group the elements of the input, apply a new name to each group, and remember the group names rather than the original input. For example, Miller (1956a) illustrated the recoding process in an experiment in which a subject learned to rename short sequences of binary digits with a single label: 00 = 0, 01 = 1, 10 = 2, and 11 = 3. This recoding

Type of Item	Structure S (syntactical)	US (unsyntactical)
N (nonsense)	5.77	7.56
W (words)	3.50	5.94

Table 5.4 *Mean Number of Trials to Achieve Perfect Reproduction*

scheme enabled the subject to remember a much longer string of binary digits than he could remember before learning to recode.

Miller (1956b) has proposed that recoding is a general strategy employed by learners to break the informational bottleneck that results when they must memorize a sequence that exceeds their memory span. The learner attempts to recode the input into a number of chunks or units whose number does not exceed his memory span. Miller refers to this form of recoding as unitization and suggests that the chunks may be unitized into higher-order chunks as well. When learning is complete, the subject has learned a hierarchy of recoded units and is able to reproduce the sequence by a reconstructive process in which the unitization rules are applied to decode the original sequence.

The plan described in the preceding paragraph seems to be mirrored in the hierarchical tree diagrams used in our earlier description of phrase structure (Fig. 5.1). This suggests the possibility that phrase structure provides the recoding plan for processing sentences, and that syntax facilitates learning because it provides a plan for recoding. In assessing this possibility, the first order of business is to determine whether the organization of sentences in memory reflects the phrase structure of English. Are the units identified by phrase structure analysis also the units of memory?

Figure 5.5 presents tree diagrams of two sentences. The first sentence has one major constituent break, between *boy* and *saved.* The second sentence has two main breaks, between *house* and *across* and between *street* and *is.* When a subject tries to memorize such sentences, does he recode the sequence of words into chunks or units consistent with the phrase structure of the sentence? To answer this question we need to specify the characteristics that distinguish a memory unit from a sequence that has not been unitized. One distinctive feature of a unit is the high degree of interdependence among its parts; if part of the unit is recalled, the remaining parts are also likely to be recalled. If the unit is composed of words that have to be emitted in serial order, the probability of recalling a word correctly should depend on the recall of the previous word. In general, the strength of a verbal unit may be measured by the probability of a transitional error (TEP), that is, the frequency with which a given word is wrong when the preceding word was correct. The TEP will be low within units and greater between units.

The foregoing was a summary of the logic underlying an experiment by Johnson (1965). Look again at Figure 5.5. Two groups of subjects learned a list of eight paired associates (see Chap. 4) following the procedure of paced anticipation. For both groups the stimuli were the digits one to eight. The responses for one group were eight sentences that had the same phrase structure as *The tall boy . . . ;*

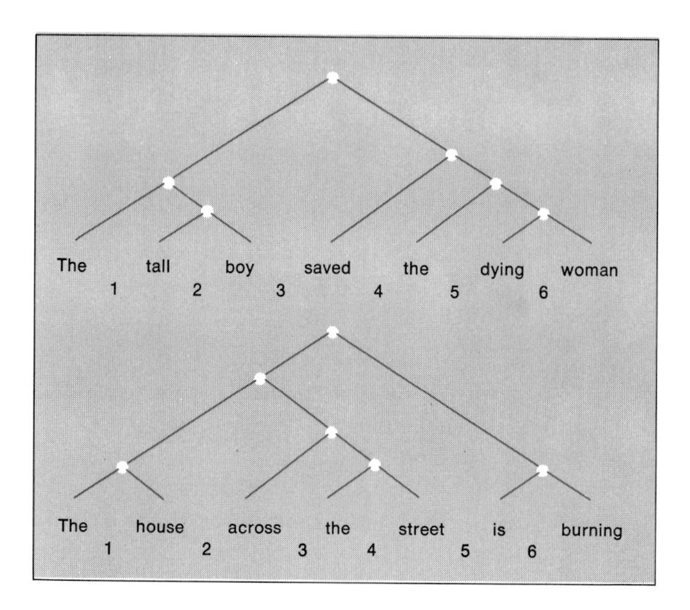

Fig. 5.5. Tree diagrams of sentences. The top diagram represents the sentences learned by one of the two groups and the bottom sentences learned by the other. The diagram is determined by the immediate constituent structure of the sentence and is a way of graphically representing the structure. The top circle or node stands for the entire sentence as a single construction, and the two lines leading from it indicate the constituents into which it is divided. (Adapted from Johnson, 1965)

the other group's responses were eight sentences with the same structure as *The house across. . . .* The subjects received 13 trials with the list.

Each sentence provides six transitions (marked in Fig. 5.5), for each of which a TEP was computed. If the sentences are recoded according to phrase structure, then *The tall boy. . .* should have been unitized into two chunks, with the first three words in one unit and the last four words in the other unit. The transitions (1, 2, 4, 5, 6) *within* these units should yield low TEP's, while the transition (3) *between* them should yield a relatively high TEP. For sentences like *The house across. . .*, the high TEP's should occur at transitions 2 and 5, since these transitions presumably bridge independent units.

Figure 5.6 shows the TEP's for sentences like *The house across the street is burning.* The TEP's at transitions 2 and 5 are significantly higher than the TEP's at other transitions. This pattern fits very well with the hypothesis that phrase structure provides the recoding plan used by the learner in trying to memorize a sentence. The memory units defined by the TEP data are compatible with the syntactic units defined by phrase structure analysis.

Consistent with the TEP data are observations reported by Wilkes and Kennedy (1969) concerning the time taken to recall single words from sentences that have been memorized. Johnson's TEP data show that the sentence is unitized so that words within a unit are dependent, while those that belong to different units are independent of one another. Suppose that after the subject has successfully memorized a sentence each word is presented individually in random order, and the subject is asked to supply the succeeding word. It is unlikely that many errors will occur, but other measures of the relationship between words are available, such

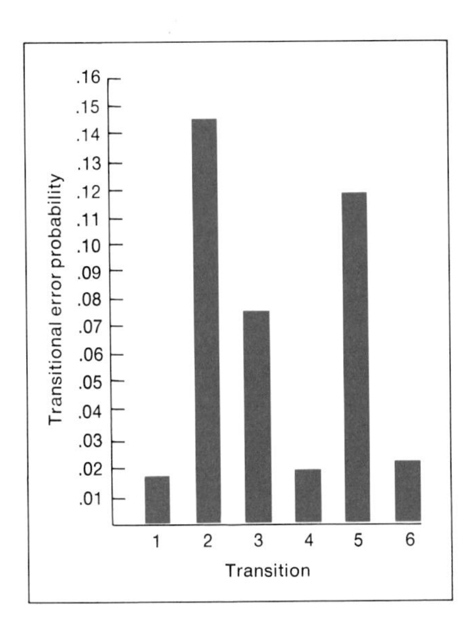

Fig. 5.6. TEP's for sentences like *The house across the street is burning.* (Adapted from Johnson, 1965)

as the latency of the response, the time taken to provide a response to the stimulus word.

Figure 5.7 shows tree diagrams for a simple declarative sentence (1) and an embedded sentence (2). Sentences like these were memorized by the method of complete presentation. Then each word was presented individually and the subject asked to give the succeeding item as quickly as possible. The response latencies are plotted in part (b) of Figure 5.7. Look first at the declarative sentence. As the tree diagram shows, this sentence has one major constituent break, between *girl* and *stole*. You will note that the response to stimulus number 4, *girl*, had the longest latency. Next, examine the embedded sentence, which has two major constituent breaks, between *plant* and *that* and between *bought* and *soon.* If you look at the latencies, you will note two peak latencies whose locations correspond to the positions of the two words, *plant* and *bought,* which border on the main constituent breaks.

Wilkes and Kennedy's (1969) latency data are consistent with Johnson's (1965) TEP data, both of which suggest that a subject memorizing a sentence recodes the sentence into units that conform to the phrase structure. But these experiments were not designed to show that this recoding plan facilitates learning. Support for this claim is provided in another of Johnson's (1968) experiments in which the subjects learned a list of paired associates consisting of numbers as stimuli and word sequences as responses. For group P the responses were acceptable English sequences which were phrase units, such as *hit the small ball.* For group NP the responses were sequences that were equally probable, but did not constitute phrase units, such as *ball hit the small.* A third group of subjects (S) learned responses consisting of scrambled sequences, such as *ball the hit small,* which are not consistent with the syntactical or statistical structure of English. Johnson reasoned that if the phrase structure of English provides the plan for recoding, and if recoding facilitates memory, group P should learn most rapidly and group S least rapidly. Group NP, which learns nonphrase units, should be intermediate between groups P and S. The results conformed to the hypothesis.

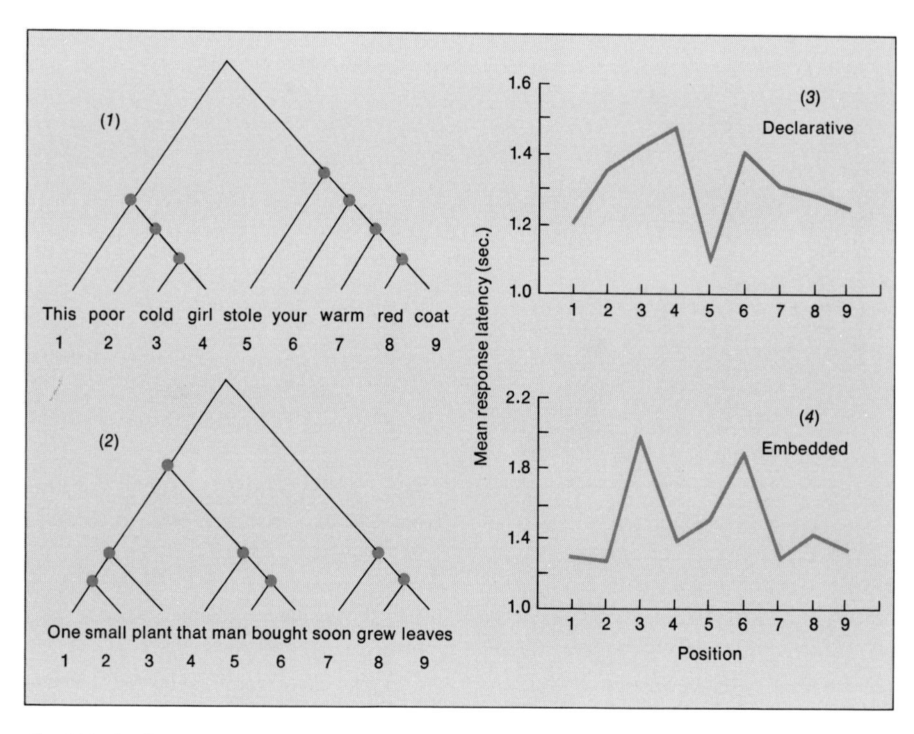

Fig. 5.7. (a) Tree diagrams illustrating constituent structure of (example) sentences: (1) simple declarative, (2) embedded. (b) Mean response latency as a function of serial position of stimulus items. (From Wilkes and Kennedy, 1969)

A supplementary finding is also worth noting. We wish to attribute the differences in rate of learning to unitization. As noted earlier, a distinctive feature of units is the high degree of interdependence among their parts. In Johnson's experiment, the words constituting the P responses should exhibit greater interdependence than the words comprising the NP and S responses. One measure of unit strength is the conditional probability that the subject will emit a perfect sequence, given that he emits at least one word correctly. A conditional probability of 1.00 would signify complete unitization or integration, while a probability of zero would signify that each word in the sequence has been encoded as an independent event. The conditional probabilities were 0.367, 0.539, and 0.679 for responses S, NP, and P, respectively. These probabilities support the claim that the differences in rate of learning are due to differences in unitization.

Association

The view of sentence learning advanced in the preceding pages does not offend common sense, but the hypothesis is notable for its disregard of a key concept in explanations of learning, *association.* A typical account of the process underlying the acquisition of a serial list of items, such as VAX, NEB, CES, MUN . . . , is that we learn a sequential chain of associations between adjacent items. Despite apparent similarities between serial learning and sentence learning, the notion of associative chaining has not figured prominently in accounts of sentence learning, which

	*old–lady** Transition 2	*lady–told** Transition 3
Without association	.0489	.0820
Prior association	.0224	.0763

Table 5.5 *Transitional Error Probabilities with and without Prior Association Learning*
* *One of the sentences used by Johnson was* The old lady told the funny story.

has been explained by a process of hierarchical organization. Nevertheless, the role of associations between words in sentences has not been totally ignored. Let us consider two studies (Johnson, 1966; Rosenberg, 1968) that examine this matter.

Both experiments were designed to study the effects of word-to-word associations on the transitional error probabilities (TEP's) within and between phrase units. Consider the sentence diagrammed in the upper half of Figure 5.5. Assume that prior to learning this sentence the subjects in Johnson's (1965) experiment learned two word-word associations, *tall–boy* and *boy–saved.* If learning a sentence entails the development of a sequential chain of word-to-word associations, then prior training with these word pairs should reduce the TEP's for the *tall boy* and *boy saved* transitions by the same amount. On the other hand, if learning of the sentence follows the unitization plan, reduction of the TEP should occur principally for the transition within the phrase unit. The TEP for the transition between phrases should not be reduced by prior association formation, because presumably the subject does not form a direct link between the two words that bridge a phrase boundary.

Experiments by Johnson (1966) and Rosenberg (1968) were based on this line of reasoning. Johnson used sentences like those shown in the upper portion of Figure 5.5. The subjects began by learning a list of word-word paired associates that bridged the second (within phrase) and third (between phrase) transitions. Then the subjects learned the digit-sentence paired associates. Johnson computed TEP data for the second and third transitions and compared the TEP's with those observed when there was no preceding associative learning. Table 5.5 summarizes the results. Statistical tests showed that the TEP for the second transition was significantly reduced by prior associative learning, but not that for the third transition. These data suggest that word-word associations may strengthen the units formed by phrase-structure recoding, but they do not provide the basis for sentence learning.

A full assessment of the role of association in sentence learning must take associative strength into account; it must examine the role of word-word bonds over a range of associative strength, including very strong associations. Rosenberg (1968) has reported data based on the learning of sentences that incorporated highly probable sequences of words, such as *The brave soldier fought the cruel war.* The TEP data provided by these sentences show evidence of the influence of associative chaining. All TEP's, *between* as well as within phrases, were lower than those for a low association sentence, such as *The rich soldier liked the green house.* Apparently very strong associative linkages can override grammatical recoding. Whether or not these associations will facilitate learning will depend on the demands of the

SAAD	—The secretary has typed the paper.
P	—The paper was typed by the secretary.
N	—The secretary hasn't typed the paper.
Q	—Has the secretary typed the paper?
NQ	—Hasn't the secretary typed the paper?
E	—The secretary did type the paper!
NP	—The paper hasn't been typed by the secretary.
PQ	—Has the paper been typed by the secretary?
PNQ	—Hasn't the paper been typed by the secretary?
EP	—The paper was typed by the secretary.
WH	—Who has typed the paper?

Table 5.6 *Sample Sentences Representing Eleven Syntactical Types*
(In the experiments by Mehler (1963) and Savin and Perchonock (1965), the different sentences did not *deal with the same subject matter.)*

learning task. If the task imposes a heavy load on memory, word-to-word associations may only interfere with the organization of memory. If the task does not strain the memory capacity, reliance on associative chaining may be an effective alternative.

Deep Structure and Memory

In our examination of phrase structure and recoding, we stressed the role of syntax in leading to unitization based on grouping of consecutive words. However, the claim of transformational grammar is that within an English sentence there are many important relations that cannot be represented by a grouping of adjacent words (a phrase structure analysis). These relations are represented in the deep structure.

The influence of deep structure on memory has been difficult to establish. The most obvious approach has been to determine whether differences in ease of learning are associated with differences in deep structure. However, sentences that represent different transformational histories may also provide different opportunities for using surface (phrase) structure in learning, so it has been difficult to avoid confounding the two (Martin and Roberts, 1966). Consequently, there does not seem to be wide agreement at present concerning the involvement of deep structure in memory. With the foregoing qualification in mind, let us consider two examples of the experimental approaches to this question.

The first experiment is a straightforward attempt to determine whether different syntactical types differ in the ease with which they are learned. Mehler (1963) had subjects try to memorize a list of eight sentences, each representing a different syntactical structure: simple active declarative (SAAD or K), negative (N), passive (P), question (Q), passive negative (PN), negative question (NQ), passive question (PQ), and passive negative question (PNQ). (Samples of these types are presented in Table 5.6.) The principal claim of transformational grammar is that these sentences should not be treated as distinct, independently derived sentence types, but rather as interrelated syntactical structures. They are related by rules that transform one structure into the other. A schematic representation of the relationships among the above syntactic types has been presented earlier in Figure

5.2. You will note that the types are separated from each other by from one to three transformations.

The list of eight sentences was presented for five alternating study and test trials. Two main findings emerged: the SAAD was learned most rapidly, and many of the errors in recalling the other syntactic types consisted of replacing the prescribed sentence type with its SAAD version. Mehler related these findings to Miller's (1962) notions about the involvement of deep structure in memory. Miller had proposed that the SAAD is the simplest syntactical structure, and that all other syntactical structures have a SAAD structure in their transformational history. In memorizing a complex sentence, the subject was presumed to decode the sentence into its SAAD form plus the transformational tags that must be applied to generate the original sentence. Therefore, Miller expected that SAAD sentences would be easiest to learn, and that errors in recall would show a shift toward the SAAD kernel.

According to this argument, deep structure is involved in memory, because we have to store more information when memorizing a complex sentence than when memorizing a simple sentence. The additional information concerning the transformations of the kernel uses up part of our limited memory capacity and makes the memory task more difficult. Presumably SAAD sentences are stored unencumbered by additional information and are therefore easier to learn than other types. It would also follow that different syntactic types should impose different loads on memory, depending on how much transformational information needs to be stored. For example, a passive sentence entails one transformation, while a negative passive entails two (see Fig. 5.2); therefore, negative passive sentences should use up more space in memory than passive sentences.

An experiment by Savin and Perchonock (1965) was designed to investigate the relationship between the storage requirements (memory load) of various sentence types and aspects of deep structure. The hypothesis was that the greater the complexity of a sentence's description, as indexed by the number of transformational rules required for its production, the greater will be the load imposed on the memory store. Savin and Perchonock examined this hypothesis with an ingenious procedure analogous to the ancient procedure for determining the volume of an object. As Archimedes noted, an object dropped into water will displace an amount of water directly related to its volume. The "water" in Savin and Perchonock's experiment was a list of unrelated words; the "object" whose volume was to be determined was a sentence of given syntactical type. The subject was shown a sentence followed by a list of unrelated words, with instructions to memorize *both* the sentence and the list. After a single presentation, the subject was asked to recall the sentence and then to recall as many of the unrelated words as possible. According to the physical analogy, the greater the amount of space in memory occupied by the sentence, the greater the number of words that should be displaced and forgotten. Thus, the hypothesis about sentence complexity and storage space leads to the prediction that sentence complexity and number of list words recalled should be related inversely—the number of words recalled should decrease as sentence complexity increases.

Table 5.6 shows the 11 sentence types studied by Savin and Perchonock. On a single trial each subject heard a sentence of one of these types followed by a list of eight words. There were 60 trials, ten with SAAD sentences, and five each with the other ten sentence types. The basic rule for predicting the results was that "whenever two sentences differ only in that one has transformations that

No. of Transformations	Sentence Type	Words Recalled
	SAAD	5.27
one	Wh	4.78
one	Q	4.67
one	P	4.55
one	N	4.44
one	QN	4.39
one	E	4.30
two	PQN	4.02
two	PQ	3.85
two	EP	3.74
two	NP	3.48

Table 5.7 *Mean Number of Words Recalled for Each Sentence Type*

are absent in the other, the one with more transformations should be harder to remember, and therefore fewer additional words should be remembered after it'' (Savin and Perchonock, 1965, p. 350).

The mean number of words recalled following each sentence type is shown in Table 5.7. The sentence types have been arranged into three categories: the kernel SAAD, the types entailing one transformation, and the types entailing two transformations. The means confirmed the hypothesis. Those sentences with one transformational operation required less storage (interfered less with recall of the words) than those with two transformations, and the SAAD was least interfering of all.

The Savin-Perchonock procedure was designed to test a particular notion (Miller, 1962) concerning the involvement of transformation rules in memory. But there is reason to doubt that the differences in number of words recalled actually reflect differences in storage. It is equally plausible to attribute the differences in word recall to differential interference from the *recall* of the sentences. All sentences may be stored in memory in the same way, but some may be easier to retrieve (recall) than others, and these may interfere less than with word recall. Evidence from more recent experiments (Epstein, 1969; Glucksberg and Danks, 1969) bolsters this interpretation. For example, Epstein (1969) showed that the Savin–Perchonock results are obtained only when the words are recalled *after* the sentences are recalled; when the subject is asked to recall the words before the sentences no differences in word recall are associated with sentence type. Therefore, we should reserve judgment about the interpretation of Savin and Perchonock's results.

In introducing this section, we noted that examination of the effects of deep structure on memory is made difficult by the fact that differences in phrase structure frequently confound the attempt. In concluding this section, let us consider a study by Blumenthal (1967) that avoids this difficulty. Examine the following sentences:

1. The child was warmed by the stove.
2. The child was warm by the stove.

Prompt Word	Sentence Structure: Standard Passive	Replaced-Agent Passive
Final noun (exp. group)	7.2	3.9
Initial noun (control group)	7.1	6.9

Table 5.8 *Mean Number of Sentences Recalled Out of Ten Possible (From Blumenthal, 1967, p. 205)*

Sentences 1 (standard passive) and 2 (agent *by*-phrase replaced with a nonagent adverbial *by*-phrase) have identical phrase structure, but very different underlying structures. The significant difference is in the relation between the noun phrase, *the stove,* and other parts of the sentence. In sentence 1 the final noun is related to the entire sentence as the logical subject—The stove warmed the child. In sentence 2 the final noun is involved in a minor relation with the rest of the sentence, serving merely as part of a phrase that acts as a verb modifier. Blumenthal asked subjects to memorize a list of five sentences like sentence 1 and five like sentence 2. These ten sentences were included in a longer list that contained 15 additional sentences of various forms. After three study trials, prompted recall of the sentences was tested. Two experimental groups received the final noun as a cue to promote recall; two control groups received the initial noun as the cue. Table 5.8 shows the mean number of sentences recalled from the set of ten. When the initial noun served as recall cue, both types of sentences were equally well recalled. Prompts which serve the same grammatical function are equally effective in promoting recall. But the story is different when the final noun serves as cue, because the prompt was much less effective for type 2 sentences. Comparable results were obtained in a subsequent study by Blumenthal and Boakes (1967).

What accounts for the difference between the level of recall of sentences 1 and 2? It is not a matter of phrase structure, since the sentences are identical in this respect. Nor are the sentences different in overall difficulty; the control data suggest they are equivalent. Blumenthal proposes that the difference reflects the different roles of the final noun in the deep structure of the sentence. When, as in sentence 1, the final noun relates to the rest of the sentence in the deep structure as subject (so that the prompt word implicated the whole sentence structure), recall was promoted. But when the prompt word implicated only part of the structure, as in sentence 2, recall was not facilitated.

Syntax and Memory

Underlying the investigation of syntax and memory is a view of memorization as an activity involving recoding or organizing the material presented for memorization. The evidence reviewed in the preceding section suggests that syntactic structure is involved in the recoding process. Syntactical structure is an important determinant of the structure of immediate memory.

Problem Type	Form of Problem	Form of Question Best?	Worst?	Average	Overall Average
I	(*a*) A better than B; B better than C	15	29	22	17
	(*b*) B better than C; A better than B	7	18	12	
II	(*a*) C worse than B; B worse than A	43	48	46	33
	(*b*) B worse than A; C worse than B	21	21	21	
III	(*a*) A better than B; C worse than B	8	10	9	10
	(*b*) C worse than B; A better than B	10	12	11	
IV	(*a*) B worse than A; B better than C	30	25	28	32
	(*b*) B better than C; B worse than A	32	43	38	
I′	(*a*) A not as bad as B; B not as bad as C	28	21	24	31
	(*b*) B not as bad as C; A not as bad as B	39	36	38	
II′	(*a*) C not as good as B; B not as good as A	14	32	23	26
	(*b*) B not as good as A; C not as good as B	26	31	28	
III′	(*a*) A not as bad as B; C not as good as B	34	45	40	40
	(*b*) C not as good as B; A not as bad as B	34	45	40	
IV′	(*a*) B not as good as A; B not as bad as C	26	30	28	28
	(*b*) B not as bad as C; B not as good as A	23	35	29	

Table 5.9 *Percentage of Errors in Solving Determinate Three Term Series Problems (From Clark, 1969b, p. 209)*

Syntax, Comprehension, and Reasoning

Considering the evidence in the previous sections showing an influence of syntax on perception and immediate memory, it is not unreasonable to expect that syntax may also affect reasoning. Everyday observations show us that people are often led to reason fallaciously merely by the way problems are worded. For example, examine the following three term problem:

If Mays is worse than Mantle
And Mantle is better than Musial
Then who is worst?
Mays, Mantle, Musial, Can't tell

The correct answer is *Can't tell*, yet many people will incorrectly select *Mays*. If the question is rephrased to ask: *Then who is best?*, the number of errors will be reduced sharply.

The three term problem has been used frequently in experimental studies of reasoning (Piaget, 1928; Hunter, 1957; Desoto *et al.*, 1965; Huttenlocher, 1968; Clark, 1969a,b). As an experimental device, it has obvious attractions. A great number of variations of the problem can be introduced and the subject's response secured and scored easily. But careful study of the three term problem is justified on other grounds as well: the problem involves an essential step in deductive reasoning. Since our aim in this chapter is to examine the influence of syntax on cognition, our discussion of the three term problem will be confined to a description of the role of syntax in its solution.

Table 5.9 shows a set of 16 variants of the three term problem. The *best* or the *worst* may be asked for each problem, to comprise a total of 32 variants.

Problem Type	Form of Problem	Form of Question: Best?	Worst?	Average	Overall Average
V	(*a*) G better than J; H better than J	4*	15	10	9
	(*b*) J better than G; J better than H	13	4*	8	
VI	(*a*) G worse than J; H worse than J	20	14*	17	14
	(*b*) J worse than G; J worse than H	7*	14	10	
VII	(*a*) G better than J; J worse than H	49*	36	42	42
	(*b*) J worse than H; G better than J	45*	37	41	
VIII	(*a*) J better than G; H worse than J	22	44*	33	35
	(*b*) H worse than J; J better than G	23	52*	38	
V′	(*a*) G not as bad as J; H not as bad as J	15*	28	22	24
	(*b*) J not as bad as G; J not as bad as H	28	25*	26	
VI′	(*a*) G not as good as J; H not as good as J	18	14*	16	19
	(*b*) J not as good as G; J not as good as H	14*	29	22	
VII′	(*a*) G not as bad as J; J not as good as H	66*	42	54	56
	(*b*) J not as good as H; G not as bad as J	66*	49	58	
VIII′	(*a*) J not as bad as G; H not as good as J	35	61*	48	45
	(*b*) H not as good as J; J not as bad as G	28	56*	42	

* The correct solution is "can't tell" to these problems and "J" to the rest.

Table 5.10 *Percentage of Errors in Solving Indeterminate Three Term Series Problems (From Clark, 1969b, p. 211)*

Table 5.10 shows a set of three term problems, containing an incomplete rank order of the three terms being compared, as in *Mays is better than Epstein, and Mantle is better than Epstein.* It is obvious who is worst, but who is best? In this respect, the rank ordering presented in the problem is indeterminate, so the correct answer is *Can't tell.* As with the determinate problems in Table 5.9, there are two forms of the question for each indeterminate problem.

In the experiments (Clark, 1969a,b) that concern us, common English names were used as the terms; for example, *if Pete isn't as good as Jack, and Jack isn't as bad as Dick, then who is best?* Each subject was given a deck of 64 cards presenting the 64 variants of the problem. On a signal every ten seconds, the subject turned a new card face up, studied the problem, and circled the answer he thought was correct. The subjects were 100 introductory psychology students.

Tables 5.9 and 5.10 show the percentage of errors in solving each of the 64 problems. There are a great many ways that we could group these data for discussion, but for present purposes it will be sufficient to emphasize only selected aspects.

In Table 5.9, compare the form of problem I with I′ and problem II with II′. You will note that the paired problems present the three terms in the same order, A, B, C and C, B, A, respectively. In addition, at least in one sense, the paired problems present the same information (for example, *A is better than B* and *A not as bad as B*). Despite these similarities between I and I′ and between II and II′, problem I proves easier than problem II, while problem I′ proves more difficult than II′ (observed most readily in the last column of Table 5.9). The same analysis and results hold for problems III, IV, III′, and IV′.

Next, consider relative difficulty as a function of the form of the question. Is it easier to solve the problem with the "best" form or the "worst" form? Table 5.9 shows that this depends on the form of the problem, since for problems I and II′ *who is best?* leads to fewer errors, while for problems I′ and II *who is worst?* leads to fewer errors.

For each pair of problems in Table 5.10, one question is answerable with a name and the other is unanswerable, the correct answer being *can't tell.* For example, for problem V (a) the answer to *who is best?* is *can't tell,* but the answer to *who is worst?* is *J.* Is it more difficult to solve an answerable or an unanswerable problem? The results show that this depends on the form of the problem. Each of the answerable problems in problems V, VI, V′, and VI′ produced more errors than the corresponding unanswerable problems. The situation is reversed for problems VII, VIII, VII′, VIII′. In each of these eight problems, the unanswerable problem produced more errors than the corresponding answerable problems.

What accounts for these results? Clark (1969b) proposes to explain the findings on the basis of two assumptions. One concerns the way in which the problem solver decodes the information provided in the premises of the problem. The other involves the way in which the problem solver searches the coded information for an answer to the question.

Clark assumes that, in his effort to understand the problem, the subject analyzes or decodes the premises into their underlying base strings. For example, underlying *John is better than Dick* are the base strings *John is good* and *Dick is good.* In addition, the two base strings are also represented as components of a comparative construction, such as *John is more good than Dick is good.* Although direct evidence of this form of linguistic processing is not available for the adult problem solvers of Clark's study, there is evidence in the verbalizations of children. The following is the verbalization of one child while attempting a three term problem: "It says that Dick is shorter than Tom, so Dick is short and Tom is short too" (Donaldson, 1963, p. 131).

The question directs the subject to search for an answer. Clark proposes that the search is for information at the level of the base structure congruent with the information asked for in the question.

> Information can only be retrieved when it is congruent with the information being sought. Furthermore, this search demands congruence, not of superficial information like words or phrases, but of underlying functional relations. For example, the proposition "John isn't as bad as Pete" implies that John is bad and Pete is bad; the question "Who is best?" requires an X fitting the description X is good. Here there is a lack of congruence of underlying functional relations in proposition and question. The question must be implicitly reformulated to read "Who is least bad?" It is only at this point that congruent information can be found and the answer retrieved (Clark, 1969b, p. 206.)

Now consider the experimental results in the light of these assumptions. Why are problems I and II′ alike in being less difficult than II and I′, respectively? Clark suggests that this is because I and II′ have one identical underlying structure and II and I′ have another identical underlying structure. Table 5.11 presents the base strings underlying the propositions in these problems. The relative number of errors for the paired problems in Table 5.11 is predictable from the base structure. For both of these structures, the frequency of errors will depend on the form of the question. The question *Then who is best?* asks for information congruent with the deep structure of problems I and II′, while the question *Then who is worst?* asks

Problem Type	Base Strings	Problem Type	Base Strings
I, II′	A is good B is good C is good	I′, II	A is bad B is bad C is bad

Table 5.11 *Analysis of Problems I, II′, I′ and II*

for information congruent with the deep structure of problems I′ and II. For this reason, the "best" question leads to fewer errors in I and II′, while the same question leads to more errors in II and I′.

The difference between the number of errors for the answerable and unanswerable problems in Table 5.10 is due to the search for information in the base strings which is congruent with the question. When the subject finds information congruent with the question, he bases his answer on it. In problems V, VI, V′, and VI′, the search of the underlying strings reveals that the series is indeterminate and the solution may be *can't tell*. Consequently, the tendency to respond *can't tell* is encouraged, leading to more correct solutions to unanswerable problems whose correct solution is *can't tell*. But the situation is reversed in problems VII, VIII, VII′, and VIII′, in which the tendency to base the answer on information congruent with the question encourages the subject to solve the problems with a specific term. For example, in problem VII′ the subject will tend to answer *who is best?* with the congruent solution *H*, whereas the correct solution is *can't tell*. Therefore, in these cases more correct solutions are obtained for the answerable problems.

You will recall that Clark allowed his subjects ten seconds for each problem. As you worked through some of the problems in Tables 5.9 and 5.10, you were probably able to solve all of them correctly. To convince yourself that these problems differ in difficulty, you must limit the amount of time allowed to each problem, or record the solution time for each problem. Clark (1969a) has reported solution times for the problems that vary in a manner consistent with the view of the problem solving process that has been presented.

Linguistic Relativity and Determinism

The experimental psychologist is typically a gradualist, advancing tentatively over the terrain that he has staked out. This predilection is apparent in the work reviewed in this chapter. But not everyone has been as restrained. We now turn briefly to an examination of a more speculative and far-reaching hypothesis about the relationship among language, perception, and cognition. According to the hypothesis of *linguistic relativity,* all of perception and thought is relative to the language of the individual. The world we perceive is a product of our language, not simply an independent existence to be perceived in the same way by everyone. Despite popular belief, it is not thought that structures language, but rather the structure of language that determines the structure of thought. Aristotle's logic would have been very different had he been a speaker of Aztec Indian language.

Whorf (1956) has been the most prominent advocate of the hypothesis of linguistic relativity. The evidence for relativity and determinism comes mainly from anthropological linguistics (crosscultural comparisons of language). The evidence consists of correlations between linguistic variations among different cultures and variations in the preferred modes of organizing perceptual and cognitive experience. As an illustration, consider the distinction made by English-language speakers between "things" and "events." We take this to be a natural distinction forced upon us by immutable reality, but Whorf (1956, pp. 214–215) contests this assertion:

> Our language thus gives us a bipolar division of nature. But nature herself is not bipolarized. If it be said that strike, turn, run, are verbs because they denote temporary or short-lasting events, i.e., actions, why then is fist a noun? It is also a temporary event. Why are lightning, spark, wave, eddy, pulsation, flame, storm, phase, cycle, spasm, noise, emotion, nouns? . . . It will be found that an "event" to *us* means "what our language classes as a verb." . . . In the Hopi language, lightning, wave, flame, meteor, puff of smoke, pulsation, are verbs—events of necessarily brief duration cannot be anything but verbs. Cloud and storm are at about the lower limit of duration for nouns. Hopi, you see, actually has a classification of events . . . by duration type, something strange to our modes of thought . . . in Nootka, a language of Vancouver Island . . . we have, as it were, a monistic view of nature that gives us only one class of words for all kinds of events. "A house occurs" or "it houses" is the way of saying "house" exactly like "a flame occurs" or "it burns."

Whorf maintains that it is because of our grammar (nouns and verbs) that we divide the world into "events" and "things," whereas the Hopi use quite another basis (their grammar classifies words by "duration" type) and the Vancouver Islanders do not distinguish at all between a "thing" and an "event." Grammar thus determines our perception of the world around us.

There are few psychologists who would subscribe to Whorf's absolute relativism. Among other reasons, their reservations reflect the difficulty of arriving at an unambiguous interpretation of the observations. Are linguistic variations responsible for perceptual-cognitive variations, as Whorf claims, or is the reverse true? Does language actually mirror the perceptual and conceptual discriminations deemed important by society? The difficulty is recognized most readily in cases involving a name and the lack of a name. The Eskimo lexicon has three words to distinguish three kinds of snow, but we have only one word. Speakers of iakuti have only a single word for both green and blue, while we have two words. How should these facts of language be interpreted? Does the lack of distinctive names mean that English speakers cannot discriminate the distinctive features of snow? Or is it simply that distinctive labels are invented only for perceptual or conceptual distinctions emphasized by members of the language group? In a society where variations of snow have little functional significance, it is unlikely that distinctive names would be invented to classify snow types. This latter interpretation is supported by a number of crosscultural studies of language and color discrimination (Brown and Lenneberg, 1961).

Arguments surrounding the hypothesis of linguistic relativity will continue. The claims of the hypothesis far exceed the objectives of the research examined in this chapter, which has the more modest aim of exploring the influence of syntactical variables on perception, memorization, and comprehension of language. Adherents to the hypothesis of linguistic relativity will find nothing in this research that disturbs their confidence, but neither are these findings likely to convert any skeptics.

Conclusions

At the beginning of this chapter we noted that psycholinguistics is the intersection of psychology and linguistics. Although we have approached this intersection from the point of view of the psychologist, there are a great many aspects of psychological endeavor that we have not described. You may wish to see the anthologies edited by Saporta (1961), Smith and Miller (1966), Lenneberg (1966), and Jakobovits and Miron (1967) for a representative sampling of the psychology of language. This chapter has been devoted exclusively to an examination of the involvement of syntax in the basic cognitive processes: perception, memory, and reasoning. Two principal objectives may be discerned in the work that has been reviewed. One aim has been to assess the psychological reality of linguistic variables, and the second has been to discover the process responsible for the effects of these variables on cognition.

In a number of places we noted that the linguist is attempting an analysis of language, not of the language user. Therefore, it was possible to suppose that the linguist's model was purely formal, that is, a systematization of linguistic relations having no psychological reality, and therefore no particular relevance for an understanding of cognition. The research reviewed in this chapter argues against this supposition, seeming to show that syntactic relationships identified by linguistic analysis are, in fact, employed in the decoding and encoding of language. The behavior of subjects in experimental situations is responsive to syntactic relationships. In this sense, we may conclude that syntactical structure has psychological reality as well as linguistic reality.

How does syntax enter into the processes of perception, memory, and reasoning? The most favored answer rests on prior assumptions about the fundamental nature of these processes. Many investigators in the field of psycholinguistics assume that recoding or reorganization plays a significant role in cognition. The subject is not viewed as a passive recipient of inputs, but is considered to be actively involved in recoding the information. Syntactic structure is presumed to provide a plan for recoding, offering a basis for grouping in speech perception, unitization in immediate memory, and analysis in reasoning involving manipulation of linguistic symbols.

Many important tasks remain for future research and analysis. A number of these merit special mention in concluding this chapter.

Most speakers and listeners are unaware of the syntactical structure of the message, and many individuals insist that they are unable to perform the kind of syntactical decoding that we have attributed to them. Therefore, one question that needs answering concerns the perception of syntax: What are the distinctive features of syntax that provide the decoder with information about syntactical structure?

Another empirical question concerns the generality of the influence of syntax. For example, it is notable that all the studies of perception and memory that we reviewed required verbatim reporting or recall; the subject had to reproduce the message word for word in correct order. Although such requirements are not rare in everyday life, there is another common situation in which the hearer is required only to reproduce the gist of the message; the criterion of performance is satisfied if the sense of the message is correctly reported. Does syntax influence this kind of report? Clark's (1969a,b) studies of reasoning suggest that syntax may also be involved in this kind of report. But more direct evidence would be desirable.

On a more theoretical plane are the important tasks of sharpening and elaborating our conceptualizations of syntactical structure and the process of organization in memory and perception. Conceptualizations of syntax are principally the business of the linguist; conceptualizations of memory and perception are principally the business of the psychologist. Developments along these lines will determine the future view of the relationship between syntax and cognition.

Glossary

Anomalous string: a meaningless sequence of words that nevertheless satisfies the syntactical requirements of English.

Deep structure: the transformational relationships between the phrase structure of a sentence and the phrase structure of other sentences that have been produced by applying a transformation rule to the original sentence.

Immediate constituent: one of two or several major constituents (phrases) of which any given sentence is formed.

Linguistic relativity: the hypothesis that all of cognition is relative to, or structured by, language.

Morpheme: a unit of linguistic analysis, the smallest meaningful component of a language.

Perceptual set: a readiness to respond selectively to some attribute of a stimulus or to one of a number of simultaneously presented stimuli.

Phoneme: a unit of linguistic analysis, a distinctive speech sound in a language.

Phrase structure: a sentence can be segmented into a hierarchically organized set of components or constituents. A familiar constituent is the phrase. This type of organizational scheme is called phrase structure.

Psycholinguistics: the interdisciplinary union of linguistics and psychology.

Recoding: the label for the variety of organizational schemes that a subject may adopt in coping with a memory task.

Transformation rule: a rule that specifies how an entire sentence may be rewritten as a different sentence, for example, a passive sentence into a passive question.

Transitional error probability (TEP): the conditional probability of an error; the probability that an error will occur depending on whether the preceding items have been missed or given correctly.

References

Bever, T.G., J.R. Lackner, and R. Kirk. The underlying structures of sentences: All the primary units of immediate speech processing. *Perception and Psychophysics*, 1969, **5**, 225–234.

Bever, T.G., J.R. Lackner, and W. Stolz. Transitional probability is not a general mechanism for the segmentation of speech. *J. exp. Psychol.*, 1969, **79**, 387–394.

Blumenthal, A.L. Prompted recall of sentences. *Journal of Verbal Learning and Verbal Behavior*, 1967, **6**, 203–206.

———, and R. Boakes. Prompted recall of sentences. *Journal of Verbal Learning and Verbal Behavior*, 1967, **6**, 674–676.

Brown, R.W., and E.H. Lenneberg. A study in language and cognition. *J. abnorm. soc. Psychol.*, 1961, **49**, 454–462.

Clark, H.H. Influence of language on solving three-term series problems. *J. exp. Psychol.*, 1969, **82**, 205–215. (b)

———. Linguistic processes in deductive reasoning. *Psychol. Rev.*, 1969, **76**, 387–404. (a)

Clifton, C., and P. Odom. Similarity relations among certain English sentence constructions. *Psychol. Monogr.*, 1966, **80** (5, Whole No. 613).

Desoto, C., M. London, and S. Handel. Social reasoning and spatial paralogic. *J. pers. soc. Psychol.*, 1965, **2**, 513–521.

Donaldson, M. *A study of children's thinking.* London: Tavistock, 1963.

Epstein, W. The influence of syntactical structure on learning. *Amer. J. Psychol.*, 1961, **74,** 80–85.

———. Recall of word lists following learning of sentences and of anomalous and random strings. *Journal of Verbal Learning and Verbal Behavior,* 1969, **8,** 20–25.

Fodor, J.A., and T.G. Bever. The psychological reality of linguistic segments. *Journal of Verbal Learning and Verbal Behavior,* 1965, **4,** 414–420.

Garrett, M., T. Bever, and J. Fodor. The active use of grammar in speech perception. *Perception and Psychophysics,* 1965, **1,** 30–32.

Gleason, J. *Introduction to descriptive linguistics.* New York: Holt, Rinehart and Winston, 1961.

Glucksberg, S., and J.H. Danks. Grammatical structure and recall: A function of the space in immediate memory or of recall delay. *Perception and Psychophysics,* 1969, **6,** 113–117.

Hunter, I.M.L. The solving of three-term series problems. *Brit. J. Psychol.,* 1957, **48,** 286–298.

Huttenlocher, J. Constructing spatial images: A strategy in reasoning. *Psychol. Rev.*, 1968, **75,** 550–560.

Jakobovits, L.A., and M.S. Miron. (Eds.) *Readings in the psychology of language.* Englewood Cliffs, N.J.: Prentice-Hall, 1967.

Johnson, N.F. The influence of associations between elements of structured verbal responses. *Journal of Verbal Learning and Verbal Behavior,* 1966, **5,** 369–374.

———. The influence of grammatical units on learning. *Journal of Verbal Learning and Verbal Behavior,* 1968, **7,** 236–240.

———. The psychological reality of phrase structure rules. *Journal of Verbal Learning and Verbal Behavior,* 1965, **4,** 469–475.

Lenneberg, E.H. Color naming, color recognition, color discrimination: A re-appraisal. *Perceptual Motor Skills,* 1961, **12,** 375–382.

———. *New directions in the study of language*. Cambridge, Mass.: M.I.T. Press, 1966.

Martin, E., and K. Roberts. Grammatical factors in sentence retention. *Journal of Verbal Learning and Verbal Behavior,* 1966, **5,** 211–218.

Mehler, J. Some effects of grammatical transformations on the recall of English sentences. *Journal of Verbal Learning and Verbal Behavior*, 1963, **2,** 346–351.

———, and P. Carey. Role of surface and base structure in the perception of sentences. *Journal of Verbal Learning and Verbal Behavior,* 1967, **6,** 335–338.

Miller, G.A. Information and memory. *Scientific Amer.*, 1956, **195,** 42–46. (b)

———. The magical number seven, plus or minus two: Some limits on our capacity for processing information. *Psychol. Rev.*, 1956, **63,** 81–97. (a)

———. Some psychological studies of grammar. *Amer. Psychologist*, 1962, **17,** 748–762.

———, and N. Chomsky. Finitary models of language users. In R.D. Luce, R.R. Bush, and E. Galanter (Eds.), *Handbook of mathematical psychology*. New York: John Wiley & Sons, 1963.

——— and E. Galanter, and K. Pribram. *Plans and the structure of behavior.* New York: Holt, Rinehart and Winston, 1960.

——— and S. Isard. Some perceptual consequences of linguistic rules. *Journal of Verbal Learning and Verbal Behavior,* 1963, **2,** 217–228.

O'Connell, D.S. Facilitation of recall by linguistic structure in nonsense strings. *Psychol. Bull.*, 1970, **73,**

Piaget, J. *Judgment and reasoning in the child.* London: Kegan, Paul, 1928.

Rosenberg, S. Association and phrase structure in sentence recall. *Journal of Verbal Learning and Verbal Behavior,* 1968, **7,** 1077–1081.

Saporta, S. *Psycholinguistics.* New York: Holt, Rinehart and Winston, 1961.

Savin, H.B., and E. Perchonock. Grammatical structure and the immediate recall of English sentences. *Journal of Verbal Learning and Verbal Behavior,* 1965, **4,** 348–353.

Smith, F., and G.A. Miller. (Eds.) *The genesis of language.* Cambridge, Mass.: M.I.T. Press, 1966.

Whorf, B.L. *Language, thought and reality.* New York: John Wiley & Sons, 1956.

Wilkes, A.L., and R.A. Kennedy. Relationship between pausing and retrieval latency in sentences of varying grammatical form. *J. exp. Psychol.*, 1969, **79,** 241–245.

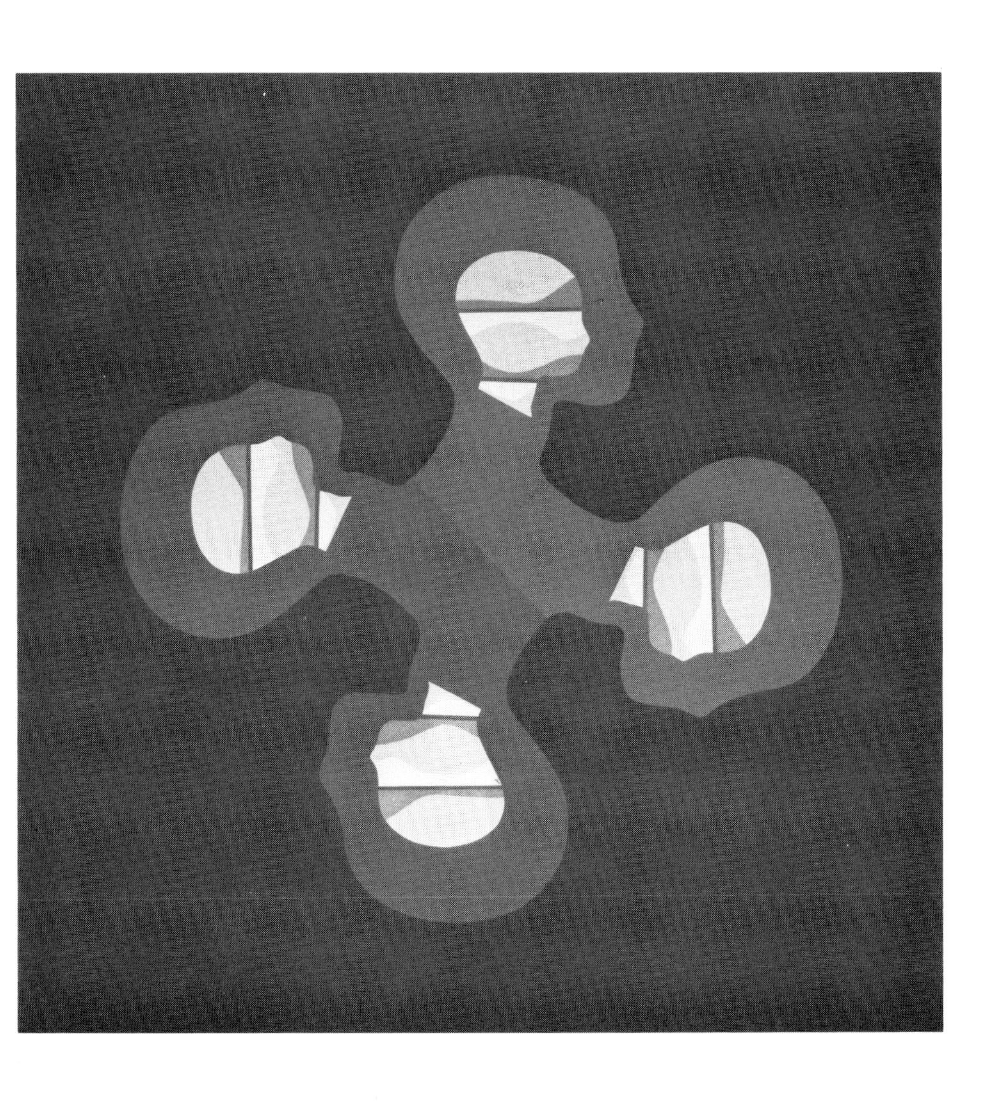

6 Regulatory Centers in the Brain: Central Mechanisms of Feeding

Eating is an overdetermined activity. We eat when we are hungry, yet we rarely pass up dessert. We may refuse to eat foods we deem unpalatable, despite gnawing sensations of hunger, yet these same foods may be considered delicacies by others for whom their availability is an inducement to eat. We often stop eating when we feel full, but overeating is not uncommon. A striking example of overeating was demonstrated by Bayer (1929) in a study of hens. First, he determined the satiety level of hens that had been allowed unlimited access to food following a period of deprivation. Once this level was determined, Bayer allowed a food-deprived hen to eat until she was sated, at which point two hungry hens were introduced. They began voracious feeding. Apparently the sight of her cronies glutting themselves was a highly effective stimulus, because the sated hen resumed eating and consumed almost 50 per cent more food. This kind of social overeating is also frequent among humans, yet there are occasions when the mere memory of yesterday's satiety is sufficient to inhibit eating today.

These commonplace examples serve to remind us that patterns of eating are influenced by environmental, social, and idiosyncratic variables. This chapter focuses on the central physiological mechanisms that regulate food intake, but in the concluding section we will consider an example of current research on obesity in humans. This research enables us to compare the behavior of humans with the behavior of animals who comprise the subject population of the physiological studies. In addition, it will afford us the opportunity to look again at the effects of social and environmental variables on eating behavior.

Central and Peripheral Factors

Our primary concern is with the physiological mechanisms that regulate food intake. Do centers in the brain regulate the onset (feeding center) and cessation (satiety center) of food intake? Before turning to the question of central regulatory centers, consider the lessons of everyday experience, which suggest that hunger and eating are regulated by peripheral factors. The most apparent of these are signals originating in the stomach. We feel hungry and know that the time to eat has arrived when the contractions associated with an empty stomach occur. We feel satisfied and stop eating when the stomach is full or distended.

These familiar observations are supported by laboratory studies of the correlation of hunger sensations with gastric motility and distension. In a classic experiment, Washburn (Cannon and Washburn, 1912) swallowed a small balloon at the end of a tube. Stomach motility was monitored by pneumographic recordings for extended periods of time before, during, and after the usual time of eating. During the recordings Washburn pressed a key when he felt pangs of hunger. Figure 6.1 illustrates the experimental arrangement. Stomach contractions and reported hunger sensations were found to coincide. These findings were confirmed and elaborated by later investigators, and provided vital support for Cannon's (1934) *local* theory of hunger which emphasized gastric motility and distension.

Contemporary students of the regulation of feeding tend to deemphasize the role of local, stomach activity in favor of regulatory mechanisms in the central nervous system. The introspective and laboratory evidence mentioned above is not denied. What is rejected is the view that peripheral processes exert a primary regulatory influence; their role is to serve as signals to centers in the brain. Also

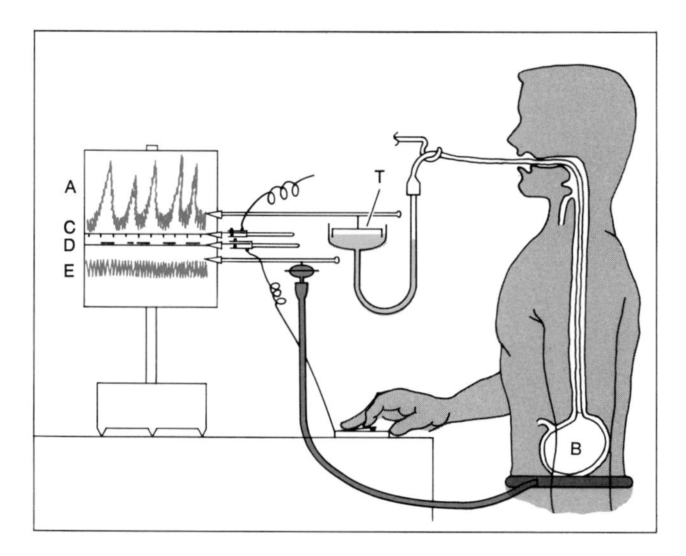

Fig. 6.1. Recording stomach contractions and reports of hunger pangs in the human observer. Changes in pressure in the stomach are represented in trace A on the revolving drum. Reports of hunger pangs are made by pressing the key; these are recorded as trace D on the drum. Gastric contractions and reports of hunger pangs correspond closely on the record.

rejected is the view that stomach motility and distension are necessary for adaptive regulation of food intake.

There are several reasons for contemporary skepticism about the local theory. Clinical and laboratory studies of humans and animals who have been subjected to denervation of the stomach (removal of the splanchnic nerves) agree that this operation has little effect on food intake or hunger sensations (for example, Harris, Ivy, and Searle, 1947; Grossman, Cummins, and Ivy, 1947). Additional evidence comes from histories of patients whose entire stomachs have been surgically removed. The esophagus is connected directly to the intestine so that ingested food is stored in the upper intestine. These patients tend to eat a greater number of smaller meals than the normal individual, but otherwise report normal sensations of hunger and regulate their total food intake without difficulty.

These observations show that sensory impulses from the stomach are not vitally involved in hunger and satiety. What about the other peripheral factors that loom so large in everyday experience? In particular, what role do taste and smell play in the regulation of food intake? No one could deny that they are significant determinants of eating, but are the taste and smell of food and the sensations associated with mastication and swallowing *essential* for normal day-to-day regulation of food intake? If these sensations were absent, would the organism retain the ability to regulate food intake? An unequivocal answer to this question is provided by Epstein and Teitelbaum (1962) in a study using the method of intragastric self-injection.

Epstein and Teitelbaum devised a method which permitted experimental rats to feed themselves, *without* accompanying sensations of taste and smell or the acts of eating, such as chewing. The animals were fitted with nasopharyngeal gastric tubes, chronic (permanent) tubes that are passed through the nasopharynx and esophagus into the stomach. After insertion into the stomach, the free end of the

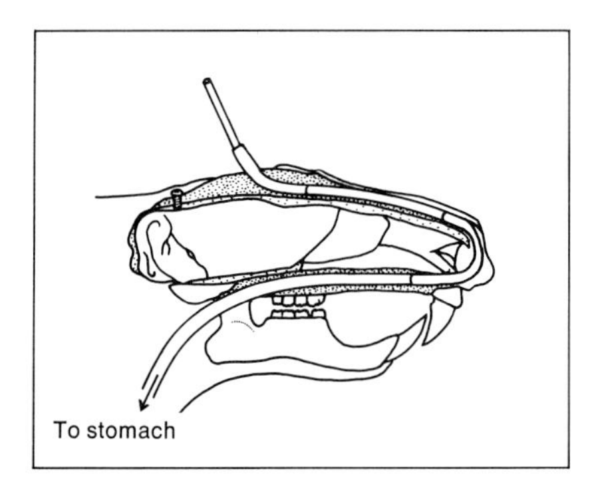

Fig. 6.2. The course of the nasopharyngeal gastric tube shown in a schematic drawing of a midsagittal section of the rat's head. (From Epstein and Teitelbaum, 1962)

tube is brought to the outside, to project upward between the animal's ears. Figure 6.2 is a schematic drawing of the arrangement. A liquid diet introduced into the tube will pass directly to the stomach, bypassing the taste and smell receptors.

Since we are concerned with *self*-regulation of food intake, a procedure is required to allow the animals to feed themselves at their own pleasure. This was accomplished in the manner illustrated in Figure 6.3, in which the gastric tube is connected to a supply of liquid diet. A bar in the animal's chamber controls the passage of liquid from the reservoir through the tube into the rat's stomach. The rat can feed itself intragastrically by depressing the bar, delivering a fixed amount of liquid directly into its stomach.

The results of this study were clear. The rats maintained themselves without difficulty, gaining weight and regulating their intake of foods for periods as long as one and one-half months. If the amount of liquid diet delivered by a bar press was halved or doubled, the rats adjusted the frequency of bar presses accordingly. If the concentration of food (nutritive density) was increased or decreased by varying the proportion of water, the rats compensated by adjusting the number of bar presses. Additional evidence that regulation was not based on secondary sensations of taste (from regurgitation into the mouth) was provided by adding a small amount of quinine to the diet. Normally, rats find the bitter taste of quinine unacceptable and refuse to eat it. But the food intake of the experimental animals was unaffected by the quinine adulterated diet, showing that no secondary taste sensations were operating.

Our first objective has been to clear the way for consideration of the role of central mechanisms in regulating food intake. It was therefore important to demonstrate that the peripheral variables under consideration are not necessary for regulation. Nevertheless, it would be incorrect to conclude that these variables are irrelevant to the general question. They may not be the essential regulatory variables, but they do moderate the effects of the central regulatory center in significant ways. This is especially true, as we shall see, in the case of taste.

The Hypothalamus

Buried deep at the base of the brain is a small region, called the *hypothalamus*, which contains a collection of cell aggregrates or nuclei. The hypothalamus accounts for less than 1 per cent of the weight of the brain. In the rat, a favorite experimental animal, it is only two to three mm. in diameter. Yet it is a vital participant in

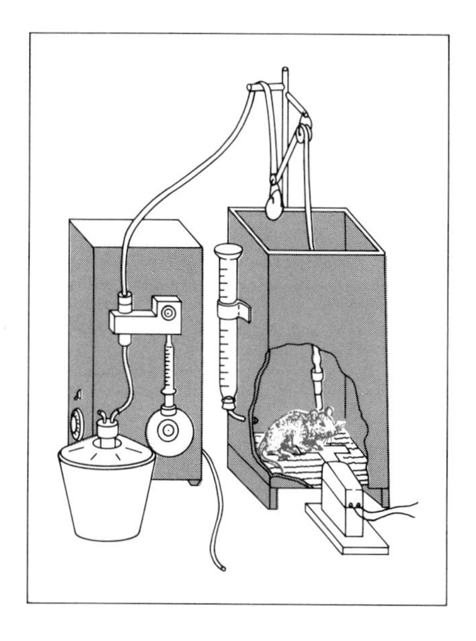

Fig. 6.3. Schematic drawing of the apparatus for intragastric self-injection by the rat. The rat presses the bar in order to activate the pipetting machine (center), thus delivering a liquid diet from the reservoir (left foreground), through the chronic gastric tube directly into its own stomach. (From Epstein and Teitelbaum, 1962)

the regulation of motivated behavior, including sexual arousal and emotion. The search for regulatory centers of food intake has also led to the hypothalamus (Fig. 6.4 will help you to locate the hypothalamus).

The hypothalamus has been subdivided into two major zones on the basis of the anatomical localization of cell concentrations. Immediately next to the tissue surrounding the ventricle (periventricular zone) is the *ventromedial* zone, while the lateralmost portion of the hypothalamus is the *lateral* zone. These zones are marked in Figure 6.4b.

The hypothalamus is the most highly vascular region of the central nervous system, with a greater density of blood vessels than any other part. This permits the hypothalamus to be influenced readily by the overall chemical state of the body. In addition, the hypothalamus has extensive neural connections with all other parts of the brain and the pituitary. These features equip the hypothalamus for its vital role.

Early Evidence of Hypothalamic Participation

The role of the hypothalamus in regulation of food intake was suspected early in the search for regulatory centers in the brain, because of certain clues. The clues came from clinical observations of *hyperphagia* (overeating) and obesity following injury or tumor growth in the region of the hypothalamus. This pathological obesity was called "Frölich's syndrome" after the medical investigator who provided the first extensive description of it in 1902. Frölich thought that the hyperphagia and obesity were caused by damage to the pituitary gland (Fig. 6.4a shows that the pituitary [hypophysis] hangs by its stalk from the hypothalamus). But other investigators argued that the locus of the affected mechanism is in the base of the brain, and that the hypothalamus is the region responsible for Frölich's syndrome. The controversy was finally resolved by the experimental studies of Camus and Roussy (1920, 1922) and Smith (1927, 1930). These investigators, working with animals, showed that surgical removal of the pituitary gland without accom-

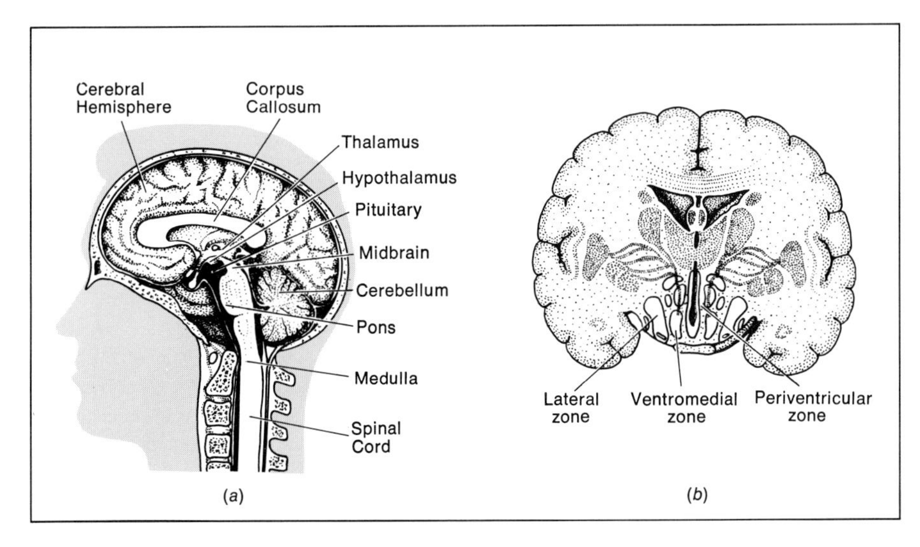

Fig. 6.4. (a) A vertical section of the human brain in its position in the skull. (b) The hypothalamus consists of a collection of nuclei (the white areas) at the base of the brain. The zones to which frequent references are made in the text are labeled "periventricular," "ventromedial," and "lateral." The basic organization of the human brain is representative of all mammalian brains including the rat's.

panying damage to the hypothalamus did not result in hyperphagia or obesity, and that lesions in the hypothalamus of an animal without damage to the pituitary gland produced obesity. These findings, and other similar results (for example, Hetherington, 1943), eliminated consideration of the pituitary gland as the cause for hyperphagia and obesity and pointed to the hypothalamus as the center responsible.

Localization of Regulatory Centers in the Hypothalamus

Early clinical observations and experimental investigations established the gross relationship between the hypothalamus and Frölich's syndrome, now called hypothalamic hyperphagia. The next step in the investigation was to determine whether the subdivided zones of the hypothalamus have distinctive parts to play in the control of feeding. Is there a hypothalamic center primarily responsible for regulation of the onset of feeding, and another for regulation of the cessation of eating? Before this question can be answered, agreement must be reached regarding which experimental observations would enable us to designate specific hypothalamic zones as feeding (start) or satiety (stop) centers.

Our description of the hypothalamic hyperphagic syndrome suggests a basis for agreement. If localized damage to a circumscribed hypothalamic zone leads to hyperphagia, then this zone may be identified as the satiety center. Conversely, if localized damage to a circumscribed area results in *aphagia* (a failure to eat even when the animal is starved and food is readily accessible), then this zone may be identified as the feeding center. These identifications are justified on the premise that the type of disruption of feeding behavior that follows damage implies the nature of the normal regulatory functions of the intact zone. For example,

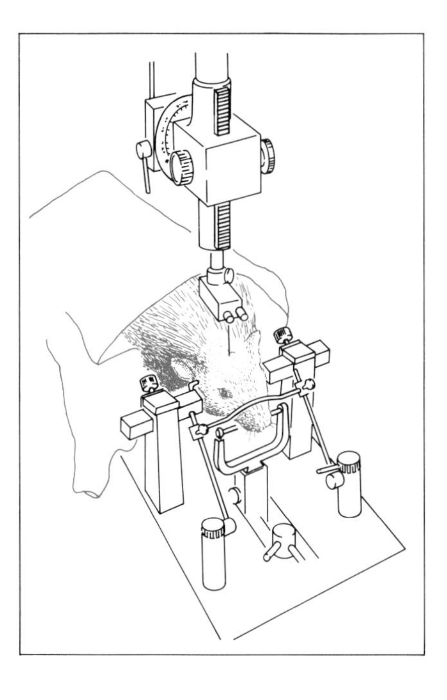

Fig. 6.5. A stereotaxic instrument for producing small areas of damage deep within the brain. The head of the anesthetized animal is fixed within a calibrated framework, and the electrode is guided into place by means of calibrated scales. (From Wickens and Meyer, 1961)

if damage to the ventromedial hypothalamic zone leads to hyperphagia, we may assume that the normal role of the intact ventromedial zone is to inhibit eating.

This argument can be extended to suggest a set of complementary observations which would help identify the regulatory roles of circumscribed zones. If we were to stimulate the hypothalamus instead of damaging it, then the zone where stimulation produces cessation of feeding may be identified as the satiety center, and the zone where stimulation produces eating may be identified as the feeding center. Thus we are seeking a set of converging results that pinpoint the regulatory functions of the hypothalamic centers. The pattern of results is summarized in Table 6.1.

Identification of these hypothetical centers requires exacting procedures. The freehand surgical procedures of the early twentieth century investigators cannot guarantee precise contact with the tiny circumscribed subdivisions of the hypothalamus. To attain such precision the investigator needs two aids: a detailed map or atlas of the brain which shows him where he is going, and a procedure for getting to the desired map location.

Both of these prerequisites have been satisfied. Atlases for the brain of the cat, monkey, rabbit, and rat have been composed. A typical map is arranged according to frontal plane sections at 0.5 or 1.0 mm. intervals from the most anterior (front) to the most posterior (rear) part of the brain. There are also atlases limited to parts of the brain. The second prerequisite has been met by development of the *stereotaxic instrument* (Fig. 6.5), which consists of a rigid metal framework within which the head of an experimental animal may be fixed. The frame is calibrated and enables the investigator to guide a fine electrode needle to any locus in the brain defined by three dimensions or coordinates: on a line between the ears (right-left or lateral dimension), on the midline of the brain (front-back or anterior-posterior dimension), and in a line perpendicular to these two planes (up-down dimension). The fine electrode needle used to penetrate the brain is

Effect on Feeding	Damage	Stimulation
Increase	Satiety center	Feeding center
Decrease	Feeding center	Satiety center

Table 6.1 *Effects on Feeding of Damage and Stimulation in Satiety and Feeding Centers*

insulated, except at its tip. Current of specified intensity and duration can be passed through the electrode to produce electrolytic lesions just around the electrode tip, or to stimulate the region.

The investigator reporting the experimental procedure usually specifies the location and type of treatment in terms of the stereotaxic coordinates. For example, "bi-lateral ventromedial lesions were produced by 1 ma. DC passed for 30 seconds through a nichrome anode placed perpendicular to the skull, 1.5 mm. posterior to the bregma, .75 mm. lateral to the midsagittal suture, and .5 mm. above the base of the brain" (Hoebel and Teitelbaum, 1966, p. 190).

With the development of brain atlases and stereotaxic instruments, evidence began to accumulate showing that centers within the hypothalamus do determine the onset and cessation of eating. The evidence has come from studies using different but complementary procedures to affect hypothalamic functions. The *lesion* treatment is used to destroy cells, the *stimulation* treatment activates cells, and the *pharmacological* treatment chemically stimulates or blocks the activity of the affected area. These studies show that two hypothalamic zones serve as regulatory centers: the lateral zone is the start (feeding) center, and the ventromedial zone is the stop (satiety) center.

The Feeding Center

Lesions in the lateral hypothalamic region have pronounced effects on food and water intake. The animal exhibits *aphagia.* It will refuse to eat, and unless tube-feeding is introduced will starve to death, despite continuous accessibility of ample provisions of food. In addition, the animal exhibits *adipsia*, refusal to drink. However, if the animal is kept alive by artificial feeding and watering, it recovers eating and drinking functions. A widely cited experiment by Teitelbaum and Epstein (1962) can serve as our introduction to the lateral hypothalamic syndrome.

Teitelbaum and Epstein used the stereotaxic instrument to produce bilateral electrolytic lesions in the lateral hypothalamus. Figure 6.6 shows photographs of the brain sections of four rats who were sacrificed in order to permit histological verification of the accuracy of the lesioning; the damaged areas are outlined in black. Earlier studies (for example, Anand and Brobeck, 1951) had already established that lateral lesions produce aphagia; Teitelbaum and Epstein were investigating the course of recovery from the effects on the lateral lesions. For this purpose the rats were also prepared for intragastric tube-feeding and watering, so that they could be kept alive during the postoperative period when they would refuse to eat or drink.

Four stages in the lateral hypothalamic syndrome were identified. In stage

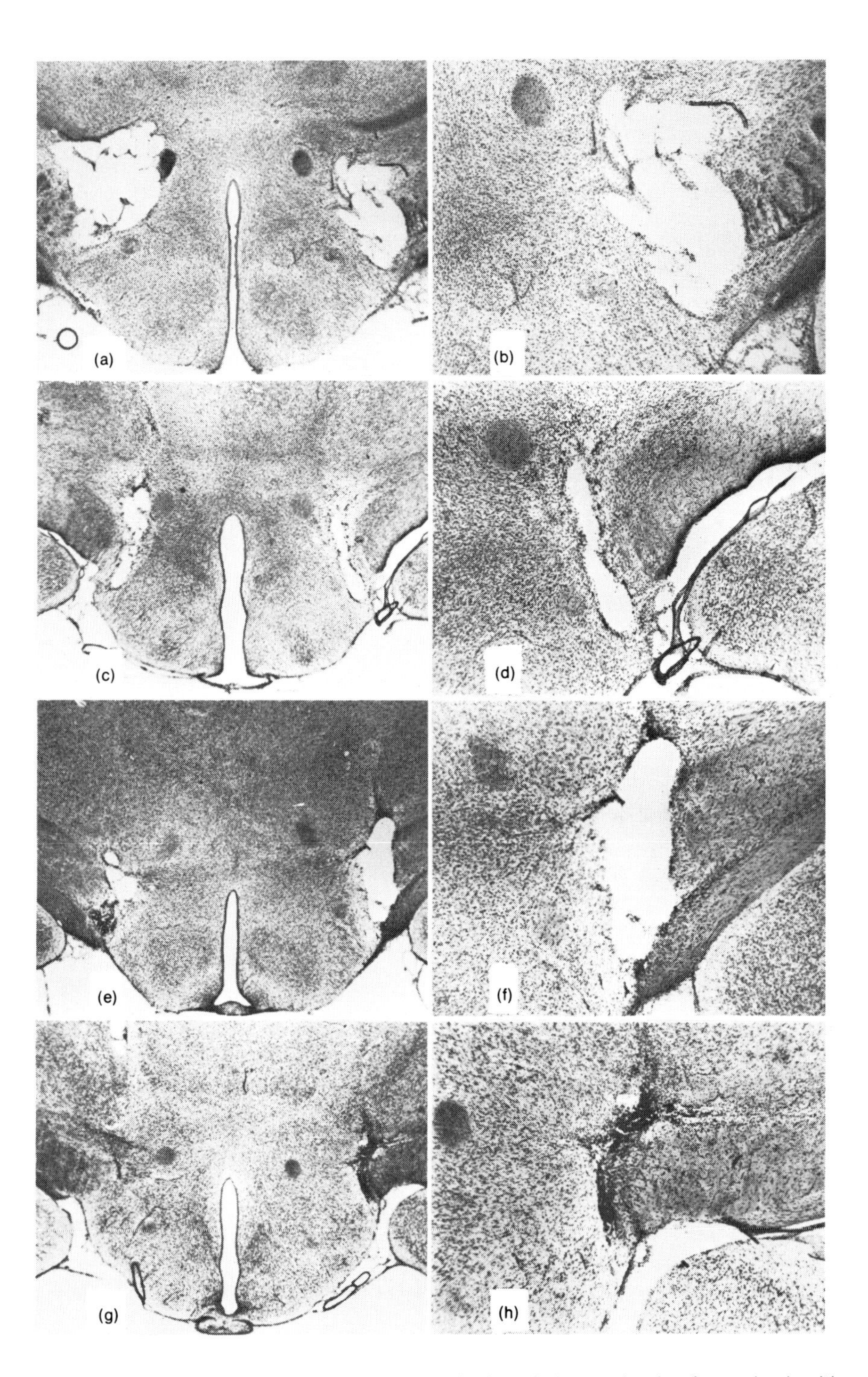

Fig. 6.6. Photomicrographs of sections through the hypothalamus showing four animals with various sized lesions. A and B represent the largest lesions; CDE and F the intermediate size and GH, the smallest ones. Variations in the size of these lesions were produced by varying the duration of the lesioning electrolitic current. (Courtesy: Richard Keesey)

I, which lasted as long as 19 postoperative days, total aphagia and adipsia were observed. The animal did not eat or drink, it lost weight steadily, and would probably have died of starvation had it not been tube-fed. Furthermore, the animal behaved as if food and water were aversive stimuli—it actively resisted oral feeding and watering.

Stage II lasted approximately until the thirty-ninth day. The animal began to eat, but only highly palatable food, and not enough to keep itself alive. The taste and smell of food initiated eating, but not sufficient eating. The animal was said to be *anorexic.* The animal continued to refuse to drink water.

During stage III the animal recovered normal patterns of food intake even when food was introduced directly into the stomach, as in the intragastric feeding experiment described earlier in this chapter. But it continued to refuse to drink, and if it were not tube-watered became dehydrated and would again refuse to eat.

In stage IV the animal began to drink water and appeared to have recovered completely. The recovery of drinking was often in two phases. In the first phase the animal seemed to be responding to dryness of mouth, drinking only during periods of eating. Unlike normal animals, the experimental animals did not respond to artificially induced dehydration by drinking. In addition, slight changes in the taste of the water produced by the addition of quinine hydrochloride completely deterred drinking. Some animals never passed through this phase; their water regulation seemed permanently impaired. Other animals passed into a stage of complete recovery.

These four stages are summarized in Figure 6.7. No time periods are shown, because the duration of the stages varies depending on the exact locus of the lesions and the amount of tissue damaged.

The chief findings of the Teitelbaum-Epstein study are worth summarizing.

1. Earlier findings regarding the role of the lateral hypothalamus were confirmed. The lateral nuclei act as a feeding center that regulates the onset of eating. If this center is damaged, eating is not initiated and the animal will probably starve to death.

2. Lesions that produce aphagia also produce adipsia—the animal refuses to drink. Thus the lateral hypothalamus is involved in the regulation of drinking as well as eating. At the same time, different recovery rates for eating and drinking suggest that the lesioned area may contain two kinds of neural elements which have independent effects on eating and drinking. This suggestion was strikingly confirmed in a series of pharmacological studies conducted by Grossman (1967, pp. 363–365).

3. The effects of the lateral lesions on food intake are not permanent; eating and regulation of food intake are recovered. Drinking and regulation of water intake are also recovered, but more slowly and not completely in all animals. The aphagia which results from lateral hypothalamic lesion is generally understood to be a consequence of the loss of regulation of food intake. The severe reduction in weight is a by-product of aphagia.

How are we to explain the recovery of food regulation? One answer is that the course of recovery from the lateral hypothalamic syndrome is a reflection of the course of recovery of adjacent brain tissue from the depressant effects of the lateral lesion. The argument is that tissue in the cerebral cortex is important in

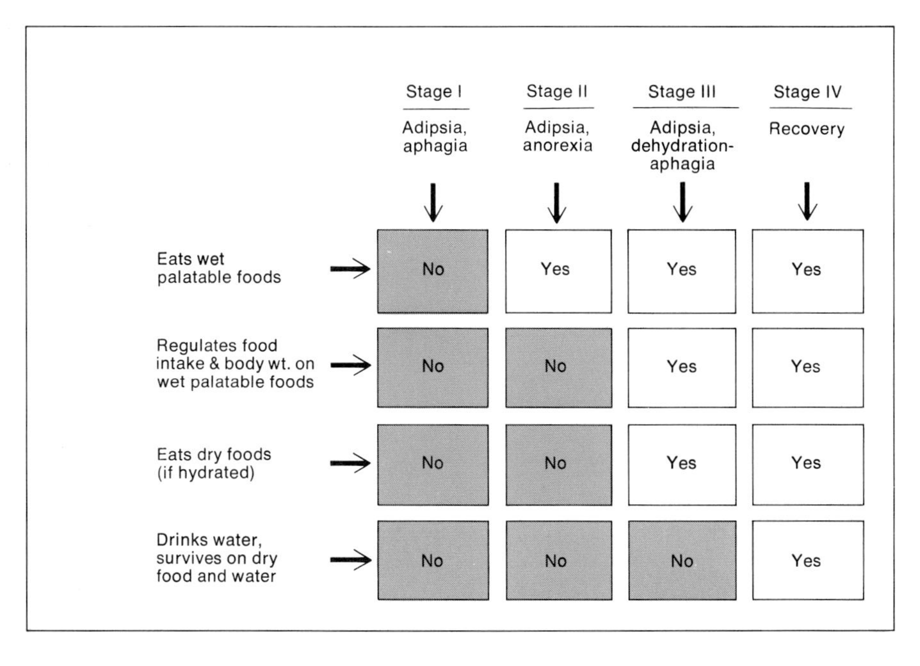

Fig. 6.7. Stages of recovery seen in the lateral hypothalamic syndrome. The critical behavioral events which define the stages are listed on the left. (From Teitelbaum and Epstein, 1962)

maintaining lateral hypothalamic activity. When a lateral lesion is made, the activity of the surrounding tissue is also depressed. As the surrounding tissue recovers, it regains the capacity for enhancing the activity of the intact lateral hypothalamic tissue, and recovery from the lateral hypothalamic syndrome occurs. This analysis of recovery is supported by several observations. If depression of cortical activity is induced in normal animals, aphagia and adipsia are observed even though the lateral hypothalamus is intact. After full recovery from the lateral hypothalamic syndrome, the syndrome is regenerated if depression of cortical activity is induced (Balinska, Buresova, and Fifkova, 1967; Cytawa and Teitelbaum, 1967).

Stimulation of the Lateral Hypothalamic Nuclei

The lesion effects confirm the expectation represented in Table 6.1. To balance the picture, we need evidence on the effect of lateral stimulation. If the correct interpretation has been made of the finding that lateral lesions inhibit eating in starving animals, lateral stimulation in sated animals should produce eating. Margules and Olds (1962) and Hoebel and Teitelbaum (1962) have reported just this effect. The typical procedure is to make chronic (permanent) implantations of electrodes in the lateral hypothalamus. The animals, after being allowed to recover from the operation, are stimulated while sated. The stimulation produces eating which begins soon after the onset of stimulation and ends when stimulation is terminated, thus confirming the other half of our prediction. The results of the lesion and stimulation studies converge to pinpoint the lateral hypothalamus as the feeding center.

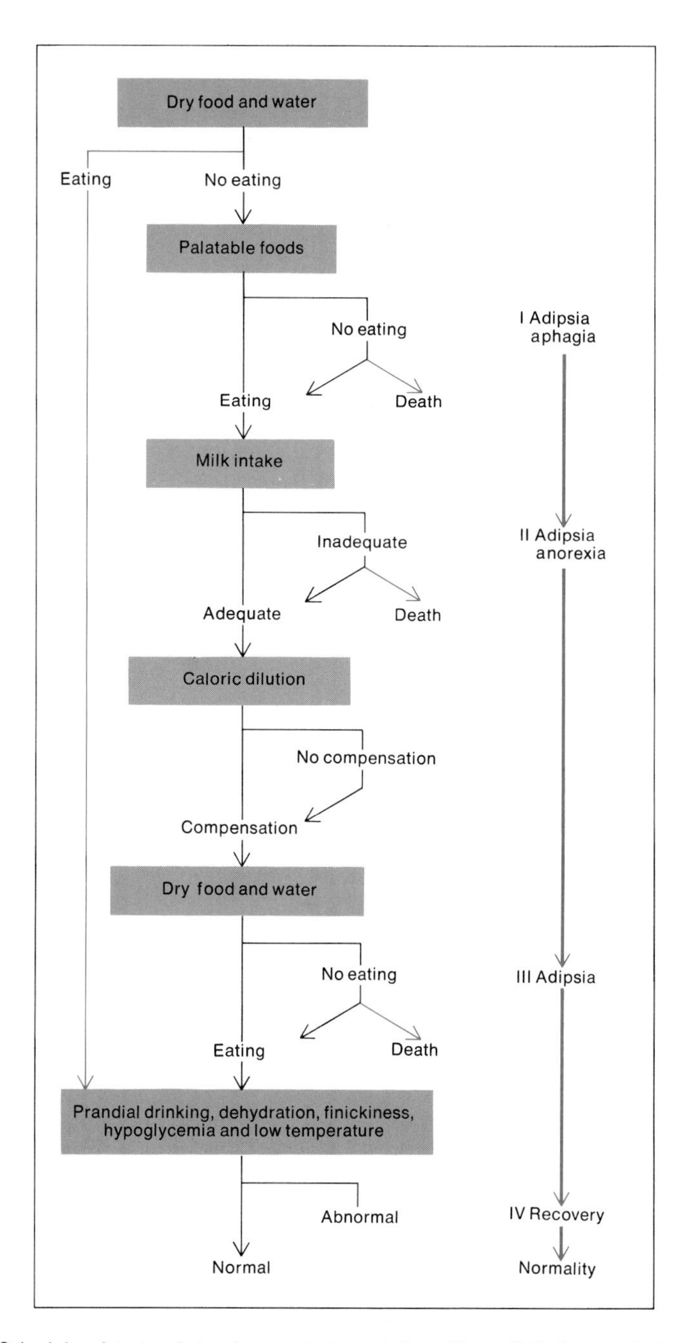

Fig. 6.8. Schedule of tests of development of regulation. (From Teitelbaum *et al.*, 1969)

An Interesting Parallel

The term "recovery" is used to describe the changes in postlesion feeding behavior because the end product is a recovery of the prelesion state of regulation. But since the lateral hypothalamic lesion eliminates regulation of feeding, the recovery period could also be viewed as developmental. This may seem little more than a semantic exchange, but it does lead to an interesting question. Are the

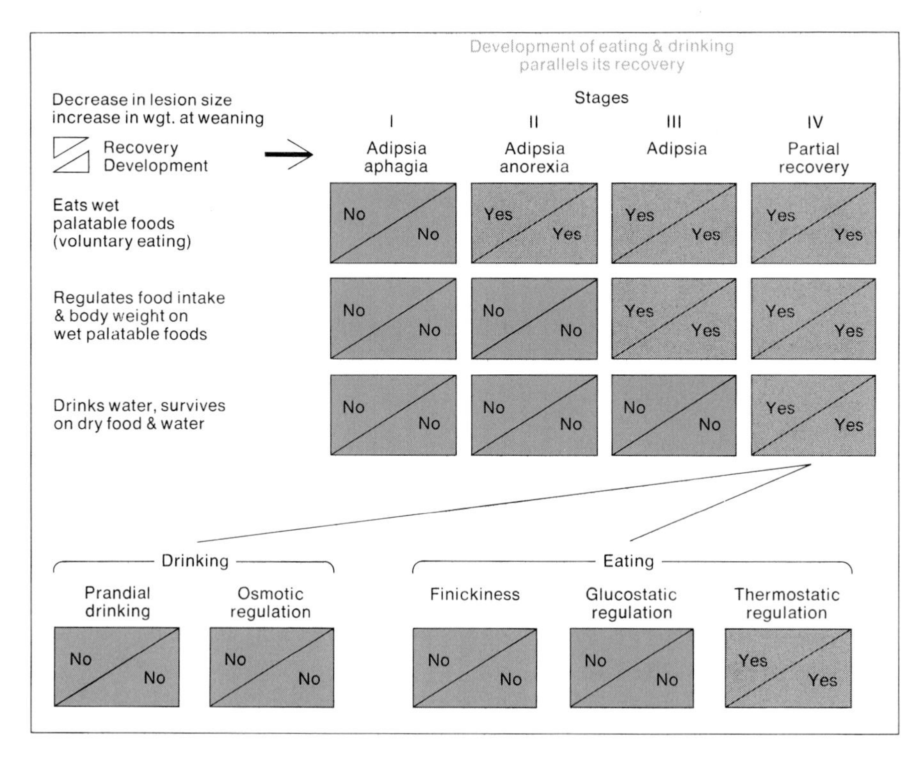

Fig. 6.9. Comparison of the development of eating and drinking in infancy and their recovery after hypothalamic lesion in the adult. The upper left half of each block represents the recovering lateral hypothalamic rat, and the lower right half the growing thyroidectomized rats. Uniform coloring in each full block indicates similar responses in recovery and development. (From Teitelbaum *et al.*, 1969)

four stages of recovery similar to the original development of feeding behavior in the normal neonatal animal? To answer this question, Teitelbaum, Cheng, and Rozin (1969) decided to examine in detail the development of regulation in infant rats.

Ordinarily dependence of the infant rat on the mother plus the rapid course of development causes great difficulties in studying the development of food regulation. Therefore, the rats in this study had their thyroid glands removed at birth in order to slow down development and enable the investigator to distinguish discrete developmental stages. These stages were distinguished on the basis of the animals' feeding or drinking on a graded schedule of tests (listed in Fig. 6.8). You will appreciate the logic of this schedule if you refer to the description of the course of recovery from the lateral hypothalamic syndrome.

The question under examination is whether normal infant rats exhibit the same order of stages in the development of regulation as do lesioned rats in their recovery of regulation. As shown in Figure 6.9, the parallel between recovery and development is perfect.

Is this parallel a result of the experimentally produced slowdown in development? It is hard to exclude this possibility entirely, but the authors do present cogent arguments to refute it (Teitelbaum *et al.*, 1969, pp. 437–439). Assuming the parallel to be genuine, why does it exist? One possibility is that the same underlying physiological changes govern normal development and recovery. Taking

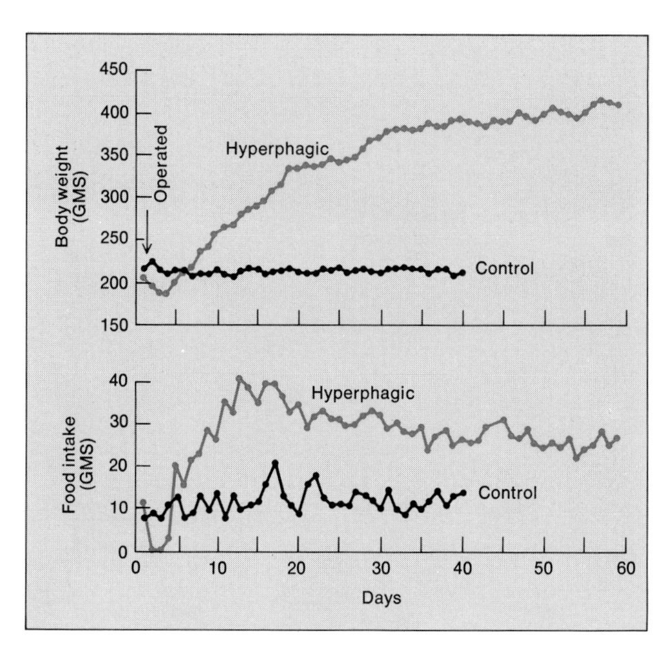

Fig. 6.10. Postoperative body weight and daily food intake of a hyperphagic animal compared to that of a normal unoperated control animal. (From Teitelbaum, 1961)

a clue from the interpretation of the recovery phenomenon described earlier, Teitelbaum *et al.* speculated that both development and recovery reflect the increased capacity of brain tissue outside the lateral and ventromedial hypothalamic zones to sustain and enhance the activity of these zones.

The Satiety Center

In renaming Frölich's syndrome as hypothalamic hyperphagia, the claim was advanced that damage to the hypothalamus was responsible for the hyperphagia and obesity. Stereotaxic studies have enabled us to be more precise, showing that damage to the *ventromedial* nuclei (see Fig. 6.4b) is critical. Lesioning of this satiety center produces hyperphagia and obesity, while stimulation leads to a decrease in food intake.

Typical consequences of a ventromedial lesion are displayed in Figure 6.10, which shows body weight and food intake for a lesioned animal and a normal unoperated control animal. It is obvious that the operated animal differs greatly from the control animal. Immediately after the operation the lesioned animal begins to eat voraciously and gains weight very rapidly. Following this *dynamic* phase, the operated animal enters a *static* phase in which food intake is reduced and weight remains stable at a high level. The fact that the animal enters a static phase does not mean that he has recovered normal regulation, because if he is subsequently deprived of food until his weight is reduced to normal and then allowed free access to food, he will renew voracious eating until his weight reaches the predeprivation level (Hoebel and Teitelbaum, 1966). A typical hyperphagic rat in the static stage and a normal control rat are pictured in Figure 6.11.

What kind of overeating is involved in hypothalamic hyperphagia? Is the obesity

Fig. 6.11. Obese rat photographed at autopsy, 8 months after operation, and its control. Hypothalamic lesions were made at the age of 4½ months. (From Hetherington and Ranson, 1942)

the result of a marked increase in frequency of eating, or is it a case of eating larger meals? Records of the eating patterns of hyperphagic rats favor the latter alternative. The hyperphagic eats the same number of meals as the normal animal, but each meal is protracted far beyond normal duration. It is as if once the animal starts to eat it cannot stop. This is precisely what one would expect if the ventromedial nucleus normally acts to inhibit the lateral hypothalamic feeding center.

This conclusion leads to another question. Does the voracious eating exhibited by the hyperphagic testify to an increased appetite? Perhaps the hyperphagic animal is not hungrier than a normal control animal; perhaps he eats more because the satiety center, which normally inhibits the feeding center, cannot function. We have all met individuals who report that they can't stop eating even when sensations of hunger are absent. This seems to be equally true for the hyperphagic animal, as may be inferred from the results of experiments that have assessed the level of hunger by observing the animal's performance on a variety of tasks motivated by hunger. Examples of such tasks are bar-pressing in the Skinner-box to receive food pellets (Chap. 12) and crossing an electrified section of a maze runway to reach food. Since the performance of normal unoperated animals on these tasks has been found to increase with the length of time the animal has been deprived of food, we may accept them as behavioral measures of the animal's motivational state.

The earliest experiment was reported by Miller, Bailey, and Stevenson (1950). In one part of their experiment animals with ventromedial lesions were compared with normal animals on a bar-pressing test. On the eleventh day after the operation, when all the animals were thoroughly satiated, they commenced a 96 hour period of food deprivation. At various times during the fast, each animal was placed in the Skinner-box for a 20 minute interval. Bar-pressing was reinforced on an interval schedule of one small pellet every five minutes. (All animals had received preliminary training in bar-pressing prior to the lesioning.)

The results are graphed in Figure 6.12, which shows the mean number of

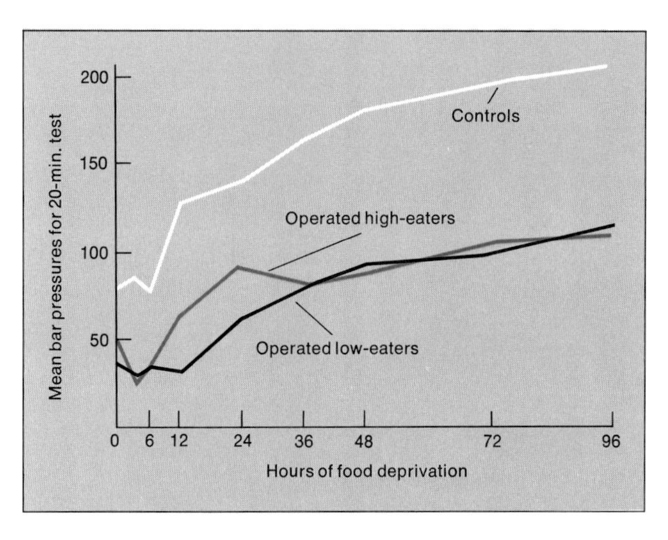

Fig. 6.12. Effect of hypothalamic lesions on the rate of bar pressing after various intervals of food deprivation. The rate of bar pressing (reinforced at 5 minute intervals) increases with hours of food deprivation; the performance of both operated subgroups is poorer than that of the control rats. (From Miller *et al.*, 1950)

bar-presses at each successive 20 minute test interval. Two aspects of the data warrant attention. First, the rate of bar-pressing by both the operated and control groups increased with hours of food deprivation, confirming our claim that this test provides a behavioral measure of hunger. Second, at each of the nine test intervals, the rate of bar-pressing for the operated animals was significantly lower than for the control animals. Similar findings, reported by Miller *et al.* (1950) for a variety of tasks, have been confirmed by subsequent investigators (for example, Teitelbaum, 1957; Grossman, 1966). Ventromedial lesions seem to produce increased food intake and obesity, but decreased hunger or motivation.

This conclusion helps make sense of another characteristic of the hyperphagic: he is a finicky eater. Stale food will be refused, except as a last resort, and diets made bitter by the addition of quinine will be rejected at levels which do not deter the unoperated normal animal. Hyperphagia and obesity are exhibited only when an appealing diet is available. This is consistent with the view that ventromedial lesions lower the motivational level, so that the incentive value (palatability) of food must be higher in order to elicit eating.

The foregoing studies have used the lesioning procedure to examine the role of the ventromedial nuclei. Consistent results have been found in studies employing electrolytic stimulation. In one experiment (Hoebel and Teitelbaum, 1962) rats were motivated to eat by being deprived of food for two days. When allowed access to food they commenced vigorous eating. Weak (0.1 ma.) ventromedial stimulation caused the rats to slow down their food intake, and higher currents (0.6 ma.) caused them to stop eating entirely. When the stimulation was discontinued there was a resumption of eating (Morgane, 1961).

The results of the stimulation studies match our expectations in showing that ventromedial stimulation produces effects opposite to those produced by ventromedial lesioning (see Table 6.1). Unfortunately, interpretation of the results is complicated by the possibility that electrical stimulation is an aversive stimulus.

This interpretation is reinforced by findings (Krasne, 1962) that rats will work to turn off ventromedial stimulation; they press a bar to escape electrical stimulation of intensity comparable to the level required to produce cessation of eating. This suggests that ventromedial stimulation is aversive, and its effects on feeding may be part of a general disruption or distraction of ongoing behavior.

Doubts created by Krasne's findings disturb the orderly pattern we have been developing. Additional evidence is needed to bolster the organization of results shown in Table 6.1. One approach currently under investigation (Beltt, 1970) is based on the following logic: if a rat will work to escape from (terminate) ventromedial stimulation, and if eating has specific effects on the level of ventromedial stimulation, then an animal that eats while it receives ventromedial electrical stimulation should terminate the electrical stimulation at a lower level. That is, the ventromedial effects of eating should combine with the effects of electrical stimulation, so that a lower level of electrical shock will elicit escape. On the other hand, if electrical stimulation of the ventromedial hypothalamus produces general response suppression, eating should not affect the escape level any more than other concurrent activities. Beltt's (1970) findings support the first alternative, providing evidence that electrical stimulation of the ventromedial hypothalamus has specific effects on feeding.

Stop and Go Signals

Now that the regulatory centers have been identified, the next objective is to determine how they operate. An appealing possibility is that these centers operate as feedback control systems. The most familiar example of such a system is the thermostat which responds to signals from the environment in order to reestablish a preselected level of environmental temperature. The two hypothalamic regulatory centers may be sensitive to some alteration in the state of the body which is correlated with food deprivation or intake. Signals (information) associated with these altered states are utilized by the regulatory centers for the purpose of reestablishing the normal bodily state.

What is the nature of these signals? Although we do not have a definitive answer, we will consider a number of possibilities.

Thermostatic Hypothesis

The signals may be changes in the temperature of the body: ". . . animals eat to keep warm and stop eating to prevent hyperthermia" (Brobeck, 1947–1948). For example, food, when it is metabolized, liberates heat in the body, and this thermal change may be detected by cells in the ventromedial hypothalamus, resulting in cessation of eating. A number of observations lend plausibility to this hypothesis. First, there is a positive correlation between feelings of satiety and elevation of body temperature. Second, variations of environmental temperature affect food intake; animals are found to eat more in cold and less in warm environments (Brobeck, 1945). Finally, in a series of studies, Andersson, Gale, and Sundsten (1964) have produced local cooling and warming of parts of the hypothalamus by permanently implanting into the brain silver *thermodes* which could then be perfused with water. The region around the thermode was cooled by perfusions of ice water and warmed by perfusions of hot water. Andersson *et al.* found that local central cooling induced eating in sated animals, while central warming inhibited eating in hungry animals.

Glucostatic Hypothesis

This hypothesis suggests that the signal utilized by the hypothalamus is a property of the blood, specifically the level of blood sugar or glucose. Glucose is essential to the nervous system; other sugars, fats, and proteins must be transformed into glucose before they can be used by the cells. Mayer (1955) has proposed that the hypothalamus contains "gluco-receptors" which are highly sensitive to the rate at which glucose passes into the hypothalamic cells. A high rate of glucose utilization in the brain activates the ventromedial hypothalamus and inhibits eating; a low rate of glucose utilization serves as a signal to initiate eating.

The glucostatic hypothesis is probably the most widely accepted of the three hypotheses discussed here; a variety of experimental observations support it. If the regulatory mechanisms are responding to rate of glucose utilization, then experimentally produced changes in the glucose level should have predictable effects on food intake. Reduction of blood sugar level by the injection of long-acting protamine insulin, should lead to an increase in food intake, while raising the level by intravenous injections of glucose should lead to inhibition of eating. In general, these expectations have been confirmed (for example, MacKay *et al.*, 1940; Hoebel and Teitelbaum, 1966).

Although these observations are consistent with the glucostatic hypothesis, they do not constitute direct evidence that the hypothalamic centers operate on glucostatic signals. Direct evidence would demand a demonstration that activity in the two hypothalamic centers is differentially responsive to changes in the level of experimentally produced glucose utilization. Precisely this sort of evidence has been provided in a series of investigations (Anand, Chhina, and Singh, 1962; Anand, Chhina, Sharma, Dua, and Singh, 1964; Oomara, Kimura, Ooyama, Maeno, Matsaburo, and Kuniyoshi, 1964; and Oomara, Ooyama, Yamamoto, and Naka, 1967).

In one study Anand *et al.* (1964) implanted microelectrodes into the hypothalamus, making possible the recording of activity from single neurons in the feeding and satiety centers of cats and dogs. Recordings from other cortical sites served as controls. The general procedure was to obtain records of unit activity and rate of glucose utilization before and after intravenous injections of glucose or insulin. The standard physiological measure of glucose utilization is obtained by determining the difference between glucose content in samples of arterial and venous blood.

The glucostatic hypothesis generates a set of predictions for this experiment.

1. Glucose infusions should lead to decreased activity in the lateral hypothalamic neurons and increased activity in the ventromedial neurons.
2. Insulin infusions should have opposite results: increased activity in the lateral hypothalamic neurons and decreased activity in the ventromedial neurons.
3. The arteriovenous glucose difference should be correlated with the changes in unit activity.

Figure 6.13 shows a sample of the experimental results. Part (a) shows the effects of glucose injections, part (b) the effects of insulin injections. The continuous lines in these figures plot neuron activity, expressed as spike frequency in ten second recording periods, against time in minutes, before and after the injection. The solid bars show the rate of glucose utilization as measured by the arteriovenous glucose

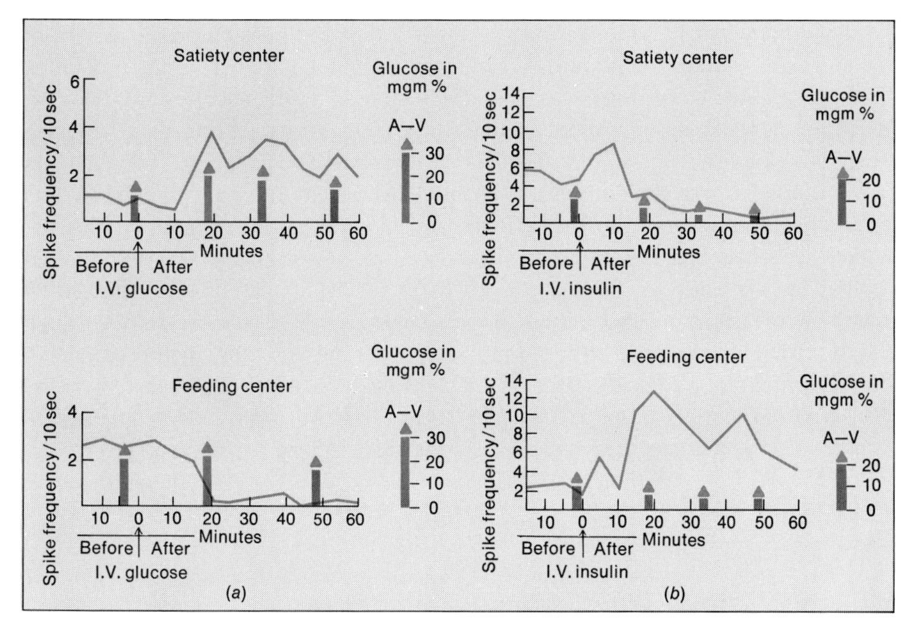

Fig. 6.13. (a) Spike frequency of a unit from the satiety center and a unit from the feeding center, from two different cats, correlated with changes in arteriovenous glucose difference, produced by intravenous infusion of glucose. The frequency of the units at any time was determined by counting the spikes for one minute and taking their mean values. The inverse relationship of changes in activity of satiety and feeding centers is well demonstrated. (b) Spike frequency of a unit from the feeding center and a unit from the satiety center, taken from two cats, showing the effects of intravenous injection of insulin. (Adapted from Anand *et al.*, 1964)

difference. Examination of Figure 6.13 shows that the three predictions were confirmed; the expected changes in neuronal activity were accompanied by appropriate differences in rate of glucose utilization. Comparable data obtained from sites in the brain other than the lateral and ventromedial hypothalamic zones did not show the same changes. These findings, confirmed by Oomara *et al.* (1964, 1967), provide strong support for Mayer's glucostatic hypothesis.

Lipostatic Hypothesis

We have considered evidence suggesting that thermostatic and glucostatic factors are the signals used by the feeding and satiety centers to regulate day-to-day food intake. There must also be some signal or information utilized by the regulatory centers in determining long-term feeding patterns. A number of related observations suggest that signals of this sort are operating.

Under normal conditions body weight is constant over long periods of time. Weight loss due to fasting or underfeeding is followed by recovery of "normal" body weight. Hyperphagic and recovered lateral hypothalamic aphagic animals stabilize at a specific weight level, although the new level is higher than preoperative in the case of the hyperphagic and lower than preoperative in the recovered aphagic.

These observations indicate that physiological signals correlated with body weight determine the interaction between the start and stop centers and assure a stable body weight. One viewpoint suggests that the physiological correlate of body weight that is monitored by the hypothalamic centers is some circulating metabolite in the blood that is associated with stored fat. At least one study (Hervey, 1959) reinforces this suggestion. Hervey united pairs of rats in parabiosis (he joined them like siamese twins so that they shared the same blood supply). Then he made a ventromedial hypothalamic lesion in one member of the pair. The result was hyperphagia and obesity in the lesioned rat, but the parabiotic partner with the intact hypothalamus ate less and showed severe weight loss. One interpretation is that the "lipostat" or fat detector in the intact hypothalamus was deceived by some circulating property of the common blood supply associated with the high fat deposits of the lesioned animal. Parabiosis is not the only experimental technique for achieving blood crossing. Other more controlled procedures have been invented (Davis and Miller, 1966; Davis, Gallagher, Ladove, and Tucausky, 1969), and experiments with these procedures may prove useful in identifying the stop and go signals.

An Alternative Viewpoint

We have described the orderly development of a network of ideas and experimental findings concerning the roles of the lateral and ventromedial hypothalamus in regulating feeding. However, remember that scientific knowledge and theory is always changing, through the discovery of new findings or the formulation of new theories to account for old data. Therefore, it should be no surprise to learn that alternative conceptualizations of the role of the hypothalamic centers in feeding have been proposed.

The view that has dominated our discussion has been that the hypothalamic centers control feeding. The dramatic weight changes accompanying damage or activation of these centers were interpreted as by-products of the feeding effects. Ventromedial lesions lead to obesity because the animal overeats, and severe weight loss accompanies lateral lesions because the animal cannot eat. Although the correlation between feeding disturbances and weight change is entirely reasonable, it does not necessarily imply a causal relationship of the sort described. Although less intuitively acceptable, it is possible that the causal chain begins at the other end: perhaps the hyperphagic eats more in order to gain weight, and the aphagic eats less in order to lose weight. Precisely this view has been proposed by Powley and Keesey (1970) in their weight regulation hypothesis.

According to this hypothesis, the ventromedial hyperphagic and lateral aphagic syndromes do *not* reflect a breakdown in the regulation of food intake. Instead, they are viewed as outcomes of *active regulation of food intake* to achieve a new body weight. When ventromedial hypothalamic lesions are made, a higher weight level is required to inhibit food intake and the animal overeats to reach that level. When lateral hypothalamic lesions are made, a lower weight level is required to keep the two control centers in balance.

To test this hypothesis, we need to distill its critical empirical implication: postoperative feeding behavior will depend on preoperative weight level. If postoperative feeding behavior subserves weight regulation, then an animal made obese prior to ventromedial hypothalamic lesions will not exhibit hyperphagia. And an animal who is starved to below normal weight prior to lateral hypothalamic lesioning will not exhibit aphagia, and may even become hyperphagic. Two experiments

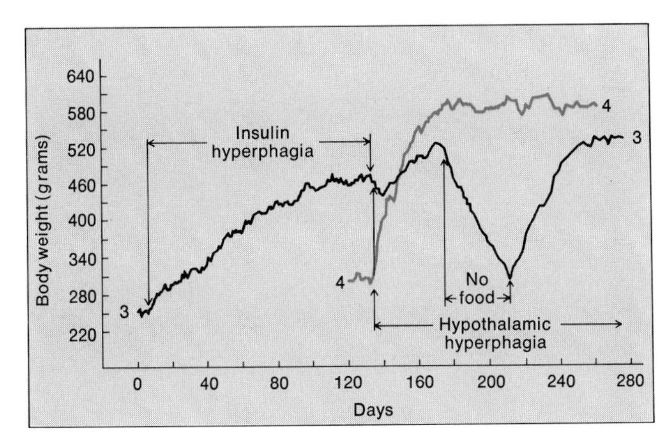

Fig. 6.14. Gradual, slight gain in weight following destruction of the ventromedial hypothalamus in a preoperatively obese rat is contrasted with the rapid, large weight gain in the same animal (3) or another (4) when they start at a normal body weight. (From Hoebel and Teitelbaum, 1966)

(Hoebel and Teitelbaum, 1966; Powley and Keesey, 1970) have shown exactly these effects.

In part of a larger experiment, Hoebel and Teitelbaum (1966) examined the effects of ventromedial lesions following experimentally induced obesity. For about four months prior to the operation, rats received daily protamine insulin injections; then ventromedial lesions were produced. Control animals did not receive preoperative insulin injections. As you may remember, insulin injections induce eating, and if continued over an extended time will lead to obesity. If the weight regulation hypothesis is correct, the postoperative feeding behavior of these animals should differ significantly from that of the control operated animals.

Figure 6.14 presents data for two animals. Animal 3 more than doubled his weight during the insulin treatment, at the time of ventromedial lesion weighing approximately 200 grams more than control animal 4. When the lesion was made, 4 showed the typical hyperphagic syndrome, overeating voraciously and gaining weight rapidly, eventually stabilizing at a high weight level. The postoperative behavior of 3 was very different. There was little evidence of hyperphagia, and weight gain was only 25 per cent of that of the control animal. To show that this was not due to ineffective lesioning, 3 was deprived of food until its body weight was reduced to the preinsulin level. When food was again made available, 3 showed the typical hyperphagic syndrome, returning to the postoperative high weight level.

The results of the Hoebel-Teitelbaum study fit the weight regulation hypothesis perfectly. Complementary results for the lateral hypothalamic syndrome have been reported by Powley and Keesey (1970), who compared the postoperative feeding behavior of two groups of rats which had sustained lateral hypothalamic lesions. One group was fed ad lib until the time of the lesion, and the other was starved to 80 per cent of normal body weight prior to the lesion. Powley and Keesey found that the effects of lateral hypothalamic lesioning were strikingly different for the ad lib and starved groups. The former displayed the typical four stage sequence from aphagia to recovery, but the starved group showed no evidence of aphagia; in fact, the lateral lesion in the starved animal seemed to produce *hyperphagia*.

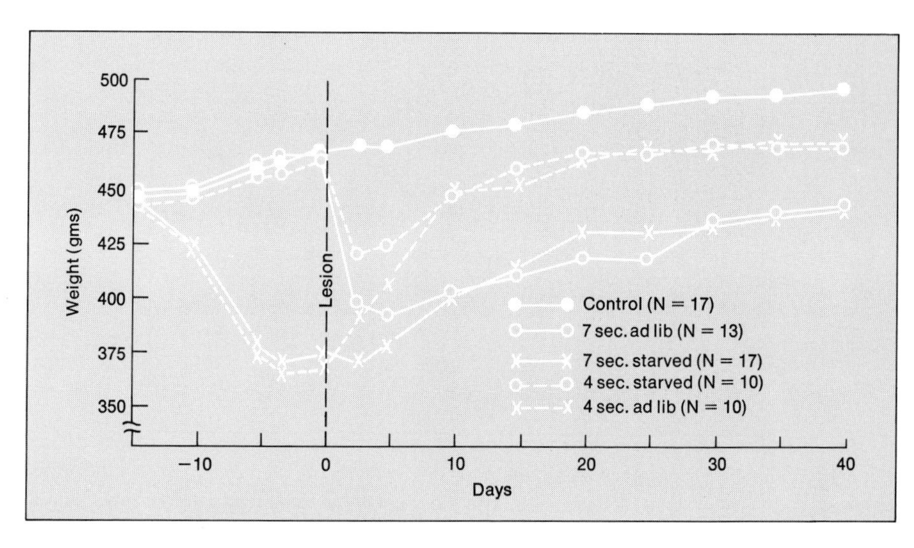

Fig. 6.15. Body weight data. The 4 sec. and the 7 sec. refer to the time parameter of the 1–ma. electrolytic lesion. The body weight of the starved groups was reduced by partial starvation prior to the time of lesioning. Ad lib groups were allowed to feed freely until the time of lesioning. (From Powley and Keesey, 1970)

This is reflected in the body weight data plotted in Figure 6.15. The two ad lib groups show a sharp postoperative drop in body weight, but the two starved groups show a rapid increase in body weight. It is also striking that the starved and ad lib animals stabilize at the same level, despite the fact that one group reaches the level by a postoperative decrease in weight, while the other attains it by gaining weight. It is as if there were a specific weight at which the actions of the two centers are in balance. This weight is at one level for intact control animals, at another level for animals with large (7 second) lesions, and still another level for animals with small lesions (4 second).

Despite the striking correlation between these data and the weight regulation hypothesis, it is too early to pass judgment. However, these findings do imply a radically different view of many of the phenomena we have described. For example, recovery from lateral hypothalamic lesion would have to be interpreted differently. In fact, the term "recovery" would no longer be an apt description of the observed behavior. Many of these implications will have to be explored before the weight regulation hypothesis can replace the established model of hypothalamic regulation.

Centrally Elicited Reinforcement and Feeding

In 1954 Olds and Milner reported a remarkable discovery: animals would learn to perform a response, if the performance led to electrical stimulation delivered to the brain. A typical experimental procedure is schematically represented in Figure 6.16. Chronic implantations of electrodes are made into the brain, and the electrodes connected to the bar in a Skinner-box so that bar-pressing leads to self-stimulation of the brain. When the electrodes are implanted in certain brain sites, the animal will learn to bar-press at high rates. These areas in which intracranial self-stimulation

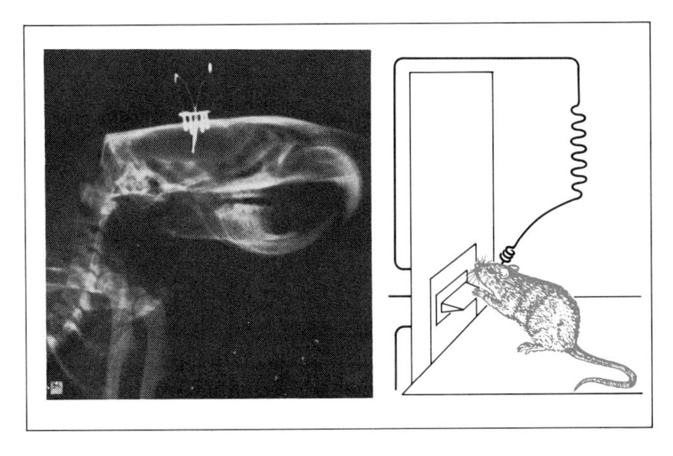

Fig. 6.16. Diagram of method of implanting an electrode in the brain and using it as a self-stimulation circuit, and an X-ray photograph showing electrode assembly in position. (From Morgan, 1961; Photo courtesy of Prof. James Olds)

leads to learning have been called "reward centers." Stimulation of other brain sites proves to be aversive (Delgado, Roberts, and Miller, 1954); the animal will learn a response that *terminates* electrical stimulation.

Intracranial self-stimulation seems to affect behavior very much like primary (biological) reinforcers, such as food and water. For example, animals in an obstruction box repeatedly crossed an electrified grid which applied aversive shock to the feet in order to obtain brain stimulation (Olds, 1961). In a Skinner-box, animals pressed one bar up to 100 times in order to gain access to a second bar with which to stimulate their brains (Pliskoff, Wright, and Hawkins, 1965). Even more compelling is the demonstration (Routtenberg and Lindy, 1965) that brain stimulation can substitute for primary reinforcement. When hungry rats were allowed a choice between brain stimulation and food, they often chose the former.

We have been concerned with the role of the lateral and ventromedial hypothalamic nuclei in the regulation of feeding. But we alluded earlier to the fact that the hypothalamus is also involved in the control of other functions, such as emotional and sexual behavior. Therefore, you might reasonably expect that these nuclei would respond significantly to intracranial self-stimulation, and that self-stimulation of these two hypothalamic sites would have different effects. These expectations are confirmed by experimental results; an experiment by Olds (1960) provides a clear example.

Olds implanted two electrode pairs in the brain of the rat, one pair in the lateral hypothalamus and the other pair in the ventromedial hypothalamus. The animal was placed in a Skinner-box that contained two bars, one connected to the lateral and the other to the ventromedial hypothalamic electrodes. Two conditions were arranged: *stimulation*, under which bar-pressing resulted in self-stimulation of the lateral or ventromedial hypothalamus, depending on which of the two bars was pressed, and *escape*, under which bar-pressing resulted in termination of the electrical stimulation. The animal's behavior was recorded under four conditions: lateral stimulation or escape, and ventromedial stimulation or escape. The behavior of the animal was found to depend on the hypothalamic locus. For the lateral location he pressed the bar to receive stimulation, but would not press the bar to deter stimulation. For the ventromedial location, the animal pressed the

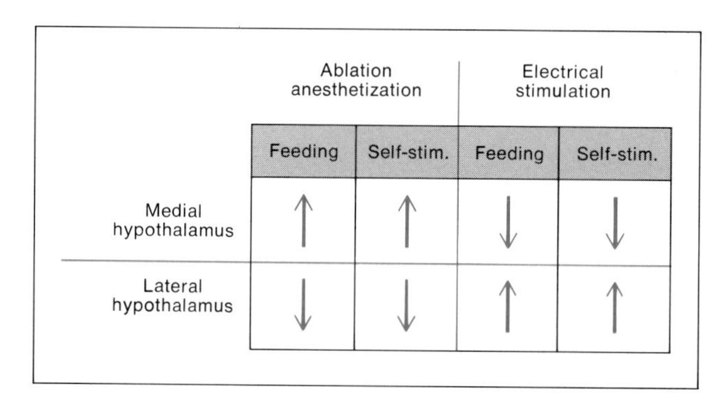

Fig. 6.17. The relationship between hypothalamic control of feeding and self-stimulation. An upward arrow means start or increase of feeding or self-stimulation, as indicated; a downward arrow means stop or decrease of these activities. Each hypothalamic manipulation that had an effect on feeding had a similar effect on lateral hypothalamic self-stimulation. (From Hoebel and Teitelbaum, 1962)

bar to terminate (escape) stimulation, but would not press the bar to receive stimulation.

Combining the results of the experiments on regulation of feeding with Olds' results, we see that the lateral hypothalamus, which excites feeding, is also a site where self-stimulation is rewarding, whereas the ventromedial hypothalamus, which inhibits feeding, is a site where self-stimulation is aversive. The covariation of feeding and self-stimulation has been confirmed in an experiment by Hoebel and Teitelbaum (1962), in which it was possible to excite or depress the ventromedial and lateral hypothalamus in the same animal independently or simultaneously. Figure 6.17 shows the effects on feeding and intracranial self-stimulation. The covariation of feeding and self-stimulation was perfect.

Electrical stimulation and pharmacological or surgical depression are experimental procedures for modifying the activity of the hypothalamic centers. But the same modifications result naturally when the organism is deprived of food or sated. Would we observe the same covariation between self-stimulation and hypothalamic activity if the latter is manipulated "naturally"? The answer provided by various investigations is affirmative. For example, an intragastric injection of food drastically decreases the rate of self-stimulation, and food deprivation leads to increasing rates of self-stimulation (Hoebel and Teitelbaum, 1962; Olds, 1958).

Olds' Theory of Reinforcement

The foregoing observations have given rise to the theory that biological reinforcers act via the self-stimulation areas of the brain. Olds and Olds (1965) have proposed that these self-stimulation areas constitute the fundamental neural mechanism for positive reinforcement. According to the theory, such primary reinforcers as food, water, and sex modify behavior—lead to learning—only because they excite sensory pathways which modulate neural activity in the self-stimulation areas of the brain.

This is a difficult thesis to establish. One line of attack has involved elaboration of the evidence that feeding and self-stimulation respond similarly to experimental manipulations. We have seen evidence that stomach distension, artificial dehydration, glucose injections, and experimentally induced obesity lead to a reduction of feeding. The opposite effect, hyperphagia, is obtained when ventromedial hypothalamic lesions are made or insulin is injected. Various investigators (for example, Hoebel, 1969) have reported that self-stimulation of the lateral hypothalamic reward center is affected in the same direction as feeding: variables that increase feeding also increase the rate of intracranial self-stimulation, and vice versa.

A related experimental approach has concerned the interaction of intracranial self-stimulation and incentive properties of food, such as taste. We will not discuss the details of these experiments (for example, Mogenson and Morgan, 1967; Phillips and Mogenson, 1968; Poschel, 1968), but we will consider the underlying logic. It is known that certain characteristics of stimuli are rewarding. If these properties have a reinforcing effect because of their action on the self-stimulation reward center, then their effectiveness should interact with the effectiveness of electrical self-stimulation. For example, eating or drinking that occurs simultaneously with self-stimulation should enhance the rewarding effects of self-stimulation. A number of investigators (Mogenson and Morgan, 1967; Phillips and Mogenson, 1968; Coons and Cruce, 1968) have demonstrated this effect. They have shown that an animal will self-stimulate at subthreshold levels of intensity (levels of electrical stimulation which do not normally elicit self-stimulation) if it is allowed to eat or drink simultaneously with self-stimulation. Furthermore, this facilitation effect will be greater if the food has positive stimulus properties (for example, sweet saccharin liquid vs. plain water). Presumably the concurrent eating or drinking enhances the activity in the reward center, thereby making rewarding self-stimulation at normally unrewarding levels.

The theory that reinforcers have their effect because they activate reward centers is under intensive investigation, and it is too early to forecast its fate. However, we may note a general implication of the theory. A long standing notion about the nature of reinforcement is embodied in the doctrine of *hedonism*: we seek that which brings us pleasure, and avoid that which brings us pain. With the advent of behaviorism, concepts such as pleasure and pain were ruled out as mentalistic, and the hedonistic theory was replaced by the drive reduction theory of reinforcement. According to this theory, motivation is based on the organism's tendency to reduce the level of drive stimulation. For example, if the organism is deprived of food, the level of hunger drive stimulation will be high, and the organism will be motivated to perform responses that lead to food and subsequent reduction of drive stimulation. Olds has argued that intracranial self-stimulation results are inconsistent with the drive reduction theory, because they demonstrate that *increases* in the level of stimulation can be reinforcing. Furthermore, reports provided by human patients undergoing neurosurgery suggest that electrical stimulation of the brain is in fact pleasurable (Heath and Mickle, 1960; Sem-Jacobson, 1959; Delgado and Hamlin, 1960). Combining these observations with the fact that there are brain sites where stimulation will be avoided seems to indicate that we are reverting to a form of dualistic hedonism.

Summary of Progress

Our principal objective in this chapter has been to examine the role of regulatory centers in the brain. Two subdivisions of the hypothalamus are vitally involved in the regulation of feeding. These two centers, operating on signals correlated with bodily states ranging from starvation to satiety, interact to regulate food intake. We have seen evidence that experimental treatments which upset the balance between these centers produce dramatic alterations in feeding. We have also described several potential signals or sources of information that may serve to enhance or inhibit the activity of these centers. Finally, we noted the striking fact that the centers involved in regulation of feeding may also be identified as reward and punishment centers.

This brief statement is a summary of impressive progress in our understanding of the physiological mechanisms that control feeding. Much remains to be done. We need to know more about the way in which the two centers cooperate to regulate feeding, and how the signals received by these centers are utilized. These and other questions will continue to capture the attention of investigators for years to come.

Obesity in Humans

We will deviate from our emphasis on physiological studies of animals and consider a number of experiments that have used the techniques of experimental social psychology to study obesity in humans (Goldman, Jaffa, and Schachter, 1968; Nisbett, 1968; Schachter, 1968; Schachter, Goldman, and Gordon, 1968; Schachter and Gross, 1968). These studies have compared the responsiveness of obese and normal human subjects to experimental variations of internal and external factors. The internal factors were stomach distension and blood sugar level; the external factors were taste and judged passage of time.

Effects of Food Deprivation and Fear

Schachter and Gross (1968) set out to examine the effects of stomach distension and blood sugar level. Obese and normal paid volunteers came to the laboratory after skipping the preceding meal. Upon arrival, half of the subjects (equally divided between the obese and the normal) were invited to eat from a tray of roast beef sandwiches until satisfied; no food was offered to the other subjects. This was the experimental procedure for manipulating stomach distension. Blood sugar level was varied by manipulating the level of fear concerning the experiment (fear is believed to liberate sugar from the liver into the blood). All of the subjects were told that the purpose of the experiment was to determine the effect of tactile stimulation on taste. It was further explained that the tactile stimulation would be electrical. Half of the subjects under each condition were informed that the experiment required a high level of electrical stimulation which might be painful; the other subjects were told that a very low level of stimulation would be used. Then the investigator explained that the experiment had a before-after design. The subject was given a box of crackers to taste and rate for 15 minutes, with the expectation that after this period the electric stimulation would be administered.

Our interest is in the effects of these variables on eating. As a measure of eating the authors simply counted the number of crackers consumed during the "taste test." Figure 6.18 shows the effects of these variables on the obese and normal subjects. They reacted very differently: obese subjects are almost unaffected by variations of stomach fullness and fear, while the same variations affect the normal subjects significantly and in the opposite directions.

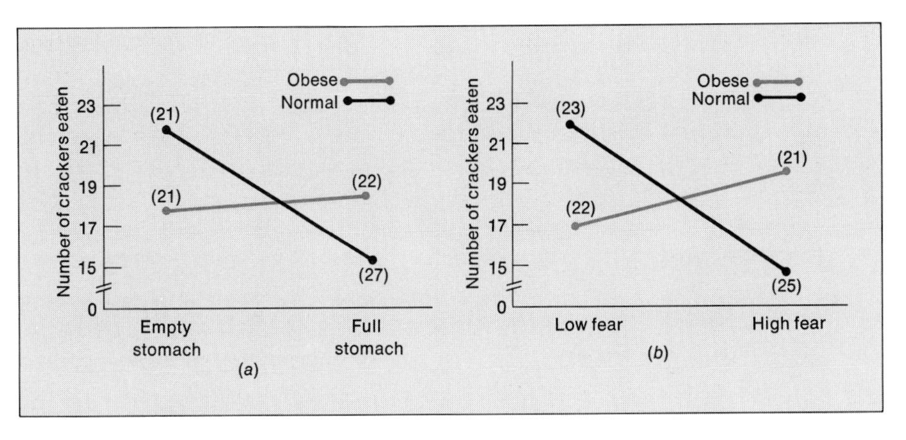

Fig. 6.18. (a) Effects of preliminary eating on the amounts eaten during the experiment by normals and obese subjects. (b) Effects of fear on the amounts eaten by normal and obese subjects. Numbers in parentheses are numbers of subjects. (From Schachter, 1968)

Effect of Time

For most of us, the passage of time is an external cue for eating: "If it's six o'clock it must be time for dinner." What would the effect be on eating if the apparent passage of time were made to differ from the true elapsed time? If you believed the hour of six had arrived when the true hour was four o'clock, would you feel hungry and ready for dinner? Schachter and Gross (1968) introduced a discrepancy between true and judged elapsed time in order to determine the degree to which the eating behavior of obese and normal subjects is controlled by the temporal cue. They rigged two clocks so that one ran at half normal speed and the other at twice normal speed. Subjects arrived in the laboratory at five o'clock and remained alone for 30 minutes. The windowless room contained only electrical equipment and either a slow or fast clock. At 5:30, when the experimenter returned to the room, the slow clock read 5:20, while the fast clock read 6:05. The experimenter carried a box of crackers from which he was nibbling. He put the box down, invited the subject to help himself to the crackers, and, after providing a self-administered personality test as a cover task, left the room.

Figure 6.19 shows the effect of the temporal cue on the amount of crackers eaten by obese and normal subjects. Again the subjects differ, but unlike the previously described study the effect of the variable is largely confined to the obese subjects, for whom cracker consumption is much greater at "6:05" than at "5:20." The "6:05" drop for normal subjects is due chiefly to several persons who refused to eat any crackers on the grounds that they might spoil their appetite for dinner.

Effect of Taste

Nisbett (1968) examined the effects of taste on the eating behavior of three groups: obese, normal, and underweight. The experiment was presented to the subjects as dealing with the relationship between hunger and the ability to concentrate. They came to the laboratory after skipping a meal, and were told that they would eat and then be tested. Ice cream was served. For half the subjects the ice cream was an excellent variety of vanilla, while for the other half it was a bitter mixture of vanilla and quinine. Immediately after eating the ice cream, all subjects

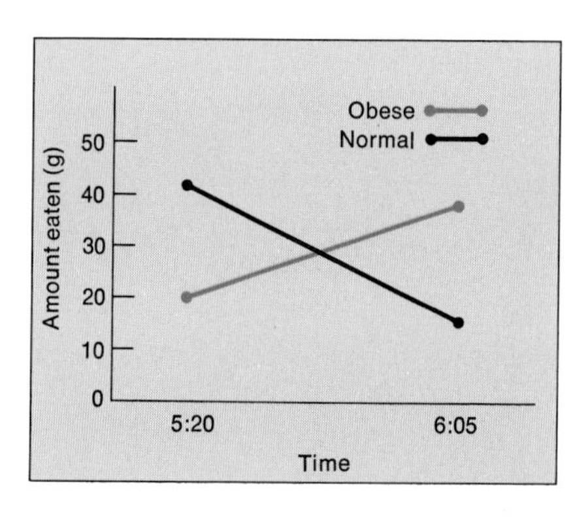

Fig. 6.19. The effects of manipulation of time on the amounts eaten by obese and normal subjects. (From Schachter, 1968)

responded to the question, "How good was the ice cream?," by rating it on a scale that ranged from "excellent" to "terrible."

Figure 6.20 shows the amount of ice cream eaten as a function of rated liking of the ice cream. The three curves for the obese, normal, and underweight persons differ significantly. For present purposes, the important finding is that the obese subjects demonstrate greater influence of their taste evaluation than do the other subjects.

In summary, the results of these studies suggest two conclusions about obese and normal persons. Correlates of feeding, such as stomach distension, play a greater role in regulating the eating behavior of normal persons than they do for obese persons. Cues such as passage of time and taste affect eating behavior to a greater extent in obese persons than in normal persons.

These studies serve to recall the observations recorded in the opening paragraphs of this chapter. Obviously, eating in man is determined by more than the responsiveness of the hypothalamic centers. At the same time, we should note that social psychological studies of the obese reveal a notable degree of similarity between the hypothalamic hyperphagic and the obese person. Both are finicky—their eating behavior is highly influenced by taste; both tend to eat when they are not hungry—a level of internal signaling, higher than for the normal, is required to inhibit eating. The theoretical significance of these similarities remains to be determined.

Glossary

Adipsia: abstention from drinking; the adipsic refuses to drink. Lateral hypothalamic lesions produce adipsia.

Aphagia: abstention from eating; the aphagic refuses to eat and behaves as if food were an aversive stimulus. Lateral hypothalamic lesions produce aphagia.

Feeding center: the zone in the hypothalamus that controls the onset of feeding. This zone, also called the start center, has been localized in the lateral hypothalamic region.

Glucostatic hypothesis: the thesis that the hypothalamic centers that control feeding behavior contain glucoreceptors that are highly sensitive to the rate at which glucose passes into the hypothalamic cells. Rates of glucose utilization are the signals used by the hypothalamic centers to regulate eating.

Hyperphagia: literally means overeating; hypothalamic hyperphagia refers to overeating that accompanies ventromedial hypothalamic lesioning.

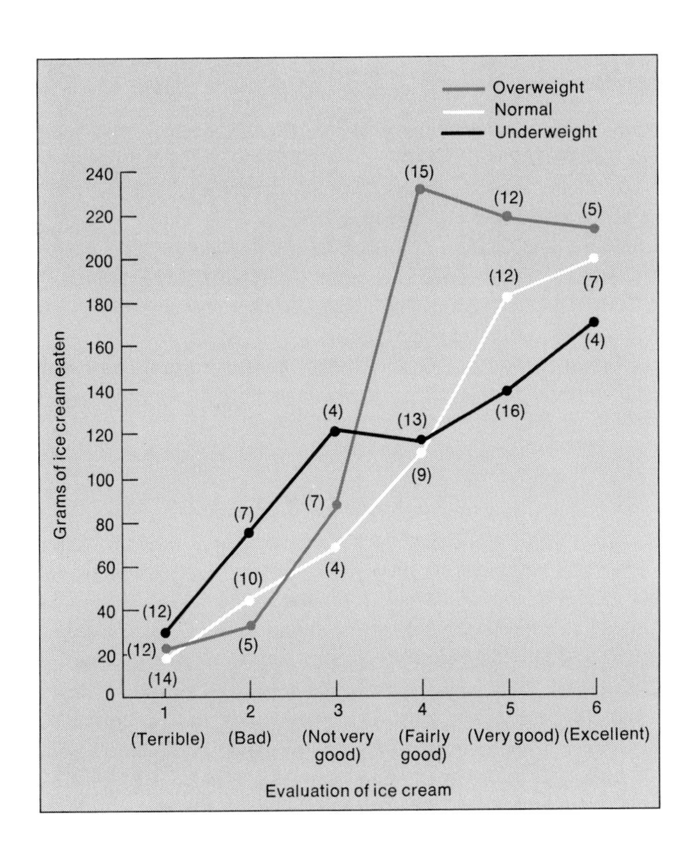

Fig. 6.20. Grams of ice cream eaten as a function of ratings of its taste. Numbers in parentheses denote *n* for each point. (From Nisbett, 1968)

Hypothalamus: a tiny, highly vascularized region at the base of the brain which is vitally involved in controlling feeding. The hypothalamus is also involved in controlling a variety of emotional responses.

Intragastric (tube) feeding: an experimental arrangement whereby food is delivered *directly* to the animal's stomach.

Lateral hypothalamic zone: the lateralmost portion of the hypothalamus (see Fig. 6.4b). This zone has been identified as the feeding (start) center.

Lipostatic hypothesis: the thesis that the hypothalamic centers that control feeding behavior respond to a circulating metabolite in the blood that is associated with stored fat.

Reward centers: intracranial self-stimulation of certain regions of the brain is reinforcing; an animal will learn to perform a response if the response is followed by intracranial stimulation. These regions are called reward centers.

Satiety center: the zone in the hypothalamus that controls the cessation of feeding. This zone, also called the stop center, has been localized in the ventromedial hypothalamic region.

Stereotaxis: a laboratory instrument that enables the experimenter to produce lesions in exactly specified brain sites.

Thermostatic hypothesis: the thesis that the hypothalamic centers that control feeding behavior respond to changes in body temperature. Body temperature changes are the signals used by the hypothalamus to regulate feeding.

Ventromedial hypothalamic zone: the zone immediately lateral to the periventricular zone (see Fig. 6.4b). This zone has been identified as the satiety (stop) center.

References

Anand, B.K., and J.R. Brobeck. Hypothalamic control of food intake. *Yale Journal of Biology and Medicine,* 1951, **24,** 123–140.

Anand, B.K., G.S. Chhina, and B. Singh. Effect of glucose on the activity of hypothalamic "feeding centers." *Science,* 1962, **138,** 597–598.

———, K.N. Sharma, and S. Dua. Activity of single neurons in the hypothalamic feeding centers: Effect of glucose. *Amer. J. Physiol.*, 1964, **207,** 1146–1154.

Andersson, B., C. Gale, and J.W. Sundsten. Preoptic influences on water intake. In M.J. Wayner (Ed.), *Thirst.* New York: Macmillan, 1964.

Balinska, H., O. Buresova, and E. Fifkova. The influence of cortical and thalamic spreading depression on feeding behavior of rats with lateral hypothalamic lesions. *Acta Biologiae Experimentalis*, 1967, **27,** 355–363.

Bayer, E. Beiträge zur Zweikomponentheorie des Hungers. *Zeitschrift Psychologie*, 1929, **112,** 1–54.

Beltt, Bruce Marshall. Specificity of inhibitory mechanism controlling food intake during hypothalamic stimulation. Unpublished doctoral dissertation, University of Wisconsin, 1970.

Brobeck, J.R. Effects of variations in activity, food intake, and environmental temperature on weight gain in albino rats. *Amer. J. Physiol.*, 1945, **143,** 1–5.

———. Food intake as a mechanism of temperature regulation. *Yale Journal of Biology and Medicine,* 1947–1948, **20,** 545–552.

Camus, J., and G. Roussy. Syndrome adipso-genital et polyurie experimentale. *Revue Neurologique*, 1920, **36,** 1201.

———. Les syndromes hypophysaires. *Revue Neurologique,* 1922, **38,** 622–639.

Cannon, W.B. Hunger and thirst. In C. Murchison (Ed.), *Handbook of general experimental psychology.* Worcester, Mass.: Clark University Press, 1934.

———, and Washburn, A.L. An explanation of hunger. *Amer. J. Physiol.*, 1912, **29,** 444–454.

Coons, E.E., and J.A.F. Cruce. Lateral hypothalamus: Food current intensity in maintaining self-stimulation of hunger. *Science*, 1968, **159,** 1117–1119.

Cytawa, J., and P. Teitelbaum. Spreading depression and recovery of subcortical functions. *Acta Biologiae Experimentalis*, 1967, **27,** 345–353.

Davis, J.D., and N.E. Miller. A technique for mixing the blood of unanesthetized rats. *J. appl. Psychol.*, 1966, **21,** 1873–1874.

———, and F. J. Gallagher, and R. F. Ladove, and A. J. Turausky. Inhibition of food intake by a humeral factor. *J. comp physiol. Psychol.,* 1970, 67, 407–414.

Delgado, J.M.R., and H. Hamilin. Spontaneous and evoked electrical seizures in animals and in humans. In E.R. Ramey and D.S. O'Doherty (Eds.), *Electrical studies on the unanesthetized brain.* New York: Paul Hoeber, 1960.

Delgado, J.M.R., W.W. Roberts, and N.E. Miller. Learning motivated by electrical stimulation of the brain. *Amer. J. Physiol.*, 1954, **179,** 587–593.

Epstein, A.N., and P. Teitelbaum. Regulation of food intake in the absence of taste, smell and other oro-pharyngeal sensations. *J. comp. physiol. Psychol.*, 1962, **55,** 753–759.

Goldman, R., M. Jaffa, and S. Schachter. Yom Kippur, Air France, dormitory food, and the eating behavior of obese and normal persons. *J. pers. soc. Psychol.*, 1968, **10,** 117–123.

Grossman, M.I., G.M. Cummins, and A.C. Ivy. The effect of insulin on food intake after vagotomy and sympathectomy. *Amer. J. Physiol.*, 1947, **149,** 100.

Grossman, S.P. Effects of adrenegic and cholinergic blocking agents on hypothalamic mechanisms. *Amer. J. Physiol.*, 1962, **202,** 1230–1236.

———. *A textbook of physiological psychology*. New York: John Wiley & Sons, 1967.

———. The VMH: A center for affective reactions, satiety or both? *International Journal of Physiological Behavior*, 1966, **1,** 1–10.

Harris, S.C., A.C. Ivy, and L.M. Searle. Mechanisms of amphetamine-induced loss of weight: Consideration of theory of hunger and appetite. *J. AMA*, 1947, **134,** 1468–1475.

Heath, R.G., and W.A. Mickle. Evaluation of seven years' experience with depth electrode studies in human patients. In E.R. Ramey and D.S. O'Doherty (Eds.), *Electrical studies on the unanesthetized brain*. New York: Paul Hoeber, 1960.

Hervey, G.R. The effects of lesions in the hypothalamus in parabiotic rats. *J. Physiol.*, 1959, **145,** 336–352.

Hetherington, A.W. The production of hypothalamic obesity in rats already displaying chronic hypopituitarism. *Amer. J. Physiol.*, 1943, **140,** 89–91.

_______, and S.W. Ranson. Hypothalamic lesions and adiposity in the rat. *The Anatomical Record,* 1942, **78,** 149–172.

Hoebel, B.G. Feeding and self-stimulation. *Ann. N.Y. Acad. Sciences*, 1969, **157,** 758–778.

_______, and P. Teitelbaum. Hypothalamic control of feeding and self-stimulation. *Science,* 1962, **135,** 375–377.

_______. Weight regulation in normal and hypothalamic hyperphagics. *J. comp. physiol. Psychol.*, 1966, **61,** 189–193.

Krasne, F.B. General disruption resulting from electrical stimulus of ventromedial hypothalamus. *Science,* 1962, **138,** 822–823.

MacKay, E.M., J.W. Calloway, and R.H. Barnes. Hyperalimentation in normal animals produced by protamine-insulin. *Journal of Nutrition,* 1940, **20,** 59.

Margules, D.L., and J. Olds. Identical "feeding" and "rewarding" systems in the lateral hypothalamus of rats. *Science*, 1962, **135,** 374–375.

Mayer, J. Regulation of energy intake and the body weight: the glucostatic theory and the lipostatic hypothesis. *Ann. N.Y. Acad. Sciences*, 1955, **63,** 15–43.

Miller, N.E., C.J. Bailey, and J.A.F. Stevenson. "Decreased hunger" but increased food intake resulting from hypothalamic lesions. *Science,* 1950, **112,** 256–259.

Mogenson, G.J., and C.W. Morgan. Effects of induced drinking on self-stimulation of the lateral hypothalamus. *Experimental Brain Research*, 1967, **3,** 111–116.

Morgane, P. J. Electrophysiological studies of feeding and satiety centers in the rat. *Amer. J. Physiol.*, 1961, **201,** 838–844.

Nisbett, R.E. Taste, deprivation, and weight determinants of eating behavior. *J. pers. soc. Psychol.*, 1968, **10,** 107–116.

Olds, J. Approach-avoidance dissociations in rat brain. *Amer. J. Physiol.*, 1960, **199,** 965–968.

_______. Differential effects of drive and drugs on self-stimulation at different brain sites. In D.E. Sheer (Ed.), *Electrical stimulation of the brain.* Austin: University of Texas Press, 1961.

_______. Effects of hunger and male sex hormones on self-stimulation of the brain. *J. comp. physiol. Psychol.*, 1958, **51,** 320–324.

_______, and P. Milner. Positive reinforcement produced by electrical stimulation of the septal area and other regions of the rat brain. *J. comp. physiol. Psychol.*, 1954, **47,** 419–427.

Olds, J., and M. Olds. Drives, rewards and the brain. In F. Barron *et al.*, *New directions in psychology*. Vol. II. New York: Holt, Rinehart and Winston, 1965.

Oomara, Y., K. Kimura, H. Ooyama, T. Maeno, I. Matasaburo, and M. Kuniyoshi. Reciprocal activities of the ventromedial and lateral hypothalamic areas of cats. *Science,* 1964, **143,** 484–485.

Oomara, Y., H. Ooyama, T. Yamamoto, and F. Naka. Reciprocal relationship of the lateral and ventromedial hypothalamus in the regulation of food intake. *Physiology and Behavior,* 1967, **2,** 97–115.

Phillips, A.G., and G.J. Mogenson. Effects of taste on self-stimulation and induced drinking. *J. comp. physiol. Psychol.*, 1968, **66,** 654–660.

Pliskoff, S.S., J.E. Wright, and D.T. Hawkins. Brain stimulation as a reinforcer: Intermittent schedules. *J. exp. Anal. of Behavior,* 1965, **8,** 75–88.

Poschel, B.P.H. Do biological reinforcers act via the self-stimulation areas of the brain? *Physiology and Behavior,* 1968, **3,** 53–60.

Powley, T.L., and R.E. Keesey. Relationship of body weight to the lateral hypothalamic syndrome. *J. comp. physiol. Psychol.*, 1970, **70,** 25–36.

Routtenberg, A., and J. Lindy. Effects of the availability of rewarding septal and hypothalamic stimulation on barpressing for food under conditions of deprivation. *J. comp. physiol. Psychol.*, 1965, **60,** 158–161.

Schachter, S. Obesity and eating. *Science,* 1968, **161,** 751–756.

———, K. Goldman, and A. Gordon. Effects of fear, food deprivation and obesity on eating. *J. pers. soc. Psychol.*, 1968, **10,** 91–97.

Schachter, S., and L.P. Gross. Manipulated time and eating behavior. *J. pers. soc. Psychol.*, 1968, **10,** 98–106.

Sem-Jacobson, C.W. Effects of electrical stimulation on the human brain. *Electroencephalography and Clinical Neurophysiology,* 1959, **11,** 379.

Smith, P.E. The disabilities caused by hypophysectomy and their repair: The tuberal (hypothalamic) syndrome in the rat. *J. AMA,* 1927, **88,** 158–161.

———. Hypophysectomy and a replacement therapy in the rat. *Amer. J. Anat.*, 1930, **45,** 205.

Stunkard, A.J., and Koch, C. The interpretation of gastric motility: I. Apparent bias in the reports of hunger by obese persons. *Arch. gen. Psychiat.*, 1964, **11,** 74–83.

Teitelbaum, P. Disturbances in feeding and drinking behavior after hypothalamic lesions. In M.R. Jones (Ed.), *Nebraska symposium on motivation.* Lincoln: University of Nebraska Press, 1961.

———. Random and food-directed activity in hyperphagic and normal rats. *J. comp. physiol. Psychol.*, 1957, **50,** 486–490.

———, M. Cheng, and P. Rozin. Development of feeding parallels its recovery after hypothalamic damage. *J. comp. physiol. Psychol.*, 1969, **67,** 430–441.

———, and A.N. Epstein. The lateral hypothalamic syndrome: Recovery of feeding and drinking after lateral hypothalamic lesions. *Psychol. Rev.*, 1962, **69,** 74–90.

Wickens, D.D., and D.R. Meyer. *Psychology.* (Rev. ed.) New York: Holt, Rinehart and Winston, 1961.

7 Sleep and Dreams

When research findings shed new light on an old problem, they are sometimes regarded as breakthroughs, and they justifiably intrigue interested onlookers as well as those who have been directly instrumental in bringing them about. Breakthroughs do not occur rapidly or simply; theoretical and experimental foundations must be laid by the hard and often disappointing work of many scientists over long years. The final results of a breakthrough are rarely obvious immediately. The airplane was invented in 1903, but 15 years later, during World War I, its possibilities were grasped by only a handful of individuals. Atomic energy was demonstrated in 1945, but today, a quarter of a century later, its full potentialities still go unrealized.

Foresight is notoriously undependable in such cases, but it appears that psychology has experienced a breakthrough of sorts. The men initially responsible were physiologists, not psychologists, but they saw the psychological implications of their work and made special efforts to bring it to psychologists' attention. It seemed to these investigators that they had discovered an objective index of dreaming. If they were correct, they had found a way for any adequately trained and properly equipped observer to know exactly when a sleeping person experiences one of those highly personal dramas of mental life that have baffled and fascinated men since the beginning of time.

How provocative their work has been can be appreciated by considering the fact that the January 1968 issue of the scientific journal, *Psychophysiology*, contains reports of 95 papers presented at a single annual meeting of the *Association for the Physiological Study of Sleep* (Foulkes and Kales, 1968). These papers range from one on sleep and dreaming in the elephant (Hartmann, Bernstein, and Wilson, 1968) to one on the dreams of pregnant women (Van de Castle, 1968).

The Lie Detector

Neither the attempt to make private mental life public, nor the idea that careful measurement of proper physiological functions is the way to do it, is completely new in psychology. The best-known illustration of this attempt is the *polygraph* (*poly* meaning many, *graph* meaning a diagram), the so-called "lie detector." A polygraph measures a variety of body functions simultaneously: *respiration* is measured with a rubber bellows strapped around the subject's chest or abdomen, *blood pressure* and *pulse* are measured with the familiar arm cuff seen in every doctor's office, and *galvanic skin response* (changes in the electrical properties of the subject's skin) is measured with finger electrodes. Other functions that are sometimes measured are skin temperature and finger or hand tremor (Fig. 7.1).

The idea behind the polygraph is that people usually react emotionally when they lie. Emotional responses are reflected in changes of body functions to which the instruments of the polygraph are sensitive. Polygraph operators who use these instruments for lie detection must be trained to distinguish among reactions that represent general emotional responsivity, imagined guilt over something that never happened, or a variety of things other than actual lying.

Dreams and Mental Life: Psychoanalysis

In ancient times dreams were commonly regarded as visitations by spirits and ghosts. Dreams have been thought to be the vehicle through which gods and

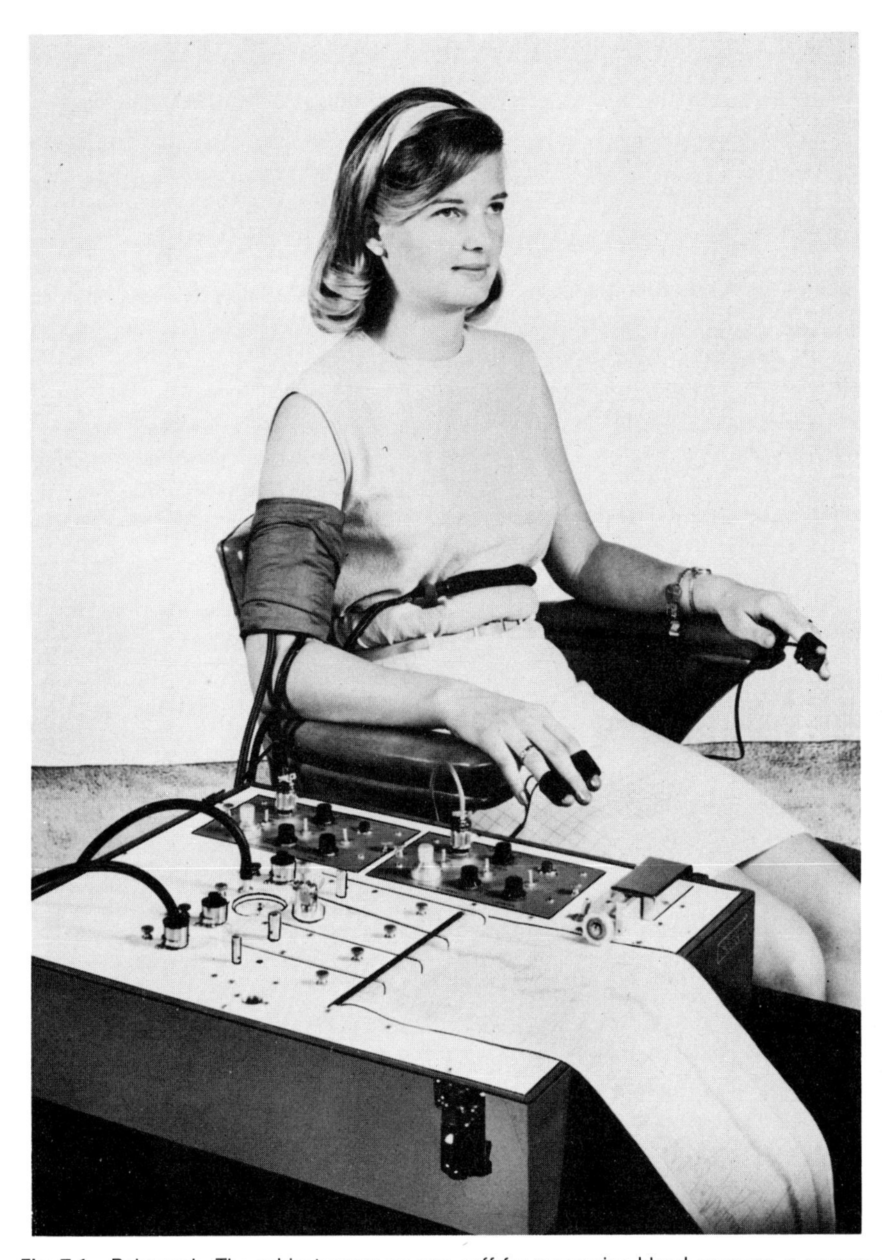

Fig. 7.1. Polygraph. The subject wears an arm cuff for measuring blood pressure, a pneumograph for measuring respiration, finger electrodes on the right hand for measuring galvanic skin responses, and a plethysmograph on the left hand for measuring heart rate. (Lafayette Instrument Co., Model 76013)

demons speak to men, and they have frequently been thought to foretell the future. Thousands of books purporting to interpret dream symbols have been produced. Artemidorus wrote such a book, *Oneirocritics*, in the second century A.D. Following the invention of the printing press in the fifteenth century, the fame of this book became worldwide (Hall, 1953b). Even today, some people rely on dreams and dream books for hints about lucky numbers in gambling and for guidance in the conduct of their daily affairs.

Dreams remained mysterious phenomena until the first major breakthrough in the early twentieth century, when Sigmund Freud published one of his most famous volumes, *The Interpretation of Dreams*. Freud saw dreams as natural products of psychological forces and mechanisms. To him, a dream was produced by conflict between the conscious, controlling forces of rational, civilized thought and the unconscious, primitive forces of man's animal heritage. The former strive to protect themselves from the latter, but the unconscious is too strong and persistent to be perpetually denied. During sleep, primitive impulses rise toward awareness and threaten to overwhelm the conscious mind. In response, the conscious mind resorts to subterfuge. It allows the impulses to enter, but clothes them in symbolic garb so that they will not be too fearful. The purpose of psychoanalysis has been to discover the techniques and devices by which this disguise takes place. Knowledge of these would make it possible to strip away the comparatively meaningless superficialities of dream reports (manifest contents) and get at their true meanings (latent contents).

Later theorists stress different functions for the dream process. C.S. Hall (1953a, b) maintains that dreams are essentially *expressive* in nature. Through dreams, the person describes what is on his mind and works out fantasy solutions to his problems. Hall feels that dreams use symbols mainly because symbolic images are often more efficient than images of the real thing. For example, the moon may be used to symbolize a variety of conceptions about women. Its monthly phases resemble the menstrual cycle, while its filling from new to full represents the filling of the woman during pregnancy. Since the moon is often regarded as inferior to the sun, it may represent the dreamer's belief that women are inferior to men. The moon changes and is therefore fickle, like the dreamer's conception of women. The weakness of moonlight represents women's frailty. All these conceptions of women may be condensed into a single symbolic object (Hall, 1953b, p. 97).

For those interested in this approach to dreams, a volume by Hall and Van de Castle (1966) provides scales for rating dream themes and contents. These scales, developed from an analysis of 1,000 dream reports provided by 100 men and women college students, represent the best available technique for the study of the contents of dream reports.

Whether a theorist regards dreams as defensive or expressive in nature, he faces certain problems when he sets out to examine them. There are two main sources of interference in his data. First is the distortion of the dream itself. Dreams do not reveal their meanings directly; their contents are often symbolic; the events they depict are not subject to the ordinary rules of logic or the restrictions of physical laws. Second, distortion is unavoidably introduced when the subject tries to remember and report dream contents.

In addition, people often forget their dreams. Some claim that they never dream, but it is most likely that nondreamers are just good forgetters, since many of them do report dreams after they have practiced remembering them for a few days. But hardly anyone remembers all his dreams; even frequent dreamers report dreams whose contents they cannot recall. Consequently, the study of dreams has been hampered by the inability of the investigator to obtain all the data he needs. Freud solved the problem in part by studying his own dreams. He knew that his own reports would be subject to some incompleteness and distortion, but felt he could rely on them more than he could on the reports of others.

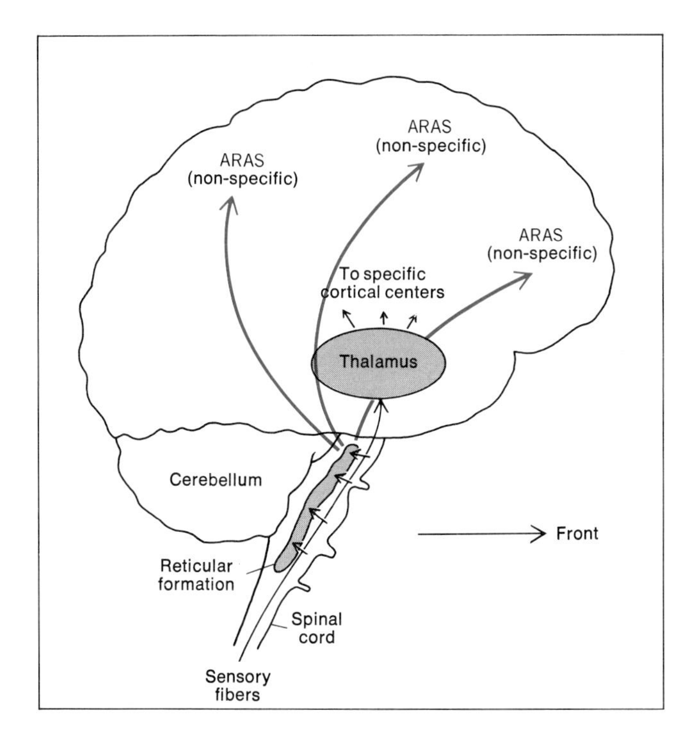

Fig. 7.2. Simplified schematic diagram of the thalamic and ascending reticular activating systems. In the former, sensory impulses are relayed by the thalamus to specific sensory centers of the cortex. The latter serve a generalized arousal function for large cortical regions. (The cerebellum, also shown in this figure, is part of the hindbrain that is a center for motor coordination, posture, and balance.)

The research summarized in this chapter has enabled investigators to tell with a high degree of certainty when a person is having particularly vivid dreams. By awakening the subject immediately, they can obtain reports of dream contents that are much less likely to be distorted or forgotten than are reports obtained on succeeding days.

To understand recent work on dreams, we must know a little about the results of research on sleep. The next section outlines some of the findings on that subject and shows how the study of sleep led to the discovery of a measure of dreaming.

Sleep

The Physiology of Sleep

Physiologically, sleep is controlled primarily by an organization of nerve cells called the *reticular activating system* (RAS). The critical segment of this system is the *reticular formation* (Moruzzi and Magoun, 1949), located in the lower central part of the brain where the nerves of the spinal cord enter (the *brain stem*). It lies anterior to (in front of) the part of the hindbrain called the *cerebellum* and below the organ known as the *thalamus* (Fig. 7.2). The thalamus relays sensory impulses from the spinal cord to specific receptive centers in the outer layer of the brain, the *cerebral cortex*. On their way to the thalamus, however, these impulses also influence the reticular formation.

Fibers extend from the reticular formation to the cortex, but, unlike fibers from the thalamus, they do not affect specific cortical centers. Rather, they spread to wide areas of the cortex. Direct, experimental stimulation of the reticular formation of a sleeping or drowsy organism does not produce a specific sensory response but a generalized awakening or arousal.

The fibers that convey impulses through the reticular formation to the cortex constitute the *ascending reticular activating system* (ARAS). There are also fibers that carry impulses from the cerebral cortex back to the reticular formation (not indicated in Fig. 7.2). These fibers complete the closed neural loop that makes up the whole RAS. Because it controls the general activity level of the cerebral cortex, the reticular activating system determines the general wakefulness or sleepiness of the organism. When the RAS activates the cortex, the organism is alert and responsive to sensory stimuli. When it does not activate the cortex and support incoming sensory impulses, the organism is asleep.

Levels of Sleep

There are borderline stages between sleeping and waking which are not easy to categorize. Anyone who has struggled to keep himself from falling asleep during a particularly dull lecture, or fought against overwhelming drowsiness while driving on the open highway, will know this. Most people have periods of daydreaming or dozing in which they are neither quite awake nor quite asleep. Even at night, one will sleep either lightly or soundly.

The electroencephalogram. Physiological research indicates that it is possible to measure various stages of sleep by recording electrical discharges of the brain. Small metal disks (electrodes), sensitive to variations of minute electrical potentials in the body, are attached to the scalp. These variations, enormously amplified, are fed to a pen-writing device that records them on paper, resulting in an *electroencephalogram* (EEG), a picture of the changes in electrical activity of the brain. Electroencephalographic records may be taken simultaneously from a number of pairs of electrodes placed at different locations on the head. The electrodes feed into a bank of amplifiers and writing units that record differences in electrical potential between pairs of electrodes. When a stimulus produces a change in the pattern of discharges recorded from one pair of electrodes, but not in the patterns recorded from the rest, the examiner infers that only the area to which that pair is sensitive has been affected. He thus studies the functions of the various regions of the brain. If he is skilled in diagnosis, he may use the EEG to provide evidence of brain tissue damage that might otherwise go undetected.

Lobes of the brain. The surface of the brain, the cerebral cortex, is a convoluted mass of nervous tissue divided into two virtually symmetrical *hemispheres*. Generally, functions on the right side of the body are controlled by the left hemisphere and functions on the left side are controlled by the right hemisphere. Each hemisphere is subdivided into *lobes* which are separated from each other by prominent fissures or *sulci*. The four main lobes, the *frontal, temporal, parietal,* and *occipital*, are shown in Figure 7.3. These cortical areas and the structures they enclose comprise the *cerebrum*, the largest portion of the human brain. The cerebel-

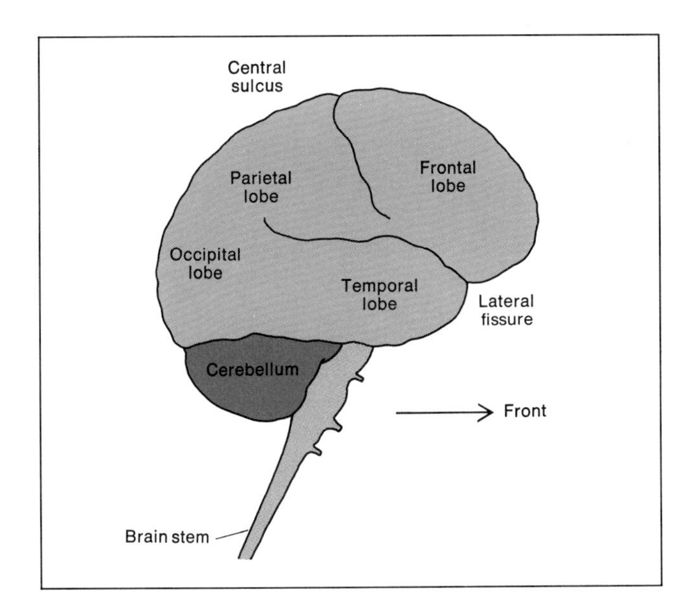

Fig. 7.3. Main lobes of the right cerebral cortex.

lum (shown in Figs. 7.2 and 7.3) lies near the brain stem, where the spinal cord enters, and is not part of the cortex. It is shown in these figures only for purposes of orientation.

Obviously, coverage of the four main lobes on both hemispheres requires at least eight electrodes. More precise localization requires an even larger number of electrodes and produces an even more complex record for analysis. Research on sleep does not require a complete map of the whole of the cortex; two or three pairs of electrodes are often sufficient.

Sleep cycles. The EEG patterns of subjects who sleep all night in the laboratory reveal four levels of sleep (Ciba Foundation, 1961; Kleitman, 1952; U.S. Department of Health, Education, and Welfare, 1966). Each level is distinguishable from the others and from the normal pattern of resting wakefulness.

When a subject is relaxed but awake, his EEG record sometimes shows *alpha* waves, regular waves of about ten cycles per second (cps) which produce pen deflections of moderate amplitude. These show up most clearly when the subject's eyes are closed. Figure 7.4a shows what a walking record looks like on an EEG recording from a single pen. When no voltage is applied to the pen, it records in a straight line. When voltage is applied, the pen swings up and down. The distance it swings is proportional to the voltage applied and is a measure of the *amplitude* or intensity of the electrical discharge from the brain. The rapidity with which the needle swings reflects the frequency of the discharges being recorded. Since the paper on the recording machine moves at a constant speed, low-frequency discharges are represented by widely spaced waves, while high-frequency discharges appear as closely spaced waves.

The first change as subjects drop off to sleep is disappearance of the alpha rhythm and its replacement by *theta* waves, which are of low to moderate amplitude and are relatively slow (four to six cps). Figure 7.4b shows how theta waves from one subject look on an EEG recording. This EEG pattern defines *stage 1 sleep.*

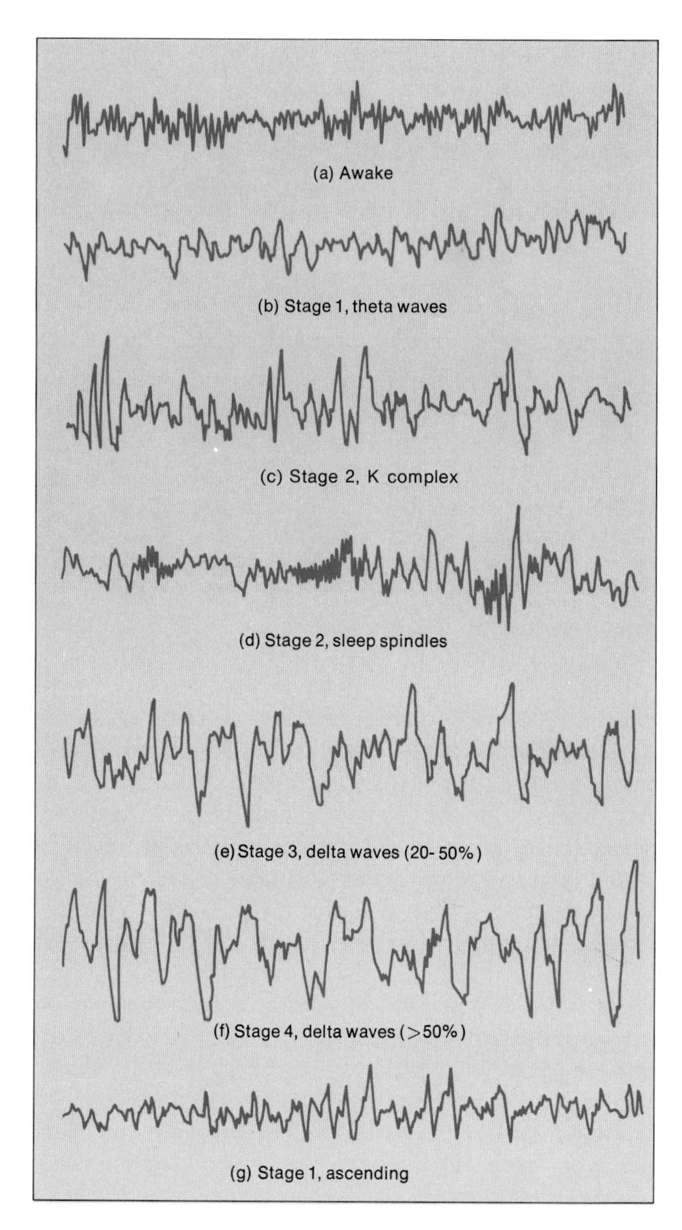

Fig. 7.4. EEG patterns at various stages of sleep. (Adapted from Rechtschaffen and Kales, 1968)

When it appears while a subject is falling off to sleep, it is called *stage 1 descending.* Subjects awakened at this time usually report that they were just going to sleep but were not yet fully asleep. When it appears while sleep is lightening, it is called *stage 1 ascending.* Interestingly, subjects awakened at this time often report that they were sleeping deeply. This is one important difference between stage 1 descending and stage 1 ascending. There are others: for example, rapid eye movements almost never occur in conjunction with stage 1 descending but are common in stage 1 ascending. For the moment, however, we are concerned only with the EEG record, on the basis of which both the descending and ascending phases of stage 1 look very much alike (compare the tracings of Fig. 7.4b and 7.4g).

The next change that is usually observed is the spontaneous appearance of slow, high amplitude waves (the *K complex*, shown in Fig. 7.4c) and the occurrence of *sleep spindles*, which look like bundles of relatively rapid, close-packed waves (Fig. 7.4d). These EEG features characterize *stage 2 sleep*, most often described as "light sleep" by subjects who are awakened.

Stages 3 and 4 are more distinguishable on the basis of EEG records than on the basis of reports by awakened subjects. Both stages are characterized by the appearance of *delta waves*, high voltage slow waves of from one to three cps. In stage 3 (Fig. 7.4e) these waves occur from 20 to 50 per cent of the time; in stage 4 (Fig. 7.4f), delta waves occupy more than 50 per cent of the record. Although stages 3 and 4 look quite different from stage 2 on the EEG record, they do not differ much from each other, and subjects awakened during stages 3 and 4 usually report having been in light sleep.

Following the appearance of stages 3 and 4, stage 2 and stage 1 reappear in that order, thus finishing a complete cycle from stage 1 (descending) through stage 4 and back to stage 1 (ascending). Cycles of EEG changes occur from four to six times in a full night's sleep (Dement and Kleitman, 1957a, b). As the cycles progress, stage 4 tends to disappear and stage 1 tends to last for progressively longer periods of time. In the last cycle or two, stages 3 and 4 may not appear at all.

Eye Movements during Sleep

The same apparatus used for amplifying and recording electrical discharges from the brain may be used to measure movements of the eyes. Electrodes are attached at the outer *canthus* (at the sides of the subject's eyes) and sometimes on the *supraorbital ridge* (the bony ridge above the eyes). These electrodes are sensitive to voltages that appear when the eyeballs move horizontally or vertically. When the voltages are amplified and recorded, the resulting *electrooculogram* (EOG) looks something like an EEG (Fig. 7.5).

Slow eye movements during sleep had been observed as early as 1922. However, in 1953 Eugene Aserinsky and Nathaniel Kleitman, from the Department of Physiology of the University of Chicago, reported periods of rapid, jerky eye movements in sleeping subjects. These periods occurred episodically, about four times during the night, the later periods appearing at somewhat closer intervals than the earlier ones. Each period lasted from 6 to 53 minutes (an average of 20 minutes) and was associated with relatively high respiratory rate, increased heart rate, and high body motility.

Furthermore, when subjects were awakened during periods of rapid eye movements (REM), they frequently reported vivid visual dreams (27 awakenings produced 20 such reports). When subjects were awakened from periods without rapid eye movements they generally did not report the occurrence of vivid dreams (23 awakenings produced only two such reports). Aserinsky and Kleitman concluded that the measurement of eye movements during sleep "furnishes the means of determining the incidence and duration of periods of dreaming." The finding that REM periods are associated with vivid visual dreaming was repeated by Dement in 1955 and has been independently confirmed by many investigators since then.

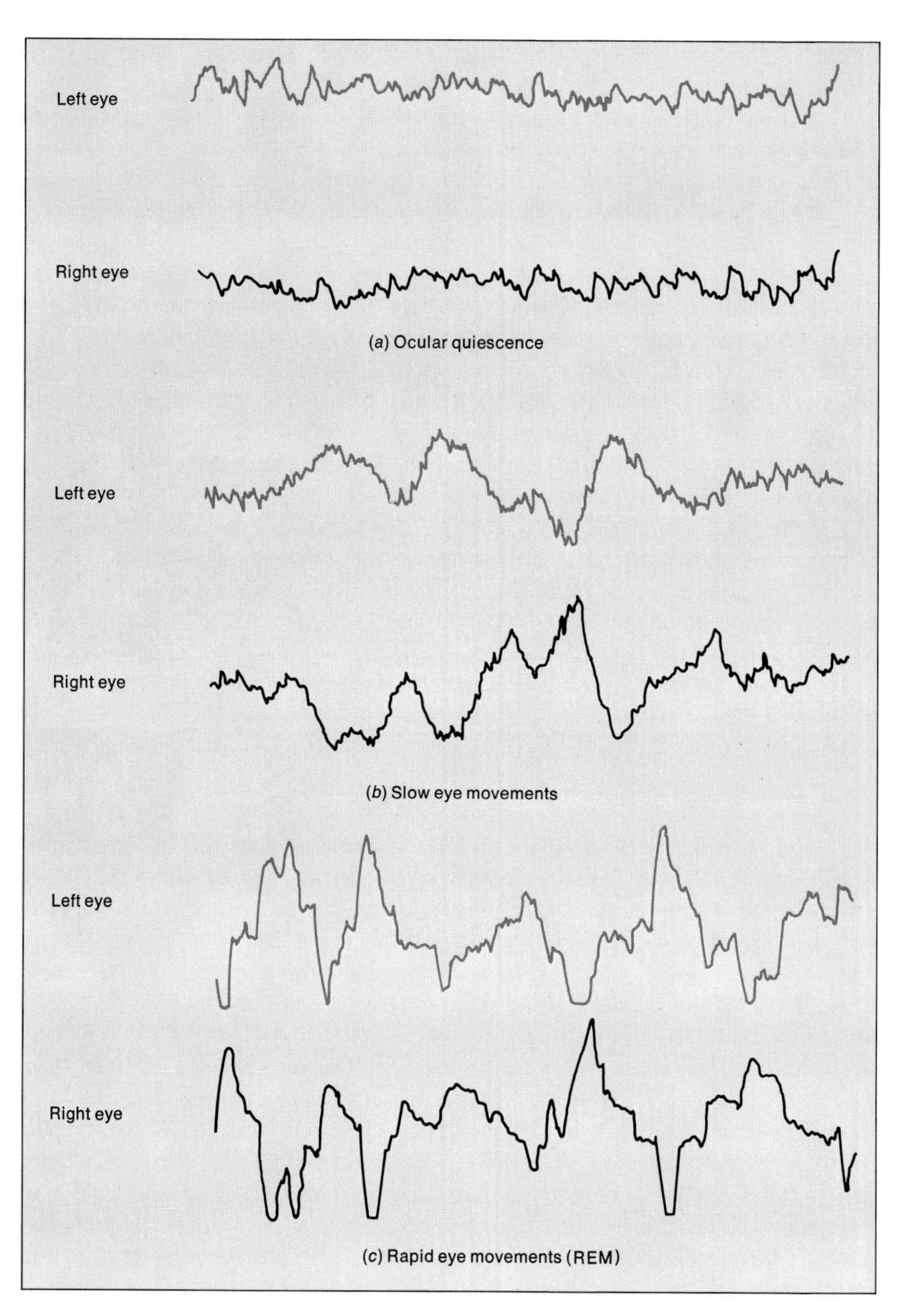

Fig. 7.5. EOG recordings of potentials associated with movements of the eyes. (Adapted from Rechtschaffen and Kales, 1968.)

REM and EEG. Rapid eye movements have been observed almost exclusively in a single stage of sleep: stage 1 ascending. They do not typically appear while the subject is going to sleep or while he is in stages 2, 3, or 4; they occur only after he comes up from the deeper levels, back through stage 1. This does not mean that stage 1 ascending is *always* characterized by rapid eye movements, for this stage also contains periods of ocular quiescence during which it is virtually indistinguishable from stage 1 descending. It only means that, for all practical purposes, REM only appears in stage 1 ascending.

Other physiological processes. Rapid eye movements are also associated with other bodily responses. The *autonomic nervous system*, which regulates the smooth muscles that control the blood vessels and the visceral organs, such as the heart, liver, lungs, and intestines, is more highly aroused during REM periods than at other times during sleep. Smooth muscles are not easily controlled voluntarily and therefore function almost automatically. The autonomic nervous system also controls the *endocrine* (ductless) glands, such as the thyroid, adrenals, and pituitary gland. One division of the autonomic nervous system, the *sympathetic nervous system*, tends to be most active during aroused organismic states (for example, during emotion). The other major division of the autonomic nervous system, the *parasympathetic nervous system*, tends to be most active when the organism is quiescent.

Subjects are also relatively insensitive to external stimulation during periods of rapid eye movements. The EEG record is likely to show signs of wakefulness, despite the fact that this is the stage from which awakened subjects are likely to report that they were sleeping deeply.

An hypothesis. It is possible to make sense of this array of correlated findings if REM periods are associated with periods of intense dreaming. A dream is a period of absorbing thought and is usually rather exciting to the dreamer. Insensitivity to external stimulation and the report of deep sleep may therefore be explained as resistance to interruption of thought processes. Activation of the autonomic nervous system (especially the sympathetic branch) may be explained as a reaction to the excitement of the dream. The wakeful EEG record may reflect the active nature of psychological processes during the dream.

The whole picture can be neatly related to Freud's earliest ideas about the function of the dream. We have already mentioned Freud's concept that ideas and fantasies that are too dangerous, frightening, or shameful to be experienced during the day press toward conscious awareness during sleep. If these were experienced directly, they would be so arousing that the person would wake up. Consequently, by distorting these ideas and fantasies, the dream keeps intolerable impulses under control and preserves sleep. (In Freudian theory, a nightmare is a dream that has been unsuccessful. The sleeper awakens because his thoughts have become so dangerous that conscious defenses must be brought into play to keep them under control.)

These are intriguing hypotheses, and it is tempting to conclude that modern research has proven Freudian theory. But there are still a great many questions to be answered, the most important of which is whether or not REM periods actually do represent dreams.

Rapid Eye Movements and Dreams

The fact that a subject reports a dream when awakened does not necessarily mean that he was actually having that dream at the time of his awakening. At least two other possibilities exist for explaining the correlation between awakening during periods of rapid eye movements and reports of dream experiences.

		REM		NREM	
		Dream Recall	No Recall	Dream Recall	No Recall
Random Schedule	PM	24	6	2	23
	KC	36	4	3	31
Patterned awakenings	DN	17	9	3	21
Instruction with random schedule	WD	37	5	1	34
Experimenter whim	IR	26	8	2	29

Table 7.1. *Dream Recall after Awakenings from REM and NREM Periods during Sleep (Adapated from Dement and Kleitman, 1957b)*

The First Possibility: Experimenter Influence

It is possible that the subject does not dream at all, but merely makes up a story that sounds like a dream. For the sake of argument, assume that people are capable of fabricating stories comparable to dream reports when they are awakened from sleep. It is still necessary to explain why a subject would make up a story instead of reporting his actual experience, and why subjects are more inclined to make up dreamlike stories when awakened from sleep with rapid eye movements than from sleep without rapid eye movements. The first explanation is easily found. Rosenthal (1966) and others (for example, Orne, 1962) have shown that subjects often produce the responses the experimenter wants. It may be that subjects in dream research produce stories only to please the examiner.

It is possible that the investigator delivers some sort of cue or hint at appropriate awakenings. Perhaps on some awakenings he says, "What were you dreaming that time?" while on others he says, "You weren't dreaming just then, were you?" Or perhaps a subtle facial expression or mannerism tells the subject: "This time I want a story from you," or "This time I'd prefer that you not report anything."

The first possibility can be tested by setting up an experiment involving no direct contact between experimenter and subject. If the experimenter is not present in the room while the subject is sleeping and does not communicate with him, the subject has no way of knowing whether or not he is expected to produce a dream on a particular awakening. If he is merely fabricating stories, it is extremely unlikely that this will take place only when he is awakened from periods of rapid eye movement sleep, for he will not know which awakenings are which.

Dement and Kleitman (1957b) tried this procedure on five subjects who were awakened by a doorbell rung by an investigator observing EEG and EOG records in another room. When awakened, the subjects spoke into a recording device near the bed, stating first whether they had just been dreaming and then relating the content of their dreams.

Two of the subjects (PM and KC in Table 7.1) were awakened in randomly determined REM and nonREM (NREM) periods. A third subject (DN) was awakened first in three REM periods, then in three NREM periods, and so on. He was not told what this pattern of awakenings would be. This procedure was included to

Subject	15 Minutes		15 Minutes	
	Right	Wrong	Right	Wrong
PM	6	2	8	3
KC	7	0	12	1
DN	8	2	5	5
WD	13	1	15	1
IR	11	1	7	3

Table 7.2. *Estimates of Dream Duration after 5 and 15 Minutes of REM (Adapted from Dement and Kleitman, 1957b)*

determine whether a subject can learn when to produce stories even without the presence of the experimenter. Subject WD was told he would be awakened *only* when he was expected to be dreaming; however, he was actually awakened on a random schedule of REM and NREM periods. Finally, subject IR was awakened according to the whim of the experimenter.

Table 7.1 shows that all subjects produced more dream reports when awakened during periods of rapid eye movements than when awakened from periods of ocular quiescence. The data speak against the notion that subjects either produced dream reports on command or learned from their own experiences how to distinguish REM from NREM periods (subject DN was no more accurate than the others, even with a pattern that he might have learned). The figures support the assertion that reports of dreams are closely associated with rapid eye movements during sleep.

The Second Possibility: Reports of Earlier Dreams

Granted the likelihood that subjects report real dreams when awakened from REM sleep, it is still possible that they are not reporting dreams actually taking place at the time they are awakened. Perhaps the physiological process associated with rapid eye movements activates a subject's memory so that he does not report a dream he has just experienced, but one he had minutes, hours, or even days before. Is there any way to prove conclusively that a dream report represents a mental event that has just taken place and not the memory of an event of some earlier time? Probably not; but it is possible to amass some rather convincing circumstantial evidence.

Dream duration. In the study reported above, Dement and Kleitman (1957b) obtained evidence relating subjects' estimates of the durations of their dreams with the actual length of eye movement periods before awakening. The investigators reasoned that, if dreams and eye movements are concurrent, subjects' estimates of dream duration and objective measures of REM duration should be closely correlated.

The subjects, awakened either 5 minutes or 15 minutes after rapid eye movements began, were asked to decide, on the basis of their recall of the dream, which duration, the shorter or longer, was correct. If "real time" and "dream time" are similar, their decisions should be accurate most of the time; if they are only guessing, only about one-half of their judgments should be accurate. The data (Table 7.2)

		Dream Content	
		Active	Passive
Eye movements	Active	42	16
	Passive	8	23

Table 7.3. *Relationship between Ratings of Dream Content and Eye Movement Records* (*Data from Berger and Oswald, 1962*)

show that subjects were generally able to choose the correct duration. One person, DN, was wrong as often as he was right in judging the longer time interval; that is, he often judged 15 minutes to be 5 minutes. The investigators interpreted this to mean that DN's dreams in these instances were actually long, but he forgot the early portions and therefore underestimated the amount of time they occupied. Even if DN is regarded as a contrary case, his judgments of shorter time periods are quite satisfactory, so that the evidence is strongly in favor of the experimental hypothesis.

Intensity and direction of eye movements. Dement and Kleitman (1957b) also correlated the intensity and direction of eye movements with reported dream content. Subjects were awakened when a specific pattern of eye movement persisted for at least one minute, and were then asked to describe in detail the dream content just before awakening. In general, vertical eye movements were associated with dream action in the vertical plane. Only one instance of pure horizontal movement was observed; this was associated with a dream of two people throwing tomatoes at each other. When their eyes were relatively quiet, subjects reported watching something at a distance or staring fixedly at some object. When mixtures of movements occurred, subjects reported looking at objects or people close to them. A check of the eye movements of awake subjects observing distant and close objects established to the investigators' satisfaction that the patterns were the same as those observed during sleep.

In another study, Berger and Oswald (1962) awakened eight volunteer subjects from REM sleep 103 times during 37 nights. Their procedure produced 89 instances of dream recall. Berger awakened the subjects; Oswald did not see the EEG or eye movement records and was not present when the dream reports were obtained. Oswald first classified the dream reports as active or passive. He then examined and classified the eye movement records which had been obtained prior to awakening without knowing which dreams went with which set of eye movements. The two sets of classifications were then compared, with the results shown in Table 7.3. Statistical evaluation of these data showed a significant correlation between dream content and eye movements.

Eye movement and dream patterns. In a more elaborate study, Roffwarg, Dement, Muzio, and Fisher (1962) investigated the relationship of dream imagery to eye movement characteristics. Twelve subjects (four women and eight men) slept a total of 38 subject nights in the laboratory and reported 121 dreams. Subjects were awakened by one investigator, who sat in another room and sounded a loud

Correspondence	Clarity Rating High	Moderate	Low (vague, fuzzy)
Good	78	71	58
Fair	11	16	16
Poor	11	13	26

Table 7.4. *Percentage of Correspondences between Actual and Predicted Eye Movements Rated Good, Fair, and Poor (Data from Roffwarg et al. 1962)* Note: *Table entries are medians to nearest whole percentages, for two judges.*

buzzer near the subject's head when a distinctive pattern of eye movements appeared on the electrooculogram. As soon as the buzzer sounded, a second investigator (who was seated in a third room and could not see the EEG and EOG records) entered the subject's room and questioned him about the contents of his dream. This investigator also obtained the subject's rating of the clarity of his own recollection of the dream.

The second investigator translated the dream records into a predicted series of eye movements. Eye movement records were then compared with these predictions, and the results rated by two judges as *good, fair,* or *poor.* Table 7.4 shows that both judges saw most matches as *good.* As might be expected, the percentage of *good* matches is highest for dreams that are well recalled by subjects and lowest for dreams that are not clearly recalled. Poor correspondence was found for about 26 per cent of vaguely described dreams, but good correspondence was found for about 78 per cent of the clearly recalled dreams. Even vaguely described dreams achieved a good match with predicted eye movements over one-half the time (58 per cent). Examples of records from a passive and an active dream are shown in Figure 7.6.

Dreams of the blind. Evidence regarding the correspondence between eye movements and dream contents might also come from studies of the blind. Sighted persons might be expected to follow dream processes with their eyes because dreams are strongly visual, and people are accustomed to using their eyes to examine visual events. However, people who have been blind for a long period of time do not use their eyes in this way; many of them report that their dreams are nonvisual in content. If rapid eye movements serve only the purpose of following dream activities, such movements should not be found in the records of persons who have been without sight for a good many years.

Berger, Olley, and Oswald (1962) submitted eight blind subjects to the usual experimental procedures. All the subjects could move their eyes voluntarily, and all reported having dreams during the investigations. However, rapid eye movements were present during dream periods only for those subjects who had been blind for less than 15 years.

These results seem consistent with the hypothesis that eye movements are related to visual dream contents. Berger and his coworkers realized, however, that lack of eye movement in the long-term blind might be due to the underdevelopment or degeneration through disuse of the nerve pathways that control voluntary move-

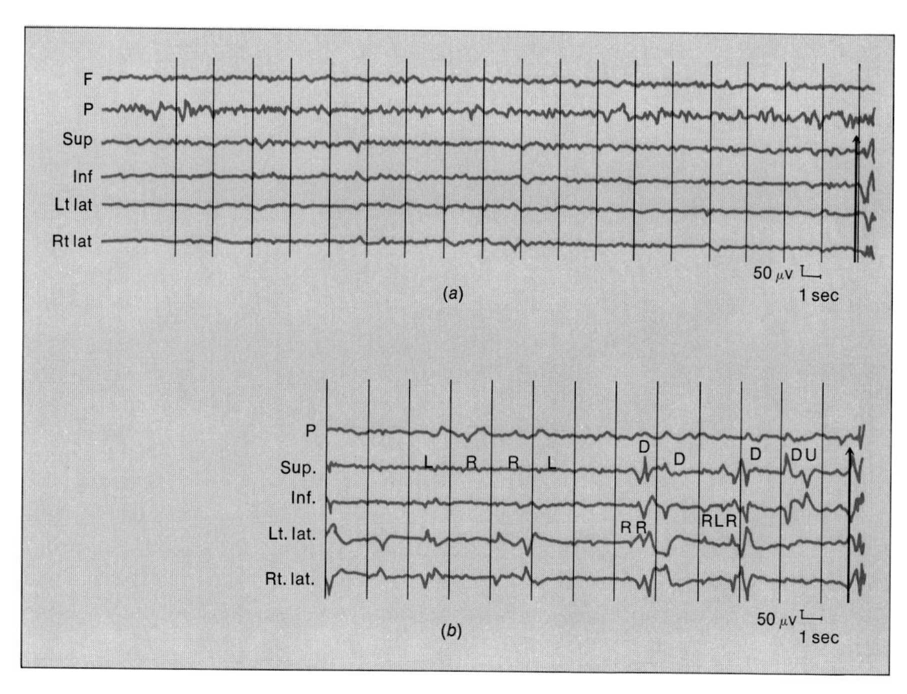

Fig. 7.6. (a) An a.c. electrooculogram of the last 40 seconds prior to an awakening. Electrode positions: *F*, frontal (EEG); *P*, parietal (EEG); *Sup.*, supraorbital; *Inf.*, infraorbital; *Lt. Lat.*, left lateral canthus; *Rt. Lat.*, right lateral canthus. The buzzer was actually sounded several seconds earlier than shown by the arrow in the record. The *P* lead shows a stage 1 sleep record. This example illustrates the finding of long stretches of REM quiescence during stage 1 sleep. When quiescence occurs after gross body movements, subjects frequently do not recall dreaming. In most other cases the subject reports visual imagery appropriate to REM quiescence. In this case, the dreamer intently watched two men holding a conversation. 7.5(b) An a.c. electrooculogram of the last 25 seconds prior to awakening (arrow). Note the variations in sequence, direction, and timing of the REMs. A diagonal deflection of the eyeballs results in a recording of concurrent vertical and horizontal deflections. The first ten seconds of the record showing to-and-fro horizontal deflections was correlated with the subject's account of being a spectator at a football game, looking at the opposite stands from one end to the other and back. He then looked down to his right to watch a cheerleader climb up into the stands in which he sat. The *P* lead shows a stage 1 sleep record. (From Roffwarg *et al.*, 1962)

ments of the eyes. That supposition would imply that eye movements might occur in the long-term blind if these pathways were adequate to the task of producing them.

Gross, Byrne, and Fisher (1965) reasoned that eye movements might appear in the records of subjects with lifelong blindness if a more direct method of measurement were used. They attached small ceramic strain gauges to the subjects' eyelids (Fig. 7.7). As these gauges flex, their electrical resistance changes in proportion to the amount of flexion. Changes in resistance are detected, amplified, and recorded on moving paper tape. The eyeball is not perfectly round; there is a bulge at the cornea. As the eyeball moves in its socket, the bulge flexes the gauge and produces a reading on the recording instrument.

Five subjects with lifelong blindness were examined with this apparatus as

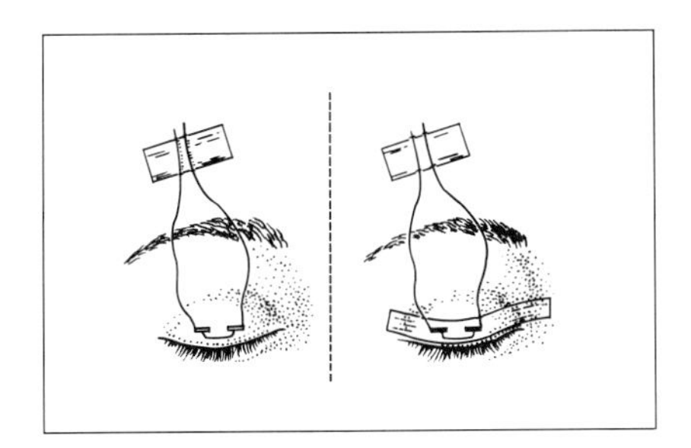

Fig. 7.7. Schema showing placement of ceramic strain gauge on the eyelid. For maximum sensitivity the center of the strain gauge overlies the medial slope of the corneal bulge: the exposed element faces outward and is given a thin coating of petroleum jelly to prevent adherence to the overlying transparent plastic tape. (From Gross *et al*, 1965)

well as with customary EOG recording instruments. When eye movements were measured with the ceramic strain gauge, all five showed rapid eye movements in stage 1 ascending sleep. Two subjects showed no EOG deflections; the other three showed deflections considerably smaller than what was recorded with the strain gauge.

These findings establish that eye movements occur even in persons who do not use their eyes for visual contact with the environment and do not experience visual dreams. The experiment confirms the notion that REMs are a universal phenomenon in sleep, whether or not visual dreaming occurs. It does not disprove the hypothesis that the eye movements of normal subjects actually scan the dream scene. It is quite possible that REMs, which are present at birth but have no initial psychological significance, are taken over and utilized for scanning as visual dreaming develops in sighted persons.

Some Additional Hypotheses

Evidence of the type described above has convinced several authorities that recorded eye movements actually result from the attempts of the dreaming subject to follow the action of his dream with his eyes. This idea was proposed by G.T. Ladd as long ago as 1892, long before modern techniques for measuring physiological functioning were invented.

If eye movements represent the type and direction of visual activity in a dream, it is possible that measures of other body functions will reflect other aspects of dream contents. Dement and Wolpert (1958) observed that the incidence of gross body movements is lower during periods of rapid eye movements than during periods just before and just after rapid eye movements. This observation suggests that body immobility results from the sleeper's thoughtful absorption in his ongoing dream. If this is so, it might be that a sudden burst of body activity during rapid eye movement sleep indicates that the dream is changing. It should follow that long, continuous dreams are accompanied by a generally low level of body activity, while a succession of brief dream episodes would be accompanied by a generally high level of body activity.

Body movements. To test this hypothesis, Dement and Wolpert (1958) collected 204 descriptions of dreams from 16 subjects and analyzed them in several

Dream Reports	Body Movements Present	Body Movements Absent
Fragmented	21	14
Continuous	10	32

Table 7.5 *Association of Body Movements with Continuous and Fragmented Dream Reports (Adapted from Dement and Wolpert, 1958)*

ways. First they selected 46 long and continuous dreams and 31 dreams that contained two or more unrelated fragments. Their purpose was to discover whether gross body movements of the sleeper signal changes in dream activity. The results (Table 7.5) showed that, in general, fragmented dreams were associated with body movements during sleep, while continuous dreams were associated with the absence of body movements. Although the correlation is far from perfect, it is clear that body movements were absent most often when subjects reported long, continuous dreams (32 times), and present most often when subjects reported fragmented, episodic dreams (21 times).

Effects of stimulation. The study just described provided the investigators with the opportunity to test some additional interesting hypotheses. It has often been said that dreams incorporate environmental stimuli, such as the sound of the alarm clock or of a passing automobile. It has also been claimed that dreams are influenced by the state of need of the dreamer; the hungry man dreams of food, the thirsty person dreams of water.

To evaluate these possibilities, Dement and Wolpert (1958) studied the effects of external and internal stimulation on dream contents. For external stimuli they used a 1,000 cycle tone, a flashing 100 watt bulb, and a spray of cold water ejected from a hypodermic syringe. They attempted to introduce the stimuli while the subject was dreaming, and tried not to awaken the subject (although they often did, especially with the cold water). Examination of dream reports indicated that, generally speaking, these stimuli were not effective in modifying dream contents.

To produce internal stimulation, several subjects were asked to restrict their intake of fluids for 24 hours before sleeping, and their dreams were studied for evidence of themes reflecting thirst. Again there was little evidence of influence on the content of the dreams reported. Dement and Wolpert (1958) commented, however, that their findings were not totally negative on this point; some dreams did seem to incorporate external and internal stimuli.

Early investigators (Calkins, 1893; Weed and Hallam, 1896) reported that less than 10 per cent of dreams they had collected showed evidence of influence by external stimuli. It is therefore entirely possible that external and internal stimulation do influence a small percentage of dreams, but popular opinion typically overestimates the degree and extent of these effects, since people remember these dreams better and are more strongly impressed by them.

Incidentally, Dement and Wolpert also used their study to reexamine the relationship between rapidity of eye movements and the degree of activity described in dream reports. Like Berger and Oswald, they found a significant correlation between the two.

More studies of stimulation. Foulkes and Rechtschaffen (1964) attempted to influence dream content by showing subjects films with either aggressive or unaggressive scenes before they went to sleep. Dreams reported during REM sleep were longer, more vivid, more imaginative, and more emotional following the aggressive than the unaggressive film, but direct incorporation of the content of either film was infrequent.

In a more impressive study, Rechtschaffen and Foulkes (1965) tried to influence dream contents by introducing visual stimuli directly on the retina. Three young adult subjects slept with their eyes taped open (not everyone can do this, but a surprising number of people can). Each subject slept for one and one-half hours with his eyes open (a vaporizer provided necessary moisture for the eyes) and one hour with his eyes closed, a sequence repeated throughout the night. During both REM and NREM sleep, stimuli of various types were presented before subjects' eyes (for example, a 6 × 9 inch card with a large black X on it; a waving white handkerchief). Each subject was awakened within ten seconds after stimulus presentation and asked what, if anything, was going on in his mind.

Apparently, sleeping subjects are functionally blind, for they reported no direct, undistorted perceptions of the stimuli. In addition, processes taking place on the retina apparently play no part in the dreaming process. If they did, one would certainly expect the retinal stimulation in this experiment to have some influence on the subjects' reports.

REMs as Dream Indicators

The evidence does not lend credence to the idea that subjects merely produce dreamlike stories to please the investigator. Even if the experimenter is not present to provide cues, subjects regularly report dreams when awakened from REM sleep; they report dreams far less frequently when awakened from NREM sleep. Duration of eye movements is consistent with the duration of dreams reported. The recorded direction of eye movements is closely associated with the actions described in dream reports. Active dreams are associated with vigorous eye movements, while passive dreams are associated with less vigorous activity of the eyes. In short, there appear to be consistent and reasonable relationships between what happens in dreams and the way the eyes move. These and related findings discredit the notion that dream reports obtained from REM sleep are memories of previous dreams, stories made up on the spot, or responses to external stimuli (Rechtschaffen, 1967).

REM Deprivation

An important point in Freud's theory was that dreams are necessary for the psychological well-being of the person. Psychoanalytic theorists liken the dream to the psychotic (bizarre and disorganized) conscious thought processes of the schizophrenic (a person so seriously disturbed psychologically as to have difficulty distinguishing clearly between fantasy and reality). (See Chap. 15.) They feel that the dream psychosis of sleep balances the emphasis on rational thinking that characterizes conscious waking life. Dreams restore psychological equilibrium by permitting limited expression of unconscious impulses.

These ideas would gain support if it could be shown that subjects deprived of the opportunity to dream exhibit disturbances of behavior that they do not exhibit under other circumstances. The first controlled study to test the hypothesis that behavior disruption follows deprivation of the opportunity to dream seemed to provide confirming evidence.

Dement (1960) had eight young men sleep through a series of consecutive nights in the laboratory. The first few nights consisted of undisturbed sleep during which the investigator simply took records of each subject's sleeping pattern and dreaming time (REM time). In the second phase of the research, subjects were "deprived" of the opportunity to dream for from three to seven nights. Every time the EEG and EOG records indicated that a subject had begun to dream he was awakened and required to sit up for a few minutes. Next were several "recovery" nights, during which subjects were again allowed to sleep without interruption. After a few days off, the subjects returned to the laboratory and underwent another series of awakenings for several consecutive nights. This time, however, they were awakened only during intervals between dream periods. Finally, the subjects underwent another recovery period of several nights' duration.

Dement noted first that, as dream deprivation progressed, the number of attempts to dream (REM periods) steadily increased; the number of awakenings necessary to prevent dreaming went up markedly. One subject quit the study altogether after three nights. Two subjects stopped after four nights of deprivation, although they later returned and completed the rest of the experiment. Some subjects showed anxiety, irritability, and difficulty in concentrating; one subject was seriously agitated. Five developed marked increases in appetite during the period of dream deprivation. During the recovery period of uninterrupted sleep, total dream time increased markedly in five of seven subjects.

In the next phase of the experiment, each subject was awakened the same number of times as he had been during dream deprivation, but only during nondream periods. None of the effects of dream deprivation were observed to result from this procedure.

This research seems to establish a genuine "need to dream" which, if frustrated, becomes more intense and disruptive of organized behavior. Before drawing that conclusion, however, consider the difficulty noted by Foulkes (1966) and by Dement (1965). When a subject is awakened from REM periods, he is deprived not only of the dream he may be having but of a particular kind of sleep (stage 1 ascending) which his body may need for purely physiological reasons. Noting experiments conducted by M. Jouvet, Foulkes pointed out that dream deprivation phenomena have been observed in cats as well as in human beings. Since there is no obvious reason why cats should have a psychological need to dream, serious doubt is cast on the validity of the purely psychological hypothesis.

Pivik and Foulkes (1966) studied reports of mental experiences following periods of dream deprivation and periods of successive awakenings from NREM sleep. The reports were rated for their dreamlike quality. For some subjects, late night dream reports were more dreamlike and REM frequency was greater following earlier REM deprivation than were late night reports and REM frequencies following earlier deprivation of NREM sleep. The authors felt that their findings supported the theory that dreams perform a necessary function, since loss of the opportunity to dream early in the night produced compensatory dreaming later on. Unfortunately, later research, using slightly different procedures, failed to confirm this finding fully (Foulkes, Pivik, Ahrens, and Swanson, 1968). Subjects' dreams on the nights after REM deprivation were not more intense; compensation in the form of progressively increasing periods of rapid eye movements did not appear significant; and subjects' waking behavior was not markedly affected. To the question "Does REM sleep deprivation constitute genuine dream deprivation?" the investigators changed their answer from its earlier tentative "yes" to an equally tentative "no."

Cartwright and Monroe (1968) varied the theme of deprivation research by asking subjects awakened from REM periods to do one of two things: report the content of their dreams or repeat lists of digits forward and backward. These investigators found that when subjects reported their dreams during awakenings, compensation (later increase in REM time) was less pronounced than when they repeated lists of digits. The investigators interpreted these results to imply that the repeating of digits counteracts the experience of fantasy by focusing attention on outside events. Since fantasy is interrupted, compensation is necessary. However, when a subject (by describing his dreams) is allowed to continue his fantasies while awake, compensation later in the night is not needed. If dream deprivation is not too great, and some allowance is made for continuing the fantasy experience, it appears that the person can make up for his loss by fantasizing in other states of sleep or while awake.

Complicating Factors

Research on REM deprivation has yet to yield conclusive findings regarding the psychological need to dream. The problem is too complex to support hope for a quick solution. One of its complexities has already been mentioned: the difficulty of determining whether observed effects are due to physiological deprivation of a particular stage of sleep or to a deprivation of the psychological functions of dreaming.

After reviewing a large body of evidence on the subject, Hartmann (1967) concluded that humans and other animals definitely require what he calls *D-state sleep* (REM sleep). Hartmann qualified his conclusion, however, by noting that subjects require other kinds of sleep as well, and will show deprivation effects when deprived of these. Hartmann further commented that establishment of a biological need for REM sleep does not answer the psychological question about the need for dreaming in itself.

Another complicating factor is *individual differences.* Some research suggests that deprivation of REM sleep has more profound effects on some subjects than on others (Cartwright, Monroe, and Palmer, 1967). In that case, it would obviously be impossible to make any generally applicable statement about the need to dream, since some people may not need to dream as much as others. While research has rather clearly established that virtually everyone dreams at least some of the time, data from nearly all the studies show that there are people who report relatively few dreams. A study by Lewis, Goodenough, Shapiro, and Sleser (1966) confirms that people who claim to be nondreamers reported fewer dreams following REM awakenings than did people who claimed that they dream frequently.

Still another problem arises from the equation: REM = dream. While it is evident that dreaming almost always accompanies periods of rapid eye movements, it is by no means certain either that dreams occur *only* during REM periods or that other forms of mental activity *do not* occur when the eyes are quiescent. There is good evidence that dreams do occur during NREM sleep, and that mental activity of some sort is continuous throughout the night.

NREM Dreams

Foulkes (1966) summarized a study by Kamiya in which 404 awakenings of subjects from sleep without rapid eye movements produced 46 per cent dream recall, a figure higher than that reported by others. Foulkes himself (1960) found 74 per cent dream recall during NREM sleep, a figure a *great deal* higher than those reported by others. (Both investigators also found over 85 per cent dream recall during REM sleep, so their findings do not challenge others in this respect.) The main reason for the discrepancies is that earlier investigators were very strict about the type of report they would accept as indicative of *dreaming*. Later investigators accepted reports of virtually all mental activities as evidence of dreaming.

Foulkes (1962) directed his attention to determining whether mental activities reported when subjects were awakened from sleep without rapid eye movements differed in any important way from mental activities reported following REM awakenings. He found that the reports of subjects awakened from NREM sleep involved less emotion, less visual and physical activity, fewer scenes and characters, less distortion of real events, and a closer relationship to recent real events, thoughts, or situations in the subject's life. For example, one subject thought of something he had learned in class, while another was thinking about a telephone call he had received earlier that night. Other studies (Foulkes and Rechtschaffen, 1964; Goodenough, Shapiro, Holden, and Steinschriber, 1959; Monroe, Rechtschaffen, Foulkes, and Jensen, 1965; Pivik and Foulkes, 1968; Wolpert, 1960; Rechtschaffen, Verdone, and Wheaton, 1963) have confirmed these differences.

Foulkes and Vogel (1965) also studied mental activities that take place at the onset of sleep, during the "resting" period of wakefulness and the descending phase of stage 1. Subjects reported a variety of thoughts and images, many of which were highly dreamlike in quality, but most of which were not strongly emotional in feeling or tone.

Coordinated muscular activities, such as sleepwalking and talking in one's sleep, are not easy to study because they do not occur very frequently. It has been found, however, that sleepwalking and sleeptalking occur predominantly when the eyes are quiet (Rechtschaffen, Goodenough, and Shapiro, 1962; Jacobson, Kales, Lehman, and Zweizig, 1965).

All stages of sleep appear to be associated with some form of psychological activity. Not all this activity is as striking, interesting, or personally revealing as REM dreams, but its presence provides convincing evidence that psychological processes are continuous, even when we are asleep and unaware of their operation.

Eye Movements and Conscious Mental Activity

If eye movements reflect mental activities that occur when subjects are not conscious, it is also possible that they reflect people's thoughts while they are awake. The eyes move when a person looks at objects in the environment, and a host of psychological researchers are devoted to the study of eye movements in visual perception (see Grunin and Mostofsky, 1968, for a bibliography). Since our interest here is not the process of perception but the process of thought, this discussion considers only studies in which the subject is instructed to engage in a certain type of thinking while the experimenter examines movements of his eyes for evidence of the process in which he is engaging.

Antrobus, Antrobus, and Singer (1964) studied the relationship among eye movements, daydreaming, visual imagery, and thought suppression. Their subjects were 24 women college students. Each subject lay on a bed and was instructed to perform mental activities. She was not told that the study concerned eye movements, but was informed that it was research on thinking and was led to believe that all the electrodes measured "brain waves."

First she was asked "to choose an important, secret wish and to freely indulge in the realization of this desire." She was assured that she would not have to reveal the actual wish she chose. Next, she was asked to engage in the same wish and then try to put it out of her mind, in other words, to suppress the wish. Each wish and each suppression period lasted one minute. The wish–suppression sequence was repeated three times for every subject. The subjects were asked to perform other mental tasks later. But first, what happened during the wish-suppression periods?

While subjects were engaging in the realization of a secret wish, the total number of seconds during which eye movements occurred averaged 37.8 per subject. (Since there were three periods of 60 seconds each, the total possible score is $3 \times 60 = 180$ seconds of ocular activity.) However, when the subjects were asked to suppress this wish, the average rose to 60 seconds of eye movements per subject. The same findings were apparent in the data on number of eye blinks, but the difference between the wish and suppression periods was not so great (average per subject when wishing = 43.1, when suppressing = 50.3). It was evident that greater activity of the eyes was associated with the effort to suppress a secret wish. What the investigators think this means will become clearer when the rest of the experiment is examined more closely.

Each subject was also asked to engage in three one minute periods of *relaxed thinking* and three one minute periods of *active thinking.* During the relaxed periods they were instructed to let their thoughts drift lazily or, if possible, to let their minds go blank. During the active periods they were told to "make their thoughts race as fast as possible, e.g., to think of as many solutions as possible to a simple everyday problem."

The total number of seconds during which eye movements occurred in the active periods averaged 51.6; during the relaxed periods the average per subject was 41.8. The eyeblink data were somewhat more impressive. During the active periods there was an average of 72.7 blinks per subject, while the average was only 38.7 during the relaxed periods.

Finally, subjects were asked to imagine specific scenes. Some of the scenes involved *motion*, such as a tennis match observed from the net, trampoline jumping, or a busy traffic intersection. The rest were *static*, such as an orange on a table in a dark empty room or a mountain on a distant horizon. Each scene was imagined twice, once with the eyes open and once with the eyes closed. The average number of seconds during which eye movements occurred under each of the various conditions of this part of the experiment is shown in Table 7.6.

The top row of the table compares eye movement scores for moving and static scenes with eyes open; the bottom row compares eye movement scores for moving and static scenes with eyes closed. In both comparisons, imagining a moving scene produced higher movement scores than imagining a scene with no motion. The vertical column on the left compares eye movement scores with eyes open to eye movement scores with eyes closed when a scene with motion is imagined. The column on the right makes the same comparison for an imagined scene without

	Motion	Static
Eyes Open	63.9	33.6
Eyes Closed	92.4	67.2

Table 7.6 *Eye Movements while Imagining Motion and a Static Scene for Three Minutes Each (Adapted from Antrobus, Antrobus, and Singer, 1964)*

motion. In both comparisons, the scores are higher when the eyes are closed than when they are open.

The average number of blinks under each of the conditions of this part of the experiment is shown in Table 7.7. Eyeblinks were more frequent when the imagined scene involved movement than when it was static. Eyeblinks also occurred more frequently when the instructions were to keep the eyes open than when the instructions were to keep them closed. (In this study, blinks were defined by EOG criteria. A blink with the eyes closed consisted of a rapid vertical eye movement and increased pressure between the upper and lower lids.)

In summary, rapid eye movements and a relatively high number of eyeblinks were found to be associated with the following experimental conditions:

1. Wish suppression.
2. Active thinking.
3. Imagining moving scenes.

The results of the experiment therefore suggest that eye movements and blinks provide a way to measure how rapidly a person's thoughts are changing. This suggestion is prompted because all three conditions are situations in which the subject was required to alter her thinking in some way. She was asked first to change from fulfilling a wish to suppressing it, next to think of many solutions to a problem, and finally imagine scenes which contained movement.

Singer and Antrobus (1965) felt the study described above to be deficient in that it permitted subjects full view of the environment. A subject might respond to instructions to suppress a thought not with mental activity but by diverting his attention to objects around him in space. To determine whether eye movements associated with thought suppression are reactions to purely internal processes, it is necessary to eliminate environmental perception. Asking subjects to close their eyes proved unsatisfactory, because some subjects display an interfering ocular tremor under this condition. The experimenters therefore employed a highly sophisticated piece of research equipment, a ping-pong ball. When cut in half and mounted on an elastic strap, the hemispheres of the ping-pong ball provide translucent eye pieces which permit the subject to see light but not external objects.

In the *imagine* condition, subjects with and without eyepieces in place were to think about a person. Sometimes they were asked to choose a person they liked; at other times they chose a person they disliked; at still other times they chose someone about whom they had no strong feelings. In the *suppress* condition, subjects were told to keep their thoughts off the person they chose.

The investigators reasoned that, if increases in eye movements were due

	Motion	Static
Eyes Open	44.4	28.5
Eyes Closed	27.6	16.2

Table 7.7 *Eye Blinks while Imagining Motion and a Static Scene for Three Minutes Each (From Antrobus, Antrobus, and Singer, 1964)*

to attentiveness to external stimuli, the increases would not occur when the subject's eyes were covered, since no external stimuli would be visible. What the investigators found was that eye movements were significantly more frequent when subjects were asked to suppress their thoughts, whether their eyes were covered or uncovered. Whether the person the subject thought of (or suppressed) was emotionally positive, negative, or neutral made no difference to the outcome.

To provide further data about the psychological processes involved, the investigators measured subjects' heart rates. If suppression is an emotional process, the attempt to suppress should activate the sympathetic nervous system and increase heart rate. However, if suppression is a purely *cognitive* activity (involving directed thinking only) heart rate should be unaffected by the effort to suppress. Singer and Antrobus (1965) found that heart rate did increase under instructions to *suppress* when the subjects' eyes were covered. When the eyes were uncovered, however, heart rate *decreased* under instructions to suppress thoughts.

The results therefore suggest the following propositions. First, conscious thought suppression is reflected in increased movements of the eyes. Second, this movement is not simply a perusal of the environment, but is probably a valid reflection of shifts in cognitive processes. Third, looking around at the environment is not a necessary condition for cognitive shifting. Fourth, although sympathetic nervous system arousal occurs when environmental scanning is impossible, such arousal is probably not essential to the process of suppression.

It appears that eye movements are valid indicators of some types of thought processes in subjects who are awake as well as in subjects who are asleep. Eye movements are not measured by most polygraph machines, but it may well be that they will be added in the future. Perhaps there is more to the old saying that the eyes are the windows of the soul than we yet fully realize.

What is a Dream?

People tend to think of their dreams as episodic, mental events that occur while they are asleep. Dreams have generally been regarded as private property, as intensely personal experiences that cannot be publicly observed or objectively measured. Many psychologists feel that private experiences of this sort are not a fit subject for science. Consequently, experimental psychologists have, until recently, spent very little of their time studying dreams.

Research in the 1950s aroused experimental interest mainly because it seemed to provide an objective definition of dreaming. It appeared to many investigators that a dream could now be defined as the appearance of REMs on the electrooculogram of a sleeping subject, a definition much more satisfactory to the experimentalist than one which regards dreams as the private experiences of the dreamer. On the basis of this definition, the study of dreams can be approached as a matter involving manipulation of records of physiological processes rather than something requiring learning about unobservable inner states or thoughts of the dreamer.

Although this approach has advantages, it tends to divert attention from the property of dreams that is most interesting to many psychologists and probably to most laymen as well. Dreams are not just the occasional sputterings of a physiological machine. They have psychological significance above and beyond what is reflected in the tracings of electrically driven pens on paper.

Research of the type described in this chapter has answered many important questions, but it has raised at least as many as it has answered. Although we know now that mental activities go on throughout sleep, we do not know how many different kinds of mental activities take place during sleep, what functions they serve, how they are related to mental processes that occur during the day, or how they influence or are influenced by the personality of the individual dreamer, by his personal modes of adjustment and adaptation.

What is needed is a strategy of research that will enable investigators to study as much of the whole person as possible without losing the value of either physiological or psychological data. Stoyva and Kamiya (1968) directed their attention to this fundamental problem and proposed such a strategy.

Their proposal employs several terms familiar to psychologists. The first is *hypothetical construct*, which might best be called a scientist's educated guess about something that cannot be directly observed. In physics, the atom and all the subatomic particles of so much interest in modern research are hypothetical constructs. In biology, the gene, ultimate carrier of hereditary traits, is a hypothetical construct. Psychology abounds with such hypothetical constructs as *associative bonds, self-concepts, habits,* and *drives.*

A hypothetical construct must be more than just an interesting idea; it must be *indexed.* That is, there must be some observable events regarded as signs of the operation of the construct. For example, expansion of a column of mercury in a thermometer provides an *index* of temperature; temperature is in turn regarded as an index of heat. The score a person achieves when he solves a set of standard problems provides an index of his intelligence. Dreams (or any mental activity, conscious or unconscious) may be regarded as hypothetical constructs which are indexed, albeit imperfectly, by both verbal reports and appropriate physiological measures.

This brings up the matter of *converging operations.* Operations converge when a variety of different measurements all support the same conclusion. Suppose a psychologist defines a dream as an emotionally arousing, visual experience that occurs during sleep. EEG records may be obtained to assess sleep (which is, of course, itself a hypothetical construct). Electrooculograms may be obtained to assess eye movements. Other physiological indicators may be obtained to determine level of emotional arousal. The subject's verbal report may be obtained to confirm whether he was actually experiencing anything at a given time, and the nature of the experience he had. Each of these procedures may be inadequate in itself to provide an index of dreaming, but when *all* outcomes conform to the requirements of the definition, the investigator may reasonably conclude that a genuine dream has taken place.

An example of how converging operations can be used to determine whether animals have visual dreams is cited by Hartmann (1967). Hartmann describes a doctoral dissertation by Vaughn (1964) in which monkeys were trained to press a bar when they saw any kind of visual image in their usually dark rooms. This training provided an index of the presence of visual imagery. Electroencephalographic and electrooculographic recordings were then set up to provide indices of sleep and dreaming, respectively. Vaughn observed that these monkeys often pressed the bar actively during REM sleep. Because different operations led to the same conclusion (converged) in this case, Hartmann decided that "there seems little reason to doubt our common-sense notions that at least some animals are capable of visual dreaming."

As he successively improves his definition and measurements of the construct "dream," the investigator enhances his own conception of the process of dreaming. Furthermore, he becomes better able to distinguish dreams from other forms of activity that take place during the night. As these distinctions become clearer, he is enabled to propose new hypothetical constructs (such as *planful thinking*) and corresponding converging operations by which they may be distinguished from dreams and more fully studied.

More importantly, in the present instance, a construct indexed by both physiological and psychological measures cannot be arbitrarily subdivided into mental and physical components. Identification of a dream as something that occurs only when *both* types of indexes reach minimal values retains the integrity of the dream process as an activity of the whole organism. It makes meaningless such questions as, "Which is more important in dreaming, physiological processes or psychological processes?" As knowledge increases, it becomes more evident that virtually all physiological processes have psychological significance, and that every psychological process has implications for some aspect of bodily functioning. The task of building a science of man that does equal justice to all his components is one of the most challenging in psychology today.

Glossary

Alpha waves: Electroencephalogram (EEG) waves of moderate amplitude, with a frequency of about 10 cps; characteristic of restful wakefulness.

Amplitude: energy intensity, represented graphically (on the EEG) by the extent of pen deflection.

Autonomic nervous system: that portion of the nervous system that regulates most of the internal organs of the body; subdivided into the sympathetic and parasympathetic systems.

Canthus: the corner where the upper and lower eyelids meet on the side of the eye.

Cerebellum: a structure at the base of the brain which regulates muscle coordination, posture, and balance.

Cerebral cortex: the outer layer of nervous tissue that covers the cerebrum.

Cerebrum: the largest segment of the brain, extending above and in front of the cerebellum; covered by the cerebral cortex.

Converging operations: the use of several independent procedures or measures to provide indicators of the presence or operation of a hypothetical construct.

Delta waves: EEG waves of high amplitude and low frequency (1–3 cps); characteristic of stage 4 sleep, but occur to a lesser extent in stage 3 as well.

Electroencephalogram (EEG): a graphic record of the electrical activity of the brain.

Electrooculogram (EOG): a graphic record of eye movements, obtained by amplifying electrical potentials at locations around the eyes.

Galvanic skin response: increase or decrease in electrical resistance of the skin; one of the functions usually measured by a polygraph and often used as an indicator of emotion or stress.

Hypothetical construct: a process or entity that cannot be observed directly but is postulated to account for observed phenomena.

K-Complex: EEG waves of high amplitude but low frequency; appear in stage 2 sleep.

Lobe (brain): a rounded portion of the cerebral cortex, usually marked off by a fissure or sulcus. The main lobes of the brain are the frontal, temporal, parietal, and occipital.

NREM sleep: periods of sleep (any stage) in which rapid eye movements are absent.

Parasympathetic nervous system: the portion of the autonomic nervous system that regulates internal body functions when the organism is not aroused.

Polygraph: a device for simultaneously measuring several physiological functions. Often erroneously called a "lie detector," the polygraph is sensitive only to physiological changes which often accompany lying.

REM sleep: periods of rapid eye movements that occur in stage 1 ascending sleep.

Reticular activating system: a complex neural organization that regulates the general state of sleep or wakefulness.

Reticular formation: a structure in the brain located near the thalamus; the reticular formation is the relay center for the reticular activating system.

Skin conductance: a measure of galvanic skin response; the reciprocal of electrical resistance.

Sleep spindles: bundles of high frequency EEG waves that become evident in stage 2 sleep.

Stage 1 sleep: the stage of sleep immediately following restful wakefulness (stage 1 descending), or preceding awakening (stage 1 ascending).

Sulcus: a shallow fissure or crevice in the cerebral cortex.

Supraorbital: above the eye.

Sympathetic nervous system: the portion of the autonomic nervous system that is most active in states of arousal, stress, or emotion.

Thalamus: a structure in the brain that relays nerve impulses to specific areas of the cerebral cortex.

Theta waves: EEG waves of low to moderate amplitude and low frequency (4–6 cps); characteristic of stage 1 sleep.

References

Antrobus, J.S., J.S. Antrobus, and J.L. Singer. Eye movements accompanying daydreaming, visual imagery, and thought suppression. *J. abnorm. soc. Psychol.*, 1964, **69,** 244–252.

Aserinsky, E., and N. Kleitman. Regularly occurring periods of eye motility and concomitant phenomena during sleep. *Science*, 1953, **118,** 273–274.

Berger, R.J., and I. Oswald. Eye movements during active and passive dreams. *Science*, 1962, **137,** 601.

———, and P. Olley. The EEG, eye movements and dreams of the blind. *Quart. J. exp. Psychol.*, 1962, **14,** 183–186.

Calkins, M.W. Statistics of dreams. *Amer. J. Psychol.*, 1893, **5,** 311–343.

Cartwright, R.D., and L.J. Monroe. Relation of dreaming and REM sleep: The effects of dream deprivation under two conditions. *J. pers. soc. Psychol.*, 1968, **10,** 69–74.

———, and C. Palmer. Individual differences in response to REM deprivation. *Arch. gen. Psychiat.*, 1967, **16,** 297–303.

Ciba Foundation. *Symposium: The nature of sleep.* Boston: Little, Brown, 1961.

Dement, W. Dream recall and eye movements during sleep in schizophrenics and normals. *J. nerv. ment. Dis.*, 1955, **122,** 263–269.

———. The effect of dream deprivation. *Science*, 1960, **131,** 1705–1707.

———. An essay on dreams. In T.M. Newcomb (Ed.), *New directions in psychology, II.* New York: Holt, Rinehart and Winston, 1965.

———, and N. Kleitman. Cyclic variations in EEG during sleep and their relation to eye movements, body motility, and dreaming. *Electroencephalography and Clinical Neurophysiology,* 1957, **9,** 673–690. (a)

______. The relation of eye movements during sleep to dream activity: An objective method for the study of dreaming. *J. exp. Psychol.*, 1957, **53,** 339–346. (b)

Dement, W., and E.A. Wolpert. The relation of eye movements, body motility, and external stimuli to dream content. *J. exp. Psychol.*, 1958, **55,** 543–553.

Foulkes, D. Dream reports from different stages of sleep. Unpublished doctoral dissertation, University of Chicago, 1960.

______. Dream reports from different stages of sleep. *J. abnorm. soc. Psychol.*, 1962, **65,** 14–25.

______. *The psychology of sleep.* New York: Charles Scribner's Sons, 1966.

______, and A. Kales. Special publication: Abstracts of papers presented to the seventh annual meeting of the Association for the Psychophysiological Study of Sleep. *Psychophysiology,* 1968, **4,** 361–398.

______, and A. Rechtschaffen. Presleep determinants of dream content: The effects of two films. *Perceptual and Motor Skills,* 1964, **19,** 983–1105.

______, and G. Vogel. Mental activity at sleep onset. *J. abnorm. Psychol.*, 1965, **70,** 231–243.

______, T. Pivik, J.B. Ahrens, and E.M. Swanson. Effects of "dream deprivation" on dream content: An attempted crossnight replication. *J. abnorm. Psychol.*, 1968, **73,** 403–415.

Freud, S. *The interpretation of dreams.* New York: Basic Books, 1955.

Goodenough, D.R., A. Shapiro, M. Holden, and L. Steinschriber. A comparison of "dreamers" and "nondreamers": Eye movements, electroencephalograms, and the recall of dreams. *J. abnorm. soc. Psychol.*, 1959, **59,** 295–302.

Gross, J., J. Byrne, and C. Fisher. Eye movements during emergent stage 1 EEG in subjects with lifelong blindness. *J. nerv. ment. Dis.*, 1965, **141,** 365–370.

Grunin, R., and D.I. Mostofsky. Eye movement: A bibliographic survey. *Perceptual and Motor Skills,* 1968, **26,** 623–629.

Hall, C.S. A cognitive theory of dream symbols. *J. gen. Psychol.*, 1953, **48,** 169–186. (a)

______. *The meaning of dreams.* New York: Harper & Row, 1953 (b)

______, and L. Van de Castle. *The content analysis of dreams.* New York: Appleton-Century-Crofts, 1966.

Hartmann, E. *The biology of dreaming.* Springfield, Ill.: Charles C Thomas, 1967.

______, J. Bernstein, and C. Wilson. Sleep and dreaming in the elephant. *Psychophysiology,* 1968, **4,** 389.

Jacobson, A., A. Kales, D. Lehman, and J. Zweizig. Somnambulism: All-night electroencephalographic studies. *Science,* 1965, **148,** 975–977.

Kleitman, N. Sleep. *Scientific Amer.*, 1952, **187,** 34–38.

Ladd, G.T. Contribution to the psychology of visual dreams. *Mind,* 1892, **1,** 299–304.

Lewis, H.B., D.R. Goodenough, A. Shapiro, and I. Sleser. Individual differences in dream recall. *J. abnorm. Psychol.*, 1966, **71,** 52–59.

Monroe, L.J., A. Rechtschaffen, D. Foulkes, and H. Jensen. Discriminability of REM and NREM reports. *J. pers. soc. Psychol.*, 1965, **2,** 456–460.

Moruzzi, G., and H.W. Magoun. Brain stem reticular formation and activation of the EEG. *Electroencephalography and Clinical Neurophysiology,* 1949, **1,** 455–473.

Orne, M.T. On the social psychology of the psychological experiment, with particular reference to demand characteristics and their implications. *Amer. Psychologist,* 1962, **17,** 776–783.

Pivik, T., and D. Foulkes. "Dream deprivation": Effects on dream content. *Science,* 1966, **153,** 1282–1284.

______. NREM mentation: Relation to personality, orientation time, and time of night. *J. consult. clin. Psychol.*, 1968, **32,** 144–151.

Rechtschaffen, A. Dream reports and dream experiences. *Experimental Neurology,* 1967, Supplement 4, 4–15.

______, and D. Foulkes. Effect of visual stimuli on dream content. *Perceptual and Motor Skills,* 1965, **20,** 1149–1160.

Rechtschaffen, A., and A. Kales. (Eds.) *A manual of standardized terminology, techniques and scoring system for sleep stages of human subjects*. Washington, D.C.: Public Health Service, U.S. Government Printing Office, 1968.

Rechtschaffen, A., D.R. Goodenough, and A. Shapiro. Patterns of sleep talking. *Arch. Gen. Psychiat.*, 1962, **7,** 418–426.

Rechtschaffen, A., P. Verdone, and J. Wheaton. Reports of mental activity during sleep. *Canadian Psychiatric Association Journal*, 1963, **8,** 409–414.

Roffwarg, H.P., W. Dement, J. Muzio, and C. Fisher. Dream imagery: Relationship to rapid eye movements of sleep. *Arch. gen. Psychiat.*, 1962, **7,** 235–258.

Rosenthal, R. *Experimenter effects in behavioral research*. New York: Appleton-Century-Crofts, 1966.

Singer, J.L., and J.S. Antrobus. Eye movements during fantasies: Imagining and suppressing fantasies. *Arch. gen. Psychiat.*, 1965, **12,** 71–76.

Stoyva, J., and J. Kamiya. Electrophysiological studies of dreaming as the prototype of a new strategy in the study of consciousness. *Psychol. Rev.*, 1968, **75,** 192–205.

U.S. Department of Health, Education, and Welfare, *Current research on sleep and dreams*. Public Health Service Publication No. 1389, Washington, D.C., 1966.

Van de Castle, R.L. Dream content during pregnancy. *Psychophysiology*, 1968, **4,** 375.

Vaughn, C. The development and use of an operant technique to provide evidence for visual imagery in the rhesus monkey under sensory deprivation. Unpublished doctoral dissertation, University of Pittsburgh, 1964.

Weed, S., and F. Hallam. A study of dream consciousness. *Amer. J. Psychol.*, 1896, **7,** 405–411.

Wolpert, E.A. Studies in psychophysiology of dreams: II. An electromyographic study of dreaming. *Arch. gen. Psychiat.*, 1960, **2,** 231–241.

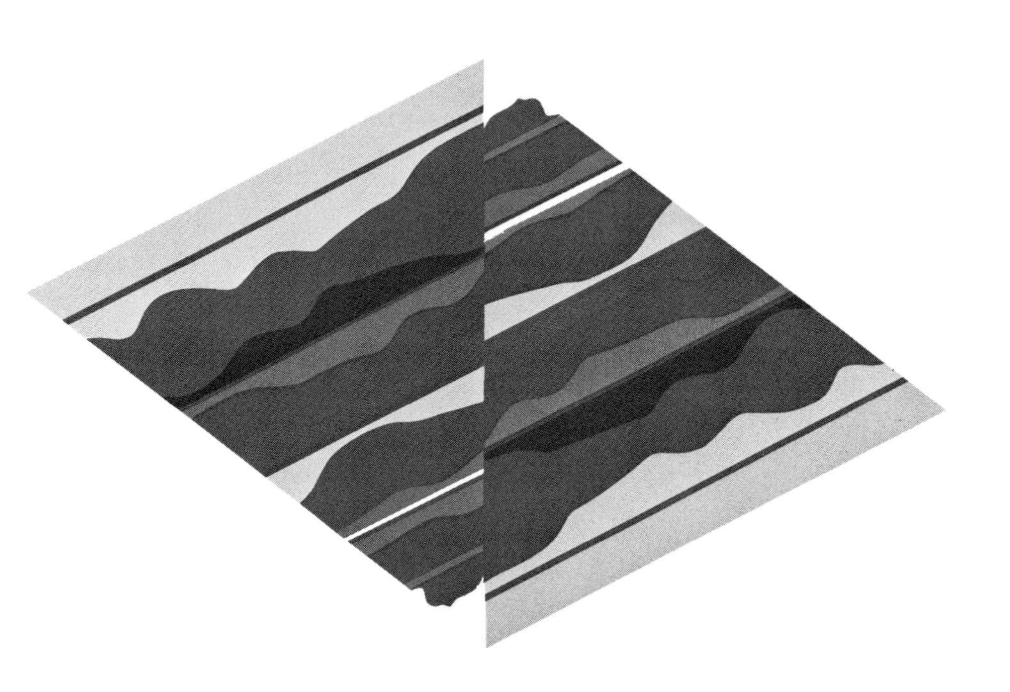

8 Stress: Things Are Not as Simple as They Seem

Science rarely produces simple answers to questions about human behavior. The body of empirical facts grows unceasingly, but psychologists continually find that the objects of their curiosity are more complex than anyone initially supposed they might be.

Events run a fairly typical course. An investigator publishes an exciting theoretical idea which promises to explain, by a revolutionary new concept, hosts of important phenomena. Other investigators become interested and begin collecting evidence on the subject. Someone eventually publishes a review of the now extensive literature and points out that much of the research is unclear; some evidence supports the theory and some does not; the whole problem is very complicated and needs to be reexamined in the light of new questions and hypotheses. The review usually contains a plea for more and better research, along with a warning that conclusions should not be drawn too hastily.

No better example exists of the progressive complication of the subject matter of psychology than the concept of *stress*. At first it seemed that this concept would tie together vast amounts of data from physiology and psychology. Stress was invoked "as a substitute for what might otherwise have been called anxiety, conflict, emotional distress, extreme environmental conditions, ego-threat, frustration, threat to security, tension, arousal, or by some other previously respectable terms" (Appley and Trumbull, 1967, p. 1). The term "stress" has been used to describe stimuli that are new, intense, rapidly changing, sudden, unexpected, persistent, conflict producing, boring, deficient, frightening, ambiguous, and absent. It has been applied to nearly all types of emotional or deviant responses and has been measured by outputs of the endocrine system, brain waves, respiration rate, electrical properties of the skin, tremors, disruptions of speech, repetitive actions, changes in reaction time, discoordination of behavior, fatigue, and rate of error production. Imagine how simple so much of psychology would be if a few basic principles accounted for all these phenomena.

Unfortunately, no such principles have emerged. Stress has turned out to be not one, but many things. Stimuli designed to be stressful do not always induce stress; a situation that is stressful for one person is not necessarily stressful for another. Furthermore, people under stress do not react in any common way. Some respond with increased heart rate but no change in galvanic skin response; some respond in precisely the opposite fashion. Some subjects display decreased accuracy and efficiency of performance under stress; some display increased accuracy and efficiency; some display increased variability of performance (both increased *and* decreased accuracy or efficiency).

Although there is little reason to hope that a simple explanation of stress phenomena will soon be found, there is also no basis for despair. A great deal is known that was not known before. A large volume of useful data has been collected, and a more accurate explication of the scope and complexity of the problem has emerged from the findings.

Two Points of View

The discussion of stress must be divided into two parts, one dealing with physiological aspects and the other dealing with psychological aspects. This division is not merely arbitrary or for convenience; it reflects distinct investigative approaches and views of the problem. Neither approach, taken by itself, is capable of dealing effectively with the whole subject of stress, though both have stimulated large quantities of research and have contributed significant findings to our store of knowledge about human behavior.

The Physiological View

It is possible to define stress solely in terms of the physiological state of the organism. A stressful stimulus may be identified as one that disrupts the organism's normal physiological equilibrium. Examples of such stimuli are electric shock, burns, disease, and prolonged or intense sensory stimulation. A stress response may be defined as any bodily reaction that acts to restore physiological equilibrium or homeostasis.

These definitions seem clear and simple enough, but they are unsatisfactory to an investigator interested in stress as a psychological phenomenon, for the subjective experience of stress is not consistently correlated with the physiological state of the organism. There is no necessary correspondence between the person's bodily state and the feelings he reports. As early as 1915, W.B. Cannon asserted that strong emotions, like pain, rage, and fear, are all accompanied by a common set of physiological conditions that prepare the organism for vigorous activity: "fight or flight." Cannon's ideas were gradually incorporated into a still commonly accepted view of emotion called activation (or arousal) theory, which leads the scientist to maintain that your physiological condition is much the same whether you are watching an exciting love scene in a movie, running a foot race, sitting in the waiting room of the dentist's office, or taking a final examination. If this were the case, your psychological experiences in all these situations should be identical. However, unless you are a most unusual person, it is highly unlikely that they are.

The Psychological View

Perhaps the inadequacy of the purely physiological view in explaining subjective responses can be overcome by defining stress in psychological terms. Unfortunately, such is not the case. Although it is obviously stressful to be forced to endure a long and boring lecture, it is also stressful to engage in hand to hand combat, to make a parachute jump from an airplane, or to appear before a judge as defendant in a lawsuit. How can one identify the common stimulus and response characteristics in all these situations? A stimulus such as a movie showing surgical removal of an eye may be very stressful to me but not at all to a physician who sees similar events every day. Overt behavioral responses to stress inducing situations are also inconsistent, not only among people but even when the same individual is exposed to a variety of presumably stress inducing situations or to the same situation a number of times.

Some investigators, recognizing these problems, have taken the position that stress exists neither in the environmental stimulus nor in the overt behavioral response the organism makes to it, but in the way the individual interprets his overall situation. One prominent investigator expressed it this way: "We cannot really speak of psychological stress without considering this [the person's] subjective evaluation, for what is stress for one may be a welcome challenge to another" (Arnold, 1967, p. 126). This approach has the merit of corresponding fairly closely to everyday experience, but it makes experimental study of stress difficult. It localizes stress in the mental (or, more technically, cognitive) processes of the organism, instead of in directly observable stimuli or in the organism's directly observable responses, thus obliging the investigator to devise techniques for discovering how his subjects interpret their situations. There still remain the problems of specifying the common features of all subjective interpretations that may be fairly regarded as stressful, and of relating these interpretations to the physiological state of the organism and to environmental conditions.

It has been noted by one authority that recent research on stress seems to show "a return to the idea that one should measure psychological variables with psychological techniques and physiological variables with physiological techniques. The two levels may reflect similar processes but there isn't necessarily a causal relationship between them" (Cohen, 1967, p. 80). This statement contains more than a hint of the doctrine of psychophysical parallelism: the philosophical assertion that mind and body are separate, noninteracting entities which nonetheless coexist in preestablished harmony. As a metaphysical statement, psychophysical parallelism leaves a great deal to be desired (where does the preestablished harmony come from?), but as a working assumption it has served psychology well on many occasions (for example, in early psychophysics). We will consider another possible relationship between physiological and psychological processes later in this chapter.

A Look Ahead

In the next section, a few studies of physiological reactivity are described to give a general picture of the directions in which this type of research on stress seems to be going. Succeeding sections examine some methodological problems of psychological research on stress and describe a program of research involving reaction to a film. Finally, a number of related research problems are touched upon briefly to provide some idea of the type and variety of research being done by other investigators.

Some Physiological Research

General Adaptation Syndrome

Perhaps the most widely publicized research on stress has been that of Hans Selye, the physician who described the general adaptation syndrome (known most commonly by its initials, GAS). Since 1936, when Selye first proposed his concept of stress, publications on the subject have been voluminous. Selye summed up his findings in a 1956 book called *The Stress of Life*.

According to Selye, the strongest argument for his concept of stress is the evidence that a common physiological state occurs in response to a variety of stress inducing agents. In broadest outline, this state has two aspects, inflammatory and anti-inflammatory. Inflammatory reactions are active defensive responses of the body that directly attack the irritant. Blood vessels dilate, and white blood cells are carried in large numbers to the site of the irritation. Connective tissues proliferate, forming a barricade against the spread of irritation. Activated by hormonal discharges, chemical substances move to the target site to neutralize poisons and kill bacteria. Anti-inflammatory reactions operate in precisely the opposite fashion. For example, they prevent proliferation of the connective tissue barrier and open the way for the spread of irritation.

The most effective bodily response to a localized stress is a combination of inflammatory and anti-inflammatory reactions. In general, the body reacts in

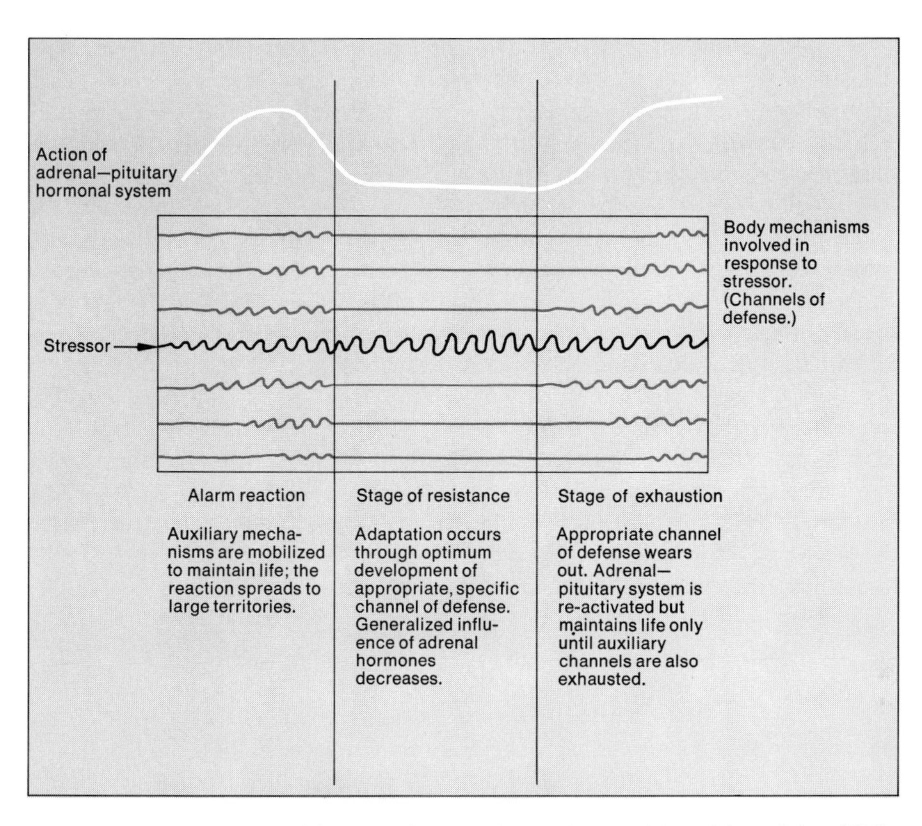

Fig. 8.1. The three stages of the general adaptation syndrome. (Adapted from Selye, 1956)

such a way as to limit stress to the smallest area in which the effects of the stress agent can be neutralized or overcome.

When it is not possible to limit the area of irritation, the stress reaction is no longer localized but involves the whole organism, giving rise to the *general adaptation syndrome* (GAS). The first stage of the GAS is the *alarm reaction*, an intense and generalized biochemical response of the body. The response affects nearly every organ; its action is mediated by the nervous system and by hormones, particularly of the pituitary-adrenal system. If the alarm reaction is unsuccessful, death of the organism or damage to some of its essential tissues (especially in the glandular, lymphatic, and gastric systems) will ensue.

Success of the alarm reaction in reducing the overall impact of the stress agent leads to *resistance*, the second stage of the syndrome. Resistance is essentially a localized and specific defense reaction concentrated on the affected area of the body. If resistance fails, the concentrated defenses of the body break down. This introduces the stage of *exhaustion*, in which the organism can no longer defend itself against the stressing agent. With no barrier to stop it, the agent is free to spread throughout the body, and when auxiliary channels of defense are exhausted, death results (Fig. 8.1).

A Revised Conception of Disease

Selye's view of stress implies that a sick person is not merely a passive host to some invading disease that runs its course and then magically dies or disappears.

The sick organism engages in an active struggle with the stress producing agent. Indeed, in some cases the stress response *is* the disease. Allergic reactions, such as hay fever, asthma, dermatitis, and conjunctivitis are, in effect, inflammatory responses to irritants, but usually irritants that are not objectively dangerous. Such diseases are not directly caused by any outside agent, but by the body's own overreaction. Allergic responses of this type are often treated by instructing the patient to avoid the substance to which his body overreacts, whether it be ragweed pollen, cats, eggs, or seafood. However, these diseases can also be treated by regulating the body's general reaction to irritating substances. One method is to inject or apply hormones, such as adrenocorticotropic hormone (ACTH), cortisone, or cortisol, to stimulate anti-inflammatory reactions.

Selye's ideas touch on important subjects, so it is not surprising that they provoked a large body of research by medical and psychological investigators. Much of this research has been devoted to testing the proposition that all forms of stress are followed by the same pattern of physiological responses. Some such generalization is strongly implied by activation or arousal theory, and is encouraged by Selye's work as well. Investigators are becoming convinced, however, that the proposition oversimplifies the actual state of affairs.

Fear and Anger

Ax (1953) attempted to induce fear or anger in subjects by exposing them to contrived situations. Fear and anger were chosen because these are most often described by advocates of activation theory as similar in their physiological bases.

Subjects were told that the study concerned physiological differences between people with and without hypertension. They were led to believe that all they would have to do was to lie on a bed and listen to music for about an hour. Instruments were attached to the subjects to measure heart rate (electrocardiogram), heart stroke volume (ballistocardiogram), respiration (pneumograph), face and finger skin temperatures, electrical conductance of the skin (galvanic skin response), muscle potential from the forehead, and blood pressure (see Chap. 7, pp. 176–180). After a 25 minute rest period had passed, subjects were exposed to fear arousing and anger arousing situations.

The fear arousing situation began with a gradually increasing electric shock to the subject's little finger. When the subject reported feeling the shock, the experimenter expressed surprise, sparks began to fly, and the subject was told that a dangerous high-voltage short circuit had occurred. After five minutes of alarm and confusion, the experimenter removed the shock wire and assured the subject that the short circuit had been repaired and all was well.

The anger arousing situation was set up by telling the subject that the operator of the recording apparatus was a person who had once been fired for incompetence and arrogance, but had to be employed temporarily because the regular operator was sick. Anger arousal began when this operator entered the room, supposedly to check the apparatus. The experimenter then left the room while the operator shut off the music, criticized the subject for being late and uncooperative, and generally subjected him to five minutes of abuse.

Ax found that physiological measures were not the same under the two experimental conditions. Anger produced higher diastolic blood pressure, more reductions in heart rate, a greater number of galvanic skin responses, and more increases of muscle tension. Fear produced a greater rise in skin conductance (an index of the amount of change in electrical resistance of the skin), a larger number of muscle tension peaks, and an increased respiration rate.

Ax compared the response profiles for fear and anger with the profiles of physiological response produced by injections of epinephrine, a hormone produced by the adrenal medulla (the central portion of the adrenal glands, which are situated on the kidneys), and norepinephrine, or noradrenaline, a close chemical relative of epinephrine that is formed at sympathetic nerve endings. The fear pattern was similar to the pattern produced by epinephrine, while the anger pattern resembled that produced by a combination of epinephrine-like and norepinephrine-like reactions.

On the basis of these results alone, Ax was not prepared to dispute activation theory, since Cannon had been concerned with visceral states, rather than with all possible physiological reactions. However, Ax did feel that his experiment demonstrated important differences between the states of fear and anger. Other investigators must have agreed with him, for Ax's experiment is frequently cited by those who work in the area of stress and emotion.

Extralaboratory Stress

The artificiality of the laboratory situation may raise doubts about the validity of Ax's findings. These may be partially dispelled by considering investigations which examined urinary secretion of epinephrine and norepinephrine by persons undergoing stress under conditions more representative of everyday experience (Hoagland, 1961; Elmadjian, Hope, and Lamson, 1957, 1958).

To test the effects of aggressive activity, a team of professional hockey players was examined before and after their games. Those who played in the most active, aggressive positions (defensemen and forwards) displayed a sixfold increase in secretions of norepinephrine after the game. The goal tender, who does not skate much but must remain constantly vigilant, showed marked increases in both epinephrine and norepinephrine excretion, but the coach, who remains on the bench and directs strategy, showed no general increases in the excretion of either substance. One player, who became involved in a fist fight and was ejected from the game, showed a twentyfold increase in epinephrine excretion and a ninefold increase in norepinephrine excretion.

Studies of amateur boxers showed that active preparation (shadow boxing) during the period of prefight apprehension was associated with high norepinephrine secretion. In addition, the higher the level of apprehension, the greater the excretion of epinephrine. The longer the contest and the closer the decision, the higher was the rate of postfight epinephrine excretion.

Examination of psychiatric patients showed that those who exhibit active, aggressive emotion excrete large amounts of norepinephrine, while those who are passive and self-effacing do not. Epinephrine excretion was found to increase in patients undergoing interviews by the hospital staff to determine the course of their stay in the hospital. In psychotherapy sessions, aggressive emotional displays were associated with increases in norepinephrine production, while tense, anxious, but passive sessions were accompanied by increases in epinephrine excretion.

Studies like these suggest differences among the physiological states accompanying various emotional and behavioral responses to stressful situations. Consequently, they speak against the idea that one's internal body state is the same regardless of the type of stress to which one is exposed.

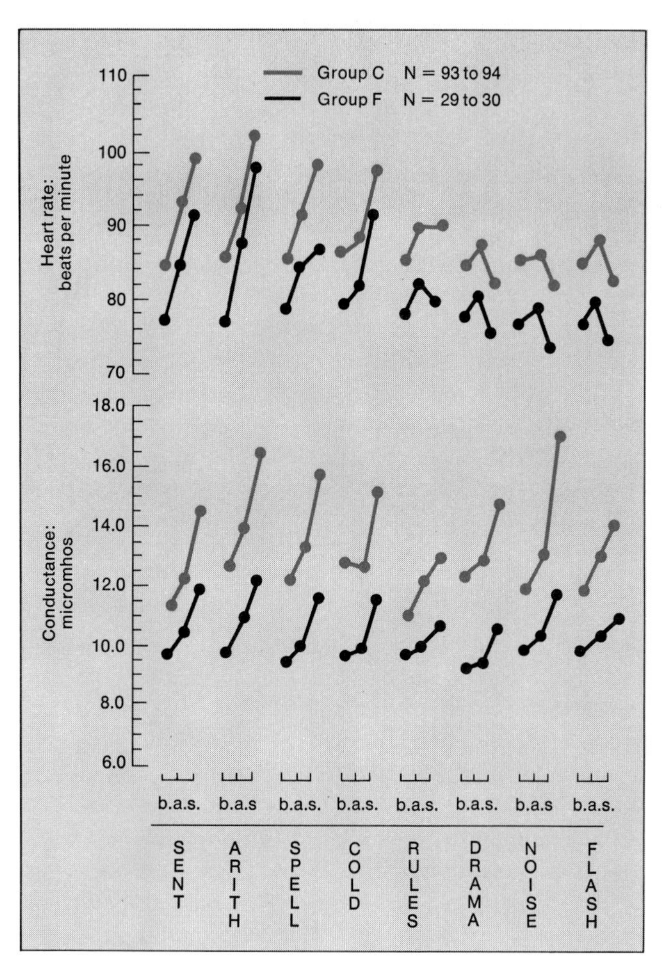

Fig. 8.2. These graphs are average response curves for heart rate and palmar conductance, for two groups of subjects under eight different stimulus conditions, indicated in the figure by single words or abbreviations. Each graph consists of three points: b, for base level, is the average prestimulus or resting value; a, for alerted level, is the average value during one minute of anticipation of the stimulus condition; s, for stress or stimulus level, is the average value during the administration of the stimulus condition. (From Lacey, Kagan, Lacey, and Moss, 1963)

Heart Rate and Skin Conductance

Lacey, Kagan, Lacey, and Moss (1963) exposed two groups of subjects to eight tasks. The groups consisted of male college students (represented by colored lines and labeled C in Fig. 8.2) and of somewhat older married men (represented by black lines and labeled F in Fig. 8.2) participating in research at the Fels Institute. The investigators measured heart rate (upper half of Fig. 8.2) and skin conductance (lower half of Fig. 8.2) during three phases of each task. Base level (b) was measured during the resting prestimulus period; alert or anticipation level (a) was measured in the period one minute before a stimulus was administered; stress level (s) was measured while the various stimuli were administered.

The lower graph shows a fairly regular pattern of skin conduction measures for all tasks. Skin conductance (the reciprocal of resistance) increases from base through alert to stress phases for both groups in nearly every instance. A similar pattern appears for heart rate on the first four tasks, but on the last four tasks heart rate increases from base to alert phases and then decreases from the alert to the stress phase. The nature of the tasks suggests the reason for these differences. The first three tasks involve mental manipulation of symbols and retrieval of stored information; none requires prolonged attention to external stimuli. In the first task (SENT), the subjects made up sentences in which each word began with the same letter of the alphabet. In the second task (ARITH), the subjects solved multiplication and addition problems "in their heads." In the third task (SPELL), words were spelled aloud in reverse order, and subjects were to rearrange the letters mentally and call out the correct word.

The cold pressor test (COLD), the fourth task, involves administration of a painfully cold stimulus to the subject's skin. This test was included to demonstrate that the same cardiac pattern occurs when a physical stimulus is "rejected" or dampened as when psychological stimuli are blocked from awareness.

By contrast, the Rules of the Game test (RULES) required subjects to listen to a prolonged description of the rules for a fictitious card game. In the DRAMA situation, subjects listened to a professional actor read the thoughts of a dying man. The NOISE situation required them to listen to white noise (a sound made up of a mixture of a wide range of audible frequencies). The FLASH situation required them to watch flashes of color at ten cycles per second. All these situations demand close attention to the environment, and all produced either a deceleration of heart beat or no noticeable change in heart rate from a to s phases.

On the basis of these findings, Lacey (1967) criticized the general view of activation theory that asserts the uniformity of physiological reactions to all forms of stress induction. He has proposed that activation processes reflect not only the intensity of response to stress, but also the intended aim or goal of the behavior (for instance, to block out or to be sensitive to environmental stimuli).

Generality or Specificity?

Despite the findings summarized above, most evidence until recent years has been consistent with the hypothesis that *arousal* and *activation* have a common core of physiological meaning (Duffy, 1962; Lindsley, 1951; Malmo, 1959). The problem with the generalized activation hypothesis is probably not that the common core does not exist, but that the hypothesis fails to pay adequate attention to additional, often highly specific, reactions to particular kinds of stress.

In part, recognition of the number and variety of possible patterns of response had to await recording instruments compact and sensitive enough to measure as many as 8 to 12 different physiological functions at once. Such instruments were not available until the discovery of the transistor and the invention of miniaturized circuitry in the 1950s and 1960s. It is no longer possible to make all-inclusive statements about the sympathetic nervous system as a whole, the pituitary-adrenal system, or even the adrenal glands themselves. The unity of stress response is not a unity of simplicity but a unity in diversity. Stress may be the common theme, but the physiological responses by which it is recognized are not simple recapitulations of the theme. They are more like unique variations which retain some fundamental similarity to the theme from which they are derived.

The Psychological Approach

In 1952, Lazarus, Deese, and Osler reviewed the research literature on stress and concluded that lack of uniformity of method and clarity of concepts had produced a situation in which it was impossible to draw firm conclusions from available data. A preliminary consideration of the problems that continue to make it difficult to conduct effective research on psychological stress provides a useful introduction to the description of specific investigations.

Finding Valid Measures

We noted previously that modern authorities prefer to identify psychological stress as an aroused internal state of the person (an intervening or mediating variable) rather than as a property of either stimuli or responses per se. The precise nature of a postulated internal state like stress may not be known, since the state itself cannot be observed directly. However, discovery of consistencies between stimulus inputs and response outputs under known conditions of stress arousal may permit us to draw reasonable conclusions about its influence on behavior. Before these discoveries can be made, it is necessary to develop measures that enable the investigator to tell with certainty when and to what degree stress is aroused in his subjects.

It is difficult to measure the internal state of stress for at least two reasons. First, the various available measures of stress do not correlate very strongly (Cowen, 1960). We cannot confidently say that a person who shows a strong response of one kind (for instance, on a measure of urinary secretion of hormones) will necessarily display a strong response of another kind (on measures of skin conductance, verbal reports of subjective experience, changes in quantity or quality of performance). A person who shows few physiological signs of fear may report that he is afraid; one who shows strong physiological evidence of emotional arousal may maintain that he is perfectly calm.

Second, we know that in various instances stress brings about better performance, poorer performance, or inconsistent changes in performance. It is possible that the relationship between stress and performance is nonlinear; that is, a steady increase in stress probably does not produce a steady increment or decrement in behavioral efficiency. It may well be that adaptation, as measured by adequacy of performance, is successful only when stress is moderate. When stress is too weak, the organism tends to ignore it. When it is too strong, the organism can no longer cope with it effectively (Janis, Mahl, Kagan, and Holt, 1969, pp. 124–141). Perhaps adaptation can be expected only when the person recognizes the existence of stress and is not prevented from overcoming its effects through appropriate adjustive maneuvers. Furthermore, everyday experience tells us that it is possible to build up resistance to environmental stimuli. An initially disturbing noise level soon comes to be completely ignored. Los Angeles smog annoys the visitor, but most long-term residents simply accept it as a mildly unpleasant fact of life. The complexity of the relationship between stress and adaptation implies that the investigator must determine for each set of research conditions, perhaps for each subject individually, what kinds of change constitute acceptable evidence of stress or threat as an internal state of the person.

In actual research, the problem of measurement is usually solved by selecting one or two conventional indexes of physiological and psychological states. In the program of research described in the next section of this chapter, measures of skin conductance and heart rate are the physiological indexes. The psychological indexes consist of subjects' reports of their emotional states.

Problems of Comparison and Control

Every study of stress requires baseline data that enable the investigator to compare responses under stressful conditions to responses under conditions that are not stressful. This seems simple enough to get; just test the subjects twice, once before and once after administration of the stressor. But what if the task is one in which subjects generally improve with practice, or in which fatigue plays an important role, so that performance might be expected to decrease as a result of repetition? In either of these cases, effects that might be attributed to stress may really be due to something else. Some of these problems may be solved by adding a control group (which is given the same test twice but not exposed to stress) to the research design. Data from such a group enable the investigator to estimate effects of variables like practice and fatigue, and to apply appropriate corrections to the data he obtains from the stressed group.

Another problem sometimes arises from the so-called *regression effect:* on almost any retest, subjects who do very well on the first administration tend to do less well on the second, while subjects who did poorly on the first administration tend to improve on the second. Since high scores tend to decrease and low scores to increase on retest, there is often a negative correlation between initial scores and scores representing the amount of change from prestress to poststress conditions (see more detailed discussion of correlation, Chap. 13, pp. 355). This correlation can be compensated for mathematically so that resulting scores are a purer measure of the effect of stress alone, but the regression effect is subtle and is frequently not taken into account in the treatment of experimental data.

Problems of Interpretation

The difficulties of research on psychological stress do not end when the investigator has selected measures and instituted procedural and statistical controls on his data. The most important problem, which still remains, consists of describing the conditions under which stress occurs and the effects it has upon behavior. That, of course, is what the research enterprise is all about.

This problem is usually solved by referring research outcomes to some more inclusive theory of behavior. For example, in his work on anticipatory fear as a determinant of postsurgical reactions of medical patients, Janis (1958) often borrowed from psychoanalytic theory. He noted, for instance, that the stress of impending surgery seemed to release formerly repressed thoughts and emotions (Chaps. 4 and 14). The release of these unconscious memories and impulses often flooded the patient with anxiety.

Many research findings may be explained by behavioristic theories. It has long been known that the initially unlearned fear response to a powerful or painful stimulus, such as electric shock, can be associated with previously neutral stimuli. After conditioning, these stimuli arouse fear in the organism whenever they are presented; the result is called a conditioned emotional response. Theoretically, its operation is analogous to the stress you would probably feel if you heard a television announcer saying that radar shows the approach of intercontinental ballistic missiles, probably carrying nuclear warheads. Though you cannot immediately perceive the forthcoming catastrophe, previously learned associations to the announcer's words touch off the internal fear you would feel.

By bringing the explanatory power of a psychological theory to bear upon his data, an investigator is led to seek relationships among his findings that might not otherwise be apparent. Later we will examine research that tests explanatory concepts derived from psychological theories.

Not all of the problems posed by research on psychological stress have been successfully solved in the research discussed in the following sections. However, a great deal can be learned even with somewhat imperfect experimental techniques, and so our attention now turns to research that has made the best use of the available methods.

Reactions to Films of Body Mutilation

Preliminary Study

One solution to many problems of stress research is to adopt a standard stress agent and use it consistently in a series of investigations; differences in research outcomes cannot then be attributed to differences in stimulus conditions. Lazarus, Speisman, Mordkoff, and Davison (1962) selected a 17 minute silent film called *Subincision* for use as a stress inducing stimulus. The film was taken by G. Roheim, an anthropologist, when he was working with the Arunta, an aboriginal Australian tribe. It depicts the ceremony that initiates young boys into manhood, a ceremony that includes, among other things, cutting into the penis of each initiate with a stone knife. Six such operations are shown during the film.

The effectiveness of the film as a stressor was tested by showing it to 35 men and 35 women college students individually after they had first seen an innocuous film on corn farming in Iowa. Skin resistance and heart rate, the two physiological records taken, were markedly affected by the film. Furthermore, changes in these measures closely paralleled the events shown in the film. Skin resistance was lowest (conductance was highest) and heart rate highest when the actual operation was being shown. Skin conductance and heart rate both decreased during a benign scene showing a hair-tying ritual. The solid curve in Figure 8.3 shows how skin conductance peaked at several critical points of the film. The inverted V's, which show the four points at which heart rate was highest, correspond to the first four critical points of the film. The lack of peaking for the fifth and sixth incisions suggests an adaptation effect on both measures.

Responses to an adjective checklist and an interview questionnaire confirmed the existence of subjective anxiety during the film. Further, after 32 subjects had seen the movie, several returned to complain about it. The investigators therefore added to the instructions a warning that the film might be upsetting and that the subject could have it stopped at any time. Following this change in procedure, eight subjects requested that the film be stopped. All in all, the investigators felt safe in considering the film an effective stress producer. Few would disagree with their conclusion. (See also Speisman, Lazarus, Davison, and Mordkoff, 1964.)

Correlations among response measures were not high. Subjects who reported feeling most anxious were not necessarily those whose skin conductance or heart rate rose to the highest levels, and vice versa. However, individuals were consistent

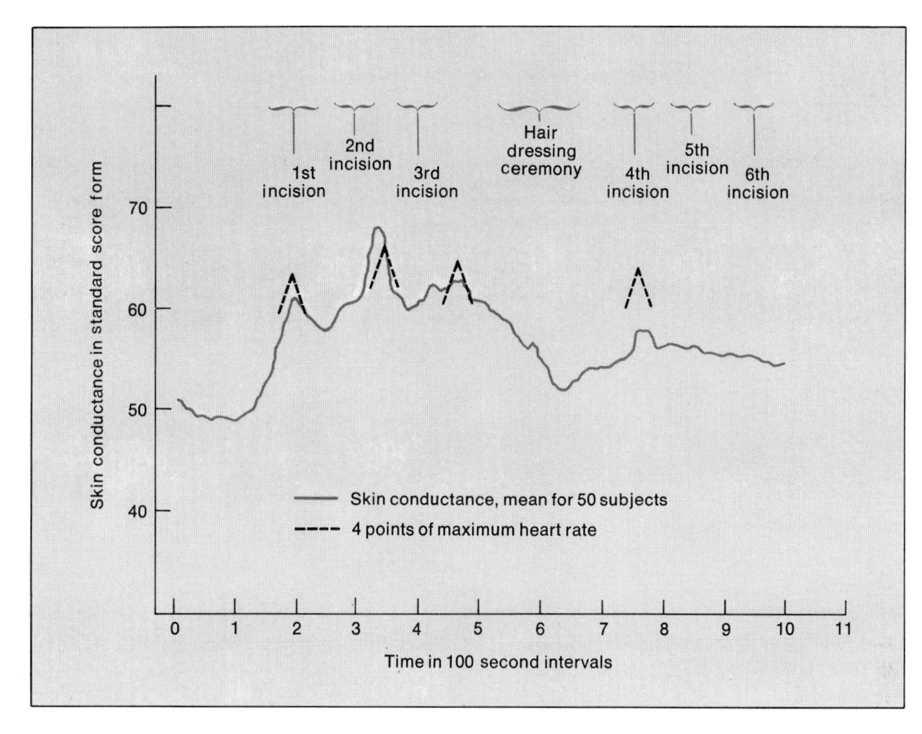

Fig. 8.3. Skin conductance in standard score form at ten second intervals, and four points of maximum heart rate, aligned with the stressor film contents. (From Lazarus, Speisman, Mordkoff, and Davison, 1962)

in their own mode of response. One subject might respond regularly with changes in skin conductance and report no subjective anxiety, while another might report high levels of anxiety and show little change in skin conductance. This type of result is typical in stress studies (Lazarus, 1967).

Manipulation of Sound Tracks

The next step in this program of stress research was to show that, given a stressor of known effectiveness, the subject's responses can be altered by manipulating the psychological conditions under which the stressor is administered. However, the number of possibilities is virtually unlimited, and the investigator must turn to psychological theory to help him decide which manipulations are most likely to be effective. Speisman, Lazarus, Mordkoff, and Davison (1964) turned to personality theory for one set of possibilities.

According to one form of personality theory, people deal with anxiety arousing or threatening thoughts and ideas by a process of *defense*. Of the many psychological defenses, the ones that seemed most used by subjects in these studies were *intellectualization* and a combination of *denial* and *reaction formation*. Intellectualization is a form of *rationalization*, a defense in which emotionally loaded material is treated as though it presented nothing more than a problem in logic, cold science, or reason. Denial, as its name implies, consists of active rejection of the emotional significance of an event. Reaction formation involves converting an emotional experience into

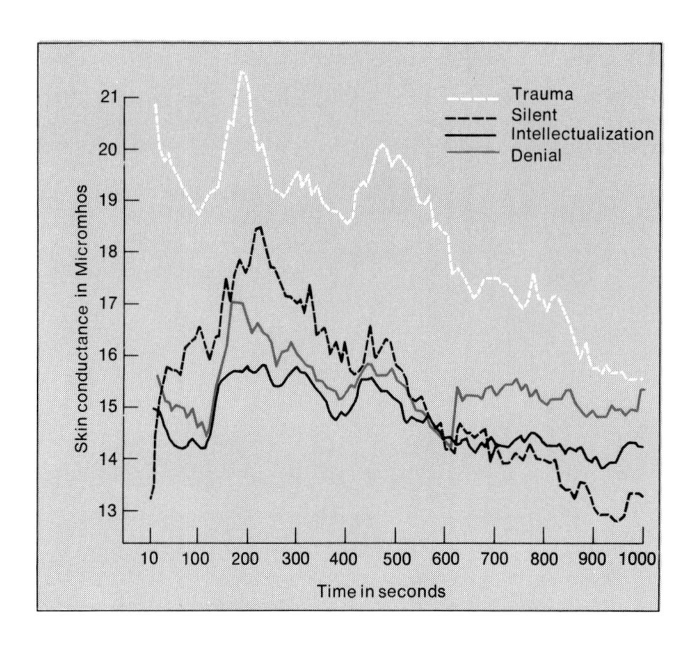

Fig. 8.4. The effects of the experimental conditions on skin conductance. (From Speisman, Lazarus, Mordkoff, and Davison, 1964)

its opposite, such as convincing yourself that you hate someone whom you really love but who does not return your affection.

Three sound tracks were created for the subincision film and compared with a silent track. One presented an intellectualized view of the ceremony. For example, at one point the commentary ran: "As you can see the operation is formal, and the surgical technique, while crude, is very carefully followed."

The second sound track encouraged denial and reaction formation by minimizing the harm and pain of the operation and by describing the events as a joyful occasion for the boys. This sound track said things like: ". . . the words of encouragement offered by the older men have their effect and the boy begins to look forward to the happy conclusion of the ceremony."

The third sound track, designed to increase stress, emphasized the pain, cruelty, danger, and primitiveness of the operation. The investigators reasoned that additional support would be gained for the idea that responses are influenced by what subjects hear if it could be shown that responses can be increased as well as decreased by manipulating the content of what is said. Figure 8.4 shows that the most striking effect was accomplished by this so-called trauma track. Skin conductance measures were consistently higher under this condition than under any others. The two defensive sound tracks yielded significantly less evidence of stress than did silent presentation of the film, but their effects were not so marked or obvious as was the effect of the attempt to increase overall stress response. Heart rate measures and reports of subjective experiences are not shown in Figure 8.4 because they did not reveal differences among experimental conditions.

This experiment shows how some responses to a stress producing agent can be influenced by the way in which the agent is interpreted by the subject. If threatening aspects of the stimulus are emphasized, stress increases. If nonthreatening alternatives are offered, stress is somewhat reduced.

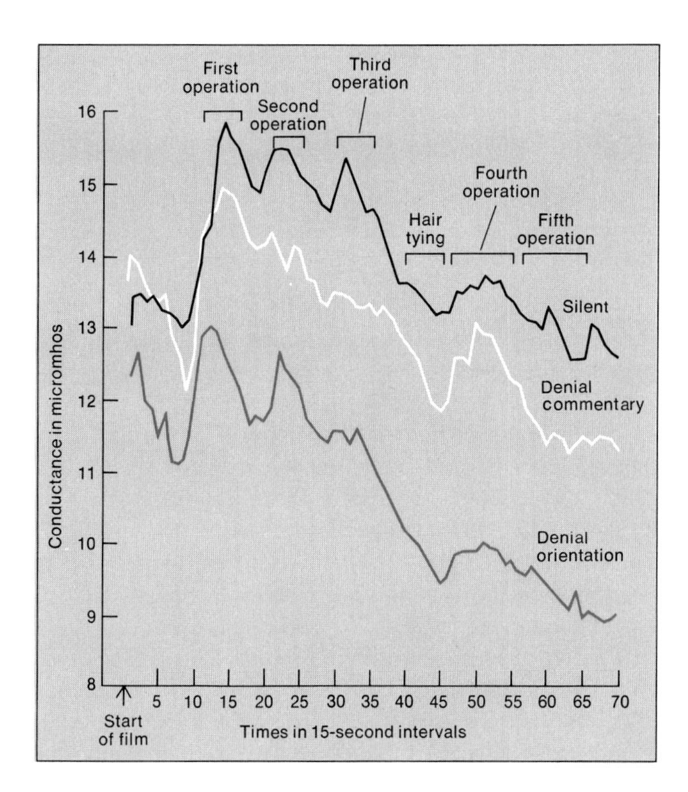

Fig. 8.5. Skin conductance curves during orientation and film periods under the experimental conditions. (From Lazarus and Alfert, 1964)

Effects of Cognitive Preparation and Personality Variables

The possibility remains that all the subject needs is a preliminary statement about the nature of the film to prepare him for its presentation. It may not be necessary to support defenses throughout its showing. To test this possibility, Lazarus and Alfert (1964) presented the film on subincision under three conditions.

The first condition (denial commentary) was the same as that described above in which the film was presented with a brief introduction and a sound track emphasizing denial and reaction formation defenses. In the second condition (denial orientation), the film was preceded by a ten minute denial and reaction formation statement which, in essence, presented the denial and reaction formation sound track before the film instead of along with it. Under the third condition the film was shown silently, with no preparation or commentary.

In general, the results demonstrated that preparation alone is not only effective in reducing stress, in some respects it is superior to the running commentary. This can be seen clearly in the skin conductance data in Figure 8.5. Lazarus and Alfert likened the influence of preparation to the effects of inoculation, which reduces susceptibility to disease if taken before exposure to disease producing agents (see Janis, 1958).

Lazarus and Alfert included in their study several measures of personality designed to assess the degree to which subjects naturally tend to employ the defense mechanism of denial. The deniers showed generally greater physiological reactivity to the film when it was run under ordinary silent conditions than did the nondeniers.

Interestingly, those who scored high on tests of denial verbally admitted less reaction on postfilm checklists and ratings than did those with lower scores on tests of denial. It appears that, in order to convince himself that he is not bothered by a stressful situation, the individual who denies reacts to it more strongly on the somatic level (Chap. 14).

Crosscultural Comparisons

It is of interest to discover whether people brought up in a different culture respond the same way as Americans do to stress, and to determine whether the personality defenses effective in reducing threat in Western society are as effective in another culture.

To examine these questions, Lazarus, Opton, Tomita, and Kodama (1966) tested 80 Japanese students and adults under conditions similar to those in the studies described above. Both students and adults were included in the study because it was felt that cultural changes introduced in Japan after World War II might have a greater effect on students' responses than on the responses of older persons. Presentation of the film was preceded by a neutral educational movie describing rice farming in Japan.

It is immediately obvious from Figure 8.6 that skin conductance values are much higher for both groups of Japanese subjects than for American subjects. Closer inspection reveals another peculiarity in the data: apparently the Japanese subjects were just as stressed by the control film as by the subincision film. In addition, while skin conductance values for American subjects generally rise to peaks during the most stressing portions of the film, few such peaks are evident in the data from either Japanese group.

During this experiment, the investigators obtained periodic verbal reports of subjective distress while the two films were being shown. The various groups of subjects were indistinguishable in these data. The Japanese reported no distress during the showing of the control film, and their reports of distress during the subincision film followed closely the content of the film.

The investigators attributed their findings to the fact that, in Japanese culture, evaluation or observation by others (as in a psychological experiment) is characteristically a threatening experience in and of itself. Additionally, Japanese are generally less accustomed than are Americans to being the subjects of impersonal psychological experiments. These two factors could well have produced a general apprehensiveness about the whole experiment in the Japanese subjects. The lack of difference between Japanese and Americans in verbal reports of subjective distress could be explained in several ways. Perhaps the Japanese were merely giving responses they thought appropriate and expected by the examiner. Another possibility is that stress, as measured by skin conductance, is not identical to stress as it is subjectively experienced by the person. At least two other possibilities exist. One is that Caucasian and Oriental subjects differ genetically in the physiological functions measured by skin conductance; the other is that differences in measurement technique account for the findings. In testing the Japanese subjects, the electrodes for measuring skin conductance were placed on the palm and wrist of one hand, while American subjects were tested with electrodes placed on both palms.

The intellectual and denial orientations preceding showing of the stress film were about as effective in reducing reactivity of the skin and reported distress and anxiety in Japanese subjects as they were with American subjects. However,

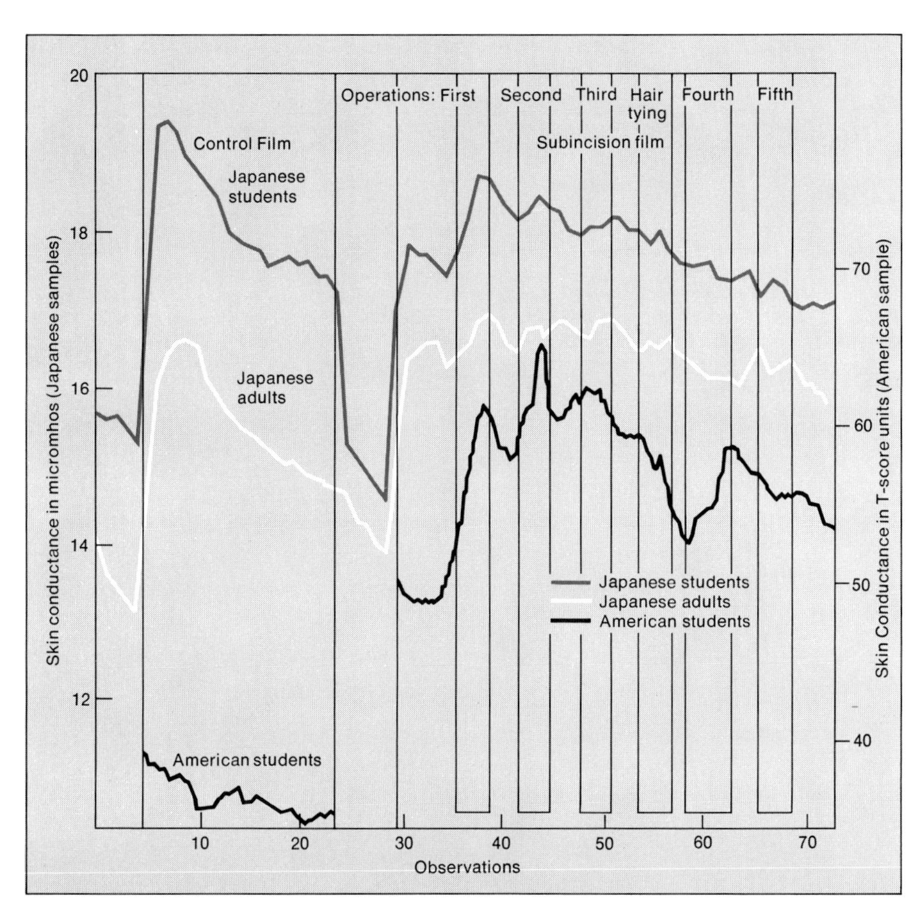

Fig. 8.6. Mean skin conductance during control and *Subincision* films and during baseline periods for Japanese students and adults and for American students. The conductance measure is the highest conductance reached during each 25 second film segment and each 25 second period during baseline periods. No recordings were made during the baseline periods for the American subjects. (From Lazarus, Opton, Tomita, and Kodama, 1966)

the trauma orientation, designed to increase stress, produced no increase among the Japanese. Indeed, the average skin conductance measure was actually *lower* under trauma conditions than it was when the film was run with no orientation. The average measures suggest that a supposedly trauma inducing orientation reduced average skin conductance slightly more than did the intellectualizing orientation. The investigators do not offer any explanation of this particular result in the report of their research. Perhaps someone who knows Japanese culture well could explain this finding, or perhaps it will remain a curiosity of scientific data that will never be satisfactorily explained.

Trials with a Different Film

To see whether cognitive factors would affect responses to a film with different stressful content, Lazarus, Opton, Nomikos, and Rankin (1965) exposed college students to a movie on industrial safety. The film shows three accidents occurring

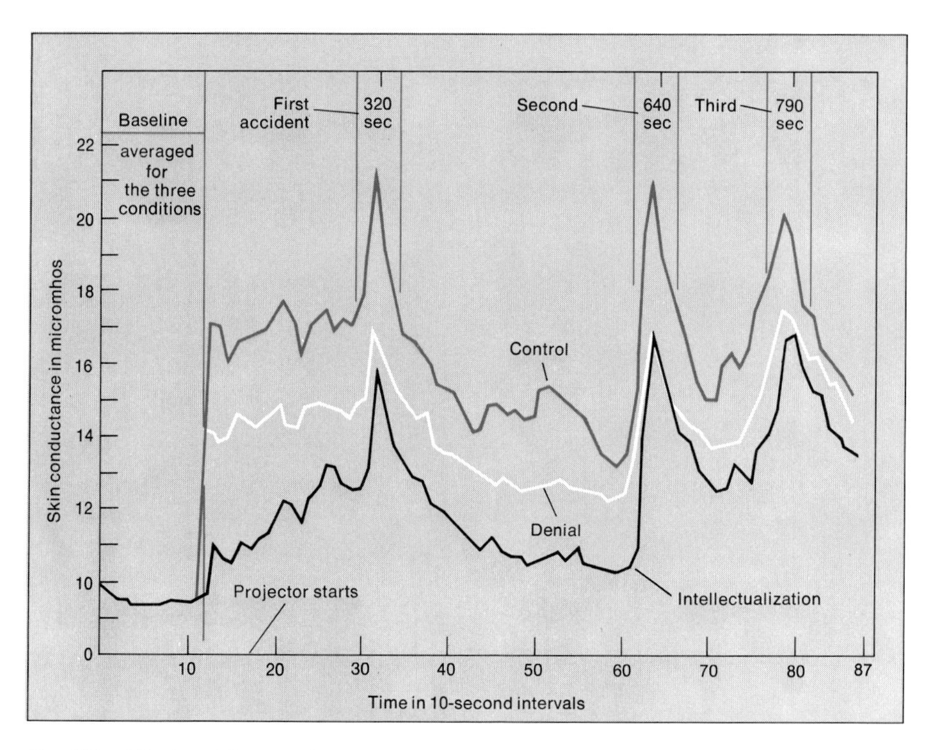

Fig. 8.7. Effects of the experimental conditions on skin conductance (baselines equalized by statistical adjustment). (From Lazarus, Opton, Nomikos, and Rankin, 1965)

in a woodshop; two involve loss of fingers in machines, while in the third a worker is run through by a board and killed.

One group saw the film under *control* conditions. Before seeing the film, they were presented with a brief descriptive summary of the first two accidents. Another group saw the film under *denial* conditions; the orientation speeches emphasized that the film is a fake, that no one is really hurt, and that the whole affair is merely designed to look as real as possible. (Note that this procedure is not the same as the denial orientation used for the subincision film, where the emphasis was upon defensive interpretation of events that are unquestionably real. Here the subjects are reminded that the events are not real at all. Since the denial statement is true it might better have been termed a reassuring orientation. By definition, the psychological term denial implies an avoidance of reality and is therefore technically inappropriate in this investigation.) A third group of subjects experienced the film following an intellectualization orientation similar to the one used in the study of the subincision film.

Figures 8.7 and 8.8 make it evident that both measures (skin conductance and heart rate) were responsive to the events of the film. It is also clear that the two orienting statements were effective in reducing reactivity, and that intellectualization was more effective than denial (or reassurance). This makes sense intuitively, since all 66 subjects were college students who might be expected to rely heavily on their intellectual resources for defense against threat.

Because the film on industrial safety deals with events that are culturally familiar to American subjects, this research shows that previous results cannot be explained on the basis of subjects' lack of familiarity with the context in which

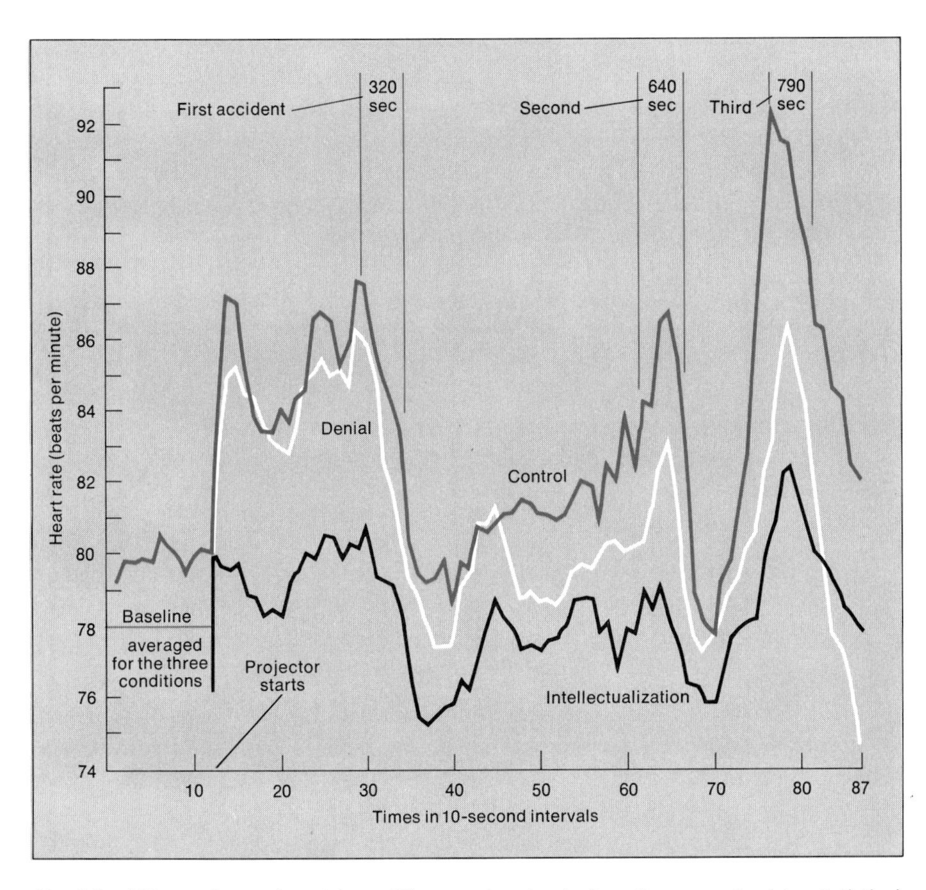

Fig. 8.8. Effects of experimental conditions on heart rate (baselines equalized by statistical adjustment.) (From Lazarus, Opton, Nomikos, and Rankin, 1965)

presumably stressful events occur. The study provides another stress agent of known properties to use in research. It also lends additional support to the hypothesis that stress responses are determined to a large extent by the way in which the subject appraises the events to which he is exposed.

Desensitization

Research on stress has been used to study the effects of psychotherapy designed to ameliorate fearful reactions of an especially disturbing nature. Such reactions appear in a variety of specific forms, called *phobias*. Claustrophobia is an overwhelming and irrational fear of enclosed spaces, acrophobia is a fear of heights, and so on. Wolpe (1958), a psychiatrist with a preference for applying the principles of traditional learning theory to the treatment of behavior disturbances, has proposed a treatment for phobias, called *densensitization*.

Desensitization consists essentially of pairing stimuli that ordinarily evoke anxiety or fear with responses that are antagonistic to anxiety, such as relaxation. The client is often asked to imagine the frightening stimulus (such as snakes, spiders, cats, people, or high places) while in a relaxed state. This is said to establish, by the principles of conditioning, a bond between the stimulus and the behavior of relaxing. Since it is difficult to be anxious while one is relaxed, this bond counteracts the preexisting bond between the stimulus and anxious behavior and eventually replaces it. It would seem that desensitization techniques might be effective as stress reducers; the following experiment was performed to evaluate this possibility.

The stress agent for which the subjects were prepared was a shortened version of the film on industrial accidents. Only a 260 second segment, showing the bloody and fatal accident in which a man is impaled by a board, was used.

One group was prepared by systematic desensitization. Each subject was first trained by a series of exercises so that he could bring about a state of relaxation virtually at will. Next he was trained to associate the relaxed state with the memory of a pleasant scene. Then the entire scene he was about to see in the film was described verbally in ten episodes, one episode at a time. After the description of each episode, the subject was asked to remember the pleasant scene and to relax. Here is one example that shows how the desensitization procedure worked (this is the seventh episode):

> Picture the workman groaning as he stumbles and falls, the board protruding from his back, blood around the board where it protrudes. Switch that off and let yourself go as limp as possible. Try to capture that heavy, dozy feeling that envelopes you when you are deeply relaxed. Let yourself go. [repeat] (Folkins, Lawson, Opton, and Lazarus, 1968, p. 104).

A second group was prepared by relaxation only. They were taught the relaxation exercises, but were provided no opportunity to associate relaxation with the events of the film. (All groups underwent three prestress sessions, so the amount of time spent in preparation was approximately the same.)

A third group was trained by cognitive rehearsal. Subjects in this group practiced imagining pleasant scenes, but were not taught relaxation techniques. The movie was then described to them episode by episode, but with no suggestion to relax. A fourth, nontreated group was exposed three times to a 32 minute talk on how to improve study habits.

The results contained a few surprises. On both self-report and skin conductance, the nontreated group displayed stronger reactions than the other three groups. That was not one of the surprises, but this was: Of the three types of preparation, the complete desensitization procedure turned out to be *least* effective, while cognitive rehearsal was the most effective. This seems to suggest that the success of desensitization therapy depends less upon conditioned responses than upon the cognitive activities of the subject. Such an explanation is consistent with the theory, proposed by Janis (1958), that mentally "working through" an anticipated stressful experience helps the individual prepare for it and results in a reduction of the amount of disturbance it causes.

How might a convinced behavior-therapist respond to this challenge of his method? Perhaps the most obvious response is that a normal person watching a brief, stressful movie is not comparable to a person who suffers from a long-lasting and disabling phobic disturbance. Furthermore, an experiment in which all subjects are exposed to identical preparation procedures (all preparations in the study were administered by tape recorder and the same tapes were used for all subjects) is not comparable to an individual therapeutic relationship. Desensitization can be effective only if the therapist is present to judge the client's level of anxiety and adjust his procedures to it. (See Davison, 1969, for additional criticism, and Folkins, Evans, Opton, and Lazarus, 1969, for replies.)

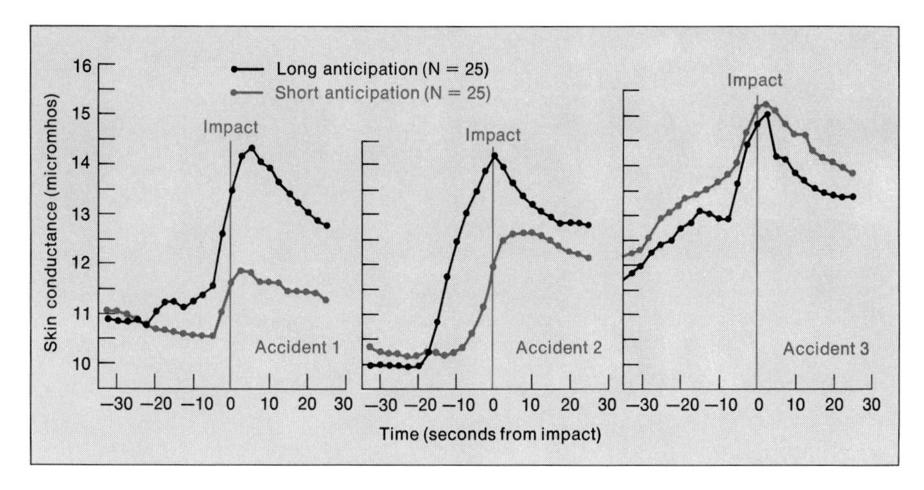

Fig. 8.9. Skin conductance of long and short anticipation treatment groups during accident anticipation and confrontation scenes. (From Nomikos, Opton, Averill, and Lazarus, 1968)

Both these criticisms attack a fundamental assumption of the research: that the conditions induced and the procedures followed were analogous to those that actually occur in the naturalistic setting of the psychological clinic. It was the investigators' opinion that the analogue is sufficiently accurate and that the study raises serious questions about the way in which desensitization therapy produces its effects. On matters such as this it is quite possible for equally competent and authoritative scientists to disagree.

Surprise and Suspense

The problem with which this next study is concerned is fairly simple methodologically, but of considerable general interest. The results are straightforward, and the study provides a good example of the use of psychological experimentation to analogize events in real life.

The stressor consisted of the industrial safety film which has already been described. Two versions of the film were prepared, a long anticipation version (LA) and a short anticipation version (SA). In the LA version, anticipation scenes (such as showing the victim's fingers approaching the blades of a milling machine) were extended to about 20 seconds each before the first two accidents were actually shown. The third accident scene was not altered.

Both skin conductance and heart rate showed marked differences in reactions to the two versions of the film. As usual, skin conductance showed the difference more clearly than heart rate (Figs. 8.9 and 8.10), and self-report measures revealed no differences between experimental conditions, although all subjects reported subjective discomfort during the film.

The skin conductance data clearly show that most of the effect of suspense occurs *before* the accidents are actually shown. Once the anticipated event takes place, reactions drop off rather quickly. The investigators would doubtless argue that this finding implies that psychological stress resides not in environmental stimuli per se, but in the experiencing organism who appraises these events.

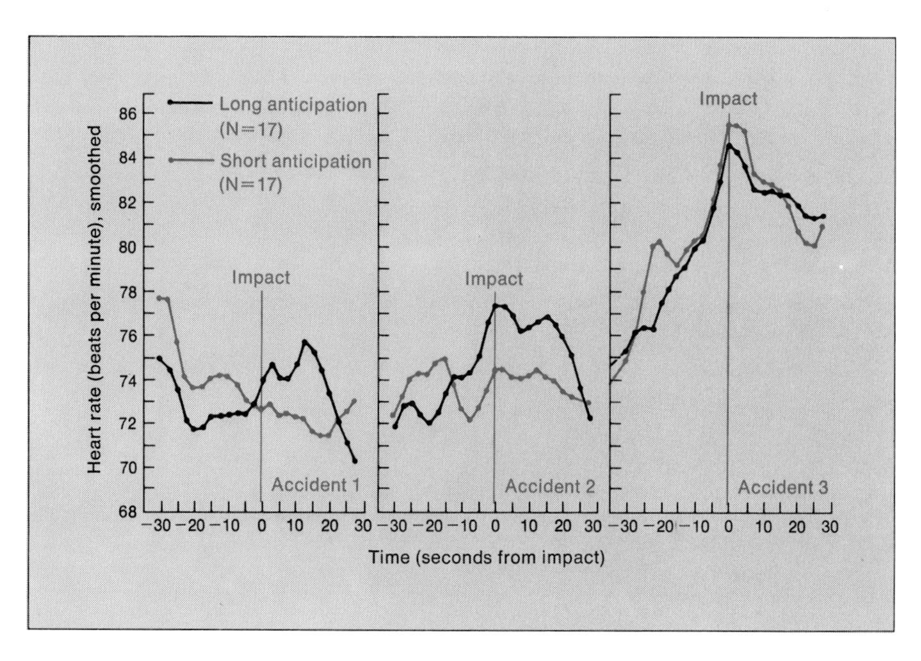

Fig. 8.10. Heart rate of long and short anticipation treatment groups during accident anticipation and confrontation scenes. Heavier lines indicate time from onset of anticipation scenes to peak response. (From Nomikos, Opton, Averill, and Lazarus, 1968)

This experimental analogue applies only to situations in which suspense is relatively brief. When anticipation time is increased, the beneficial inoculative effects of the "work of worry" may ameliorate some of the less pleasant responses to come (Janis, 1958). Exactly when, how, and under what conditions this occurs must remain an open question for future investigators.

An Effort To Integrate

In an attempt to tie together a large body of research on stress, Lazarus (1966) proposed a set of integrating concepts for summarizing findings and discussing issues. Lazarus maintained that it is most proper to think of stress as a general concept that refers to a large, amorphous subject of interdisciplinary interest. Analysis of stress from a strictly psychological point of view deals with a more specific problem, that of *threat*. Threat is the (not necessarily conscious) anticipation of harm. *Anticipation* refers to the person's cognitive appraisal of a situation, and *harm* is anything that thwarts one's motives. Thus, a person is under psychological stress (experiences threat) when he expects that he will be prevented from maintaining or attaining a necessary or desired state.

Lazarus emphasizes the coping aspects of responses to threatening situations (see also Lazarus and Opton, 1966). He argues that different appraisals of a threat producing stimulus result in different reactions to the same stimulus. One set of coping responses involves direct actions, such as attack and avoidance, which may bring into play the emotions of anger or fear. Another set of coping reactions involves defensive reappraisals, such as scapegoating, rationalization, and denial. A third set of coping reactions is characterized by a state of *anxiety*, an intense, fearlike condition that occurs when threat is not clearly delineated and when action or defensive reappraisal are not possible. Anxiety and action, or anxiety and defense, are interchangeable to some extent. Successful action or defense reduces anxiety; the failure of action or defense increases it.

Lazarus argues that physiological responses to stress are part of the total stimulus situation and must also be appraised by the subject. These responses are part of a feedback system: psychological appraisal of an initial stimulus produces stress, then stress produces physiological changes, and these are in turn monitored and appraised psychologically. The postulation of continuous interaction between physiological and psychological processes provides an alternative to psychophysical parallelism of the type suggested earlier in this chapter. It incorporates ideas suggested by others (Mandler and Uviller, 1958; Korchin and Heath, 1961) and is consistent with research showing that the quality of emotional experience is largely determined by the way in which an individual interprets his own physiological state (Schachter and Singer, 1962).

Finally, Lazarus maintains that the commonly reported failure of response measures to correlate significantly in stress states should not be viewed pessimistically. What may prove to be most important is not a subject's overall level of general stress, but the *pattern* of stress responses he exhibits. Each type of indicator may reflect a specific type of transaction between the individual and the situation to which he is exposed. In that case, each type of coping may be associated with a qualitatively different pattern of physiological and psychological response. Once basic patterns are identified, consistencies and correlations that are not apparent now will become evident.

These ideas are still somewhat speculative. However, they are consistent with much of the available evidence, and they hold out hopeful prospects for future research. Buttressed by a carefully collected body of empirical facts, they may prove to be extremely valuable as integrating concepts.

Related Research

In the laboratory, stress has been induced by plunging the arm into frigid water, exposing subjects to heat, cold, noise, noxious chemical stimulation, pressure to perform more efficiently or to conform to normally unacceptable attitudes, fear of failure, rejection, or abandonment, disturbing movies, forcing subjects to lie, telling them they are mentally ill, administering electric shock, and by a host of other techniques too numerous to mention. Field studies of stress cover a wide variety of situations, including exposure to extreme heat and cold, physical exertion and fatigue, being interviewed by an important person, dental surgery, prolonged isolation, living in a new environment, space flight, anticipating surgery, military combat, auto racing, parachute jumping, near drowning, test taking, fear of death, disasters such as fires, earthquakes, bombings, floods, and tornadoes, and physical disability. In September 1969, almost an entire issue of the popular magazine *Psychology Today* was devoted to discussions of studies of this type.

Obviously, it is not possible to review or summarize all this work here. This section merely touches upon a few subjects of particular interest to give you some idea of what else is going on in the field.

Isolation Phenomena

An extremely popular subject for research on stress has developed around the study of the effects of sensory isolation on behavior (Brownfield, 1965; Zubek, 1969). These effects were first demonstrated convincingly by Bexton, Heron, and Scott (1954), who placed subjects in isolated cubicles for periods of two to three days. The subjects reclined on comfortable beds and all their physiological needs were cared for; however, their vision was limited by translucent goggles, and the only sound they could hear was the noise of temperature regulating equipment in the cubicle. Their arms were swathed in bandages to prevent tactual exploration of the environment.

The effects were dramatic. Subjects complained of inability to concentrate, confusion, and emotional instability. Most experienced visual hallucinations: visions of people, animals, landscapes, or geometric figures appeared before them and could not be consciously controlled. The subjects' ability to perform intellectual tasks decreased; they became disoriented in space and time.

Of particular concern in the 1950s were reports that American prisoners in Korea were being "brainwashed" by their captors, their morale destroyed, their belief systems altered, and their patriotism undermined. Reports of prison experiences suggested that isolation was used by the North Koreans to influence prisoners to sign false confessions or betray their comrades. Heron (1961) had found that exposure of subjects in sensory deprivation to propaganda about clairvoyance, telepathy, and ghosts was effective in altering their beliefs and attitudes. Consequently, there seemed to be a basis for believing that something of great importance was at stake in these investigations.

By 1961, it became evident that the problem of isolation is exceedingly complex. Kubzansky and Leiderman (1961) noted, for example, that results differ depending upon whether stimulation is reduced in intensity or merely reduced in patterning. Some studies (Vernon, McGill, and Schiffman, 1958; Heron, 1961) revealed that visual hallucinations occur less frequently when visual stimuli are completely absent (when the subject wears a blindfold) than when visual stimuli are present but depatterned (when he wears translucent goggles). It was also impossible to say whether deprivation in some sense modalities is more effective than deprivation in others, or whether deprivation occurs only when all senses are affected. Furthermore, measures of responses were so varied and unsystematic that there was no basis for comparing results among studies. Finally, individual differences among subjects made generalization a hazardous venture. In short, things were not as simple as they had once seemed.

The study of reactions to altered sensory environments has obvious relevance to understanding the concept of stress. Not only does it involve psychological factors, but neurophysiologists were quick to see its pertinence to their interests. For example, Lindsley (1961) related deprivation effects to the functioning of the reticular activating system (Chap. 7), noting that the system can produce arousal not only when stimuli act upon it from without, but also when it is deprived of the level of sensory input to which it is adapted.

Neurophysiological explanations of sensory deprivation phenomena generally emphasize self-regulatory processes. Prolonged reduction of sensory inputs below normal values either increases organismic sensitivity to spontaneous neural discharges ("noise") that normally go unnoticed, or raises the level of such activity to compensate for loss of input from the environment. Some investigators have noted the similarity of responses under conditions of sensory deprivation to behavior in the normal state of light sleep (Chap. 7), and have suggested that the physiological states in the two cases are much the same (Cohen, 1967). More psychologically oriented theorists have pointed to the organism's tendency to maintain order in its perceptual world, and have noted that sensory deprivation produces a state of disorder which the subject attempts to eliminate with self-generated stimuli (Bruner, 1961; Freedman, Grunebaum, and Greenblatt, 1961; Freedman, Grunebaum, Stare, and Greenblatt, 1962). Others have proposed that subjects may be responding to the social situation of an experiment in which they know they are expected to produce bizarre behavior (Orne and Scheibe, 1964; Pollard, Uhr, and Jackson, 1963; Jackson and Kelly, 1962; Jackson and Pollard, 1962). Still others claim that sensory deprivation weakens rational controls over behavior (so-called secondary processes) and permits more primitive mental activities (so-called primary processes, which involve a large component of imagery) to dominate behavior. Such theorists see sensory deprivation as an analogue of states that produce pathological behavioral disturbances like schizophrenia (Kubie, 1961; Goldfried, 1960; Rapaport, 1958; Goldberger and Holt, 1958). For still more theoretical possibilities see Freedman (1961), Held (1961); Riesen (1961), and Teuber (1961).

These views are by no means mutually incompatible. All are doubtless "correct" in some sense of the word. As with all research on stress, the difficulty is not that there are no explanations, but that there is no obvious way to integrate them into a single, unified theory.

Attention and Psychophysiological Interaction

Routtenberg (1968) has suggested that physiological arousal from the reticular activating system serves to prepare and organize response sequences. Teichner (1968) has observed, however, that alertness in response to stress is not simply a matter of generalized wakefulness; the alert organism attends to some stimuli but not to others. (Easterbrook, 1959, and Korchin, 1962, have made similar observations.) The state of attention implies not only activation of some parts of the brain but inhibition of others, a process that might be called *tuning*. An important characteristic of a tuned organism is its *bandwidth*, the breadth or narrowness of the range of stimuli to which it will respond. Teichner hypothesized that bandwidth is inversely related to level of activation: increases in activation (stress) produce narrower attentional bandwidth; decreases in activation broaden bandwidth. Narrow attentional bandwidth raises both the sensitivity and selectivity of additional processes; the organism pays closer attention to a relatively narrow stimulus field.

Complex tasks require broad bandwidths for their solution, because the organism must attend to many things at once, and this theory predicts that subjects will have greater difficulty performing such tasks when stress is high than when it is low. Actually, the theory proposes an optimal combination of attention level and bandwidth for performance on every task. Deviation from optimum in either direction should therefore produce decrements in performance.

This theory is consistent with a large body of research, and it leads to predictions about the effects of physiological and psychological conditions on behavior. Some of these predictions have been subjected to experimental validation, and the theory appears to provide a good starting point for future research.

Psychosomatics

No discussion of stress can be complete without some mention of the use of the concept in the field of psychosomatic medicine. During the 1920s a number of papers were published espousing the view that the stresses and strains of life can produce physiological changes which may lead to actual physical disease (Murphy, 1949). Growing recognition of the importance of emotional factors in the production of some forms of physical disease culminated in the publication of an historic volume, *Emotions and Bodily Changes*, by H.F. Dunbar (1935). The journal *Psychosomatic Medicine* was founded in 1939, and the field of psychosomatics was soon recognized as one of considerable interest to medicine and psychology alike.

One of the early ideas in psychosomatics was that each psychosomatic illness is caused by a distinctive form of emotional disturbance. Here are some examples of associations that have been postulated: duodenal ulcer—ambition, underlying dependency with conscious emphasis on independence, fear of assuming authority; asthma—insecurity, fear of loss of love and protection by others; rheumatoid arthritis—independence, overconscientiousness, self-sacrificing tendencies, adherence to routine (Coleman, 1956, pp. 232–233). The doctrine that particular emotional constellations are associated with particular somatic manifestations is called the specificity hypothesis, and is consistent with the traditional medical doctrine that every disease has its own cause.

As time passed, the specificity hypothesis came to be severely criticized (Kubie, 1953; Grinker, 1961; White, 1956). Although the doctrine of specificity has not been completely abandoned, a large number of authorities now recognize that people who develop the same physical symptoms may have very different problems of personality, and that the same problem of personality may produce quite different arrays of symptoms in different individuals.

Psychosomatic research poses special problems for the psychological investigator. Virtually all the studies examined in this chapter have dealt only with short-term reactions to stressful situations. But psychosomatic processes exert their influence over periods measured in years rather than in minutes or hours. Of course, ethical considerations place severe restrictions on any research that might attempt to produce psychosomatic illness in human subjects. Aside from these, it is simply not technically feasible to devise and execute studies that manipulate the life conditions of human beings over long enough periods of time to test most hypotheses about the origins of psychosomatic disease.

Occasionally, impressive research has been conducted with animals. Brady, Porter, Conrad, and Mason (1958) exposed pairs of monkeys to a shock avoidance apparatus. One animal of each pair (the "executive") was taught to control shock presentation by pressing a lever within 20 seconds before shock onset. If he pressed the lever in time, neither animal was shocked; if he did not, both were shocked. Although both animals were shocked equally, physiological disturbances were evident only in the "executives" who controlled the presence or absence of shock. Every one of these animals (four altogether) died as a result of extensive gastrointestinal ulceration. Similar physiological symptoms were not found in the control animals, even though they had been exposed to the same restraints and physical stimuli as the experimental subjects.

Perhaps the most striking demonstration of the influence of psychological factors on somatic states is the "sudden death" phenomenon, observed by Richter while he was studying survival swimming in water at various temperatures (Richter, 1957). Richter noticed that domesticated laboratory rats would swim in a tank for hours when escape was impossible. Wild rats, however, would often swim to the bottom of the tank and die within minutes. Autopsies revealed that these rats did not drown; they died of cardiac arrest due to massive discharge of vagus nerves (a pair of nerves that supply the abdominal and thoracic regions with autonomic fibers). A critical experiment was performed in which it was found that wild rats, familiarized with the apparatus and procedures through preliminary training in handling and rapid immersion, swam as long as domesticated rats. This experiment demonstrated that psychological factors may sometimes be powerful enough to bring about or avert the death of an organism. The idea that some people may will their own deaths or the deaths of others, and that death may be caused by hopelessness as well as by physical disease, has been in existence for centuries. Rarely, however, has it been possible to demonstrate the force of experience in altering physiological states. Knowing the power of these factors makes it easier to see why stress responses must be understood in the science of behavior.

Ethical Considerations

Before concluding this chapter, a few words should be said about the methods used in research on stress. It has probably occurred to you that some of the experiences to which subjects are exposed in this research are rather extreme and severe. Recall that in the early studies of the effectiveness of the subincision film it became necessary to allow subjects to request that the film be discontinued, because so many previous subjects had complained about it. After this procedure was introduced several subjects expressed the level of their discomfort by requesting discontinuation. Other forms of stress induction are just as effective in producing distress. Some subjects become seriously upset when they are told that their responses to a test indicate that they are likely to fail in college, or that they are homosexual or mentally ill.

There are ways to reduce the impact of most such research procedures. If a subject is to experience electric shock or other unpleasant stimuli, he can be informed of the possibility in advance and have the opportunity to refuse to participate or to quit the experiment at any time without penalty. If the experiment involves feeding back to the subject false information about his performance on some test, he can be reassured and told the true purpose of the experiment after data have been collected from him. If his level of arousal is high, time can be allowed after the experiment for individual counseling and tension reduction.

Many techniques for inducing stress and similar psychological states, such as aggression and cognitive dissonance (Chaps. 9 and 10), raise serious ethical questions about the limits within which psychological research should be confined, and psychologists themselves are becoming greatly concerned about the effects their experiments have on research subjects (Baumrind, 1964; Kelman, 1967, Milgram, 1964; Stricker, Messick, and Jackson, 1969; Seeman, 1969). A large number of universities, hospitals, and research institutions have permanent committees to evaluate the ethical aspects of all proposed projects that use human beings as subjects. The American Psychological Association acts upon complaints of unethical behavior. In any good university, graduate students in psychology are taught an attitude of respect for their subjects.

Most investigators feel their obligations strongly and take them seriously, but there is no way to guarantee that all studies give due and proper consideration to ethical matters. In the final analysis, the best protection against abuse is the conscience of the individual scientist, who must realize that, like any human endeavor, psychology cannot progress if it does violence to the basic principles of concern for the welfare of one's fellow men.

Glossary

ACTH: adrenocorticotropic (or adrenocorticotrophic) hormone; a substance which stimulates the adrenal gland.

Adrenal glands: paired ductless glands adjacent to the kidneys; active in stress and emotion.

Anti-inflammatory reaction: response of the body (largely by way of the production of ACTH) which inhibits inflammatory reactions to stress or injury.

Anxiety: a fearlike reaction, the source or cause of which usually cannot be readily identified.

Arousal: a generalized state of organismic activation produced by stress.

Cortex: the outer surface of an organ (e.g., adrenal cortex).

Cortisol: a hormone produced by the adrenal cortex.

Cortisone: a hormone produced by the adrenal cortex.

Denial: a form of personality defense that involves refusal to recognize or acknowledge the occurrence or emotional significance of threatening events.

Desensitization: a technique developed by Wolpe for treating anxiety reactions (such as phobias) by conditioning associations between fear provoking stimuli and relaxation responses.

Epinephrine: adrenaline; a hormone of the medulla of the adrenal glands; mediates the action of nerve impulses.

General adaptation syndrome: a sequence of stages of organic adjustment to stress, consisting of the alarm reaction, the stage of resistance, and the stage of exhaustion.

Hormone: a chemical substance produced within a specific organ of the body and carried through the body from the site of its production to affect remote, and often grossly generalized, body functions.

Inflammatory reaction: response of the body to stress; characterized by swelling, reddening, heat, and pain.

Intellectualization: a form of rationalization in which emotionally threatening occurrences are treated as though they were merely logical or intellectual exercises.

Medulla: the central or core tissue of an organ (e.g., adrenal medulla).

Norepinephrine: noradrenaline; a hormone that is chemically similar to adrenaline, but about which relatively less is known.

Personality defense: any of several psychological processes that reduce the emotional impact of threatening perceptions or experiences (see as examples, denial, rationalization, intellectualization. (See also Chap. 14).

Phobia: an intense and irrational fear of a specific type of object or situation.

Psychosomatics: the study of the influence of emotion on bodily states, particularly in cases where the result is bodily disorder or illness (psychosomatic medicine).

Rationalization: a personality defense by which the emotional impact of threatening events is partly neutralized by inventing reasonable explanations for the events.

Reaction formation: a personality defense which converts a distressing emotion into a facsimile of its opposite (for example, hate into overprotective love).

Regression effect: the tendency for extreme scores to approach the mean more closely when subjects are tested more than once.

Skin conductance: a measure of the capacity of the skin to transmit electrical energy; the reciprocal of electrical resistance.

References

Appley, M.H., and R. Trumbull. (Eds.) *Psychological stress: Issues in research.* New York: Appleton-Century-Crofts, 1967.

Arnold, M. Stress and emotion. In M.H. Appley and R. Trumbull (Eds.), *Psychological stress: Issues in research.* New York: Appleton-Century-Crofts, 1967.

Ax, A.F. The physiological differentiation between fear and anger in humans. *Psychosom. Med.*, 1953, **15,** 433–442.

Baumrind, D. Some thoughts on ethics of research: After reading Milgram's "Behavioral study of obedience." *Amer. Psychologist*, 1964, **19,** 421–423.

Bexton, W.H., W. Heron, and T.H. Scott. Effects of decreased variation in the sensory environment. *Canadian Journal of Psychology*, 1954, **8,** 70–76.

Brady, J.V., R.W. Porter, D.G. Conrad, and J.W. Mason. Avoidance behavior and the development of gastroduodenal ulcers. *J. exp. Anal. of Behavior*, 1958, **1,** 69–72.

Brownfield, C.A. *Isolation: Clinical and experimental approaches*. New York: Random House, 1965.

Bruner, J.S. The cognitive consequences of early sensory deprivation. In P. Solomon *et al.* (Eds.), *Sensory deprivation*. Cambridge, Mass.: Harvard University Press, 1961.

Cannon, W.B. *Bodily changes in pain, hunger, fear, and rage.* (2nd ed.) New York: Appleton-Century-Crofts, 1929. (1st ed. 1915)

Cohen, S.I. Central nervous system functioning in altered sensory environments. In M.H. Appley and R. Trumbull (Eds.), *Psychological stress: Issues in research*. New York: Appleton-Century-Crofts, 1967.

Coleman, J.C. *Abnormal psychology and modern life*. (2nd ed.) Chicago: Scott, Foresman, 1956.

Cowen, E.L. Personality, motivation, and clinical phenomena. In L.H. Lofquist (Ed.), *Psychological research and rehabilitation*. Washington, D.C.: American Psychological Association, 1960.

Davison, G.C. A procedural critique of "Desensitization and the experimental reduction of threat." *J. abnorm. Psychol.*, 1969, **74,** 86–87.

Duffy, E. *Activation and behavior*. New York: John Wiley & Sons, 1962.

Dunbar, H.F. *Emotions and bodily changes*. New York: Columbia University Press, 1935.

Easterbrook, J.A. The effect of emotion on cue utilization and the organization of behavior. *Psychol. Rev.*, 1959, **66,** 183–201.

Elmadjian, F., J.M. Hope, and E.T. Lamson. Excretion of epinephrine and norepinephrine in various emotional states. *J. clin. Endocrinology*, 1957, **17,** 608–620.

______. Excretion of epinephrine and norepinephrine under stress. In G. Pincus (Ed.), *Recent progress in hormone research*. New York: Academic Press, 1958.

Folkins, C.H., K.L. Evans, E.M. Opton, Jr., and R.S. Lazarus. A reply to Davison's Critique. *J. abnorm. Psychol.*, 1969, **74,** 88–89.

Folkins, C.H., K.D. Lawson, E.M. Opton, Jr., and R.S. Lazarus. Desensitization and the experimental reduction of threat. *J. abnorm. Psychol.*, 1968, **73,** 100–113.

Freedman, S.J. Perceptual changes in sensory deprivation: Suggestions for a conative theory. *J. nerv. ment. Dis.*, 1961, **132,** 17–21.

Freedman, S.J., H.V. Grunebaum, and M. Greenblatt. Perceptual and cognitive changes in sensory deprivation. In P. Solomon *et al.* (Eds.), *Sensory deprivation*. Cambridge, Mass.: Harvard University Press, 1961.

______, and F.A. Stare. Imagery in sensory deprivation. In L.J. West (Ed.), *Hallucinations*. New York: Grune & Stratton, 1962.

Goldberger, L., and R.R. Holt. Experimental interference with reality contact (perceptual isolation): Method and group results. *J. nerv. ment. Dis.*, 1958, **127,** 99–112.

Goldfried, M.R. A psychoanalytic interpretation of sensory deprivation. *Psychological Record*, 1960, **10,** 211–214.

Grinker, R.R. The physiology of emotions. In A. Simon, C.C. Herbert, and R. Straus (Eds.), *The physiology of emotions*. Springfield, Ill.: Charles C Thomas, 1961.

Held, R. Exposure–History as a factor in maintaining stability of perception and coordination. *J. nerv. ment. Dis.*, 1961, **132,** 25–32.

Heron, W. Cognitive and physiological effects. In P. Solomon *et al.* (Eds.), *Sensory deprivation.* Cambridge, Mass.: Harvard University Press, 1961.

Hoagland, H. Some endocrine stress responses in man. In A. Simon, C.C. Herbert, and R. Straus (Eds.), *The physiology of emotions.* Springfield, Ill.: Charles C Thomas, 1961.

Jackson, C.W., Jr., and E.L. Kelly. Influence of suggestion and subjects' prior knowledge in research on sensory deprivation. *Science*, 1962, **132,** 211–212.

Jackson, C.W., Jr., and J.C. Pollard. Sensory deprivation and suggestion. *Behavioral Science*, 1962, **7,** 332–342.

Janis, I. *Psychological stress: Psychoanalytic and behavioral studies of surgical patients.* New York: John Wiley & Sons, 1958.

———, G.F. Mahl, J. Kagan, and R.R. Holt. *Personality: Dynamics, development, and assessment.* New York: Harcourt, Brace & World, 1969.

Kelman, H.C. Human use of human subjects: The problem of deception in social psychological experiments. *Psychol. Bull.*, 1967, **67,** 1–11.

Korchin, S.J. Anxiety and cognition. Paper presented at the Martin Scheerer Memorial Meeting, University of Kansas, 1962.

———, and H.A. Heath. Somatic experience in the anxiety state: Some sex and personality correlates of autonomic feedback. *J. consult. Psychol.*, 1961, **25,** 398–404.

Kubie, L.S. The problem of specificity in the psychosomatic process. In F. Deutsch (Ed.), *The psychosomatic concept in psychoanalysis.* New York: International Universities Press, 1953.

———. Theoretical aspects of sensory deprivation. In P. Solomon *et al.* (Eds.), *Sensory deprivation.* Cambridge, Mass.: Harvard University Press, 1961.

Kubzansky, P.E., and P.H. Leiderman. Sensory deprivation: An overview. In P. Solomon *et al.* (Eds.), *Sensory deprivation.* Cambridge, Mass.: Harvard University Press, 1961.

Lacey, J.I. Somatic response patterning and stress: Some revisions of activation theory. In M.H. Appley and R. Trumbull (Eds.), *Psychological stress: Issues in research.* New York: Appleton-Century-Crofts, 1967.

———, J. Kagan, B.C. Lacey, H.A. Moss. The visceral level: Situational determinants and behavioral correlates of autonomic response patterns. In P.H. Knapp (Ed.), *Expression of the emotions in man.* New York: International Universities Press, 1963.

Lazarus, R.S. Cognitive and personality factors underlying threat and coping. In M.H. Appley and R. Trumbull (Eds.), *Psychological stress: Issues in research.* New York: Appleton-Century-Crofts, 1967.

———. *Psychological stress and the coping process.* New York: McGraw-Hill, 1966.

———, and E. Alfert. Short-circuiting of threat by experimentally altering cognitive appraisal. *J. abnorm. soc. Psychol.*, 1964, **69,** 195–205.

Lazarus, R.S., J. Deese, and S.F. Osler. The effects of psychological stress upon performance. *Psychol. Bull.*, 1952, **49,** 293–317.

Lazarus, R.S., and E.M. Opton, Jr. The study of psychological stress: A summary of theoretical formulations and experimental findings. In C.D. Spielberger (Ed.), *Anxiety and behavior.* New York: Academic Press, 1966.

Lazarus, R.S., E.M. Opton, Jr., M.S. Nomikos, and N.O. Rankin. The principle of short-circuiting of threat: Further evidence. *J. Pers.*, 1965, **33,** 622–635.

Lazarus, R.S., E.M. Opton, Jr., M. Tomita, and M. Kodama. A crosscultural study of stress-reaction patterns in Japan, *J. pers. soc. Psychol. Monogr.*, 1966, **4,** 622–633.

Lazarus, R.S., J.C. Speisman, A.M. Mordkoff, and L.A. Davison. A laboratory study of psychological stress produced by a motion picture film. *Psychol. Monogr.*, 1962. **76** (34, Whole No. 553).

Lindsley, D.B. Common factors in sensory deprivation, sensory distortion, and sensory overload.

In P. Solomon *et al.* (Eds.), *sensory deprivation.* Cambridge, Mass.: Harvard University Press, 1961.

———. Emotion. In S.S. Stevens (Ed.), *Handbook of experimental psychology.* New York: John Wiley & Sons, 1951.

Malmo, R.B. Activation: A neurophysiological dimension. *Psychol. Rev.*, 1959, **66,** 367–386.

Mandler, J.M., and E.T. Uviller. Automatic feedback, the perception of autonomic activity. *J. abnorm. soc. Psychol.*, 1958, **56,** 367–373.

Milgram, S. Issues in the study of obedience: A reply to Baumrind. *Amer. Psychologist*, 1964, **19,** 848–852.

Murphy, G. *Historical introduction to modern psychology.* New York: Harcourt, Brace & World, 1949.

Nomikos, M.S., E.M. Opton, Jr., J.R. Averill, and R.S. Lazarus. Surprise versus suspense in the production of stress reaction. *J. pers. soc. Psychol.*, 1968, **8,** 204–208.

Orne, M., and K. Scheibe. The contribution of non-deprivation factors in production of sensory deprivation effects. *J. abnorm. soc. Psychol.*, 1964, **68,** 3–12.

Pollard, J.C., L. Uhr, and C.W. Jackson, Jr. Studies in sensory deprivation. *AMA Arch. gen. Psychiat.*, 1963, **8,** 435–434.

Rapaport, D. The theory of ego autonomy: A generalization. *Bull. Menninger Clinic*, 1958, **22,** 13–35.

Richter, C.P. On the phenomenon of sudden death in animals and man. *Psychosom. Med.*, 1957, **19,** 191–198.

Riesen, A.H. Studying perceptual development using the technique of sensory deprivation. *J. nerv. ment. Dis.*, 1961, **132,** 21–25.

Routtenberg, A. The two-arousal hypothesis: Reticular formation and limbic system. *Psychol. Rev.*, 1968, **75,** 51–80.

Schachter, S., and J.E. Singer. Cognitive, social, and physiological determinants of emotional state. *Psychol. Rev.*, 1962, **69,** 379–399.

Seeman, J. Deception in psychological research. *Amer. Psychologist*, 1969, **24,** 1025–1028.

Selye, H. *The stress of life.* New York: McGraw-Hill, 1956.

Speisman, J.C., R.S. Lazarus, L. Davison, and A.M. Mordkoff. Experimental analysis of a film used as a threatening stimulus. *J. consult. Psychol.*, 1964, **28,** 23–33.

———. Experimental reduction of stress based on ego-defense theory. *J. abnorm. soc. Psychol.*, 1964, **68,** 367–380.

Stricker, L.J., S. Messick, and D.N. Jackson. Evaluating deception in psychological research. *Psychol. Bull.*, 1969, **71,** 343–351.

Teichner, W.H. Interaction of behavioral and physiological stress reactions. *Psychol. Rev.*, 1968, **75,** 271–291.

Teuber, H.L. Sensory deprivation, sensory suppression, and agnosia: Notes for a neurologic theory. *J. nerv. ment. Dis.*, 1961, **132,** 32–40.

Vernon, J.A., T.E. McGill, and H. Schiffman. Visual hallucinations during perceptual isolation. *Canadian Journal of Psychology*, 1958, **12,** 31–34.

White, R.W. *The abnormal personality.* (2nd ed.) New York: Ronald Press, 1956.

Wolpe, J. *Psychotherapy by reciprocal inhibition.* Stanford, Calif.: Stanford University Press, 1958.

Zubek, J.P. *Sensory deprivation: Fifteen years of research.* New York: Appleton-Century-Crofts, 1969.

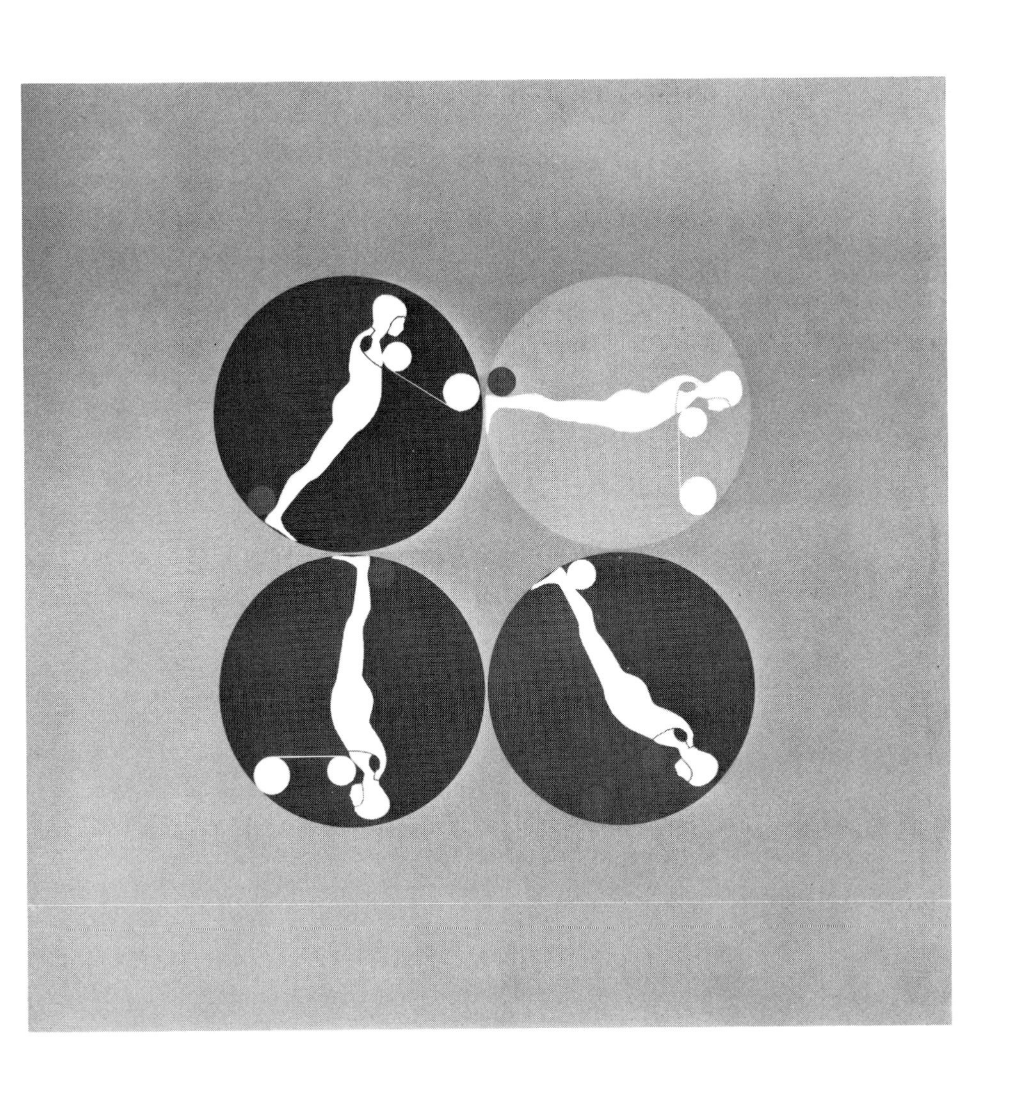

9 Models of Aggression

This chapter concerns some aspects of human aggression, exhibited in the behavior of individuals. The term "aggression" is used in a descriptive rather than an evaluative sense. We define it as behavior whose chief objective is to inflict harm, pain, or damage on another person or inanimate object.

In normal usage, the label of aggression is rarely applied to pain or damage producing acts that are judged to be justified. Only when the act seems unjustified are we inclined to designate it as aggression. Normal usage, therefore, presupposes an evaluation of the act. For example, even a casual observer of international affairs will recognize that one nation's aggression can be another nation's self-defense. Disagreement about designation of an act as aggressive arises out of concern with moral and legal implications.

Our definition omits the criterion of justification. This does not mean that the distinction between justified and unjustified acts has no significance in the analysis of aggression. In fact, we will present experimental evidence that an individual's interpretation of the context of justification determines the likelihood that he will behave aggressively. However, in accordance with our definition, we do *not* restrict the term to unjustified acts.

Aspects of Aggression

Intentionality

Perhaps you have noticed a potential difficulty in the definition. It proposes to consider as aggression only harm producing acts that reflect an *intention* to harm. Some psychologists (for example, Buss, 1961, pp. 1–2) have objected to this emphasis on intentionality. They have argued correctly that only the form of the action and its consequences can be observed directly, while intention must be inferred. The argument concludes with the claim that a definition of aggression limited to observable attributes is the only safe one.

Despite this objection, most students of human aggression (for example, Berkowitz, 1962, 1965; Bandura and Walters, 1963) do include intentionality as a criterion of aggression. We need intentionality as a basis for excluding many acts that would not be regarded as aggressive according to common sense. Accidental pain or damage producing acts are the most obvious examples. The form and consequences of these acts may be indistinguishable from genuine aggression except for the presumption of intentionality in the latter case.

Instrumentality

This chapter focuses on the type of aggression which has as its immediate and ultimate objective the inflicting of pain or damage. Very little is said about the type of aggression that serves to further a more constructive objective. These acts, performed because they are instrumental in achieving an explicitly formulated goal, are characterized by the aggressor's professing not to dislike the victim. For example, when a parent spanks his child, he may say, "This hurts me more than it does you." We are justifiably skeptical concerning this claim, and the victim is certainly not much consoled. Nevertheless, the aggressor is probably describing his intentions honestly. The aggressive act is not an end in itself, but is instrumental in achieving a goal: improvement of the child's subsequent behavior.

Trained Aggression

We also have little to say about trained aggression. The actions of the combat soldier exemplify this category. One Sunday afternoon before your television screen will prove that the professional football player ranks a close second. These men have been taught the techniques of aggression, and have been disciplined to aggress. Their aggression does not reflect individual initiative, but the acting out of behavior patterns required by a societally sanctioned role. Only when the soldier or football player deliberately violates the rules that normally constrain him, or when he transfers his aggressive behaviors to outside settings, would his behavior be a matter for discussion in this chapter.

The Instinct to Aggress

The natural state of man is war. This was the opinion of philosopher and political theorist Thomas Hobbes (1588–1679). Man is instinctively aggressive and warlike, and without societal restraints would be continually at war with his fellows. The notion that man is born with a programmed impulse to aggress is uncommonly resilient. Three centuries after Hobbes, Albert Einstein (1933), at the request of the League of Nations, exchanged correspondence with Sigmund Freud on the question: "Is there any way of delivering mankind from the menace of war?" Upon considering the reasons for war, Einstein concluded that "only one answer is possible." Man, in Einstein's view, is impelled by an innate "lust for hatred and destruction." Freud concurred. In his reply to Einstein, he wrote that man has "an active instinct for hatred and destruction" (Freud, 1959), thus echoing the three centuries old opinion of Hobbes. This view of human aggression has its adherents among contemporary writers, including Ardrey (1966), Lorenz (1966), and Storr (1968).

The instinct hypothesis of human aggression also has its vigorous critics (for example, Berkowitz, 1969, 1970; Scott, 1958; Montagu, 1968). According to them, the claims of the instinct theorist are based principally on unjustified analogies between animal and human behavior. Similarity between the behavior patterns displayed by two species, such as Lorenz's Greylag goose and man, does not necessarily imply identical underlying causes. Furthermore, the critics claim similarities between behavior patterns often become apparent only when dissimilar aspects of the behavior are ignored. The instinct theorist is accused of engaging in "word magic," glossing over important differences in behavior by applying the same descriptive labels to them.

The instinct hypothesis has been discussed in a number of books intended for the general reader (Ardrey's *The Territorial Imperative*, 1966, and Morris' *The Naked Ape*, 1968). As a result, the controversy has spilled over into the book review pages of the popular press. Although the last word on the issue has not been heard, it may safely be said that the dominant view among psychologists who favor the experimental approach is opposed to the instinct hypothesis of human aggression. Perhaps we reject the instinct hypothesis in part because it offends our optimism about human potentialities; this has been one of the counterarguments of the instinct theorist. But the principal reason for objecting to the instinct hypothesis is that the evidence is inconclusive.

What would constitute evidence of an instinct to aggress? Klineberg (1954), a social psychologist, suggests that the evidence would consist of demonstrations of the validity of the following three claims:

1. The behavior pattern is found universally among the members of the species.
2. The behavior pattern occurs without opportunity to learn.
3. The behavior pattern has a unique physiological basis.

Insofar as human aggression is concerned, positive evidence is lacking on all three counts. In one sense, it is a pity that aggression cannot be referred to an instinctual base. An instinct theory has the appeal of most simplistic theories. (Instinct theory does not have to be simplistic, but when the theory is worked out in detail it generally loses its appeal for most of its original adherents.) Abandonment of instinct theory is especially disappointing when we learn that there is no other single hypothesis that can replace it as an explanation of aggression. On the contrary, there is widespread agreement that the roots of aggression, the form it assumes, and the likelihood of its occurrence cannot be understood in terms of a single principle.

This chapter focuses on one of many factors that may affect aggression significantly. It examines the influence of observing aggression on the individual's acquisition and performance of aggressive behavior. The role of observed aggression has been of great interest to psychologists who have favored a learning theory approach to aggression. In addition, as we shall make explicit in the concluding section, investigations of observed aggression may have important implications for a much debated current social issue: the effects of violence portrayed in mass media.

Models of Aggression

Imitation, the sincerest form of flattery, is also an effective factor in shaping behavior. In fact, imitation often regulates behavior despite the wishes of the model. "Do as I say, not as I do" is a partially facetious admonition to children. Imitation has been called "vicarious or no-trial" learning. Unlike other instances of learning that represent changes in performance as a function of reinforced practice, successful imitation can lead to acquisition of a novel behavior pattern without prior performance of the behavior (Chap. 12). The response and its consequences, such as reward or punishment, are experienced vicariously through observation of the model.

In the preceding section we concluded that evidence supporting the instinct hypothesis of human aggression is not convincing. The major alternative would seem to be that aggression is learned. However, the learning of aggression must be quite different from the learning of behavior patterns that are deliberately taught. One possibility is that aggressive behavior patterns are acquired by observation and imitation. The following pages describe a series of experiments concerned with the effects on young children of the observation of aggressive and nonaggressive models. These studies examine the effects of live models as well as filmed models, and investigate cases in which aggression pays off, as well as cases in which the model's aggression is punished. Finally, several studies will be described that examine the effect of observation of one specific pattern of aggressive behavior on the probability of occurrence of another type of aggressive behavior.

Transmission of Aggression through Imitation

The first objective is to determine whether novel patterns of aggressive behavior can be acquired through imitation. Affirmative evidence would supply the essential foundation for the view that imitation is one of the origins of aggression. Two experiments by Bandura, Ross, and Ross (1961, 1963) are widely cited in this context.

The subjects in these experiments were nursery school children with a mean age of 52 months. The experiments followed the same general plan. In the first stage, the children observed the behavior of a real or filmed model. The situation was arranged so that observation of the model seemed to the child to be incidental to the main task. The child did not reproduce the model's behavior *during* the observation period. When the observation period was concluded, the children were introduced to another setting that was similar to the setting of the model's behavior. However, the model was *absent*. In this setting, the child was subjected to mild frustration. Then the child was left alone to play freely.

The principal question was this: If the child has observed the model engaging in *novel* aggressive acts, that is, aggressive behavior patterns not present in the child's preexperimental response repertoire, will the child tend to imitate these behavior patterns in the absence of the model?

Live models. In the first experiment, Bandura *et al.* (1961) compared the imitative behavior of three groups of children assigned to three different conditions of observation. One experimental group was exposed to a live adult model who behaved aggressively. A second experimental group was exposed to the same model engaging in nonaggressive behavior. The third group, assigned to the control condition, received no prior exposure to an adult model.

In the first stage of the experiment, the child was brought into the room together with the model. Both child and model were invited to play in separate corners of the room. The child's game was a quiet paper and paste activity that earlier had been found to be very appealing to the child. The "toys" provided for the model's play were a tinker toy set, a mallet, and a five foot inflated Bobo doll.

With children in the nonaggressive condition, the model played quietly with the tinker toys, completely ignoring the mallet and doll. With children in the aggressive condition the model started the same way, but after a minute of subdued play began a sustained attack on the Bobo doll. The attack was characterized by distinctive, unconventional aggressive patterns.

> The model laid Bobo on its side, sat on it and punched it repeatedly in the nose. The model then raised the Bobo doll, picked up the mallet and struck the doll on the head. Following the mallet aggression, the model tossed the doll up in the air aggressively and kicked it about the room. This sequence of physically aggressive acts was repeated approximately three times interspersed with verbally aggressive responses such as, "Sock him in the nose . . . ," "Hit him down . . . ," "Throw him in the air . . . ," "Kick him . . . ," "Pow . . .," (Bandura *et al.*, 1961, p. 576).

Thus, in this first stage, the children observed the model's behavior in the absence of any instructions to observe or imitate him. There was no opportunity to engage in imitative behavior during the observation. After ten minutes, the child

Response Category	Experimental Groups Aggressive	Nonaggressive	Control
Complete imitation	10.4	0.7	0.9
Partial imitation	16.9	8.3	13.5
Nonimitative aggression	14.1	10.9	12.2

Table 9.1 *Mean Aggression Scores for Experimental and Control Subjects*

was taken to a second room, leaving the model behind. This room contained many attractive toys with which the child was invited to play. But as soon as the child became engrossed in play, the experimenter interrupted, explaining that she had decided to reserve these toys for another child. However, the subject could play with any of the toys in the next room. This room, the final test room, contained a variety of toys that could be used to display imitative and nonimitative aggression, as well as nonaggressive behavior. Aggressive toys included the Bobo doll and the mallet among others, such as dart guns. The 20 minutes that the child spent in the room was fractionated into five second intervals, for a total of 240 time units for each child. During this period the child was continuously observed through a one-way mirror and his behavior scored for the occurrence of imitative and nonimitative aggression.

Table 9.1 shows the frequency of occurrence of three kinds of responses: complete imitation of the model's aggressive behavior pattern, for example, sitting on the doll and punching it in the nose; partial imitation, for example, striking objects other than the Bobo doll aggressively with the mallet; and nonimitative aggression, that is, aggressive acts not displayed by the model.

Can novel aggressive behavior patterns be acquired merely through observation? The answer provided by Table 9.1 is plainly affirmative; children exposed to the aggressive model imitated the model's behavior. At the same time, these patterns of behavior were very rare among the experimental children who observed the nonaggressive model and the control children who did not observe any model. The degree of imitation represented in the complete imitation category of Table 9.1 is vividly portrayed in Figure 9.1. The top row shows the aggressive model's behavior; the second and third rows show the imitative aggressive behavior of two of the children. The fact that aggressive patterns matching the specific aggressive sequences of the model occurred very rarely in the nonaggressive and control groups bolsters the conclusion that these patterns are indeed transmitted by imitation, since they did not occur spontaneously in the absence of prior observation.

In general, children exposed to the nonaggressive model behaved differently from children assigned to the aggressive model. For example, children who observed the nonaggressive model spent more than twice as much time as those in the aggressive condition simply sitting quietly without playing with any of the toys. Observation of the subdued behavior of the nonaggressive model seems to have exercised a general inhibitory effect, so that these children exhibited a smaller range of behaviors.

Live and filmed models. Direct observation of live behavior is only one of the channels through which a model's behavior may be transmitted to the child.

The role of imitation transmission of novel responses

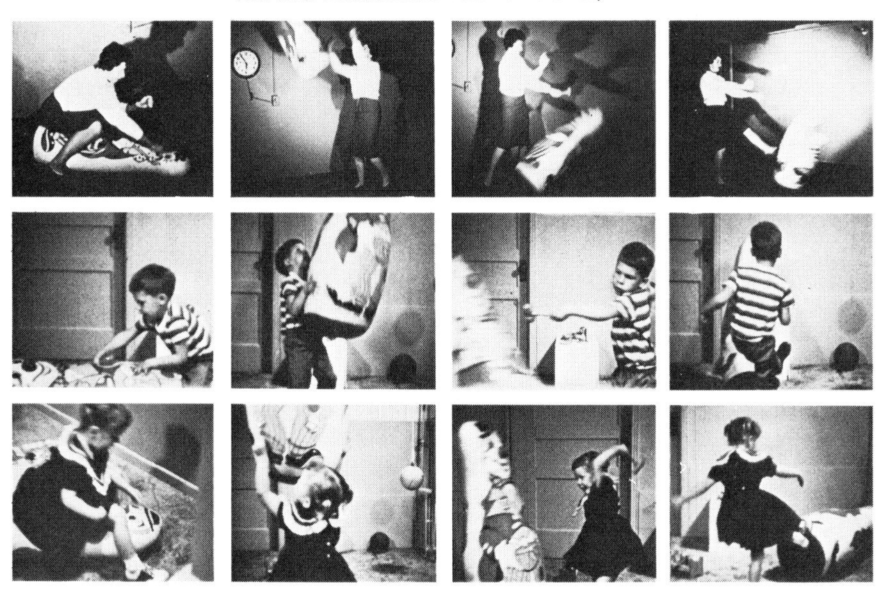

Fig. 9.1. Photographs of children reproducing the aggressive behavior of the female model they had observed on film. (From Bandura, Ross, and Ross, 1963a)

An equally important channel is provided by filmed portrayals of aggressive models. Bandura, Ross, and Ross (1963a) compared the effects of observation of a live model with the effects of observation of two filmed versions of the model. One of the films simply pictured the live model's behavior; the other presented a cartoon version of the model's behavior. In all cases, the model's behavior was aggressive in the manner described for the earlier experiment. Different groups of children were assigned to four conditions of observation: live aggression, realistic film aggression, cartoon film aggression, and control, no observation of aggression.

The experiment was designed to answer two questions. Can aggressive behavior patterns be acquired by observation of filmed aggression? Does the likelihood of imitation depend on the reality of the model? The answers are plainly indicated by experimental results. The mean total number of aggressive behavior episodes was 83, 92, 99, and 54 for the real-life, realistic film, cartoon, and control conditions, respectively. Obviously, observation of filmed aggression greatly increased the likelihood of aggression. As in the earlier experiment, this increase was not simply due to a general reduction of the inhibition against aggression; a significant portion of the increase was occasioned by the occurrence of specifically imitative aggressive patterns. The frequency of imitative aggressive episodes was 21, 16, 12, and 3 for the real-life, realistic film, cartoon, and control conditions, respectively. There appears to be a trend for the frequency of imitative behaviors to be greater in direct relation to the reality of the model. But, in fact, only the difference between the live and cartoon models passes the test of statistical significance. The differences between the real-life and realistic film model, and between the latter and the cartoon model, are not great enough to achieve statistical significance. Thus the expectation that imitative aggression would be positively related to the reality status of the model was only partially supported.

The Influence of Reinforcement Contingencies

The two experiments described above establish that novel forms of aggressive behavior can be learned by imitation. In these studies, the model's behavior was not followed by any particular consequences. In other words, the model was neither positively reinforced (rewarded) nor negatively reinforced (punished) for behaving aggressively. Typically, aggressive behavior occurring outside the laboratory does not elicit a neutral reaction; it is either applauded or disapproved. In a series of studies, Bandura, Ross, and Ross (1963b) and Bandura (1965) examined the effect of vicarious reinforcement on the learning and performance of aggressive behavior.

In the first experiment, four groups of children were tested for occurrence of imitative aggression following observation of a film. In the rewarded aggression condition, the children observed a five minute filmed episode of a model engaging in physical and verbal aggression toward another individual. The model's aggression was successful and his behavior was explicitly rewarded and approved. In the punished aggression condition the children observed the same film, except that the ending was changed to show the aggressive behavior displayed by the model severely punished. The remaining two groups were assigned to control conditions which did not provide exposure to aggression. Children in the nonaggressive model control condition observed the same two persons engaged in vigorous but *non*aggressive play with the same objects used in the aggressive films; children in the no model control condition had no prior exposure to the model. It may seem that a more appropriate control would provide observation of filmed aggression without specification of any consequences. This condition was not included because other evidence suggested that, in the absence of depicted punishment, subjects assumed that the aggression was sanctioned and approved by the experimenter, thus transforming the condition into one of implied reward.

The films were observed under the same conditions that prevailed in the earlier studies. The children were not instructed to learn the filmed behavior patterns, nor was there opportunity to reproduce the behaviors during observation of the film. The test for delayed imitation took place in another room containing all the toys needed to reproduce the model's aggressive behavior, as well as a variety of toys for eliciting nonaggressive responses. Unlike the subjects in the earlier studies, these children were not frustrated. They were simply left in the test room for 20 minutes and their behavior was rated in five second segments.

Our principal interest is in the effect of observed response consequences on the imitative learning of aggression. The investigators expected that acts of imitative aggression would occur most frequently following observation of rewarded aggression. The prediction for the punished aggression condition is not so straightforward, since two conflicting influences are present under this condition. Inasmuch as mere observation of aggression is sufficient to enhance the likelihood of its occurrence, observation of punished aggression may produce both eliciting and inhibiting effects on imitation. Therefore, a conservative prediction is indicated. The punished aggression condition should yield no more imitative aggressive responses than the nonaggressive model condition. The experimental results confirmed these predictions. The average imitative aggression scores were 15.4, 8.4, and 7.2 for the rewarded aggression, punished aggression, and nonaggressive conditions, respectively. The no model control group yielded 5.3 "imitative" responses.

There are two major possibilities for explaining the effect of observed response consequences on the frequency of imitative responses. One alternative is that the observed reinforcement contingencies affect the likelihood that the novel behavior patterns will be *learned*. It might be that a greater number of the novel aggressive patterns are learned when the model is rewarded rather than punished. Another alternative is that the observed reinforcement contingencies affect the likelihood that the novel behavior patterns will be *performed*. According to this alternative, the aggressive behavior patterns are learned or transmitted equally well under all conditions of reinforcement, reward, punishment, or no consequences, but the tendency to perform the aggressive behavior will depend on its consequences for the model. Observation of rewarded aggression disinhibits or releases the response and encourages performance of imitative aggression. Observation of punished aggression inhibits performance.

It is not possible to decide between these interpretations on the basis of the child's performance on a single postobservation test. Another step must be added, as in the following experiment by Bandura (1965a).

The first stage of the experiment involved observation of filmed aggression directed at the steadfast victim of earlier experiments, the Bobo doll. The aggression consisted of four highly novel forms of behavior (for example, the model threw rubber balls at the doll, accompanying each hit with an aggressive "Bang"). Three different groups of nursery children observed the same film, which varied only in the ending. For one group the film ended with the model receiving material and social rewards as a consequence of his aggressive acts. A second group saw the model receiving corporal punishment and a scolding. For the third group the film ended without portraying any particular reward or punishment.

In the second stage the child was observed for ten minutes in a test room. The number of different physical and verbal aggressive imitative responses recorded during this period was the performance measure.

To this point, the experiment is similar to the earlier study. The third stage was the added step introduced to help decide between the learning and performance interpretations. After the ten minute performance test was concluded, the experimenter entered the room with an assortment of treats and toys. The child was informed that the experimenter wanted to see how well he could reproduce the aggressive model's behavior. He was told that he would receive a toy and a treat after each reproduction. Bandura reasoned that providing the positive incentive would "activate into performance what the children had learned through observation . . . it was assumed that the number of different physical and verbal imitative responses reproduced by the children under the positive-incentive condition would serve as a relatively accurate index of learning" (1965a, pp. 591–592).

With this assumption in mind, two contrasting predictions can be derived from the learning and performance hypotheses.

The learning hypothesis. The introduction of positive incentives in the third stage should not affect the relative frequency of occurrence of imitative aggression. On the performance test (second stage), imitative aggressive responses should be most frequent for the rewarded aggression condition, least frequent for the punished aggression condition, and intermediate for the no consequences condition. The same should be true for the learning test (third stage).

The performance hypothesis. The introduction of positive incentives for

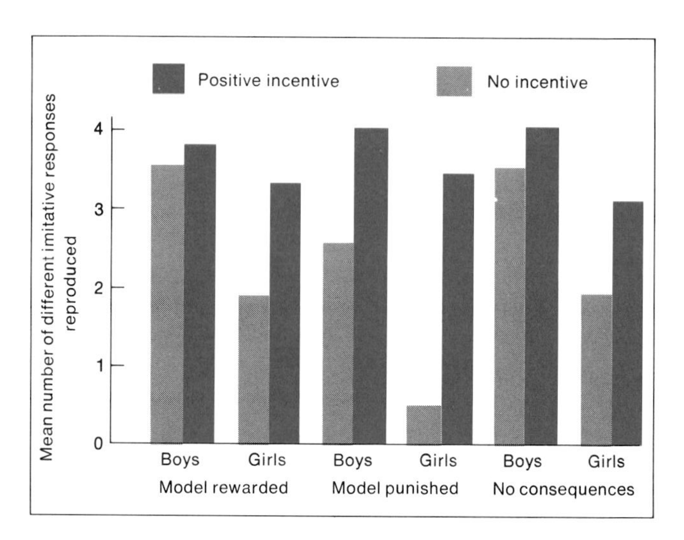

Fig. 9.2. Mean number of different matching responses reproduced by children as a function of positive incentives and the model's reinforcement contingencies. (From Bandura, 1965)

imitative aggression should wipe out the differences observed among the three conditions on the second stage. This hypothesis assumes that the second stage differences represent only differences in performance, while learning is assumed to be at the same level for all three groups. Therefore, in the third stage, when the groups are provided with a positive incentive for performing imitative aggression, all three groups should perform at the same level.

The results are graphed in Figure 9.2. The gray bars show the mean number of imitative responses produced by the children in the second stage; the responses are graphed separately for boys and girls. The figure shows that imitative aggression is more frequent following observation of rewarded aggression than following observation of punished aggression. Observation of aggression without consequences is as effective as observation of rewarded aggression, probably because of the tendency to construe absence of punishment as implied approval. Figure 9.2 also shows that under all reinforcement conditions boys reproduce more aggressive acts than do girls.

The colored bars in Figure 9.2 show the frequency of imitative aggression when positive incentives are introduced in the third stage. Three observations may be made. First, positive incentives led to increased frequencies of imitative aggression under all conditions for boys and girls. Obviously, the degree of imitative learning is not reflected accurately by the performance scores of stage two.

Second, the difference between frequency of imitative responses for boys and girls was reduced significantly by the introduction of incentives. Thus the second stage differences do not necessarily imply better imitative learning by boys. It seems just as likely that the difference in imitative aggression reflects a difference in learned inhibition against the performance of aggression. Physical aggression is rarely approved in girls, so the girls' performance during stage two is inhibited. However, when powerful positive incentives and adult approval are introduced in stage three, the girls are disinhibited and prove that they have not lagged behind in learning the patterns of aggressive behavior.

Third, the introduction of positive incentives completely eliminated performance differences between the rewarded aggression and punished aggression conditions. This outcome conforms to the performance hypothesis of the effects of observed reinforcement. Reinforcements administered to the model influence the observer's behavior chiefly by inhibiting or stimulating performance. Imitative learning, on the other hand, does not require positive reinforcement of the model.

Generalization of Learned Aggression

Nonimitative aggression. The experiments described in the previous sections have concentrated on imitative aggression. They have shown that aggressive behavior may be acquired by imitation of observed aggression. Neither practice at the time of observation nor reinforcement of the observer's behavior is necessary. This section shifts from imitative aggression to the occurrence of aggression which has *not* been modeled for the subject. Does observation of aggression increase the likelihood of aggressive acts that are not portrayed by the model? It also looks at the effect of training in one form of aggressive behavior, verbal aggression, on the occurrence of a different, untrained form of aggressive behavior, physical aggression.

Experiments by Lövaas (1961a, b) and Loew (1967) bear on this question. The subjects in Lövaas' experiments were children of ages four to seven. The first experiment (Lövaas, 1961a) was designed to determine whether exposure to filmed aggression would lead to a preference for performing nonimitative aggressive responses in a two-choice situation in which the alternative was a comparable nonaggressive act. Children observed one of two films for five minutes. One film was an edited commercial cartoon showing one humanlike cartoon figure engaging in almost continual aggression against another. The other was a nonaggressive film depicting cartoon-character bears engaging in pleasant, humanlike play.

Following this observation period, two mechanical toys were presented alongside each other for free play. Each child had already been familiarized with the toys, and it had also been established that the children assigned to the two films did not differ in their preference for the two toys in advance of the film. The doll toy consisted of two boy dolls facing each other. The doll on the right held a stick in its hand. When the child depressed a lever protruding from the front of the toy box, this doll would raise its arm with the stick and clout the other doll on the head. The ball toy consisted of a lever and a wooden ball enclosed in a cage. Depression of the lever made the ball go through the cage and back, through obstacles, to its original position. Both toys were connected to electric counters, so that the number of lever presses was counted automatically. The play period lasted four minutes.

Does exposure to filmed aggression enhance the observer's tendency to respond aggressively in nonimitative ways? In the context of Lövaas' experiment, our question may be phrased as follows: given a choice between aggressive and nonaggressive play, will children who have observed filmed aggression engage in more aggressive play (doll toy) than children who have observed filmed nonaggressive behavior? The answer is shown in Table 9.2. The aggressive film group had almost twice as many responses as the nonaggressive group to the aggressive doll toy.

This finding shows, first, that observation of filmed aggression enhances the tendency to aggress even when imitation is not possible. It is important to remember that, prior to the film, the children in both groups gave similar numbers of responses

	Mean Responses on Toy		
	Dolls	Ball	Sum
Aggressive film	98.2	99.5	197.7
Nonaggressive film	58.6	142.1	200.7
Sum	156.8	241.6	

Table 9.2 *Responses on Dolls and Ball Following Aggressive and Nonaggressive Films (From Lövaas, 1961b)*

to the doll toy. Second, note in Table 9.2 that the total number of responses was virtually the same for the two groups. Observation of filmed aggression did not raise the overall level of responding; the increase was confined to the aggressive response.

In all but one of the experiments considered thus far the form and likelihood of aggressive behavior has been affected simply by exposing the child to the behavior of others. These experiments are particularly important in showing that aggression can be learned even when it is not taught. The subjects were not instructed to aggress, nor were they reinforced for engaging in aggressive behavior. Now we are going to focus on the generalization of aggression: Will a subject rewarded for performing a specific aggressive response show a greater tendency to aggress in other ways? Both experiments concern the effect of reinforcement of verbal aggression on the subsequent occurrence of physical aggression.

Reinforced generalization. Lövaas (1961b) studied this question with children of ages three to seven. The experimental procedure had three stages. First, the children were invited to play freely with the doll toy and the ball toy. This period, lasting three minutes, was necessary to determine the existence of any preexperimental preferences for one of the toys. No initial preference was found; the children played equally often with both toys. The second stage was designed to reinforce either aggressive or nonaggressive verbal behavior. The child was seated in front of a "talk-box" that displayed two dolls, one very dirty, "the bad doll," and the other neat and clean, "the good doll." A chute at the side of the box could be used to deliver trinkets (reinforcements). The children received the following instructions:

> This is a talk-box; when you talk to this box, it will give you toys right here [points to reinforcement tray]. Now see here are two dolls. This [pointing] is the good doll; this [pointing] is the bad doll. Say "good doll" [if necessary coaches S to say, "good doll"; this response is also reinforced]. See what the box gave you; this is your toy to keep. Now you sit here and tell the box all about the dolls; tell the box what is going to happen to the dolls (Lövaas, 1961b).

One group of children was reinforced (received trinkets) for aggressive verbal responses, such as derogatory remarks, and the other group was reinforced for nonaggressive verbal responses. Figure 9.3 shows that the procedure was successful in shaping the child's verbal behavior. By the end of the training period, the children reinforced for aggressive responses (AV group) were responding only aggressively,

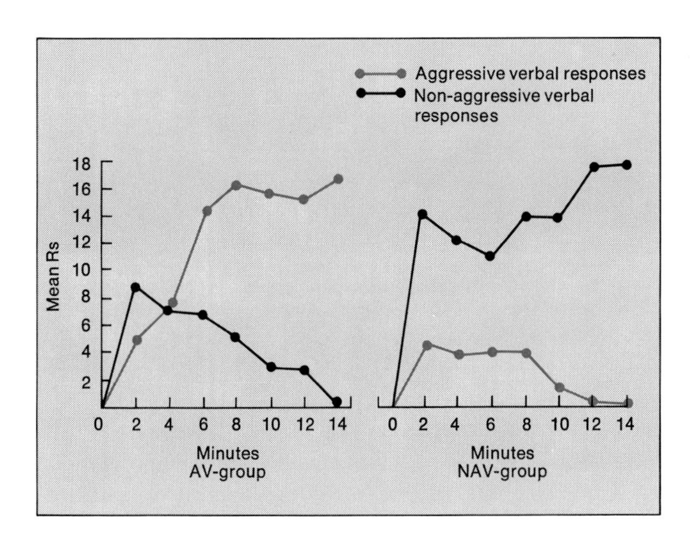

Fig. 9.3. Mean number of aggressive and nonaggressive verbal responses over successive two minute periods in the verbal conditioning period. Aggressive verbal conditioning group presented separately from the nonaggressive verbal conditioning group. (From Lövaas, 1961b)

and the children reinforced for nonaggressive responding (NAV group) were giving only nonaggressive responses.

The third stage was designed to determine the effect on physical behavior of training of verbal behavior. Does reinforcement of verbal aggression result in a generalization effect, leading to an increase in the frequency of physical aggression? To find an answer, the children were invited to play with the doll toy and ball toy once more. Table 9.3 shows the mean proportion of aggressive responses before and after verbal conditioning. Before verbal conditioning, the two groups did not differ. About 55 per cent of the total number of responses were made to the doll toy. The critical test is provided by the response proportions after conditioning. Table 9.3 shows that reinforcement of verbal aggression did lead to a significant increase in physical aggression, from 55 per cent to 78 per cent, while the change following nonaggressive conditioning was negligible.

Results very similar to Lövaas' have been reported by Loew (1967) for adult subjects. Briefly, Loew found that adults who are rewarded for choosing hostile, aggressive words on a multiple choice test will, on a subsequent test, administer more intense electric shocks to another person than will subjects who have received prior reinforcement for nonaggressive verbal choices. The generalization effect reported by Lövaas is not confined to children or to physical aggression directed against inanimate objects. Although electric shock was not actually being transmitted, the subject in Loew's experiment believed that he was administering painful shocks to another person.

Long-Term Retention of Imitative Aggression

If you have been evaluating the implications of laboratory studies of imitative aggression for understanding aggressive behavior patterns outside the laboratory, you may have noted one important difference between the experimental and extraexperimental situations. The former provide an opportunity for imitation very

	Before Verbal Conditioning	After Verbal Conditioning
Aggressive conditioning	55.2	78.4
Nonaggressive conditioning	55.4	59.4

Table 9.3 *Mean Proportion of Aggressive Responding Before and After Verbal Conditioning (From Lövaas, 1961b)*
Note: Proportion = 100 × total R's on doll total R's on doll + ball.

soon after the moment of observation, but rarely in the natural setting may the observer engage in imitative behavior immediately following observation. Therefore, if observational studies are confined to the condition of immediate testing, the data would have limited application outside the laboratory. Will imitative aggression occur if the test for imitation is administered after an extended interval following the time of original observation? Hicks (1965, 1968) has studied this question in two experiments. One experiment (Hicks, 1965) exposed four groups of children (mean age of 61 months) to filmed aggression in a simulated television program. The aggressive episode was patterned after the Bobo doll sequence. Each group observed a different model: adult male, adult female, peer (child) male, or peer female. A control group of children was not exposed to the film. Following observation of the film, all subjects were mildly frustrated and then tested for imitative aggression following the procedure used by Bandura *et al.* (1963). As in the earlier studies, Hicks found significantly greater imitation scores for the children who observed filmed aggression. These groups yielded an average number of 16 imitative aggressive responses, while the control group exhibited no responses that were similar to those executed by the model. Approximately six months after their exposure to the film the children were retested. They were *not* reexposed to the film, but were returned to the test room, mildly frustrated, and then observed for the occurrence of imitative aggression. Once more the children who had been exposed to the film were found to display significantly more imitative aggression than the controls, although the frequency of imitative behaviors was much lower than the first test. A further finding was that retention loss from the immediate to the delayed test was least for the children who observed the adult male model.

Hicks' study suggests that the effects of observing aggression are retained over long intervals of nonrehearsal. However, interpretation of Hicks' studies in terms of long-term retention of initiative aggression must be qualified by the recognition that this second testing was, in fact, a *retest* rather than a delayed test—the experimental subjects had been given what amounted to a "practice trial" immediately after having observed the model. Recall and reproduction of these responses may then not have been based on the initial *observation* alone, but also on the subjects' recall of their previous performance of the acts. This distinction is important for the assessment of the social effects of media aggression, since, as was noted earlier, violent actions in films and television programs are not likely to be "practiced" immediately after they have been seen. Research comparing retention of practiced versus unpracticed responses is needed in order to determine the permanence of aggression learning from observation of the media.

Conditions of Aggression

Assume that the individual has acquired patterns of aggressive behavior. What conditions are likely to elicit these behavior patterns? In their now classic monograph, *Frustration and Aggression*, Dollard, Doob, Miller, Mowrer, and Sears (1939) advanced the claim that the *sole* antecedent condition of aggression is frustration: ". . . the occurrence of aggressive behavior always presupposes the existence of frustration," and also that "the existence of frustration always leads to some form of aggression" (p. 1). These sweeping claims have not passed unchallenged. Critics (for example, Bandura and Walters, 1963; Buss, 1961) have presented evidence of aggression without frustration and of frustration without ensuing aggression. Even the staunchest proponents of the frustration–aggression hypothesis (Berkowitz, 1962, 1970) have abandoned the original form of the hypothesis in favor of the weaker claim that frustration is *one* of the antecedents of aggression. One may feel inclined to accept this proposition uncritically, since it is after all a modest claim entirely compatible with daily observation. Nevertheless, we should point out that, despite its reasonableness, it has limited scientific utility unless it is elaborated to include a statement specifying the conditions under which one may expect that frustration will lead to aggression.

What Is Frustration?

For Dollard *et al.* (1939, p. 7), frustration was "an interference with the occurrence of an instigated goal-response at its proper time in the behavior sequence." Frustration is the blocking of behavior before it can culminate in achievement of the goal. A number of points should be made about this apparently straightforward definition. First, the goal-response may be blocked at several distinct points in the sequence of behavior. Consider the following hypothetical illustration: Tommy hears the ringing bell of the ice cream truck and heads outdoors, money in hand, to buy his favorite ice cream bar. But it is not to be: (1) Before Tommy can reach the truck, his mother calls him back. The instrumental response is blocked. (2) Or he reaches the truck to discover that the supply of his favorite flavor has been exhausted. Presentation of the reinforcer is blocked. (3) Or, cruelest of all, Tommy secures the ice cream bar, but before he can begin eating he trips and the ice cream bar is ruined. The consummatory response is blocked. Tommy's misadventures illustrate that the blocking operation constituting frustration can occur at various stages during the goal directed behavior sequence.

The second point is that there are a variety of operations that can block the response. For example, blocking of the instrumental response may result from the introduction of barriers, or from failure to perform the instrumental response successfully, or from the introduction of conflict, such as, "Tommy, remember, you were saving that money for the movies."

One other aspect of the definition of frustration has been stressed by Berkowitz (1970). Frustration is the blocking of ongoing goal directed behavior; blocking is frustrating only if the person continues to aspire to the goal despite the block. If the goal is abandoned, frustration does not result. Suppose I am waiting at the bus stop and see the bus approaching, but instead of stopping, the bus speeds by. I have been blocked, but whether or not I have been frustrated will depend on the circumstances. Suppose that as the bus draws near I recognize

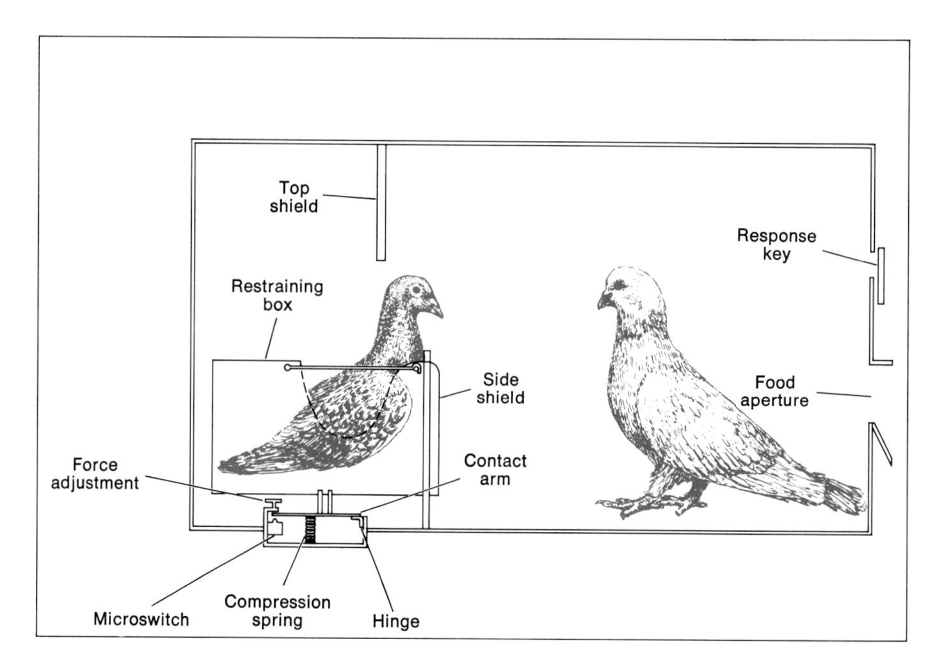

Fig. 9.4. Schematic of the apparatus for measuring attack. The experimental chamber was 25 × 14 × 14 inches high. Plexiglas shields at the top and on the sides of the restraining box prevented the experimental pigeon from getting behind the target pigeon. (From Azrin *et al.*, 1966)

the destination notice, *TO GARAGE*. Under these circumstances, I will abandon my goal of boarding the bus and the blocking will not lead to frustration. On the other hand, suppose the destination of the bus is also my own. In that case I will anticipate boarding the bus and, being blocked, I will experience frustration.

Frustration Can Lead to Aggression

Let us consider a sample of the experimental evidence that shows a relationship between frustration and aggression. We have selected three diverse examples dealing with aggression in animals, children, and adults.

Extinction induced aggression. In reviewing Tommy's difficulties we noted that one form of blocking is failure to provide the expected reinforcer. The extinction procedure commonly used in experiments on learning provides an experimental analog of Tommy's fate. This procedure involves termination of the delivery of reinforcement after an organism is conditioned to perform a response leading to that reinforcement. If extinction, or withholding of the reinforcement, is frustrating, it could lead to aggression. Azrin, Hutchinson, and Hake (1966) investigated this possibility in an ingenious series of experiments.

A pair of pigeons was placed into the experimental apparatus shown in Figure 9.4. One of the pigeons (the target or victim) was an innocent bystander in a restraining box; the other pigeon was the active subject. In the first part of the experiment both pigeons were in the box with the food delivery mechanism disconnected. The pigeons were observed, to determine the frequency of spontaneous aggression. Then the passive pigeon was removed and the other pigeon was trained in an alternating cycle of reinforcement and extinction sessions. The first ten responses the pigeon made after a tone sounded were rewarded by food, followed by a five minute period of no reward. The pigeon was trained to keypeck only immediately following the tone, and never during extinction. At that point the target pigeon was returned to the box, and the cycle of reinforcement–extinction was continued.

The results were dramatic. When extinction was initiated the trained pigeon responded by attacking the target pigeon. Extinction induced frustration led to aggression.

> The usual burst of key pecks occurred [following the tone]. . . . The pigeon attacked the target shortly after the last response of the burst . . . attack consisted of strong pecks at the throat and head . . . especially around the eyes. The feathers of the target bird were often pulled out. . . . Frequently, the attack was preceded and accompanied by a deep-throated sound (Azrin *et al.*, 1966, pp. 194–195).

There is no mistaking the pigeons's reaction. All 18 pigeons who were tested aggressed more during extinction than during the preliminary no reinforcement phase. Comparable results were obtained in another experiment which tested pigeons ten months old who had been reared in isolation from other pigeons. Apparently the aggressive response to extinction does not depend on a prior history of competition over food and reinforcement.

Frustration of instrumental responses. A study by Mallick and McCandless (1966) illustrates the relationship between frustration and aggression when the blocking occurs during the instrumental segment of the goal directed sequences. Third grade children were promised a nickel for each of five moderately simple block construction tasks that they could complete in cooperation with another child. The other child was actually a confederate of the experimenter. Half of the subjects were assigned to a frustration condition, in which the confederate acted clumsily and prevented the subject from completing any of the tasks. In addition, the confederate directed sarcastic, teasing remarks at the subject. The other subjects were assigned to a nonfrustrative condition in which the confederate helped the subject complete all the tasks.

In order to exhibit the frustration–aggression relationship, each subject was given an opportunity to aggress against the confederate. The subjects were allowed to administer electric shocks to the confederate, with the assurance that the confederate would not know the identity of his aggressor. No limit was imposed on the number of shocks that could be administered (shock was not actually delivered); the number of "shocks" was taken as the measure of aggression. The results were clear. Frustrated subjects administered significantly more shocks than nonfrustrated subjects.

The catharsis hypothesis. The Mallick-McCandless study reported another finding of interest. There is a popular opinion that the acting out of aggressive impulses is "cathartic," leading to a reduction of the instigation of further aggression. This opinion has generated a widespread expectation that the incidence of unwanted, dangerous aggression resulting from frustration will be reduced if the person is given a chance to "let off steam" by engaging in socially sanctioned, harmless aggression. Mallick and McCandless examined this belief. Between the frustrating block building task and the aggressive shock administration stages of

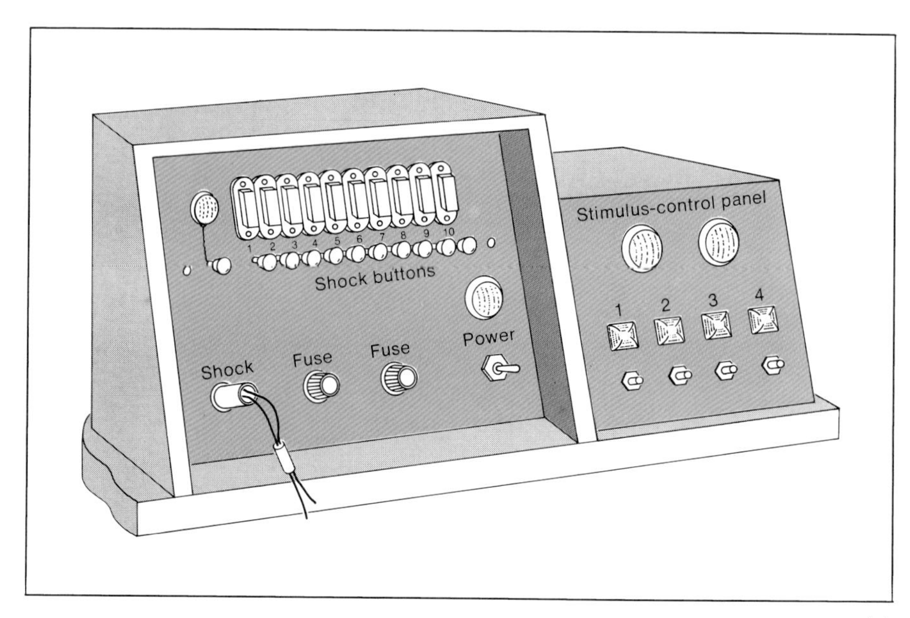

(a)

(b)

Fig. 9.5. Aggression machine: (a) subject's side; (b) accomplice's ("victim's") side. (From Buss, 1961)

the experiment, the experimenters interposed one of three types of activity: shooting a play gun at drawings of human and animal figures, shooting at a bullseye target, or solving simple arithmetic figures. If the catharsis hypothesis is correct, we would expect these interpolated activities to influence the subject's response to the opportunity to shock the confederate (for example, the first activity should have a cathartic effect leading to reduction of aggression). However, Mallick and McCandless found no evidence of any effect of these interpolated activities. Later we will say more about the catharsis hypothesis.

The Aggression Machine

One restriction in designing a study of the frustration–aggression hypothesis involving human subjects stems from concern with the victim. We cannot deliberately arrange a situation that would cause pain or harm, although these consequences are exactly those specified by our definition of aggression. One solution has been to use inanimate objects as the target of aggression, such as the Bobo doll. However, eventually the investigator must examine aggressive behavior that is directed toward persons. This study requires a mode of physical behavior that satisfies the definition of aggression without actually harming the victim. A second demand is common to most analytic experimentation. Differences in levels of the dependent variable (aggressive response) must be expressed in quantitative terms. In the present context, a quantifiable intensity dimension of aggression is required. This would enable the investigator to arrange aggressive responses of a specific type on a dimension of intensity, and to specify each intensity level quantitatively. The "Aggression Machine" was designed by Buss (1961) to satisfy these requirements.

The apparatus is pictured in Figure 9.5. The mode of aggression is administration of electric shock. The victim is actually a confederate of the experimenter. The subject is instructed to play the role of an experimenter in a learning task, his goal being to teach the victim a concept. The subject can present stimuli by depressing the buttons on the right-hand panel. The victim can respond by causing one of two response lights to flash. The subject is instructed to flash the "Correct" light whenever the victim makes a correct response. However, when the victim makes an incorrect response, the subject is to press one of the ten shock buttons, and thus deliver a shock to the victim. The intensity of shock ranges from very mild to painful, depending on the button selected. At the start of the experiment, the subject is himself shocked from several buttons so that he may develop an idea of the shock intensity scale. This procedure also has the effect of convincing him that the machine does indeed deliver shocks. In fact, however, the victim receives no shock, since the electric connection is broken before the "learning" task begins. In order to maintain realism, the victim emits gasps or groans when shock buttons are pressed. The number of the button that the subject presses is flashed on a translucent screen on the victim's side so that it may be recorded.

The Aggression Machine provides a quantitative measure of physical aggression without danger to the victim. Various versions of the apparatus have been used in studies of aggression. One study (Buss, 1963) examined the frustration–aggression hypothesis using college students as subjects and victims. The subject, told that his goal was to teach the victim a concept, presented a series of stimuli to which the accomplice responded in a preprogrammed way. Despite the experimenter's assurance to the subject that the task was easy, the accomplice persisted in making errors. Consequently, the subject was frustrated by the victim's apparent inability to learn. In order to enhance the goal striving, the subjects were offered a variety of incentives for successful teaching, such as earning money or obtaining a better grade. Control subjects were not offered any incentives, and in addition were told that the concept was very difficult and it was likely that the pupil (victim) would need as many as 75 trials to learn it.

There were six blocks of ten trials during which the accomplice committed 26 errors. Experimental and control subjects did not differ on the first block. The average shock intensity was about 2.5 on the scale, a level that is not painful. The control subjects remained at this level throughout the trials, but the experimental subjects behaved differently. During the third block, by which time they had been led to expect learning, the experimental subjects diverged from the control subjects and began increasing the shock level, going to successively higher levels in the ensuing blocks. During the last block the subjects administered painful shocks to the victim. These were shocks at intensity levels which the subjects themselves had previously experienced as painful. Since a mild, innocuous shock would have been just as informative to the victim, we may reasonably conclude that the delivery of intense shocks was punitive in intent and not simply intended to instruct. Frustration led to aggression.

When Does Frustration Elicit Aggression?

The results of these three experiments and other similar studies show that frustration *can* elicit aggression. Nevertheless, there is also widespread agreement that frustration does not inevitably lead to aggression. An important objective for future research is specification of the conditions that affect the likelihood that aggression will follow frustration.

Instrumental value. In the studies we have considered, aggression had no instrumental value. These were cases of aggression for its own sake, since aggression was not instrumental in removing or alleviating the frustrating condition. It is reasonable to suppose that, when aggression has high instrumental value, it is more likely to be elicited by frustration. An experiment by Buss (1966a) confirmed this expectation.

Response strength of aggression. Many experiments show wide individual differences among subjects who receive the same frustration treatment. One interpretation of this is that the aggressive response occupies a different rank in the response hierarchies of various subjects. For some subjects aggressive behavior is the predominant response, while for others it has a low probability of occurrence, relative to other available responses. But the relative strength of a response is not permanently fixed, and the likelihood that frustration will elicit aggression may depend on the *current* response strength of aggression.

An experiment with seven to nine year old children, conducted by Davitz (1952), provides supportive evidence. The experiment was in four stages: (1) free play, (2) training in either aggressive or nonaggressive play, (3) frustration (blocking of the consummatory response), and (4) free play. Davitz reported that subjects trained in aggressive play engaged in more aggressive free play following frustration than the subjects who were trained nonaggressively. Furthermore, most of the children who were trained nonaggressively showed no increase in aggressive play from the pre- to postfrustration free play period. Thus, the likelihood of frustration leading to aggression depended on the potency or response strength of aggressive behavior patterns at the time of frustration.

Availability of aggression—eliciting stimuli. Certain objects have powerful associations with aggression. As a result of their history, these objects may become aggression eliciting stimuli. This does not mean that exposure to these stimuli always elicits aggression. Everyone has been exposed to a gun without experiencing the impulse to aggress, and the same is true for other aggression–eliciting stimuli. Nevertheless, under certain conditions, exposure to these stimuli may encourage aggression. When frustration is involved, the presence of aggression–eliciting stimuli may interact with it to increase the likelihood of aggression.

An experiment by Berkowitz and LePage (1967) illustrates this effect. In part of the study, three groups of college students were aroused to anger by an unjustifiably large number of electric shocks administered to them by another subject (actually an accomplice of the experimenter). Then, under a reasonable pretext, the subjects were given an opportunity to shock their tormenter (counteraggression). For one group, a rifle and a shotgun were on the table near the subject's shock key. The second group had two badminton racquets on the table, and for the third the table was bare of objects. Berkowitz and LePage found that the subjects exposed to the weapons administered the greatest number of shocks. The other two conditions resulted in lower numbers of shocks and did not differ from each other. The effectiveness of the weapons as eliciting stimuli was further increased if they were identified for the subject as belonging to the accomplice.

Berkowitz and LePage's (1967) results are compatible with the hypothesis that the likelihood and nature of the aggressive response to frustration may be influenced by stimuli associated with aggression, and that such stimuli may serve to bring the aggressive response to the top of the response hierarchy. A good deal of future research will be needed to clarify this notion of aggression–eliciting stimuli and to specify the mechanisms by which these stimuli interact with frustration or anger.

Other Antecedents of Aggression

Frustration has been discussed in some detail because it has been a principal concern of students of aggression. However, very few investigators would claim that frustration is the only antecedent of aggression, or that aggression is the inevitable response to frustration. At least two other major causes of aggression, attack and pain, have been identified, and these factors would have to be considered in a full discussion of individual aggression.

Vicarious Aggression: Catharsis or Stimulation?

The Catharsis Hypothesis

Earlier in this chapter we considered evidence showing that patterns of aggressive behavior can be acquired by imitation of observed aggression. This section considers another aspect of observing aggression. Consider an individual who is angered (instigated to aggression), and who then observes other people engaging in aggressive behavior. What effect will the vicarious experience of aggression have on the expression of aggression? Will vicarious aggression reduce the probability of further aggression, or will it stimulate aggression? As noted previously, the possibility that observation of aggression reduces further aggression is usually attributed to a process called *catharsis*, first defined by Aristotle in his analysis of tragedy in the *Poetics*. Aristotle proposed that one of the functions of tragedy is to provide the audience with an opportunity to discharge the tragic emotions of fear and grief. This discharge comes about because the audience experiences the emotions along with the actors; the audience has a *cathartic* experience. In a similar vein, it has been suggested that observation of aggression may result in a draining of the reservoir of aggression. The vicarious experience is presumed to be an occasion for catharsis and a condition leading to reduction in the likelihood of further aggression.

The catharsis hypothesis was part of Freud's theory, and it also played a role in the behavioristic analysis of aggression proposed by Dollard *et al.* (1939, pp. 53–54). The hypothesis also has many adherents outside psychology. For example, spokesmen for the television industry often counter criticisms of violence in programing with the claim that exposure to repeated displays of violcncc and aggression has a socially desirable effect. The viewer allegedly discharges his aggressive impulses while observing televised aggression, consequently reducing the likelihood of aggression being discharged in socially undesirable ways.

Methodological considerations. The minimal experimental design for study of the catharsis hypothesis compares two groups of subjects. In the initial step, all subjects are angered. Then the experimental subjects view a film depicting aggression, while the control subjects view a neutral film. Finally, the subjects are provided with an opportunity to express aggression. Comparisons between behavior of the experimental and control subjects during the last stage provide the data for evaluating the catharsis hypothesis. The hypothesis requires that the experimental subjects exhibit less aggression than the control subjects.

Two points need clarification before the experimental literature is considered. First, it may seem, even before new evidence is introduced, that the catharsis hypothesis is contradicted by earlier studies showing an *increase* in aggression following observation of filmed or modeled aggression. This conclusion is unwarranted, since the earlier studies did not test the effect of vicarious aggression on *previously aroused* anger or instigation to aggression. The subjects in the experiments of Bandura, Ross, and Ross (1961, 1963) observed the films while in a neutral emotional state. The frustration treatment was introduced *after* observation of aggression. Therefore, these experiments do not test the catharsis hypothesis.

Second, the catharsis hypothesis requires that subjects who have observed filmed aggression exhibit less aggression than control subjects. At the same time, this outcome need not conclusively establish the hypothesis. Reduced aggression could be explained without recourse to the catharsis hypothesis. As one alternative, observation of aggression may arouse anxiety and inhibit expression of aggression.

Experimental investigations. The early history of the catharsis hypothesis has been reviewed by Buss (1961, Chap. 5) and Berkowitz (1962, Chap. 8). Early experimental investigations of the effects of *observed* aggression were rare, so we will concentrate on more recent work, beginning with an experiment by Feshbach (1961). Male college students were assigned to one of four conditions: insult (angered) versus noninsult and aggressive film versus neutral film. Students assigned to the insult condition were subjected to unwarranted and extremely critical remarks that disparaged their intellectual competence and emotional maturity. Previous studies (Feshbach, 1955) had shown that this treatment arouses hostility toward the experimenter. Subjects assigned to the noninsult condition were treated in a neutral manner. Then the subjects viewed one of two films. One was a film clip showing a violent prizefight sequence from the motion picture *Body and Soul;* the other was a neutral film depicting the consequences of the spread of rumors in a factory. As a rationale for presentation of the film, all the subjects were told that they would be asked to judge the personality of its main character.

When the film was completed the subjects filled out a questionnaire concerning the main character. At this point the experimenter left the room and was replaced by a new experimenter, who explained that the psychology department wished to learn students' opinions of the value of participating in psychological experiments. A questionnaire was administered dealing with the subject's attitude toward the experimenter and the experiment. Each question had six alternative answers from which the subject selected one. (The alternatives ranked in aggressive intent from one, least aggressive, to six, most aggressive.) The subjects' response to this questionnaire provided the measure of aggression.

Feshbach predicted that the insulted group exposed to the fight film would exhibit less aggression toward the experimenter than the insulted group exposed to the neutral film. This would represent the cathartic effect of vicarious aggression. On the other hand, the noninsulted group exposed to the fight film should show more aggression than the noninsulted group exposed to the neutral film. This prediction is not derived from the catharsis hypothesis, but it is one of the implications of the observation studies and is consistent with the hypothesis that viewing aggression stimulates aggressive behavior, even when frustration does not occur.

The experimental results conformed to the catharsis hypothesis. The mean aggression score for insulted subjects who viewed the fight film was significantly lower than the score for the insulted group who viewed the neutral film. Furthermore, most of the subjects (20 of 26) assigned to the insult–fight film condition yielded aggression scores below the median (fiftieth percentile) for the entire insult group, while most of the subjects (22 of 29) assigned to the insult–neutral film condition yielded aggression scores above the median. The second half of Feshbach's prediction, involving the noninsulted groups, was not supported. Comparable aggression scores were obtained following the fight film and the neutral film.

By contrast, other investigators, such as Walters and Thomas (1963), have succeeded in demonstrating the stimulating effect of vicarious aggression for nonangered subjects. The subjects included high school students, college students, and older persons. Using a version of Buss' Aggression Machine, Walters and Thomas compared the shift in level of shocks that the subject administered to another "subject" (confederate) in a learning task. In the first of three stages the subjects administered electric shock (as in previously described procedures). Then one group of subjects witnessed a scene depicting a switchblade knife fight between two adolescent boys taken from the film, *Rebel Without a Cause*. The other group viewed an educational film depicting adolescents engaged in cooperative art work. Finally, the subjects returned to the Aggression Machine to continue the learning task. The results were clear: The group that watched the knife fight punished the confederates' learning errors more severely, using a significantly higher intensity level of electric shock than the group that watched the neutral film.

Putting together the results of Feshbach's and Walters' studies, it would appear that the effect of observed aggression depends in part on the emotional state of the observer. It seems that when the observer is in a neutral, nonangered state (as in the Walters and Thomas study), observation of aggression acts as a stimulant. The group in Feshbach's research that was not insulted but did view the fight film did not however show increased aggression, which suggests that this hypothesis is incomplete. On the other hand, if the observer has been aroused at the time of observation (as in Feshbach's research), then the instigation to aggress is probably reduced by the observation of aggression.

How general is this conclusion? Is it confirmed under a wide range of conditions, or is it confined to highly specific conditions? Are there, in fact, conditions under which observation of aggression leads to increased aggression in angered persons?

Catharsis or Inhibition?

Justification of aggression. One aspect of observed aggression that might be expected to affect the postobservation response of the angered subject is the perceived justification of the aggressive act. This consideration is especially important in light of the alternative interpretation of the "cathartic" reduction of aggression. According to this alternative, aggression is reduced not because of a cathartic purging, but because observation has aroused guilt or anxiety feelings which inhibit expression of aggression. The importance of this distinction is not exclusively theoretical. For those who wish to apply laboratory data to an evaluation of the effects of mass media, it makes a considerable difference whether the effect is cathartic or inhibitory. In the latter case, the aggressive drive remains undiminished, and variables that *disinhibit* the anxiety or guilt feelings associated with aggression will lead to increased aggression following observation. One disinhibiting factor may be the degree of justification provided by the context of aggression. A context that justifies the aggressive act may serve to remove the inhibitions and allay the anxieties otherwise evoked by witnessing aggression, and the result could be enhanced rather than reduced postobservation aggression.

Berkowitz and his associates (1963, 1965a) have examined the justification factor in a series of experiments. The general procedure compared postobservation aggression of subjects who witnessed justified and unjustified aggression with the behavior of a control group which did not observe aggression. College students were shown a film of a brutal prizefight after having been angered by the experimenter or treated in a neutral manner. For half of the subjects the film was preceded by a synopsis which portrayed the victim in highly unfavorable terms, making it clear that he had received his just deserts. The other subjects received a synopsis which portrayed the victim sympathetically and made it appear that the beating was undeserved. After the movie, subjects were allowed to aggress against the experimenter. Berkowitz *et al.* found that observation of justified aggression led to increased levels of aggression in angered subjects, thus suggesting that justification of aggression tends to remove inhibitions against aggression. Furthermore, this finding reinforces the suspicion that the reduction in aggression reported by Feshbach (1961) may have been due to inhibition rather than catharsis.

Observation of pain cues. Hartmann (1969) has examined another condition of observed aggression. Hartmann notes that an aggressive behavior sequence generally contains two distinctive events, the instrumental aggressive act of the agent and the pain reactions exhibited by the victim. In many of the earlier studies, such as those on imitative aggression, pain cues were absent, and in other studies, such as those depicting fight scenes, the pain cues were not isolated. Hartmann designed a procedure to test the independent effects of observed aggression and observed pain cues. The subjects were male adolescents who had been committed to an institution for juvenile delinquents. In the first stage, all subjects took a so-called social judgment test. Each subject's performance was evaluated by another "subject" who remained out of sight in another room. This "fellow subject" was, in fact, a fictitious individual whose presumed responses to the experimental subject

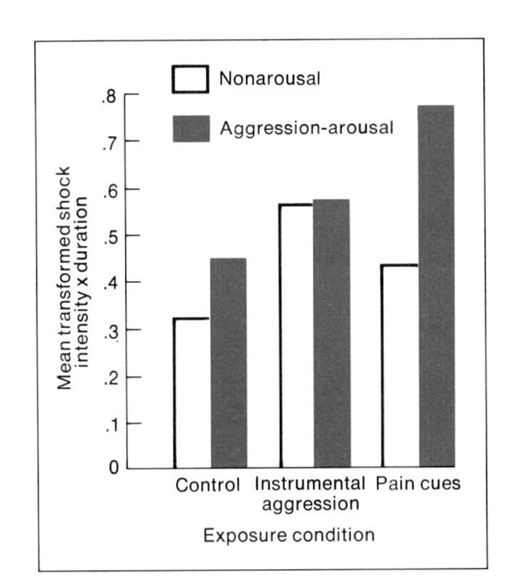

Fig. 9.6. Mean transformed shock intensity × duration for subjects viewing the control film, the instrumental aggression film, and the pain cue film. (From Hartmann, 1969)

were played on tape. Half the subjects received highly critical and derogatory evaluations; the rest received neutral evaluations. In the second stage, the subjects viewed a two minute film under the guise of a test of attention. Three versions of the film were prepared. The first minute, which was the same in all versions, showed two boys shooting baskets on a basketball court. After the first minute the three films diverged: the control film showed the boys engaged in an active cooperative game; the instrumental aggression film showed an argument develop, culminating in a fight (the film focused on the aggressor's responses, like flying fists, angry expressions); the pain cue film focused on the victim's verbal and gestural pain reactions. In the third stage of the experiment the subjects were given the opportunity to administer sanctioned and anonymous punishment to their evaluator. The task and experimental arrangement were patterned after Buss' learning task, using the Aggression Machine.

The Aggression Machine provides two measures of aggression: the intensity of shock and its duration. In Figure 9.6 we see a combined intensity × duration measure for each of the six conditions. Look first at the data for aggression arousal. The catharsis hypothesis predicts that aroused subjects exposed to filmed aggression will exhibit less aggression than aroused subjects who observe a neutral film. Obviously, the opposite was true in Hartmann's study. Observed aggression, whether focused on instrumental acts or pain cues, led to increased aggression.

Next, compare the differences between the control and the two experimental films, first for the aggression-arousal, then for the nonarousal condition. When the subject is aroused, focus on the victim's pain leads to greater stimulation of aggression than focus on the aggressive act. The reverse is true for nonaroused subjects; their aggression scores were higher following observation of instrumental aggression. In fact, nonaroused subjects who observed the pain cue film did not differ from the aroused subjects who viewed the neutral film.

Hartmann's findings concerning the effect of pain cues are generally consistent with the results of earlier investigators, such as Patterson *et al.* (1967), Feshbach *et al.* (1967), and Buss (1966b). A coherent account of these results has yet to be developed. We need a theoretical formulation which will explain why pain cues act to inhibit postobservation aggression in nonaroused subjects, and to stimulate aggression in aroused subjects.

Let us return to the question that opened this section. Does observation of aggression reduce or enhance the likelihood of aggression in an aroused observer? We have probably not heard the last word on this matter, but whatever future research may reveal, one conclusion may be confidently offered today. Observation of aggression frequently leads to increased aggression. A reduction of aggression may also occur under certain circumstances, but it is not at all clear that this reduction is due to catharsis.

Violence and the Mass Media

Those with a penchant for labeling historical periods may call the present time the Age of Violence. Whether we deserve this distinctive appellation can be debated, but there is little doubt that our times rival any other in expression of concern about violence. All levels of government and society have expressed alarm about the frequency, intensity, and character of violence. An excellent series of discussions of violence in America can be found in the report to the National Commission on the Causes and Prevention of Violence (Graham and Gurr, 1969). This report provides a valuable reminder that violence in the form of criminal, political, and economic activities has been a pervasive feature of United States society. It also makes clear that the causes of violence are varied and complex.

These observations help in maintaining a balanced perspective when considering the effects of violence in the mass media. No reasonable person would attribute violence in society entirely to the effects of observation of mass media aggression. The issue is whether media violence contributes significantly to the intolerably high rate of violence in society. Would the character and quality of life be better if violence and aggression were only rarely portrayed in fictional televised or filmed presentations? What facts are available to help find the answer? There seem to be four principal observations that figure prominently in discussions of the question:

1. Content analysis of media programing in the 1960's has consistently shown that violence and aggression are the most frequent methods of resolving conflicts or gaining objectives.
2. Violence and aggression are depicted in the media as the procedures that are most likely to succeed in achieving objectives.
3. Television viewing is becoming an increasingly prominent activity; for many people, viewing time is exceeded only by time spent in work (or school) and sleep.
4. Experimental investigations have shown that observation of aggression leads to imitative aggression and enhances nonimitative aggression.

What conclusion can be drawn from these facts?

The answer will depend on your willingness to generalize laboratory findings regarding the effects of observation to the case of the confirmed television viewer in his living room. The situations obviously differ. To begin with, the sequence and timing of events that characterize the laboratory experiment are not found often in daily life. Second, the aggressive episodes are usually presented in the context of a narrative plot. Third, the viewer rarely has the opportunity to aggress immediately after viewing, nor is he able to engage in anonymous aggression without threat of retaliation. Finally, there is the obvious difference in frequency and regularity of exposure. Given these differences, may the results of laboratory studies be applied to an analysis of media effects? An affirmative answer means that there is a case for indicting the television industry for inciting violence. However, if generalization from the laboratory is unwarranted, then there is no firm basis for attributing the occurrence of violence to the effects of observed media violence. (For a discussion of the validity of applying laboratory findings to natural settings, see Chap. 11.)

The question of generalization has been vigorously debated by critics and advocates of mass media (Lawson, 1968), but it is unlikely that the disagreement can be resolved by debate. The matter, after all, is empirical, and can be answered only by experiment. This becomes clear if the question is formulated in the following way: In an experiment designed to capture the salient characteristics of mass media observation, will the major findings of the earlier laboratory studies be replicated? There is no way to answer this except by appropriate experimentation, and it seems apparent that social psychologists will move in this direction.

In the absence of agreement regarding the implications of laboratory findings, policies governing mass media programing are usually made on the basis of intuition. But intuition can be misleading. For example, the policies regulating the content of television programing specify that wanton violence should not be exhibited; only justified violence is permitted. Furthermore, portrayal of the victim's suffering is to be minimized. On first impression, these would seem to be laudable guidelines, but actually they prescribe the very conditions which laboratory research has identified as leading to postobservation increases in aggression. It is no empty caveat to conclude that more research is urgently needed.

Glossary

Aggression: behavior whose chief objective is to inflict harm, pain, or damage on another person or an inanimate object.

Aggression Machine: an experimental apparatus used in studying aggression against humans. The aggressive act is administration of electric shock of varying intensity. The "victim" is an experimental accomplice who does not actually receive the shock.

Catharsis: literally, a purging; used in two principal ways: (a) acting out an emotion purges the individual and reduces the likelihood of further instigation to act in a similar way; (b) vicarious participation in an emotional experience through observation of others purges the witness of the emotion.

Frustration–aggression hypothesis: the hypothesis that frustration leads to aggression. In its unmodified form, frustration is the sole antecedent of aggression and aggression always follows frustration.

References

Ardrey, R. *The territorial imperative*. New York: Atheneum, 1966.

Azrin, N.H., R.R. Hutchinson, and D.F. Hake. Extinction-induced aggression. *J. exp. Anal. of Behavior*, 1966, **9,** 191–204.

Bandura, A. Influence of model's reinforcement contingencies on the acquisition of imitative responses. *J. pers. soc. Psychol.*, 1965, **69,** 589–595. (a)

———. Vicarious processes: A case of no-trial learning. In L. Berkowitz (Ed.), *Advances in experimental social psychology*. Vol. 2. New York: Academic Press, 1965. (b)

———, D. Ross, and S.A. Ross. Imitation of film-mediated aggressive models. *J. abnorm. soc. Psychol.*, 1963, **66,** 3–11. (a)

———. Transmission of aggression through imitation of aggressive models. *J. abnorm. soc. Psychol.*, 1961, **63,** 575–582.

———. Vicarious reinforcement and imitative learning. *J. abnorm. soc. Psychol.*, 1963, **67,** 601–607. (b)

Bandura, A., and R.H. Walters. *Social learning and personality development.* New York: Holt, Rinehart and Winston, 1963.

Berkowitz, L. *Aggression: A social psychological analysis.* New York: McGraw-Hill, 1962.

———. The concept of aggressive drive: Some additional considerations. In L. Berkowitz (Ed.), *Advances in experimental social psychology.* Vol. 2. New York: Academic Press, 1965. (b)

———. The frustration-aggression hypothesis revisited. In L. Berkowitz (Ed.), *Roots of aggression: A re-examination of the frustration-aggression hypothesis.* New York: Atherton Press, 1970.

———. Simple views of aggression. *Amer. Scientist*, 1969, **57,** 372–383.

———. Some aspects of observed aggression. *J. pers. soc. Psychol.*, 1965, **2,** 359–369. (a)

———, R. Corwin, and M. Heironimus. Film violence and subsequent aggressive tendencies. *Public Opinion Quarterly*, 1963, **27,** 217–229.

Berkowitz, L., and A. LePage. Weapons as aggression-eliciting stimuli. *J. pers. soc. Psychol.*, 1967, **7,** 202–207.

Berkowitz, L., and E. Rawlings. Effects of film violence on inhibitions against subsequent aggression. *J. abnorm. soc. Psychol.*, 1963, **66,** 405–412.

Buss, A.H. The effect of harm on subsequent aggression. *J. exp. Res. Pers.*, 1966, **1,** 249–255. (b)

———. Instrumentality of aggression, feedback, and frustrations as determinants of physical aggression. *J. pers. soc. Psychol.*, 1966, **3,** 153–162. (a)

———. Physical aggression in relation to different frustrations. *J. abnorm. soc. Psychol.*, 1963, **67,** 1–7.

———. *The psychology of aggression.* New York: John Wiley & Sons, 1961.

Davitz, J.R. The effects of previous training on postfrustration behavior. *J. abnorm. soc. Psychol.*, 1952, **47,** 309–315.

Dollard, J., L. Doob, N. Miller, O. Mowrer, and R. Sears. *Frustration and aggression.* New Haven, Conn.: Yale University Press, 1939.

Einstein, A. *Why war?* Letter to Professor Freud. International Institute of Intellectual Cooperation, League of Nations, 1933.

Feshbach, S. The drive-reduction of fantasy behavior. *J. abnorm. soc. Psychol.*, 1955, **50,** 3–11.

———. The stimulating vs. cathartic effects of a vicarious aggressive activity. *J. abnorm. soc. Psychol.*, 1961, **63,** 381–385.

———, W.E. Stiles, and E. Bitter. The reinforcing effect of witnessing aggression. *J. exp. Res. Pers.*, 1967, **2,** 133–139.

Freud, S. *Why war?* Letter to Professor Einstein. In J. Strachey (Ed.), *Collected papers of Sigmund Freud.* Vol. 5. New York: Basic Books, 1959.

Graham, H.D., and T.R. Gurr. (Eds.) *The history of violence in America.* New York: Bantam, 1969.

Hartmann, D.P. Influence of symbolically modeled instrumental aggression and pain cues on aggressive behavior. *J. pers. soc. Psychol.*, 1969, **11,** 280–288.

Hicks, D. Imitation and retention of film-mediated aggressive peer and adult models. *J. pers. soc. Psychol.*, 1965, **2,** 97–100.

———. Short- and long-term retention of affectively varied modeled behavior. *Psychon. Sci.*, 1968, **11,** 369–370.

Hobbes, T. *Leviathan.* First edition, London, 1651. Repr. in B. Rand (Ed.), *Modern classical philosophers.* Boston: Houghton Mifflin Co., 1936.

Klineberg, O. *Social psychology*. New York: Holt, Rinehart and Winston, 1954.

Lawson, O.N. (Ed.) *Violence and the mass media*. New York: Harper & Row, 1968.

Loew, C.A. Acquisition of a hostile attitude and its relation to aggressive behavior. *J. pers. soc. Psychol.*, 1967, **5,** 335–341.

Lorenz, K. *On aggression*. New York: Harcourt, Brace & World, 1966.

Lövaas, O.I. Effect of exposure to symbolic aggression on aggressive behavior. *Child Develpm.*, 1961, **32,** 37–44. (a)

______. Interaction between verbal and nonverbal behavior. *Child Develpm.*, 1961, **32,** 329–336. (b)

Mallick, S.K., and B.R. McCandless. A study of catharsis of aggression. *J. pers. soc. Psychol.*, 1966, **4,** 591–596.

Montagu, M.F. Ashley. (Ed.) *Man and aggression*. New York: Oxford University Press, 1968.

Morris, D. *The naked ape*. New York: McGraw-Hill, 1968.

Patterson, G.R., R.A. Littman, and W. Bricker. Assertive behavior in children: A step toward a theory of aggression. *Monographs of the Society for Research in Child Development*, 1967, **32,** No. 5, 1–43.

Scott, J.P. *Aggression*. Chicago: University of Chicago Press, 1958.

Storr, Anthony. *Human aggression*. New York: Atheneum, 1968.

Walters, R.H., and L.E. Thomas. Enhancement of punitiveness by visual and audiovisual displays. *Canadian Journal of Psychology*, 1963, **17,** 244–255.

______, and C.W. Acker. Enhancement of punitive behavior by audiovisual displays. *Science*, 1962, **136,** 872–873.

10 Decision and Dissonance

Thomas Armstrong, a physician with a deep interest in religion, mysticism, and the study of unidentified flying objects, has become convinced that Mrs. Marian Keech receives messages from outer space through the medium of automatic writing. Dr. Armstrong and his wife, who is as convinced as he, meet frequently with Mrs. Keech. Through her they learn something of the language of the people of the planet Clarion, they are told of the superiority of life on that planet, and they hear of the prospect of miracles to come on this earth. Unobtrusively, the Armstrongs recruit disciples, and soon a small but devoted group meets more or less regularly with Mrs. Keech to learn what the mysterious correspondents from outer space have to reveal.

Among other things, they are informed that in about three months, on December 21, a catastrophe will occur. Except for a few isolated places in the Rockies, the Catskills, and the Allegheny mountains, America will be inundated by a vast sea. The continent will split, and a new, purified race will inhabit the earth. As the chosen and enlightened few, Mrs. Keech and her group will be preserved from this disaster. Just before the flood they will be removed from danger by flying saucers that will take them to safety on other planets in other solar systems.

Believing that these events will take place exactly as predicted by (or through) Mrs. Keech, the group prepares for its date with destiny. Dr. Armstrong composes a press release announcing the forthcoming cataclysm. Mrs. Keech gives lectures to interested groups. The followers study even more carefully the lessons they have learned from the space people. Members of the group volunteer to type and mimeograph teaching materials. They give up smoking, drinking, and the eating of meat. As the time grows shorter, some quit their jobs and sell their property. Student members neglect their classwork and risk antagonizing friends and families; all endure public ridicule. A few days before the disaster is expected, Dr. Armstrong is discharged from his job in a university health service because of his beliefs. None of these things matter, for the end is near at hand, and the flood will make all sacrifices worthwhile.

Throughout the period of intense preparation, the group makes few attempts to win converts. They are instructed by the space people that those who are to be saved will appear of their own accord. All the group can do is announce the prophecy and stand ready to accept those who come voluntarily and in obvious sincerity. All who approach the group are carefully screened, tested, and examined. Newspaper reporters are discouraged, and no photographs are allowed.

On December 17, four days before the expected flood, Mrs. Keech receives a message that a flying saucer will land in her back yard at 4:00 P.M. to pick up the faithful believers. The group assembles and, according to instructions, prepares by removing all metal from their persons, including watchbands, zippers, clasps, bobby pins, and belt buckles. Everyone is ecstatic. But four o'clock comes and goes; five o'clock comes and goes. Finally, at five-thirty, they give up. Although their faith is shaken, they conclude that this has been a practice session—merely a preparation for the real thing.

At midnight, Mrs. Keech receives another message: a flying saucer is now on its way. The group prepares again, this time waiting outside in the cold winter night until about 3:00 A.M., when yet another message tells them to go back inside and rest. Another practice session has taken place. The group is urged to secrecy, but it remains willing to accept new members who seem genuine in their wish to join.

At 10:00 A.M. on December 20, Mrs. Keech receives still another message, telling her that the long awaited saucer will arrive at midnight. The group gathers and calmly awaits their final moment of salvation. The next day is the day of the flood; this time the prophecy must come true. By 11:30, all are prepared and waiting. The minutes pass. Midnight comes and goes, and a message is received that the plan has been slightly delayed. At 12:30 there is talk of a miracle. At 2:30 A.M., a message tells the group to break for coffee. By about 4:00 A.M. it becomes apparent that no saucer is to come. The prophecy has failed.

Under the circumstances, what would be the rational course of action for Mrs. Keech and her followers to take? Prophecies had been made, on the basis of which some people had radically altered their lives. Yet not a single material prediction had been borne out; not one publicly verifiable prophecy had been fulfilled. Most would say that the only sensible thing would be to admit that the prophecy had been wrong, that a terrible mistake had been made. Face the facts, swallow one's pride, pick up the pieces, and start life over again. Indeed, that is what some of Mrs. Keech's followers did. Many others, however, did not.

At 4:45 on the morning of the twenty-first, while the discouraged group discussed its problem, Mrs. Keech announced that she had received a momentous message. In substance, it said that the force for Good of this group had been so great that the Almighty had called off the flood and saved the world from destruction. The efforts of the group had not been in vain after all.

What is now the sensible and rational course? Now that face has been saved, would it not be best simply to accept this message and quit the cause? The group actually decided something quite different. They renounced secrecy and exposed themselves to the full view of the public. They called all the news services to announce their revelation. Secret documents and tape recordings were opened to public scrutiny. More than ever convinced of the righteousness of their cause, the group wanted the world to know of the miracle it had brought about.

Later, two additional predictions were disconfirmed. An attempt to record voices from space on December 22 produced a blank tape, and an expected public visit from the space people on Christmas Eve failed to materialize.

The rapid succession of disconfirmations finally had its effect. Despite the publicized miracle, no new converts had been won. Under threat of police action and possible commitment to a mental institution, Mrs. Keech took flight. Nevertheless, she continued to receive messages and to report them to her followers by mail. Dr. Armstrong and his wife sold their house and embarked on a tour of the country, preaching the doctrine of flying saucers. The group disbanded, and the entire episode was closed.

As strange as they may seem, the events described above actually took place (although, of course, the names are all fictitious). Our story is a brief summarization of the report of a naturalistic study by Festinger, Reicken, and Schachter (1956), described in detail in a book called *When Prophecy Fails*.

How can we explain the fact that, as disconfirmation of a belief system grows, the intensity of faith in the disconfirmed system may tend not to decrease in accordance with the evidence, but to increase out of all proportion to what can be justified on rational grounds? A possible answer to that question is taken up in the balance of this chapter.

The Theory of Cognitive Dissonance

Consonance and Dissonance

We generally expect people to behave in ways consistent with their beliefs, and to harbor only beliefs, attitudes, and thoughts that are consonant with each other. Given no outside restraints on his behavior, we expect the person who goes to church regularly to agree with the beliefs of the religious group to which he belongs. Conversely, we expect the person who espouses religious causes to go to church or to display in public concrete behavioral evidence of his commitment. We expect the professed Democrat to support and vote for Democratic candidates for political offices. Our expectations are confirmed when the student who preaches pacifism burns his draft card and goes to prison rather than serve in the armed forces. In short, we expect consonance between behavior and belief.

Similarly, if someone says that black people are not as intelligent as white people, it is almost certain that he regards blacks as inferior in other ways as well. It would not be consonant for him to maintain that, despite their intellectual inferiority, blacks are just as competent physicians, lawyers, judges, or company presidents as whites. If a politician advocates maximum military preparedness as the best policy for preserving peace, it is likely that he also believes it unwise to increase federal spending on public health and welfare, for he will see these as demands that compete with and threaten to reduce the size of the military budget. In short, we expect, and usually find, consonance within a person's belief systems, as well as between his beliefs and actions, and among his actions on various occasions.

However, we also know of situations in which consonance does not exist. The narcotics addict goes on taking drugs even though he knows they are harmful and wants to quit. The same people who profess on Sunday to believe the ten commandments proceed on Monday to break most of them. The political speaker tells us his nation is dedicated to world peace, and then justifies a war that lasts for over 15 years. The group described at the beginning of this chapter believed sincerely that a flood would occur on December 21. When their beliefs were contradicted by reality, their faith lost its consistency with observable facts. All such cases display a characteristic called *cognitive dissonance* (Festinger, 1957).

In this context, cognition means knowledge one has about himself or the world in which he lives. Dissonance exists when cognitive elements are mutually contradictory, that is, when an individual "knows" two things that are inconsistent.

The word "knows" is placed in quotation marks in the preceding statement because it refers not only to formal academic or factual scientific knowledge, but also to the "knowledge" one has of one's own feelings, beliefs, attitudes, opinions, actions, and expectations. I know, in a formal sense, that two plus two equals four and that I have an appendix. I "know," in quite a different sense, when I am hungry or in pain. I "know," in still another way, that I am a decent person who would not intentionally harm anyone. This last kind of knowledge is part of what is often called the self-concept, which has become quite important in recent research on cognitive dissonance. All forms of knowledge are incorporated in the term "cognition" as it is used in the theory of cognitive dissonance.

Dissonance as Drive

The state of cognitive dissonance produces discomfort. In fact, dissonance acts as a *drive* which must be reduced. It exerts pressure on the person to bring about and maintain consonant relations among his cognitions of himself, his behavior, and the world about him.

There are many ways to eliminate cognitive dissonance. The person may change his beliefs about himself: for example, the jilted lover may come to believe that he did not really care much for the girl who turned him down. He may change his own behavior: someone who believes he is overweight may cut down on his intake of food. He may change his perception of reality: a patient with a terminal illness may convince himself that he suffers only from fatigue.

The group described at the beginning of this chapter resolved dissonance between their beliefs and the failure of reality to confirm their faith by adding a new element to their belief system: the assertion that the catastrophe had been called off because of their own good works. So effective was this resolution of dissonance for some of the members that it changed the character of the group from a semisecret organization retiring from public view to an openly proselytizing band who published their miracle to the world.

Which form of dissonance reduction will be adopted in any given case depends upon the nature of the situation and the particular kinds of people involved. For present purposes, details and refinements are less crucial than the general principles of dissonance theory. However, the importance of the situation in which dissonance occurs may be appreciated by considering two examples: a person who buys a house which he later discovers to have been badly misrepresented by the agent who sold it, and a person who does not feel ill but has been told by his physician that he has a potentially serious disease, such as diabetes or a heart condition. In the first example, distortion of reality is difficult; the house has been bought and the roof is threatening to collapse. It is easier to reduce dissonance by changing one's opinion, reassuring oneself that a weak roof is not a serious fault and can be easily repaired, than by asserting that rotten wood and wet ceilings are signs of structural strength. Distortion of reality is easier in the second example. After all, the person feels no symptoms, and doctors do make mistakes: there is probably no serious illness after all.

Another factor that needs to be borne in mind is the relative importance of a given state of dissonance to the person who experiences it. If you order a particular food at a restaurant, expecting it to taste especially good, and find it disappointing, dissonance is present but probably not severe. However, if you get your first F on an exam in college after having received nothing but A and B grades in high school, dissonance is likely to be marked and much more difficult to resolve.

Some Unexpected Implications

These proposals sound so acceptable that it is not unreasonable to ask at this point whether dissonance theory has anything unique to offer, anything that differs from what common sense alone tells us ought to be true. In answer to this, at least two propositions are implied by dissonance theory that do not follow from ordinary, everyday, common assumptions about human behavior. The first proposition is that, contrary to what common sense tells us, there are many situations in which behavior determines thought, rather than the reverse.

Thought and behavior. People generally believe that mental events precede and in some way determine the course of most human actions. At least since the days of Aristotle it has been assumed that man, the rational animal, directs his own behavior by his thoughts. For centuries, Western philosophers have wrestled with the problem of describing how this process occurs. The problem is by no means insignificant, for our belief in the person's capacity to plan his own behavior, to anticipate the consequences of his own actions, lies at the foundation of our legal and moral conceptions of responsibility and free will. A certain discomfort arises when we entertain the possibility that our belief may be incorrect.

Given a person who behaves in a way that is contrary to his own convictions, but who does not deny his own behavior, the dissonance thereby created can only be reduced by altering belief. In this situation, belief must change: it must follow behavior and become consonant with it. Thus, a person forced by group pressure to engage in an act that he regards as wrong (for example, a boy who steals something as a way of getting into a gang he wants to join) will tend to regard the act as less wrong after committing it than he did before committing it. In a subsequent section, we examine experimental evidence on this point.

Dissonance and reward. The second proposition that is implied by the theory of cognitive dissonance, but that does not correspond to the dictates of common sense, is that reinforcement or reward and punishment often play only a secondary role to the tendency to reduce cognitive dissonance in determining belief structure.

One of the oldest ideas in psychology is that behavior can be manipulated by regulating the administration of rewards and punishments. The doctrine of *hedonism*, that man seeks pleasure (reward) and avoids pain (punishment), is traceable to the ancient Greeks. It appears in most obvious form in early scientific psychology as Thorndike's *law of effect* (1911). Variations are implied in Freud's *pleasure principle* and in modern theories of reinforcement as the primary determinant of learning. Recent discoveries of "pleasure centers" in the brain have added new interest to hedonistic explanations of behavior (see Chap. 6).

Dissonance theory, which of course deals with cognition (thought processes) rather than with overt behavior, argues that rewards and punishments may influence how a person acts in public, but not necessarily what he thinks about his actions. A payment of money may induce a person to display behavior inconsistent with his beliefs, but if the payment is large enough dissonance will not be aroused and his inward beliefs will not change. In effect, the reward itself acts as a dissonance reducing factor; the person justifies his behavior on the grounds that "I only did it for the money." It is the effect of reward on cognition that is psychologically critical.

Cognitive dissonance is most likely to occur when rewards are inadequate to justify behavior that is inconsistent with belief. For example, a soldier, who has been taught all his life that it is wrong, is forced to injure others in combat. Since his tangible rewards are not often very great, he must amend his belief system. He must come to think that it is all right to injure others when you are fighting for your country, when your own life is endangered, or when you are being a good soldier and obeying orders. The principle that cognitive factors are more critical than reward and punishment does not apply only to human beings; the weaknesses of simple reward theory can be demonstrated in experiments on animals as well.

The next section examines some of the evidence presented in support of the theory of cognitive dissonance (for a more complete bibliography see Margulis and Songer, 1969). Following that, some criticisms of both the theory and the research it has stimulated are considered. Finally, we will examine more recent evidence and some proposed modifications of theory.

Research on Cognitive Dissonance

Forced Compliance

Perhaps the best known of the early investigations is one on "forced compliance," reported by Festinger and Carlsmith in 1959. The term refers to all situations which elicit "public compliance without private acceptance" (Festinger, 1957, p. 87), no matter how this state of affairs is brought about. In this experiment it was induced by deceiving subjects as to the purpose of the study and the part they were to play in it.

Each subject was first required to spend one hour performing tasks intended to be as repetitive, dull, and meaningless as possible: filling a box with spools, turning pegs one-quarter turn. The subject was then told that the experiment was over, although of course it had scarcely begun. Next the subject was told that he was needed to help run more subjects by introducing them to the tasks he had just performed himself. He was to tell these subjects (actually confederates of the experimenters) that the tasks are interesting, fun, exciting, and intriguing. This is where dissonance comes in.

One group of subjects was told they would be paid $1.00 for the job (low reward); another group was told they would be paid $20.00 (high reward). This was part of the deception, too; when the experiment was over, subjects were asked to return the money (which they all did willingly). A control group did not contact any "new" subjects and was not offered any money; they simply sat for four minutes after completing the tasks.

After the subjects had completed their assignments, they were interviewed by another investigator with questions about how enjoyable the initial tasks were, how important the research is to science, how willing they would be to participate in a similar experiment in the future, and how much they felt they had learned from their participation in the study. The last question was included for its value in differential prediction of outcomes. Only the first three were expected to produce differences among groups.

The theory of cognitive dissonance leads to two main predictions. First, since cognitive dissonance causes belief to conform to behavior, subjects who were forced to comply should find the experiment more interesting and more important, and be more willing to participate again in the future, than subjects who were not forced to comply. Second, however, if reward modifies dissonance, as specified by the theory, this effect should be apparent only in the data from the group receiving the lower reward ($1.00). Since the group that thought it was being paid $20.00 for helping out had a ready-made excuse for claiming that the dull tasks were interesting, these subjects should experience little dissonance and should rate the experiment about the same way as the control subjects.

Figure 10.1 shows that these predictions were confirmed. The dissonant ($1.00) group, represented by the middle bar in each case, rated the experiment as more enjoyable and important and expressed greater willingness to participate in the future than did the other two groups. "Common sense," or simple hedonism, would lead us to expect the group given the larger reward to show greater enthusi-

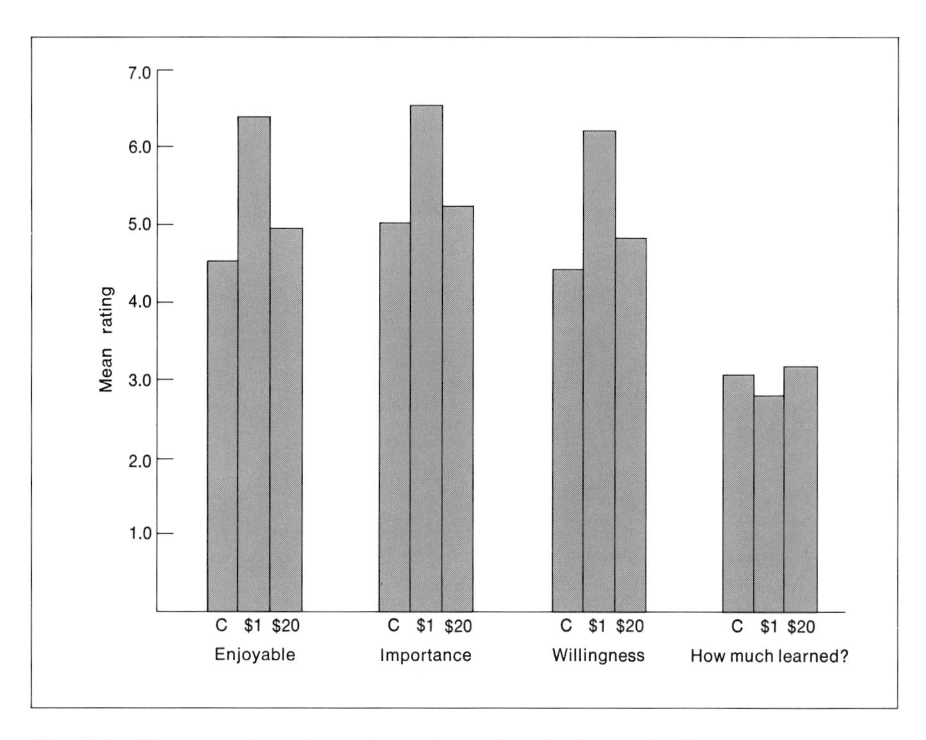

Fig. 10.1. Responses to post-experimental questions in the study of cognitive dissonance. (Constant of +5 added to data from first and third questions for graphic purposes. Data from Festinger and Carlsmith, 1959).

asm. That expectation is not borne out by the data, and common sense is disconfirmed. As predicted, there were no differences in responses to the fourth question (how much learned). This question was included to show that the results were not simply due to a general tendency of the $1.00 group to give higher ratings to all questions, regardless of content.

Additional studies on forced compliance have used experimentally organized discussion groups in which subjects are rewarded for advocating points of view dissonant with their own beliefs, or punished for failing to comply with dissonance producing requirements (Burdick, 1955; McBride, 1954, summarized in Festinger, 1957, pp. 99–104). Janis and King (1954) found that a subject who improvises a speech supporting a point of view with which he personally disagrees will change his private opinion in a direction favoring the position advocated in the speech (see also King and Janis, 1956).

Davidson (1964) had subjects listen to a presentation by a (fictitious) person in the next room who was made to sound rather likable. The investigator then cajoled his subjects into reading aloud a derogatory statement about that person while the subjects thought the other person was actually listening. As expected, liking for the fictitious person decreased under these conditions; the subjects' opinions came to conform to the statements they had been induced to make.

Cohen (1962) conducted an experiment similar in conception to the one by Festinger and Carlsmith on forced compliance, but subjects wrote essays and were paid smaller amounts ($.50 to $10.00). The results generally confirmed the prediction that increasing attitude change accompanied decreasing incentive for engaging in counterattitudinal (dissonant) behavior.

In 1966, Carlsmith, Collins, and Helmreich reported an experiment much like the one by Cohen, but with one important difference. In their study, one group was required to speak directly to another person when making counterattitudinal statements, while a second group wrote anonymous counterattitudinal essays. As predicted, the data from the face-to-face condition showed the operation of dissonance reduction. Also as predicted, reward effects operated straightforwardly (greater reward produced greater attitude change) when subjects wrote anonymous essays for which they were not held personally responsible. This experiment anticipates later developments in the theory of cognitive dissonance which are considered in a subsequent section of this chapter.

Postdecision Processes

The theory of cognitive dissonance emphasizes that every complex decision involves dissonance. Choosing one alternative over another necessarily means giving up the anticipated advantages associated with the abandoned possibility. At the same time, one obliges oneself to accept the disadvantages of the choice that was made. This creates postdecision dissonance: a feeling of discomfort, of uncertainty about the correctness of the choice, perhaps even of regret. Some modern business firms aid their customers to overcome postdecision dissonance by providing them with literature which says something like: "Congratulations! You have shown the good judgment to buy a genuine Gizmo widget, the finest widget in the world!" Thus reassured, the customer feels satisfied that his decision to buy a Gizmo instead of a Framis was correct.

Postdecision regret. Festinger and Walster (1964) conducted an experiment to show that decision is often followed by regret. Sixty-eight college women first rated 12 photographs of hair styles according to how much they would like to have their own hair done in each style. They next *ranked* the hair styles under two different conditions. Before ranking the photographs, subjects in one subgroup (the "regret" group) were told that they would later choose between two of the hair styles they had previously rated as attractive and be given a free haircut and set for their trouble. The two styles from which they would later choose were marked during their ranking of the 12 photographs. After ranking the photographs, these subjects selected the style they wanted for themselves.

Subjects in the control group ranked the hair styles *before* they knew that they could select one for themselves; the pair from which these subjects could choose was not marked in advance of the selection procedure.

In this experiment, dissonance was expected to arise as a natural consequence of the decision making process. Subjects in the "regret" group, however, had a chance to express their dissonance by changing their choice of hair style. The investigators reasoned that subjects in the "regret" group actually made three implicit or explicit choices. Their first choice came when they initially *rated* the hair styles for attractiveness, and their second when they subsequently *ranked* the hair styles (remember, only these subjects were told at this point that they would get one free). They made their third choice when they were asked to select a hair style for themselves. Subjects in the other group made only the first and third choices described above, for they did not know at the time of the intervening ranking procedure that they would receive a hair set free.

The comparison of interest is the number of changes in decisions between the initial ratings and the actual selections made. If "regret" operates, the group making three decisions should show more reversals (more frequent ultimate selection of the alternative initially rated lower) than the group making only two decisions. In the "regret" group, the reversal rate was higher (62 per cent); the reversal rate in the control group was 28 per cent.

A final set of ratings was obtained from both groups to confirm that dissonance did, in fact, take place in all subjects. When initial and final ratings were compared, both groups showed the expected increase in attractiveness of the chosen alternative and decrease in attractiveness of the rejected alternative.

Postdecision information seeking. A well-known piece of research by Ehrlich, Guttman, Schonbach, and Mills (1957) was designed to show that postdecision dissonance is followed by selective information seeking. In other words, the person who has made an important decision should seek out information that supports his choice and avoid information suggesting that a different choice would have been more favorable. The investigators reasoned that the purchase of a new car involves a decision of considerable personal importance, and should result in predictable postdecision behavior. Specifically, the person who has recently purchased a car should recognize and recall advertisements for the brand he purchased better than advertisements for other brands he had seriously considered.

The investigators interviewed 125 car owners, 65 of whom had purchased their cars four to six weeks before the study (recent purchasers). The data partially confirmed the hypothesis, in that recent purchasers claimed to have recognized and read more advertisements of their brand than of other brands, while such differences were not apparent in the data from subjects who had owned cars for a longer period of time. However, several other predictions were not clearly confirmed by the data.

These findings are typical (see also Adams, 1961; Engel, 1963; Feather, 1963; Jecker, 1964; Mills, Aronson, and Robinson, 1959; Rosen, 1961). Festinger (1964, p. 64) admitted that the data on postdecision processes are not always convincing; he proposed that other factors must be considered before the postdecision process can be fully understood. He noted, for instance, that a person may actually seek out dissonant information following a decision if he feels confident that he can cope with it successfully and thus nullify its effects. Canon (1964) devised an experiment to test this idea.

The subjects (80 college men) read four "case studies" describing business problems in the belief that they were helping to develop materials for a new course. The first three cases were used to establish a necessary condition for the experiment. After each subject read a case and selected from the alternate choices provided what he thought was an appropriate solution to the problem, he was handed a slip which ostensibly informed him of the correctness of his choice. Half of the subjects were told that their choices were correct and that most other subjects had been wrong (high confidence induction); the rest were told that their choices were incorrect and that most others had made the correct choices (low confidence induction).

When the choices for the fourth case were made, the subjects were told that this time they would not receive information about their correctness, but should prepare to justify their decisions by writing essays defending them. To aid in writing the essays, copies of five articles would be made available. The titles of the (actually nonexistent) articles implied that two were in favor of solution A, two were in favor

	Confidence		
	High	Low	Mean
Highly Useful	−14.3	+ 5.9	− 4.2
Less Useful	+ 8.2	+29.6	+18.9
Mean	− 3.0	+17.8	

Table 10.1 *Average Preference for Consonant over Dissonant Articles (From Canon, 1964)*
Note: A plus sign indicates preference for consonant articles; a minus sign indicates preference for dissonant articles.

of solution B, and one was neutral. Subjects were asked to evaluate these articles, indicating the degree to which they wanted to read each one. Half of the subjects in each "confidence" group were told that their essays would be part of a written debate in which they would be required to answer questions challenging their decision. It was assumed that these subjects would find the prospect of reading articles valuable in preparing their essays, so this was designated the "highly useful" condition. The rest of the subjects were simply told they would write an essay presenting their case. They had no reason to anticipate opposition, so this was designated the "less useful" condition. Actually, the required essays were never written, for the experiment was over once subjects' evaluations of the articles had been obtained.

Of main concern is the rating of preference for consonant and dissonant articles by members of the various experimental groups; these are shown in Table 10.1. The strongest preference for consonance is evidenced by low confidence subjects with less use for available information. Subjects with high confidence for whom the available articles are highly useful actually show a preference for dissonant material. Festinger argued that coping with and arguing against dissonant information serves the purpose of mastering dissonance. Thus, the data may not contradict the general theory. It might be more correct to say that they supplement it by adding a new dimension which could be called "personal relevance." As we shall see, addition of this new dimension constitutes one of the most important later revisions of dissonance theory.

Commitment. There is another aspect of the postdecision process that must be considered if the theoretical picture is to be complete. It appears that personal commitment to a decision is essential for the arousal of dissonance (Brehm and Cohen, 1962). There will be no dissonance if a decision makes no appreciable difference to one's future behavior. A student who must complete a graduation requirement by taking one of two equally appealing courses will not experience dissonance if the choice is a matter of indifference; he will graduate whichever course he chooses, so long as he is equally capable of passing them both. Under these circumstances, the student is not so much "making a decision" as "stating a preference" (Festinger, 1964, p. 156).

The type of decision to which dissonance theory applies is that in which different implications follow from each alternative. The situation might be accurately exemplified by the student who must decide whether to go on to graduate study. His decision is almost certain to have a profound effect upon his future behavior, and dissonance is highly probable.

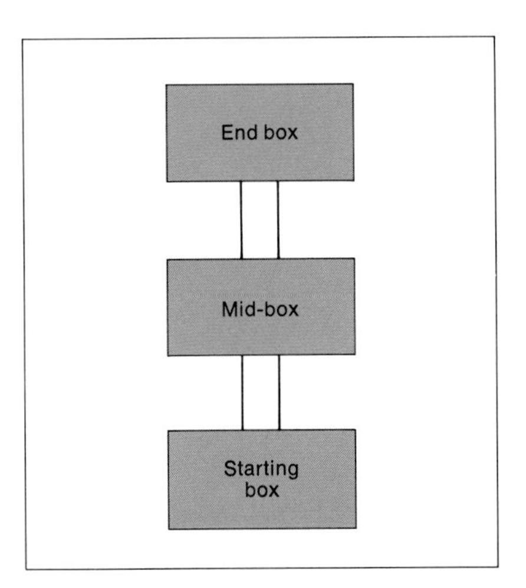

Fig. 10.2. Design of maze for first study of effect of effort on learning.

The postdecision process is not yet clearly understood. A good deal more carefully designed research must be completed before its complexities are finally unravelled.

Effort and Value

Another important set of investigations has been developed around the idea that organisms learn to value positively that which they must work to obtain, not that which rewards them (as common sense suggests). The inspiration for this proposition comes from the theory of cognitive dissonance, which implies that positive value is consonant with a high level of effort, while negative value is not.

Several experiments have been conducted to demonstrate the validity of this proposition. The first, and still one of the best known, is a study by Aronson and Mills (1959) in which college women were required to undergo an "initiation" in order to become members of groups discussing the psychology of sex. For some of the subjects the initiation was intended to be highly embarrassing. For example, they were required to recite a list of obscene words in the presence of the male experimenter. A second group underwent a milder initiation, reciting a list of sex related words that were not obscene, and a third group underwent no initiation at all. The subjects then listened to a (rather mild) tape recording of a discussion held by the group they had just joined. As expected, the girls who had undergone the severe initiation rite rated the discussion as more interesting than did the girls in the other two conditions.

Although a number of variations on this basic theme have been played by many investigators (Aronson, 1961; Brehm, 1959, 1960; Zimbardo, 1965; Gerard and Mathewson, 1966), our attention will be restricted to two of the more ingenious. These were reported by Festinger in 1961 and are of interest not only because they deal with the effort-value relationship, but also because they represent an attempt to apply the principles of the theory of cognitive dissonance to research on the most common laboratory subject in psychology: the white rat.

It has been known for years that responses learned under conditions of partial (less than 100 per cent) reinforcement resist extinction longer than do responses

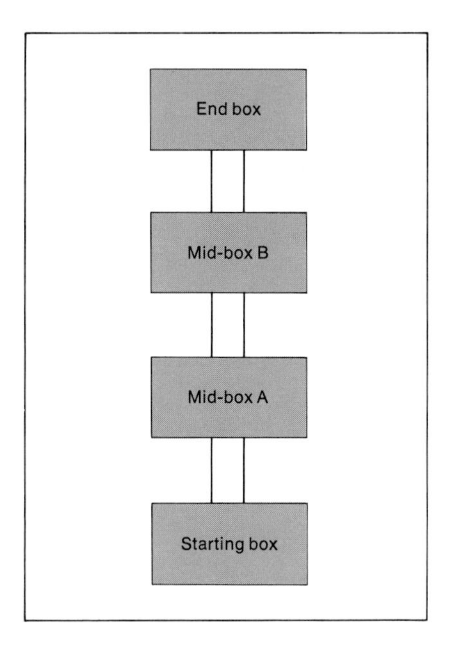

Fig. 10.3. Design of maze for second study of effect of effort on learning.

learned under conditions of 100 per cent reinforcement (Chap. 12). Resistance to extinction is measured by the number of nonreinforced trials which continue to elicit a previously learned response, and it has generally been assumed that the determinant of resistance in partial reinforcement research is the ratio of unrewarded trials to total trials in the initial learning situation. Festinger argued that a more important determinant is the amount of effort required. The greater the effort, the greater the resistance to extinction. His explanation also accounts for the observation that delay of reinforcement increases resistance to extinction. Animals forced to wait for reward must endure more to achieve it, so the reward becomes more valued.

To demonstrate the dissonance theory point of view, a simple maze of the type shown in Figure 10.2 was constructed. Food was available at all times to all animals in the end box. The midbox was associated with 100 per cent reinforcement for one group of animals, 50 per cent reinforcement for another group, and with delay, but no reinforcement, for a third group. After a number of training trials, extinction trials were run, but only from the starting box to the midbox. Greatest resistance (faster running for more trials) to extinction was shown by the group that had received no reinforcement in the midbox; least resistance was shown by animals that had received 100 per cent reinforcement at the midbox. These findings were true regardless of whether or not the animals were hungry during the extinction trials. What appears to have happened is that the nonreinforced group, who were simply delayed in the midbox while on their way to reinforcement (which was always available in the endbox), learned to prefer the midbox because they had to exert effort to get there.

A second demonstration of preference for the place where effort is required used a slightly more complicated apparatus and procedure (Fig. 10.3). In this study, one group of animals (A) was delayed in midbox A, allowed to run through midbox

B, and fed in the end box. A second group (B) was allowed to run through midbox A, but was delayed in midbox B before being allowed to continue to the endbox, where it, too, was fed.

Extinction trials were run only between midbox A and midbox B, which means that group A was running *away* from a delay box, while group B was running *toward* a delay box. If a preference had developed for the place at which delay occurred, group B should show greater resistance to extinction than group A. That is, in fact, what the data showed. It was obviously not difficult for Festinger to see these findings as confirming the principle that animals as well as men come to love things for which they have worked or suffered.

Criticisms of the Theory

No sooner was the theory of cognitive dissonance promulgated (in 1957) than it was attacked. Asch (1958) pointed out that the results yielded by the studies cited were generally confirming, but weak and inconsistent. The complexity of the situations with which research on cognitive dissonance concerns itself is so great that alternative explanations for the outcomes are nearly always available. The studies are too heterogeneous in design and content; they represent a collection of miscellaneous research, rather than a systematic program of investigation. Furthermore, the theory itself is crude and primitive. It does not distinguish clearly between dissonance reduction and personality defense (see Chaps. 8 and 14), nor does it provide any clear-cut way for the independent investigator to identify a truly dissonant situation. Asch decided that dissonance is an interesting theory, but must be regarded as *not proven* by the evidence available at the time.

Asch had only the earliest data on which to base his judgment; however, a similar verdict was delivered by Chapanis and Chapanis (1964) six years later, after considerably more research had been completed. As might be expected, their criticisms were more specific and detailed. Some of their objections were theoretical; some were methodological. The following sections focus on some of the methodological criticisms, because these are most relevant to the purpose of this text; they point out dangers inherent in many types of psychological research.

Methodological Objections

Effectiveness of manipulations. Any research that proposes to study an internal state of the organism, like cognition, must provide evidence that the desired state actually does exist in the experimental subjects. Few studies of cognitive dissonance provide such evidence. For example, in Aronson and Mills' (1959) study of the effect of initiation rites on interest in a group discussion, the group of girls who had to recite obscene words in the presence of the investigator was presumed to have undergone an embarrassing experience. But were they really embarrassed? Perhaps reading obscene words aroused their interest in sex, making the ensuing discussion seem more exciting than it would have otherwise. Would another group who had to experience electric shock to get into the discussion have displayed the same high level of interest? Another quite different possibility is that the girls were embarrassed by their initiation, but were so relieved to discover that the real discussion was actually rather dull that their ratings reflected relief or tension reduction rather than dissonance (Haber, 1970). There is no way of knowing whether these explanations are correct, since the necessary evidence is not available.

Furthermore, to be convincing, such research must not only demonstrate that it has aroused the desired variable, it must show that it has *not* aroused some other process that could also account for the outcome. For instance, in the above study, it is insufficient to show only that the girls were embarrassed; it is also necessary to show that they were *not* made more interested in the topic. Both processes can easily operate at the same time. Similarly, a study that requires a subject to endure pain to achieve a goal leaves doubt as to whether it is pain or the goal that makes the behavior occur. Unless the two are separated experimentally, it is impossible to tell which is the more important.

Treatment of data. A serious objection to at least a few studies is that data from some subjects were not employed in statistical analyses of research outcomes. For example, in the research on recognition of automobile advertisements, as many as 82 per cent of the cases were rejected for various reasons in some statistical comparisons. Subjects in other studies were shifted from one group to another after the data had been collected.

This criticism raises a serious methodological point, for subjects' responses in psychological research often appear to reflect failure to understand instructions or to take them seriously. For instance, if an investigator sees a subject answering questionnaire items without reading them, he feels justified in regarding these data as invalid and discarding them. This practice is dangerous because it is all too easy to extend the procedure to the point where all responses inconsistent with the investigator's expectations are regarded as invalid and discarded. Such practices would produce a science in which disconfirmation never occurred, and in which it would be impossible to apply the principles of strong inference.

The best solution to the problem of invalid data is for the investigator to specify objective criteria for exclusion of responses *before* he sees any subjects. If that is not possible (as is often the case), data should be excluded before the results are analyzed, and subjects should never be transferred from one group to another simply because the investigator suspects that they did not respond appropriately to the experimental conditions. Any other procedures necessarily lead to suspicion of conscious or unconscious biasing of outcomes.

Operational ambiguities. Finally, there is the problem of lack of operational clarity in many of the terms used in dissonance theory. The theory often uses familiar words in strange ways, and many important definitions are phrased so ambiguously that independent investigators cannot devise adequate tests of propositions derived from the theory. For example, Festinger and Carlsmith's (1959) study of "forced compliance" did not actually force anyone to do anything. Subjects were tricked into cooperating with the investigators, believing they would be paid for their services. Furthermore, the tasks they performed at the beginning of the experiment were supposed to be extremely dull, uninteresting, and boring, but even subjects in the control group found them only "slightly boring," according to their own ratings. Finally, the concept of reward is unclear. Subjects who expected to be paid $1.00 for a few minutes work probably did not regard this as inadequate reward. It is almost certain that subjects who were told they would be paid $20.00 just to tell someone the tasks were interesting would regard the whole situation as implausible; the magnitude of the reward is so great as to raise the specter of doubt. In any case, there is no way of knowing with certainty how the rewards were regarded, for no data were collected on this point.

Replies to Criticism

Few recent psychological theories have generated the hostility aroused by the theory of cognitive dissonance, but few have been as productive of empirical research (McGuire, 1966). Certainly the crudity of the theory and the relative underdevelopment of techniques of experimentation in the fields of social psychology and personality make it almost impossible to design definitive and absolutely convincing research (Aronson, 1969). Nevertheless, some methodological criticisms have been answered, and the theory has not been clearly disconfirmed.

Criticism of the study of initiation rites was partially answered in a study by Gerard and Mathewson (1966) in which some subjects endured severe shock but did not regard it as a form of initiation into a group. Other subjects endured severe shock as a prerequisite to group membership. All subjects then listened to a recorded group discussion and rated its attractiveness. Those who experienced shock as an initiation requirement rated the discussion as more attractive than did those who did not regard it as a form of initiation.

The Festinger and Carlsmith (1959) experiment has been repeated with more reasonable rewards, and the results remain consistent with those of the original study (Cohen, 1962; Carlsmith, Collins, and Helmreich, 1966). Festinger himself has admitted that the term "forced compliance" is probably unfortunate (Festinger, 1964, p. 46), and it is clear, even in his earlier writings, that he never intended it to refer only to situations in which the person is literally forced to behave in certain ways. (Indeed, as we shall see, the belief that one is free to choose not to engage in dissonant behavior is important in determining the degree of dissonance one experiences.)

It is true that any given study of cognitive dissonance can be attacked on grounds of methodological inadequacy. Such attacks usually maintain that the conditions under which the study was run do not eliminate all possible plausible alternative explanations of the results. The merit of dissonance theory, however, is simplicity. To accept all the proposed alternatives is to accept a hodgepodge of possibilities; to accept dissonance theory is to accept a single, unified explanation that accounts for a variety of phenomena as can no other single point of view.

There is also the argument that, while no single study may be convincing, the sheer weight of accumulated evidence is overwhelming. Research techniques may not yet have reached the point where it is possible to prove the validity of the theory of cognitive dissonance beyond the slightest question of doubt. Until they do, an investigator may choose to ignore the theory, but this seems unwise. Although only modest proof exists of the theory's correctness, results of nearly all studies have been consistently favorable; clear-cut disproof does not exist.

Many investigators feel that it is more reasonable to ask, "Under what conditions do the effects predicted by the theory of cognitive dissonance occur?" than to ask whether cognitive dissonance is real (Aronson, 1969). Consider the dispute over whether learning is a function of reinforcement or of effort expended. Perhaps the issue is not "Which is more important?" but "Under what conditions is one more important than the other?" Most research on cognitive dissonance since 1965 seems to have adopted this general strategy. Instead of attempting to prove the validity of the theory, it has concentrated on discovering the properties of situations that arouse dissonance. The next section presents a few examples of this type of research.

	Incentive	
	$ .50	$2.50
No choice	1.66	2.34
Free decision	2.99	1.64

Table 10.2 *Attitude Scale Means after Subjects Wrote Essays Favoring Ban on Certain Campus Speakers (From Linder, Cooper, and Jones, 1967)*
Note: The higher the scale number, the less the objection to the speaker ban.

Conditions Affecting the Magnitude of Dissonance

Reinforcement and Dissonance Reduction

We have already examined a study by Carlsmith, Collins, and Helmreich (1966) which showed that subjects who had to make face-to-face counterattitudinal statements displayed dissonance effects (greater attitude change for smaller reward), while subjects who merely wrote anonymous counterattitudinal essays displayed straightforward reinforcement effects (greater attitude change for greater reward). This study is important because it shows how the approach to investigation of cognitive dissonance has changed, and suggests the type of variables that have become progressively more interesting to investigators (see also the preceding discussion of the study by Canon, 1964). These variables have to do with degree or kind of the subject's personal involvement in the experimental situation. Generally, the greater that involvement, and the more it touches the subject's self-concept, the greater is the effect of cognitive dissonance (Aronson, 1969).

Linder, Cooper, and Jones (1967) report two experiments bearing on this point. Knowing that college students were generally opposed to laws forbidding political nonconformists from speaking on campus, the investigators asked four groups of students to write forceful and convincing essays in favor of such laws. Following the writing, subjects expressed their opinions about such laws on a seven point rating scale, from "completely justified" to "not justified at all." The subjects believed they were participating in a survey to establish policy on the issue.

One-half of the subjects had been told they were entirely free to participate or refuse to participate in the research; the rest were simply instructed to write the required essays. Half the subjects in each of these two groups were paid $.50; the other half were paid $2.50. Payment was provided before the essays were written.

The investigators expected to find that subjects who felt they had decided freely to participate and were provided minimal incentive would show relatively positive attitudes in the postessay ratings, because dissonance would be highest for them. The same attitude changes should appear for subjects who felt they had no choice but were provided with higher incentive payments; they would not experience dissonance, but would respond in a straightforward way to the level of reward received. The results, which are in line with expectations, are shown in Table 10.2. Relatively higher values were expected in the lower left and upper right corners of this table.

A second experiment of similar design dealt with the issue of the university's *in loco parentis* regulations. One group was treated as though it were expected

	Incentive	
	$ .50	$2.50
No choice	2.68	3.46
Free decision	3.64	2.72

Table 10.3 *Attitude Scale Means after subjects Wrote Essays Favoring* In Loco Parentis *Regulations (From Linder, Cooper, and Jones, 1967).*
Note: The higher the scale number, the less the objection to in loco parentis *regulations.*

to write counterattitudinal essays in favor of these regulations, while members of the other group were told that they had complete freedom to decide whether or not to participate. Incentive conditions were the same as in the first study, and the predictions were identical. The results parallel those of the first study (Table 10.3).

The dissonance theory explanation of these results is that the drive to reduce dissonance is strongest when a person feels he has chosen freely to engage in dissonant behavior, while the effects of rewards are strongest when the person feels he has little freedom to determine this choice. In other words, dissonance operates when personal psychological involvement is strong; reward operates when personal involvement is weak.

Anticipated Effects of Behavior

Nel, Helmreich, and Aronson (1969) reasoned that dissonance would be greatest when a person feels that his dissonant actions are likely to produce serious effects of a type that violate the dictates of his own conscience. You should not change your own beliefs as a result of making a speech advocating a life of crime to an audience of criminals, even though you really believe that crime does not pay. You know that your actions are not likely to affect this audience, so dissonance is not aroused. Presenting the same speech to a group of policemen might make you feel embarrassed or uncomfortable, but is again unlikely to change your own ideas. You would not find it necessary to think more favorably about crime because you would not expect your views to be taken seriously by your audience, and therefore no harm is done.

Suppose, however, that you gave the same talk to a group of predelinquent 11 year old boys. Now you would be doing something that affects important beliefs about yourself. Your self-concept probably includes the belief that you would not intentionally lead another person who is not your enemy into harmful behavior. In this case you would be talking to an audience that might take you seriously, and you would feel responsible for any trouble they might get into as a result of your counterattitudinal activity. This situation would be truly dissonant.

One way to reduce dissonance would be to modify your view of reality. If a boy in the audience later got into trouble, you might convince yourself that he probably would have done so anyway; his mind was made up before he listened to you. Another method would be to change your own beliefs, to decide that some criminal behavior is not so bad after all, especially if it is petty and no one is physically injured in the process. It is this latter form of dissonance reduction that interested Nel, Helmreich, and Aronson.

	Expected Audience		
Payment	Pro	Con	Neutral
$ .50	0	0	D
$5.00	R	0	0

Table 10.4 *Design of Experiment on Effect of Expected Impact on Response to Dissonance and Reward*

They selected college women who had expressed themselves as opposed to legislation legalizing marijuana. Each subject made a videotape in favor of legalizing the drug. Some believed the tape would be shown to a student audience agreeing with it (pro-audience); some believed it would be shown to an audience disagreeing with it (con-audience); some were told it would be shown to an uncommitted audience (neutral). Half the subjects in each audience condition were paid $.50 (inadequate reward); half were paid $5.00 (adequate reward).

The design of the experiment is shown in Table 10.4. From the above arguments, it is easy to see that maximum change of speakers' beliefs due to dissonance reduction is expected in cell D. Subjects in this condition made a counterattitudinal statement to a group they believed might be influenced, and were inadequately rewarded for their efforts. Subjects in cell R were also expected to show some attitude change, due to the operation of reward. Although they were making a counterattitudinal statement, it was to a sympathetic audience, and they were reasonably well rewarded for doing so.

The results are easily summarized. Subjects in cell D showed markedly greater attitude changes toward the counterattitudinal position they advocated than did subjects in any of the other experimental conditions. Although reward effects were not demonstrated in cell R, the main point of the study seems to be made: degree of dissonance, as measured by amount of dissonance reducing change in beliefs, is apparently determined by the extent to which dissonant behavior threatens the person's concept of himself as a decent human being who avoids behavior that is harmful to others.

Individual Differences

Some aspects of dissonance theory have as yet been barely touched upon experimentally. Theorists have long recognized two particularly difficult factors that complicate the issue. The first is availability to the subject of dissonance reducing alternatives that the investigator may not take into account in the design of his study. The second is the tendency of subjects to employ response modes consistent with their own personalities.

Hamilton (1969) gave students false and unfavorable feedback about their own personalities and, in effect, offered four different types of response to the dissonance thus created. The four possible responses were: *conformity* (change of self-evaluation to correspond with the false feedback), *underrecall* of the feedback after a period of time, *rejection* of the person who provided the feedback (a fictitious "graduate student" who supposedly scored the tests), and *devaluation* of the source of feedback (personality tests).

Among other things, Hamilton found that subjects who responded with conformity generally did not respond with rejection, indicating that these are probably alternate means of resolving dissonance which may reflect individual response preferences (Steiner, 1966). By contrast, the correlation between rejection and devaluation was positive and moderately high (about .60), suggesting that these two types of responses can be used together. Thus, there are probably different patterns of personally preferred responses to cognitively different situations, but we do not yet know all the possibilities that people tend to employ.

Hamilton incorporated several tests of personality into his investigation, and found a few relationships between scores on these measures and responses to cognitive dissonance. Since these relationships are complex and better regarded as suggestive rather than conclusive in nature, they need not be detailed here. The problem of the relationship between personality structure and preference for mode of response to cognitive dissonance remains wide open to future investigators.

Conclusion

A theory may be scientifically valuable not because it is easily proven or disproven, but because it provokes thought, challenges old concepts, and stimulates research. Such is the case with the theory of cognitive dissonance. It has aroused heated controversy and inspired investigators to question established viewpoints, devise ingenious new experiments, and open up new fields of psychological inquiry.

In a review of the literature, Aronson (1969) noted that the theory of cognitive dissonance is "primitive" and lacking in "elegance and precision," yet its impact on psychology has been great. Since, like all science, psychology benefits greatly from the type of innovation introduced by the theory of cognitive dissonance, we shall conclude this introduction as Aronson concluded his review. "Happily, after more than 10 years, it is still not proven; all the theory does is generate research."

Glossary

Cognition: thought, thinking, ideation, knowledge.

Cognitive dissonance: inconsistency, incongruence, or contradiction between beliefs, between beliefs and behavior, or between beliefs and reality.

Counterattitudinal: opposed to existing attitudes or beliefs.

Drive: a motivational force, the strength of which is reduced by successful goal directed behavior.

Extinction: *see* Glossary, Chapter 1.

Hedonism: the doctrine that behavior is motivated by the desire to seek pleasure and avoid pain.

Reinforcement: *see* Glossary, Chapter 1.

References

Adams, J.S. Reduction of cognitive dissonance by seeking consonant information. *J. abnorm. soc. Psychol.*, 1961, **62,** 74–78.

Aronson, E. Progress and problems. In R. Abelson, E. Aronson, W. McGuire, T. Newcomb, M. Rosenberg, and P. Tannenbaum (Eds.), *Theories of cognitive consistency: A source book*. Chicago: Rand McNally, 1968.

________. The effect of effort on the attractiveness of rewarded and unrewarded stimuli. *J. abnorm. soc. Psychol.*, 1961, **63,** 375–380.

———. The theory of cognitive dissonance: A current perspective. In L. Berkowitz (Ed.), *Advances in experimental social psychology.* New York: Academic Press, 1969.
———, and J. Mills. The effect of severity of initiation on liking for a group. *J. abnorm. soc. Psychol.*, 1959, **59,** 177–181.
Asch, S.E. Review of L. Festinger, A theory of cognitive dissonance. *Contemporary Psychol.*, 1958, **3,** 194–195.
Brehm, J.W. Attitudinal consequences of commitment to unpleasant behavior. *J. abnorm. soc. Psychol.*, 1960, **60,** 379–383.
———. Increasing cognitive dissonance by a *fait accompli. J. abnorm. soc. Psychol.*, 1959, **58,** 379–382.
———. Postdecision changes in the desirability of alternatives. *J. abnorm. soc. Psychol.*, 1956, **52,** 384–389.
———, and A.R. Cohen. *Explorations in cognitive dissonance.* New York: John Wiley & Sons, 1962.
Burdick, H. The compliant behavior of deviates under conditions of threat. Unpublished doctoral dissertation, University of Minnesota, 1955.
Canon, L.K. Self-confidence and selective exposure to information. In L. Festinger, *Conflict, decision and dissonance.* Stanford: Stanford University Press, 1964.
Carlsmith, J.M., B.E. Collins, and R.L. Helmreich. Studies in forced compliance. *J. pers. soc. Psychol.*, 1966, **4,** 1–13.
Chapanis, N.P., and A. Chapanis. Cognitive dissonance: Five years later. *Psychol. Bull.*, 1964, **61,** 1–22.
Cohen, A.R. An experiment on small rewards for discrepant compliance and attitude change. In J.W. Brehm and A.R. Cohen, *Explorations in cognitive dissonance.* New York: John Wiley & Sons, 1962.
Davidson, J.R. Cognitive familiarity and dissonance reduction. In L. Festinger, *Conflict, decision and dissonance.* Stanford: Stanford University Press, 1964.
Ehrlich, D., I. Guttman, P. Schonbach, and J. Mills. Post-decision exposure to relevant information. *J. abnorm. soc. Psychol.*, 1957, **54,** 98–102.
Engel, J.F. Are automobile purchasers dissonant consumers? *Journal of Marketing*, 1963, **27,** 55–58.
Feather, N.T. Cognitive dissonance, sensitivity, and evaluation. *J. abnorm. soc. Psychol.*, 1963, **66,** 153–163.
Festinger, L. *Conflict, decision and dissonance.* Stanford: Stanford University Press, 1964.
———. The psychological effects of insufficient rewards. *Amer. Psychologist*, 1961, **16,** 1–11.
———. *A theory of cognitive dissonance.* Stanford: Stanford University Press, 1957.
———, and J.M. Carlsmith. Cognitive consequences of forced compliance. *J. abnorm. soc. Psychol.*, 1959, **58,** 203–210.
Festinger, L., and E. Walster. Post-decision regret and decision reversal. In L. Festinger, *Conflict, decision and dissonance.* Stanford: Stanford University Press, 1964.
Festinger, L., H.W. Riecken, and S. Schachter. *When prophecy fails.* Minneapolis: University of Minnesota Press, 1956.
Freedman, J.L. Attitudinal effects of inadequate justification. *J. Pers.*, 1963, **31,** 371–385.
Gerard, H.B., and G.C. Mathewson. The effects of severity of initiation on liking for a group: A replication. *J. exp. soc. Psychol.*, 1966, **2,** 278–287.
Haber, R.N. Personal communication to authors, 1970.
Hamilton, D.L. Responses to cognitive inconsistencies: Personality, discrepancy level, and response stability. *J. pers. soc. Psychol.*, 1969, **11,** 351–362.
Janis, I.L., and B.T. King. The influence of role-playing on opinion change. *J. abnorm. soc. Psychol.*, 1954, **49,** 211–218.
Jecker, J.D. Selective exposure to new information. In L. Festinger, *Conflict, decision and dissonance.* Stanford: Stanford University Press, 1964.
King, B.T., and I.L. Janis. Comparison of the effectiveness of improvised versus non-improvised role-playing in producing opinion changes. *Hum. Relat.*, 1956, **9,** 177–181.

Linder, D.E., J. Cooper, and E.E. Jones. Decision freedom as a determinant of the role of incentive magnitude in attitude change. *J. pers. soc. Psychol.*, 1967, **6,** 245–254.

Margulis, S.T., and E. Songer. Cognitive dissonance: A bibliography of its first decade. *Psychol. Rep.*, 1969, **24,** 923–935.

McBride, D. The effects of public and private changes of opinion on intragroup communication. Unpublished doctoral dissertation, University of Minnesota, 1954.

McGuire, W.J. Attitudes and opinions. In P.R. Farnsworth, O. McNemar, and Q. McNemar (Eds.), *Annual review of psychology*. Vol. 17. Palo Alto, California: Annual Reviews, 1966.

Mills, J., E. Aronson, and H. Robinson. Selectivity in exposure to information. *J. abnorm. soc. Psychol.*, 1959, **59,** 250–253.

Nel, E., R. Helmreich, and E. Aronson. Opinion change in the advocate as a function of the personality of his audience: A clarification of the meaning of dissonance. *J. pers. soc. Psychol.*, 1969, **12,** 116–124.

Rosen, S. Post-decision affinity for incompatible information. *J. abnorm. soc. Psychol.*, 1961, **63,** 188–190.

Steiner, I.D. Personality and the resolution of interpersonal disagreements. In B.A. Maher (Ed.), *Progress in experimental personality research*. Vol. 3. New York: Academic Press, 1966.

Thorndike, E.L. *Animal intelligence*. New York: Macmillan, 1911.

Zimbardo, P.G. The effect of effort and improvisation on self persuasion produced by role playing. *J. exp. soc. Psychol.*, 1965, **1,** 103–120.

11 Naturalism in Psychology

Ecology is the study of interrelationships of organisms and their natural environments. In the biological sciences, ecologists study the adaptations of animals' organic structures and behavior patterns to the demands and resources of their surroundings. For example, although gibbons and gorillas belong to the same biological family (*the anthropoids*), they are structurally and behaviorally quite different. An ecological point of view accounts for such differences by emphasizing the adaptations of these creatures to their characteristic habitats. Gibbons, whose small size and long arms suit them admirably for arboreal existence, live almost exclusively in trees, but are awkward when moving about on the ground. Gorillas spend most of their time grubbing about on the forest floor for food. They are massively built and function well on the ground, but are not capable of swinging from limb to limb like their more agile relations.

Biologists know that the study of organisms is incomplete without serious consideration of the environments in which organisms live. The same is true of the study of human behavior. Much of what people do represents the adjustment of behavior to environmental conditions and demands. It is from this premise that the naturalistic approach in psychology is derived.

Environmentalism in Psychology

Laboratory and Naturalistic Environmentalism

Psychologists have long been interested in the influence of environmental conditions on behavior, as indicated in examples provided by research on learning. When studying the behavior of rats in mazes, the psychologist varies the surroundings (for example, the form of the maze) and observes how the rats' behavior changes as a result of these variations. In studies of human verbal learning, environmental control consists of varying the conditions under which stimuli are learned (for example, the length or content of stimulus words and the lengths of time stimuli are presented to the subjects).

These are not *naturalistic* studies, for they are carried out in the laboratory rather than in the settings of everyday life. In recent years, a number of psychologists have claimed that some problems of great interest to psychology cannot be solved by laboratory methods (Sells, 1966; Willems, 1965; Willems and Raush, 1969). To answer such questions it is necessary for the investigator to get out into the natural environment of schools, grocery stores, and bowling alleys, the real and complicated world of people conducting the everyday business of life.

It may seem inappropriate to describe a school or factory as "natural," since both are man-made. The forest, the plains, a riverbank, or a stretch of mountainous terrain are obviously "natural" environments, while a city, a grocery store, or an office building seem less so because they are planned and constructed to serve specific purposes. As the naturalistic psychologist uses the term, however, the word "natural" does not mean "wild, uncultivated, or uncivilized." It more nearly means "uninfluenced by experimental intervention." Thus, a courtroom is man-made, but a court in session is a natural behavior setting so long as nothing is done to interfere with its functioning for purposes of experimentation. Even biological ecologists do not confine their interests to animals in forests, plains, or mountains. They are as interested in how Norway rats adapt to the man-made environment of the large city as in how various kinds of monkeys are suited for lives in trees or on the open plains.

Molecular and Molar Approaches

In psychology, laboratory scientist and naturalist agree that the proper way to learn about human behavior is to study how it responds to changes in environmental conditions. However, they disagree on one important matter. Classical laboratory experimentation has long been identified with what is sometimes called an elementaristic or molecular strategy (Chap. 1). The elementarist wishes to work with the simplest units he can find, like the *stimulus-response* bond, which some psychologists call a *habit*. Such a bond is inferred when a particular stimulus in the environment, like food, consistently brings about a particular response, like eating, from an appropriately motivated organism. From the elementaristic standpoint, complex habits consist of combinations of elementary stimulus-response bonds.

The psychologist who prefers naturalistic methods usually views his subject from a more *molar* standpoint. He looks at whole systems of the environment and of behavior, rather than at the parts that make them up. From the molar standpoint, an environment is not an assemblage of physical stimuli, but a total pattern of possibilities for behavior. The same pattern of possibilities may exist in a variety of different physical settings. A religious service may be held in a brick building, a wooden building, or even an open field. A teen-ager may study as effectively in a quiet library or while riding on a noisy bus, even though the specific stimuli to which he is exposed in the two situations are quite different.

Similarly, to the naturalist, behavior is not an assemblage of simple habits but a set of action patterns, no part of which can be understood except as it relates to the rest. The same purpose may be served by many different specific behaviors, as when a child checks his rote memorization of the product of six times four by adding six to itself four times and then by adding four to itself six times. By the same reasoning, a single act may serve several purposes. When a young man takes a girl out to dinner he accomplishes a good deal more than mere satisfaction of his hunger drive. The relationship between molar and molecular approaches to the study of behavior will be clarified in succeeding sections, where the discussion turns to analysis of specific research findings.

Behavior in Natural Settings

Evidence from the study of animals in confinement indicates that the behavior one sees exhibited by the caged rat or the chimpanzee in the zoo does not represent the behavior of these animals in their natural environments. For example, it has been shown that wild rats and mice that are captured and brought into the laboratory find it rewarding simply to exert control over their environment (Kavenau, 1964, 1969) even when their responses lead to apparently contradictory effects or conditions. A wild rat placed on a motor-driven activity wheel which it can turn off will "immediately and invariably" turn the motor off when the experimenter turns it on. A rat on an activity wheel which it has turned on itself, but which is then turned off by the experimenter, immediately turns the motor back on. A rat which can operate a switch to adjust the light level in its cage will generally turn the light off if the experimenter turns it on. This is not unusual because nocturnal animals prefer the dark, but unexpectedly, if the experimenter should turn the light off, the rat usually turns it right back on. It is often a matter of weeks before the animal "gives in" and ceases to oppose the arbitrary schedules imposed upon him.

Laboratory animals are usually carefully inbred to represent pure genetic strains. From the point of view of classical experimental procedures, inbreeding of subjects is highly desirable, as is the fact that "standard" experimental animals are brought up under nearly ideal conditions: they are well fed, their cages are kept clean, they are disease-free, and they have all been exposed to the same sets of stimuli. The experimenter can use such subjects in research without fear that his results reflect the operation of uncontrolled organismic or developmental factors. From a naturalistic point of view, however, inbreeding and perpetual confinement are disadvantageous. They produce species which are not typical of those existing in the wild and are probably incapable of surviving outside of the laboratory (Lockard, 1968).

What is true of rats and mice is true of other animals as well. Reports of the differences between the behavior of chimpanzees in confinement and in the wild have been brought to public attention by articles in *National Geographic* (Goodall and Van Lawick, 1963; Van Lawick-Goodall and Van Lawick, 1965). An extensive article in *Life* (Morris, 1968) expressed the concerns of many zoologists over the fact that behavior displayed by caged animals in zoos does not represent the typical characteristics of the animals, but their distress and discomfort in response to physical and psychological imprisonment.

The value of naturalistic research in providing solutions to some types of human problems has been convincingly demonstrated (Beecher, 1956; 1959a, b; 1960). Beecher observed the reactions of men wounded in combat and of civilian patients in the naturalistic setting of surgical wards to various compounds that had been found in controlled laboratory experiments to relieve pain. He discovered that many such compounds failed to relieve the suffering of surgical patients, while some substances with no medicinal properties whatsoever (*placebos*) often achieved the purpose successfully on the wards. Beecher further noted that the psychological significance of an injury or illness in the life situation of the patient is far more potent in determining how much pain he experiences than is the severity of damage to his body or the type of drug he is given for its relief. Soldiers with severe wounds that signified the desirable prospect of honorable escape from the dangers of combat suffered noticeably less from their bodily conditions than did civilians for whom surgery meant the threat of financial sacrifice and disruption of previously satisfying, dependable life processes.

Measurement and the Observation of Behavior

In the laboratory. When an experimenter decides to examine a particular kind of behavior, he takes great care to arrange for its objective and reliable measurement. Often he must choose among several alternatives. For example, as a measure of the learning of a conditioned response, he may count the number of trials to successful continuous performance. Conversely, he may observe the rate at which unsuccessful performances (errors) decrease with successive exposure to the conditioning stimulus, or he may measure the rate at which the learned response disappears, or *extinguishes*, when reinforcement for successful performance is withheld. Similarly, when a psychologist constructs a scale to measure an attitude (like prejudice), a trait (like extroversion), or a capacity (like intelligence), he is careful to identify the particular behavior that will serve as the appropriate index. He may ask the subject whether he agrees with a series of prejudicial statements about members of minority groups. He may provide statements describing activities that involve mingling with other people on close personal terms, and ask the subject whether each statement describes him. He may pose a series of problems for the subject to solve.

In all such situations, the investigator knows before he begins his study what units he will use for measuring behavior. Learning is measured by units like *trials to correct performance, rate of error production,* or *trials to extinction.* Other psychological tests use units such as *items agreed with, activities liked,* or *problems correctly solved.*

In nature. Everyday behavioral phenomena rarely come in easily measurable packages. A salesman's success may be partly measured by the volume of his sales, but how does one evaluate the image of the company he projects? A worker's productivity on an assembly line may be measured by the number of units he turns out per hour, but is a fast worker who is frequently absent from his job and gets along poorly with his boss better or worse than a slow worker who is dependable and well-liked?

People do not naturally express their traits and skills as specific responses to verbal statements. A prejudiced person does not go around saying, "I think black people are dirty." An introvert does not go about telling everyone, "I like to work with ideas rather than objects." Even a highly intelligent person spends most of his time doing things that can be accomplished by people who are somewhat mentally retarded. The units of the laboratory and testing room simply do not lend themselves to measurement of behavior as it occurs in nature. Where are appropriate units to be found? The naturalist's answer is "in nature itself" (Barker, 1963a). The first task is to acquire records of behavior as it occurs in natural situations. Next, these records must be examined to discover the units by which naturally occurring behavior may be measured.

The record of behavior. To be useful, a record of behavior must be objective, unobtrusive, and complete. An *objective* record validly reports events as they actually occurred, with a minimum of bias or distortion. An *unobtrusive* record does not interfere with or influence the events being recorded. Obtrusive measurement in the study of behavior is exemplified by the newspaper or television reporter who interrupts rescue workers at a flood scene to ask what they are doing. Unobtrusive measurement might be exemplified by observations of prison life made by a person who has introduced himself into prison as an inmate. A *complete* record includes all necessary details for proper evaluation of recorded material.

It is not easy to obtain behavior records that fulfill all these criteria. Completeness and objectivity might be assured by employing banks of movie cameras and tape recorders to transcribe behavior, but such methods would hardly be unobtrusive in a classroom or church service; in a courtroom they would simply not be tolerated. Completeness and objectivity of sound recording could be assured by the use of miniature tape recorders (Schoggen, 1964), but these machines have the irritating property of being as sensitive to unwanted sounds as they are to those one wishes to preserve. The sound of a passing truck can easily blot out the words one wants most to save. In any case, tape recorders do not respond to visual inputs, which are essential to a complete record of behavior.

The most satisfactory instrument for recording behavior is the human observer. He is the only one capable of focusing several sensory channels on an observed event and producing a single, continuous record of their measurements. Obviously, the human recorder is not perfect; it undoubtedly misses some events, distorts others, and misinterprets some of the things it observes. Nevertheless, a human being can provide data of a type unavailable from any presently made mechanical or electronic equipment, and the human observer can be trained to enhance his value as a measuring device. Human beings can be taught how to look at behavior, just as they can be taught how to observe cells through a microscope or how to appreciate the regularities of composition and design of a leaf or a work of art.

The care actually taken in the collection of naturalistic data is suggested by the following summary of procedures and rules that are taught to one group of trained observers (Barker and Wright, 1955, pp. 214–218; Wright, 1967).

An observation is not to last more than 30 minutes, during which time the observer is to take notes sufficient to permit "near duplication of all verbal behavior." The observer is to attend not only to the behavior of the person observed but also to his situation, that is, to other conditions that make a difference or are necessary to his behavior; the record should also include a detailed description of the scene as it exists before observation begins. The record must be continuous and unbroken, without gaps; the observer should regard all behavior as interesting and report everything that occurs. Events should not be separately timed; instead the observer should indicate the passage of time at one minute intervals. Negative statements ("Sally did not answer") should be avoided; positive statements ("Sally continued to play with her doll in silence") are to be used whenever possible. The observer should note *how* behavior occurs as well as simply *what* behavior occurs, and at the same time remain descriptive and avoid theoretical interpretation. It is necessary to note whether an action is undertaken quickly or slowly, sadly, or gaily, matter-of-factly, or with painstaking care. However, it is not acceptable to report that "Mike cried because his sister had hurt his feelings" or that "George's self-esteem was shattered by the teacher's remark." Such statements do not describe what was observed but reflect the observer's personal explanations of what he saw.

The observer dictates or writes the first version of his complete report as soon as possible after the observation period is completed. This report is then scrutinized by another observer, who questions the first observer about ambiguities or omissions in the narrative. On the basis of this interrogation, the report is revised and clarified. The revised report is then examined, and a final revision prepared.

There is still the problem of the possible obtrusiveness of the observer. Observations of behavior would lose much of their value if the very presence of an observer changes the natural patterns of behavior that he wishes to record. Fortunately, observer influence, like observer error, can be minimized. Willems (1965) reports that observer influence is least when the subject is young, when he is in a group, and when he has had time to adapt to the observer's presence. An observed child engaged in stealing checked to see if anyone else was watching besides the observer (who was not regarded as a threat) and went ahead with the theft. In general, experienced observers report that their effect on the behavior of their subjects is far less than even the observers themselves initially expected.

Specimen records. One product of the effort to obtain objective records of natural behavior is a report called a *specimen record*. "A specimen record is a sequential account of a long segment of a person's behavior and situation as seen and described by a skilled observer. It reports in concrete detail a stream of behavior and psychological habitat'' (Barker, Wright, Barker, and Schoggen, 1961). The most extensive specimen records, each of which describes a full day's activity, are made by teams of five to nine observers who take turns throughout the day. A single daylong specimen record has been published as a book under the title *One Boy's Day* (Barker and Wright, 1951). Other examples of specimen records can be found in the book, *The Stream of Behavior,* (Barker, 1963).

Specimen records can be used to answer a variety of questions, such as, "How often does a specific kind of event, such as frustration, occur, and what are its consequences?'' There have been many studies of frustration conducted in the laboratory. In a famous one by Barker, Dembo, and Lewin (1943), children were first allowed to play with a set of attractive toys. Later they played again in the same room, but this time some of the most attractive toys were blocked off by a wire screen; *frustration* consisted of preventing the subjects from playing with the toys they liked. The result was that the children's play became less constructive and more typical of the play of younger children; they *regressed* by behaving in less mature fashion. This type of experiment shows a clear relationship between an independent variable (frustration) and a dependent variable (regression) which might be difficult to demonstrate outside of the laboratory. However, it does not tell how often frustration occurs in everyday life, nor how frequently regressive behavior occurs in response to frustration when frustration occurs in natural settings. To answer these questions it is necessary to examine evidence of the type provided by specimen records.

Fawl (1963) analyzed 16 daylong specimen records for evidence of frustration, or blocking of goals, in the daily lives of children. Even though he used what he considered a liberal definition of the term, he found fewer incidents of frustration than he anticipated (a mean of 16.5 incidents per child per waking day). Furthermore, he could find no evidence that frustration in daily life is consistently followed by any signs of disturbance such as aggression or regression.

In light of these findings, the laboratory situation appears to represent a special case of frustration. It is possible that the conditions imposed in laboratory study provide a close approximation to those relatively rare real-life situations that do, in fact, lead to behavior disturbance or, in extreme cases, neurosis and psychosis. If so, the laboratory experiment serves a useful purpose and increases our understanding of the processes by which abnormally inefficient psychological states are generated, but it may not show how frustration occurs and affects behavior in the course of everyday life.

The Units of Behavior

Laboratory studies often give the impression that behavior proceeds serially and consecutively, in a straight line from one stimulus and its appropriate response to the next stimulus and its appropriate response. While traversing a maze, the organism moves in linear fashion from one choice to the next until it reaches the goal or endpoint of the single correct path. If behavior in natural settings occurs in this way, it should be fairly easy to identify its units, since these will simply be responses to specific stimuli, and their direction toward some goal will be apparent.

Studies of specimen records reveal that observers can reliably identify units of behavior in the actions of persons in natural settings (Dickman, 1963; Barker, 1963b), but the units are not simple sequences of stimuli and responses. Natural behavior units are called *behavior episodes*; here are examples of two behavior episodes that take place in less than half a minute. The setting is a drugstore where Maud, a five year old girl, sits at the fountain waiting to order a treat promised by her mother. Next to Maud sits her two year old brother, Fred; next to him sits their mother (Barker, 1965).

	Episode
I. Pretending to use lipstick	From her jeans' pocket Maud now took an orange crayon. She brushed it across her lips as if it were a lipstick.
II. Watching girl eat soda	Maud then leaned over, sliding her arms along the counter, as she watched a man serve a strawberry soda to his blond, curly-headed, three-year-old girl. Maud seemed fascinated by the procedure; she took in every detail of the situation.

This example is useful for purposes of illustration because it contains a rather clear demarcation between episodes. However, it does not represent the way such episodes usually appear in records of behavior. Analysis of more than 200 hours of specimen records, including 18 daylong records, showed that only 27 per cent (about one-fourth) of all behavior episodes occurred in this way. Seventy-three per cent overlapped with at least one other episode. For example, during one period, Maud engaged in three episodes simultaneously: she watched the other girl eating a soda while she ate her own ice cream cone and tried to get her mother's attention (Barker and Wright, 1955). The way in which behavior episodes overlap and subsume each other is shown in the upper part of Figure 11.1. A particularly inclusive episode is marked by the letter I at the top of the figure.

Naturalistic observation of behavior shows that everyday activities are not strung out on the time dimension like beads on a string. They more frequently occur in overlapping clusters: " . . . behavior episodes do not move along Indian file, but, rather, one, two, or three abreast quite irregularly" (Barker, 1968, p. 148). Since this is not the way behavior is made to occur in laboratory experiments or in responses to most psychological tests, serious consideration must be given to the possibility that data from these sources destroy essential attributes of psychological phenomena and paint a false picture of behavior in extralaboratory situations.

Another well-accepted notion about behavior is that every action, or response, occurs in reaction to some stimulus. Consequently, the tester or experimenter conventionally studies behavior by arranging series or sequences of stimuli and observing the responses that occur as each stimulus is presented. Barker and his co-workers examined specimen records for evidence of relationships between inputs to the behaving organism and resulting episodes. They discovered two important things. First, the episodes did not appear as reactions to specific inputs (Fig. 11.1). A whole series of inputs would frequently be followed by a paucity of episodic outputs (region a in Fig. 11.1), or a relatively small number of inputs would be followed by a massive production of behavior episodes (region b in Fig. 11.1).

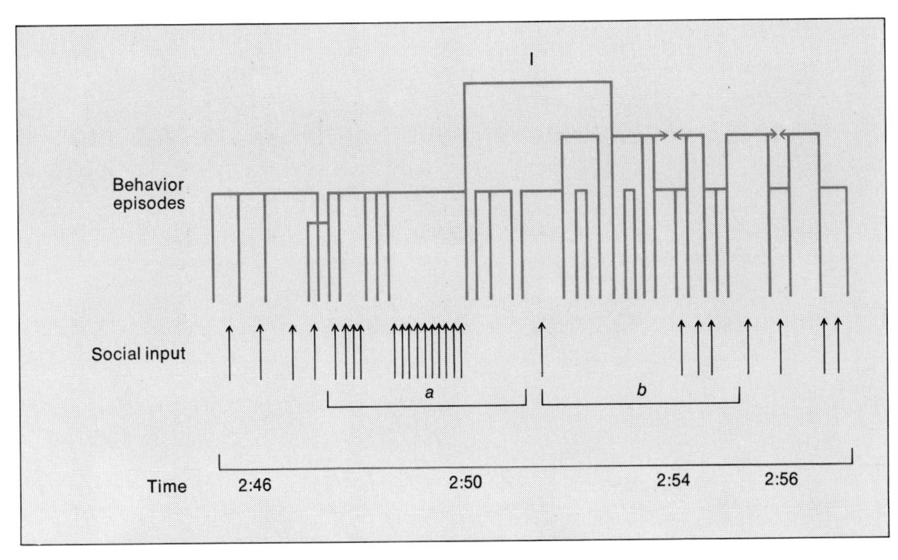

Fig. 11.1. Inputs and behavior episodes as Maud gets a treat at the drugstore. (From Barker, 1965)

Second, they noticed that there was no necessary congruence or similarity between stimuli applied to the subject and behavior emitted by the subject as a result of their application. In Maud's case, for example, the following social inputs from her mother *did* elicit episodes congruent with the nature of the input:

Input (Mother)	*Episode (Maud)*
We'll all go to the drugstore.	Entering the drugstore.
Pushes Maud toward a stool.	Moving toward stool.
What do you want, Maud?	Choosing treat (soda).

The following social inputs produced episodes that were *not* congruent with the nature of the input:

Input (Mother)	*Episode (Maud)*
Not now; you're not having a comic now.	Continues looking at comic (previous episode).
Oh, you don't want a soda.	Continues choice of soda (previous episode).
Fred snatches Maud's coat.	Ignores Fred.

In large samples of children's behavior, it has been found that about one-half of all social inputs elicit congruent episodes (Barker, 1968). The 26 social inputs that occurred during the 11 minute observation of Maud, Fred, and their mother are reproduced in Table 11.1. These are the same incidents recorded as social inputs in Figure 11.1. Those that elicited congruent behavior episodes are marked with asterisks.

*Mother:	"We'll all go to the drugstore."
Mother:	"Not now; you're not having a comic now."
Mother:	"Leave things [Christmas cards] alone."
Mother:	"Come on now, get your coat off."
Mother:	"Maud, come back and sit down."
*Mother:	Pushes Maud toward the stool.
*Mother:	"Now you sit here."
*Mother:	"What do you want, Maud?"
Mother:	"Oh, you don't want a *soda*."
Mother:	"No, you don't get a soda."
Mother:	"What do you want?"
Mother:	"You don't want a soda. Besides you wouldn't drink it if you had it."
Mother:	"Do you want a coke?"
Mother:	"Do you want an ice cream cone?"
*Mother:	"*Do* you want an ice cream cone?"
Clerk:	"What flavor, Maud?"
*Clerk:	"Vanilla, that's the white one."
Clerk:	"Don't eat Fred's cone."
Mother:	"Come on. Get your coat on, Maud."
*Mother:	Refuses Maud's whispered request.
Fred:	Snatches Maud's coat.
Clerk:	"Hi, Maud," as she ruffles Maud's hair.
Mother:	"Come on."
Mother:	Pushes Maud toward her coat.
*Fred:	Asks Maud for gum (from gum-machine).
*Mother:	Urges children from store with words and motions.

Table 11.1 *Social Inputs as Maud Gets a Treat at the Drugstore*
** Inputs that elicited congruent behavior.*

A Brief Rejoinder

This chapter presents the naturalistic view of behavior, with minimal consideration of objections that might be raised by those who study psychology in more traditional ways. However, a moment's attention to some of these objections can be instructive.

Since analysis of Maud's behavior fails to show clear congruence between social inputs and behavior episodes, it is tempting to conclude that the stimulus-response model is therefore inadequate for explaining behavior that occurs in natural settings. The correctness of this conclusion depends upon the correctness of the equations:

social input = stimulus;
behavior episode = response.

Neither equation is valid. Maud was exposed to a great many more stimuli than those included or emphasized in the specimen record. Two stimuli mentioned in that record but not given adequate emphasis as possible influences on Maud's behavior are the comic book and the other little girl's soda. A brightly colored comic book has considerable power to attract and hold a child's attention. Maud's continued examination of the comic book despite her mother's statement, "You're not having a comic now," is therefore not an example of incongruence between stimulus and response. In fact, Maud's behavior (continued looking at comic) is highly congruent with the stimulus properties of the comic book itself. Maud probably did what any organism would do in the presence of more than one stimulus; she reacted to the more attractive stimulus with the response that was easiest to produce. (It was easier for her to continue looking at the comic because she was already doing it; to obey her mother would have required effortful initiation of a completely new response sequence.)

Maud's desire for a soda is also easily explained as a response to the stimulus of the other little girl's soda. The naturalistic analysis of the incident does not include this object in its description of social inputs, and is therefore incomplete. Furthermore, the specimen record does not describe other possibly effective stimuli in the environment. Advertisements for sodas may have been prominently displayed near the counter; Maud may have overheard someone else talking about sodas; she may have seen a picture of a soda in the comic book. As a description of all stimuli in the environment to which it was possible for Maud to respond, the specimen record is woefully inadequate. Consequently, it is not surprising that real and consistent stimulus-response relations cannot be observed in the report. Even so-called "elementaristic" psychology does not deny that the natural world consists of complex patterns of stimulation, or that conflicts among responses often result from competition among stimuli in natural settings. It is precisely his recognition of the complexity of stimulus-response relations in the real world that causes the elementarist to insist that research be conducted in the laboratory. Only there is it possible to reduce this complexity to manageable proportions so that the investigator can describe completely the stimuli to which his subject is exposed and the responses his subject produces.

Much the same arguments apply to the equation of episodes with responses. Maud's continuing to look at the comic is not counted by the naturalist as a new episode; neither is her repeated desire for a soda. Both actions involve responses, however. As Maud looks from one picture to the next she responds to the stimuli in the comic book. When she insists on the soda, she responds again to the stimulus that determined her choice in the first place. Simply because an easily observed response to her mother's statements or to Fred's snatching of her coat did not appear does not mean that Maud did not react to these stimuli. Had the investigator taken appropriate measures of physiological reactions of the type usually associated with emotional arousal, he might have observed very strong reactions. Since such reactions are just as much *behavior* as more obvious actions of the body, the specimen record can be justifiably criticized as providing an incomplete account of responses, just as it provides an incomplete description of the stimulus situation.

Differences between naturalism and elementarism can be resolved by recognizing that each views the same sets of events in different but equally defensible ways. To argue that only naturalism is correct is like saying that all one needs to understand a house is a molar diagram of its floor plans. This is true only if one does not care whether his house is built of brick, wood, or chicken wire. On the other hand, to say that the laws of stimulus-response relations are the only correct laws in psychology is like saying that all one needs to understand a house is a knowledge of how to lay bricks, pound nails, and saw wood. These are indeed necessary skills, but even the best craftsman in the business cannot build a house until he knows where to put the bathroom and the kitchen.

The naturalist is correct when he says that there are important molar aspects of behavior which deserve to be studied and understood in their own right, and which must be described in terms other than stimulus-response relations. The experimental analyst is correct when he points out that it is always possible to break down observations of behavior into simpler units. Both are wrong if they assert that one approach is more complete, accurate, objective, or correct than the other.

Ecological Units: Behavior Settings

Environment and Ecology

The term *environment* is often used in psychology as though it referred only to the physical structures and forces that surround and impinge upon the organism. It is not this sense of the word that is employed by those who study psychology naturalistically. The word more accurately means *all* conditions in the organism's surroundings that influence or modify its behavior. It therefore refers not only to physical structures and forces, but to social and cultural conditions as well. The natural environment of a basketball game includes not only the nets, ball, stadium, players, and officials, but also the formal regulations by which the game is played, the principles of effective offensive or defensive movement, the encouragement players receive from spectators, and the generally agreed upon standards of fair play and sportsmanlike conduct.

There is an orderly relationship between molar behavior and environment (Gump, Schoggen, and Redl, 1957, 1963), but it is as difficult to explain this relationship in purely physical terms as it is to explain the Smith family's custom of eating in the dining room by saying that their house has aluminum siding. What is needed in a naturalistic psychology is a unit which can be used for describing the environment. One such unit is the *behavior setting.*

Here are several behavior settings that occurred in a small American town in the early 1960's:

1. American Legion dinner and business meeting.
2. High school Latin class trip to convention at State College.
3. Ruttley's Jewelry and Watch Repair Shop.
4. Household auction sale.
5. High school boys' basketball game.

How does one identify a part of the environment as a behavior setting? In Barker's words,

> A behavior setting has both structural and dynamic attributes. On the structural side, a behavior setting consists of one or more standing patterns of behavior-and-milieu, with the milieu circumjacent and synomorphic to the behavior. On the dynamic side, the behavior-milieu parts of a behavior setting, the synomorphs, have a specified degree of interdependence among themselves that is greater than their interdependence with parts of other behavior settings (1968, p. 18).

Obviously this definition requires elaboration.

When Barker says that a behavior setting has both *structural* and *dynamic* attributes, he means that it can be described both as an organized arrangement of actions and objects and as a set of forces that resist disruption and maintain the integrity of the setting. A business meeting or a basketball game has obvious structural attributes; both consist of arrangements of actions, objects, and people. A business meeting usually has a chairman, located behind a table or lectern but facing the rest of the group. The chairman directs discussion by determining who shall speak on what subjects, and manages the decision making processes of the organization. The structure of a basketball game may be identified by describing the arrangement of the court, the equipment used, and the positions and roles played by athletes, coaches, officials, and spectators.

The dynamic attributes of a behavior setting are the relationships that hold the setting together as a cohesive unit. Interdependence occurs in a variety of ways. It is high when the same people use the same objects in the same physical space at the same time; it is also high when specific behaviors are closely interconnected and leadership is constant. Interdependence is high in a business meeting for all these reasons; the constancy of population, physical-temporal location, and leadership is apparent. Interconnected behavior is evident in the relevance of each member's contribution to the contributions of others, and in the extent to which each item of business is related to the next. Interconnectedness is also high in a basketball game, since everyone's actions are determined by the actions of others present in the setting.

To be described as a behavior setting, a part of the environment must qualify structurally as a *behavior-milieu synomorph*. Barker uses *milieu* as a close synonym for environment, although milieu usually refers to immediate surroundings, while environment may refer to a much broader class of influences as well. Synomorph is not a word you are likely to find in your dictionary. It is a composite of the prefix *syn* (along with; together) and the combining form *morph* (shape; structure; type; form). When the milieu includes physical features, such as boundary lines, school bells, seating arrangements, and so on, to which the actions of people conform, synomorphy exists. If a group of boys simply run about at random on a basketball court and do not throw the ball toward the baskets or observe the boundaries of the court, their behavior is not synomorphic with the milieu, at least so far as the setting "basketball game" is concerned. In a true behavior setting, environmental arrangements and behavior patterns coincide.

Circumjacent, another composite word used in Barker's definition (*circum:* around; *jacent:* lying), means enclosing or encompassing. The boundaries of a behavior setting surround it in time and space. A class is in session continuously from 2:00 P.M. to 2:50 P.M. on certain days of the week in a particular physical location. Beyond these boundaries, the setting does not exist. Boundaries need not be only physical or temporal; a person who does not know the rules of chess is outside the boundary of the setting "chess game" even if he moves the pieces around on the board.

Population Density

Population figures tell how many people occupy a community, but these figures alone do not contain enough information to be useful in most naturalistic research. A large number of people occupying a sufficiently large space may be no more crowded than a small number of people in a much more limited area. Of greater

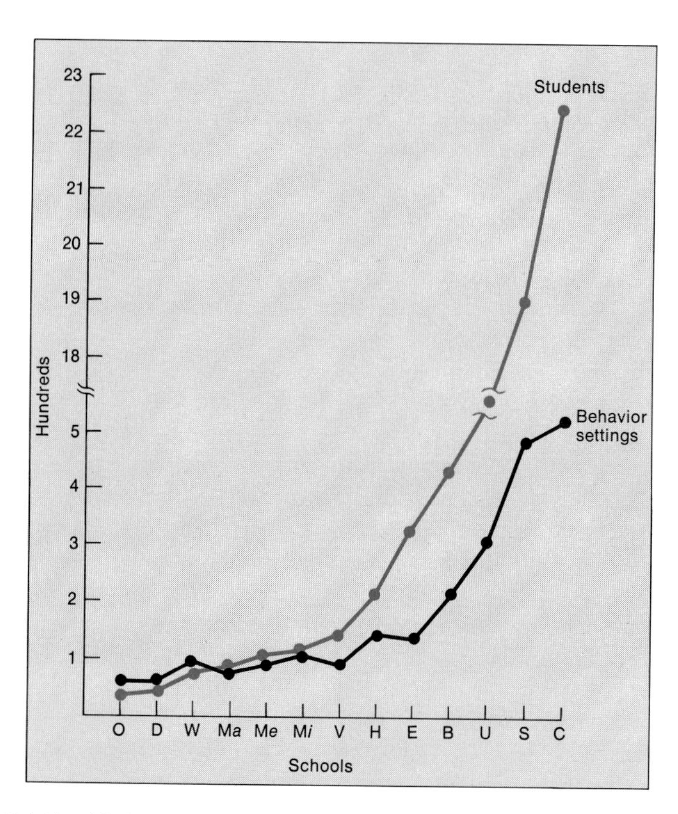

Fig. 11.2. Relationship between population and number of behavior settings in 13 high schools. (From Barker and Barker, 1964)

interest is a measure of *population density*, the number of people per unit of space. Ecological psychology is concerned with number of people per behavior setting. Consequently, the index that interests the ecological psychologist is derived by dividing population by number of behavior settings. The higher this number, the more "crowded" available behavior settings tend to be. Barker and Barker (1964) reported the relationship between population and the number of behavior settings in 13 high schools. These data are graphically presented in Figure 11.2.

As number of students increases, the number of behavior settings also increases. That is to be expected, because large schools offer more opportunities than small schools. However, the rates of increase (the upward slopes of the curves) are by no means the same. As school population goes beyond about 200, behavior settings increase more slowly than number of students. Consequently, there are more students per setting in the large schools than in the smaller schools; population density is higher in the larger schools.

Behavior settings may be classified into types (for instance, football games and baseball games are both outdoor athletic contests). A count of the varieties of behavior settings in the large and small schools of Figure 11.2 revealed that differences are not very great. The smallest school (0) offers 29 varieties of behavior settings; the largest (C) offers only 43. There are relatively few differences among schools on this score, and many of the additional behavior settings in large schools simply repeat the contents of other settings without adding anything substantially different to the types of opportunities offered by the environment.

Density and Behavior

The presence and activity of at least a minimal number of participants is a necessary condition for the continued functioning of a behavior setting. So long as congruence exists between the tasks to be performed and the behavior of the available participants, the setting continues to function. Congruence between setting requirements and activities of participants may be maintained even when population density falls below or rises above the optimum level. A baseball game can be played with only six on a team, but only if each player assumes a greater share of active responsibility than he would in a game with the optimal nine on each side. A baseball game can also be organized with 25 players on each team, but a great many people are likely to end up on the sidelines as spectators or substitutes.

When population density is low (below the optimal number for maintaining the setting), it is necessary to keep as many inhabitants as possible functioning. Consequently, means are found for correcting or bypassing deficiencies in the participants. Rules may be modified (no hitting to right field) and inhabitants who might otherwise be unacceptable are admitted to the setting. Barker notes that in the town of Midwest (his name for Oskaloosa, Kansas) a four person ball game of nine year olds can arrange to include a four year old or even a mother as a participant. Including an additional, though inadequate, player produces a sufficiently better game to justify the special allowances that must be made for his deficiencies.

In general, "the prevailing forces in undermanned behavior settings are inward; they press behavior, materials, and processes into more appropriate formats within the setting; they are centripetal . . . the direction of forces within optimally manned behavior settings is more often centrifugal; they shunt some components, both inhabitants and milieu components, out of the setting . . ." (Barker, 1968, p. 182). The individual in the undermanned setting experiences pressure toward participation in the form of invitations, demands, and exhortations to engage in important activities. His personal reaction is a heightened sense of obligation and responsibility to the setting.

The satisfactions experienced by persons in undermanned settings differ from the satisfactions realized by inhabitants of overpopulated settings. In undermanned settings (such as in smaller schools), satisfactions are most likely to be derived from being wanted or needed, being active, and assuming a high level of leadership and responsibility. In settings that occur in an overpopulated environment (such as a large school), satisfactions are most likely to derive from being a spectator rather than from being an active, involved participant (Barker and Gump, 1964).

A Look at Some Data

Participation in interschool events. Barker and Hall (1964) collected data from 218 high schools and counted the number of students in each school participating in district competitions and conferences involving dramatics, musical performances, journalism, and student government. They calculated the rates of participation per thousand students and plotted these figures against school size (Fig. 11.3). The results are clear: participation rate is lowest in large schools, where population density is high, and highest in smaller schools, where behavior settings are undermanned. Interestingly, the participation rate is relatively low in the very smallest schools (class 1, mean population 42), but even in these schools it is higher than for schools in classes 5 through 9 (populations over 300).

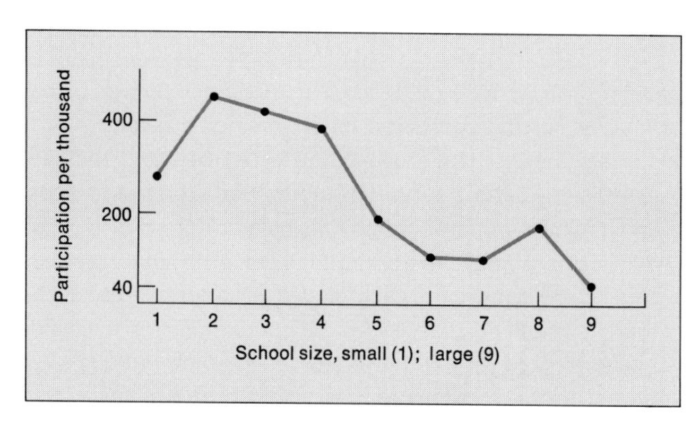

Fig. 11.3. Participation of high school students in district meetings. (From Barker and Hall, 1964)

Participation in extracurricular activities. By examining reports of extracurricular activities in yearbooks for 36 high schools, Barker and Hall (1964) were able to relate participation with school size (Fig. 11.4). In this case, they plotted mean number of activities per student on the ordinate. Again the results clearly show that participation by individual students is greater in small schools than in large schools.

Level of participation. Gump and Friesen (1964a) surveyed the Junior classes in one large school (794 Juniors) and four small schools (fewer than 40 Juniors in each). Each student was presented with a list of the behavior settings in his school and was asked, "Were you there?" Next he was asked to describe what he did in each setting he had entered.

The 794 Juniors of the large school had been exposed to 189 settings, while the approximately 23 Juniors in each small school were exposed to an average of 48 settings. As might be expected, the results showed that the settings of the large school were much more densely populated (36 per behavior setting) than those of the smaller schools (11 per behavior setting). What is of special interest are the differences in *how* students participated in these behavior settings.

Each student's reported activity in each setting was rated according to its degree of importance to the setting. For example, being a spectator is usually relatively unessential to the program of the setting, while being an actor in a play or a member of the football team is rated high, because actors and athletes are essential to the production of plays and football games. Highly responsible participations are called *performances*.

Figure 11.5 summarizes the average data on number of performances per student in the large and small schools. Since number of performances is an index of responsibility, it is evident that students in the underpopulated settings assume more responsibility for the behavior settings they enter than do students in the more densely populated school.

Satisfactions. Gump and Friesen (1964b) selected 88 Juniors from the large school to match 88 Juniors in the smaller schools in sex, I.Q., and race. These students reported what their participation in behavior settings had meant to them. A coding scheme was devised for classifying responses, and two coders scored the data.

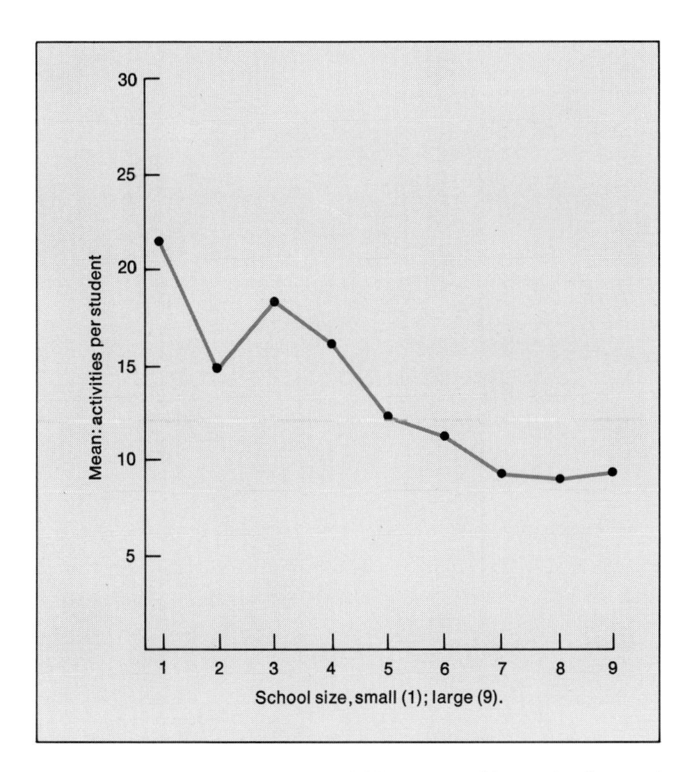

Fig. 11.4. Mean number of extracurricular activities reported by graduating seniors in schools of different sizes. (From Baker and Hall, 1964)

Small school Juniors more frequently reported satisfaction from demonstrating or improving some kind of competence, from meeting challenges and making significant contributions, from being valued by others, from activity as such ("I like to swim"), and from moral or spiritual improvement. Juniors in the large school more often reported satisfaction dealing with vicarious (nonperformance) enjoyment, with belonging to large groups, with learning about their immediate surroundings, and with gaining "points" for participation. In general, students in the large school also reported a narrower range or variety of types of satisfaction than did students in the small schools. These findings confirm the expectation that population density affects the experiences as well as the actions of the inhabitants of behavior settings.

Forces exerted on inhabitants. In a rather complex study, Willems (1964) examined students' experiences of personal attraction or external pressure toward participation in available behavior settings. Using data obtained from individual interviews and rating methods, he found, as expected from behavior setting theory, that students from small schools reported more of both types of forces than did students from large schools.

Willems was particularly interested in a subgroup of "marginal" students, people most likely to drop out of high school. These students are characterized by low I.Q. and poor academic performance, their fathers are in nonprofessional occupations, and neither parent has completed high school (Thomas, 1954). A sample of such students from both large and small schools was included in Willems'

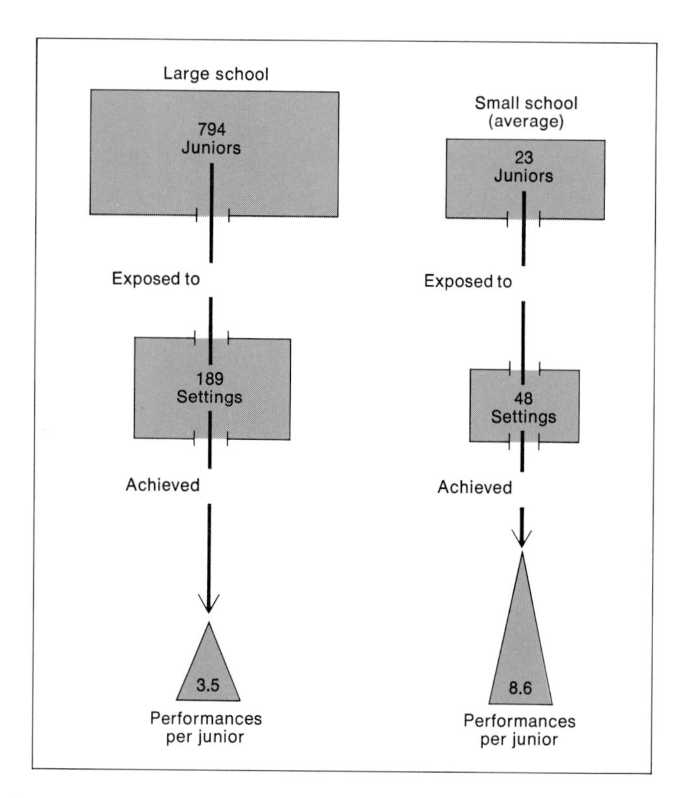

Fig. 11.5. Number of performances per student in schools of different sizes. (From Gump and Friesen, 1964)

investigation. He found that marginal students in small schools experienced as many forces toward participation as did nonmarginal students in these schools. However, in the large school, marginal students experienced fewer forces than did nonmarginal students. Willems also noted that student responses in small schools reflected more felt responsibility and obligation; in the large school, a sizable group of outsiders reported no felt responsibility.

Willems repeated this study in 1965 with new samples of subjects (Willems, 1967). The results were the same as in the earlier study and may therefore be regarded as highly dependable.

Other Matters of Interest

Much of the data reported above has been gathered in a single, large-scale, systematic research effort by a fairly cohesive group of investigators. It is of interest to consider examples of research that deals with naturalistic problems in other contexts.

Research in Industry

Indik (1963) summarized a large body of industrial research relating organization size to behavior. He cited research showing that lateness and absence rates are higher, while morale is lower, in larger industrial organizations. There is also a relationship between organization size and individual output or productivity. It appears that there are optimal sizes for industrial organizations, above or below which productivity per worker declines markedly. In addition, as organization size increases, group cohesiveness decreases.

From his own data, Indik (1964) found that, as organization size increases, the ratio of supervisors to workers tends to decrease systematically. He also found that member participation decreases as organization size increases. That is, number of absences and resignations go up while attendance at voluntary meetings goes down (Indik, 1965). Findings such as these further confirm the strength of the influence of environment on behavior.

Porter and Lawler (1965) surveyed 108 studies of relations between organization structure and behavior in business and industry. They noted that job satisfaction increases steadily as level of management increases; higher level managers regularly report greater job satisfaction than lower level managers and rank and file workers. This finding is not a purely American phenomenon; it "tends to be a worldwide fact of industrial organizations" (Porter and Lawler, 1965, p. 27). They also concluded that job level affects the amount of information a person receives on his job, the types of interpersonal relationships he forms, and the nature of the decisions he makes. Further, staff managers, who determine policy but do not directly supervise production, derive less satisfaction from their jobs and exhibit different patterns of behavior than do line managers, who directly supervise workers. Finally, at the blue collar level, size of subunit in which the employee works is an important organizational variable. Small subunits are characterized by higher job satisfaction, lower absence rates, lower turnover rates, and fewer labor disputes.

In short, a large body of evidence from research in business and industry shows that the behavior and psychological experiences of individuals are strongly influenced by forces that originate in the natural environment. Findings from this type of research closely parallel findings from studies of behavior settings in schools.

The parallel has been noted by Wicker (1968), who obtained data similar to those of Gump and Friesen (1964b) in the research on satisfaction described earlier in this chapter. Wicker found that the most important determinant of students' personal experiences was their *level of performance* in a given behavior setting. In other words, *what* the student did in the setting was generally more important than the size of the school or whether the setting was overmanned or undermanned. Performers expressed more satisfaction than spectators in all instances. Wicker related these results from studies of high school to results from studies in industry like those described above. It is logical that high level managers should be more satisfied with their jobs than lower level employees, because managers, like performers in high school settings, occupy positions of greater responsibility and therefore benefit personally from their relatively greater importance to the setting. It also makes sense that blue collar workers are generally more satisfied in small subunit settings than in large groups, because small subunits give each worker a greater opportunity to assume responsibility. Advocates of the naturalistic approach regard such parallels as supporting their contention that the science of psychology will remain incomplete until it takes these forces fully into account.

Descriptive and Manipulative Techniques

In virtually all the research described so far, the investigators have studiously avoided intruding upon, managing, or manipulating the behavior and behavior settings that interested them. They elected to proceed in this way because they wanted their results to reflect behavior as it actually occurs in real life, not as it can be made to occur in an artificial environment.

However, not all research in natural settings is nonmanipulative. In fact, premeditated experimentation can serve a highly useful purpose in a naturalistic psychology. Examples of manipulative research are described in the following sections to show how such research is conducted and what its contributions can be.

Power and performance in games. Gump and Sutton-Smith (1955) arranged an experiment in a camp for boys to test the effects of environmental conditions on behavior. The environment was manipulated by devising two variations of a single game, Pom-Pom-Pullaway. In the basic game, the person who is *It* stands in the center of a field while others stand in a safe area at one end of the field. At a given signal, players at the end of the field attempt to cross to the safe area at the other end. If tagged by *It* while crossing the field, a player is out.

In one version of this game (called Black Tom) *It* was given considerable power; *It* gave the signal that required the others to run, and could therefore come fairly close to a player he wished to tag before giving the signal to run. In the other version of the game (called Dodge the Skunk) *It* had low power; the rest of the players were permitted to run at will.

The boys did not know they were in an experiment, but games were arranged so that boys of high skill (fast runners) and low skill (slow runners) had the opportunity to be *It* in both kinds of game. As expected, all *Its* had more success (number of tags) playing Black Tom than playing Dodge the Skunk.

Of special importance is the fact that manipulation of game structure permitted some unskilled boys who might never succeed otherwise to experience success in the role of *It*. However, the investigators noted that several such boys experienced a considerable sense of failure when playing Dodge the Skunk; eight of 20 games which used unskilled boys as *It* had to be stopped because "further play would have been painfully discouraging." Furthermore, taunting and disparagement of *It* (such as "Oh, Peter's easy to beat") and conspiracies against the leader were more frequent when *It* had low power than when *It* had high power.

Commenting later on this experiment, Gump and Kounin (1959) noted that manipulation of the game settings permitted the investigators to observe behavior in situations that practically never occur in real life. Observation of the unrestricted play of boys reveals that unskilled boys rarely get involved in games they cannot manage, and when they do, they generally avoid difficult roles. Consequently, if an investigator wants to see what happens when an unskilled person is put into a position of low power, he must arrange that situation himself. The likelihood of observing this pattern of relationships in nature is so small that attempts to study it by purely observational methods would be close to futile. (Notice that the same argument applies to the studies of frustration cited earlier in this chapter.)

Bystander intervention. Four studies of reactions to apparent emergencies serve as final examples of controlled research on complex environmental variables. These studies are important because they exert a high degree of control over experimental conditions and are on a subject of current general social interest.

Public attention is frequently captured by accounts of situations in which witnesses to an emergency have failed to respond by giving or seeking help. A famous case of this sort involved Kitty Genovese, a young woman stabbed to death in the middle of a residential street in New York City. It was later discovered that 38 people had observed the attack, yet no one had attempted to assist her or even called the police. Whatever other conclusions about human nature one may wish to draw from this case, two investigators saw in it the suggestion of an hypothesis best described as "ecological" in nature (Darley and Latané, 1968b). The hypothesis is simply that "the more bystanders to an emergency, the less likely, or the more slowly, any one bystander will intervene to provide aid." The logic behind it is that responsibility is diffused when others are present, and pressures to intervene are therefore diminished.

To test this hypothesis, Darley and Latané (1968a) had subjects (college students) appear for an experiment in which they were asked to talk about their personal problems. The subject was placed in a small room by himself and told that he would talk to other students over an intercom system. Actually, there were no other subjects; the "others" were tape recordings prepared by the experimenters. The subject was told that each person would first talk briefly about his problems, and each would then comment on what the others had said; when each person spoke everyone else could hear what was said, but only one person's microphone would be *on* at any given time. He was also told that the experimenter would not be listening to anything that was said. Some subjects were led to believe they were in two-person groups, some were supposedly in three-person groups, and others thought they were in six-person groups.

During the first part of the experiment, the simulated confederates as well as the real subject described problems of adjustment to college life. The first confederate said, among other things, that he was subject to seizures. In the second phase of the study, the first confederate began his comments in an ordinary voice; then he began to act as though he were having a seizure on the spot. He called for help several times and claimed he was about to die.

The effect of this was to leave the real subject feeling that he was in an emergency situation. If he believed himself to be in a two person group, he was effectively alone, because the experimenter was not supposed to be listening and the only other person around was the one in trouble. The subject was given up to six minutes to leave the room and seek help (it would have done no good to talk into his microphone, since he believed it to be *off*). As soon as the subject left the room (or after six minutes had passed), the experiment was terminated.

Of the subjects who thought they were alone, 85 per cent reported the emergency (average time, 52 seconds); of the subjects who thought they were in three person groups, 62 per cent reported the emergency (average time, 93 seconds); of the subjects who thought they were in six person groups, only 31 per cent reported the emergency (average time, 166 seconds). Other variables, such as sex of subject, sex of "victim," composition of the groups, and personality of subject did not correlate with these outcomes. The investigators observed that subjects who did not report the apparent emergency were not apathetic or indifferent. They expressed considerable concern over the "victim" after the experiment; evidently they had been in severe conflict over whether or not to report the incident, and had deliberately decided not to do so.

Incidentally, all subjects were later informed of the true nature of the experiment and all reported that they found it interesting. The reader may decide for himself whether the deceptions involved in contriving the artificial emergency situation raise ethical questions about the conduct of some forms of psychological research (see Chap. 8).

The second experiment on bystander intervention was similar to the first, except that the subject was in the same room with other members of the group (Latané and Darley, 1968). In this research, the subjects were sent to a "waiting room" where they were to fill out a questionnaire. Some subjects were in the room alone; some were in the company of two experimental confederates; others were with two naive subjects like themselves.

While the subjects worked on their questionnaires, smoke was introduced into the waiting room through a ventilator. All behavior and conversation was observed through a one-way mirror, and, again, the subject was given six minutes to leave the room and report the emergency.

Eighteen of the 24 subjects in the *alone* condition reported the smoke (median time, about two minutes). Only one out of ten subjects who were in the room with two stooges reported the smoke (the stooges, of course, made no move to report it). Three of the eight groups made up of three naive subjects each reported the smoke. The investigators had predicted that the presence of apparently nonresponsive bystanders would inhibit individual action, and the evidence was clearly in their favor.

In a third experiment (Latané and Darley, 1969), subjects were led to believe that a lady in an adjacent room had fallen and hurt her ankle. Seventy per cent of the subjects who heard the accident while alone in a waiting room offered to help the victim. In the presence of a nonresponsive bystander (a stooge of the experimenter), however, only 7 per cent of the subjects intervened. In the presence of another stranger (not a pretrained stooge), only 8 of 40 subjects intervened. The response rate in the presence of a friend was higher than the rate with strangers or a stooge, but not quite as high as when the subject was alone.

Finally (Latané and Darley, 1969), 92 thefts of a case of beer were staged in a beverage store in New York. The beer was "stolen" while the manager was ostensibly in the back of the store checking his stock. On half the occasions, one real customer was at the checkout counter during the theft; 65 per cent of these customers reported it. On the other occasions, two real customers were at the checkout counter during the theft; 56 per cent of these groups reported it.

The difference between 65 per cent and 56 per cent does not seem very great, but bear in mind that twice as many people actually witnessed each theft in the two customer situations. Ordinary logic would lead us to expect more frequent reporting under these conditions. We would naively suppose that if one witness did not report it, the other surely would, making the chances of reportage twice as great. Apparently, such is not the case. The chances of the theft being reported were slightly lower when two people saw it than when only one saw it.

On the basis of these studies, the investigators concluded that "failure to intervene may be better understood by knowing the relationship among bystanders rather than that between a bystander and the victim." In short, when individual forces conflict with environmental pressures, the environment wins out.

Although these studies on bystander intervention were conducted as contrived experiments, they are clearly concerned with behavior in natural settings. Like the experimental study of children's games, they enable investigators to examine responses to situations that rarely occur in real life. Unlike other naturalistic studies, however, they permit no estimate of the actual frequency of such situations, and make no allowance for alternative responses that are usually available in natural situations. They show "what would happen if . . . ," but not how often conditions comparable to those set up in the laboratory really occur. Both types of information are needed in a psychology that wishes to call itself complete.

Glossary

Behavior episode: the unit of behavior as it occurs in natural settings, usually identified by trained judges.
Behavior setting: a unit of the natural environment; a behavior setting provides all the conditions necessary for conduct of a specific type of activity.
Circumjacent: enclosing, encompassing, surrounding.
Ecology: the study of the system of organism-environment relations that determine the forms of biological adaptation.
Frustration: blocking of goal directed behavior.
Milieu: the immediate, nearby environment.
Molar: in psychology, a viewpoint that emphasizes study of wholes and configurations (opposed to *molecular*).
Molecular: in psychology, a viewpoint that stresses study of the simplest possible units of behavior (opposed to *molar*); elementarism. (*See* Glossary, Chap. 1.)
Natural: the environment that exists independently of investigators' intentions to study its effects on behavior.
Naturalism: the viewpoint that stresses the need to study behavior in nonlaboratory environments.
Performance: participation in behavior essential to the operation of a behavior setting.
Placebo: a nonactive substance administered as if it were active medication.
Specimen record: a sequential record describing behavioral events occurring in a specified setting at a specified time; specimen records are prepared by trained human observers.
Synomorph: similarity of form between behavior and environment; for example, pedestrians' routes follow the boundaries of the sidewalks.

References

Barker, R.G. *Ecological psychology*. Stanford: Stanford University Press, 1968.
_______. Explorations in ecological psychology. *Amer. Psychologist*, 1965, **20,** 1–14.
_______. (Ed.) *The stream of behavior*. New York: Appleton-Century-Crofts, 1963. (a)
_______. The stream of behavior as an empirical problem. In R.G. Barker (Ed.), *The stream of behavior*. New York: Appleton-Century-Crofts, 1963. (b)
_______, and L.S. Barker. Structural characteristics. In R.G. Barker and P.V. Gump, *Big school, small school*. Stanford: Stanford University Press, 1964.
Barker, R.G., and P.V. Gump. *Big school, small school*. Stanford: Stanford University Press, 1964.
Barker, R.G., and E.R. Hall. Participation in interschool events and extracurricular activities. In R.G. Barker and P.V. Gump, *Big school, small school*. Stanford: Stanford University Press, 1964.
Barker, R.G., and H.F. Wright. *One boy's day*. New York: Harper & Row, 1951.
_______. *Midwest and its children*. New York: Harper & Row, 1955.
Barker, R.G., T. Dembo, and K. Lewin. Frustration and regression. In R.G. Barker, J.S. Kounin, and H.F. Wright (Eds.), *Child behavior and development*. New York: McGraw-Hill, 1943.
Barker, R.G., H.F. Wright, L.S. Barker, and P. Schoggen. *Specimen records of American and English children*. Lawrence: University of Kansas Press, 1961.
Beecher, H.K. Generalization from pain of various types and origins. *Science*, 1959, **130,** 267–268. (a)

———. Increased stress and effectiveness of placebos and "active" drugs. *Science*, 1960, **132** (3418), 91–92.

———. *Measurement of subjective responses*. New York: Oxford, 1959. (b)

———. Relationship of significance of wound to pain experienced. *J. AMA*, 1956, **161,** 1609–1613.

Darley, J.M., and B. Latané. Bystander intervention in emergencies: Diffusion of responsibility. *J. pers. soc. Psychol.*, 1968, **8,** 377–383. (a)

———. When will people help in a crisis? *Psychol. Today*, 1968, **2** (7), 54–57, 70–71. (b)

Dickman, H.R. The perception of behavioral units. In R.G. Barker (Ed.), *The stream of behavior*. New York: Appleton-Century-Crofts, 1963.

Fawl, C.L. Disturbances experienced by children in their natural habitats. In R.G. Barker (Ed.), *The stream of behavior*. New York: Appleton-Century-Crofts, 1963.

Goodall, J., and H. Van Lawick. My life among wild chimpanzees. *National Geographic*, 1963, **124,** 272–308.

Gump, P.V., and W.F. Friesen. Participation in nonclass settings. In R.G. Barker and P.V. Gump, *Big school, small school*. Stanford: Stanford University Press, 1964. (a)

———. Satisfactions derived from nonclass settings. In R.G. Barker and P.V. Gump, *Big school, small school*. Stanford: Stanford University Press, 1964. (b)

Gump, P.V., and J.S. Kounin. Issues raised by ecological and "classical" research efforts. *Merrill-Palmer Quart.*, 1959, **6,** 145–152.

———. Milieu influences on children's concepts of misconduct. *Child Develpm.*, 1961, **32,** 711–720.

Gump, P.V., and B. Sutton-Smith. The "It" role in children's games. *American Association of Group Workers*, 1955, **17,** 3–8.

Gump, P.V., P. Schoggen, and F. Redl. The behavior of the same child in different milieus. In R.G. Barker (Ed.), *The stream of behavior*. New York: Appleton-Century-Crofts, 1963.

———. The camp milieu and its immediate effects. *J. soc. Issues*, 1957, **13,** 40–46.

Indik, B.P. Organization size and member participation. *Hum. Relat.*, 1965, **18,** 339–350.

———. The relationship between organization size and supervision ratio. *Admin. Sci. Quart.*, 1964, **9,** 301–312.

———. Some effects of organization size on member attitudes and behavior. *Hum. Relat.*, 1963, **16,** 369–384.

Kavanau, J.L. Behavior: Confinement, adaptation, and compulsory regimes in laboratory studies. *Science*, 1964, **143** (3605), 490.

———. Behavior of captive white-footed mice. In E.P. Willems and H.L. Raush (Eds.), *Naturalistic viewpoints in psychological research*. New York: Holt, Rinehart and Winston, 1969.

Latané, B., and J.M. Darley. Bystander "apathy." *Amer. Scientist*, 1969, **57,** 244–268.

———. Group inhibition of bystander intervention in emergencies. *J. pers. soc. Psychol.*, 1968, **10,** 215–221.

Lockard, R.B. The albino rat: A defensible choice or a bad habit? *Amer. Psychologist*, 1968, **23,** 734–742.

Morris, D. The shame of the naked cage. *Life*, 1968, **65** (19), 70–86.

Porter, L.W., and E.E. Lawler, III. Properties of organization structure in relation to job attitudes and behavior. *Psychol. Bull.*, 1965, **64,** 23–51.

Schoggen, P. Mechanical aids for making specimen records of behavior. *Child Develpm.*, 1964, **35,** 985–988.

Sells, S.B. Ecology and the science of psychology. *Multivariate Behavioral Research*, 1966, **1,** 131–144.

Thomas, R.J. An empirical study of high school drop-outs in regard to ten possibly related factors. *J. educ. Sociol.*, 1954, **28,** 11–18.

Van Lawick-Goodall, J., and H. Van Lawick. New discoveries among Africa's chimpanzees. *National Geographic*, 1965, **128,** 802–831.

Wicker, A.M. Undermanning, performances, and students' subjective experiences in behavior settings of large and small schools. *J. pers. soc. Psychol.*, 1968, **10,** 255–261.

Willems, E.P. An ecological orientation in psychology. *Merrill-Palmer Quart.*, 1965, **11,** 317–343.
———. Forces toward participation in behavior settings. In R.G. Barker and P.V. Gump, *Big school, small school.* Stanford: Stanford University Press, 1964.
———. Sense of obligation to high school activities as related to school size and marginality of student. *Child Develpm.*, 1967, **38,** 1247–1260.
———, and H.L. Raush. (Eds.) *Naturalistic viewpoints in psychological research.* New York: Holt, Rinehart and Winston, 1969.
Wright, H.F. *Recording and analyzing child behavior.* New York: Harper & Row, 1967.

12 The Control of Behavior

This chapter considers a line of research and application that has been gaining momentum since the early 1950s. The concepts and methods of operant conditioning which originated with a laboratory rat in a box have now been applied in schools, industry, and hospitals. At a time when single-minded theories of psychology are being abandoned in favor of freewheeling eclecticism, subscribers to the concepts and methods of operant conditioning have redoubled their enthusiasm and optimism regarding the sufficiency and efficacy of their approach.

Anticipations of contemporary procedures of operant conditioning can be noted in the work of the early investigators of animal behavior, particularly Thorndike (1874–1949). Nevertheless, it has been the work of B.F. Skinner (1938, 1953, 1959, 1966, 1970) that has provided the fundamental outlook, concepts, and procedures of the modern operant approach.

Our discussion of the operant approach is in four parts. The first section describes basic types of operant conditioning, the principal variables that are manipulated, and the concepts employed. Next, distinctive features of the operant analysis of behavior are contrasted with those of other experimental approaches. Then several examples of application of operant techniques to modification of extralaboratory behavior are described. Our examples will include applications to the training of mental retardates and to the practice of psychotherapy. Finally, a number of contrasting evaluations of the theoretical and practical significance of operant conditioning are considered.

Operant Conditioning

Operant behavior is characterized by interaction between behavior and environment. The organism operates on the environment and the consequences of the operation modify its behavior. This may sound very much like a description of everyday purposive behavior, but the investigator of operant conditioning eschews the concept of purpose. In his denial of this conventional concept, the operant behaviorist agrees with proponents of traditional stimulus-response theory, such as J.B. Watson (1878–1958) and C.L. Hull (1884–1952) (See Chap. 1). For the operant analysis of behavior, it is sufficient to describe a sequence of contingencies or probabilistic relationships between observable events. In the typical experimental model of operant behavior, three contingencies are involved: the initial probability of occurrence of a behavioral response in the absence of consequences, the probability that a response will have a consequence, and the modification of response frequency as a result of the consequences of responding.

The standard experimental arrangement for studying operant behavior includes three components: some device which the organism can manipulate or operate, a device to record the frequency of manipulations, and a programming device to control the occurrence of response consequences according to a preset schedule. An arrangement that meets this description was invented by Skinner to study operant behavior in the rat. The basic apparatus is an experimental chamber which is bare except for a bar protruding from one of the walls and a food receptacle directly below it. The bar can be connected to a reservoir of food pellets so that when pressed it will deliver food to the receptacle. Each bar-press is automatically recorded to provide a cumulative record of the number of responses per unit of time. This experimental arrangement is pictured in Figure 12.1a. Obviously, details of the experimental chamber vary to accommodate differences among animals and

(a)

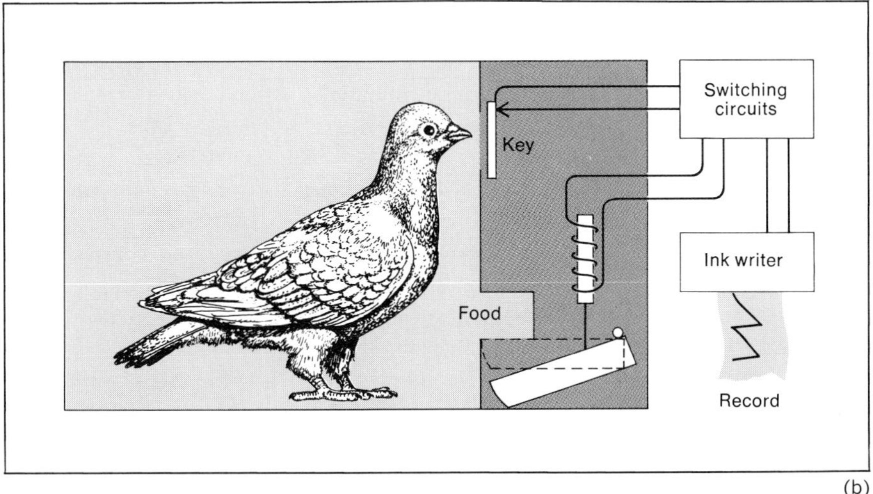

(b)

Fig. 12.1. (a) A Skinner box, illustrated here, is a device that automatically delivers a pellet of food whenever the bar is pressed. Each depression of the bar activates a mechanism that moves an ink pen, which makes a special mark on a continually moving piece of paper. The marks can then be counted to determine the frequency of the responses. In the foreground you can see the bar, while the feeding mechanism is located in the back area. (From Anliker and Mayer, 1956) (b) Diagram of a Skinner box for a pigeon. (From Dews, 1955)

experimental objectives; Figure 12.1b shows an arrangement for studying pigeons. An electric key has replaced the bar and pecking has replaced bar-pressing. The pigeon is probably the favorite organism for laboratory study of operant behavior, since it is a tireless performer who can sustain a very high rate of responding for long periods of time.

Now let us consider a simple experimental demonstration of operant conditioning. The aim is to show that the consequences of responding control behavior. The first step is to determine the probability of occurrence of the response in

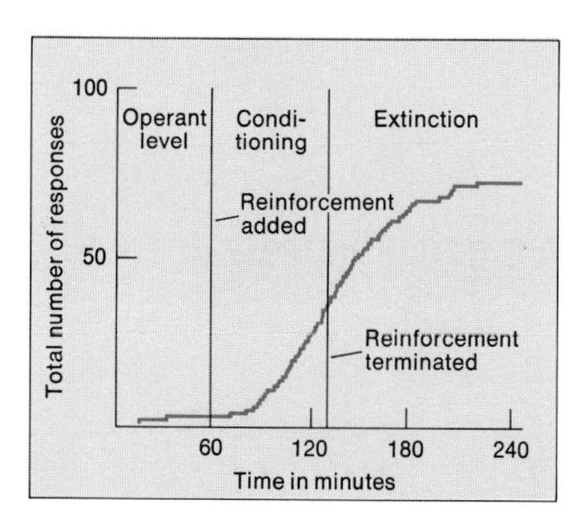

Fig. 12.2. A cumulative record showing the operant level, conditioning and extinction of an individual rat's bar-pressing response. Each time the rat responds, the curve moves up a notch. Note that initially, when no reinforcement is given the rat responds infrequently. This rate of responding represents his operant level. The introduction of reinforcement is withdrawn, the rate of responding gradually declines until the rat is responding at approximately his initial operant level. (From Kendler, 1968)

question prior to introduction of response-contingent consequences. A hungry rat is placed in the experimental chamber, with the food delivery mechanism disconnected. The rat is observed to wander about the chamber in aimless exploration, examining the bar and occasionally depressing it. This rate of bar-pressing is the *operant level* or baseline frequency of the response, that is, the rate of occurrence in the absence of experimenter controlled consequences. Once the operant level is determined, the conditioning procedure is initiated. The food delivery mechanism is connected and programmed to deliver a pellet of food each time the bar is depressed. (The rat has been previously trained to eat from the feeder to which the pellets are delivered.) At the outset this change does not affect the animal's behavior, but after a while the cumulative response record shows a sharp increase in rate of bar-pressing. When a high rate of responding has been achieved, the food delivery mechanism is disconnected again so that bar-presses do not lead to food delivery. The rate of bar-pressing then gradually declines, eventually returning to the operant level observed in the first stage. Withdrawal of the food constitutes the *extinction* procedure. The course of events in this experiment is graphed in Figure 12.2.

In this example, the rat's operation on the environment (bar-pressing) resulted in consequences that significantly modified the rate of responding. Response consequences that have this effect are called *reinforcements*. Two reinforcement schedules were introduced, continuous reinforcement and extinction. In the former, every response was followed by reinforcement, while in the latter reinforcements were always omitted. These all-or-none conditions are limiting cases; the more typical situation is intermittent reinforcement. Sometimes a response pays off and other times it does not. Observations of real life indicate that intermittent schedules of reinforcement may be highly effective. Two or three coin returns following widely separated telephone calls are sufficient to insure an almost involuntary probe of the coin return receptacle following every telephone call.

Schedules of Reinforcement

In the laboratory, intermittent reinforcement is arranged by schedules that select the responses which are to be reinforced. There are several basic schedules of intermittent reinforcement.

Interval schedules. In a *fixed* interval schedule, a response is reinforced only if a specified period of time has elapsed since the last reinforcement. The interval is constant throughout the experiment. Thus, if the fixed interval is ten minutes, responses occurring in the ten minutes following the previous reinforcement are not reinforced. The first response following the conclusion of the interval is reinforced and a new interval is initiated.

The *variable* interval schedule is a modification of the fixed interval schedule. As with the fixed interval, presentation of reinforcement is contingent on elapsed time, but the duration of the interval will vary from one interval to the next. For example, in a five minute variable interval schedule, the schedule may assign reinforcements with the following temporal spacings (seconds) and sequence: 6, 50, 170, 770, 530, 24, 290, 410, 100, 650. The intervals are of variable duration, averaging five minutes (300 seconds).

Ratio schedules. This schedule selects the response to be reinforced by specifying a ratio between number of responses and reinforcement. For example, a "fixed ratio five" schedule requires that exactly every fifth response be reinforced. A "variable ratio five" schedule requires an average of five responses per reinforcement, but the number of responses between reinforcements will vary.

Although ratio schedules may appear complex, they are not uncommon in real life. The fixed ratio schedule is the piecework arrangement used in some industries, in which the worker is paid according to an agreed upon ratio of output to payoff. The variable ratio schedule characterizes the reinforcement schedule of many gambling devices, such as the "one-armed bandit." Both of these schedules are designed to produce a high rate of responding and strong resistance to extinction. The addicted gambler is testimony to the effectiveness of this design.

Differential reinforcement schedules. This schedule is based on the temporal spacing of responses, with reinforcement contingent on the absence of the response for a specific interval. For example, a bar-press is followed by food only if the rat has not executed the response in the preceding 30 seconds.

These basic reinforcement schedules select the responses that will be reinforced according to the number of responses emitted, the temporal spacing of responses, or the temporal spacing of reinforcements. By combining these programs, even more complex schedules can be arranged. (Ferster and Skinner, 1957, describe 16 different schedules.) The basic schedules have distinctive effects on the rate of operant conditioning. A number of the differences among them can be seen by comparing the records presented in Figures 12.3 and 12.4.

Intermittent reinforcement schedules are much more effective than continuous schedules in maintaining the response after reinforcement has been withdrawn (during the extinction period). Ratio schedules are especially notable for this characteristic. Skinner (1957) has reported that the pigeon whose performance is graphed in the right half of Figure 12.4 emitted 73,000 key pecks during the first four and one-half hours of the extinction period. Evidence of the persistence of the conditioned response has been found as late as six years after prolonged reinforcement on a variable ratio schedule.

Shaping

A response can be reinforced only after it has occurred. Combined with the observation that the operant level of the response is usually very low, this indicates

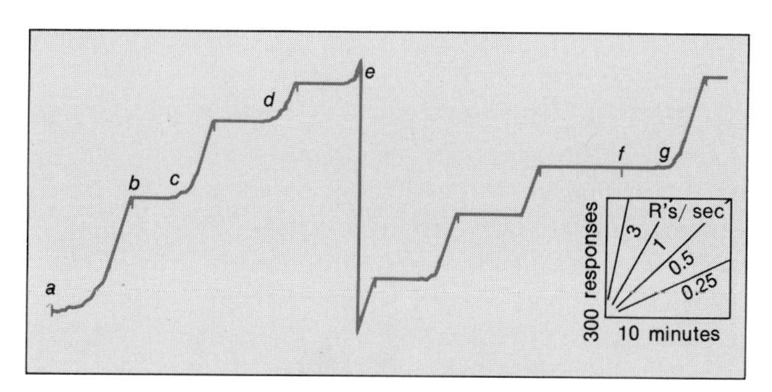

Fig. 12.3. Characteristic performance by pigeon under fixed-interval reinforcement. (From Skinner, 1959) The experimental session begins at *a*. The first reinforcement will not occur until ten minutes later, and the bird begins at a very low rate of responding. As the ten minute interval passes, the rate increases, accelerating fairly smoothly to a terminal rate at reinforcement at *b*. The rate then drops to zero. Except for a slight abortive start at c, it again accelerates to a high terminal value by the end of the second ten minute interval. A third fairly smooth acceleration is shown at *d*. (At e the pen instantly resets to the starting position on the paper.) The overall pattern of performance on a fixed-interval schedule is a fairly smoothly accelerating scallop in each interval, the acceleration being more rapid the longer the initial pause.

a potential problem for the operant conditioner. If the response is initially rare, a good deal of time may be wasted waiting for it to occur. Furthermore, since the intervals between responses are long, the effect of single reinforcements may be dissipated. The problem is most obvious in the case of a response with an original probability of zero for the particular organism, that is, a response which has never been observed to occur. How can an investigation of the effects of reinforcement contingencies proceed if the response does not occur?

The solution is provided by the method of *shaping*. The investigator does not wait for spontaneous occurrence of the response, but instead shapes the response by reinforcing successive approximations of it. This procedure is illustrated in the following description of shaping the key-pecking response in the pigeon.

> To get the pigeon to peck the spot as quickly as possible we proceed as follows: We first give the bird food when it turns slightly in the direction of the spot from any part of the cage. This increases the frequency of such behavior. We then withhold reinforcement until a slight movement is made toward the spot. This again alters the general distribution of behavior without producing a new unit. We continue by reinforcing positions successively closer to the spot, then by reinforcing only when the head is moved slightly forward, and finally only when the beak actually makes contact with the spot. We may reach this final response in a remarkably short time. A hungry bird, well adapted to the situation and to the food tray, can usually be brought to respond in this way in two or three minutes (Skinner, 1953, p. 92).

The method of shaping allows the investigator to build up a relatively complex response in a short time, even if the initial probability of the response is zero. Successful shaping depends on a combination of judgment and timing. The experimenter must judge accurately which specific behaviors constitute components of

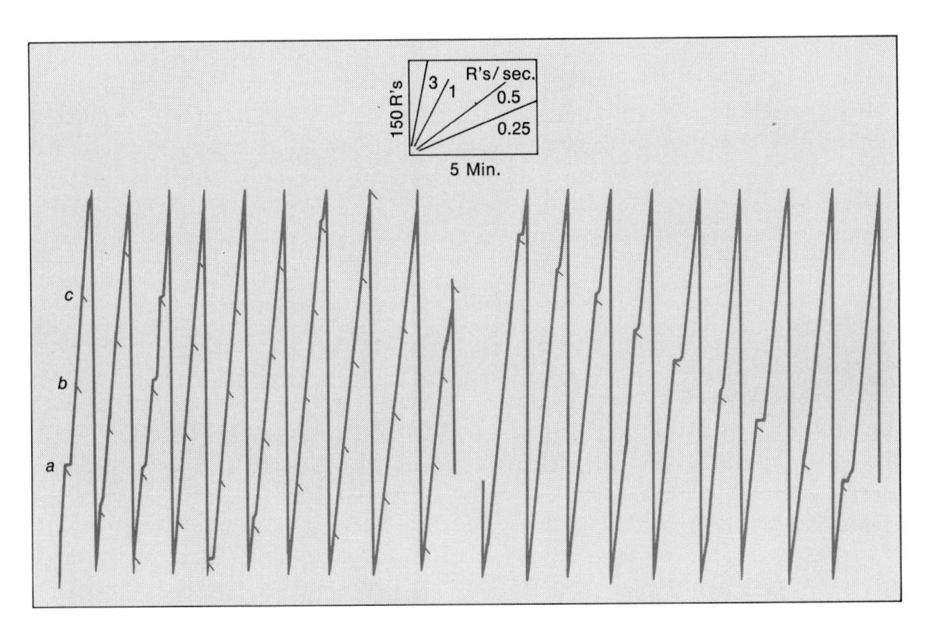

Fig. 12.4. Typical performance by a pigeon under fixed-ratio reinforcement. At the left every 210th response is reinforced; at the right every 900th response. The reinforcements occur at the pips (*a, b, c* and elsewhere). The overall rate of responding is high. Most of the pauses occur immediately after reinforcement. (From Skinner, 1959)

the final integrated response, and he must be equipped to deliver reinforcements, without delay, following the desired behaviors.

In the preceding example, behavior was deliberately shaped to conform to a preselected pattern. However, behavior is shaped by reinforcement contingencies no matter what the experimenter's objectives may be. The intentions of the experimenter are important only insofar as he schedules the reinforcements, but the effect of reinforcements does not depend on his intent. This claim is substantiated by the experimental development of "superstitious" behavior (Skinner, 1948; Morse and Skinner, 1957; Herrnstein, 1966). The basic procedure is to deliver reinforcements at fixed short intervals *with no reference whatsoever to the subject's behavior.* The result is that the subject (pigeon, rat) behaves as if there were a causal relation between its behavior at the time of reinforcement and the presentation of reinforcement. For example, if a pigeon has been executing a counterclockwise turn at the time that reinforcement was delivered, this response will be strengthened and become part of the pigeon's behavioral repertoire. It is as if the pigeon has a superstitious belief in the efficacy of turning. This superstition results from the purely accidental shaping of behavior by reinforcements presented without concern for behavior.

Stimulus Control

In real life, operant behavior is not emitted indiscriminately. It is generally recognized that the operant response is not likely to pay off under all circumstances. A smile usually indicates that social approach will be followed by reinforcement; a frown is a condition under which reinforcement is less likely. Every child learns to discriminate subtle stimuli in the parent's expressions, and eventually his behavior may come to be controlled by the presence of these stimuli. These kinds of operant behavior are called *discriminated operants* and they are said to be under *stimulus control*. The laboratory procedure for establishing discriminated operants calls for differential reinforcement in which the reinforcement depends upon stimuli present during responding. For example, reinforcement may be made contingent on the presence of a green light. When the light is red, reinforcement is omitted. The animal will learn to respond when the light is green and will respond only rarely when the light is red; the operant is under stimulus control.

A more impressive example of discriminated operants under stimulus control is provided by introducing two different reinforcement schedules in the presence of different stimuli. For example, a pigeon's pecks may be reinforced under a fixed ratio schedule when the light is green and under a fixed interval schedule when the light is red (Dews, 1956). Stimulus control will be exhibited in the different patterns of responding, appropriate to the two schedules, that occur in the presence of the different lights.

Establishment of stimulus control defines the state of selective attention. To say in the operant analysis that an organism is attending to a stimulus is to say that the stimulus controls the response. "In general an organism attends to an aspect of the environment if independent variation or independent elimination of that aspect brings about variations in the organism's behavior" (Reynolds, 1961, p. 203).

Discrimination and Generalization

The training involved in establishing stimulus control often affects the tendency to respond to stimuli other than the discriminative stimuli. There is a spread of effect of reinforcement, called *stimulus generalization*, to other stimuli that vary along some dimension of the original stimulus. One procedure reinforces responses in the presence of a single stimulus value, such as a 1,000 cycle tone, according to a variable interval schedule. (This insures a high rate of responding after reinforcement has been discontinued.) No other tone is present during the conditioning procedure. When a high rate of responding has been reached, reinforcement is discontinued. The original stimulus tone and a number of tones varying in frequency are then presented individually in irregular order. Figure 12.5a shows the generalization gradients obtained by Jenkins and Harrison (1960) with five pigeons. The figure shows the per cent of total responses given to the discriminative stimulus of 1,000 cycles (S^D) and the generalization stimuli ranging from 300 to 3,500 cycles. The points in the lower right corner show the outcome when the "negative" stimulus (S^Δ, no tone) is presented. The generalization gradient shows maximal responding for S^D, with decreasing proportions of responses as the stimulus becomes increasingly different from the training stimulus. Farthing and Hearst (1968) have also reported analogous extinction gradients. First they reinforced pecks only in the *absence* of a vertical line; responses in the presence of a vertical line displayed on the face of the key were never reinforced. Then they varied the slope of the line in the generalization test. An extinction gradient emerged: response rate was lowest for the vertical line and increased as the difference in slope between the test and training line increased (see Fig. 12.5b). Similar results have been reported by Jenkins and Harrison (1962), Guttman and Kalish (1956), and Honig, Boneau, Burstein, and Pennypacker (1963).

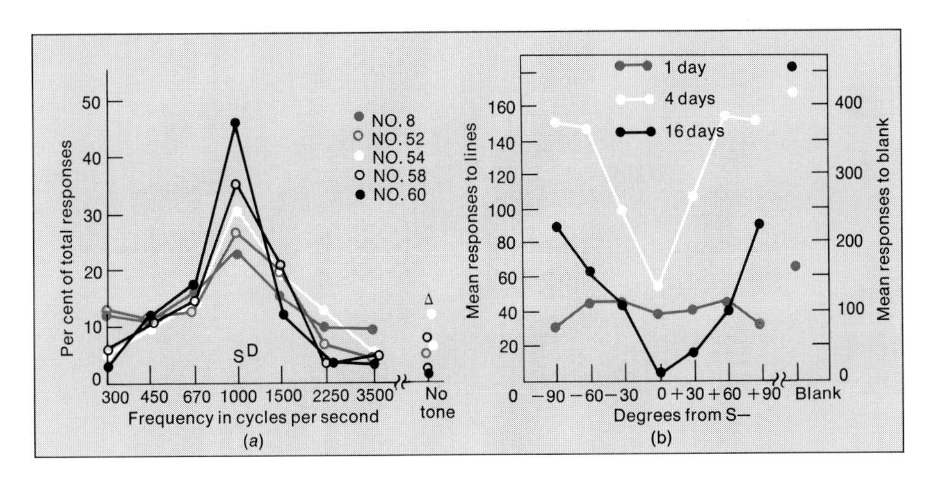

Fig. 12.5. (a) Generalization gradients following differential training with a 1000 cps tone as S^D, no tone as S^{Δ}. Individual gradients are based on the means of three generalization tests. (From Jenkins and Harrison, 1960) (b) Generalization of extinction. The average number of pecks in the presence of each text stimulus (slope of line displayed on key). Pecking had been reinforced in the absence but not in the presence of a vertical line (S −). Three groups of pigeons had received, respectively, one, four, and sixteen days of training. The height of the curve for the four day group was affected by the unusually high rate shown by one bird. Note that a reduced scale has been used for pecks on the blank key (S +), to the right.

Conditioned Reinforcement

The behavior shaping reinforcements discussed thus far have been primary biological reinforcers. However, there is an important class of stimuli whose capacity to reinforce behavior is acquired. These are called *conditioned reinforcers*, since they acquire their capacity to reinforce as a result of a history of association with a primary reinforcer. Money is probably the most obvious example of a conditioned reinforcer. Although improved procedures for demonstrating conditioned reinforcement have been devised, as in Findley and Brady (1965), a simple illustration will suffice. First, a light is paired with food delivery, which serves to establish the light as a conditioned or secondary reinforcer. Then the light is used as an intermittent reinforcement to condition other behavior. Zimmerman (1963) and Kelleher (1966) have demonstrated the effectiveness of conditioned reinforcers established with this procedure.

Aversive Control

We have described the effects of positive reinforcement in controlling behavior. But behavior may also be modified by the introduction of negative reinforcement, in which case it is under the control of *aversive stimuli*. Exposure to aversive stimuli can modify behavior in several ways. Behavior followed by withdrawal of the aversive stimulus is increased. Exposure to aversive stimuli increases the rate of occurrence of escape behavior, because the consequent reduction in aversive stimulation is reinforcing. In addition, behavior that delays or forestalls occurrence of the aversive stimulus is reinforced. The rate of *avoidance* behavior is increased.

As was true for positive reinforcement, stimuli not originally aversive may

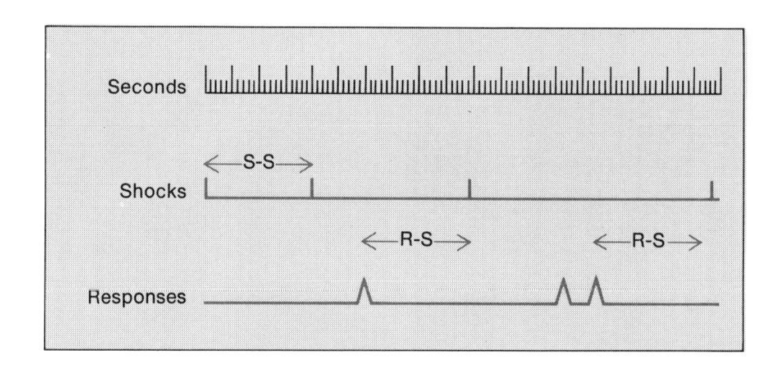

Fig. 12.6. A diagrammatic representation of the avoidance procedure. S-S indicates the shock-shock interval; R-S indicates the response-shock interval. (From Sidman, 1966)

become aversive as a consequence of pairing with primary aversive stimuli. Such stimuli may be called *conditioned aversive* stimuli.

Electric shock is frequently used as the aversive stimulus for animal subjects in avoidance training. For example, a rat is placed in an experimental chamber whose floor is made of a grid of stainless steel rods. The rods may be electrified to deliver a brief but discomforting shock to the rat's feet; two recycling timers program the shocks. When the animal does not press the bar, the time interval between shocks (shock–shock interval) is specified by one timer. The shock can be postponed by pressing the bar; the response–shock interval is determined by the second timer. By pressing the bar, the animal ensures that the second timer cannot deliver a shock before the response–shock interval has elapsed. Figure 12.6 is a diagrammatic representation of the procedure. In this example, both the shock–shock and response–shock intervals are four seconds in duration. If the animal does not press the bar, shock recurs at four second intervals; if the bar is depressed, shock is delayed for four seconds beginning with the response.

Under these conditions, the animal learns to press the bar and avoid the shocks. In this kind of avoidance training situation, the animal typically does not go for a long time without shock. In a study by Sidman (1966) using shock–shock and response–shock intervals of 15 seconds, the longest period that the animal went without shock was four minutes. There is also a tendency for the response rate to decrease in the course of long sessions. One explanation of these observations is that successful avoidance eliminates the stimuli that reinforce the response. Consequently, extinction occurs. The avoidance response is restored by reoccurrence of the aversive stimulus.

These events have obvious analogs in human behavior. For example, to avoid the onset of allergic symptoms the patient is instructed to take certain medication after meals. At first the instructions are followed religiously and symptoms do not occur. After a while the patient begins to skip doses, with the inevitable consequences. Successful avoidance of allergic symptoms following medication eliminated the aversive stimulus that reinforced the response (self-medication), leading to weakening of the response. Reintroduction of the aversive symptoms is usually enough to reinstate the response.

In the case of escape and avoidance, exposure to aversive stimuli increased the rate of responding. But there is an obvious instance of aversive control, of which punishment is an example, that is accompanied by a decrease in rate of responding. When a response is followed by a stimulus that reduces the subsequent probability of the response, the response is said to be punished and the stimulus is a punisher. Punishment leads to suppression of responding.

A typical procedure is illustrated in a study by Holz and Azrin (1963). First a high rate of key-pecking was established by reinforcing the response on a differential reinforcement schedule: a response was reinforced if 30 seconds or more had elapsed since the preceding response. Next the punishment procedure was introduced. The same reinforcement schedule was maintained, but electric shock was administered for each key peck. The result was an immediate reduction in the rate of responding.

Characteristics of Operant Analysis

Emphasis on Observables

You may have noted that all the terms in operant analysis refer to conditions or events that are directly observable. Many concepts that are part of commonsense psychology and which figure importantly in our accounts of daily behavior are not directly observable. The concept of purpose or intention is an example. If a man is observed to walk a direct route from his doorstep to the mailbox, where he deposits a letter, we explain his behavior by remarking that he wanted to post a letter. In the case of avoidance behavior, we might be inclined to say that the rat presses the bar in order to avoid the shock. This assertion introduces a mediating purpose to explain the behavior, but operant analysis denies the scientific utility of such concepts, claiming they are actually imprecise references to observable contingencies that shape behavior. "Statements which use such words as 'incentive' or 'purpose' are usually reducible to statements about operant conditioning . . . to bring them within the framework of natural science" (Skinner, 1953, p. 87). This act of translation presumably has the effect of externalizing the concept and making it amenable to scientific research (one illustration was noted earlier in the redefinition of attention in operant terms).

There is a second class of unobservable concepts that do not originate in commonsense psychology. These are called intervening constructs, and their origins are in scientific theories of psychology. The behavioristic theories of learning advocated by Hull (1952) and Tolman (1959) are studded with intervening constructs which refer to unobservable events that occur between the directly observable stimulus and response (see Chap. 8). Behavior is initiated by environmental stimuli and physiological states; certain processes intervene, and behavior emerges. Examples are Hull's concept of "habit strength" and Tolman's concept of "expectancy." According to these views, repeated pairings of a stimulus and response lead to a buildup of habit strength or development of an expectancy, and these intervening processes are responsible for changes in the power of the stimulus to elicit a response. Intervening variables abound in the theories of Hull and Tolman (see Hilgard and Bower, 1966, Chaps. 6 and 7), and they sustain a large portion of the explanatory burden.

Operant analysis provides a sharp contrast to these approaches by striving to formulate a pure stimulus-response account of behavior which avoids intervening variables. The aim of operant analysis is to describe and explain behavior in terms of observable contingencies without reference to unobservable intervening processes.

Deemphasis of Theory

The 1940s and 1950s were periods of great ferment among psychologists interested in the study of learning, involving extensive theory building and testing. Proponents of rival theories took issue with each other in the laboratory and in argument. An excellent book published at the height of this period (Osgood, 1953) reviews many of the controversies. Despite the enthusiasm which was generally evident, not everyone felt the game to be worth the prize. In 1950 Skinner authored an article titled: "Are Theories of Learning Necessary?" The question was plainly rhetorical, since little time was wasted in informing the reader that it should be answered negatively. This low regard for theory continues into the present. The operant analysis of behavior aspires to be an *a*theoretical descriptive approach. Depreciation of theory arises from several considerations:

> A science of behavior must eventually deal with behavior in its relation to certain manipulable variables. Theories—whether neural, mental, or conceptual—talk about intervening steps in these relationships. But instead of prompting us to search for and explore relevant variables, they frequently have quite the opposite effect . . . the principal function of learning theory to date has been, not to suggest appropriate research, but to create a false sense of security, and unwarranted satisfaction with the status quo (Skinner, 1950, p. 194).
>
> Research designed with respect to theory is also likely to be wasteful. That a theory generates research does not prove its value unless the research is valuable. . . . It is possible to design significant experiments for other reasons and the possibility to be examined is that such research will lead more directly to the kind of information that a science usually accumulates (Skinner, 1950, p. 194).

In brief, the operant analyst feels that pursuit of theory is likely to lead us down the primrose path to unobservables. Having been thus seduced, we will be blinded to the theory's flaws and inhibited from recognizing the virtues of other approaches, questions, and methods.

The discussion has thus far considered two of the *meta*theoretical principles of the operant analysis (emphasis on observables, deemphasis of theory). These are principles that guide the analysis and exercise a selective influence on the kinds of propositions advocated. Next we turn to several methodological characteristics of the experimental approach of the operant analysis.

The Free Operant

In order to clarify the distinctive feature of operant conditioning, it is useful to contrast operant conditioning with classical conditioning (Chap. 1). Suppose that a puff of air is directed to a subject's eye. The subject will blink. The air puff is the unconditioned stimulus and the eyeblink is the unconditioned response. Next, a tone of specified frequency is sounded preceding the puff, and this pairing of tone (conditioned stimulus) and puff is repeated in a series of trials. Eventually the tone comes to elicit the eyeblink before the puff is delivered. It is obvious in this situation that the conditioned eyeblink has been elicited by a specific stimulus.

The circumstances are quite different for operant conditioning, in which it is assumed that the stimulus is unknown and irrelevant to an understanding of operant behavior. The operant responses are not elicited by known stimuli; rather, they are *emitted*. In classical conditioning, reinforcement (unconditioned stimulus) is correlated with the stimulus (conditioned stimulus); for example, in the Pavlovian experiment, food is correlated with the bell. In operant conditioning, reinforcement is correlated with the response. The analysis of operant behavior emphasizes the effects of the consequences of behavior on future emission of the behavior, rather than the effects of antecedent stimuli in eliciting behavior.

The laboratory examples have concentrated on a class of responses frequently called *free operants*, responses whose completion leaves the organism free to emit the response again and for which rate of responding is a suitable measure. Rate of responding is uniquely preferred as a dependent variable in the analysis of operant behavior. In this respect, operant conditioning experiments differ from most other learning studies, which allow the subject to supply only one response per trial. This is true of classical conditioning as well as instrumental learning studies characterized by the rat who runs a maze to find food in the goal box. Common measures of conditioning are changes in the speed or amplitude of response measured over a large number of trials. There are no distinct trials in the operant conditioning paradigm, and rate of responding is the principal datum. It is contended that rate of responding holds out the best promise of exhibiting the principles of behavior.

Emphasis on Single Organism Research

The aspiration of operant analysis is to control behavior. If this can be accomplished, the operant analyst feels that the important contingencies have been identified and behavior has been explained. Therefore, the design of operant behavior research ignores conventional scientific wisdom which prescribes testing of large groups and reporting averaged group performance. Group averages often fail to reproduce the performance of any single individual in the group, and consequently have little predictive value for the individual. Control of individual behavior provides the most convincing demonstration that the behavior is understood, and group averages contribute little to this objective. Experiments designed to study operant behavior use single subjects, or very few subjects, whose behavior is studied intensively. The claim is that precise identification of the contingencies that control the behavior of a single subject contributes more to general understanding than the imprecise specification of variables allowed by the necessarily less intensive study of large groups.

Related to the use of single subjects is an atypical attitude toward statistical analysis. Data generated in typical psychological experiments involving large numbers of subjects yield conclusions only to complex statistical analyses. The combination of different conditions and the variability between and within subjects' performance often make it impossible to say precisely what significant results have been obtained. Therefore, statistical analysis is a necessary adjunct to the research process. Research on operant behavior is notable for its neglect of statistical analysis. Skinner (1966, p. 20) describes the state of affairs:

> Much of this is lacking in the experimental analysis of behavior, where experiments are usually performed on a few subjects, curves representing behavioral processes are seldom averaged, the behavior attributed to complex mental activity is analyzed directly, and so on. The simpler procedure is

possible because rate of responding and changes in rate can be directly observed, especially when represented in cumulative records. The effect is similar to increasing the resolving power of a microscope: a new subject matter is suddenly open to direct inspection. Statistical methods are unnecessary. When an organism is showing a stable or slowly changing performance, it is for most purposes idle to prove statistically that a change has indeed occurred.

Modification of Human Behavior

Our description of the techniques and concepts of operant conditioning referred to examples from human behavior as analogs of the behavior of the rat or pigeon in the experimental chamber. The implication is that the analysis of operant behavior illustrated in laboratory investigations of animal behavior can also be applied to human behavior in natural settings. Advocates of the operant approach do not shrink from this implication. Reports of the application of operant techniques in school and hospital settings have been published in large number. Several of these reports are described in this section.

Effect of Social Reinforcement on Isolate Behavior

There are obvious differences among children in the frequency and quality of social interactions with other children. These differences are readily observed in a nursery school setting. In some cases a child will display an undesirable degree of social isolation from his peers. Two studies by Allen, Hart, Buell, Harris, and Wolf (1964) and Hart, Reynolds, Baer, Brawley and Harris (1968) applied operant conditioning procedures to modify the behavior of a nursery school isolate. The aim of the studies was to demonstrate that controlled social reinforcement contingent on social interaction would increase the frequency of these interactions.

The child in the study by Allen *et al.* was 4.3 years old. The procedures were carried out in the nursery school setting. The child, who had a good repertoire of physical and mental skills, interacted freely with adults but seldom with children. If adult interaction was not possible, she would stand and look from a distance at ongoing activity, or retire to a make-believe bed to "sleep." By the sixth week of school she began to exhibit a variety of nervous mannerisms, and the experimental effort to modify her behavior was initiated at this time.

The first stage of the experiment established the operant level of social interaction. For five days, the child was carefully observed and an objective record obtained of the actual amounts of time she was spending with children, adults, and alone. The second stage introduced the reinforcement procedures. For six days the teacher administered social reinforcement in the form of attention whenever and *only* when the child interacted with other children; interactions with the teacher herself were not reinforced. The third stage of the experiment reversed the procedure. Solitary activity and contact with adults were exclusively reinforced, while interaction with children was ignored. After a five day reversal period the previous reinforcement contingencies were reintroduced. Over a period of nine days, the continuous schedule of reinforcement was gradually shifted to an intermittent schedule that provided the amount of social reinforcement normal for the group.

Figure 12.7 shows the percentage of time spent in interaction with adults

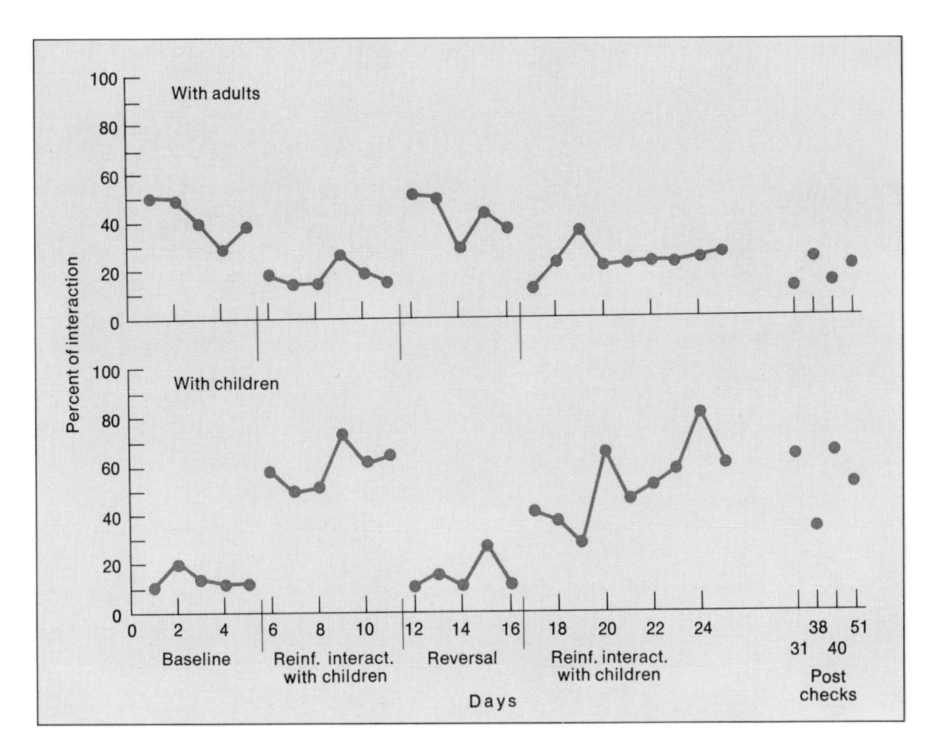

Fig. 12.7. Percentages of time spent in social interaction during approximately two hours of each morning session. (From Allen, Hart, Buell, Harris, and Wolf, 1964)

(upper half) and children (lower half) during each two hour daily session. The baseline data show that the operant level of interaction with children was about 10 per cent, and that about 40 per cent of each daily session was spent in interaction with adults. Introduction of social reinforcement in the second stage increased the percentage of time spent in interaction with children to 60 per cent. Reversal of reinforcement contingencies reversed the development of the desired social interaction; the earlier isolate behavior reappeared. Reintroduction of the previous reinforcement contingencies on the seventeenth day led to a new increase in interaction with children. The experiment was discontinued after the twenty-fifth day, but postexperimental checks were made 6, 13, 15, and 26 days afterward. The results, appearing in the right-hand portion of Figure 12.7, showed that the increased level of interaction with children was maintained in the absence of experimental intervention.

This experiment shows that controlled schedules of reinforcement can modify behavior in a naturalistic setting. The evidence is supplied by the pattern of responding that accompanied manipulations of the reinforcement contingencies. The rise and fall of response frequency accompanying the introduction and withdrawal of reinforcement constitutes the argument for the efficacy of reinforcement. By demonstrating that the newly established response rates return to base levels when reinforcement is withdrawn, the experiment established the critical role of reinforcement. In a sense, this reversal test is a form of control procedure in which the subject serves as his own control.

The same experimental design was used in a subsequent study by Hart *et*

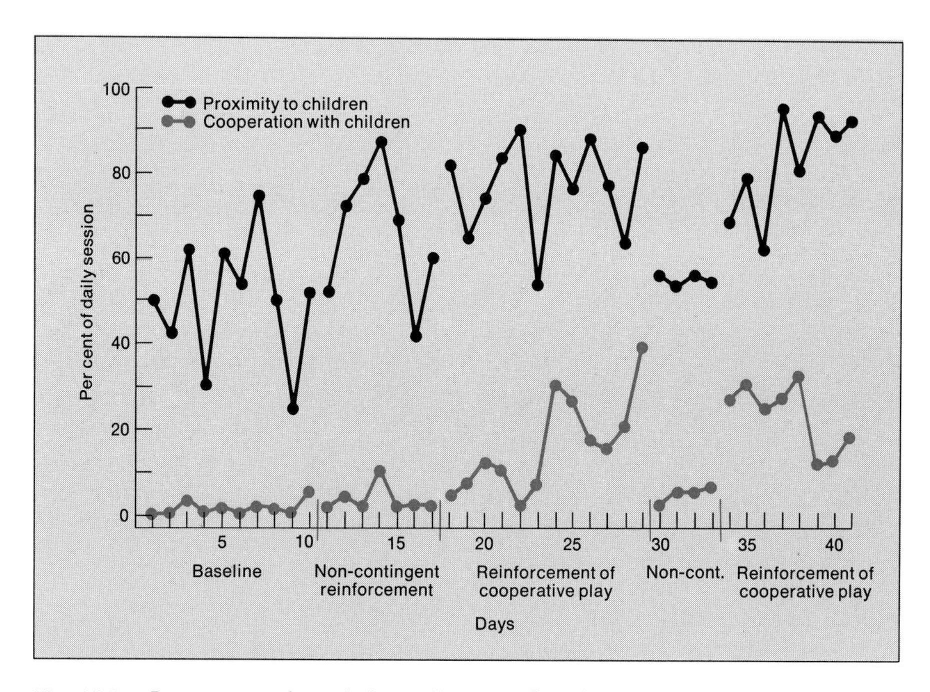

Fig. 12.8. Percentages of proximity and cooperative play over sequential experimental conditions. (From Hart, Reynolds, Baer, Brawley, and Harris, 1968)

al. (1968). Again the subject was a nonsocial nursery school girl. Although this child had frequent contact with other children, the contacts were brief and characterized by uncooperative and aggressive behavior. The major response variables in this experiment were cooperative play and proximity to other children.

The first stage of the experiment determined the baseline of responding. Figure 12.8 shows that although the subject spent a good deal of time near other children (within three feet of another child indoors, and within six feet outdoors), cooperative play was usually absent.

The next stage introduced a noncontingent reinforced schedule. Unlike the reversal stage in the previous experiment, this treatment did not involve systematic differential reinforcement of other than the desired behavior. Instead, social reinforcement in the form of attention and approval was presented at random intervals, without regard for the behavior that might be occurring at those times. Figure 12.8 shows that noncontingent reinforcement had no effect on the occurrence of cooperative play.

In the third stage, social reinforcement was made contingent on the occurrence of cooperative play. Since the baseline rate of cooperative play was very low, it was necessary to prime other children to initiate cooperative play and to use the shaping procedure. The subject was reinforced for successive approximations of the desired behavior. "Shaping meant that Martha was initially reinforced for all responsive verbalizations in proximity to children, subsequently only for such verbalization in potentially cooperative situations, and finally (by the seventh of this 12-day period) only for full-blown cooperative play" (Hart *et al.*, 1968, p. 74). Figure 12.8 shows that reinforcement of cooperative situations led to clear increases in rate of cooperative play. From an initial baseline of approximately zero, the daily percentage rose to 40 per cent; proximity to other children also increased.

When noncontingent reinforcement was reintroduced on day 30, both proximity to children and cooperative play dropped almost to baseline levels. When the contingent schedule was restored, cooperative play reappeared. (The last three data points, showing a drop, were obtained with a different procedure).

Both experiments provide evidence that important features of social behavior can be modified significantly by applying the techniques and principles of operant conditioning. Two additional aspects of the findings are worth noting. First, the results reported by Allen *et al.* (1964) for the differential reinforcement schedule show that behavior may occur at a low rate because the prevalent reinforcement contingencies maintain a high responding rate for competing behavior. Thus, sympathetic attention given to the isolate may reinforce the isolation behavior, precluding the appearance of peer directed behavior. Second, the results reported by Hart *et al.* (1968) show that the *amount* of reinforcement is not always critical in determining behavior modification. More important is the *scheduling* of reinforcement. Although reinforcements were considerably more frequent under the noncontingent schedule, only the contingent schedule modified behavior.

Reinforcement Control of Generalized Imitation

This section describes two experiments dealing with the control of imitation. Interest in imitative behavior arises partly because imitation figures prominently in the process of socialization and language development, and partly because the imitative capability is often assumed in instructional procedures. Imitation is not a specific behavior, but a class of behaviors whose defining characteristic is topographical similarity between behavior of model and behavior of observer. In this respect, studies of imitation differ from the studies examined thus far, which considered the effect of reinforcing a *specific* response on the rate of occurrence of that specific response. However, in order to demonstrate imitation, it must be shown that there is a generalized tendency to respond similarly to the model, a claim that cannot be advanced if the response in question has been directly reinforced. Therefore, in these studies, the evidence consists of the increased frequency of a response that is topographically similar to the model's response, but which has *not* been directly reinforced. Other imitative responses are reinforced, and evidence of conditioned imitation is sought in the amplified rate of the unreinforced response.

In the first study, by Baer and Sherman (1964), the subjects were nursery school children with the typical imitative abilities of young children. In the second study, by Baer, Peterson, and Sherman (1967), the subjects were mentally retarded children who had never been observed to perform a distinctly imitative response. in both experiments the investigators sought to determine whether the likelihood of imitative behavior could be modified by reinforcement.

Conditioning of imitation in normal children. The model in the first study was an animated talking puppet (shown in Fig. 12.9) capable of four responses: nodding his head, opening and closing his mouth, bar-pressing on a puppet-scaled apparatus, and talking. The child sat facing the puppet. A bar-pressing device, identical to the puppet's except for size, was located near the child.

The first phase of the experiment assessed the operant level of imitative bar-pressing. The puppet engaged the child in friendly, approving conversation for a period of 15 to 30 minutes. During the conversation the puppet pressed his bar,

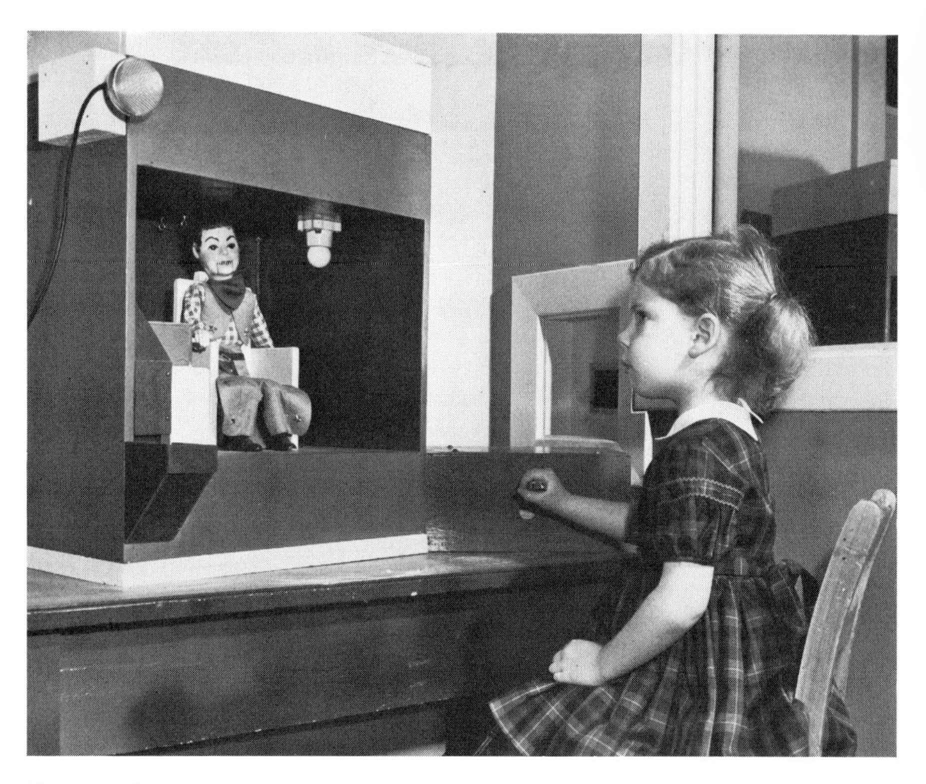

Fig. 12.9. The mechanized puppet in an "attentive" position. (From Baer, 1962)

sometimes as frequently as three times per second. None of the subjects displayed imitative bar-pressing.

After the operant level was established, the puppet stopped bar-pressing and began presenting a series of other responses, including nodding, mouthing, and uttering a variety of nonsense statements. At the beginning of the series the puppet introduced each response by asking, "Can you do this?" If the response was imitated, the puppet reinforced the child's response with verbal approval, such as, "Very good." After a while the prefatory question was eliminated, but still the child would invariably imitate all the responses. At that point, the puppet resumed bar-pressing. The puppet continued to display the other responses from time to time, and imitation of these responses was always reinforced, but imitation of bar-pressing was *never* reinforced.

The important datum in the experiment was the rate of imitative bar-pressing. Baer and Sherman (1964, p. 41) explain the logic of the experiment this way:

> An increase over operant level in this never-reinforced bar-pressing by the child, especially insofar as it matched the puppet's bar-pressing, would be significant: it would be attributable to the direct reinforcement of the other responses (nodding, mouthing, and verbal). These responses have very slight topographical resemblance to bar-pressing; they are like it essentially in that they all are imitative of a model's behavior. Thus an increase in imitative bar-pressing by the child would indicate that similarity of responding per se

was a functional dimension of the child's behavior, that is, similarity of responding could be strengthened as could responding itself.

In brief, increased bar-pressing would signify that the child had been conditioned to imitate.

Of the 11 children studied, seven exhibited an increased rate of bar-pressing. Evidence that this constituted imitation was provided by the temporal contiguity of the child's and the puppet's response. With rare exception, the child's bar-pressing response would immediately follow a bar-pressing response by the puppet. Following the design of the studies described in the previous section, Baer and Sherman introduced two additional procedures to establish that the generalized imitative bar-pressing depended on reinforcement of the other imitative responses. In the extinction procedure, the puppet stopped giving reinforcement for imitation of the previously reinforced responses. In the "time-out" procedure, the puppet stopped performing the previously reinforced set of responses, but social reinforcement was continued, noncontingent on imitation. Both procedures led to weakening of imitative bar-pressing. Finally, when the original reinforcement schedule was resumed, imitative bar-pressing reappeared at the previously conditioned rate.

Conditioning of imitation in retardates. Nursery school children begin this experiment with a history of imitation. Would the same results be obtained with subjects who had no prior history of imitation? Baer, Peterson, and Sherman (1967) examined this question with three institutionalized children, 9 to 12 years of age, who were profoundly retarded. These children had never been observed to perform an imitative response, either spontaneously or following a verbal command.

The general plan of the experiment was the same as in the first imitation study. The subjects were seen at mealtime. The experiment began by reinforcing a series of imitative responses with mouthfuls of food. However, unlike the normal children in the earlier experiment, the retarded children required a shaping procedure. The initial responses were taught in the following way: The experimenter performed a response, such as hand raising, accompanied by the words, "Do this." When the subject failed to comply, the experimenter reached out, took the subject's hand, and raised it, immediately reinforcing the response with food. Gradually, the shaping procedure was faded out until the subject performed an unassisted imitative response whenever the experimenter provided the discriminative stimulus, "Do this." When the subject reached this stage, tests for imitation of other actions were introduced. Certain actions were performed by the experimenter which, if imitated, were deliberately *not* reinforced. These tests established the extent to which imitation had been successfully conditioned. After the test phase, nonreinforcement of all imitative behavior was instituted. In this phase (DRO, for differential reinforcement of other behavior) the experimenter reinforced all behavior other than imitation. Finally, contingent reinforcement of imitation was resumed.

Figure 12.10 shows the results for one subject. The pattern of responding should be familiar. The lines on the left show that the initial procedures succeeded in establishing imitation of unreinforced responses in a child who had never before exhibited such behavior. The DRO phase shows that previously nonreinforced imitative responses fell off markedly when nonimitative behavior was temporarily reinforced. The lines on the right show that nonreinforced imitation again increased dramatically when reinforcement for imitation of specific responses was reintroduced. In another part of the experiment, the investigators showed that the newly

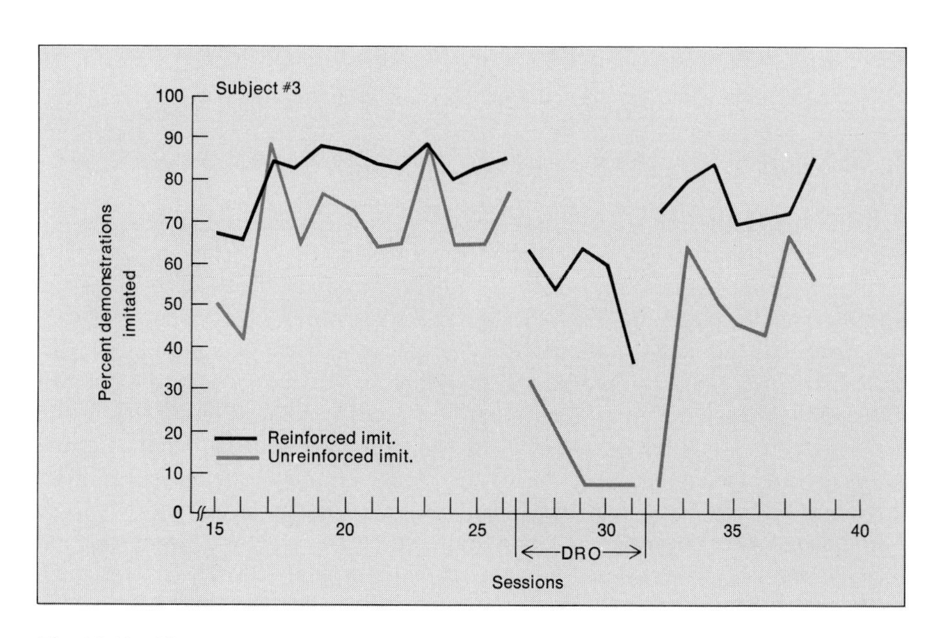

Fig. 12.10. The maintenance and extinction of reinforced and unreinforced imitation in a retarded subject. During the DRO period all behavior other than imitation was reinforced. (From Baer, Peterson, and Sherman, 1967)

acquired imitative tendency would transfer without loss to another model, thus enhancing the potential instructional value of the newly acquired imitative ability.

Modification of Psychotic Behavior

Psychosis is a psychiatric category that includes a wide variety of symptom constellations (see Chap. 15). The symptoms take the form of highly deviant, sometimes bizarre behaviors. But however bizarre the acts of the psychotic may be, they are behavioral responses, and their rate of occurrence should be subject to the control of reinforcement contingencies. By controlled scheduling of reinforcement, it should be possible to modify the behavior of the psychotic. The term *psychotherapy* is used to refer to procedures calculated to modify the behavior of neurotic and psychotic individuals; psychoanalytic therapy is one example. Do the methods and principles of operant conditioning provide another basis for therapy? Skinner (1959, pp. 182–219) has unequivocally advanced this claim. The study described next illustrates how the symptomatic verbal behavior of psychotic patients may be modified by application of operant techniques.

The study was conducted by Ayllon and Haughton (1964) in a psychiatric hospital. The subject was a 47 year old woman diagnosed as chronic schizophrenic who had been in the hospital for 16 years. Despite varied efforts by the hospital staff, the patient's verbal behavior was preoccupied with a delusion of royalty.

> The content of her verbal behavior was characterized by frequent references to "Queen Elizabeth," "King George," and the "Royal Family." A sample of her talk is as follows: "I'm the queen . . . the Queen wants to smoke . . . how's King George, have you seen him?" . . . The staff stated that references to herself as "the Queen" had been virtually her only topic of

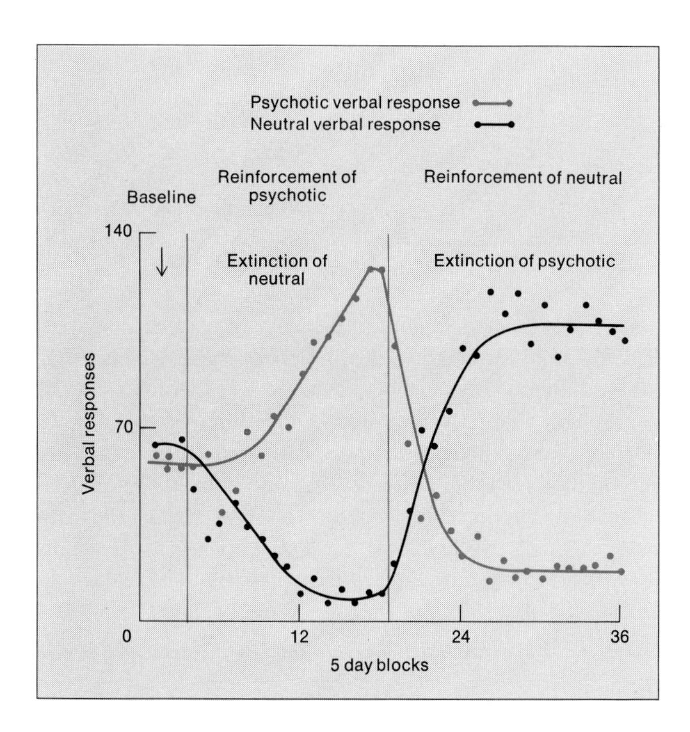

Fig. 12.11. This figure shows that the baseline (first period) included both psychotic and neutral verbal behavior in equal strength. The second period shows that reinforcement increased psychotic verbal behavior while extinction decreased the neutral. The third period shows that in reversing this procedure the neutral verbal behavior increased while the psychotic verbal behavior decreased. (From Ayllon and Haughton, 1964) (Additional information and related research are found in Ayllon and Azrin, *The Token Economy: A Motivational System for Therapy and Rehabilitation*, New York: Appleton-Century-Crofts, 1968.)

conversation for the eight years immediately prior to the investigation (Ayllon and Haughton, 1964, p. 90).

The aim of the study was to determine whether the patient's verbal behavior could be modified. First the baseline frequency of occurrence of psychotic and neutral verbal behavior was determined. Next, for 75 days, psychotic verbal behavior (references to royalty) was reinforced, while neutral verbal behavior ("It's nice today") was extinguished. Reinforcement was in the form of attention, social approval, and offers of cigarettes. Extinction was in the form of withdrawal of attention, indifference, and withholding of cigarettes. Finally, in the third period, the reinforcement contingencies were reversed: psychotic verbal behavior was extinguished, and neutral verbal behavior reinforced.

Figure 12.11 shows the results of this experiment. The frequencies of psychotic and neutral verbal responses are plotted for the three experimental periods. The figure shows that the absolute and relative frequency of psychotic verbal behavior was altered dramatically by varying the reinforcement contingencies. So far as the goal of therapy is concerned, it should be noted that psychotic verbal behavior was sharply reduced by the end of the third period, so that it comprised only a small fraction of total verbal behavior.

This study is illustrative of a growing number of reports of the application

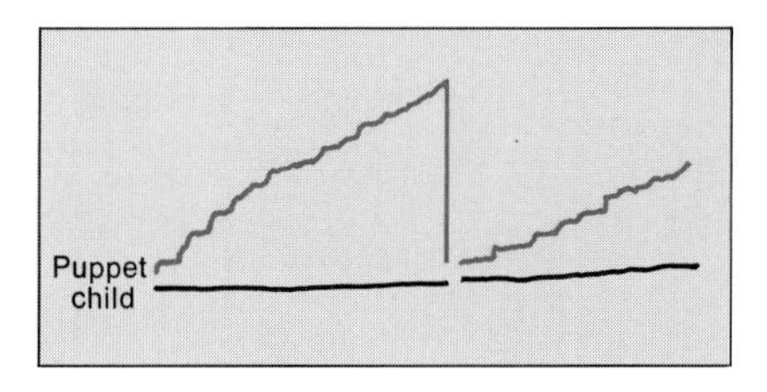

Fig. 12.12. The development of generalized bar-pressing; one subject in the Baer-Sherman study. (From Baer and Sherman, 1964)

of operant techniques to modification of behavior of psychiatric patients (Bandura, 1969, Chaps. 4-6). Apart from the contribution of these studies to the welfare of individual patients, the results have suggested to the operant analyst that behavior disorders are originally shaped by reinforcement contingencies. Complicated theories to account for the development of the behavior seem unnecessary to him, as does the assumption that aberrant behavior is a sign of malfunctioning in the underlying psychic processes. According to the operant analyst, psychiatric patients are not suffering the anxiety of psychological conflict or the pain of childhood trauma. In Skinner's words, "What they are suffering from in fact is very bad schedules of reinforcement" (Hall, 1967, p. 70).

Evaluations

The principles and techniques of operant conditioning have been presented uncritically here, but the procedures and claims of the operant analyst have not passed without criticism. In fact, the challenge of operant analysis to the established procedures of experimental psychology and to the theories and procedures of clinical psychology has made it a prime target for criticism.

Questions of Methodology

The design of operant research substitutes intrasubject replicability for the conventional use of control groups, and visual examination of data curves for statistical analysis. Both of these practices are severely criticized by other experimental psychologists. Neglect of statistical analysis often leaves it up to the investigator's judgment to determine whether a significant change in frequency of responding has occurred. For example, look at Figure 12.12, taken from the Baer-Sherman study of imitation; it shows the bar-pressing responses for the puppet and one child. Is this the record of one of the seven children who displayed conditioned imitation, or one of the four who did not? There is a barely discernible trend in the child's response, but is it a significant departure from no change? Baer and Sherman thought so, but in the absence of statistical evidence there is obvious room for doubt. The problem of evaluating small changes is further compounded when performance is variable during the baseline period. In this case, visual inspection cannot inform us whether the change that accompanies reinforcement procedures exceeds the variability in the absence of reinforcement. In summary, critics of operant methodology doubt the reliability of the data.

The operant analyst can have only one response to this criticism: better control of reinforcement contingencies will bring more precise control of behavior. The fault is not in our data, but in our reinforcers. A similar explanation is offered to account for replicative failures. For example, in the Baer–Sherman study, the failure of four of the eleven children to develop imitative bar-pressing is attributed to the inadequacy of reinforcers, while the seven successes are assumed to result from application of the same reinforcers. It seems reasonable for the critic to conclude that the experimenter is not controlling the response, in which case the seven successes do not necessarily signify control by reinforcement contingencies. They may simply be due to the effect of unidentified variables that are correlated with the reinforcement procedures in some of the cases. Control conditions are needed that will establish that behavior changes are indeed due to experimenter controlled reinforcements. The need is especially obvious when the reversal procedure is not used.

Questions of Sufficiency

The reinforcement principle was not discovered by the operant conditioner, nor is the study of operant behavior without precedent. The reinforcement principle has always been implicit in the conduct of human affairs, especially in child-rearing practices, and its application to the shaping of behavior has probably always been part of the technology of animal training. What is new in operant analysis is the scientific refinement of the reinforcement principle, and the claim that the pigeon in the experimental chamber presents an analog for all human behavior. The operant analyst states that the only useful business of psychology is the study of operant behavior and the only fruitful procedures are those of operant research (Hall, 1967; Evans, 1968). It is here that most other psychologists part company with him. There is wide agreement that operant behavior is an important class of behavior, but there is also widespread skepticism regarding the claim that all behavior can be represented by the operant model.

Questions of Efficacy

The acid test of operant analysis is the control of behavior. A number of representative examples of operant control of behavior were described earlier. Despite these demonstrations, many psychologists concerned with the development and modification of human behavior continue to question the efficacy of operant techniques. One doubt that is voiced frequently concerns the durability of the modification. Are changes induced by operant conditioning enduring, or are they confined to the duration of the experiment? If uncontrolled *pre*experimental reinforcement contingencies did not support the desired behavior, isn't it likely that uncontrolled *post*experimental reinforcement contingencies will also fail to maintain it? In that event, extinction will occur; the modification will be transient.

Another question in the same vein concerns the generality of the conditioned modification. Is the modification restricted to the original experimental setting, or has a generalized modification been achieved? This question is most crucial in evaluating therapeutic efficacy. How will the conditioned isolate child behave outside the nursery school setting, in a situation such as a birthday party in a child's home?

These questions are empirical issues that can be decided by experiment. Unfortunately, studies utilizing operant techniques have rarely proceeded beyond the demonstration of behavior modification to answer these questions. Nevertheless, we can anticipate how the operant analyst would reply to these criticisms. The durability of the change will depend on the schedule of reinforcement that has been used to establish the new response. If a continuous reinforcement schedule is used, extinction will be rapid when the changeover to the natural schedule occurs.

But if the behavior has been gradually shifted to an appropriate intermittent schedule, such as variable interval, extinction will be retarded, and the modification may be maintained.

In many cases the modification may be long-lasting even without careful management of reinforcement contingencies. Modification of the subject's behavior often results in modification of the naturally occurring schedule of reinforcements. The new behavior brings the individual into situations where other reinforcers can take over to maintain the behavior. For example, modification of the isolate child's behavior exposes the child to the reinforcement inherent in cooperative play. These reinforcers maintain the new behavior when experimenter controlled reinforcers are withdrawn.

The extent to which the change can be generalized may depend on the selection of an appropriate discriminative stimulus. If the stimulus is unlikely to be present in the natural setting, the response is not likely to occur. However, if the stimulus that sets the occasion for the response in the experimental setting is also present in other situations, the response will generalize to these extraexperimental circumstances. These claims are consistent with the general view of operant behavior, but experimental verification of them is needed.

Another aspect of the efficacy question concerns efficiency. Is the operant technique efficient? Does it yield enough change per unit of effort? In one study (Sherman, 1965), operant techniques were applied to reinstate verbal behavior in a psychiatric patient with a 45 year history of mutism. After 30 weeks of shaping, involving three 45 minute weekly sessions with the experimenter, the patient was able to utter one nonimitative verbal response, "food." No doubt the event was dramatic, coming as it did after a 45 year silence. Still, the achievement hardly provides grounds for optimism about the efficacy of operant techniques.

Concern with efficacy in the above sense is certainly legitimate, but it is obviously difficult to settle the argument without prior agreement about the magnitude of change that will be acceptable as a standard of efficacy. A change of the magnitude demonstrated in Sherman's experiment may not seem very great, but if continued application of reinforcement techniques eventually yielded rapidly accelerating and self-sustained growth in the patient's usable vocabulary, there would be little doubt that the operant approach to this type of problem has merit in the long run.

Another much more complex question concerning the efficacy of operant methods asks whether operant techniques are more effective than other techniques that have been proposed for modifying behavior. This question is complicated not only by disagreements over *how* change should be brought about, but by differences of opinion about what sorts of changes are required. For example, if a person complains of severe anxiety, the operant analyst would approach the problem entirely differently from the psychoanalytic therapist or the therapist who uses nondirective counseling techniques. The operant analyst might regard the patient's complaints as purely verbal behavior to be dealt with by extinction (for instance, by simply ignoring all the patient's expression of distress) or by aversive conditioning (for instance, by delivering a slight shock to the patient every time he says he is anxious). In addition, the operant therapist would probably introduce a program of positive reinforcement for all verbal expressions of good feeling and well-being. By these devices he might seek to change the client's behavior so that he no longer complains of troublesome feelings.

In contrast, the psychoanalyst and nondirective therapist would induce the subject to talk at length, not only about his symptoms but about all the events in his life. These therapists would regard their client's anxiety as a real, though internal, psychological state which signals the existence of more pervasive personality conflicts. It is toward these conflicts, rather than the anxiety itself, that attention would be directed. Even complete disappearance of complaints of anxiety would not signify success of the treatment, so long as these deeper conflicts remain unresolved. By the same token, resolution of conflicts need not result in immediate reduction of anxiety, for the client will sometimes find it necessary to undertake reorganization of his total life pattern, which cannot be accomplished without considerable emotional turmoil.

It is obvious that treatment techniques can be compared only when there is agreement about what is to be changed, and when the comparison concerns only the relative efficiency with which the desired change is brought about by alternative techniques. Since operant treatment disavows concern for "inner" or "mental" states, and since other forms of therapy disavow concern for overt behavior per se, agreement on goals is virtually impossible. Conclusive tests of relative efficacy cannot be conducted until these fundamental theoretical differences are resolved.

Questions of Value

The complaint is often expressed (Krutch, 1953; Rogers, 1956) that operant analysis is incompatible with cherished beliefs concerning human freedom and personal dignity. Man's potentialities are proscribed by reinforcement contingencies. The quality of inner-directedness is denied, and it is implied that any behavior can be shaped by skillful manipulation. The critic is distressed, but not surprised, to learn that Skinner's (1948) fictional utopia, *Walden Two*, is a controlled society.

These complaints have not passed unheeded. Skinner (1959) has responded in a series of articles dealing with freedom and control of human behavior: the arguments of the critics begin with the implicit premise that is certainly wrong, that, except for self-serving intervention by external agents, man's behavior is spontaneous and uncontrolled. However, systems of child rearing, education, and social ethics exert powerful control over man's behavior. Add the ubiquitous controls inherent in social interactions to these formal controls, and it is plainly wrong to contend that man is uncontrolled. Therefore, in asserting that behavior is controlled the operant analyst is only making explicit that which is unalterable fact. In proposing that behavior is controlled by reinforcing contingencies, he is trying to replace vaguely conceived notions of control with a scientific conception. There is no virtue in ignorance, and freedom cannot be genuine if it is based on a denial of the real forces that shape behavior. Freedom is not insured by refusing to intervene in the process that controls behavior, since such refusal entrusts our fates to adventitious control. The real issue is not whether behavior should be controlled or uncontrolled, but rather, "What kind of control, by whom, and for what purpose?" Operant analysis proposes an answer to the first part of the question, but the latter two parts cannot be answered by science; they are questions for society.

Glossary

Conditioned reinforcer: a stimulus that has become effective as a reinforcer because it consistently precedes another reinforcer.

Continuous reinforcement: reinforcement of every response within the prescribed class.

Cumulative record: a record in which total responses are plotted as a function of time.

Differential reinforcement schedule: a schedule of reinforcement in which the presentation of a reinforcer depends on the temporal spacing of responses.

Discriminated operant: a response whose occurrence has been made to depend on the presence of a specific stimulus.

Extinction: withdrawal or discontinuation of the reinforcement leading to reduction in rate of responding.

Intermittent reinforcement: the class of reinforcement schedules in which reinforcers do not follow every response.

Interval schedule: a schedule of reinforcement in which the reinforcements are presented on the basis of time elapsed, for example, every five minutes, or on an average of every five minutes.

Operant level: the rate at which responses occur before they have been reinforced.

Ratio schedule: a schedule of reinforcement in which the reinforcements are presented on the basis of the number of responses, for example, a reinforcement for every five responses, or a reinforcement for every five responses on the average.

Reinforcer: a stimulus (such as food) that modifies the probability of occurrence of the response that preceded it.

Shaping: gradual formation of a response by reinforcing successive approximations of the response until the desired response unit is developed.

Stimulus generalization: the spread of effect of reinforcement from the original discriminative stimulus to other stimuli that vary along some dimension of the original stimulus.

References

Allen, K.E., B.M. Hart, J.S. Buell, F.R. Harris, and M.M. Wolf. Effects of social reinforcement on isolate behavior of a nursery school child. *Child Develpm.*, 1964, **35,** 511–518.

Anliker, J., and J. Mayer. An operant conditioning technique for studying feeding-fasting patterns in normal and obese mice. *J. appl. Psychol.*, 1956, **8,** 667–670.

Ayllon, T., and E. Haughton. Modification of symptomatic verbal behavior of mental patients. *Behavior Research and Therapy*, 1964, **2,** 87–97.

Baer, D.M. A technique of social reinforcement for the study of child behavior: Behavior avoiding reinforcement withdrawal. *Child Develpm.*, 1962, **33,** 847–858.

———, and J.A. Sherman. Reinforcement control of generalized imitation in young children. *J. exp. Child Psychol.*, 1964, **1,** 37–49.

Baer, D.M., R.F. Peterson, and J.A. Sherman. The development of imitation by reinforcing behavioral similarity to a model. *J. exp. anal. of Behavior*, 1967, **10,** 405–416.

Bandura, A. *Principles of behavior modification.* New York: Holt, Rinehart and Winston, 1969.

Dews, P.B. Studies on behavior: I. Differential sensitivity to pentobarbital of pecking performance in pigeons depending on the schedule of reward. *Journal of Pharmacology and Experimental Therapeutics*, 1955, **113,** 393–401.

———. Studies on behavior: II. The effects of pentobarbital, methamphetamine and scopolomine on performances in pigeons involving discriminations. *Journal of Pharmacology and Experimental Therapeutics*, 1956, **115,** 380–389.

Evans, R.I. *B.F. Skinner: The man and his ideas*. New York: Dutton, 1968.

Farthing, G.W., and E. Hearst. Generalization gradients of inhibition after different amounts of training. *J. exp. anal. of Behavior*, 1968, **11,** 743–752.

Ferster, C.B., and B.F. Skinner. *Schedules of reinforcement*. New York: Appleton-Century-Crofts, 1957.

Findley, J.D., and J.V. Brady. Facilitation of large ratio performance by use of conditioned reinforcement. *J. exp. anal. of Behavior*, 1965, **8,** 125–129.

Guttman, N., and H. Kalish. Discriminability and stimulus generalization. *J. exp. Psychol.*, 1956, **51,** 79–88.

Hall, M.H. An interview with "Mr. Behaviorist," B.F. Skinner. *Psychology Today*, 1967, **1** (5), 65–70.

Hart, B.M., N.J. Reynolds, D.M. Baer, E.R. Brawley, and F.R. Harris. Effect of contingent and noncontingent social reinforcement on the cooperative play of a preschool child. *J. appl. Behavior Analysis*, 1968, **1,** 73–76.

Herrnstein, R.J. Superstition: A corollary of the principles of operant conditioning. In W.K. Honig (Ed.), *Operant behavior: Areas of research and application*. New York: Appleton-Century-Crofts, 1966.

Hilgard, E.R., and G.H. Bower. *Theories of learning*. (3rd ed.) New York: Appleton-Century-Crofts, 1966.

Holz, W.C., and N.H. Azrin. A comparison of several procedures for eliminating behavior. *J. exp. anal. of Behavior*, 1963, **6,** 399–406.

Honig, W.K., C.A. Boneau, K.R. Burstein, and H.S. Pennypacker. Positive and negative generalization gradients obtained after equivalent training conditions. *J. comp. physiol. Psychol.*, 1963, **56,** 111–116.

Hull, C.L. *A behavior system: An introduction to behavior theory concerning the individual.* New Haven, Conn.: Yale University Press, 1952.

Jenkins, H.M., and R.H. Harrison. Effect of discrimination training on auditory generalization. *J. exp. Psychol.*, 1960, **59,** 246–253.

———. Generalization gradient of inhibition following auditory discrimination learning. *J. exp. anal. of Behavior*, 1962, **5,** 435–441.

Kelleher, R.T. Chaining and conditioned reinforcement. In W.K. Honig (Ed.), *Operant behavior: Areas of application and research*. New York: Appleton-Century-Crofts, 1966.

———. Conditioned reinforcement in chimpanzees. *J. comp. physiol. Psychol.*, 1957, **50,** 571–575.

Kendler, H.H. *Basic psychology*. (2nd ed.) New York: Appleton-Century-Crofts, 1968.

Krutch, J.W. *The measure of man*. Indianapolis: Bobbs-Merrill, 1953.

Morse, W.H., and B.F. Skinner. A second type of superstition in the pigeon. *Amer. J. Psychol.*, 1957, **70,** 308–311.

Osgood, C.E. *Method and theory in experimental psychology*. New York: Oxford University Press, 1953.

Reynolds, G.S. Attention in the pigeon. *J. exp. anal. of Attention*, 1961, **4,** 203–208.

Rogers, C.R., and B.F. Skinner. Some issues concerning the control of human behavior: A symposium. *Science*, 1956, **124** (3231), 1057–1066.

Sherman, J.A. Use of reinforcement and imitation to reinstate verbal behavior in mute psychotics. *J. abnorm. Psychol.*, 1965, **70,** 155–164.

Sidman, M. Avoidance behavior. In W.K. Honig (Ed.), *Operant behavior: Areas of research and application*. New York: Appleton-Century-Crofts, 1966.

Skinner, B.F. Are theories of learning necessary? *Psychol. Rev.*, 1950, **57,** 193–216.

———. *The behavior of organisms*. New York: Macmillan, 1938.

———. *Contingencies of reinforcement: A theoretical analysis*. New York: Appleton-Century-Crofts, 1970.

———. *Cumulative record*. New York: Appleton-Century-Crofts, 1959.

———. The experimental analysis of behavior. *Amer. Scientist*, 1957, **45,** 343–371.

———. Operant behavior. In W.K. Honig (Ed.), *Operant Behavior: Areas of research and application*. New York: Appleton-Century-Crofts, 1966.

———. *Science and human behavior*. New York: Macmillan, 1953.

———. "Superstition" in the pigeon. *J. exp. Psychol.*, 1948, **38,** 168–172.

———. *Walden Two*. New York: Macmillan, 1948.

Tolman, E.C. Principles of purposive behavior. In S. Koch (Ed.), *Psychology: A study of a science*. Vol. 2. New York: McGraw-Hill, 1959.

Zimmerman, J. Technique for sustaining behavior with conditioned reinforcement. *Science*, 1963, **142** (5), 682–684.

13 Body Experience

Interest in particular psychological phenomena is sometimes aroused by observation of extreme, unusual, or atypical behavior. Close and unprejudiced examination of the actions of psychologically disturbed persons usually reveals that these people deviate from normality more in degree than in kind. Consequently, principles and concepts originally proposed to explain abnormal psychological states are often found to apply to normal behavior as well. By studying behaviorally abnormal individuals, an investigator may observe, in exaggerated form, many of the characteristics or traits of normal persons. The condition of the person with a serious somatic or psychological disorder is sometimes regarded as a "natural experiment," the production by nature of a state of affairs that cannot be duplicated in the laboratory.

An interest in unusual or atypical phenomena is not unique to psychology. Geologists learn about the structure of the earth by studying such abnormalities as earthquakes and volcanic activities. Sociologists and anthropologists learn principles of social or cultural organization by examining societies during periods of change or adaptation. A large amount of medical knowledge of the functioning of the human brain has been gained from studying the effects of damage to that organ from disease, accident, or congenital anomaly. It is likely that Hippocrates in the fifth century B.C. could state emphatically that epilepsy is a disorder of the brain, and not the result of visitation by the gods, only because he had studied the effects of cranial damage on Greek warriors in the field of battle.

Most theories of personality in modern psychology are products of efforts to explain the behavior of seriously disturbed individuals. Originally intended to aid the clinician in diagnosing and treating neuroses and psychoses, these theories have yielded insights into more normal behavior processes and have stimulated a great deal of provocative, if not always entirely convincing, research.

The study of body experience began in much the same way. Interest was aroused when disturbances of body perception were observed in persons suffering from physiological or functional disorders. These observations led to the formulation of theories and construction of psychological measuring instruments designed to reveal how people perceive their own bodies and how the body enters into the structure and function of the human personality. Although progress in this field of study has not been rapid, psychologists' interests have been stirred in recent years, and it is likely that the future will see the production of more careful research on the problem than has appeared in the past.

Disturbances of Body Experience

Phantom Body Parts

In the sixteenth century, Ambroise Paré (1510–1590), a French neurosurgeon, reported the occurrence of *phantom limbs* in patients who had suffered amputations of extremities. Similar phenomena were observed and described in the nineteenth century by an American physician, S. Weir Mitchell (1829–1914). A person has a phantom limb when he experiences sensations that apparently come from a missing arm or leg. Phantom limbs occur not only for body parts that have been completely lost, but for body parts that are still present, though incapable of providing sensation; such a condition exists in persons whose spinal cords have

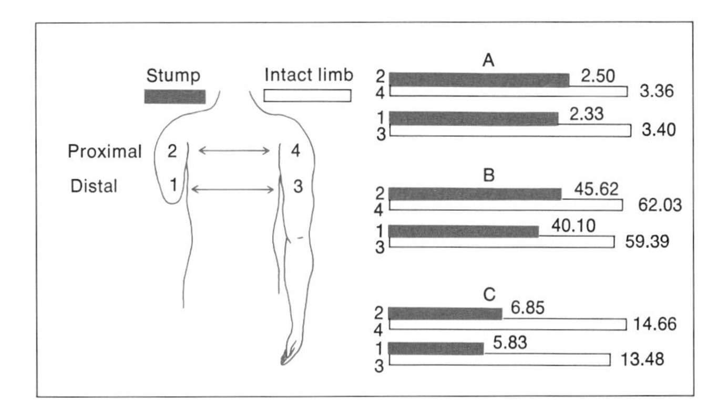

Fig. 13.1. Mean thresholds on proximal and distal portions of stump and intact limb. (A) Light-touch threshold, in log milligrams; (B) two-point discrimination in millimeters; (C) point localization, in millimeters. (From Haber, 1958)

been transected (cut through) as a result of injury or accident. Furthermore, phantoms occur for body parts other than arms, legs, hands, and feet. There have been reports of phantoms following the removal or denervation of many body organs, including teeth, nose, penis, and breasts.

Although phantom body parts occur as the result of change or damage to the body, they are distinctly psychological phenomena. The person experiences sensations from, or the possibility of controlling, a body part that cannot be felt or controlled because it is missing or lacks adequate supplies of functioning nerves. A phantom may lead a patient whose leg has been amputated to fall down when he inadvertently tries to place his weight on a foot that is not there.

Modern authorities regard phantom sensations as the expected consequence of sudden denervation of a body part. Phantom sensations tend to disappear with time, and adaptation is usually complete within a matter of weeks or months. Few phantoms are painful, and those which are tend to be irritating and annoying rather than agonizing. There is evidence that severely painful phantoms occur only in persons whose cases are complicated by other problems of psychological adjustment (Kolb, 1954, 1959, 1962).

Interest in phantom phenomena has been expressed mainly by those who encounter them in the clinical situation, and there has been little controlled psychological research on the subject. A review of a few well-executed investigations, however, will show how much can be gained from careful study of persons with phantom limbs.

Stump Sensitivity

Haber (1955, 1958) examined the tactile sensitivity of the stumps of 24 men who had undergone above the elbow amputations of one arm. Using classical psychophysical methods (Chap. 1), he tested each subject for sensitivity to light touch (by applying the tips of a set of hairs, called Von Frey hairs, to the skin), for two point threshold (the minimum distance at which two stimulated points are perceived as two points instead of one), and for ability to localize a single stimulated point accurately on the skin. Measures were taken at both proximal and distal locations: *proximal* means near the trunk (locations 2 and 4 in Figure 13.1); *distal*

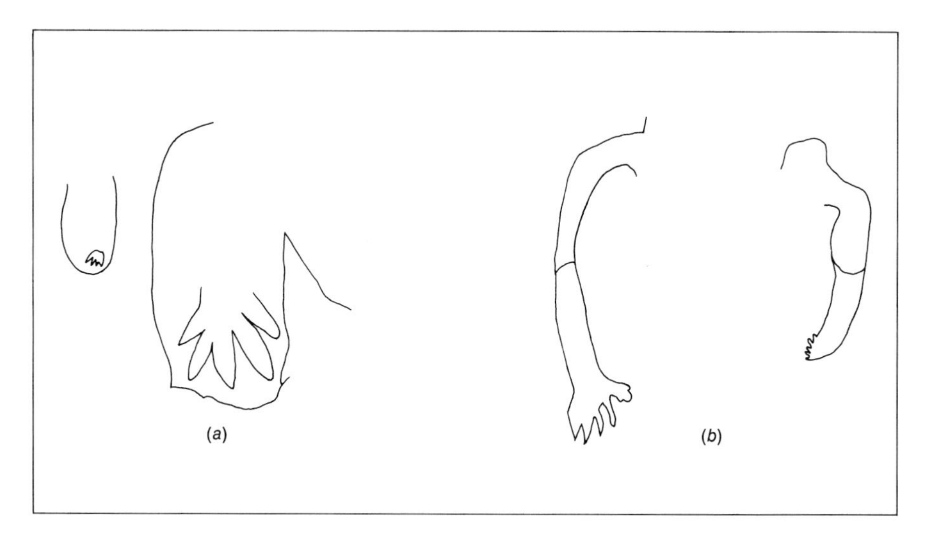

Fig. 13.2. Drawings of (a) "telescoped" phantom arms and (b) extended phantom arms. (From Haber, 1955)

means away from the trunk, i.e., at the end of the stump on the amputated side (locations 1 and 3 in Figure 13.1).

The bar graphs in Figure 13.1 show the results of these measurements. On all three sensory functions, amputated limbs (solid bars) are more sensitive than the intact limbs of the same men. Furthermore, there is a general and significant tendency for the distal area of the stump to be more sensitive than the proximal region of the amputated arm (location 1 vs. location 2).

Haber compared these data with similar data derived from tests of the intact arms of men without amputations. In all instances, findings from the nonamputee group matched those from the *intact* arms of the men with amputations. This means that the amputee group differences between sound limbs and stumps were not due to decreased sensitivity of intact arms, but represented a true rise in level of stump sensitivity. Haber also found that his subjects reported two distinct types of phantoms. The *extended* phantom feels as though it protrudes beyond the point of amputation; the *telescoped* phantom feels as though the extremity (hand) is either inside the stump or partially protruding from it. Some of his subject's drawings of extended and telescoped phantoms are reproduced in Figure 13.2

Telescoping is a rather common experience, since phantoms generally tend to disappear in a proximal-distal manner. That is, parts near the trunk, which are least densely represented in the sensory-motor cortex of the brain, tend to disappear first, while parts further from the trunk (like hands and fingers), which are most densely represented in the brain, disappear last. Haber found that the difference in touch sensitivity between sound limb and stump was greater for subjects who reported telescoped phantoms than for those who reported extended phantoms. He interpreted these findings as suggesting that the distal portion of the amputated arm tends to take over the sensory functions of the lost hand. His suggestion might be tested in future research by observing subjects with telescoped and extended phantoms to determine whether those with telescoped phantoms actually use their stumps more like hands.

In another phase of this study, in which Haber (1958) interviewed his subjects about their phantom experiences, he was impressed by the remarkable similarity of their reports of phantom limb sensations. Despite a wide variety of physical conditions preceding the loss, and despite considerable variation in subjects' personalities, all appeared to experience phantoms in very much the same way. Only one of 24 subjects reported pain. Most described the sensations as "pins and needles," "as if asleep," "vibrating," "electricity," or "tingling." Haber felt that phantoms do not represent idiosyncratic modes of adjustment, but result from the central nervous system's continuing to function as if the missing limb were present even after it has been lost.

A similar point of view is evident in the work of Simmel (1956a, b, 1958, 1959, 1961, 1962, 1963), who studied the occurrence of phantoms in a variety of subjects and found that, when limbs are lost early in life (before the age of about 5) or are denervated gradually (as in Hansen's disease), rather than suddenly, phantom sensations do not occur. These results are somewhat surprising, because phantom sensations are generally regarded as the normal consequence of the loss of body parts.

Simmel reasoned that people ordinarily build up *body schemata*, psychological ground plans of their own bodies, which enable them to judge accurately the position of their bodies in space and the localization of stimuli on the surface of their bodies. The schemata serve as guides to behavior and interpretive devices for organizing incoming sensations. When a limb or other body part is removed or paralyzed, sensory data from the affected body part suddenly cease, but the schemata, which have been built up gradually over years of experience with the body in space, continue to operate just as before. Consequently, the person feels phantom sensations until the schemata have time to adjust to the changes in peripheral stimulation. Young children do not experience phantoms because they have not yet built up stable body schemata, and amputation does not disrupt any well-established psychological processes in these subjects. Patients with Hansen's disease do not experience phantoms because they lose their extremities so slowly that adjustments of the schemata incorporate changes in sensation without interference.

Hemiplegia

Psychologists are indebted to the work of a British neurologist, Henry Head (1861–1940), for the idea that some central organization represents the body and the relationships among its parts. Head derived his theory primarily from the study of persons who had suffered damage to the brain. Injury to that vital organ has a variety of effects on behavior. Intellectual functioning may be impaired, memory may be weakened, language functions may be disturbed, and emotional responsiveness may be affected. In addition, defects in awareness and perception of the body may develop, particularly in cases of *left hemiplegia*: paralysis or weakness of the left side of the body due to damage to the right side of the brain. (Most nerve fibers cross the midline of the body in transit to the brain.)

One of the most striking distortions of body perception is the condition known as *anosognosia*, described in 1914 by Babinski (1857–1932), a French neurologist. The patient who displays anosognosia refuses to admit that he is paralyzed, although the evidence of his disability is there before his very eyes. Anosognosia is an extreme instance of a more general phenomenon known as *denial of illness*, in which the patient refuses to acknowledge the reality or implications of his actual bodily state (Weinstein and Kahn, 1955).

To explain observations of difficulties experienced by his patients, Head proposed the concept of body schemata (1920). He saw these schemata both as structures and as processes: *structures* because they are organizations that give form to experiences, and *processes* because they are continuously modified by new stimulation as it enters the complex central sensory-motor system. Head maintained that any current stimulation of the body comes into immediate contact with already existing schemata, and the relationship established between the two gives meaning to the stimulation.

If you close your eyes, you may be aware of a general field of sensation from your body. This is a rather clearly organized field from which, if necessary, you can specify whether your legs are crossed or straight, where your hands are, and which sensations come from your head, stomach, or back. If you suddenly raise one arm above your head, you introduce into this field a new sensation, a *proprioceptive* (self-generated) stimulus. Even though you cannot see your arm, you know where the sensation comes from and what it means because it enters an organized field of existing sensations that gives it meaning. This is a simple way of illustrating how the organized *structure* of the body schemata enables a person to make sense of incoming stimuli.

If you keep your arm up for awhile, and the position is not too uncomfortable, you will notice that the whole field of sensation changes to incorporate or adapt to this altered position. The stimulation from your arm no longer requires attention; it has been integrated into the whole field of experience. This adaptation illustrates how the body schemata act as *processes* by integrating new stimulation. Of course, when you bring your arm back down new proprioceptive stimuli enter the field. These are in turn interpreted in terms of their relationship to the modified schemata, and you immediately realize that your arm has changed position relative to the rest of your body.

Disturbances of body schemata in patients with hemiplegia were studied by Bender, Shapiro, and Schappell (1949), who compared subjects' responses to single and double pinpricks. Single stimulation yielded evidence of cutaneous sensory defect in 29 of 50 patients; double stimulation yielded evidence of defect in 44 of 50 patients. Two main forms of defect were found when double stimulation was employed. *Extinction* occurred when the subject failed to report one of the pinpricks, even though he was known to be capable of experiencing both, when they were administered separately; *displacement* occurred when the patient localized a stimulus in the wrong place on his body. Extinction and displacement did not occur randomly. There was a definite pattern to the direction in which displacement took place and to the disappearance of one stimulus in extinction. In general, the *face* appeared to be dominant over all other parts of the body. If the subject were stimulated on both the cheek and the hand, extinction would occur only for the stimulus on the hand. If displacement occurred, the stimulus on the hand would be reported as having been administered to the face.

The dominance pattern was more extensively studied by Bender, Green, and Fink (1954) in a wider variety of subjects, using touch rather than pinprick as the cutaneous stimulus. Patients with brain damage were found to display dominance of face and genital regions, and the hand was found to be the least dominant part of the body. Normal children displayed the same dominance pattern, but they could learn correct responses and overcome the pattern, while the brain damaged could not. Dominance patterns did not appear strongly in the responses of normal adults or subjects with schizophrenia, a severe disturbance of behavior often thought of as a "mental illness" (see Chap. 15).

In short, damage to the brain produces a characteristic pattern of body sensation similar to that displayed by immature organisms. Normal and "mentally ill" adults do not display this pattern strongly; there is no reason why they should, since neither group shows evidence of neurological retardation or pathology. As Head suggested, there appears to be some underlying organization of body experience in the central nervous system. Apparently the structure of this organization is ordinarily concealed, but is evident in children and emerges clearly in those who have suffered damage to the brain.

Psychiatric Disorders

Although patients with serious functional disturbances of behavior, such as schizophrenia, do not show the dominance pattern characteristic of patients with brain damage, psychiatrically disturbed individuals frequently report distortions of body experience. Many psychotic persons feel they are suffering from horrible (but nonexistent) body diseases, that their bodies are rotting or being eaten away, that parts of their bodies are distorted in shape or size, or that they are, in fact, dead.

Excerpts from a case study reported by Schilder show how far these disturbances may go. The patient is a woman of about 45: "When I get this anxiety state I cannot walk further. I run into myself. It breaks me into pieces. . . . I have no weight. . . . When I am melting I have no hands. . . . Sometimes the roof of my skull flies away" (Schilder, 1950, pp. 159–160). Once the patient's skull fell from her body and lay before her feet; she was in danger of stepping on it. Sometimes her body flies up and down; the upper and lower parts separate. She hears the voice of the devil frequently.

Even less serious psychological conditions are often associated with disturbances of body experiences. Severe attacks of anxiety may be accompanied by dizziness, nausea, and feelings of weakness or loss of control over internal and external body organs. Symptoms of hysteria, a neurotic disturbance of personality, often include strange sensations, or even complete loss of sensation, in various parts of the body. Nearly everyone is familiar with the experience of *depersonalization*, the sudden loss of identity between the self and the body. The victim in cases of acute crisis often reports later that he felt as though he were outside of his body watching his own behavior take place as if it were automatic. The psychological basis of these disorders is confirmed by the fact that most of them can be produced or eliminated by hypnosis, a procedure that requires no physiological intervention on the part of the investigator.

Distortions of the body are often used by artists to convey particular emotional states. A significant portion of the tension displayed in Rodin's famous statue, "The Thinker," results because it feels unnatural for the ordinary person to assume the position portrayed by the statue (Fig. 13.3). Heironymous Bosch, a medieval painter, used extensive symbolic body distortion in his paintings to display the follies of mankind. Figure 13.4 shows a portion of his triptych, "The Garden of Delights," which contains numerous representations of distorted body experiences.

Artistically talented psychiatric patients often use painting as a way to describe their personal feelings. Figure 13.5 shows a detail from one such painting by a young man. The white boundary at the bottom of the picture is a portion of his

Fig. 13.3. Auguste Rodin's "The Thinker." (Rodin Museum, Philadelphia)

skull, which has been cut open. Inside, he is seen as a lizard being picked at by crows, as a patient in bed, as a specimen in a test tube, as a victim of a torture machine, and as the observer of his own arm, which he has evidently denuded of flesh.

Body Image

A well-known theorist, Paul Schilder, was impressed by similarities between the behavior of patients who experience phantom body parts or suffer damage to the brain and people whose disturbances of behavior are more purely psychological in origin. For example, he saw in denial of illness a bodily counterpart of the

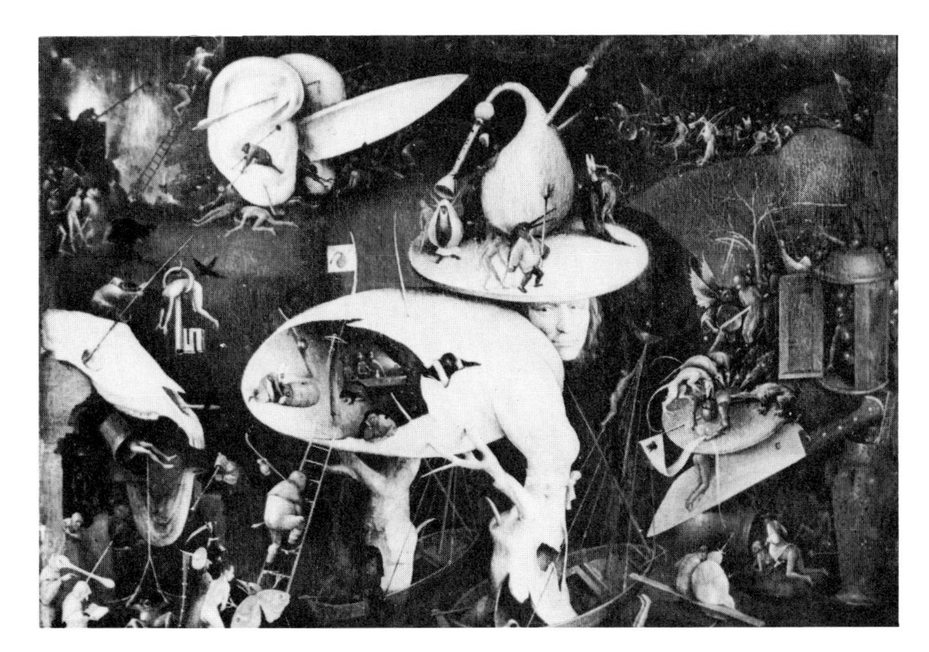

Fig. 13.4. Detail of the right panel from Triptych of The Garden of Earthly Delights, showing the purposeful, though obscure, use of extreme body distortions in artistic production. (photo: MAS, Barcelona) Prado, Madrid.

psychological mechanism of repression, a mental process by which a person forces out of conscious awareness and into the unconscious memories, thoughts, and wishes too shameful or frightening to bear (see Chaps. 4 and 14).

Schilder conceived the idea that each person develops a mental picture of himself, a *body image*. This image is not merely a schematic diagram of the body and its parts, but has emotional significance and is part of the total personality of the individual. Schilder also proposed that certain regions of the body are especially strongly represented in the body image. He reflected the influence of psychoanalysis on his thinking by maintaining that the oral, anal, and genital regions (the *erotogenic* or *erogenous* zones) are particularly prominent. Furthermore, Schilder proposed that the body image is not necessarily held within the confines of the physical body itself. During intimate social contact, one's body image may extend outward and incorporate the body image of another person. In more ordinary circumstances, the body image incorporates the clothes one wears, the cigarette extending from the mouth, or the pencil or wrench with which one manipulates objects in the environment.

These provocative ideas have been highly influential in stimulating the development of a variety of techniques for measuring body image and its relation to other psychological variables. Because of the lack of uniformity concerning which specific techniques are best for assessing body image, the next three sections of this chapter are devoted to a selective description of some of the more interesting and popular methods that have been proposed and subjected to empirical evaluation.

Draw-a-Person Technique

In 1949, Karen Machover published what was to become a highly influential, albeit controversial book, *Personality Projection in the Drawing of the Human Figure.*

Fig. 13.5 Detail from "The Maze," showing a portion of a patient's skull sawn open to portray his own fantasies. (From Carstairs, 1963)

Her thesis was that, when a subject draws a picture of a human body, he actually provides a picture of his own personality. His way of approaching the task and the final product of his efforts reveal his inner feelings about himself, his emotional conflicts, and his typical modes of adaptation to the environment. Machover's theories were not buttressed by strong research support, but her ideas were intriguing, and the draw-a-person technique rapidly became a popular test of personality and body image.

As it is typically administered, the draw-a-person test is a *projective technique*, which means a task that is relatively free of constraint and leaves the subject at liberty to express his own attitudes, beliefs, and personality in his performance. The draw-a-person test (the DAP) is administered in such a way as to allow the subject to produce any kind of drawing he wishes. He is merely given a pencil and sheet of paper and asked to draw a picture of a person. If he asks questions, such as, "Do you want a man or a woman?" the examiner replies, "Anything you like," or "Whichever you choose." Sometimes, if a subject draws only a bust, the examiner will make note of this and hand the subject another sheet of paper, asking him to draw a full figure. After the first figure is completed, the subject is given another sheet of paper and asked to draw a figure "of the opposite sex." Both drawings are usually used in evaluating personality.

Examples of the first drawings produced by two normal college men under standard testing conditions are presented in Figure 13.6. The drawing on the left was judged to show moderate disturbance of body image, while little or no evidence of such disturbance was inferred from the drawing on the right.

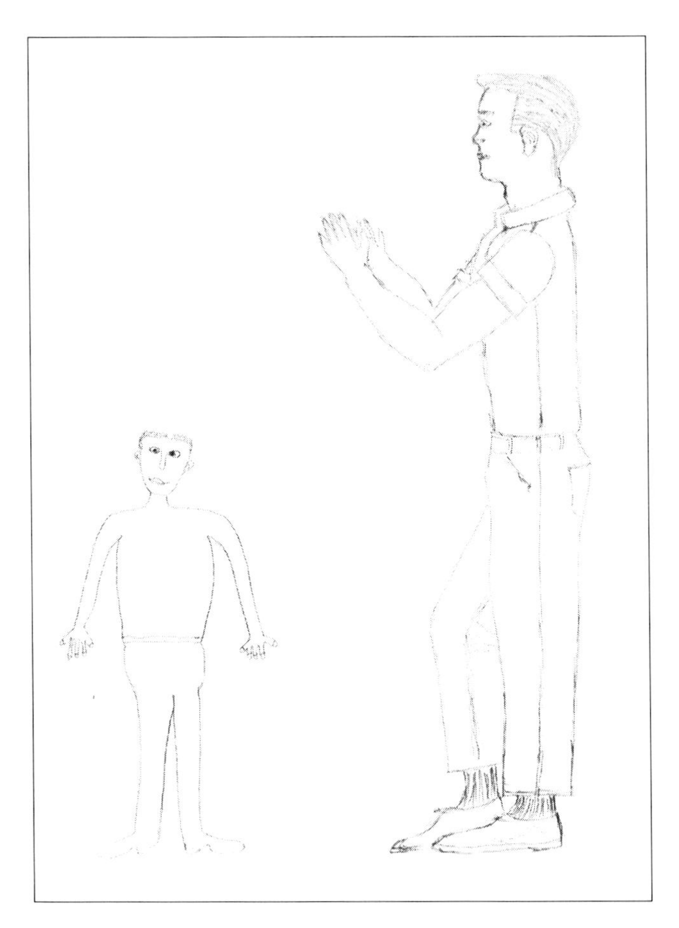

Fig. 13.6. Figure drawings produced by two college men. The one on the left was judged to show moderate disturbance of body image.

Research on the DAP

As might be expected, the prospect of a relatively simple test of personality was of considerable interest to a large number of psychologists, particularly those who wished to learn more about the body image. There is every reason to suppose that projections of personality into drawings of the human figure are heavily affected by the image one has of one's own body. In 1957, Swensen reviewed 87 scientific publications on the draw-a-person technique. The same author reviewed 126 additional publications in 1968, while Roback, devoting himself to a similar task, reviewed 79.

It is obviously not possible to summarize such a large body of research here. However, by considering a single hypothesis and some of the attempts to confirm it, a great deal can be learned about how some psychologists work and how complex an apparently simple proposition about human behavior can become when it is subjected to close scientific scrutiny. The hypothesis examined, that of *isomorphism* (*iso*-means *equal* or *alike; morph*-means *form*), is that the form or shape of a figure drawing displays at least the most important forms or features of the person's actual body, such as its general shape or proportions.

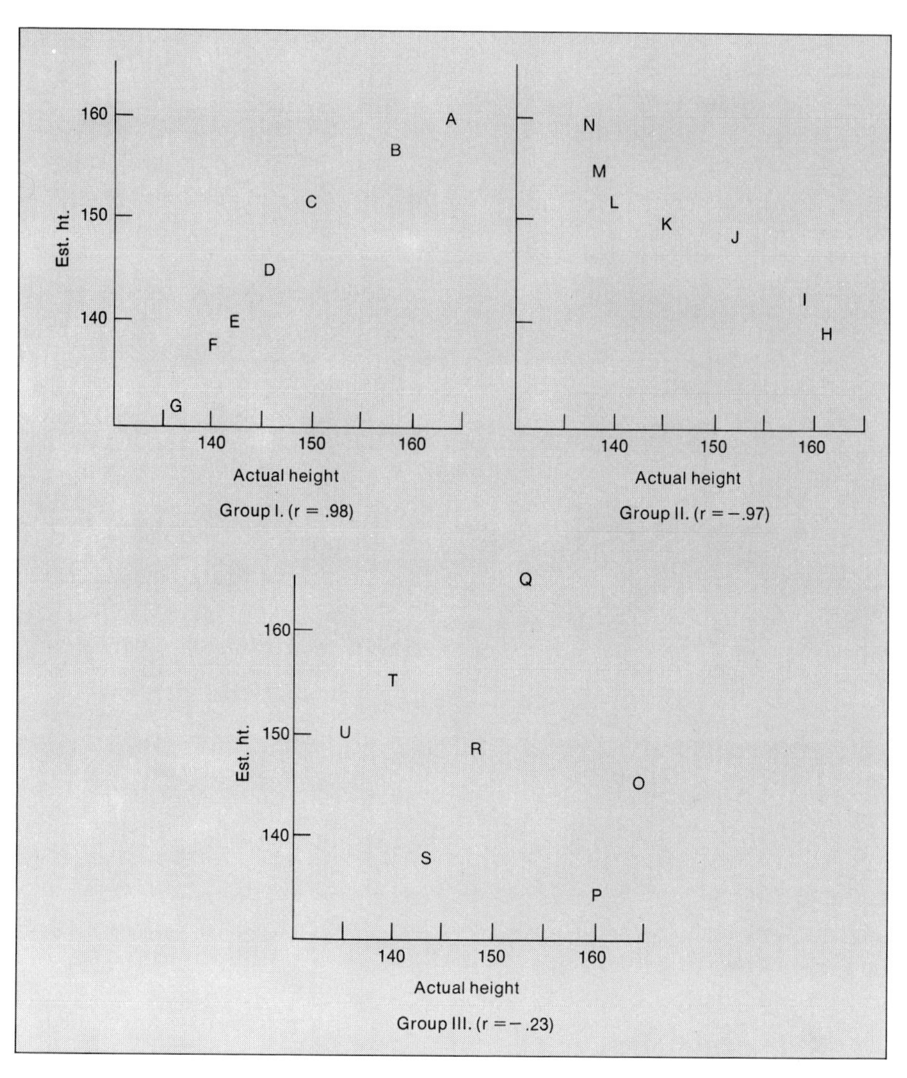

Fig. 13.7. Scattergrams for correlation coefficients (*r*) representing strong positive, strong negative, and unsystematic correlations.

A study of children's drawings. Silverstein and Robinson (1961) asked children in the sixth grade of a public school to draw a whole person and then a person of the other sex. After the drawings were completed, the children estimated their own height and weight and were asked how tall they would like to be and how much they would like to weigh. Finally, each child's actual height and weight were determined.

These children's drawings were measured for height, and an estimate of weight was obtained from each. "Weight" was estimated by multiplying height by the square of the width of the drawing at the waistline, which produces an estimate of the volume the figure would occupy if it were actually three-dimensional. Use of the estimate is justified by the everyday observation that body volume is closely correlated with body weight (a large person weighs more than a small one). The main question was whether taller and heavier children drew taller and heavier figures.

To answer it, the investigators calculated *correlation coefficients* to represent the degree of correspondence between actual body measurements and measurements of the figures drawn by each child.

To determine the correlation between actual height and height of figure, the two sets of measures are paired for each subject, and mathematical formulas are applied to obtain an index which may range from +1.00 (perfect correspondence) through 0.00 (randomness) to −1.00 (perfect negative correspondence). Suppose that the taller children drew the taller figures, while the shorter children drew the shorter figures; the correlation in this event would be positive and close to 1.00. However, if the relationship were reversed and the taller children drew the shorter figures, and vice versa, the correlation would be negative and close to 1.00. If there were no relationship of any kind between children's actual heights and the heights of the figures they drew, the correlation value would be close to zero. Diagrams (called scattergrams) for various degrees of correlation are shown in Figure 13.7. The hypothetical subjects are represented by the letters A through U. A high positive correlation shows up as a nearly straight line from the lower left to the upper right of the scattergram. A high negative correlation produces a nearly straight line from the upper left to the lower right, while a random correlation shows as an unorganized display. The actual values of the correlation coefficients that summarize the data are shown in each part of Figure 13.7. We have had occasion to consider values of correlation coefficients in several previous chapters, and Chapter 14 shows how important they are in the study of other aspects of personality.

The values of the correlation coefficients that Silverstein and Robinson calculated between the actual heights and weights of the children and the heights and weights of the two figures each of them drew were very low, ranging from −.23 to −.11. There was virtually no correspondence between actual body characteristics and the characteristics of the drawings. This does not indicate that the children simply did not know how big they were, because the correlation between estimated and actual height was .86, and the correlation between estimated and actual weight was .95.

Can the hypothesis now be rejected with certainty? The answer has to be "no," because there are other possible reasons for failure of the study to confirm it. For instance, perhaps the hypothesis is correct for adults but not for children. Or it may be that people represent things about their bodies other than height and weight in their drawings. It is necessary to study the problem further.

A study of drawings from adults. Apfeldorf and Smith (1966) had 52 women college students provide drawings of the human figure. One week later, these same students were photographed. Drawings and photographs were presented to judges, whose task was to attempt to match the drawings with the photographs.

For various reasons that need not concern us here, the number of drawings and photographs used was reduced to 25 pairs. Five photographs and five drawings were presented at a time, and it was found that the judges' overall average accuracy was about 1.2 correctly matched drawings and photographs in each set of five pairs. This is not very high, and the investigators were far from eager to conclude that their results lend strong support to the hypothesis of isomorphism between the real body and drawings of the human figure.

Further investigations. The two studies already considered may be enough to convince many people that the hypothesis of isomorphism can be discarded with a fair degree of certainty. Others might point out that the tests of the hypothesis have not been entirely fair. Apfeldorf and Smith's study used only drawings produced by women, and its judges did not really see the women who produced the drawings; they judged only photographs.

Another objection might be that there would be no special reason in either study for subjects to project their bodies into their drawings. After all, despite its general importance, the body is rarely the center of attention for a physically healthy person. It may be reasonable to expect someone who has something wrong with his body to express his concern in a drawing, but it is not logical to expect *everyone* to do so. An obvious way to test this proposal is to examine drawings produced by persons with physical disabilities. One would think that if anyone is going to project the real features of his body into his drawing of the human figure, it would be a person who has a physical disability. There have been a number of studies of this type.

Unfortunately for the status of the hypothesis of isomorphism, none of these studies showed clear evidence of differences between drawings produced by persons with and without physical disabilities. Silverstein and Robinson (1956) found few significant differences between drawings produced by children with and without physical disabilities; even experienced judges were unable to tell which drawings came from which group. Schmidt and McGowan (1959) found that judges could identify drawings by persons with disabilities at a rate about 8 per cent better than chance would allow. Johnson and Wawrzaszek (1961) found that judges could identify drawings by children with disabilities at a rate about 12 per cent better than could be achieved by random guessing. Centers and Centers (1963) found that even when amputee children were specifically instructed to "draw yourself," judges were only about 18 per cent more accurate than chance. Many of the self-portraits of the amputee children in this study included both arms, thus eliminating the most obvious clue to identity of the subjects. Since the children were not questioned about their drawings, there is no way of knowing why this occurred. It does indicate that even when a child is asked to draw himself, he may not do so with a high degree of accuracy.

Children's drawings of themselves and others. Although most of the results in the studies outlined above were statistically significant, none were of great magnitude. Even under the apparently ideal conditions in which children with missing limbs were asked to draw themselves, judges were not very successful in matching drawings with the subjects who produced them. These studies provide almost no support for the hypothesis that freely produced drawings of the human figure reflect the body attributes of the persons who produce them. Indeed, they may raise the question of whether drawings of the human figure convey anything psychologically meaningful. Perhaps a closer examination of the features of such drawings can provide some clues.

Gellert (1968) collected a series of drawings from 68 boys and 83 girls, 5.6 to 12.8 years of age. First each child drew a picture of a man, next he drew a picture of himself, and finally he drew an agemate of the other sex. The first picture was scored for intelligence according to standards established in 1926 by F.L. Goodenough, who discovered that maturity of drawing of the figure of a man could be assessed objectively and used as a measure of intellectual ability. The other two drawings were evaluated by a number of scores, such as measures of proportion, amount and accuracy of detail, height, symmetry, and quality of lines.

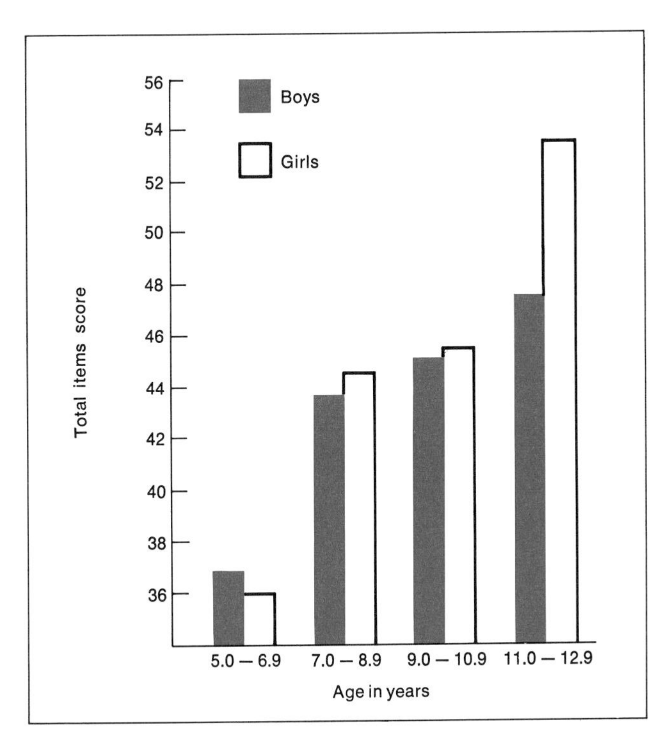

Fig. 13.8. Development in detail and accuracy of children's drawings of themselves. (Data from Gellert, 1968)

First, it is important to note that the children's drawings showed steady improvement with age; older children drew more detailed, accurate, symmetrical, and better proportioned figures than did younger children. Figure 13.8 shows how one of these scores (called the *total items* score), measuring accuracy and detail, increased with age. It seems clear that figure drawings at least measure something connected with maturity and differentiation of thought (Harris, 1963). (It is likely that the relative superiority of girls' drawings at ages 11 and 12 reflects their closer proximity to puberty than boys at that age.)

Second, this study again revealed no correlation between subjects' *actual* heights and the heights of their portraits. Thus, it fails to support the hypothesis of isomorphism, at least with regard to height.

Finally, the study contains some interesting data on consistency of drawing performances. The correlation between drawings of the self and drawings of an agemate of the other sex was .78 on the overall measure of detail and accuracy. The correlation on the same measure between self-drawings produced in the initial study and self-drawings produced one day to one week later was .88. These high values indicate that graphic and expressive styles of the children are consistent from one drawing to the next.

It therefore appears that the figure drawing technique does reveal something stable and important about the growing child. Apparently figure drawings provide some index to children's developing awareness of the body's structure and components. In addition, they probably reflect children's increased ability to control their own bodies in the production of more carefully executed pictures. If there is one thing the studies do not show, it is that children produce anything like accurate photographic representations of their own bodies.

Artistic Skill

If drawings of the human figure do not present an accurate picture of the body of the person who produces them, perhaps it is because other factors complicate the situation. Many persons who are asked to draw the human figure complain that the task is too difficult for them. Perhaps drawings do not reflect the body or personality of the subject, but primarily his artistic ability or skill.

The possibility that an artistic factor is involved in the drawing task is suggested first by the fact that psychologically untrained judges have often been able to evaluate drawings just as effectively as trained judges. Perhaps the judges actually evaluate the artistic merits of drawings (which would theoretically be obvious to anyone) rather than any special psychological "signs" or "indicators" which can be recognized only by the specially trained. Further evidence comes from studies that compare psychologists' ratings of drawings with independent ratings of artistic quality. In one study, Feldman and Hunt (1958) asked two art instructors to rate various body parts for drawing difficulty. They then examined figure drawings for "signs" of emotional disturbance of the type mentioned by Machover (erasures, distortion, heavy shading) and found that body parts which are most difficult to draw are the ones most likely to be judged as showing signs of emotional disturbances. Other studies on the same subject have yielded results consistent with those of Feldman and Hunt (Whitmyre, 1953; Sherman, 1958a, b).

Nichols and Strümpfer (1962) correlated a large number of measures of drawings obtained from 90 patients in a VA hospital and 107 college men. They grouped the correlations by a mathematical technique called *factor analysis* and determined that most of the differences among drawings could be accounted for by "general quality." Furthermore, they concluded that the overall quality of a person's drawings is probably not related to his psychological adjustment. Nichols and Strümpfer were reluctant to call this pervasive factor "artistic quality," for the term *artistic* is too ambiguous. Nevertheless, it is apparent that the factor is one of skill rather than personality. If the DAP is to be used as a measure of personality, skill in drawing must be taken into account when interpretations are made.

Status of the Draw-a-Person Technique

The studies cited above by no means cover the field of research on the draw-a-person technique, but they may be taken as typical. The conclusions to which they lead are certainly consistent with those that have been drawn from more extensive surveys of the available literature.

While some people may represent personal body characteristics in drawings of the human figure, the hypothesis of isomorphism has been firmly rejected as a principle of behavior that applies to all persons. The factor of overall quality of drawing seems to be the most important cue to which judges respond when evaluating figure drawings. Overall quality, in turn, seems to depend upon the skill of the subject and the varying degrees of difficulty with which different body parts can be drawn. Research on the psychological significance of specific signs (shading of hair, concealment of hands, and so on) cannot be effectively conducted unless quality of drawings and the fact that some body parts are more difficult than others to draw are taken into account (Swensen, 1968).

Lack of firm research support for hypotheses derived from assumptions about the meaning of human figure drawings has not prevented psychologists from using

Fig. 13.9. Example of an inkblot, of the type used in projective tests of personality.

the draw-a-person technique as a diagnostic device. This is in part because the test is quick and relatively easy to administer, and the busy clinician finds such devices attractive. Mainly, however, the draw-a-person technique continues to be popular because it is intuitively appealing. The approach *seems* like a good idea, and some experienced clinicians are capable of using it with remarkable effectiveness in arriving at descriptions of individual subjects. Despite the volume of research that has been conducted on this method of personality assessment, it still remains to be determined whether and how drawings of the human figure express the characteristics of the persons who produce them.

Body Image Boundaries

In 1958, Fisher and Cleveland published reports of research on a projective measure of one aspect of the body image: its function as a psychological boundary between the self and the environment. These investigators proposed that each person experiences himself as existing *within* his own body. The body therefore serves as a kind of protective screen which preserves personal integrity and relates the self within to the environment without. Fisher and Cleveland further proposed that the boundary properties of the experienced body are revealed in a person's responses to inkblots, such as those used in the Rorschach or Holtzman Inkblot technique (Fig. 13.9).

Inkblot tests are projective techniques in which the subject is asked to describe what he sees in, or can "make out of," a meaningless (though usually symmetrical) blob of ink on a piece of paper. The test is based on the proposition that responses to such objectively meaningless stimuli contain projections of the subject's personality. After all, if the blot has no meaning itself, where can a response come from except the memory, thoughts, and fancies of the subject?

Not all responses to inkblots reflect boundary properties of the body, but of those that do, Fisher and Cleveland recognize two types. *Barrier* responses emphasize the separation of self from environment, and are illustrated by responses which emphasize boundary definiteness (for example, an armored car, a man covered with a blanket, a fort). *Penetration of boundary* responses emphasize the disruption or breakdown of a barrier (a bullet penetrating flesh, a torn coat, a fleecy cloud). Notice that the responses do not have to mention the body or its parts; it is assumed that attitudes and feelings about the body are also projected into perceptions of nonbody objects.

Fisher and Cleveland have reported a host of studies on barrier and penetration scores. Their survey of research from 1958 to 1967 alone contains 106 references. On the basis of their review of the literature, these authors conclude that "the state of the individual's boundaries seems to be a fundamental modifier which plays a role in the entire continuum from physiological reactivity to social interaction" (Fisher and Cleveland, 1968, p. 394).

Body Image Boundaries and Body Experience

Interest in body image boundaries has been extensive. Barrier and penetration scores have been correlated with everything from locus of bodily symptoms of physical illness to behavior in small groups. For present purposes, one set of investigations will be representative of many others.

These studies were designed to establish the existence of a relationship between the barrier score and reports of actual body experience (Fisher and Fisher, 1964). In each study, about 100 college subjects were first administered an inkblot test to establish their barrier scores.

Study I. In this research, subjects were asked simply to sit for five minutes and report any prominent body sensations that occurred. They made their reports by checking on a sheet of paper one of four body regions: skin, stomach, muscle, and heart. For each subject, the sum of sensations reported from skin and muscle was designated the *exterior* score; the sum of sensations reported from the stomach and heart was designated the *interior* score. The final score for each subject was the difference between exterior and interior scores, calculated so that a high positive score represented relative prominence of exterior sensations.

When this score was correlated with the barrier scores, the resulting coefficient was .33. This value is statistically significant for the size of the group studied (it is unlikely to have occurred by chance), but it is not very large.

Study II. Subjects in this research were asked to reminisce about 30 situations (when you were angry, when you were tired, when you felt very successful, and so on). For each reminiscence they reported whether their main sensations came from the skin, stomach, muscles, or heart.

Again, the exterior minus interior score was correlated with barrier scores from the inkblot test. In one group, the value of the correlation was .15 (not significant); in a second group, the correlation was .47. This study therefore produced conflicting results.

Study III. In this investigation, subjects swallowed a large capsule which they were told contained a harmless drug that could nonetheless produce a variety of body sensations. Actually, the capsule contained an inert substance. Fifteen minutes later, each subject reported on the effects of the drug by checking a list of skin, muscle, heart, and stomach sensations.

A low but significant correlation (.33) was found between reports of exterior symptoms and barrier scores for male subjects only. The correlation for women was .11.

Study IV. In the final study of the series, subjects were shown a list of 20 phrases describing sensations from various parts of the body ("skin itch," "stomach full," "heart pounding," "muscle stiff"). After a one minute exposure to the list, subjects were asked to recall as many phrases as they could. This time the exterior minus interior score correlated .52 with barrier scores in one group and .38 with barrier scores in a second group.

Conclusions from the Studies

These investigations established the existence of modest positive correlations between reports of body sensations and inkblot responses that are scored for evidence of concentration upon the barrier properties of the body image boundary. The student may find it disappointing that the correlation figures are not higher; it would certainly be easier if the values were closer to .7 or .8. However, the results of these studies are typical, not only of much research on the body image, but of research on personality in general. They allow the investigator to make broadly applicable statements about relationships among variables, but they are too low to permit specific predictions in individual cases.

Verbal Measures

Little use has been made of direct verbal techniques in the study of body experience. A questionnaire has been developed to measure subjects' satisfaction with their bodies (Jourard and Remy, 1957; Jourard and Secord, 1954, 1955; Secord and Jourard, 1953), and attempts have been made at applying word association techniques to assessing the importance of the body in the personality (Secord, 1953). Judging by the decreasing use of these instruments in recent scientific literature, little has come of these efforts. Psychologists' attention has been largely directed toward the more subtle and romantic projective approaches, such as the draw-a-person technique and responses to inkblots.

Despite current general rejection of verbal techniques, they merit more than casual mention. A particularly promising device is the basically simple method called *associative listing*. It consists of asking the subject to name a given number of items of a particular kind (such as occupations, colors, or automobiles). Bennett (1960) had three groups of subjects list ten names of body parts. The subjects were 110 workers from an electronics plant and a hospital, 29 persons who were blind from birth, and 83 patients with schizophrenia. What concerned the investigator was possible differences in the type and location of body parts that would be listed. Bennett considered his study to be an investigation of body *concept* (the way one thinks about his body) rather than body *image* (the way one imagines or perceives his body to be), but it is obviously relevant to any discussion of body experience as a whole.

The major finding from this investigation was that some parts of the body were significantly more frequently mentioned by blind subjects than by sighted subjects. In Figure 13.10, the parts more frequently mentioned by both groups

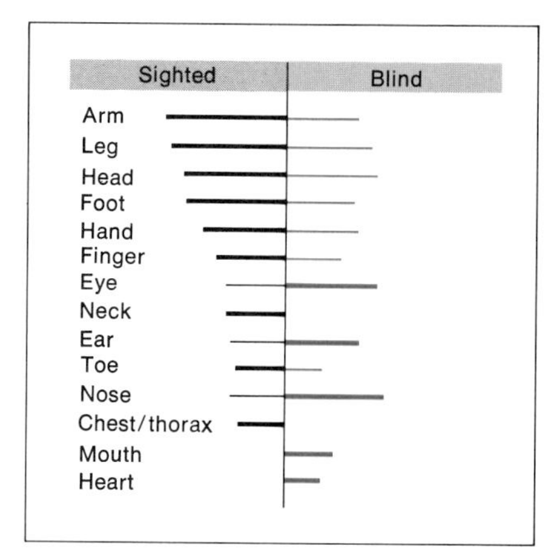

Fig. 13.10. Comparison of the frequency of mention of body parts by blind and sighted persons. (From Bennett, 1960)

are depicted by heavy lines; the length of each line represents the frequency of mention of each part. Notice the general tendency for the blind to mention portions of the face, such as eye, ear, nose, and mouth. Notice also the tendency for sighted subjects to place greater emphasis upon organs of active environmental contact, such as arm, leg, hand, and finger.

A second finding of considerable interest was that differences between listings provided by schizophrenic and normal subjects were negligible. Although many schizophrenics claim to have bizarre body experiences, no gross distortions of body concept were evident in this research. You may recall that Bender and his co-workers, working with double simultaneous tactile stimulation, also failed to discover differences between schizophrenics and normal adults. It appears that some aspects of body experience are relatively immune even to rather severe disturbances of the personality.

Perception of Body Parts

An entirely different approach to the study of body experience has been taken by investigators who try to determine how accurately and by what means people perceive the physical properties of their own bodies as objects in space. In this type of research it is not uncommon to require a subject to estimate the lengths of parts of his own body, or to judge the distances between pairs of stimulated points on the surface of the body. The investigator often tries to alter subjects' perceptions by manipulating the conditions under which they are made.

For example, Werner, Wapner, and Comalli (1957) and Wapner, Werner, and Comalli (1958) had subjects estimate the widths of their heads. Half the judgments were made while the examiner touched the subjects' temples lightly with his fingertips; the other half were made without touch. (Subjects' eyes were closed throughout the procedure.) Head width was estimated as smaller when touch was present.

In a closely related experiment, Humphries (1959) had subjects judge apparent arm length with and without administration of light touch to the fingertips (arms extended forward, eyes closed). Fourteen of 16 subjects reported that the touched arm felt shorter than the untouched arm. Shontz (1969) had subjects make judgments of forearm length under similar conditions. About two-thirds of his subjects reported that their arms felt shorter when touched lightly than when untouched.

These findings suggest that body parts are experienced as smaller when the boundary of the body is emphasized or called to attention by stimulation. Evidently some sort of *contrast effect* is involved, for the influence of stimulation of the body boundary seems to depend upon the experience of an actual *change* in body articulation. Extensive studies of judgments of distances on the body have shown no differences between estimates of head width by persons whose heads are continuously articulated by the wearing of glasses and persons who do not wear glasses. Neither have appreciable differences been found between judgments provided by subjects for whom distances on the body are defined only by two point touch, and judgments provided by other subjects for whom body distances are defined only by verbal description (Shontz, 1969).

Fuhrer and Cowan (1967) found that subjects' estimates of upper arm and hand length became larger after these parts were actively moved by the subject. Wapner, McFarland, and Werner (1963) found that an arm extended toward open environmental space is experienced as longer than an arm extended toward a wall one foot away. Other studies have shown that arm length is perceived as greater when the subject is instructed to point to an object in the distant environment than when he is not so instructed (Wapner and Werner, 1965), and that apparent arm length is greater when the subject uses his hand for actively touching objects than when his hand is passively touched by objects or no touch at all is involved (Schlater, Baker, and Wapner, 1969).

Porzemsky, Wapner, and Glick (1965) found that when subjects are asked to point toward a target, the experience of arm length and target distance can be altered by asking subjects to assume either a *polarized* or *depolarized* attitude. In the polarized attitude, the subject is asked to think of a separation and independence between self (arm) and object (target); in the depolarized attitude he thinks of self and object as psychologically fused. It was found that the arm seems slightly shorter in the polarized state than in the depolarized state. As in the articulation phenomenon, it is probably the *change* of attitude that makes the difference in this research. The observed differences might not occur in a study that uses one set of subjects in the polarized attitude and a different set in the depolarized attitude; this possibility remains open for investigation.

Bauermeister, Wapner, and Werner (1967) tilted subjects to the right and left in a chair. While tilted, the subjects adjusted a luminous rod to apparent correspondence with their longitudinal body axis. Apparent body position was uniformly found to be displaced from actual body position in the direction of body tilt; that is, subjects overestimated the extent of tilt they actually experienced.

Finally, Fink and Shontz (1960) found that subjects with hemiplegia underestimated distances on their bodies more than did subjects with illnesses not involving the central nervous system or subjects with no physical disabilities. Underestimation in the hemiplegics was peculiar to stimuli on the body and did not simply represent a tendency for them to produce smaller responses to all objects; they were just as accurate in judging distances between visually perceived points in the environment as were subjects in the other two groups. Strangely enough, constriction of responses in subjects with hemiplegia was not confined to parts of the body affected by the disability (hemiplegia affects either the right or left side of the body), but occurred for estimates of body distances on both sides of the body.

Apparently a number of factors are capable of influencing estimates of distances on the body, not the least of which is the method by which estimates are obtained (Shontz, 1969). For example, it makes a difference whether subjects are asked to adjust simple markers on a rod to indicate their judgments, or are required to select from an array of pictures of body parts the one that most closely matches a particular distance on their own bodies. Differences in body perception between schizophrenic and nonschizophrenic subjects are demonstrable only when the latter (configurational) method is used. When the measurement situation contains no actual representations of body parts to be judged, schizophrenics are as accurate as normal subjects.

Other measurement conditions also affect judgments of distances on the body. Estimates of distances on the body are more sensitive to starting position effects than are estimates of lengths of nonbody objects. The starting position effect is the difference between a subject's responses when the apparatus he adjusts is initially set in different positions. If the apparatus is set at an initial value which is too small or too low, responses tend to underestimate stimulus magnitudes; if the initial value is too large or too high, responses tend to overestimate stimulus magnitudes. Relative underestimation of body distances also occurs when subjects make their judgments by drawing pictures of their own bodies to specific scale or estimate body distances as percentages of total body height, instead of adjusting markers on a rod.

There seems to be no one right way to measure perception of the body. The best one can do is to establish a set of standard measurement conditions and use these conditions consistently in a systematically designed series of investigations. Shontz (1969) defined one such set of conditions and tested a large number of normal subjects with his apparatus. He found that errors in judgments of a sample of distances on the body assumed a characteristic pattern in which head width and forearm length were consistently overestimated, while hand and foot length were consistently underestimated (Fig. 13.11). Note that the only marked difference between sexes occurs for the stimulus *waist width*, which women tend to overestimate more than men.

This pattern remained stable even when measurement conditions were systematically varied from those defined as *standard*. On the basis of several experiments, Shontz concluded that his data are consistent with the proposition that judgments of distances on the body are made by a somewhat different perceptual process than are judgments of comparable distances in nonbody space. Judgments of distances on the body appear to be strongly influenced by cognitive schemata of the type proposed by Head and discussed earlier in this chapter. By contrast, judgments of distances in the environment are more strictly determined by information available in the stimulus itself; in that sense, they are less *subjective* and more *objective* than judgments of distances on the body.

Shontz found no correlation between accuracy of judgment of distances on the body and traits of personality. He contended that the experience of the body as a physical object in space is quite different from the experience of the body as a part of the personality or self. He also maintained that different techniques of research are needed for the study of these two kinds of body experience.

Conclusion

Interest in the psychological study of body experience began with observation of disturbances of body experience in patients with amputations (phantom limbs), damage to the brain (anosognosia), and schizophrenia (bizarre beliefs about body

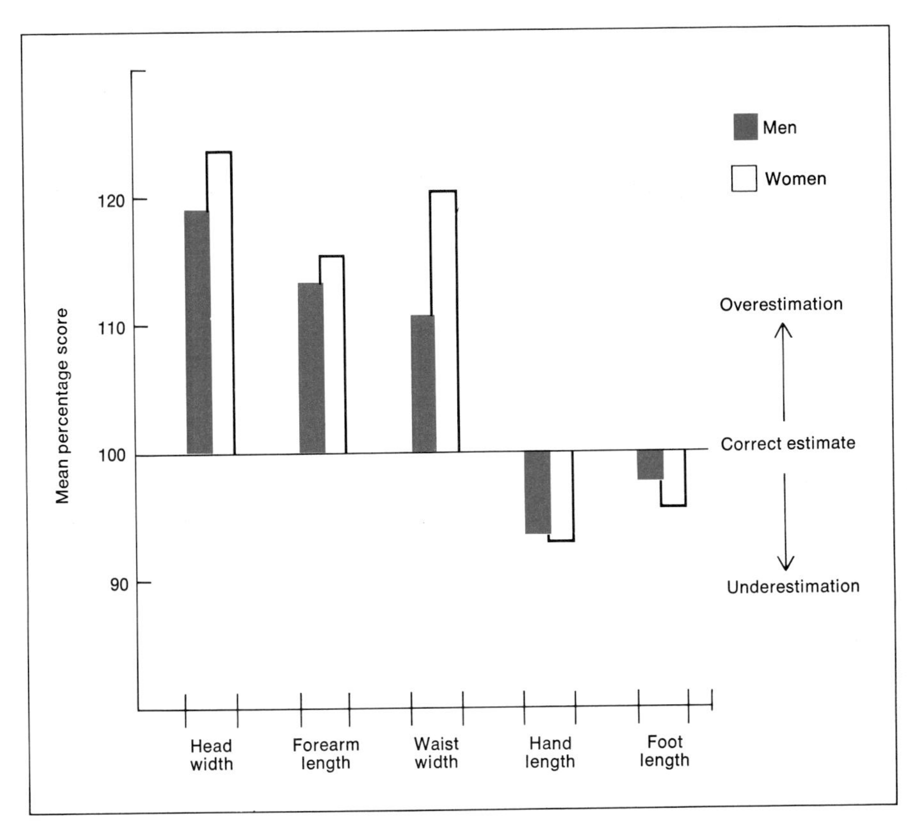

Fig. 13.11. Tendencies to overestimate or underestimate distances on the body. Estimates expressed as percentages of actual body distances. (From Shontz, 1969)

states). Clinical observation led to the hypothesis that body perception is guided by cognitive schemata, central processes that provide psychological models or maps of body structure and movement. The theory of body schemata was extended and elaborated to include the idea that body experience has emotional significance and plays an important part in development of the personality through the mechanism of the body image.

The draw-a-person technique was invented as a projective device for studying personality, and has been used extensively in body image research. It has long been known that children's drawings of the human figure provide reasonably accurate estimates of intellectual development, and there is evidence that children's individual graphic styles are consistent from drawing to drawing over at least a short period of time. However, there is no strong evidence to indicate that people portray their own bodies when they produce projective drawings of the human figure. Judgments of personality based on human figure drawings seem to reflect level of artistic skill at least as much as the personality of the subject. Nonetheless, the draw-a-person technique is still a popular diagnostic instrument in the clinical situation. It has intuitive appeal, and some clinicians are capable of using it effectively for arriving at descriptions of personality.

Body image boundary scores derived from projective responses to inkblots have also proved popular in research. These scores have been shown to correlate modestly with a number of other psychological variables. The relationships are often statistically significant, but not of sufficient magnitude to support predictions about individuals.

Verbal techniques for assessing body experience enjoyed a short period of popularity but have not been exploited to the fullest extent possible. The technique of associative listing appears to have especially interesting potential.

Studies of perception of body part sizes and body distances reveal that body perception is influenced by a variety of factors, including changes in articulation of the body surface, active movement of body parts, relation of the body to the environment, attitudes, and conditions under which measurements are taken.

Research of several types suggests that such functional psychiatric disorders as schizophrenia do not typically affect body perception adversely. This is somewhat surprising, since it has been known that schizophrenic individuals frequently report severe distortions of body experience. At the same time, the finding makes some sense, for, unlike the person with anosognosia, the schizophrenic is often quite capable of managing the everyday affairs of life (such as eating, walking, and reaching) that require reasonably accurate body perception for their successful execution. Apparently it is possible for a person to experience considerable subjective confusion about his own body and still be able to produce adequate objective judgments of his body's physical characteristics (Cappon and Banks, 1965).

It has not been possible in this chapter to narrow our interests to a specific problem and trace a single line of investigation from beginning to end. Instead, it has been necessary to examine a variety of approaches, each of which attempts with varying degrees of success to study body experience in its own way. That is partly because psychology has not yet developed adequately effective techniques for assessing body experience. The body is an extremely complex stimulus object, and theorists who say that body experience is an important factor in virtually everything we do are probably largely correct.

Oddly enough, research interest in the problem of body experience has been quite recent in psychology. Directly relevant investigations are almost absent from the scientific literature before about 1950. Therefore, it is perhaps not surprising that so many of the studies available are somewhat weak when judged by the standards of mature scientific method. The subject of body experience poses a host of problems for the psychological investigator. Enough is known to make the subject interesting and to pose a sizable challenge for future investigators. Hopefully, in the next few years, that challenge will be successfully met.

Glossary

Anosognosia: denial of illness, especially of hemiplegia.

Barrier responses: responses to inkblots that reflect separation of the self from the external environment and imperviousness of the body image boundary.

Body image: a hypothetical "mental picture" of the body that is important in personality development and functioning.

Body schema (pl., schemata): a psychological representation of the location and position of body parts in space.

Contrast effect: the enhancement of one stimulus by virtue of its difference from or opposition to another.

Correlation coefficient: an index of the degree of relationship between pairs of measures; perfect correlation is indicated by coefficients of $+1.00$ and -1.00; a coefficient of zero corresponds to no relationship.

DAP: the draw-a-person test, a projective technique to measure body image.
Depersonalization: loss of the integrity of the self-body relationship; sense of detachment of self from body.
Displacement: localization of a stimulus in the wrong place on the body; displacement occurs in the direction of the most dominant region of the body schema.
Distal: distant; away from the center of the body.
Dominance: a structural principle of body schema organization; the head is the most dominant body region.
Erogenous (erotogenic) zones: regions of the body which produce sexual excitation when stimulated.
Extinction (perceptual): failure to perceive one of a pair of stimuli, both of which can be perceived when presented separately (not to be confused with the extinction procedure in conditioning; see Glossary, Chap. 1).
Hemiplegia: paralysis or weakness of the right or left side of the body.
Isomorphism: having the same, equivalent, or closely analogous form.
Penetration responses: responses to inkblots that indicate weakness of the body image boundary and vulnerability of the self to environmental stimuli.
Phantom limb: the experience of sensations from an absent or denervated arm or leg; phantoms also occur (though less frequently) for other body parts that are removed or denervated.
Projective test (or technique): an unstructured task, employing ambiguous stimuli; the subject's behavior on such a task reveals his personality characteristics.
Proprioceptive: self-generated.
Proximal: close by; near the center of the body.
Repression: forceful exclusion from consciousness of threatening thoughts or memories; a personality defense (see Glossary, Chap. 8).
Schizophrenia: see Glossary, Chapter 15.
Telescoping: the feeling that the phantom extremity of a lost limb exists within the remaining stump of the limb.

References

Apfeldorf, M., and W.J. Smith. The representation of the body self in human figure drawings. *J. proj. tech. and pers. assess.*, 1966, **30,** 283–289.

Bauermeister, M., S. Wapner, and H. Werner. Method of stimulus presentation and apparent body position under lateral body tilt. *Perceptual and Motor Skills*, 1967, **24,** 43–50.

Bender, M.B., M.A. Green, and M. Fink. Patterns of perceptual organization with simultaneous stimuli. *AMA Arch. Neurol. Psychiat.*, 1954, **72,** 233–255.

Bender, M.B., M.F. Shapiro, and A.W. Schappell. Extinction phenomenon in hemiplegia. *AMA Arch. Neurol. Psychiat.*, 1949, **62,** 717–724.

Bennett, D.H. The body concept. *J. ment. Sci.*, 1960, **160,** 56–75.

Cappon, D., and R. Banks. Orientational perception. II. Body perception in depersonalization. *Arch. gen. Psychiat.*, 1965, **13,** 375–379.

Carstairs, G.M. Art and psychotic illness. *Abbottempo*, 1963, **1** (3), 15–31.

Centers, L., and R. Centers. A comparison of the body images of amputee and non-amputee children as revealed in figure drawings. *J. proj. tech. and pers. assess.*, 1963, **27,** 158–165.

Feldman, M.J., and R.G. Hunt. The relation of difficulty in drawing to ratings of adjustment based on human figure drawings. *J. consult. Psychol.*, 1958, **22,** 217–219.

Fink, S.L., and F.C. Shontz. Body image disturbances in chronically ill individuals, *J. nerv. ment. Dis.*, 1960, **131,** 234–240.

Fisher, S., and S.E. Cleveland. *Body image and personality.* (2nd rev. ed.). New York: Dover, 1968.

Fisher, S., and R.L. Fisher. Body image boundaries and patterns of body perception. *J. abnorm. soc. Psychol.*, 1964, **68,** 255–262.

Fuhrer, M.J., and C.O. Cowan. Influence of active movements, illumination, and sex on estimates of body-part size. *Perceptual and Motor Skills*, 1967, **24,** 979–985.

Gellert, E. Comparison of children's self-drawings with their drawings of other persons. *Perceptual and Motor Skills*, 1968, **26,** 123–138.

Goodenough, F.L. *Measurement of intelligence by drawings*. New York: Harcourt, Brace & World, 1926.

Haber, W.B. Effects of loss of limb on sensory functions. *J. Psychol.*, 1955, **40,** 115–123.

———. Reactions to loss of limb: Physiological and psychological aspects. *Ann. N.Y. Acad. Sciences*, 1958, **74,** 14–24.

Harris, D.B. *Children's drawings as measures of intellectual maturity*. New York: Harcourt, Brace & World, 1963.

Head, H. *Studies in neurology*. Vol. II. London: Oxford University Press, 1920.

Humphries, O.A. Effect of articulation of finger tip through touch on apparent length of outstretched arm. Unpublished master's thesis, Clark University, 1959.

Johnson, O.G., and F. Wawrzaszek. Psychologists' judgments of physical handicap from H-T-P drawings. *J. consult. Psychol.*, 1961, **25,** 284–287.

Jourard, S.M., and R.M. Remy. Individual variance score: An index of the degree of differentiation of the self and the body image. *J. clin. Psychol.*, 1957, **13,** 62–63.

Jourard, S.M., and P.F. Secord. Body cathexis and the ideal female figure. *J. abnorm. soc. Psychol.*, 1955, **50,** 243–246.

———. Body size and body cathexis. *J. consult. Psychol.*, 1954, **18,** 184.

Kolb, L.C. Disturbances of the body image. In S. Arieti (Ed.), *American handbook of psychiatry*. Vol. 1. New York: Basic Books, 1959.

———. *The painful phantom*. Springfield, Ill.: Charles C Thomas, 1954.

———. Phantom sensations, hallucinations and the body image. In L.J. West (Ed.), *Hallucinations*. New York: Grune and Stratton, 1962.

Machover, K. *Personality projection in the drawing of the human figure*. Springfield, Ill.: Charles C. Thomas, 1949.

Nichols, R.C., and D.J.W. Strümpfer. A factor analysis of draw-a-person test scores. *J. consult. Psychol.*, 1962, **26,** 156–161.

Porzemsky, J., S. Wapner, and J.A. Glick. Effect of experimentally-induced self-object cognitive attitudes on body and object perception. *Perceptual and Motor Skills*, 1965, **21,** 187–195.

Roback, H.B. Human figure drawings: their utility in the clinical psychologist's armamentarium for personality assessment. *Psychol. Bull.*, 1968, **70,** 1–19.

Schilder, P. *The image and appearance of the human body*. New York: International Universities Press, 1950.

Schlater, J., A.H. Baker, and S. Wapner. Body perception as a function of self-world orientation. Paper presented at the meeting of the Eastern Psychological Association, Philadelphia, April 1969.

Schmidt, L.D., and J.F. McGowan. The differentiation of human figure drawings. *J. consult. Psychol.*, 1959, **23,** 129–133.

Secord, P.F. Objectification of word-association procedures by the use of homonyms: A measure of body cathexis. *J. Pers.*, 1953, **21,** 479–495.

———, and S.M. Jourard. The appraisal of body cathexis: Body cathexis and the self. *J. consult. Psychol.*, 1953, **17,** 343–347.

Sherman, L.J. The influence of artistic quality on judgments of patient and non-patient status from human figure drawings. *J. proj. Tech.*, 1958, **22,** 338–340. (a)

———. Sexual differentiation or artistic ability? *J. clin. Psychol.*, 1958, **14,** 170–171. (b)

Shontz, F.C. *Perceptual and cognitive aspects of body experience*. New York: Academic Press, 1969.

Silverstein, A., and H. Robinson. The representation of orthopedic disability in children's figure drawings. *J. consult. Psychol.*, 1956, **20,** 333–341.

———. The representation of physique in children's figure drawings. *J. consult. Psychol.*, 1961, **25,** 146–148.

Simmel, M.L. The absence of phantoms for congenitally missing limbs. *Amer. J. Psychol.*, 1961, **74,** 467–470.

———. The conditions of occurrence of phantom limbs. *Proceedings of the American Philosophical Society*, 1958, **102,** 492–500.

———. On phantom limbs. *Arch. Neurol. Psychiat.*, 1956, **75,** 637–647. (a)

———. Phantom experiences following amputation in childhood. *Journal of Neurology and Neurosurgery*, 1962, **25,** 69–78.

———. Phantoms in patients with leprosy and in elderly digital amputees. *Amer. J. Psychol.*, 1956, **69,** 529–545. (b)

———. Phantoms, phantom pain and "denial." *Amer. J. Psychotherapy*, 1959, **13,** 603–613.

———. Psychological aftereffects of amputation. *Rehab. Couns. Bull.*, 1963, **6,** 75–83.

Swensen, C.H., Jr. Empirical evaluations of human figure drawings. *Psychol. Bull.*, 1957, **54,** 431–466.

———. Empirical evaluations of human figure drawings: 1957–1966. *Psychol. Bull.*, 1968, **70,** 20–44.

Wapner, S., J.H. McFarland, and H. Werner. Effect of visual spatial context on perception of one's own body. *Brit. J. Psychol.*, 1963, **54,** 41–49.

Wapner, S., and H. Werner. *The body percept*. New York: Random House, 1965.

———, and P.E. Comalli, Jr. Effect of enhancement of head boundary on head size and shape. *Perceptual and Motor Skills*, 1958, **8,** 319–325.

Weinstein, E.A., and R.L. Kahn. *Denial of illness*. Springfield, Ill.: Charles C Thomas, 1955.

Werner, H., S. Wapner, and P.E. Comalli, Jr. Effect of boundary on perception of head size. *Perceptual and Motor Skills*, 1957, **7,** 69–71.

Whitmyre, J.W. The significance of artistic excellence in the judgment of adjustment inferred from human figure drawings. *J. consult. Psychol.*, 1953, **17,** 421–422.

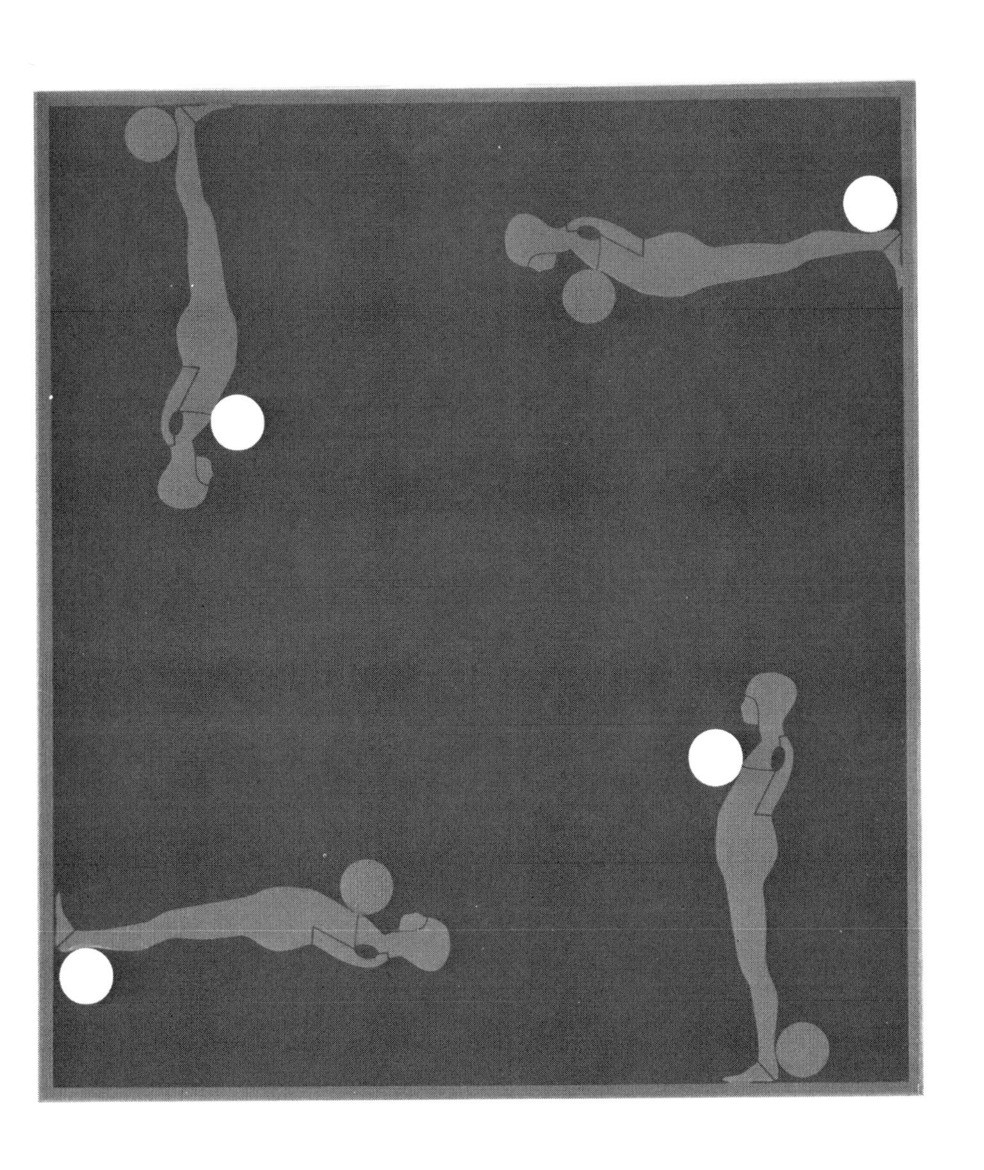

14 Individual Differences in Repression-Sensitization

Evolutionary theory teaches that biological survival is possible only for species that achieve adequate functional adaptation to their environments. A species becomes extinct when it is no longer structurally and behaviorally capable of sustaining its own existence in a constantly changing and none too friendly world. To early students of behavior, it seemed that same rule applied to individual human beings. Those who come to satisfactory terms with their environments survive successfully; those who fail fall by the wayside.

The apparent parallel between laws that determine the survival of species and those that determine the success of individuals intrigued Francis Galton (1822–1911), a brilliant mathematician and a half cousin of Charles Darwin. Galton was interested in the study of genius, which he regarded as an especially successful form of adaptation determined by hereditary factors (Boring, 1929). Though not in the mainstream of the psychology of his day, Galton anticipated important later developments in the study of behavior, and is now regarded as one of the founders of the important branch of psychology known as the study of individual differences, or sometimes as the correlational approach (Cronbach, 1957).

Another pioneer in the study of individual differences was an American psychologist, James McKeen Cattell (1860–1944). Cattell studied for three years with Wilhelm Wundt, one of the founders of experimental psychology (Chap. 1), but Cattell's interests were much different. Wundt devoted his energy to discovering universal psychological laws, principles that apply with minimum error to all persons. He followed the course established by Fechner, who felt that his famous psychophysical equation stated a universal relationship between mind (perception) and matter (stimulus). Cattell, however, was less concerned with discovering, for example, the average reaction time of a large group of subjects, than he was in trying to determine why it is that some persons typically and consistently react quickly while others, equally consistently, react slowly.

Cattell's most important contribution was his keen perception of the possibility of using laboratory techniques for assessing individual differences in behavioral capacities and skills. He showed how the power of the psychophysical methods (see Chap. 1) could be applied to answer questions raised by evolutionary doctrine but never before taken seriously by experimentalists. Cattell coined the term *mental test* and published many papers on the subject of psychological measurement.

The first practical mental test was developed by a French psychologist, Alfred Binet (see Chap. 1). Binet set himself the task of identifying children who could be expected to experience difficulty in ordinary classroom activities because of their lack of intellectual capacity. He first tested large numbers of children on many different tasks, using these data to establish the ages at which each task could be successfully performed by most normal children; that is, he *standardized* his test. Using the standards or *norms* derived from these investigations, he could compare the performance of any child with the performances of others of that age and determine whether this particular child was markedly above or below the standard for his age.

Mental testing received a boost in public popularity in World War I, when psychological tests were first given to large numbers of military personnel. The number and variety of available tests had multiplied many times over by the time of World War II. Since the 1940s, tests have been routinely employed not only to assess intelligence but to evaluate personality, aptitudes, achievement, and mental health. Today they are used by the military, in schools and universities, in industry, clinics, mental hospitals, and vocational guidance centers. It would be a rare person who grows up in the modern world without ever being exposed to a psychological test.

Practical applications of the principles of psychological measurement are most obvious and therefore most familiar to the general public. But tests serve the science of psychology in ways that are less well publicized, though no less important to the understanding of human behavior. It is axiomatic that a theoretical concept becomes useful only when it has been identified with specific, objective indices of its presence or magnitude. Consequently, much of the history of psychology consists of investigators' efforts to objectify theoretical ideas by developing appropriate operations for measuring them.

This chapter describes the development of a single test, designed to measure the personality dimension called *repression-sensitization*. The following section outlines early theoretical and experimental work that led to construction of the test. A brief summary of about four years' research on the test follows. Next, several specific investigations are examined in somewhat greater detail. Finally, an overview summarizes work with the test and examines its contribution to psychological science.

Background

Psychoanalytic Theory

The concept of repression was promulgated by Freud, who gave it a central place in his theory of the unconscious. Psychoanalytic theory proposes that repression is the primary form of psychological defense against instincts and impulses that are unacceptable to conscious awareness. These impulses and instincts, the most important of which Freud believed to be sexual in nature, press outward from the id (the hypothetical reservoir of psychic energy) toward overt expression. Their force is brought to bear on the ego (postulated to be the managerial or executive branch of the personality), which must respond to them in some way.

In making its response, the ego must take into account two other sets of determinants, one of which (the superego) is another hypothetical, internal, psychological structure. The superego is often equated with what we familiarly experience as the conscience: the "inner voice" that tells a person what is right and wrong, good and bad, meritorious or meritricious. However, it is more correct to say that the superego is the irrational or unreasonable component of the conscience, making demands which stem from punishments received early in childhood and cannot be altered by reason or rational argument. Ethical and moral judgments logically derived from an explicit system of value judgments can also be considered part of the conscience, but (unless they are merely rationalizations) they need not involve superego activity.

When the superego reacts negatively to an impulse from the id, it threatens the ego with punishment. The threat appears in the form of *anxiety*, a nameless, objectless sense of fear or danger that seems to come from nowhere and continues despite all efforts to control it by conscious mental activity. In response to anxiety, or to signs that anxiety is about to appear, the ego takes action against the dangerous impulse. It uses a portion of the energy available to it to force the impulse back into the unconscious id, from which it came; in short, it institutes repression.

The effect of repression is to create between id and ego forces a dynamic balance that is delicate and easily upset. When the ego relaxes, as when a person sleeps, repressed impulses express themselves symbolically in his fantasies and dreams (see Chap. 7). Even when the person is awake, an event or stimulus that reactivates the repressed impulse may allow the id to overcome the ego temporarily and activate impulsive behavior (for which the superego then makes the person feel guilty or ashamed). To prevent such slips, the ego develops other defenses, such as projection (ascribing to others impulses that are really our own), rationalization, and denial (see Chap. 8). These defenses are sometimes referred to as *secondary* defenses, because they protect and preserve the primary repressive balance but do not deal directly with the dangerous impulse.

Besides the intrapsychic forces of the id and superego, the ego must contend with external reality. Conditions in the environment may dictate the need to abort impulse expression. Unless they arouse the forces of the superego, however, such conditions do not impose the additional necessity for repression; *suppression*, a more temporary delaying tactic, is available. A person suppresses when he consciously and deliberately contains an impulsive action, such as the desire to strike someone who has just insulted him.

Freud, and theorists influenced by him, were convinced that the mechanism of repression lies behind all serious personality disturbances. The methods of most forms of psychotherapy devised by these theorists are designed first to aid the client in relieving the impacted emotional pressure of repressive conflict, and second to develop new ways of evaluating and expressing impulses and biological drives. It is easy to see how development of an objective index of an individual's tendency to repress would contribute to our understanding of personality processes.

Perceptual Defense

Experiments performed in the late 1940's seemed to demonstrate that perception is not a straightforward, mechanical process of registering and interpreting stimuli from the environment, but is strongly influenced by the needs, motives, and values of the perceiver (Bruner and Goodman, 1947; Bruner and Postman, 1947a). Subjects in one such experiment were presented with stimulus words on a tachistoscope, a device for presenting visual stimuli at brief exposure times of controlled duration. Two weeks before the tachistoscopic testing, a pretest of the words had shown which were most and least threatening for each subject. (Degree of threat was measured by reaction time to a word association test; the longer the reaction time, the greater the presumed threat; see Chap. 4.) There was a significant relationship between degree of threat and tachistoscopic exposure required to enable subjects to recognize words the second time they were presented.

The concept of repression leads us to expect that subjects will require longer tachistoscopic exposure times to recognize threatening words than nonthreatening stimuli, but such is not universally the case. Some subjects actually require less recognition time for threatening words. When subjects respond in the expected fashion (requiring longer recognition times for threatening stimuli), the phenomenon is called *perceptual defense*; when they respond in the opposite way, the phenomenon is called *perceptual vigilance* (Bruner and Postman, 1947b). Subjects who react with perceptual vigilance came to be called sensitizers.

Although considerable controversy arose over the adequacy of methods used to demonstrate the influence of personality on perception, research on the relation between the two continued unabated. Studies using a variety of subject groups and many different measures of perception and personality turned up consistently significant findings. Subjects who perceived threatening stimuli less accurately or with greater difficulty showed tendencies toward blocking, repressing, and avoiding threatening stimuli in other contexts as well. Subjects who perceived threatening stimuli more accurately or with less difficulty showed general tendencies toward sensitization and approach (or attraction) when faced with conflict arousing stimuli (Byrne, 1964).

Two conclusions seemed justified by the accumulating data. First, it seemed that experimental studies had revealed the existence of important individual differences in defensive style. Second, it appeared that the concept of repression tells only half the story. Personality defense may also take the form of vigilance, sensitization, or hyperreactivity to threat. It looked very much as though people can be meaningfully described along a continuum of defensive style, at one end of which are the extreme repressors, at the other end the extreme sensitizers, and in the middle those who use both defenses about equally.

The next step is to develop a convenient, efficient, and valid measuring instrument by which a person's general tendency to repress or sensitize can be measured in standard fashion. Byrne undertook this task, and the next section describes briefly how he went about it.

Measurement of Repression-Sensitization

The Minnesota Multiphasic Personality Inventory (MMPI) seemed a good place to start with the attempt to measure repression-sensitization. This test consists of 550 statements which the subject marks *true* or *false* according to the way each applies to him. The MMPI, originally designed to aid in identifying various types of behavior disturbances in patients requiring psychiatric help, was initially given to samples of normal persons and persons known to display specific kinds of behavior disorders (such as hysteria, depression, and schizophrenia). Statistical techniques were used to discover which items were answered differently by clinical and nonclinical subjects, and scoring keys were set up to evaluate responses from subjects tested later. In each instance when a subject's response differs from that expected from a normal population but is the same as that given by one of the clinical groups, one point is scored on the appropriate clinical scale.

An important feature of the MMPI is that item content per se makes no difference whatsoever in the scoring. The nature of the test is such that saying *true* to an item like "I feel fine" can as easily contribute to a high score on a clinical scale as saying *true* to an item like "I think I am going crazy." In principle, all that matters is whether a particular response does or does not conform to responses given by normal or disturbed subjects in the original standardizing samples.

In its standard form, the MMPI consists of ten clinical scales (Hysteria, *Hy*; Depression, *D*; Hypochondriasis, *Hs*; Psychasthenia, *Pt*; Psychopathic deviate, *Pd*; Masculinity-femininity, *Mf*; Paranoia, *Pa*; Schizophrenia, *Sc*; Hypomania, *Ma*; and Social introversion, *Si*) and four other scales: a measure of the number of "don't know" or "cannot say" responses; the L scale, designed to detect lying; the F scale, designed to assess response validity; and the K scale, designed to measure the subject's tendency to suppress responses that do not present him in a favorable light. It was not long, however, before the number of scales increased tremendously.

Agreement indicates sensitization:	
*158.	I cry easily.
321.	I am easily embarrassed.
362.	I am more sensitive than most other people.
555.	I sometimes feel that I am about to go to pieces.
Agreement indicates repression:	
36.	I seldom worry about my health.
160.	I have never felt better in my life than I do now.
242.	I believe I am no more nervous than most others.
379.	I very seldom have spells of the blues.

Table 14.1 *Sample Items from the Repression-Sensitization Scale*

** Item numbers are those in the booklet form of the MMPI, New York: The Psychological Corp., 1943.*

The MMPI handbook, published in 1960, lists 213 scales purporting to measure everything from ego strength, college achievement, and intelligence, to social status, aging, and low back pain (Dahlstrom and Welsh, 1960).

A number of attempts have been made to measure personality defenses with the MMPI. Among them were efforts to measure repression-sensitization by combining total scores from several MMPI scales (Gordon, 1957, 1959; Altrocchi, Parsons, and Dickoff, 1960). This procedure poses technical problems, because a deviant response to one item on the MMPI often adds to the score on several clinical scales. Byrne (1961) corrected for this in his version of the repression-sensitization scale by substituting a scoring system in which each item is counted only once. The original version of Byrne's scale contained 156 scorable items and 26 buffer items (items that are not scored but are included in a psychological test to make its purpose less obvious).

To give you an idea of the nature of the test for repression-sensitization, Table 14.1 reproduces eight items. Answers of *true* to the first four indicate sensitization; answers of *true* to the last four indicate repression. The test is scored so that a high total score indicates sensitization, while low total score represents repression.

Byrne, Barry, and Nelson (1963) later reduced the number of scorable items on the repression-sensitization (R-S) scale from 156 to 127 by examining the relationship between scores on individual items and scores on the test as a whole. In other words, they conducted an *item analysis* based on a study of the internal consistency of the test. An item is consistent (and therefore deserves retention) if the subjects who answer it in the repressor direction also achieve low scores on the total test, indicating that they are high on repression. An inconsistent item elicits responses not in accord with subjects' scores on all items combined.

To appreciate the meaning of this kind of internal consistency, suppose you constructed a test to measure how well a class had learned the material in Chapter 1 of this book. If your test were given to a large, heterogeneous group, you would certainly find that some students answer most items correctly, while a few answer most items incorrectly. If you took all the A papers and all the D and F papers and examined the distribution of correct and incorrect answers for one test item only, you should find that the A students answered the item correctly with much more frequency than students with overall grades of D or F.

Obviously, an item that all students answer correctly, regardless of their overall grade, does not contribute to your final assessment of individual differences; it is "too easy." An item missed by virtually all students is not much good either; it is "too hard." An item that is missed or passed about equally by A students and by D and F students also fails to show discriminatory power. The content of such an item might be irrelevant to the purpose of the test, or it might be on a topic that is covered extensively in another course. A question on Darwin may measure whether a student has taken a course in biology rather than whether he has studied the first chapter of this book.

An item incorrectly answered by A students and correctly answered by D and F students is clearly unsatisfactory, since it discriminates in the wrong direction. Such might be the results for a question that is intrinsically ambiguous. For example: Research on obstacle perception shows that sighted persons can avoid obstacles successfully when auditory cues are eliminated—*true* or *false*? Although the expected answer is false, brighter students may observe that the question does not exclude the possibility that the sighted persons are using vision; it does not specifically state that they are blindfolded. Sensing a trick question, these students may answer *true*, while other students who do not see the ambiguity reply *false*. This type of question penalizes the persons who should be getting high scores, and is therefore inconsistent with the purpose of the test.

By eliminating test items that show signs of inconsistency with total scores, the test's discriminatory power can be improved. With all items pulling in the same direction, individual differences are more marked; the overall range of scores is greater, and confidence in their meaning increased.

Testing the Test

It is not enough merely to assemble a group of items and call them, collectively, a test of repression-sensitization. No matter how sound the rationale behind it, a new test must prove its worth in several ways before it can be regarded as an acceptable measure of a psychological variable. The new instrument must pass several tests itself, and extensive research is often required to establish that it has done so. The item analysis of the R-S scale described above was one such test.

In addition, a new measuring instrument must be shown to be *reliable* and *valid*. Both these terms have more than one meaning, so each is dealt with separately in the following pages.

Reliability

The term *reliability* has two conventional meanings in psychological measurement. One meaning stresses the level of agreement between two presumably equivalent measures of the same variable. My watch is reliable if it consistently agrees with the time shown by the clock on the wall. Note that accuracy or correctness (validity) is not at issue here; both timepieces may be 25 minutes fast or slow. All that matters, in terms of reliability, is whether two separate measures of the same thing yield closely similar assessments. (The second meaning, involving stability over time, will be covered later.)

Equivalent forms and split-half reliability. Sometimes an investigator initially constructs two separate versions (or forms) of the same test, so that agreement reliability may be conveniently assessed by comparing subjects' performances on these presumably equivalent measures. However, research with the repression-sensitization scale approached determination of this type of reliability in a slightly different way. Equivalent forms were arbitrarily constructed by dividing the overall scale in half; even-numbered items were assigned to one half, odd-numbered items to the other half. Subjects' scores on both halves of the test were then correlated to assess the level of agreement of the scores. Because reliability values are influenced by the number of items in a scale, an additional correction was applied to the data, but details of the correction procedure are of no concern here. Bear in mind that a correlation coefficient of +1.00 represents perfect agreement, −1.00 represents perfect disagreement, and a correlation of zero indicates no agreement, that is, a random relationship between scores on the two halves of the test (see Chap. 13).

The split-half reliability of the original 156 item R-S scale was .88 (133 subjects); the split-half reliability of the revised 127 item scale was .94. These values are quite satisfactory for a psychological test and provide strong evidence that the R-S scale is reliable, at least according to one meaning of the term. The coefficient of split-half reliability is sometimes referred to as a coefficient of internal consistency. The logic of the split-half procedure is similar to the logic of item analysis.

Interjudge, interscorer, interrater agreement. Many psychological tests are easily scored; the examiner merely counts the number of responses that correspond to those specified on a standard scoring key. When this is the case, the test constructor often does not bother to test interscorer agreement. He simply assumes that his data are "objective," that independent scorers will be sufficiently accurate in applying the key to produce identical data. When the subjects record their responses directly on standard test forms that are scored by a reliable machine, this assumption is usually safe.

Some types of psychological tests, however, require that agreement be determined between judges' ratings of subjects' behaviors. Drawings of the human figure, specimens of handwriting, or responses to inkblots do not yield easily scored answers. It is usually necessary to submit records of subjects' behaviors on projective tests to judges trained to assess responses in standard ways (for example, according to the amount of body image disturbance displayed in human figure drawings; see Chap. 13). Each judge independently evaluates a series of records, and the correlation between the judges' evaluations establishes the agreement reliability of the test.

Stability over time. The second general meaning of reliability emphasizes the stability or constancy of a measure over a period of time. A measure of intelligence is not very useful if the values it yields change by 20 or 30 points over a two week period between testings. Similarly, it is not very helpful to characterize someone as a repressor on the basis of his test score if two weeks later he seems to respond like a sensitizer. When a test purports to measure a stable psychological characteristic, evidence must be adduced to show that scores on the test do not shift radically over a period of time.

Stability is usually assessed by test-retest procedures, in which subjects are readministered the same test after a suitable interval of time. The test-retest reliability of the original form of the R-S scale was reported to be .88 after six weeks. The test-retest reliability of the revised scale was .82 after three months. Both values are satisfactory as indices of temporal stability.

There are situations in which a high level of temporal stability is not desirable (Shontz, 1965). A test designed to measure variations of mood from day to day should not yield the same score for every subject on every testing. Before he can assess the reliability of his instrument, the test constructor must know something about the expected properties of the variable he hopes to measure.

Validity

The problem of validity is much more complicated than that of reliability. The classical question of validity was: Does the test measure what it is supposed to measure? Later investigators realized that this question oversimplifies the matter by suggesting that it is possible to answer with a simple yes or no. Behind the classical question lies another, more realistic question: How do we know when a test measures what it is supposed to measure?

There are at least four ways of answering this (Cronbach and Meehl, 1955); consequently, it is possible to consider at least four types of validity. They are concurrent validity, predictive validity, content validity, and construct validity. When we measure variables that are of primarily theoretical interest, construct validity assumes overwhelming importance. Indeed, most of the balance of this chapter describes efforts to assess the construct validity of the repression-sensitization scale.

Concurrent and predictive validity. One way to determine whether an instrument measures something accurately is to compare it with a presumably better measure of the same thing. I may validate my watch against the clock on the wall if I have good reason to believe that the wall clock is a better measure of time than my watch. If I wish to validate the clock on the wall, I will have to find a better measure still. I might call the telephone company or tune a good radio receiver to WWV, the radio station of the U.S. Bureau of Standards.

By the same logic, a psychologist could validate a newly devised test of intelligence against an already existing, well-accepted test of intelligence. Subjects would be given both tests, and their scores on the two correlated. The higher the correlation, the more valid the new test.

Why would one take the trouble to make up a new test if a usable one already exists? Sometimes there is reason to believe the new instrument is actually better than the one against which it is initially validated. If an existing test penalizes deaf people by requiring the examiner to read instructions aloud, a new test that replaces oral instruction with printed instructions or that substitutes nonvocal items may be more valid. Binet initially validated his tests against teachers' ratings of pupil performance; later, his scale became the standard against which new tests of intelligence were evaluated.

Another reason for developing new tests is simply to make the process of measurement more efficient. If it takes one hour to administer an existing test to one subject, a new test that measures the same factors and can be given to a large group in 20 minutes promises great savings of time and effort.

In each case, the measurement against which a new test is validated is called the *criterion* (pl., *criteria*). Both concurrent and predictive validity require use of a criterion. The difference between the two approaches is essentially that concurrent validity uses a contemporaneous standard, while predictive validity employs a criterion that does not become available until after the test has been administered. For example, a college aptitude test, a scale to predict success in psychotherapy, or a test designed to select employees who will be most productive must be validated against information that becomes available only some time after the predictive instrument is used. In its published standards for educational and psychological tests, the American Psychological Association (1966) discusses concurrent and predictive validity under the single heading of criterion-related validity. Combining the two forms makes sense, because it is not always easy to distinguish between them in actual practice.

The repression-sensitization scale is not designed to predict the future occurrence of any specific level of achievement or type of activity, so the question of predictive validity does not arise. Studies are cited later in which R-S scores are used to predict subjects' responses in other testing situations. Though predictive in the broadest sense of the term, these studies are best regarded as evaluations of construct validity. Their purpose is to clarify the *theoretical* status of the repression-sensitization dimension by testing inferences derived from the same set of assumptions about personality that led to construction of the R-S scale. That is, they are intended to test the theory of repression as much as to evaluate the specific scale in question. Strictly speaking, predictive validity is involved only when the purpose of the test is the forecasting of a predesignated type or level of behavior of a very specific character.

A test of the concurrent validity of the repression-sensitization scale requires a criterion of repression. Since there is no Bureau of Standards for Psychology to provide criteria against which new tests may be validated, acceptable criteria are hard to find. Nonetheless, a few studies may be cited to show how substitute criteria may be used even where no agreed upon scientific standards exist.

In earlier research, Ullmann (1960) reported the development of a 43 item MMPI scale designed to measure what he called Facilitation-Inhibition. Ullman's scale had been validated against ratings of case history records (Ullman, 1957), and it appeared to measure the same dimension as the R-S scale. Since Ullman's scale is scored in the opposite direction to the R-S scale, a high negative correlation would indicate that they do, in fact, measure the same personality dimension. In a study of 64 subjects, the actual correlation was −.76, a rather satisfying confirmation of the investigator's expectations. Independent replication of this study by Bernhardson (1967) produced a correlation of −.75 between the two scales in a sample of 92 subjects, further supporting the contention that both measure the same variable.

Tempone (1964) used psychiatrists' ratings of patients as a criterion against which to validate scores on the repression-sensitization scale. He found correlations of .35 between these ratings and scores on the original version of the scale and .38 between the ratings and scores on the revised scale. Neither of these values is statistically significant for the size of the sample (18 patients). It is not easy to decide on the basis of Tempone's study whether the repression-sensitization scale is valid or invalid. The number of subjects is small, and no data were presented to permit evaluation of the interjudge (agreement) reliability of the psychiatrists' ratings of patient characteristics. The investigator himself expressed reluctance to accept psychiatric ratings as a completely valid criterion.

To complicate matters, Tempone's research provided fairly strong evidence of the *content validity* of the R-S scale. Before considering the evidence, it is necessary to describe briefly the meaning of this term.

Content validity. A test has content validity when the items it contains adequately represent the variable the test is intended to measure. It is usually easier to detect the absence of content validity than to assess precisely the degree of its presence. A test of arithmetic skill that requires the subject to spell words is obviously low in content validity. However, even an arithmetic test that asks the subject to solve mathematical problems may be low in content validity if the problems are expressed in such complex language that the subject spends most of his time figuring out what they say.

A common way to evaluate the content validity of an instrument like the repression-sensitization scale is to ask expert judges, familiar with the theoretical basis of the test, to evaluate the items. In the research described above, Tempone had nine psychiatrists identify the responses they thought represented repression. Agreement on an item was defined as concurrence by at least seven of the nine judges. Agreements corresponding to the scoring rules were evident on 72 per cent of the items in the original scale and 90 per cent of the items in the revised scale. Although some items did not produce agreement (28 per cent and 10 per cent on the two forms of the test), none produced agreement on a response opposite to that specified by the scoring key. These data show that nearly all the items on the revised R-S scale clearly reflect the repression-sensitization dimension. Apparently about 10 per cent of the items are ambiguous, but none actually contradicts the purpose of the test.

Construct Validity

For a test designed to measure a theoretical variable, by far the most important form of validity is construct validity. As implied by the name, the procedures of construct validity evaluate not only the test but also the theoretical construct the test is supposed to measure. A test of repression-sensitization is of little value unless the person's score tells us something more than that he responded in particular ways to particular stimuli. Both repression and sensitization are, after all, regarded as defense mechanisms, devices or processes by which people handle their anxieties. If the theoretical dimension represented by the R-S scale is a valid dimension in personality, and if the R-S scale actually measures along that dimension, it should be possible to generate hypotheses and predictions about how people who obtain high or low scores on the scale will act in other situations. If these hypotheses are confirmed in actual research, both the scale and the construct it represents gain credibility. If they are not confirmed, either the theory or the scale must be revised to conform more closely to actual research outcomes.

Byrne (1964) described a number of studies designed to establish the construct validity of the R-S scale, with conclusions that are briefly summarized in the following paragraphs. The succeeding section of this chapter takes up in greater detail some investigations that were conducted after Byrne's review of the literature was published.

Repressors (low scorers on the R-S scale) tend to suppress the memory of threatening material. They require longer exposure times than sensitizers to recognize threatening words following failure. Repressors report experiencing less anxiety in stressful situations, and they dislike humor to a greater extent than do sensitizers. Repressors are more self-satisifed, while sensitizers describe themselves in negative, self-depreciatory ways. Contrary to expectations, high scores on the R-S scale (indicating sensitization) have been found to coincide with evidence of psychological maladjustment. Paper and pencil tests have shown scores on the R-S scale to be positively correlated with tendencies toward alcoholism, anxiety, emotional instability, social withdrawal, and maladjustment. Byrne rightly pointed out that repressors would not be expected to agree on a paper and pencil test that anything is wrong with them. By definition, a repressor does not admit his problems; it is therefore quite possible that the picture he presents of himself in most tests of personality is inaccurate (see Byrne, Golightly, and Sheffield, 1965).

Byrne summarized his review of the literature by pointing out that research on repression-sensitization began with two basic propositions. The first was that individuals may be arranged along a continuum according to whether they tend, at one extreme, to avoid threatening stimuli (repressors), or, at the other extreme to approach threatening stimuli (sensitizers). The second was that maladjustment should be greatest for persons at both extremes of the continuum and smallest for persons in the middle range. He concluded that the first proposition had been strongly supported by the data, but that the second had not.

It certainly does not seem that these findings lend strong support to the theory of repression originally outlined in psychoanalytic theory. First, they suggest that repression is not a simple on-off event that is either present or absent in a given individual, but instead is one end of a continuum that extends from denial of impulses to its opposite, exaggeration of impulses. Psychoanalytic theory recognized the possibility that a person may deal with anxiety by approach, rather than by avoidance. Such behavior is often called counterphobic; it might be exemplified by the person who decides to study veterinary medicine in the hope that it will help him overcome a longstanding fear of animals. But psychoanalytic theory does not place as much emphasis upon such activity as the R-S scale would seem to indicate is necessary.

Second, these studies indicate that, contrary to the expectations of psychoanalytic theory, repression does not produce maladjustment; in fact, quite the contrary. Sensitizers consistently show less positive self-regard and a greater tendency to be maladjusted than do repressors.

The correspondence between what psychoanalytic theory says ought to happen and what actually happens in research is obviously not very close. A decision must therefore be made. Is psychoanalytic theory wrong, or is the R-S scale simply invalid as a measure of repression? Before attempting to answer, let us examine a few more studies that use the R-S scale.

Further Research

Psychological Adjustment

Feder (1967) attempted to overcome the objection that many measures of adjustment are paper and pencil tests on which repressors are likely to falsify responses in order to conceal their problems. He administered the R-S scale to 78 adult patients hospitalized for psychiatric disturbances (maladjusted), and 83 patients hospitalized only for medical-surgical reasons (comparison group). The highest scoring 40 per cent of all subjects were identified as sensitizers; the lowest scoring 40 per cent were identified as repressors. If there were no relationship between repression-sensitization and level of adjustment, equal numbers of medical-surgical and psychiatric patients should appear at both ends of the scale; the

	Repression	Sensitization
Medical-surgical	49	19
Psychiatric	15	45

Table 14.2 *Occurrence of Repression and Sensitization in Groups of Medical-Surgical and Psychiatric Patients* (Adapted from Feder, 1967.)

number of subjects in each cell of Table 14.2 should be nearly the same. As you can see, the numbers are by no means equal. Medical-surgical patients are designated repressors to a much greater degree than are psychiatric patients. Psychiatric patients, in turn, are much more often in the sensitizer category. This demonstrates that even when an independent empirical criterion of maladjustment is used, an association exists between disturbance of behavior and scores on the R-S scale.

Tempone and Lamb (1967) compared R-S scores for 175 clinical outpatients (maladjusted) and 459 college students. The average score for the outpatients was 58.11, while the average for the college students was 36.75. Again it is evident that maladjustment is associated with a tendency to sensitize. In a second part of the same study, the responses of 58 outpatients in a mental health clinic to a test involving incomplete sentences were rated for evidence of psychological conflict. (Incomplete sentences tests are semiprojective devices which require subjects to finish sentences like: I . . . ; My future . . . ; I feel. . . .) Conflict ratings within the maladjusted group correlated .73 with R-S scores; the higher the rating, the higher the R-S score (the stronger the tendency to be a sensitizer).

Thelen (1969) compared the R-S scores of college students who sought help at the university mental health clinic with the scores of students who did not seek such help. The mean score for the help seekers was 62.03; the mean score for the other students was 42.43. Among those in therapy, R-S scores tended to be lower for subjects who quit therapy soonest and higher for those who continued through the program.

Byrne, Steinberg, and Schwartz (1968) found that high scorers on the R–S scale complained of greater frequencies of tension headaches, colds, nausea, emotional difficulties or problems, heart palpitations, accidents, illnesses in general, and visits to physicians.

The existence of a positive correlation between maladjustment and the tendency to sensitize has been firmly established in several studies. The question is not, "Does such a correlation exist?" but, "What does it mean?" Tempone and Lamb (1967) suggested that low scores on the R-S scale do not reflect defensive repression but merely normal adjustment. Dublin (1968) has made a similar suggestion; he found that sensitizers were anxious and hesitant in responding to ambiguous stimuli, but that repressors did not differ from subjects who scored in the middle range of the R-S scale. Thelen (1969) went even further and speculated that the difference between sensitizers and repressors is not a difference in level of adjustment, but in willingness to face problems. Sensitizers may only seem more maladjusted because they are more able to deal honestly with the real difficulties of human existence.

Thelen's ideas receive support from an interesting source: the opinions of subjects who take the R-S scale. Lefcourt (1966) asked repressors and sensitizers what they thought the test was about and what they thought a person would be like who gave responses opposite to their own. Repressors saw the scale as a test of mental health and described those who answer in the opposite way as ill, abnormal, and "away from reality." Sensitizers saw the scale as a test of emotionality, honesty with oneself, and seriousness. They described repressors as liars, people who are not too bright, and conservatives.

It is one thing to say that maladjusted persons obtain high scores on sensitization, since there is some basis in clinical experience and personality theory for arguing that behavior disturbance often results from the collapse of psychological defenses. However, it is quite another thing to say that people who score high on the R-S scale are necessarily maladjusted. There is no experimental basis for assuming that people who do not typically rely on repression for protection against their own experiences are psychologically disturbed. Repression may ward off personality breakdown at the expense of the richness and wholeness of psychological experience. Weak defenses may increase vulnerability to internal and external stimuli but allow for a fuller, more complete, and more satisfying existence in the long run. More is said on these matters later.

Anxiety

In his 1964 review of the literature, Byrne took cognizance of the fact that both the R-S scale and Ullman's Facilitation-Inhibition Scale correlate at extremely high levels (between .85 and .95) with measures of anxiety (see also Sullivan and Roberts, 1969). In 1967, Golin, Herron, Lakota, and Reineck also reported a correlation of .87 between R-S scores and scores on the Manifest Anxiety Scale, a popular test of anxiety derived from the MMPI (Taylor, 1953). On the basis of a complex analysis of scores from several tests, Golin *et al.* suggested that both scales measure anxiety or proneness to emotionality. This may be another way of saying that a high score on the R-S scale indicates that defenses are weak or absent, so that anxiety is directly experienced rather than kept under control.

The possibility that repressors actually experience anxiety but simply refuse to admit it verbally has been examined in a few studies. In an investigation on stress (described in more detail in Chap. 8), Lazarus and Alfert (1964) found evidence that subjects who verbally denied experiencing anxiety displayed higher levels of physiological reactivity to a stressful film than did subjects who admitted feeling anxious. Later analysis of data from several similar studies showed that, while repressors generally show about the same physiological responsiveness to stress as sensitizers, repressors consistently *report* feeling less stress (Weinsten, Averill, Opton, and Lazarus, 1968).

In a group of 35 psychiatric patients, Lomont (1965) found the usual high correlation (.76) between R-S scores and a self-report measure of anxiety. Lomont also measured anxiety less directly by examining subjects' responses to a word association test for evidence of disturbance. Some of the signs of disturbance on this test are long reaction time, blocking (inability to respond), and unusual, bizarre, or vulgar responses. The correlation between anxiety measured indirectly and R-S scores was −.45; that is, sensitization was associated with *less* disturbance of response to threatening words. Lomont felt his results support the contention that repressors are anxious but cannot admit it. Sensitizers' behavior on the word association test is less disturbed because the sensitizer admits his psychological tensions and is therefore able to manage them successfully.

	Repressors	Sensitizers
Disgusted	.34*	.06
Entertained	.02	.33*
Anxious	.25	.67*
Bored	−.15	−.57*
Angry	.36*	.00

Table 14.3. *Correlations among Self-Reports of Reactions to Sexually Arousing Stimuli by Repressors and Sensitizers* (From Byrne and Sheffield, 1965)

* Statistically significant.

Other Drives

Hostility. Parsons and Fulgenzi (1968) formed mixed five person groups of college men who had been identified as repressors, sensitizers, and neutrals by their scores on the R-S scale. The groups were assigned the task of producing a combined story about a picture they were shown. While they worked on the task, three observers rated the amount of hostility expressed in the interaction. Later, subjects rated themselves and others in the group on hostility. Although the repressors rated themselves as less hostile and aggressive, they actually displayed the most hostility in the work situation.

Sexuality. Byrne and Sheffield (1965) had repressors and sensitizers read sexually arousing passages from novels. The subjects then reported the extent to which they were sexually aroused by the passages and the extent to which they felt disgusted, entertained, anxious, bored, and angry. Ratings of arousal were correlated with ratings of all other reactions, with the results shown in Table 14.3.

The pattern in these data is clear. Sexual arousal in repressors tended to go along with increased anger and disgust, while in sensitizers it tended to be associated with reduced boredom, increased entertainment, and heightened anxiety. It looks as though repression involves a tendency to regard sexual feelings as unwelcome, while sensitization is based on the expectation that such feelings are desirable, even if the experience of them temporarily heightens anxiety.

Pain. Hare (1966) administered painful electric shocks to subjects at 30 second intervals and found a slightly negative relationship between physiological reactivity to shock and scores on the R-S scale. That is, repressors tended to react somewhat more strongly on the physiological level than did sensitizers. Furthermore, subjects who reported consciously trying to avoid thinking about the coming shocks had significantly lower (more repressive) scores on the R-S scales than subjects who did not try to avoid thinking about them. In this respect, Hare's findings are consistent with those of studies on other drives. However, Hare raised an interesting question. If subjects who achieve low scores on the R-S scale *consciously* avoid stimulation, are they really *repressing?* Psychoanalytic theory postulates that repression must be an unconscious process to be effective. Ego defenses are built upon self-deception, and one cannot deceive himself by purely conscious mental activity. Hare's observation suggests that the R-S scale does not measure defense mechanisms, but what might more accurately be called "adaptive styles" or "generalized behavior tendencies." Let us keep this suggestion in mind for later discussion.

I never hesitate to go out of my way to help someone in trouble. (*true*)
I am sometimes irritated by people who ask favors of me. (*false*)
I like to gossip at times. (*false*)
I never resent being asked to return a favor. (*true*)

Table 14.4 *Examples of Items in Crowne and Marlowe's Scale of Social Desirability*

Social Desirability

There is one more possibility to be considered. The tendency to "repress," as measured by the R-S scale, may not be so much a reflection of defense or life style as it is a measure of the degree to which the person is trying to put up a good front by saying only desirable things about himself. A scale to measure such tendencies was developed by A.L. Edwards (1957, 1959). Joy (1963) found a correlation of −.91 between scores on this scale and the R-S scale, strongly suggesting that repression does represent an attempt to appear in a favorable light. Byrne (1964) reported several other investigations that yielded similar results. The matter would seem to be settled.

However, objections were raised to Edwards' scale on the grounds that it contains items with strong pathological implications. Crowne and Marlowe (1960) developed a new social desirability scale containing items with culturally approved answers but without implications of abnormality. Examples of four items from this scale, with the socially desirable responses indicated in parentheses, are shown in Table 14.4

Byrne (1964) reported a correlation of −.37 between the Crowne-Marlowe scale and the R-S scale. Silber and Grebstein (1964) reported correlations of −.32 and −.48 in two samples of medical students, and of −.39 in a sample of undergraduates. Feder (1967) found a correlation of −.45 in a mixed group of adult subjects who were hospitalized for medical-surgical and psychiatric conditions. These correlations are not extremely high, but they are fairly stable from study to study and are well within the range of values taken seriously by investigators in the field of personality.

As a group, these studies of social desirability show that low scorers on the R-S scale avoid responses that tend to imply behavioral maladjustment. They tend to behave so that they appear in a socially desirable light. Whether this is because they are, in fact, remarkably well-adjusted and actually do behave in socially desirable ways cannot be said with certainty.

By contrast, sensitizers seem to prefer answers that are not socially favored and that reveal maladjustment. Whether they exhibit these preferences because they are maladjusted and behave in undesirable ways also cannot be said with certainty. Other evidence indicates that we must be extremely careful about generalization along these lines. The final section of this chapter presents an attempt to integrate the findings from research on the repression-sensitization scale. At this point, it is best to delay the matter temporarily and to examine two more studies.

Group Behavior in Problem Solving Situations

Cohen and Foerst (1968) made up five man groups of subjects, homogeneous with respect to scores on the R-S scale: repressors worked only with repressors, sensitizers worked only with sensitizers. The groups were required to solve problems in two types of enforced communication networks. In the *wheel* network, four subjects can communicate only with the fifth subject, who is at the center of the wheel. The fifth subject, however, can communicate with all others in the group. This structure is conducive to centralized activity in which the man at the center organizes information sent to him and delegates responsibilities to other group members. In the *completely connected* network, every subject can communicate freely with every other member of the group. Centralization is not imposed, although the group itself may decide to use only some of the channels available and may deliberately centralize its own operations.

In the first part of the experiment all the groups were given experience with the wheel network, and the problems they solved were fairly simple (involving identification of symbols). The task in the second part of the experiment remained simple but the groups were organized into completely connected networks. Finally, in a third part of the experiment, the task was made much more complex, but the completely connected network was retained. Complex tasks are best solved by a centralized structure such as the wheel network. It was therefore of interest to see whether repressors and sensitizers differed in their ability to adopt the more appropriate wheel structure.

They did. The following brief portraits of the behavior of the two kinds of groups were drawn up by the investigators to summarize their complex findings:

> R groups tend to (a) settle more quickly on stable ways of working; (b) resist changes to traditional ways of behaving in the face of environmental change; (c) behave as if environmental change is smaller than it is; (d) quickly redevelop stable patterns of problem-solving following change; (e) become secure earlier in their environment; (f) exhibit a low rate of increasing efficiency over time because they start at a higher level; and (g) produce more stable role specialization earlier. S groups tend to (a) take longer to settle on stable ways of working; (b) be highly susceptible to disruptions in ways of behaving in the face of environmental change; (c) behave as if environmental change is larger than it is; (d) develop stable patterns of problem-solving following change slowly; (e) become secure later in their environment; (f) exhibit a high rate of increasing efficiency over time because they start at a lower level; and (g) produce later and less stable role specialization (Cohen and Foerst, 1968, p. 215).

REM Deprivation

Chapter 7, on sleep and dreams, describes research that has demonstrated a high correlation between rapid eye movements during sleep (REM) and active dreaming. That chapter also discusses studies in which subjects were deprived of the opportunity to dream; they were awakened by the experimenter just as REM activity began. This procedure generally increases the frequency of occurrence of

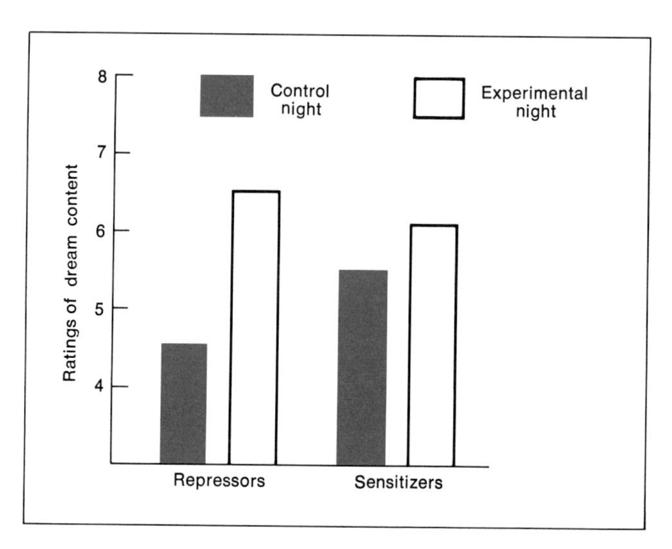

Fig. 14.1. Ratings of dream contents reported by repressors and sensitizers in the study of REM deprivation. (Data from Pivik and Foulkes, 1966)

REM periods later in the night and causes subjects to report experiences that are more dreamlike, i.e., more hallucinatory, and more bizarre.

Pivik and Foulkes (1966), reasoning that repressors and sensitizers should respond differently to REM deprivation, selected ten low scorers and ten high scorers on the R-S scale and subjected both groups to dream deprivation. On the experimental night, the first four REM periods were interrupted at the first sign that active dreaming was taking place. The fifth REM period was allowed to continue for five minutes; then the subject was awakened and asked what he was just thinking about. On the control night, early night dreaming was not interrupted. Except for a single occasion (when he was awakened during an REM period to provide a dream report), the subject's sleep was disturbed only between periods of REM activity.

Half the repressors and half the sensitizers were subjected first to the experimental treatment and then to the control conditions; the remaining subjects were run in the reverse order. The subjects themselves did not know which night was which. Subjects' verbal reports were rated on an eight point scale designed to measure the dreamlike quality of fantasy productions.

Average ratings of late night dream reports on experimental and control nights are shown in Figure 14.1. This graph shows the tendency in both groups for dreams to be more intense (dreamlike) on the experimental night than on the control night. It also shows that the effect of deprivation is greater for repressors than for sensitizers; only data from repressors passes the test of statistical significance. Notice that sensitizers tended to report more intense dreams on the control night. This is consistent with the general hypothesis that sensitizers are typically more "in touch with" their internal psychological processes.

Is it possible that repressors' dreams are just as intense as sensitizers' dreams, but repressors simply choose not to report their experiences? That does not seem likely, in view of the fact that repressors' reports on deprivation nights are actually slightly *more* intense than sensitizers' reports. Apparently, repressors do not resist reporting intense dreams when they have them.

Could repressors' dreams on control nights be just as intense as sensitizers' dreams, but forgotten by the repressors? Perhaps repressors' control night dreams are not intense enough to break down repressive barriers. Their deprivation night dreams, being even more intense, are strong enough to cross the threshold of repression and therefore come through to conscious memory. This hypothesis is plausible, but could only be tested if we could assess dream intensity independently of subjects' verbal reports. As yet, no sufficiently sensitive technique is available for doing so.

Although the data are not conclusive, they are certainly consistent with the notion that repressors typically minimize the intensity of their own inner lives. They are also consistent with the proposal that repressions tend to break down under severe pressure, resulting in a flood of impulses into awareness.

Unfortunately for our purposes, the study cited above did not include a third "recovery" night in its procedure. The theory of repression would lead us to expect some rather specific findings from such a night. Most particularly it would lead us to expect repressors (but not sensitizers) to return to a very low level of dream intensity following their deprivation-induced outburst of dream activity. If dream deprivation does release threatening impulses in the repressive subject, it is likely that this outburst would be succeeded by an even stronger reconstruction of the repressive barrier. The construct validity of the R-S scale would be considerably enhanced by data that confirmed this prediction.

Conclusions

Difficulties inherent in the theory of repression itself make it impossible to draw a clear conclusion about whether the R-S scale measures what it is supposed to measure. It could be said that the scale has been shown to be invalid. Theoretically, repression is a mechanism of defense against natural and basically normal impulses. Too much defensiveness leads to a state of conflict and alienation from one's true self, a condition that practically defines psychological ill health. But sensitization denotes awareness and acceptance of impulses, accessibility to consciousness of the full reality of inner mental life. A sensitizer should therefore be the picture of psychological well-being, aware of the forces that activate his own behavior and free to experience all things. Yet all the evidence points in the opposite direction. Sensitizers consistently show more signs of maladjustment than repressors. Consequently, predictions from theory are contradicted by empirical data, and the scale must be judged to have failed in its purpose.

However, the same theory permits us to argue that the R-S scale has shown the theory of repression to be perfectly correct. Psychoanalysts have long maintained that psychological defenses are necessary for successful adjustment to life in a civilized society. One must learn to control his impulses and prevent them from gaining the upper hand. Only through a modicum of repression is it possible to hold the instinctual life in check. The psychoanalyst can argue that we should expect repressors to be well adjusted because they have developed the capacity to deny primitive impulses immediate expression (a distinguishing characteristic of the strong ego). Sensitizers are poorly adjusted either because they have failed to develop adequate defenses or because stressful life events have weakened their defenses and unleashed forces too strong for the ego to control.

The present situation is therefore one in which differential prediction is impossible. Repression may either be a sign of neurosis or of successful adaptation.

Sensitization may result from insight and acceptance of self, in which case it is a sign of good adjustment, or from the ego's weakness and incapacity to deal with instinctual demands, in which case it is an indication of poor adjustment. If the validity of a test to measure the defense mechanism of repression is to be established beyond question, it will be necessary for distinctions to be made between healthy and neurotic repression and between healthy and neurotic sensitization. Differential predictions of behavior will then become possible.

As suggested previously in this chapter, it is perhaps best, for the moment, to regard the R-S scale not as a measure of defense, but as an index of a generalized attitude toward inner experiences, and perhaps toward external stimuli as well. Low scorers on the R-S scale seem to prefer to avoid these experiences; high scorers seem to prefer to approach them. Among the benefits gained from avoidance are increased self-satisfaction, a superficial appearance of successful adaptation, and enhanced efficiency of goal directed behavior. Among the disadvantages are the strong possibility of self-deception and a sterile inner life. The benefits of sensitization are probably a sense of freedom from social restraint, a belief that one is honest with oneself, and a feeling that life is being lived to the fullest extent possible. The disadvantages are that the sensitizer is as susceptible to intense unpleasant feelings as he is to intensely pleasurable ones, that he is likely to be regarded as maladjusted (especially by avoiders), and that he is likely to be conscious of feelings of dissatisfaction with himself.

Fortunately, few of us have to make the choice between total repression or sensitization; most people obtain scores in the middle of the R-S scale. The vast majority seems to achieve a modicum of control over themselves without serious loss of sensitivity to their inner impulses. It is quite likely that balanced adjustment is best in the long run.

Glossary

Anxiety: see Glossary, Chapter 8.

Completely connected network: group structure in which all subjects can communicate freely with each other (see Wheel network).

Construct validity: the degree to which scores on a test may be regarded as an index of a theoretical variable or hypothetical construct (see Glossary, Chap. 7, hypothetical construct).

Content validity: the degree to which the items of a test convey or express the intended characteristics of a theoretical construct (see Glossary, Chap. 7, hypothetical construct).

Criterion: a standard of accuracy; the concurrent or predictive validity of a test is demonstrated by showing that scores on the test correlate strongly with scores on the criterion (see Glossary, Chap. 13, correlation coefficient).

Ego: in psychoanalytic theory, the mediating and directive agency of the personality. Among other things, the ego institutes personality defenses (see Glossary, Chap. 8, personality defense).

Id: in psychoanalytic theory, the source of instinctual drives.

Item analysis: a test of the consistency of responses to individual test items with total scores on the test.

Norms: an array of scores obtained by testing a large number of people; norms provide the standards against which later individual performances on the test are evaluated.

Perceptual defense: delayed recognition of threatening stimuli.

Perceptual vigilance: a reduction of recognition time when threatening stimuli are presented.

Primary personality defense: see Repression.
Psychoanalysis: see Glossary, Chapter 1.
Reliability: an index of agreement between equivalent tests of the same characteristic, between independent judgments of subjects' performances, or between successive administrations of the same test over a period of time.
Repression: a personality defense (see Glossary, Chap. 8) in which threatening thoughts or memories are forcefully excluded from conscious awareness; often called the primary personality defense. Also, the general tendency to avoid threatening or conflict arousing stimuli.
Sensitization: the general tendency to approach threatening or conflict arousing stimuli.
Standardization: the process of acquiring norms (see Norms).
Superego: in psychoanalytic theory, the irrational conscience, derived from childhood experiences of parental punishment and praise.
Validity: see construct validity, content validity, and criterion.
Wheel network: group structure in which all members but one can communicate freely only with the remaining subject (see Completely connected network).

References

Altrocchi, J., O.A. Parsons, and H. Dickoff. Changes in self-ideal discrepancy in repressors and deniers. *J. abnorm. soc. Psychol.*, 1960, **61,** 67–72.

American Psychological Association. *Standards for educational aod psychological tests and manuals.* Washington, D.C.: American Psychological Association, 1966.

Bernhardson, C.S. The relationship between facilitation-inhibition and repression-sensitization. *J. clin. Psychol.*, 1967, **23,** 448–449.

Boring, E.G. *A history of experimental psychology.* New York: Appleton-Century-Crofts, 1929.

Bruner, J.S., and C.C. Goodman. Value and need as organizing factors in perception. *J. abnorm. soc. Psychol.*, 1947, **42,** 33–44.

Bruner, J.S., and L. Postman. Emotional selectivity in perception and reaction. *J. Pers.*, 1947, **16,** 69–77. (b)

———. Tension and tension release as organizing factors in perception. *J. Pers.*, 1947, **15,** 300–308. (a)

Byrne, D. Repression-sensitization as a dimension of personality. In B.A. Maher (Ed.), *Progress in experimental personality research.* Vol. 1. New York: Academic Press, 1964.

———. The repression-sensitization scale: Rationale, reliability, and validity. *J. Pers.*, 1961, **29,** 334–349.

———, and J. Sheffield. Response to sexually arousing stimuli as a function of repressing and sensitizing defenses. *J. abnorm. Psychol.*, 1965, **70,** 114–118.

Byrne, D., J. Barry, and D. Nelson. Relation of the revised repression-sensitization scale to measures of self-description. *Psychol. Rep.*, 1963, **13,** 323–334.

Byrne, D., C. Golightly, and J. Sheffield. The repression-sensitization scale as a measure of adjustment: Relationship with the CPI. *J. consult. Psychol.*, 1965, **29,** 586–589.

Byrne, D., M.A. Steinberg, and M.S. Schwartz. Relationship between repression-sensitization and physical illness. *J. abnorm. Psychol.*, 1968, **75,** 154–155.

Cohen, A.M., and J.R. Foerst, Jr. Organizational behaviors and adaptations to organizational change of sensitizer and repressor problem-solving groups. *J. pers. soc. Psychol.*, 1968, **8,** 209–216.

Cronbach, L.J. The two disciplines of scientific psychology. *Amer. Psychologist*, 1957, **12,** 671–684.

———, and P.E. Meehl. Construct validity in psychological tests. *Psychol. Bull.*, 1955, **52,** 281–302.

Crowne, D.P., and D. Marlowe. A new scale of social desirability independent of psychopathology. *J. consult. Psychol.*, 1960, **24,** 349–354.

Dahlstrom, W.G., and G.S. Welsh. *An MMPI handbook*. Minneapolis: University of Minnesota Press, 1960.

Dublin, J.E. Perception of and reaction to ambiguity by repressors and sensitizers. *J. consult. clin. Psychol.*, 1968, **32,** 198–205.

Edwards, A.L. Social desirability and personality test construction. In B.M. Bass and I.A. Berg (Eds.), *Objective approaches to personality assessment*. Princeton, N.J.: Van Nostrand, 1959.

———. *The social desirability variable in personality assessment and research*. New York: Dryden, 1957.

Feder, C.Z. Relationship of repression-sensitization to adjustment status, social desirability, and acquiescence response set. *J. consult. Psychol.*, 1967, **31,** 401–406.

Golin, S., E.W. Herron, R. Lakota, and L. Reineck. Factor analytic study of the Manifest Anxiety, Extraversion, and Repression-Sensitization scales. *J. consult. Psychol.*, 1967, **31,** 564–569.

Gordon, J.E. Interpersonal predictions of repressors and sensitizers. *J. Pers.*, 1957, **25,** 686–698.

———. The stability of the assumed similarity response set in repressors and sensitizers. *J. Pers.*, 1959, **27,** 362–373.

Hare, R.D. Denial of threat and emotional response to impending painful stimulation. *J. consult. Psychol.*, 1966, **30,** 359–361.

Joy, V.L. Repression-sensitization and interpersonal behavior. Paper presented at the meeting of the American Psychological Association, Philadelphia, August 1963.

Lazarus, R.S., and E. Alfert. Short-circuiting of threat by experimentally altering cognitive appraisal. *J. abnorm. soc. Psychol.*, 1964, **69,** 195–205.

Lefcourt, H.M. Repression-sensitization: A measure of the evaluation of emotional expression. *J. consult. Psychol.*, 1966, **30,** 444–449.

Lomont, J.F. The repression-sensitization dimension in relation to anxiety responses. *J. consult. Psychol.*, 1965, **29,** 84–86.

Parsons, O.A., and L.B. Fulgenzi. Overt and covert hostility in repressors and sensitizers. *Perceptual and Motor Skills*, 1968, **27,** 537–538.

Pivik, T., and D. Foulkes. "Dream deprivation": Effects on dream content. *Science*, 1966, **153,** 1282–1284.

Shontz, F.C. *Research methods in personality*. New York: Appleton-Century-Crofts, 1965.

Silber, L.D., and L.C. Grebstein. Repression-sensitization and social desirability responding. *J. consult. Psychol.*, 1964, **28,** 559.

Sullivan, P.F., and L.K. Roberts. Relationship of manifest anxiety to repression-sensitization on the MMPI. *J. consult. clin. Psychol.*, 1969, **33,** 763–764.

Taylor, J.A. A personality scale of manifest anxiety. *J. abnorm. soc. Psychol.*, 1953, **48,** 285–290.

Tempone, V.J. Some clinical correlates of repression-sensitization. *J. clin. Psychol.*, 1964, **20,** 440–442.

———, and W. Lamb. Repression-sensitization and its relation to measures of adjustment and conflict. *J. consult. Psychol.*, 1967, **31,** 131–136.

Thelen, M.H. Repression-sensitization: Its relation to adjustment and seeking psychotherapy among college students. *J. consult. clin. Psychol.*, 1969, **33,** 161–165.

Ullman, L.P. Clinical correlates of facilitation and inhibition of response to emotional stimuli. *J. proj. Tech.*, 1957, **21,** 399–403.

———. An empirically derived MMPI scale that measures facilitation-inhibition of recognition of threatening stimuli. *Research Report of the Veterans Administration Center at Palo Alto*, No. 10, 1960.

Weinstein, J., J.R. Averill, E.M. Opton, Jr., and R.S. Lazarus. Defensive style and discrepancy between self-report and physiological indexes of stress. *J. pers. soc. Psychol.*, 1968, **10,** 406–413.

15 The World of Schizophrenia

In a study of personal values, 73 psychologically normal adults ranked 24 descriptive items according to their relative importance. An item was judged important if the subject felt that personal loss of the function it mentioned would pose a serious threat to him. Half the items described bodily functions (ability to walk, use of body from the neck down, vision, control of bladder); the other half described psychological and social functions (ability to think, religion, freedom, sanity).

Of all 24 items, the two most important turned out to be *sanity* and *ability to think*. Thirty-one subjects in this study were patients hospitalized with chronic physical illnesses, people with paralyses, amputations, or neurological diseases, who actually suffered severe physical losses of the types described in many of the items. Even to them, sanity and ability to think were more important personal values than such functions as hearing, general physical health, or use of the body (Shontz, Fink, and Hallenbeck, 1960).

Of all personal tragedies that can be imagined, the most frightening is probably the prospect of going crazy. Even psychiatric patients in mental hospitals express negative attitudes toward insanity, and make a point of describing themselves as average individuals (Giovanni and Ullman, 1963). There is sound basis for dreading the loss of sanity. No group of people, with the possible exception of those with leprosy (Hansen's disease), has been less understood or more severely persecuted than those whom society has seen fit to call "insane." The insane have most frequently been regarded as possessed by demons, devils, or evil spirits. They have been subjected to torture and burned at the stake as witches. It has long been the practice to taunt, jeer at, annoy, and injure the insane, for they have been thought of as soulless animals, incapable of human feeling or rational thinking.

Confinement to an institution has rarely provided a solution to the problem of behavioral disturbances, for only recently have institutions attempted to supply even barely tolerable conditions for human existence. The English word *asylum* conveys the apparent intention of society to protect inmates from abuses. But it is likely that asylums were initiated to protect society from people it regarded as dangerous or undesirable, rather than the reverse. We still refer to a noisy, disorganized, dirty, and unpleasant place as bedlam; the word is a contraction of St. Mary's of Bethlehem, the name of an early English asylum for the insane.

In the modern world, the term *insanity* has complex legal connotations and usages, but it is rarely employed in polite society to describe the condition of a person whose behavior is so disordered as to appear frightening, dangerous, or strange. The well-educated twentieth century man describes disturbed behavior as sickness, and he expects such sickness to be understood and treated by a member of the medical profession (usually a psychiatrist) or by a clinical psychologist. He demands that the mentally ill be "cured," not exorcised, punished, or killed. He is even willing to forgive serious antisocial behavior if it can be shown that the person who committed it was not responsible for his own actions because he was mentally ill.

The Disease Model

Development

The transition from the demonic conception of insanity to the disease-oriented conception so prominent today came about largely because of the successes of medical science in the eighteenth and nineteenth centuries. Not only had medicine succeeded in identifying and curing or preventing many abnormal physical conditions, it had firmly established that at least some disorders of behavior are the result of specific somatic (bodily) disease. Research by Krafft-Ebbing (1840–1902) in 1897 strongly suggested that a common form of insanity, known as general paresis, is the result of earlier syphilitic infection; by 1913 the correctness of Krafft-Ebbing's conclusion was beyond doubt. In the beginning of the twentieth century, Alois Alzheimer (1864–1915), a German neurologist. identified changes in the cerebral cortex tissues of patients with schizophrenia and raised hopes that eventually a neurological basis would be found for all conditions of mental derangement (Kety, 1959).

To facilitate the process of identifying the various forms of mental disease, Emil Kraepelin (1856–1926) undertook the task of symptom classification. He developed a system of psychiatric categories that is still highly influential in the practice of medicine and clinical psychology. Almost simultaneously, Sigmund Freud developed the psychoanalytic school of thought, which proposed systematic psychological explanations for various types of behavior disturbance, and recommended a specific form of treatment for a large number of such conditions.

Add to these developments the farsighted action of Phillipe Pinel (1745–1826), a French physician who freed the insane from their institutional chains and developed treatment routines for their care as sick people; the pioneering work of Dorothea Dix (1802–1887), who fought diligently for more considerate treatment of all institutionalized persons; and the efforts of Clifford Beers (1876–1943), who founded the mental hygiene movement in the United States. These combined forces produced radical changes in society's attitudes toward and management of its behaviorally disturbed members.

Dissatisfaction with the Disease Model

The behaviorally disturbed are far better treated now that their conditions are regarded as illnesses rather than evidence of possession by supernatural forces. Yet many modern authorities are unhappy with the current situation, arguing that to explain deviant behavior by attributing it to illness is to ignore some important social and psychological facts. Furthermore, they assert that the evidence which supports the disease model is far too weak to bear the weight of inference that has been heaped upon it by its advocates.

O.H. Mowrer (1960), a learning theorist, has strenuously objected that the concept of mental illness is wrongly used to absolve people of the necessity for feeling guilt. It leads us to ignore the fact that human behavior has moral implications. There are actions, such as hurting others deliberately and unnecessarily, for which we should feel guilty. What is called mental illness may actually result from a person's inability to accept real and unexpiated guilt. The "cure" for mental problems is not to reduce the experience of guilt by telling a client that he is merely sick, but to encourage the client to confess and make restitution for his past errors in behavior, and to teach him how to avoid such errors in the future.

The most forceful attacks on the disease model of abnormal behavior have been launched by T.S. Szasz (1960, 1961 a,b). Szasz, a psychiatrist himself, has argued that the label of mental illness is a social judgment, not a medical diagnosis. A person does not catch or get a mental illness; he does not transmit it to others. Rather, he demonstrates by his actions that he has failed to learn the rules by which the game of life is played; his failure displays itself in the problems he experiences in living and in the unacceptability of his actions to others.

Szasz regards the concept of mental illness as a dangerous "myth" which differs only slightly from the religious and mystical myths it has replaced. Ascribing deviant behavior to illness and expecting a doctor to cure it with pills or psychological therapy is fundamentally not very different from ascribing it to demons to be exorcised by priests or shamans through magic, prayer, or incantation. Both approaches assume the action of some outside force, agent, or enemy; both ignore the difficult personal, social, and ethical conflicts that must be resolved on their own terms if psychological well-being is to be genuine.

Along similar lines, Sarbin (1967, 1969) has argued that the phrase "mental illness" is not a description of a real entity, but an historically valuable metaphor that has been misused in recent years. He traced the term back to the sixteenth century, when it was used to fend off the Inquisition, which saw behavior disturbance as evidence of demonic possession and was inclined to treat the disturbed as evil beings. What was called sickness of the soul in the sixteenth century later became sickness of the mind. However, mental illness is still a pejorative, degrading, and stigmatizing appellation, and mental hospitals continue to segregate undesirable persons from the rest of society (Goffman, 1961).

Albee (1968) has noted that the disease concept leads to the funneling of economic resources into support for medical programs and forms of laboratory research that have little relevance to the real problems of disturbed people. What Albee calls the Mental Health Establishment is committed to "treatment" in "hospitals" and "clinics" by medically trained personnel, and is threatened by the possibility that psychological knowledge may prove this approach wrong. Albee regards the alleviation of disturbed psychological states as an educative, not a curative, enterprise. He suggests a new kind of institution, a psychological service center where existing psychological knowledge of learning processes can be effectively applied by competent, psychologically trained technicians and rehabilitation personnel to modify the behavior of those who require help.

Wolfer (1969) summed up the fundamental argument by pointing out that the real question is whether problem behavior is to be dealt with directly as such, or is to be regarded as merely symptomatic of some vaguely understood, but presumably more important, underlying process called disease. Since attempts to identify and treat underlying disease processes have been largely unsuccessful, it makes no difference whether these processes are assumed to be mental or physical in nature. The contention of modern learning theorists that problem behavior can be successfully altered by direct manipulation renders the disease concept obsolete. At best it has become superfluous; at worst it is misleading and actually harmful.

Schizophrenia: A Case in Point

Psychosis

Of the various forms psychological disturbance may take, schizophrenia is generally regarded as the most serious. Schizophrenia does not mean split personality. It is a form of *psychosis*, which is any state in which a person's actions become so divorced from reality as to be incomprehensible to others. *Organic* psychoses are caused by bodily conditions, such as damage to the brain from disease, poison, or penetrating head wounds. Schizophrenia is usually called a *functional* or *psychogenic* psychosis, because it has no known physical basis and is believed to represent a serious psychological failure in functional adaptation to the demands of the environment. Schizophrenia is further identified as an *ideational* disorder, since its effects are most obvious in the thought processes of the disturbed individual. So-called *affective* disorders, like manic-depressive psychosis, are more evident in the feeling state of the person, who may be overly excited and happy (manic phase) or excessively melancholy and sad (depressive phase), but remains in ideational contact with the world around him.

Psychoses as a group are distinguished from the neuroses, which are also functional behavior disturbances. A neurosis is characterized generally by the person's intense struggle to adjust, and by his retention of the ability to communicate effectively with others. In the chapter on stress (Chap. 8), we considered briefly one form of neurotic symptom: the phobia, in which the person suffers inexplicable and overwhelming fears of specific things, like cats, spiders, or worms, or certain kinds of situations, like being in a crowd or in a high place. Almost everyone experiences some mild forms of temporary neurotic disturbance at some time in his life. However, most people manage to come to terms with themselves and their environments so that these disturbances do not prevent them from functioning effectively and generally feeling satisfied with their existence.

For that matter, almost everyone experiences psychotic states. Overconsumption of alcohol, marijuana, or LSD produces a virtually psychotic state; a high fever can bring on delirium. In fact, everyone who dreams knows what the psychotic condition is like. As we saw in the chapter on sleep (Chap. 7), many theorists feel that normal dreaming provides a necessary avenue for the psychotic discharge of unresolved tensions. In some ways, the normal dream provides a model for understanding schizophrenia, for it often appears that the schizophrenic lives in a private dream world which has become more real for him than the world the rest of us know and experience.

Varieties of schizophrenia. Clinicians usually distinguish among several forms of schizophrenia, but only two of the many possible distinctions need concern us here. One is the distinction between *paranoid* and *nonparanoid* states; the other is the distinction between *process* and *reactive* conditions.

Paranoid schizophrenia is distinguished by the systematic, but nonetheless bizarre and rigid, character of the person's belief system. The paranoid often has the notion that he is unusually important (delusions of grandeur) and that a special group of enemies is out to destroy him at all costs (delusions of persecution). For example, he may believe that he knows the details of a secret plot to overthrow the government, and that enemy agents are everywhere, trying to prevent him from thwarting their plans. Everything that happens, no matter how trivial or irrelevant, is forced to fit into the delusional system (ideas of reference). If a passing acquaintance says, "How are you?" the remark is taken as evidence that poison has been injected into the schizophrenic's food, and the question was asked only to ascertain whether the poison has begun to take effect. Furthermore, the paranoid schizophrenic frequently creates events and experiences that occur only to him. While awake, he hallucinates visions, voices, and mysterious forces much as others hallucinate sensory experiences in dreams. All these are made part of the scheme of his delusional beliefs.

Nonparanoid forms of schizophrenia are displayed in a variety of ways. Language disturbances, disorganized thought, emotional flatness or apathy, childlike behavior, inappropriate affect, unsystematized hallucinations, and bizarre actions are common evidences of these forms of psychosis. The distinction between paranoid and nonparanoid forms of schizophrenia is important, because paranoids generally show less psychological deficit, less disorganization of thought, and less deterioration of condition over time than do schizophrenics of other types (Lang and Buss, 1965).

Cutting across the paranoid-nonparanoid distinction is the distinction between process schizophrenia and reactive schizophrenia. Process schizophrenia shows itself as a long-term, progressive deterioration of psychological organization. Reactive schizophrenia occurs more suddenly, often in response to an identifiable, precipitating life event, such as the death of a parent, loss of a job, or physical illness. Reactive schizophrenia generally involves greater agitation and a more rapid deterioration of behavior. Process and reactive schizophrenia probably represent the extreme ends of a continuum rather than two distinct and qualitatively different modes of maladjustment (Herron, 1962). Nevertheless, patients at the two extremes have been shown to differ on physiological and psychological measures as well as in life histories. The prognosis is much more favorable for reactive schizophrenia than for process schizophrenia, even though the apparent severity of behavior disturbance is often greater in the former.

The problem of classification. A description of the various types of psychological disorders (such as that presented above) gives the impression that people fall neatly into groups. Actually, it is rare for a person to show only one kind of behavior disturbance. Classification of various types of disorder reflects the clinician's concern with psychopathology (literally, mind sickness) and his effort to identify the forms that mental disease may take, just as the physician identifies the various forms of bodily disease, such as measles, mumps, or chicken pox.

The process of deciding which type of psychopathology a disturbed person presents is called by a term borrowed from medicine: *psychodiagnosis*. A large part of the training of psychiatrists and clinical psychologists is devoted to mastering the diagnostic art. The function of diagnosis is to facilitate making judgments about people. The clinician may be called upon to make a legal determination of a person's sanity, to decide whether a person is competent to function independently in society, or to determine whether an inmate should be kept on a locked ward or permitted freedom to walk about the grounds. By assigning diagnostic labels to people, the clinician justifies his decisions; he feels that these labels reveal something about their behavior and general competence (Zigler and Phillips, 1961 a).

Unfortunately, empirical evidence does not confirm the validity of most diagnostic labels as descriptions of actual behavior (Zigler and Phillips, 1961 b). In general, it is safe to say that a person diagnosed as schizophrenic has at some time in his life displayed bizarre behavior and has convinced others that he is incapable of getting along in the everyday world. Beyond that, the diagnosis of schizophrenia tells very little about his actual way of life.

Behavioral Differences between Schizophrenics and Normals

Since people are not labeled as schizophrenic unless they have already demonstrated that they differ from others, it is not surprising that schizophrenics behave differently from more typical subjects on psychological tests. However, diagnosis is a highly subjective process, and controlled laboratory procedures are needed to discover in a systematic way how the behavior of people who are called schizophrenic differs from that which we are willing to accept as normal.

Response to censure and criticism. Buss and Lang (1965) reviewed the experimental literature in an effort to evaluate the similarities and differences between the behavior of schizophrenic and normal subjects. First they examined the hypothesis that schizophrenics are more than usually sensitive to social censure and criticism. In most studies of this hypothesis, social censure consisted of mild punishment administered by telling the subject that his response to some task (for example, a learning and memory task) is wrong or incorrect. The performance of schizophrenic subjects under these conditions has generally been found to deteriorate, thus seeming to support the social censure hypothesis.

However, Buss and Lang found that the social censure hypothesis was too narrow to explain all available data. There is strong evidence that many other affective (emotion arousing) and symbolic stimuli which do not involve social censure also produce poorer performance by schizophrenic subjects. Examples of such stimuli are pictures of human figures, as opposed to pictures of squares, circles, and triangles; apparently schizophrenic deficit occurs in response to any stimulus that is emotionally arousing. Deering (1963) found that schizophrenics gave more associations to both pleasant and unpleasant affective words than did normal subjects; there was no difference between groups in the number of associations attributed to neutral words. It may be that symbolic stimuli elicit a larger number of irrelevant associations in schizophrenic subjects, and that these extraneous associations interfere with their ability to organize their responses effectively (see Fuller and Kates, 1969; Schwartz and Rouse, 1961).

Several investigations have shown that, on many tasks, mild punishment of wrong responses (censure) actually improves schizophrenics' performances to the point where they behave as effectively as normal subjects. Buss and Lang suggested that this may occur because punishment helps the schizophrenic recognize errors and eliminate irrelevant associations that interfere with effective performance. Poor performance from schizophrenics is most obvious when they are required to attend to more than one stimulus at a time, when they must shift attention frequently, and when they must select weak but task relevant stimuli from an array of irrelevant stimuli. Physiologically, schizophrenics show generally high levels of muscular tension and cardiovascular activity; however, they fail to react as quickly or as intensively as normal subjects to stressful stimuli.

Variability of response. A characteristic feature of schizophrenia is the high level of intraindividual variability of response. This is evident on physiological measures as well as on psychological tests, where inconsistency of performance is also marked. The schizophrenic will frequently perform very well on one test of intelligence and very poorly on another, or produce incorrect responses to easy questions and correct responses to very difficult questions.

Lang and Buss (1965, p. 97) summarized their own interpretation of the findings in this way:

> The associations of schizophrenics are idiosyncratic and deviant, and they deteriorate performance because they serve as distractors. Schizophrenics

> have difficulty in focusing on relevant stimuli and excluding irrelevant stimuli, in maintaining a set over time, in shifting a set when it is necessary, in instructing themselves and in pacing themselves, and generally in performing efficiently. . . . These difficulties are pervasive, occurring over a wide range of perceptual, motor, and cognitive tasks.

Lang and Buss speculated that schizophrenics suffer a fundamental sensorimotor defect; they suggested that the ascending reticular activating system (Chap. 7) is implicated as a possible source of the difficulty. For the moment, it is not necessary to concern ourselves with whether schizophrenia represents a disorder of the nervous system or is more accurately described as a functional disturbance of behavior that results from faulty learning. It is enough simply to show that laboratory studies reveal unusual features in schizophrenic behavior.

Problems of generality. If results from the studies summarized above are to be generalized, an important, but unfortunately highly questionable, assumption must be granted. The assumption that the subjects of these studies are representative of schizophrenics everywhere is almost certainly invalid for several reasons.

First, samples in many of these studies probably do not include adequate numbers of severely disturbed individuals. Investigators usually cannot collect data from persons who are mute, stuporous, seriously out of contact with reality, or likely to become assaultive. Such subjects are therefore not represented in most research.

Second, samples in these studies probably do not include adequate numbers of the less severely disturbed. A large number of unrecognized or "subclinical" schizophrenics avoid commitment by concealing their symptoms from public view or by finding ways of living that do not threaten others, and hence are regarded as merely strange or eccentric. Such persons would not come to the attention of the investigator.

Third, the samples in these studies may not represent *any* psychologically meaningful population. The group to which the results of most such studies generalize with least difficulty is the population of testable inmates of state-operated mental hospitals in the United States. Most subjects therefore come from the lower socioeconomic classes, and all are products of modern western civilization.

It may be that what is presented as evidence of a common, underlying disease is really evidence of the failure of modern urban society to provide adequate conditions for development of appropriately adaptive behaviors, especially in its poor and disadvantaged groups. If that is the case, schizophrenia is neither a bodily nor a mental illness, but a behavioral by-product of social injustice and cultural intolerance.

Social and Cultural Considerations

Statements like those above open up whole new fields for study. The purposes of this book (one of which is to serve as an introduction to specifically psychological research) permit no more than passing mention of these important fields of investigation, which have developed their own methods and theories. An introduction to them may be found in the collection of papers, *Changing Perspectives in Mental Illness* (Plog and Edgerton, 1969). However, proper appreciation is to be gained only by taking appropriate courses in sociology and anthropology, subjects which are becoming increasingly necessary for students who wish to understand all aspects of abnormal behavior.

The sociological approach. In the study of mental illness, the sociologist usually has attempted to determine whether the causes of behavior disturbances can be found in the structure and organization of society itself. An early example of such research is the study by Faris and Dunham (1939) which examined the incidence of mental illnesses in large urban areas and found that, except for the manic-depressive psychoses, high rates of mental illness were clearly concentrated in the center of the city in areas marked by poverty, substandard housing, ethnic conflicts, unstable families, and mobile populations. These findings suggested a close relationship between social class and mental illness; they raised the possibility that mental illness is the product of poor social conditions.

Later work by Dunham (1969), one of the co-authors of the earlier study, showed that this pattern has been changing since World War II. It now appears that rates of mental illness are becoming more homogeneous throughout urban areas. There are many possible reasons for the change, but the important thing is that the more recent findings cast doubt on conclusions drawn from earlier work; they raised grave questions about the actual significance of living conditions and cultural organizations as explanations for mental illness, particularly schizophrenia.

Although the search for specifically social causes of deviant behavior continues, the study of factors like social mobility, degree of integration of persons into larger social units, and anomie (loss of social support for regulation of personal behavior) accounts for a large portion of sociologists' interests today. New techniques and theories for the study of these factors are developing rapidly.

The anthropological approach. The work of the sociologist and the cultural anthropologist overlap considerably in the study of mental illness. Both seek to relate behavioral disturbances to the structure and processes of the society in which the disturbances take place. In somewhat oversimplified fashion, we may say that the sociologist tends to use data gathered from our own society as source material, while the cultural anthropologist concerns himself somewhat more extensively (and by different methods) with descriptions of cultures other than our own.

Historically, anthropological interest in abnormal behavior was aroused by such contributions as Ruth Benedict's famous book, *Patterns of Culture* (1934). Benedict proposed that different cultures support and devalue different types of behavior; consequently, "normal" actions in one culture will be "abnormal" in another. For example, aggressive behavior that is admired in a warlike tribe may be regarded as seriously deviant in a tribe that prohibits expressions of hostility. Indeed, a whole culture may be "sick" by western standards if it encourages behavior (such as suspiciousness and delusions of personal grandeur) that we have found to be indicative of mental illness.

Ideas like these are now regarded as dangerous oversimplifications of the complex relationship between culture and behavior (Wallace, 1969; Opler, 1969). Nevertheless, it was theories like Benedict's that awakened anthropological interest in the study of mental illness. There remains much to be learned about the rate of occurrence and the forms of behavior disturbances in cultures other than our own. It is the anthropologist who sets himself the task of learning these things.

Similarities between Schizophrenics and Normals

The idea that schizophrenia is a kind of sickness leads naturally to a search for differences between schizophrenics and normal people. Unfortunately, it also causes investigators to ignore what may be fundamental similarities between the behaviors of these two groups. A growing group of investigators feels that these similarities should not be ignored. It is a matter of no small significance that, under certain conditions, schizophrenics perform as effectively as nonschizophrenics.

A Proposal

What would happen if we abandoned the assumption that schizophrenics differ from nonschizophrenics? What if a program of research were organized around the proposition that schizophrenics are fundamentally the same as everyone else, and react in perfectly rational ways to the situations in which they find themselves? If the disease conception of schizophrenia were correct, such a program would be doomed to failure. If schizophrenia is as fundamentally disruptive of the total personality as has always been thought, disorganization should be evident in everything the schizophrenic does; attempts to explain his behavior from rational premises should prove fruitless.

However, as we have seen, schizophrenia may not be a disease or a sickness. It may be better described as a demonstration of a person's inability or unwillingness to live in normal society. What are commonly called "symptoms" may really be communications to oneself and others that the way of life prescribed by the world in which one lives has become unbearable. If that is so, removal of the person who displays schizophrenic behavior from the pressures and demands of everyday affairs should markedly reduce his personal distress and psychotic symptoms. Protest in the form of pathological behavior should then become necessary only when the person is threatened with the possibility of return to "normal" life.

The restorative effects of removal from society should not be immediate, however, for the prospect of commitment to a mental hospital poses a serious threat in itself. Very few people (no matter how disturbed their overt actions) delight in the expectation of being called insane and locked up in a hospital ward with crazy people. The schizophrenic seems to want and need a life that is more protective and less demanding than the lives most of us prefer, but he does not want it at the cost of personal freedom or self-respect.

We can therefore expect that many people institutionalized for behavior problems will at first try to appear as normal as possible in order to convince the authorities that incarceration is unnecessary. Most new inmates quickly learn that the way to accomplish this is not by fighting or becoming hostile, since institutions know very well how to handle people who behave this way. The newcomer accomplishes release by admitting that he once was sick and maintaining that he is rapidly returning to a state of mental health as a result of the help he has received in the institution.

Inmates who fail to learn this, or who carry it off poorly, eventually become absorbed into the institutional structure. They become oldtimers who have learned that a moderately satisfying life can be lived in a mental hospital if one knows the ropes. The transition from newcomer to oldtimer produces profound changes in attitudes and behavior. The knowledgeable oldtimer does not seek out doctors or social workers, for he knows that they possess the power to disrupt his life by forcing him to leave the institution. He realizes that his *modus vivendi* is secure only so long as others believe that he is sick and requires institutional care. At the same time, he cannot appear to be too sick or he will lose his privileges, be given unpleasant treatments, be transferred to a less desirable ward, or perhaps even be locked up in a solitary cell. In short, the oldtimer, in finding a way of life that suits both him and society, behaves in perfectly rational, adaptive ways. He does what anyone would be expected to do in similar circumstances, he does it intelligently, and he may even do it deliberately (Braginsky, Braginsky, and Ring, 1969).

Evidence from Research

If this conception of psychotic behavior is correct, it should be possible not only to demonstrate differences between the behavior of oldtimers and newcomers, but to manipulate conditions in such a way as to alter these behaviors in predictable ways. Several investigations have explored these possibilities.

Test-taking behavior. Braginsky, Grosse, and Ring (1966) prepared two forms of a 30 item test made up of items from the Minnesota Multiphasic Personality Inventory (Chap. 14). The test items were not particularly symptom oriented, although a few did describe somewhat unusual states. (Examples: Sometimes when I am not feeling well I am cross. I wish I were not bothered by thoughts about sex. My skin seems to be unusually sensitive to touch. I have had some unusual religious experiences.)

The only difference between the two forms of the test was that one was labeled "Mental Illness Test" while the other was labeled "Self-Insight Test." Inmates taking the mental illness test were told that people who answer True to a great many items are mentally ill and likely to remain in the hospital for a long period of time; people who answer False to a great many items are likely to be in for a short time. Inmates taking the self-insight test were told that True answers reflect self-knowledge and people who answer True to many items would probably not remain in the hospital for a long time, while people who answer False to many items show lack of self-knowledge and would probably remain in the hospital for a long time. Both forms of the test were given to groups of newcomers (patients hospitalized for less than three months and for the first time) and oldtimers (patients hospitalized for more than three months, the majority for more than three years).

If it is true that newcomers wish to leave the institution, they should produce more True responses to the self-insight than to the mental illness test, even though the items are identical on both tests. If oldtimers wish to remain in the institution, they should produce more True responses to the mental illness than to the self-insight test. Figure 15.1 shows that these expectations are borne out by the data. The first pair of bars represents the average number of True responses given by newcomers; the second pair represents the average number of True responses given by oldtimers. The third pair represents the average number of True responses given by a comparison group of oldtimers who were given the two tests but told nothing about the supposed meanings of True and False answers. There are ten subjects in each group.

It is obvious that newcomers presented themselves as insightful rather than as mentally ill, while the oldtimers presented themselves as mentally ill. Data from

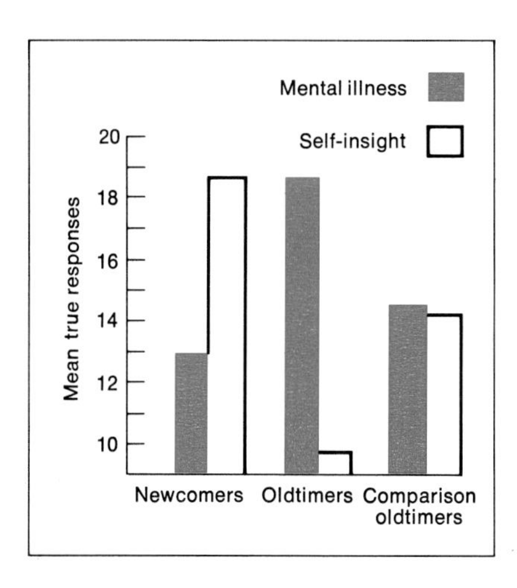

Fig. 15.1 Mean number of True responses as a function of patient type and alleged purpose of text. (Data from Braginsky, Braginsky, and Ring, 1969)

the comparison group show that these tendencies (at least among the oldtimers) do not simply result from the different labels assigned to the tests, but are attributable to the explanations of test purposes provided by the experimenter; the alleged purposes of the tests were not explained to subjects in the comparison group.

In a somewhat similar study, Fontana and Gessner (1969) examined 75 psychiatric patients (mixed diagnoses) by asking them to provide self-reports of pathological symptoms. Twenty-four were told that the test was for research purposes, but the outcome might influence the decision to discharge them. Another group of 24 was also told that the test was for research purposes, but that the outcome might influence the decision to transfer them to another institution (something the patients would wish to avoid). The remaining 27 subjects were told only that the test was being administered for research purposes.

Briefly stated, the results were as follows. Patients in the *transfer* condition presented themselves as significantly less pathological than patients in the *research* condition. This finding is in accord with expectations based on the assumption that transfer is undesirable and can be avoided by not looking too sick. Under the *discharge* condition, patients judged to be most fully disabled presented themselves as more pathological than they did under the other two conditions, but patients judged to be only partially disabled presented themselves as less pathological than under the other conditions. These findings are consistent with the idea that people with severe behavior disturbances do not wish to leave the protection of the hospital environment, while people whose disturbances are less completely disabling do wish to leave.

Patients diagnosed as psychotic consistently presented themselves as less pathological than patients diagnosed as nonpsychotic. This suggests that the "sicker" one is, the less sick one wishes to appear to others. It is consistent with the results of research by Giovanni and Ullman (1963), described earlier in this chapter, which showed that people generally avoid identifying themselves publicly as seriously mentally ill. It is also consistent with data reported by Mahrer, Mason, Kahn, and Projansky (1967), who found that, in a sample of 284 psychiatric patients, 25 per cent reported fewer than 10 (of a possible 180) symptoms on a checklist, 50 per cent reported fewer than 20 symptoms, and 75 per cent reported fewer than 33 symptoms.

	Conditions		
	Discharge	Determination	Informational
Psychopathology*	3.70	2.63	3.66
Hospital control †	4.20	2.83	4.10

* Range 1–5
† Range 1–8.
Table 15.1. *Mean Psychiatric Ratings of Patients' Psychopathology and Need for Hospital Control According to Experimental Conditions (Adapted from Braginsky and Braginsky, 1967)*

Interview behavior. The next investigation was designed to determine whether the impression management evident in the study of test-taking would appear in a face-to-face situation with a person in authority (Braginsky and Braginsky, 1967). Thirty oldtimers were brought to an interview room for a two minute examination by a psychologist which consisted mainly of questions about how the inmate was feeling.

On their way to the examination room, ten subjects were told that the purpose of the interview was probably to determine which patients are ready for discharge; ten were told that the purpose was probably to determine which patients should be on locked (undesirable) and open (desirable) wards; ten were told the interview was probably just to find out how patients are feeling and getting along in the hospital. The person who conducted the interviews did not know which subjects had been assigned to which condition.

Tape recordings of all interviews were submitted to three staff psychiatrists who had no prior knowledge of the experiment and were unfamiliar with the patients. The psychiatrists rated each interview on degree of psychopathology displayed (1: low; 5: high) and on amount of hospital control the patient needs (1: low, discharge; 8: closed ward, continual observation). The investigators predicted that subjects in the second condition (ward determination) would be rated lower than patients in either of the other two conditions. These patients would desire the freedom of the open ward and would therefore present themselves as relatively free from pathology and relatively low in need for confinement. By contrast, patients in the *discharge* condition would present themselves as higher in pathology and in need of control because they wish to remain in the institution. Those in the *informational* condition were expected to sense a threat of discharge (since mental status interviews of this type are frequently used for evaluating readiness for release), and were therefore expected to behave in much the same way as those who were told that discharge was a possible outcome of the interview.

The results of the interview ratings were in accord with expectations (Table 15.1). Patients in the ward determination group were rated as less pathological and less in need of hospital control than patients in either of the other two conditions.

Reaction time. Fontana and Klein (1968) wished to discover whether some of the laboratory findings regarding the so-called "schizophrenic deficit" might be

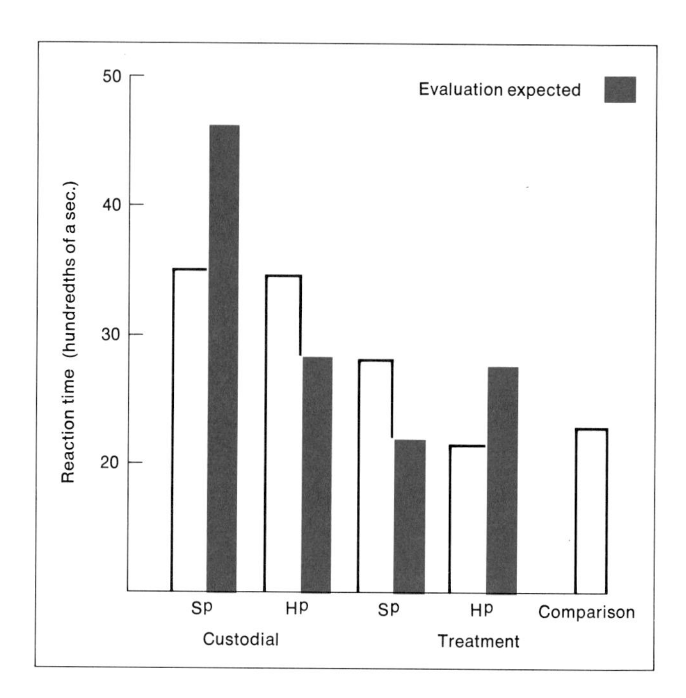

Fig. 15.2. Overall mean reaction times for subjects who expect and who do not expect their performances to be evaluated. (Data from Fontana and Klein, 1968)

explained by patients' tendencies to present themselves in ways that are personally advantageous. Using a test developed in another investigation (Fontana, Klein, Lewis, and Levine, 1968), patients were divided into groups of *healthy presenters* (HP—persons who report few symptoms of psychopathology) and *sick presenters* (SP—persons who report many symptoms of psychopathology). HP and SP subjects were selected from groups of *custodial* patients, who were not receiving treatment but were merely being housed by the institution, and *treatment* patients, who were on active programs of therapy. A comparison group was made up of ten hospital employees who knew that their performances on the experimental task would be compared with the performances of patients.

The experimental task was a simple reaction time procedure in which the subject is required to respond as quickly as possible to a stimulus (in this case an auditory click) presented by the examiner. Reaction time is commonly used in laboratory studies of schizophrenia, and is regarded as being particularly sensitive to schizophrenic disturbance.

Ten *practice* trials were administered, then 11 *prebreak* trials were administered, followed by a brief break in the testing procedure. Finally, 11 *postbreak* trials were administered. About half the schizophrenic subjects were told in advance that they would receive information about their performances during the break in testing. These patients were informed during the break that they were doing about as well as most patients on the assigned task.

The results indicated that performance evaluations had no noticeable effect on the data. Patterns and levels of performance were the same in the postbreak period as in the prebreak period (Fig. 15.2 shows the overall mean reaction times for the various research groups).

More important than evaluation per se was whether or not subjects expected their performances to be evaluated. Look first at the data for custodial patients. Notice that the performances of SP who expected to be evaluated are poorer (longer reaction time) than the performances of those who did not expect to be evaluated. Notice also that the performances of HP who expected to be evaluated are better than the performances of those who did not expect evaluation. These data can be explained by proposing that the expectation of evaluation exaggerates preexisting tendencies in custodial patients. Patients who wish to be seen as sick behave in a more sickly fashion, but patients who wish to be seen as healthy behave in a more healthy fashion.

The data for patients in treatment shows that the differences between treatment patient groups are in directions precisely contrary to those evidenced by custodial patients. SP in treatment perform *better* when they expect to be evaluated; HP perform more poorly when they expect to be evaluated. Why should this be so?

The investigators suggest that patients in treatment wish to appear deserving of their status. To remain in treatment requires that one be sick, but not too sick. If an SP in treatment gets worse, his treatment may be regarded as unsuccessful and he will lose his favored place in the institution, so he does better when he expects his performance to be evaluated. By contrast, an HP in treatment who does too well faces the threat of discharge, so he does worse when he expects to be evaluated.

Incidentally, you may have noticed that patients in treatment generally show shorter reaction times than custodial patients, which suggests either of two hypotheses. One (the more obvious) is that patients in treatment once had slower reaction times but have improved as a result of therapy. An alternate hypothesis is that only patients who show least disturbance of behavior are selected for treatment in the first place. Indirect evidence suggests that the latter is as likely to be correct as the former. Sinnett and Hanford (1962) found that patients who were the most popular with other patients and were best liked by physicians were the ones most likely to be given therapy. Manis, Houts, and Blake (1963) found that patients whose beliefs about mental illness are most strongly influenced by the beliefs of the staff are the ones who respond most favorably to hospitalization. Apparently, cooperativeness and a desire to please those in authority are attributes of behavior as important within the walls of mental institutions as they are outside them.

Behavior outside the laboratory. Hersen (1969) described the failure of an attempt by a mental hospital staff to install an independent living, or self-care, unit in the institution. A self-care unit is designed to aid patients in making the transition from hospital to community after their period of treatment has been completed. Patients are given considerable freedom to arrange their own schedules and manage their own affairs. In this particular instance, failure to establish the unit was primarily due to patient unwillingness to participate. One patient summarized the typical response by saying, "I came here because I'm sick and need treatment. If I could be on Self-Care, I wouldn't need the hospital, and I would go home." Hersen concluded that this attitude represents inmates' desires to use the hospital as an escape from the harsh realities of life; many patients avoid responsibility for solving problems by hiding behind the socially acceptable facade of illness.

Zlotowski and Cohen (1968) examined the effects of a forthcoming change in hospital organization on patients' behaviors, as reflected in nurses' ratings. They found that patients who were better adjusted before the reorganization showed increased disturbance of behavior, while patients who were initially more poorly adjusted showed improvement. These changes were stable enough to remain significant three months later. In effect, these findings suggested that poorer patients view any change as an improvement, while better adjusted patients, being relatively satisfied with things as they are, see change as disruptive and threatening, a sign of rejection by the hospital.

Braginsky, Holzberg, Ridley, and Braginsky (1968) asked patients to describe a typical 24 hour day in the hospital. They found that three types of patients could be identified: warders, workers, and mobile socializers. As suggested by the names assigned, warders spend much of their time on the wards and relatively little time at work or off the ward socializing. Workers spend much of their time on jobs, while socializers move around the grounds a good bit and spend a great deal of time with friends.

Time spent on the ward correlated with patient attitudes that stressed differences between patients and normal people, the immutability of the patient's condition, the need to suffer, and a desire to be left alone. Work time was correlated with somewhat similar attitudes which, however, emphasized the need for comfort and a desire for greater freedom to enter and leave the hospital at will. Mobile socializers stressed similarities between patients and normal people, opposition to social restriction and loss of civil liberties, the temporary nature of patient status, and the need for comfort and enjoyment while in the hospital. Patients who spent a great deal of time on the wards tended not to enter psychotherapy. Patients who socialized a great deal did tend to enter psychotherapy, and also tended to have the highest discharge rate. Entrance into psychotherapy was not correlated with amount of time spent working or apparent degree of behavior disturbance.

In other research, Braginsky, Braginsky, and Ring (1969) found that patient visibility (being remembered by the psychiatrists) is related to style of adaptation, but not to degree of psychopathology. Male patients remained invisible by staying on the wards and socializing less; women remain invisible by staying off the wards through involvement with either socializing or work. Visible patients were found to have a higher rate of discharge from the hospital than invisible patients.

The same investigators presented evidence that patients in a mental hospital behave more similarly to the way they acted on weekends than to the way they acted during the week in the period before they were hospitalized. Furthermore, it was generally found that patients (especially those who have other patients or expatients for friends) often tend to view the hospital more as a retreat or resort than as a place to go for cure of a disease: "a relatively large portion of admissions to the hospital are indeed friends and enter the hospital together, not because they simultaneously 'caught' schizophrenia but simply because they wanted to enjoy together the resort potentials of the mental hospital" (Braginsky, Braginsky, and Ring, 1969, p. 156).

Are Schizophrenics Normal?

The studies outlined above establish that there is empirical merit in the hypothesis that people who are labeled schizophrenic nonetheless adapt effectively and intelligently to situations in which they are placed. Shall we now argue that it is no longer feasible to consider schizophrenics to be different in any respect from normal people?

Such a radical position scarcely seems justified. None of the studies proves beyond question that schizophrenia does not involve disease of some sort. What they do demonstrate is that it is often just as reasonable to ascribe normal as abnormal motives to schizophrenic behavior. They show that the dominant disease-oriented conception of schizophrenia is limited in its ability to explain a large part of what schizophrenics actually do in their everyday lives. They also show that, even if schizophrenia is a disease, it is not one that sets its victims apart from the rest of mankind. It does not necessarily disrupt behavior totally or deform the whole personality.

Retorts and Counterarguments

Any student who has come this far in his introduction to psychology should realize that few matters are settled quickly or simply in the science of behavior. Just as there are those who radically oppose the idea that schizophrenia is an illness, there are also those who vigorously support it. Support for the disease conception assumes two forms: logical and empirical. Both forms of argument are considered briefly in the following sections.

Logical Arguments

One set of arguments attacks the conception of disease that is assumed by those who reject the explanation of behavior disorder in terms of illness. According to this argument, the term disease means "any marked deviation, physical, mental, or behavioral, from normally desirable standards of structural and functional integrity" (Ausubel, 1961). Consequently, it is appropriate to call behavior disturbance disease, whether or not it has a basis in physical states (see also Sarason and Ganzer, 1968).

Dissatisfaction with the disease concept seems to have arisen, in large part, as a reaction against two major trends in the handling of behavior disorders (Ausubel, 1961). The first trend has been toward strict reservation to medically trained personnel of the right to treat such disorders. Clinical psychologists (who receive their training in departments of psychology and usually possess the Ph.D. degree) resent restrictions placed upon their activities by medically dominated institutions and antiquated laws. They feel that, by proving behavior disorders to be defects in learning, they can establish more effectively their own right to assume full responsibility for treatment procedures. This reaction can be seen most clearly in the case presented by Albee (1968) outlined at the beginning of this chapter.

The second major trend, which exists within clinical psychology itself, has been toward repudiation of the relevance of moral judgment and personal responsibility in the assessment of behavior. Many authorities feel that elimination of the disease concept will restore to psychology interest in values and ethics. This reaction is most forcefully expressed by Mowrer (1960) and by Szasz (1960, 1961a, 1961b), whose positions were also outlined at the beginning of this chapter.

Briefly, the counterargument to these assertions is that both trends can be overcome without abandoning the disease concept. First there is precedent, in such professions as dentistry, for the development of nonmedical specialties whose practitioners treat recognized diseases. There is no reason why psychology should not seek similar status. Second, there is no necessary contradiction between the concept of disease and the belief that people are responsible for their own actions. A distinction can be made between behavior that arises from mental illness and behavior that stems from immorality or willful misconduct. But even if it were true that mental illness results from immoral actions, the disease is just as real and the person just as much in need of therapy. Treatment is not denied a person with syphilis just because he may have contracted it in a way that might be judged immoral.

Another set of logical arguments has been developed around the proposition that, whether or not the disease concept is correct, it works fairly well in actual practice. According to this view, it is not the concept of mental illness that must be changed, but the condemnation, punishment, and social rejection that is aroused when the term is used (Ellis, 1967).

There are, in fact, people who are not responsible for their own disordered behavior who must be incarcerated to protect themselves and others. The label "mentally ill" enables society to identify such people and to perform its protective function effectively. In some cases, application of the label may produce in a person a sense of shame and loss of self-respect. However, in other cases, telling a person that he is mentally ill, and not sinful or evil as he originally supposed, produces relief from misery, a feeling of exoneration, and increased self-regard.

Similarly, the label "mental illness" may induce some people to avoid admitting their problems. At other times, however, telling a person that he is mentally ill causes him to admit for the first time in his life that he really does have problems that ought to be solved.

The label may sometimes be used to control nonconforming, but actually creative, behavior. Any radical thinker can be called sick, and subsequently ignored or incarcerated. However, this is not the fault of the label itself. Unconventional people have always been rejected in some way. Eliminating the concept of mental illness will not increase society's willingness to accept nonconformity. If the term is used properly, no injustice will be done, for there is no reason to believe that a neurotic or psychotic person is necessarily more creative or constructively innovative than one who is psychologically healthy.

Empirical Arguments

Potentially more convincing than purely logical debates, which sometimes degenerate into unproductive semantic quibbles, are arguments based on empirical findings. A number of such arguments have been marshaled by Rimland (1969). Since the disease concept has not been pressed to its limit in preceding sections of this chapter, it is appropriate to finish this discussion of schizophrenia by briefly summarizing the points Rimland makes.

Rimland noted that the terms "functional" and "psychogenic" are often used simply to conceal our ignorance of the true causes of behavior. Our knowledge of the operation of the nervous system and of the biological bases of behavior is still so incomplete that it is, at best, premature to rule out physical factors as causes of behavior disturbances. When we do so, we divert attention from such important factors as endocrine balance, nutritional deficit, possible influence of viruses, and so on.

Studies of twins reared apart which show that only one becomes schizophrenic are often cited as evidence that schizophrenia is not biologically caused. However, a review of many such cases (Pollin, Stabenau, and Tupin, 1965) showed that the ultimately schizophrenic twin often weighed less than his sibling at birth. This hints at the possibility of constitutional differences (perhaps beginning in the prenatal environment) that may well be crucial to the later appearance of schizophrenia.

Most research on the psychological causes of behavior disorder is purely correlational and permits no firm conclusions to be drawn. For example, Rimland cites one study (Beisser, Glasser, and Grant, 1966) which found that children of behaviorally disturbed mothers show a greater rate of behavioral deviation than children of normal mothers. The findings, based on interviews with the mothers, were seen as supporting the proposition that family milieu contributes significantly to the mental health of its members. Rimland noted that they also support at least two other propositions, neither of which was considered by the investigators. The first is that behaviorally disturbed mothers are poor judges of their children. The second, and more important from Rimland's point of view, is that children inherit the tendency to behavior disorder from their parents. Most studies that purport to prove the psychogenic basis of behavior disorder do not actually eliminate the possibility of physical causes (as is required by the method of strong inference, Chap. 1); they simply ignore it.

Properly controlled studies of the effectiveness of psychotherapy with schizophrenics consistently fail to show significantly greater improvement in treated groups than in nontreated groups. Introduction of biochemical methods, by contrast, reduced the number of hospitalized patients in this country by 83,000 between 1955 and 1965. Drugs are now available that produce realistic psychoses. Reserpine produces depression in some subjects that cannot be distinguished from the "real" thing; amphetamine produces effects that are nearly indistinguishable from paranoid schizophrenia.

Studies of the incidence of schizophrenia and of its symptoms show remarkable statistical stability over time and across cultures. A person with an identical twin, who is schizophrenic is known to have a 67 to 86 per cent likelihood of developing schizophrenia himself; a person with an ordinary sibling who is schizophrenic has only a 5 to 14 per cent likelihood of becoming schizophrenic. Even when children of schizophrenic mothers are adopted into homes without schizophrenia, they show a higher incidence of behavior disturbance than adopted children of nonschizophrenic mothers (Heston, 1966; also relevant is Higgins, 1966). The extensive literature on the subject of heredity in mental disorder is fairly consistent in its implications. Evidence for the heritability of schizophrenia is sufficiently strong to be accepted as virtually conclusive (Murray and Hirsch, 1969). The problem for future research is therefore to determine not whether a predisposition to schizophrenia is inherited, but how it is inherited and how the predisposition is affected by environmental factors.

Research has linked reduction of wheat consumption in Finland, Norway, and Sweden during World War II with reduction in hospital admissions for schizophrenia (Dohan, 1966). Other research has related schizophrenia to celiac disease, a disorder that involves unusual sensitivity to wheat and certain other grains. Favorable results have been reported in treating schizophrenia with massive doses of niacin, a B vitamin (Hoffer and Osmond, 1966). These and similar results suggest the possibility that the disease results from the inability of certain individuals to utilize certain specific nutritive substances effectively.

A Final Note

Our present state of knowledge is such that it would be misleading to claim that anyone knows either the cause or cure of schizophrenia. Productive research and provocative arguments have been generated both by the assumption that schizophrenia is a disease and by the assumption that it is not. Evidence that bodily states affect psychological functioning is incontrovertible. Evidence that psychological factors are important determinants of behavior is equally strong.

It would be convenient if science could produce some simple cure for the troubles that beset us, both as individuals and as a society. It would be comforting to think that some day our problems can be made to disappear simply by ingesting a pill or by reciting magical incantations before a psychiatrist.

Hope and optimism are beneficial, for even false hope can make realistic progress possible in the long run. At the same time, we must not expect too much too fast. The human organism is an intricate, complex, and altogether wonderful creature. If we expect human behavior to be simply explained or easily understood, we are certain to be disappointed. Problems in living, sin, guilt, and ethical and moral values are as real and potent in the daily lives of men as are disorders of the heart, brain, and genes. All these pose real problems for the scientist, and each must be dealt with in its own terms.

Glossary

Affective: emotional.

Disease model: the viewpoint that disturbances of behavior are symptoms of mental or physical illness and therefore require medical treatment.

Manic-depressive psychosis: psychosis (*q.v.*) marked by extremes of emotion, affect, or mood.

Paranoid: characterized by suspiciousness, delusions of persecution and grandeur, and ideas of reference.

Process schizophrenia: long-term, progressive deterioration of behavior and thought (*see also* schizophrenia, reactive schizophrenia).

Psychiatrist: a medically trained specialist in the treatment of "mental illness."

Psychogenic: of psychological origin.

Psychosis: a severe form of behavior disturbance, usually involving markedly unrealistic behavior.

Reactive schizophrenia: schizophrenia (*q.v.*) of sudden onset, with a high level of agitation and rapid deterioration of behavior.

Schizophrenia: a form of psychosis characterized by disturbances of thought, hallucinations, delusions, bizarre behavior, and extreme withdrawal.

References

Albee, G.W. Conceptual models and manpower requirements in psychology. *Amer. Psychologist*, 1968, **23,** 317–320.

Ausubel, O.P. Personality disorder is disease. *Amer. Psychologist*, 1961, **16,** 69–74.

Beisser, A.R., N. Glasser, and M. Grant. Level of psychosocial adjustment in children of identified schizophrenic mothers. *California Mental Health Research Digest*, 1966, **4,** 113–114.

Benedict, R. *Patterns of culture*. Boston: Houghton Mifflin, 1934.

Braginsky, B.M., and D.D. Braginsky. Schizophrenic patients in the psychiatric interview: An experimental study of their effectiveness at manipulation. *J. consult. Psychol.*, 1967, **31,** 543–547.

———, and K. Ring. *Methods of madness: The mental hospital as a last resort*. New York: Holt, Rinehart and Winston, 1969.

Braginsky, B.M., M. Gross, and K. Ring. Controlling outcomes through impression-management: An experimental study of the manipulative tactics of mental patients. *J. consult. Psychol.*, 1966, **30,** 295–300.

Braginsky, B., J. Holzberg, D. Ridley, and D. Braginsky. Patient styles of adaptation to a mental hospital. *J. Pers.*, 1968, **36,** 283–298.

Buss, A.H., and P.J. Lang. Psychological deficit in schizophrenia: Affect, reinforcement, and concept attainment. *J. abnorm. Psychol.*, 1965, **70,** 2–24.

Deering, G. Affective stimuli and disturbance of thought processes. *J. consult. Psychol.*, 1963, **27,** 338–343.

Dohan, F.C. Wheat "consumption" and hospital admissions for schizophrenia during World War II. A preliminary report. *Amer. J. clin. Nutrition*, 1966, **18,** 7–10.

Dunham, H.W. City core and suburban fringe: Distribution patterns of mental illness. In S.C. Plog and R.B. Edgerton (Eds.), *Changing perspectives in mental illness*. New York: Holt, Rinehart and Winston, 1969.

Ellis, A. Should some people be labeled mentally ill? *J. consult. Psychol.*, 1967, **31,** 435–446.

Faris, R.E.L., and H.W. Dunham. *Mental disorders in urban areas: An ecological study of schizophrenia and other psychoses*. Chicago: University of Chicago Press, 1939.

Fontana, A.F., and T. Gessner. Patients' goals and the manifestation of psychopathology. *J. consult. clin. Psychol.*, 1969, **33,** 247–253.

Fontana, A.F., and E.B. Klein. Self presentation and the schizophrenic "deficit." *J. consult. clin. Psychol.*, 1968, **32,** 250–256.

———, E. Lewis, and L. Levine. Presentation of self in mental illness. *J. consult. clin. Psychol.*, 1968, **32,** 110–119.

Fuller, G.D., and S.L. Kates. Word association repertoires of schizophrenics and normals. *J. consult. clin. Psychol.*, 1969, **33,** 497–500.

Goffman, E. *Asylums*. New York: Doubleday, 1961.

Giovanni, J.M., and L.P. Ullman. Conceptions of mental health held by psychiatric patients. *J. clin. Psychol.*, 1963, **19,** 398–400.

Herron, W.G. The process-reactive classification of schizophrenia. *Psychol. Bull.*, 1962, **59,** 329–343.

Hersen, M. Independent living as a threat to the institutionalized mental patient. *J. clin. Psychol.*, 1969, **25,** 316–318.

Heston, L.L. Psychiatric disorders in foster home reared children of schizophrenic mothers. *Brit. J. Psychiat.*, 1966, **112,** 819–825.

Higgins, J. Effects of child rearing by schizophrenic mothers. *J. Psychiat. Res.*, 1966, **4,** 153–167.

Hoffer, A., and H. Osmond. *How to live with schizophrenia*. Hyde Park, N.Y.: University Press, 1966.

Kety, S.S. Biochemical theories of schizophrenia: Part I. *Science*, 1959, **129,** 1528–1532.

Lang, P.J., and A.H. Buss. Psychological deficit in schizophrenia: II. interference and activation. *J. abnorm. Psychol.*, 1965, **70,** 77–106.

Mahrer, A.R., D.J. Mason, E. Kahn, and M. Projansky. The non-Gaussian distribution of amount of symptomatology in psychiatric patients. *J. clin. Psychol.*, 1967, **23,** 319–321.

Manis, M., P.S. Houts, and J.B. Blake. Beliefs about mental illness as a function of psychiatric status and psychiatric hospitalization. *J. abnorm. soc. Psychol.*, 1963, **67,** 226–233.

Mowrer, O.H. "Sin," the lesser of two evils. *Amer. Psychologist*, 1960, **15,** 301–304.

Murray, H.G., and J. Hirsch. Heredity, individual differences, and psychopathology. In S.C. Plog and R.B. Edgerton (Eds.), *Changing perspectives in mental illness*. New York: Holt, Rinehart and Winston, 1969.

Opler, M.K. Anthropological contribution to psychiatry and social psychiatry. In S.C. Plog and R.B. Edgerton (Eds.), *Changing perspectives in mental illness*. New York: Holt, Rinehart and Winston, 1969.

Plog, S.C., and R.B. Edgerton. (Eds.) *Changing perspectives in mental illness*. New York: Holt, Rinehart and Winston, 1969.

Pollin, W., J.R. Stabenau, and J. Tupin. Family studies with identical twins discordant for schizophrenia. *Psychiatry*, 1965, **28**, 119–132.

Rimland, B. Psychogenesis versus biogenesis: The issues and the evidence. In S.C. Plog and R.B. Edgerton (Eds.), *Changing perspectives in mental illness*. New York: Holt, Rinehart and Winston, 1969.

Sarason, I.G., and V.J. Ganzer. Concerning the medical model. *Amer. Psychologist*, 1968, **23**, 507–510.

Sarbin, T.R. On the futility of the proposition that some people be labelled "mentally ill." *J. consult. Psychol.*, 1967, **31**, 447–453.

———. The scientific status of the mental illness metaphor. In S.C. Plog and R.B. Edgerton (Eds.), *Changing perspectives in mental illness*. New York: Holt, Rinehart and Winston, 1969.

Schwartz, F., and R. Rouse. The activation and recovery of associations. *Psychol. Issues*, 1961, **3**, Monograph 9.

Shontz, F.C., S.L. Fink, and C.E. Hallenbeck. Chronic physical illness as threat, *Archives of Physical Medicine and Rehabilitation*, 1960, **41**, 143–148.

Sinnett, E.R., and D.B. Hanford. The effects of patients' relationships with peers and staff on their psychiatric treatment programs. *J. abnorm. soc. Psychol.*, 1962, **64**, 151–154.

Szasz, T.S. The myth of mental illness. *Amer. Psychologist*, 1960, **15**, 113–118.

———. *The myth of mental illness*. New York: Hoeber, 1961. (b)

———. The uses of naming and the origin of the myth of mental illness. *Amer. Psychologist*, 1961, **16**, 59–68. (a)

Wallace, A.F.C. Cultural change and mental illness. In S.C. Plog and R.B. Edgerton (Eds.), *Changing perspectives in mental illness*. New York: Holt, Rinehart and Winston, 1969.

Wolfer, J.A. Concerning the concern over the medical model. *Amer. Psychologist*, 1969, **24**, 606–607.

Zigler, E., and L. Phillips. Psychiatric diagnosis: A Critique. *J. abnorm. soc. Psychol.*, 1961, **63**, 607–618. (a)

———. Psychiatric diagnosis and symptomology. *J. abnorm. soc. Psychol.*, 1961, **63**, 69–75. (b)

Zlotowski, M., and D. Cohen. Effect of environmental change upon behavior of hospitalized schizophrenic patients. *J. clin. Psychol.*, 1968, **24**, 470–475.

Author Index

Ahrens, J. B., 194, 203
Albee, G. W., 396, 409
Alfert, E., 384
Allen, K. E., 328, 331, 340
Altrocchi, J., 376
American Psychological Ass'n., 391
Ames, E. W., 37, 55
Adams, J. S., 276, 287
Alfert, E., 219, 234
Alzheimer, A., 395
Anand, B. K., 150, 160, 161, 172
Anderson, B. C., 159, 172
Angyal, A., 16
Anliker, J., 317
Antrobus, J. S., 197–199, 202, 204
Apfeldorf, M., 355, 356
Appley, M. H., 206, 233
Archer, J. E., 86, 110
Archimedes, 131
Ardrey, R., 239, 263
Aristotle, 2, 137, 257, 272
Arnold, M., 207, 233
Aronson, E., 276, 282–285, 287, 288
Artemidorus, 177
Aserinsky, E., 183, 202
Ausubel, O. P., 409
Averill, J. R., 225, 226, 235, 384, 392
Ax, A. F., 210, 211, 233
Ayllon, T., 340
Azrin, N. H., 252, 253, 263, 325, 341

Babinski, 347
Bacon, F., 3, 20
Baer, D. M., 328, 330–333, 340, 341
Bailey, C. J., 157, 173
Balinska, H. O., 153, 172
Bamber, D., 79
Bandura, A., 238, 241, 243–246, 250, 251, 258, 263, 264, 340
Banks, R., 366, 367
Barker, L. S., 295, 302, 311
Barker, R. G., 294–297, 300–304, 311
Barnes, J. M., 90–93, 110
Barnes, R. H., 173
Barry, J., 376
Bauermeister, M., 367
Baumrind, D., 231, 233
Bayer, E., 144, 172
Beecher, H. K., 311, 312
Beers, C., 395
Beltt, B., 159, 172
Bender, M. B., 348
Benedict, R., 401
Bennett, D. H., 361, 367
Berger, R. J., 188, 189, 192, 202
Berkeley, G., 58, 97
Berkowitz, L., 238, 239, 251, 257, 258, 260, 264
Bernhardson, C. S., 380, 391
Bernstein, J., 176, 203
Bever, T. G., 117, 119, 121, 140, 141
Bexton, W. H., 228, 233
Binet, A., 15, 372
Bitter, E., 261, 264
Bjork, R. A., 101, 102, 110
Blake, J. B., 407
Blumenthal, A. L., 132, 133, 140

Boakes, R., 133, 140
Boneau, C. A., 322, 341
Boring, E. G., 27, 42, 55, 372
Bosch, H., 349
Bossom, J., 71, 74, 79
Bousfield, W. A., 107, 110
Bower, G. H., 27, 325
Bower, T. G. R., 39–41, 48–50, 55
Brady, J. V., 223, 230, 233
Braginsky, B. M., 403–405, 408
Brawley, E. R., 328, 330, 341
Brehn, J. W., 277, 287
Brennan, W. M., 37, 55
Bricker, W., 261, 265
Briggs, G. E., 90, 110
Brobeck, J. R., 150, 159, 172
Bronowski, J., 19, 26
Brown, R., 26, 103–105, 110
Brown, R. W., 138, 140
Brownfield, C. A., 228, 233
Bruner, J. S., 229, 233, 374, 391
Buell, F. R., 328, 329, 340
Burdick, H., 274, 287
Buresova, O., 153, 172
Burnham, C., 79
Burstein, H. R., 322, 341
Buss, A. H., 238, 255, 256, 258, 259, 261, 264, 398–400
Byrne, D., 375, 376, 381–386, 391
Byrne, J., 190, 203

Calkins, M. W., 192, 202
Calloway, J. W., 173
Camus, J., 147, 172
Cannon, W. B., 144, 172, 207, 233
Canon, L. K., 276, 277, 283, 287
Cappon, D., 366, 367
Carey, P., 117, 122, 141
Carlsmith, J. M., 273–275, 282, 283, 287, 288
Carroll, L., 123
Carstairs, G. M., 352, 367
Cartwright, R. D., 195, 202
Casey, A., 50, 55
Castor, 106
Cattell, J. M., 15, 372
Centers, L., 356, 367
Centers, R., 356, 367
Chamberlin, T. C., 20
Chapanis, A., 287
Chapanis N. P., 287
Cheng, M., 155, 173
Chhina, G., 160
Chomsky, N., 115, 141
Ciba Foundation, 181, 202
Cicero, 106
Clark, H. H., 134–137, 139, 140
Clemes, S., 95–98, 100, 110
Cleveland, S. E., 359, 360, 367
Clifton, C., 117, 140
Cohen, A. M., 387, 391, 392
Cohen, A. R., 274, 277, 282, 288
Cohen, S. I., 209, 229, 233
Cohn, D., 408
Coleman, J. C., 230, 233
Collins, B. E., 275, 282, 283, 287
Conrad, D. G., 230, 233
Coons, E. E., 167, 172
Cooper, J., 283, 288
Copernicus, 3
Corwin, R., 260, 264
Cotzin, M., 20, 21, 23, 24, 26, 27
Cowen, E. L., 214, 233
Crafts, 20, 22, 26
Cronbach, L. J., 372, 379, 391
Crowne, D. P., 386, 391
Cruce, J. A., 167, 172
Cummins, G. M., 144, 172
Cupid, 2
Cytawa, J., 153, 172

Dahlstrom, W. G., 376, 392
Dallenbach, K. M., 20, 21, 23, 24, 26, 2[illegible] 86, 111
Danks, J. H., 132, 141
Darley, J. M., 309, 310, 312
Darwin, C., 3, 4, 372, 377
Davidson, J. R., 274, 288
Davis, J. D., 162, 172
Davison, L. A., 216–218, 224, 233, 234
Davitz, J. R., 256, 264
Deering, G., 399
Deese, J., 214, 234
Delgado, J. M., 165, 167, 172
Dembo, T., 295, 311
Dement, W., 183, 186–188, 191, 192, 194, 202–204
Descartes, R., 3, 30
Desoto, C.M., 134, 140
Dews, P. B., 317, 322, 340
Dickman, H. R., 295, 312
Dickoff, H., 376, 391
Dix, D., 395
Dollard, J. L., 251, 258, 264
Donaldson, M., 136, 140
Doob, L., 251, 264
Dua, S., 160, 172
Dublin, J. E., 383, 392

Duffy, E., 213, 233
Dukes, W. F., 94
Dunbar, H. F., 230, 233
Dunham, H. W., 401

Easterbooks, J. A., 229, 233
Ebbinghaus, H., 83, 84, 86, 110
Ebenholtz, S. M., 64, 65, 67, 68, 79
Edgerton, R. B., 400
Edwards, A. L., 386, 392
Ehrlich, D., 276, 287
Einstein, A., 239, 264
Ekstrand, B. R., 85, 110
Elmadjian, F., 211, 233
Elmes, D. G., 101, 110
Engel, J. F., 276, 288
Epstein, A. N., 146, 147, 150, 152, 153, 172, 173
Epstein, W., 31, 40, 50, 53, 55, 63, 73, 79, 101, 102, 110, 124, 132, 140, 141, 144
Evans, K. L., 224, 233
Evans, R. I., 340
Ewart, P., 73, 79

Fantz, R. L., 32–37, 55
Faris, R. E., 401
Farthing, G. W., 322, 340
Fawl, C. L., 295, 312
Feather, N. T., 276, 288
Fechner, G., 4–6, 8, 9, 11, 14, 26, 27, 372
Feder, C. Z., 382, 383, 386, 392
Feldman, M. J., 358, 367
Ferster, C. B., 341
Feshbach, S., 258–261, 264
Festinger, L., 72, 79, 269, 270, 273–277, 282, 288
Fifkova, E., 153, 172
Findley, J. D., 323
Fink, S. L., 348, 367, 394, 414
Fisher, C., 188, 189, 203, 204
Fisher, R. L., 360, 367
Fisher, S., 359, 360, 367
Fiss, H., 80
Fodor, J. A., 117, 119, 141
Foerst, J. R., 387, 392
Folkins, C. H., 224, 233
Fontana, A. F., 404–406
Foulkes, D., 176, 193, 194, 196, 203, 388, 392
Freedman, J. L., 288
Freedman, S. J., 229, 233
Freud, S., 15, 26, 84, 94, 110, 178, 185, 193, 203, 239, 258, 264, 272, 373, 374, 395
Friesen, W. F., 304, 306, 307
Fulgenzi, L. B., 385, 392
Fuller, G. D., 399

Galanter, E., 12–14, 26, 106, 141
Gale, C., 159, 172
Galileo, 3
Gallagher, R. J., 162
Galton, F., 372
Ganzer, V. J., 409
Garret, M. T., 117, 120, 122, 141
Gilbert, E., 356, 357, 368
Gerard, H. B., 282, 288
Gessner, T., 404
Gibson, E. J., 46–49, 51, 55, 56
Gibson, J. J., 38, 45, 54, 55
Gilbert, R. W., 20, 26
Giovanni, J. M., 394, 404
Gleason, J., 114, 141
Glucksberg, S., 95, 99, 100, 111, 132, 141
Goffman, E., 396
Goldberger, L., 229, 233
Goldfried, M. R., 229, 233
Goldman, K., 168, 173
Goldman, R. M., 168, 172
Goldstein, K., 16
Golightly, C., 382, 391
Golin, S., 384, 392
Goodall, J., 312
Goodenough, D. R., 195, 196, 203, 204
Goodenough, F. L., 356, 368
Goodman, C. C., 374, 391
Gordon, A., 168, 173
Gordon, J. E., 376, 392
Gottleib, N., 69–71, 73, 74, 79
Graham, H. D., 262, 264
Grebstain, L. C., 386, 392
Green, M. A., 348, 367
Greenblatt, M., 229, 233
Gregory, R. L., 31, 55
Grinker, R. P., 230, 233
Gross, J., 190, 191, 203
Gross, L. P., 168, 169, 173
Grossberg, R., 55
Grosse, M., 403
Grossman, M. I., 144, 172
Grossman, S. P., 152, 158, 172
Grunebaum, H. V., 229, 233
Grunin, R., 196, 203
Gump, P. V., 300, 303–308, 311, 312

Gurr, T. R., 262, 264
Guttman, I., 276, 287
Guttman, N., 322

Haber, R. N., 288
Haber, W. B., 345, 346, 368
Hake, D. F., 252, 263
Hall, C. S., 27, 177, 178, 203
Hall, E. R., 303–305, 311
Hallenbeck, C. E., 394, 414
Hallum, F., 192, 204
Hamilton, D. L., 285, 286, 288
Hamlin, H., 167, 172
Handal, S., 134, 140
Hanford, D. B., 407
Hare, R. D., 385, 392
Harris, C. S., 73, 79
Harris, D. B., 357, 368
Harris, F. R., 328–330, 341
Harris, S. C., 144, 172
Harrison, R. H., 322, 323, 341
Hart, B. M., 328–330, 341
Hart, M. H., 328, 341
Hartmann, D. P., 260, 261, 264
Hartmann, E., 176, 195, 201, 203
Harvey, W., 3
Haughton, E., 340
Hawkins, D. T., 165, 173
Hay, J., 74, 75, 79
Head, H., 347–349, 368
Hearst, E., 323, 340
Heath, H. A., 227, 234
Heath, P., 55
Heath, R. G., 167, 172
Hein, A., 76, 77
Heironimus, M., 260, 264
Held, R., 69–74, 76, 77, 79, 229, 234
Helmreich, R., 275, 282–285, 287, 288
Heron, W., 228, 233, 234
Herrnstein, R. J., 27, 341
Herron, E. W., 384, 392
Herron, W. G., 398
Hersen, M., 407
Hershenson, M., 37, 55
Hervey, G. R., 162, 173
Hess, E. H., 26
Hetherington, A. W., 148, 157, 173
Hicks, D., 250, 264
Hilgard, E. R., 27, 325, 341
Hillix, W. A., 27
Hippocrates, 344
Hoagland, H., 211, 234
Hobbes, T., 239, 264
Hochberg, J. E., 43, 53, 55
Hoebel, B. G., 150, 153, 156, 160, 16[illegible] 166, 173
Holden, M., 196, 203
Holt, R. R., 214, 229, 233, 234
Holz, W. C., 325, 341
Holzberg, J., 408
Honig, W. K., 322, 341
Hope, J. M., 211, 233
Horowitz, L. M., 105, 111
Houston, J. P., 91, 111
Houts, P. S.,
Howard, I. P., 63, 79
Hull, C., 16, 17
Hull, C. L., 316, 325, 341
Hunt, R. G., 358, 367
Hunter, I. M. L., 134, 141
Hunter, W. S., 97, 111
Hutchinson, R. R., 252, 263
Huttenlocher, J., 134, 141

Indik, B. P., 306, 307, 312
Irwin, J. M., 88–90, 92, 111
Isard, S., 117–120, 123, 124, 141
Ivy, A. C., 144, 172

Jacobovitz, L. A., 139, 141
Jacobson, A., 196, 203
Jacobson, A. L., 18, 26
Jackson, C. W., 229, 233–235
Jackson, D. N., 231, 235
Jaffa, M., 168, 172
James, W., 14, 18, 30, 53, 55, 85, 103, 111
Janis, I., 214, 215, 219, 224, 226, 234, 274, 288
Jecker, J. D., 276, 288
Jenkins, H. M., 322, 323, 341
Jenkins, J. G., 86, 111
Jenkins, J. J., 99, 111
Jensen, H., 196
Jessop, T. E., 79
Johnson, N. F., 126–129, 141
Johnson, O., 92, 111
Johnson, O. G., 356, 368
Jones, E. E., 283, 288
Jourard, S. M., 361, 368
Jouvet, M., 194
Joy, V. L., 386, 392
Jupiter, 2
Julesz, B., 44, 55

Kagan, J., 55, 212, 214, 234

Kahn, E., 404
Kahn, R. L., 347, 368
Kales, A., 176, 182, 184, 196, 203, 204
Kalish, H., 322
Kamiya, J., 196, 200, 204
Kates, S. L., 399
Kavenau, J. L., 291, 312
Keesey, R., 151, 162–164, 173
Kelleher, R. T., 323, 341
Kellogg, W. N., 21, 26
Kelly, E. L., 229, 234
Kelman, H. C., 231, 234
Kendler, H. H., 341
Kennedy, R. A., 126–128, 141
Keppel, G., 91, 92, 109, 111
Kessen, W., 37, 55
Kety, S. S., 395
Kidd, A. H., 55
Kimura, K., 160, 173
King, B. T., 275, 288
King, L. J., 95, 99, 100
Kirk, R., 121, 140
Klein, E. B., 405, 406
Kleitman, N., 181, 183, 186–188, 202, 203
Klineberg, O., 239, 265
Kling, J. W., 30, 55
Kodama, M., 220, 221, 234
Kohler, I., 59, 63, 64, 73, 80
Kolb, L. C., 345, 368
Korchin, S. G., 227, 229, 234
Kosinin, J. S., 308, 312
Kraepelin, E., 395
Krafft-Ebbing, 395
Krantz, D. H., 13, 26
Krasne, F. B., 159, 173
Krutch, J. W., 341
Kubie, L. S., 229, 230, 234
Kubzansky, P. E., 228, 234
Kuniyoshi, M., 160, 173

LaBerge, D., 101, 110
Lacey, B. C., 212, 213
Lacey, J. I., 212, 234
Lackner, J. R., 121, 140
Lockard, R. B., 312
Ladd, G. T., 191, 203
Ladove, R. F., 162
Lakota, R., 384, 392
Lamb, W., 383, 392
Lamont, J. F., 384, 392
Lamson, E. T., 211, 233
Lang, P. J., 398–400
Latané, B., 309, 310, 312
Lawler, P., 307, 312
Lawson, K. D., 224, 233
Lawson, O. N., 263, 265
Lazarus, R. S., 214, 216–227, 233–235, 384, 392
Lefcourt, H. M., 383, 392
Legrand, R., 101, 110
Lehman, D., 196, 203
LePage, 257, 264
Leiderman, P. H., 234
Lenneberg, E. H., 138–141
Levine, L., 406
Lewin, K., 295, 311
Lewin, Kurt, 16
Lewis, E., 406
Lewis, H. B., 195, 203
Lewis, M., 37, 55
Linder, D. E., 283, 288
Lindy, J., 165, 173
Lindsley, D. B., 213, 228, 234
Lindzey, G., 27
Littman, R. A., 261, 265
Loew, C. A., 247, 249, 265
London, M., 134, 140
Lorenz, K., 239, 265
Lovass, O. I., 247–250, 265
Luce, A. A., 79

M.S.A. Barcelona, 351, 368
Machover, K., 351, 352, 358, 368
Mack, A., 72, 80
MacKay, E. M., 160, 173
MacKinnon, D. W., 94, 111
Maeno, T., 160, 173
Magoun, H. W., 179, 203
Mahl, G. F., 214, 234
Mahrer, A. R., 404
Mallick, S. K., 253, 265
Malmo, R. B., 213, 235
Mandler, G., 26, 108, 111
Mandler, J. M., 227, 235
Manis, M., 407
Margulis, D. L., 153, 173
Margulis, S. T., 272, 288
Marlowe, D., 386, 392
Martin, E., 130, 141
Marx, M. H.,
Mason, D. J., 404
Mason, G., 94, 111
Mason, J. W., 230, 233
Matasaburo, J., 160, 173
Mathewson, G. C., 282, 288
Mayer, J., 160, 161, 173, 317
McBride, D., 274, 288

McCandless, B. R., 253, 265
McCrary, J. W., 97, 111
McGill, T. E., 228
McGovern, J. M., 91, 111
McGowan, J. F., 356, 368
McGuire, W. J., 282, 288
McNeill, D., 103–105, 110
Meehl, P. E., 379, 391
Mehler, J., 117, 122, 130, 131, 141
Melton, A. W., 88–90, 92, 111
Melville, H., 19
Messick, S., 231, 235
Meyer, D. R., 149, 173
Meyers, W., 55
Mickle, W. A., 167, 172
Milgram, S., 231, 235
Miller, G. C., 106, 111, 115, 117–120, 123–125, 131, 132, 139, 141
Miller, N., 251, 264
Miller, N. E., 157, 158, 162, 165, 172, 173
Mills, J., 276, 288
Milner, P., 164, 173
Miron, M. S., 139
Mitchell, S. W., 344
Moffett, A., 37, 55
Mogenson, G. J., 167, 173
Molyneaux, 30
Monroe, L. J., 195, 196, 202, 203
Montagu, M. F., 239, 265
Moore, R. W., 37, 55
Mordkoff, A. M., 216–218, 234
Morgan, C. W., 167, 173
Morgan, P. J., 158, 165, 173
Morris, D., 239, 265, 312
Morse, W. H., 341
Moruzzi, G., 179, 203
Moss, C. E., 95, 111
Moss, H. A., 212, 234
Mostofsky, D. I., 196
Mowrer, O. H., 251, 264, 395, 409
Munsinger, H., 37, 55
Murphy, G., 27, 230, 235
Murray, H., 19, 26
Muzio, J., 188, 204

Nako, F., 160, 173
Nel, E., 284, 285
Nelson, D., 376, 391
Nichols, 358, 368
Nisbett, R. E., 168, 171, 173
Noble, C. E., 86, 111
Nomikos, M. S., 221–223, 225, 226, 235
Norman, D. A., 106, 111

O'Connell, D. S., 124, 141
Odom, P., 117, 140
Ogle, K. N., 61, 80
Olds, J., 153, 164–167, 173
Olds, M., 166, 173
Olley, P., 189
Ono, H., 79
Oomara, Y. H., 160, 161, 173
Ooyama, T., 160, 173
Opler, M. K., 401
Opton, E.M., 220–226, 233–235, 384,
Ordy, J. M., 33, 34, 55
Orne, M. T., 186, 203, 229, 235
Osgood, C. E., 85, 111, 326, 341
Osler, S., 105, 111, 214, 234
Oswald, I., 188, 189, 202

Palmer, C., 195, 202
Paré, A., 344
Park, J., 40, 50, 55
Parson, O. A., 376, 385, 391, 392
Patterson, G. R., 261–265
Pavlov, I., 16
Pearlstone, Z., 105, 111
Pennypacker, H. S., 322
Perchonock, E., 130–132, 141
Peterson, L., 82, 83, 111
Peterson, M. J., 82, 83, 111
Peterson, R. F., 331, 333, 340
Phillips, A. G., 167, 173
Phillips, L., 398
Piaget, J., 134, 141
Pick, H., 74, 75, 79
Pinel, P., 395
Pivik, T., 194, 196, 203, 388, 392
Plato, 3
Platt, J. R., 20, 26
Plog, S. C., 400
Pollard, J. C., 229, 234, 235
Pollux, 106
Porter, L. W., 307, 312
Porter, R. W., 230, 233
Postman, L., 55, 92, 93, 111, 374, 391
Pribram, K. H., 106
Pliskoff, S. S., 165, 173
Poschel, B. P., 167, 173
Powley, T. L., 162–164, 173

Projansky, M., 404
Prytulak, L. S., 105, 111
Psyche, 2

Rankin, N. O., 221–223, 234
Ranson, S. W., 157, 173
Rapaport, D., 94, 111, 229, 235
Rausch, D. S., 91, 111
Raush, H. L., 290, 313
Rawlings, E., 264
Rechtschaffen, 184, 193, 196, 203, 204
Redl, F., 300
Reed, H., 101, 111
Reicken, H. W., 269, 288
Reineck, L., 384, 392
Rekosh, J., 72, 79
Remy, R. M., 361, 368
Reynolds, G. S., 322, 328, 341
Rice, C. E., 21, 26
Richter, C. P., 230, 231, 235
Ridley, D., 408
Riesen, A. H., 229, 235
Riggs, L. A., 30, 55
Ring, K., 403, 404, 408
Rivoire, J. L., 55
Roback, H. B., 353, 368
Roberts, K., 130, 141
Roberts, L. K., 384, 392
Roberts, W., 165, 172
Robinson, E. E., 20, 22, 26
Robinson, H., 276, 288
Robinson, H. A., 354–356, 368
Rock, I., 63, 73, 80
Rodin, 349, 350, 368
Roffwarg, H. P., 188, 189, 204
Rogers, C. R., 341
Roheim, G., 216
Rosen, S., 276, 288
Rosenberg, S., 129, 141
Rosenthal, R., 19, 26, 186, 204
Rosenzweig, S., 94, 111
Ross, D., 241, 243, 244, 258, 264
Ross, S. A., 241, 243, 244, 258, 264
Roussy, G., 147, 172
Routtenberg, A., 165, 173, 229, 235
Rozin, P., 155, 173
Russell, W. A., 99, 111

Sairn, H. B., 130–132, 141
Sarason, I. G., 409
Sarbin, T. P., 396
Schachter, I., 168–170, 172, 173, 227, 235, 269, 288
Schappell, A. W., 348, 367
Scheibe, K., 229, 235
Schiffman, H., 228, 235
Schilder, P., 349–351, 368
Schmidt, L. D., 356, 368
Schnierla, T. D., 20, 22, 26
Schoggen, P., 295, 300, 311, 312
Schonbach, P., 276, 288
Schontz, F., 364, 365, 367
Schwartz, M. S., 383, 391
Scopas, 106
Scott, J. P., 239, 265
Scott, T. H., 228, 233
Searle, L. M., 144, 172
Sears, R., 251, 264
Secord, P. F., 361, 368
Seeman, J., 231, 235
Sells, S. B., 312
Selye, H., 208, 210, 351
Sem-Jacobson, C. W., 167, 173
Sensen, M. von, 30, 55
Sinnett, E. R., 407
Shapiro, A., 195, 196, 203, 204
Shapiro, M. F., 348, 367
Sharma, K. N., 160, 172
Sheffield, J., 382, 385, 391
Sherman, J. A., 331–333, 341
Sherman, L. J., 358, 368
Shontz, F., 394, 414
Shontz, F. C., 379, 392
Sidman, M., 324, 341
Silber, L. D., 386, 392
Silverstein, A., 354–356, 368
Simmel, M. L., 347, 368
Simon, T., 15
Simonides, 106
Singer, J. E., 227, 235
Singer, J. L., 197–199, 202, 204
Singh, B., 160, 172
Skinner, B. F., 17, 40, 316, 325–327, 341, 342
Sleser, I., 195, 203
Smith, F., 139, 141
Smith, P. E., 147, 173
Smith, W. J., 355, 356, 367, 368
Songer, E., 272, 288
Speisman, J. C., 216–218, 234, 235
Stare, F. A., 229, 233
Stark, K., 92, 111
Stechler, G., 37, 56
Steinberg, M. A., 383, 391

Steiner, I. D., 285, 288
Steinschriber, L., 196, 203
Stevens, S. S., 10, 11, 26
Stevenson, J. A. F., 157, 173
Stiles, W. E., 261, 264
Stolz, W., 121, 140
Storms, L. H., 99, 111
Storr, A., 239, 265
Stoyva, I., 200, 204
Stratton, G. M., 58–60, 63, 73, 80
Stricher, L. J., 231, 235
Strümpfer, D., 358, 368
Sullivan, P. F., 384, 392
Sundsten, J. W., 159, 172
Supa, M., 20, 21, 24, 27
Sutton-Smith, B., 308
Swanson, E. M., 194, 203
Szasz, T. S., 395, 396, 409
Swenson, C. H., 353, 358, 368

Taylor, J. G., 72, 80
Teichner, W. H., 229, 235
Teitelbaum, P., 144, 146, 147, 150, 152–156, 158, 160, 163, 166, 172, 173
Templeton, W. B., 63, 79
Tempone, V. J., 380, 381, 383, 391
Teuber, H. L., 229, 235
Thelen, M. H., 383, 392
Thomas, L. E., 259, 265
Thomas, R. J., 305, 312
Thorndike, E. L., 272, 288, 316
Tolman, E. C., 325, 342
Tomita, M., 220, 221, 234
Trumbull, R., 206, 233
Tulving, E., 105, 108, 111
Turausky, A. J., 162
Turvey, M. T., 101, 111

Udelf, M. S., 33, 34, 55
Uhr, L., 229, 234, 235
Ullman, L. P., 394, 404
Ullmann, L. P., 380, 384, 392
Underwood, B. J., 78, 80, 90–93, 109–111
U. S. Dept. of Health, Education, & Welfare, 181, 204
Uviller, E. T., 227, 234

Van de Castle, 176, 178, 203, 204
Van Lawick, H., 312
Van Ormer, E. B., 86, 111
Vaughn, C., 201, 204
Venus, 2
Verdone, P., 196, 204
Vernon, J. A., 228, 235
Vesalius, 3
Vogel, G., 196, 203

Walk, R., 46–49, 51, 55, 56
Wallace, A. F. C., 401
Wallace, J. G., 31, 55
Walls, G. L., 73, 80
Walster, E., 275, 288
Walters, R. H., 251, 259, 264, 265
Wapner, S., 367
Washburn, A. L., 144
Watson, J. B., 17, 18, 316
Watson, R. I.,
Wawrzaszek, F., 356, 368
Weber, S. H., 4–6, 8, 14, 26
Weed, S., 192, 204
Weiner, B., 94, 101, 111
Weinstein, E. A., 347, 368
Weinstein, J., 384, 392
Welsh, G. S., 376, 392
Werner, H., 367
Wertheimer, M., 15
Wheaton, J., 196, 204
White, R. W., 230, 235
Whitmyre, J. W., 358, 368
Whorf, B. L., 137, 138, 141
Wickens, D. D., 149, 173
Wicker, A. M., 307
Wilkes, A. L., 126–128, 141
Willems, E. P., 290, 294, 305, 306, 31
Wilson, C., 176, 203
Wittlinger, R. P., 101, 111
Wolf, M. M., 328, 329, 340
Wolfer, J. A., 396
Wolpe, J., 223, 235
Wolpert, E. A., 191, 192, 196, 203, 204
Woodworth, R. S., 7, 27
Worchel, P., 20, 23, 27
Wright, H. F., 294–296, 311, 313
Wright, J. E., 165, 173
Wundt, W., 14, 15, 372

Yamamoto, T., 160, 173
Yates, F. A., 106, 111

Zeller, A. F., 94, 111
Zigler, E., 398, 399
Zimbargo, P. G., 288
Zimmerman, J., 323
Zlotowski, M., 408
Zubek, J. P., 78, 80, 228, 235
Zweizig, J., 196, 203

Subject Index

Absolute threshold, 8, 11–13
Activation theory of emotion, 207–213
Acuity grating, 33
Adaptation, 31, 60–79
  degree of transformation, 65
  duration of exposure, 66
  effective stimulus, 66–69
  locus, 73–76
  movement and intention, 69–73
  perceptual development, 76–78
  rate, 66–68, 78
Adipsia, 150–156, 170
Aftereffect measure, 60–61
Affective disorder, 397
Aggression, definition, 238
Aggression machine, 254–255, 263
Alarm reaction, 209
Alpha waves, 201
Anosognosia, 347, 366
Anomalous string, 118
Anorexia, 152
Anthropological linguistics, 138
Anxiety, 373–374
Anxiety and repression-sensitization, 384
Aphagia, 150–156, 170
  recovery from aphagia, 150–153
  stages in recovery, 152
Art and behavior disorder, 349–352
Associations in sentences, 128–130
Atlas of brain, 149
Attention, 229–322
Attitude change and dissonance, 274–275, 283–285
Autonomic nervous system, 185
Aversive stimuli, 323–325
Aversive control, 323–325
Avoidance training, 324

Barrier response in inkblot test, 359–361, 366
Base structure and reasoning, 136
Behaviorism, 17, 25
Behavior episodes, 296–298, 311
  and social inputs, 296–298
  stimulus-response relationships, 298–299
Behavior in nature, 291–292
Behavior modification, 328–338
  generalized imitation, 331–334
  isolate behavior, 328–331
Behavior settings, 300–301, 311
  and population density, 302–306
Big school vs. small school, 303–306
Binocular disparity, 44
Blood sugar level, 160–161, 168
Blocking and frustration, 251–252
Body experience
  evaluation of research, 364–366
  projective techniques, 351–361
  verbal measures, 361–364
Body image, 350–351, 366

Body movements during dreams, 191–192
Body-part perception, 363–365
Body schemata, 347–349, 364–366
Boundary response in inkblot test, 359–361
Bystander intervention, 308–310

Catharsis and aggression, 253–254, 257–263
Cerebral cortex, 180–181
Cerebellum, 180, 201
Classical conditioning, 16, 25
Click displacement, 120–121
Clustering, 107–108, 109
Commitment and dissonance, 277
Concurrent validity, 380–381
Conditioned reinforcer, 323–340
Conditioned response, 16, 25, 326–327
Conditioned stimulus, 16, 25, 326–327
Conditioning of imitation
  in normal children, 331–333
  in retarded children, 333–334
Conscious correction in adaptation, 62–63
Constancy, perceptual, 39–42, 48–50, 78
Constant error, 7, 25
Construct validity, 381–382, 390
Contextual associations, 91
Continuous reinforcement, 340
Converging operations, 200–201
Cognitive dissonance, 270–286
  as drive, 270–271
  individual differences, 285
  theory, 270–271
Corneal reflection, 32, 54
Correlation, 215, 354–355, 366
Cumulative record, 316–321, 340

Dark rearing, 51–52
Deep structure, 121–123, 130–133, 136–137
Definition, psychology, 18–19
Degree of learning, 94–95
Delta waves, 183–201
Denial, 217–218, 232
Dependence hypothesis, adaptation, 66
Deprivation of REM, 193–195
Depth cues, 43–44
Desensitization, 223–225, 232
Depersonalization, 349, 367
Detection threshold, 12, 25
Difference limen, 7, 11–13
Discrimination and generalization, 322–323
Discriminated operant, 322, 340
Disease model of schizophrenia, 394–
  arguments favoring, 409–411
  objections, 395–396, 409
Dissonance and reward, 272, 283–
  273–274
Distortions of the body in art, 349–35
Disuse hypothesis, 85, 109
Draw-a-person technique, 351–352, 3
  artistic skill, 358
  evaluation of research, 358–359
  research with adults, 355, 358
  research with children, 354–3
  356–358
  research with disabled subjects, 356
Dream reports
  and effect of stimulation, 192–193
  experimenter influence, 186–187
  of earlier dreams, 187–188
Dreams as symbols, 178
Dualism, 3

Ear-eye, 75–76
Ear-hand coordination test, 74–76
Eating, social, 144
Eating in humans
  and fear, 168
  and food deprivation, 168
  and test, 169
  and time, 169
Ecology, 290
Efferent readiness, 72, 79
Egocentric localization, 71, 79
Electroencephalogram, 180–183, 201
  and stages of sleep, 181–183
Electrooculogram, 193, 201
Empiricism, 53, 54
Environment and molar behavior, 300–301
Escape training, 324
Ethical considerations in stress researc
  231–232
Evolution, 3, 372
Extinction, 318–322, 340
Extinction gradients, 322–323
Extinction-induced aggression, 252–253
Eye-hand coordination, 69–71, 73–75
Eye-head, 75–76
Ego, 373–374
Eye movements
  during sleep, 183–185
  during thinking, 196–199
Fear vs. anger, 210–211
Fear and conditioning, 215

Fear and psychoanalytic theory, 215
Fechners Law, 5–6
Feeding center, 144, 148–149, 150–156, 167–168, 170
Figure-ground perception, 31
Flying saucers, 268–269
Forced compliance, 273–275
Fovea, 54
Form discrimination, 35–36
Free association, 96, 99–100
Form preference
  complexity, 36–37
  novelty, 36
Free operant, 326–327
Free recall, 107–108, 109
Frölich's syndrome, 147
Frustration and aggression, 251–257
  availability of stimuli, 256–257
  hypothesis, 251–263
  in lab vs. extralaboratory, 295
  instrumental value, 256
  response strength, 256
Frustration of instrumental responses, 253
Frustration, defined, 251
  types of frustration, 251–252
Frustration and regression, 295
Functionalism, 4, 25

Galvanic skin response, 176–177, 202
Ganzfeld, 72
General adaptation syndrome, 208–209, 232
Generalization of aggression, 247–249
Gestalt psychology, 15–16, 25, 119
Glucoreceptors, 160
Glucostatic hypothesis, 160–161, 170
Glucose utilization, 160–161

Habit strength, 325
Head-Hand, 75–76
Heart rate during stress, 212–213, 216–223
Hedonism, 167, 272, 286
Hemoplegia, 347–349, 367
  related to body schemata, 348
Human recorder, 293–294
Hunger sensations, 144–145
Hyperphagia, 147–148, 170
Hypnosis, 95
Hypothalamus, 146–147, 171
Hypothalamic hyperphagia, 148, 156–159
  and motivation, 157–158
  and ventromedial lesioning, 156
  and ventromedial stimulation, 158
Hypothetical construct, 202

Id, 373–374
Ideational disorder, 397
Imagining and eye movements, 197–199
Imitation and aggression, 240
  and reinforcement control, 331–334
Immediate constitutent, 115, 140
Independence hypothesis, adaptation, 66
Industry, size and performance, 306–307
  and satisfaction, 307
Information theory, 13–14
Inkblot test, and body image, 359–361
  and actual body experience, 360
Insanity, 394
Instinct to aggress, 239–240
Intellectualization and stress, 217–218, 232
Intelligibility and syntax, 118
Interference theory, 86, 109
Interscorer agreement, 378
Interval schedule, 340
Intervening variables, 325
Intracranial self-stimulation, 164–167
Intragastric tube feeding, 145–146, 150, 171
Introspection, 14, 26
Isolate behavior, 328–331
Isomorphism hypothesis, 353, 355–356

Justification of aggression, 260
Just noticeable difference, 5, 26

Language and thought, 137–138
Lateral hypothalamic syndrome, 150–156
  lesion effects, 151–153
  stimulation effects, 153
Lateral hypothalamic zone, 147, 171
Learning theory, 326
Linguistic determinism, 137–138
Linguistic relativity, hypothesis, 137–138, 140
Lipostatic hypothesis, 161–162, 171
Long-term memory, 83

Maladjustment and repression, 381–384
Manipulation in naturalistic psychology, 308–311
Mass media effects, 250, 258, 262–263

Mediated association, 98–100, 110
Memory load and syntax, 131–132
Memory systems, 82, 106–107
method of analytic substitutions, 106–107
method of loci, 106–107
Mental illness, 394–396
anthropological view, 401–402
criticisms of concept, 395–396
sociological view, 401
Mental testing, 15, 372–373
Method of adjustment, 8, 26, 30
Method of constant stimuli, 6–8
Method of free association, 15
Method of limits, 8, 26
Method of paired comparisons, 8
Method of ranking, 9
Method of single stimuli, 26
Minnesota Multiphasic Personality Inventory, 375–376
Molecular vs. molar, 291–311
Models of syntax, 115–117
generative, 116–117
left-to-right, 115
Movement, active vs. passive, 70–72, 76–78
Movement parallax, 44–46, 54
and visual cliff, 47–48, 51–52

Nativism, 53, 54
Naturalistic environmentalism, 290
Naturalism vs. elementarism, 291, 299–300, 311
Newly seeing, vision of, 30–31
Nonimitative aggression, 247–249
Non-REM dreams, 196, 202
Not remembering, 84, 103–105

Obesity in humans, 168–170
Obtrusiveness of observer, 293–294
Observed aggression, 240
and justification, 260
and pain cues, 260–261
effect of observed rewards, 244–247
film models, 242–243
generalization, 247–249
live models, 241–243
retention of effects, 249–250
Obstacle detection in blind, 20–24
Olds' theory of reinforcement, 166–167
Operant conditioning, 17, 316–318
compared to classical, 326–327
Operant analysis
de-emphasis on theory, 326
emphasis on observables, 325–32
single organism research, 327–32
the free operant, 326–327
Operant level, 318, 328, 340
Optic array, 31
Optical texture, 44, 54
and visual cliff, 47–48, 51–52
Organization of memory, 106–109, 1

Pain cues and observed aggres
260–261
Paired associates learning, 86
Parabiosis, 162
Participation in school activities, 303–
Passive forgetting, 84
Perceptual defense, 374–375, 390
Perceptual set, 122, 140
and deep structure, 122
Perceptual units, 119
Phantom limb, 344–347, 367
Phobia, 223–225, 232
Phrase structure, 115, 119–121, 124–1
132–133, 140
Pituitary gland and obesity, 147–148
Point of subjective equality, 7, 11, 26
Polygraph, 176–177, 202
Population density, 301–306
and behavior in settings, 303
and satisfactions, 303–305
participation, 303–304
Postdecision information seeking, 27
277
Postdecision regret, 275–276
Posthypnotic amnesia, 95–98, 110
Power in games, 308
Preoperative weight level, 162–164
Proactive inhibition, 92–93, 101–103
Problem solving in groups, 387
Projection, 355–356
Projection of personality, 359
projective test, 367
Proprioceptive shift, 73–75, 79
Psychiatric disorder and body perceptio
349–350
Psychoanalysis, 15, 26
theory of dreams, 176–178, 185, 193–
194, 215
theory of repression, 373–374, 382
Psychodiagnosis, 398, 400
Psycholinguistics, 114, 140
Psychophysical methods, 6–10

Psychophysical parallelism, 208
Psychosis
a behavioristic view
varieties, 396–398
Psychosomatics and stress, 230–231, 232
Purpose, 325

Rapid eye movement (REM) 183–185
and dream pattern, 188–189
and dreams, 185–191
and intensity of dream, 188
deprivation, 193–196
dreams of the blind, 189–191
Ratio scale, 11
Ratio schedule, 340
Reaction formation, 217–218, 232
Reaction time and anxiety, 96
Readiness to perceive, 72
Recoding, 124–128, 140
Recovery and development of feeding, 154–156
Reduction of dissonance, 271, 283–285
Regression effect, 215, 232
Reinforcement
differential reinforcement of other behavior, 33–334
noncontingent, 330–331
positive and negative, 323–324
primary and conditioned, 323
schedules, 318–322
Reinforcement and observed aggression, 244–247
Relearning, 82
Reliability of a test, 377–379, 391
REM deprivation
and dreaming, 193–196
and repression-sensitization, 387–389
Repression, psychoanalytic theory, 374–375, 389–390, 391
Resistance to stress, 209
Response competition, 87–94, 110
Response latency and syntax, 127
Repression and memory, 84, 94–100
mediated association, 98–100
posthypnotic amnesia, 95–98
Repression-sensitization, measurement, 375–382
Repression-sensitization scale, 376–382
Reticular activating system, 179–181, 202
Retinal image orientation, 58
Retrieval and forgetting, 85, 103–105
Retroactive interference, 86–92, 110
intrusions, 88–89
two factor theory, 87
Reversal procedure, 329
Reward, 272
Reward centers, 164–167, 171
Rewrite rules, 116

Satiety center, 144, 148–149, 156–159, 167–168, 171
Satisfaction and population density, 304–305
Satisfaction and performance, 307
Savings measure, 83
Schedules of reinforcement, 318–322
Schizophrenic vs. normal
reaction time, 405–406
response to censure, 399
response variability, 399–400
similarities, 402–409
Schizophrenics' behavior in vs. out of hospital, 407–408
Schizophrenic impression management, 404–407
Schizophrenics, old-timers vs. newcomers, 403–404
Schizophrenia, types
nonparanoid, 397
paranoid, 397
process, 398
reactive, 398
Self-produced movement vs. passive, 76–78
Sensitizers vs. repressors, 382–387
and anxiety, 384
and hostility, 385
and maladjustment, 382–385
and problem solving, 387
and REM deprivation, 387–389
and response to pain, 385
and sexuality, 385
and social desirability, 386
Sensory deprivation, 78, 228–229
Serial position curve, 97–98, 110
Shape constancy, 39–42, 54
in infants, 40–42
Shadowing speech, 118
Shape, objective, projective, 38
Shape-slant relationship, 40–42
Shaping, 330, 340
Short-term memory, 82, 110
Signal detection, 12–13
Single organism research, 327–328
Size constancy, 48, 54
in infants, 48–50

Size-distance relationship, 50
Skin conductance during stress, 212–213, 216–223, 232
Skinner box, 316–17
Sleep cycles, 181–183
Sleep and forgetting, 85–86
Social desirability, 387
Specimen record, 294–297, 311
Stability of a test, 378
Stages of sleep, 180–183
Statistical constraints in language, 115, 123
Stereotaxic instrument, 149–150, 171
Steven's law, 10
Stimulation and dreaming, 192–193
Stimulus control, 321–322
Stimulus generalization, 322–323, 340
Stomach motility
  and eating, 168–170
  and hunger sensations, 144–145
Stop and go signals, 159–162
Stress
  and cognitive preparation, 219–223
  and performance, 214
  and personality variables, 219–220
  anticipation of harm, 226–227
  cross cultural comparisons, 220–221
  extralaboratory, 211
  physiological correlates, 210–213
  physiological view, 207–213
  psychological view, 207–208, 214–217
Strong inference, 19–20, 26
Stimulus-preference method, 31–32, 54
Stress reaction to film, 216–223
Stump sensitivity, 345–347
Subincision film, 216–218
Subjective organization, 108, 110
Superego, 373–374
Surprise and suspense, 225–226
Synomorphs, 300–301, 311
Syntax and learning, 123–124

Taste and smell, 145–146
Thalamus, 179–180, 202
Thermostatic hypothesis, 159–160, 1
Thought and behavior, 271–272
Three-term problem, 134–137
Tip of the tongue phenomenon, 85, 105, 110
Trained aggression, 239
Transformational rules, 116–117, 132, 140
Transitional error probability, 125–129–130, 140
Two-point thresholds, 345–346

Unconditional (unconditioned) respo 16
Unconditional (unconditioned) stimu 16
Unitization in memory, 125–128
Unlearning of associations, 88–93, 1
Up-down inversion, 58–60
Units of behavior, 295–296

Validity of a test, 379–382
  concurrent, 379–380
  construct, 381–382
  content, 381
  predictive, 379–380
Verbal aggression, 248–249
Vicarious aggression, 257–262
Violence and mass media, 262–263
Visual acuity, 33–35, 54
Visual angle, 54
Visual capture, 75
Visual cliff, 46–48, 50–52, 55, 77
Visual direction, 59
Voluntary forgetting, 100–103

Weber's Law
Wedge prism, 31, 60–61
Weight loss, 152
Weight regulation hypothesis, 162–164
Wish suppression and eye moveme 197–199